"[A] POLISHED AND GRIPPING HISTORY . . .
The best account yet of the most momentous event
in the modern Middle East."

—FAREED ZAKARIA, Editor, *Newsweek International*

"Masterful and thrilling . . . Oren's beautifully modulated account of the war,
which is drawn from the historical archives of four countries, offers an
implicit explanation of the inability or refusal of the U.S. and other Western
countries to take Osama bin Laden seriously before September 11."

—*National Review*

"The Six-Day War had, and still has, a great influence on Israel,
its neighbors, and the current events in the Middle East. Michael B. Oren
has presented a detailed and multi-perspective picture of the events and
dynamics of that period. It is a significant step toward a better understanding
of our national and regional history. Hopefully, such understanding may
assist us in reaching peace in the Middle East."

—EHUD BARAK

"Mr. Oren brings a novelist's flair to recounting [the circumstances]
and to the war itself. His meticulous research cuts through the
propagandized histories on all sides."

—*The Wall Street Journal*

"The most comprehensive chronicle of this crucial
turning point in contemporary Middle East history.
Six Days of War is an elegantly detailed, often riveting account."

—*Chicago Sun-Times*

Please turn the page for more reviews. . . .

"THE FINEST BOOK EVER ON THIS SUBJECT."

—The New York Post

"[The] definitive history of the
1967 Arab-Israeli war and its aftermath."

—New York magazine

"The historical debate about the 1967 war in the Middle East grows ever
sharper because the consequences of Israeli victory extend to the present.
Michael Oren's balanced and detailed book is based on archival sources and
throws much new light on the Israeli conquest of the Arab territories and the
reaction, above all, within the United States government."

—WM. ROGER LOUIS, Author of
The British Empire in the Middle East, 1945–1951

"*Six Days of War* scores highly in telling an extremely complicated story
within a narrative which, despite being loaded with a crushing volume of
research, reads at times like the breeziest blockbuster."

—*The Financial Times*

"The reunification of Jerusalem is just one of the tantalizing tales in
Six Days of War. . . . The book is the most comprehensive report yet
about what many believe is Israel's greatest military triumph."

—*The Miami Herald*

"One of the most valuable recent works on the subject."

—*Library Journal*

Please turn the page for more reviews. . . .

Six Days
of War

By Michael B. Oren
The Origins of the Second Arab-Israeli War

Six Days of War

*June 1967
and the Making of the
Modern Middle East*

MICHAEL B. OREN

PRESIDIO
PRESS

BALLANTINE BOOKS • NEW YORK

A Presidio Press Book
Published by The Random House Publishing Group
Copyright © 2002, 2003 by Michael B. Oren

All rights reserved under International and Pan-American Copyright Conventions.
Published in the United States by The Random House Publishing Group,
a division of Random House, Inc., New York, and simultaneously in Canada by
Random House of Canada Limited, Toronto.

Presidio Press and colophon are trademarks of Random House, Inc.

www.ballantinebooks.com

Library of Congress Control Number: 2003103713

ISBN 0-345-46192-4

This edition published by arrangement with Oxford University Press.

Cover photo: Col. Motto Gur (turning, with field phone) addressing Israeli troops
from the Mount of Olives, The Dome of the Rock below. (Israel Government Press)

Manufactured in the United States of America

First Presidio Press Edition: June 2003

3 5 7 9 10 8 6 4

For my wife, Sally,
and for our children—Yoav, Lia, and Noam.

Each We seized for his sin and against some We unleashed a storm. Some were seized by the cry and some the earth swallowed and some We drowned. God would never wrong them, but they wrong themselves.

The Qur'an, 29:39

But though they roar like breakers on a beach, God will silence them. They will flee like chaff scattered by the wind or like dust whirling before a storm.

Isaiah, 17:13

CONTENTS

LIST OF MAPS

ACKNOWLEDGMENTS

T
HOUGH MY NAME APPEARS as the author of this book, and I take sole responsibility for its contents, *Six Days of War* represents the efforts, the expertise, and the dedication of many esteemed individuals.

I wish to thank, firstly, those archivists and archival assistants who facilitated my research at various libraries around the world: Regina Greenwell at the Lyndon B. Johnson Presidential Archive; Patrick Hussey in Washington, D.C.; Michael Helfand at the UN Archive in New York; Alexey Kornilov and Masha Yegorova in Moscow; Gilad Livne and Eliahu Shlomo at the Israel National Archives; Michael Tzur at the IDF Archives, Col. Yoram Buskila and Capt. Michal Yizraeli at the Israel Air Force Historical Wing.

Throughout the research and writing of the book, I received invaluable input from fellow scholars. Thanks are due to Ambassador Richard B. Parker, scholar-in-residence at the Middle East Institute, Yigal Carmon, President of MEMRI, Dr. Abdel Monem Said Aly, Director of the Al-Ahram Center for Political and Strategic Studies, Zaki Shalom of Ben-Gurion University, Eyal Sisser of the Dayan Center of Tel Aviv University, and Dan Schueftan, Arie Morgenstern, and Rabbi Isaac Lifshitz, all of the Shalem Center. Thanks to Eran Lerman for his critical reading of the text. I wish to express special gratitude to two colleagues whose advice and support have seen me through the many vicissitudes of this project—to Hebrew University Professor Avraham Sela and to Mor Altschuler, also of the Shalem Center.

For feedback on my writing, suggestions on phrasing and sources, and the occasional morale boost, I was able to turn to a number of knowledgeable friends, among them Yossi Klein Halevi, Jeremy Herman, Sharon Friedman, Matthew Miller, Jonathan Karp, John Krivine, Joseph Rothenberg, Danny Grossman, Isabella Ginor, Kenneth Weinstein, Zion Suliman, the Hon. A. Jay Cristol and, as always, Jonathan Price and Naomi Schacter-Price. I warmly thank them all.

I have been blessed—it is the only word for it—with a team of committed and talented research assistants without whom this book could not have come to life. My deepest appreciation goes to Moshe Fuchsman, Yemima Kitron, Elisheva Machlis, and Alexander Pevzner. Thanks are also due to editorial assistants Aloma Halter and Michael Rose, and to graphic artist Batsheva Kohay. I am particularly indebted to Noa Bismuth, whose devotion, energy, and skills proved utterly indispensable.

I want to warmly thank my editor, Peter Ginna, for his unswerving commitment to this book, and to the others at Oxford University Press—Tim Bartlett, Helen Mules, Sara Leopold, Furaha Norton, Kathleen Lynch, and Ruth Mannes—who patiently saw it through publication. Thank you, too, Glenn Hartley, head of Writers Representatives, my excellent agent.

The book is dedicated to my family, my wife and children, for whom no mere acknowledgement can suffice. The same holds for my parents, Marilyn and Lester Bornstein, and my sisters, Aura Kuperberg and Karen Angrist, and their husbands.

I wish also to thank my "family" at the Shalem Center, the educational and research institute where I am a Senior Fellow, and under whose auspices this book was researched and written. To those staff members who aided me in myriad ways, to Marina Pilipodi, Rachel Cavits, Naomi Arbel, Carol Dahan, Dina Blank, Yehudit Adest, Biana Herzog, Laura Cohen, Dan Blique, Michal Shaty, Anat Tobenhouse, Einat Shichor, Ina Tabak—thank you all. My appreciation goes to David Hazony and Josh Weinstein, on whose sage advice I have often relied, and to Yishai Haetzni and Shaul Golan, the executives who shared with me the vision of this book and so often made the impossible happen. Special gratitude is reserved for Daniel Polisar, the Academic Director of Shalem, who stood behind this project from inception to publication, and to our indefatigable publicist, Deena Rosenfeld-Friedman. The members of the Shalem Board of Trustees—and especially Allen H. Roth and William Kristol are thanked for their unflagging support and advice. Finally and most ardently, my thanks go to Yoram Hazony, President of Shalem, and to the head of its Board, Roger Hertog, for their generosity, their inspiration, and leadership.

The 1967 war is, at base, a saga not of books and documents, but of people, many of whom I have had the pleasure and honor to meet. To exceptional individuals such as Abba Eban and Miriam Eshkol, Indar Jit Rikhye, Muhammad al-Farra and Suliman Marzuq, Joseph Sisco, the Rostow brothers, Eugene and Walter, Eric Rouleau and Vadim Kirpitchenko, I can only say that I owe you a great deal, and so does history.

A NOTE ON SOURCES AND SPELLINGS

MANY AND DIVERSE SOURCES were employed in the writing of this book. The bulk of the research is based on diplomatic papers from archives in North America, Britain, and Israel, observing the thirty-year declassification rule. The protocols of Israeli Cabinet meetings remain for the most part classified, however, as do all but a segment of Israel Defense Forces papers. Archives in the Arab world are closed to researchers, though several private collections—Cairo's Dar al-Khayyal, for example—are accessible. Also, a significant number of Arabic documents fell into Israeli hands during the war, and can be viewed at the Israel Intelligence Library. Russian language documents are, in theory, available at archives in Moscow, though these are poorly maintained and highly limited in their holdings. The French files from 1967 have not yet been released to the public.

In the notes, names of archives are abbreviated as follows:

BGA	Ben-Gurion Archives
FRUS	Foreign Relations of the United States
IDF	Israel Defense Forces Archives
ISA	Israel State Archives
LBJ	Lyndon Baines Johnson Presidential Library
MPA	Mapai Party Archives
NAC	National Archives of Canada
PRO	Public Record Office (FO=Foreign Office, CAB=Cabinet Papers, PREM=Prime Minister's Office)

SFM   Soviet Foreign Ministry Archives
UN   United Nations Archives
USNA   United States National Archives
YAD   Yad Tabenkin Archive

Oral history interviews represent another important source for the book. The majority of these were conducted by the author, though in several highly sensitive cases, the author provided written questions to a research assistant who, for reasons of personal security, wished to remain anonymous. I have attempted to interview as many of the war's principal figures as possible. Several, such as Gideon Rafael and Kings Hussein and Hassan, passed away during the course of my research; others—Ariel Sharon and Yasser Arafat, for example—declined to be interviewed.

Transliteration, particularly in Arabic, presents a formidable challenge, as names often have both popular and literary spellings. For clarity's sake, preference is given to the former. Thus: Sharm al-Sheikh rather than Sharm al-Shaykh, Abu 'Ageila and not Abu 'Ujayla. Personal names are also formally transliterated except in cases in which the individual was accustomed to a specific spelling of his or her name in English. Some examples are Gamal Abdel Nasser (instead of Jamal 'Abd al-Nasir), Yasser Arafat (Yasir 'Arafat), and Mohammad El Kony (Muhammad al-Kuni). Many place names—Cairo, Jerusalem, Damascus—have been preserved in their English equivalents, rather than in the original Arabic or Hebrew.

FOREWORD

THE WAR OF ATTRITION, the Yom Kippur War, the Munich massacre and Black September, the Lebanon War, the controversy over Jewish settlements and the future of Jerusalem, the Camp David Accords, the Oslo Accords, the *Intifada*—all were the result of six intense days in the Middle East in June 1967. Rarely in modern times has so short and localized a conflict had such prolonged, global consequences. Seldom has the world's attention been gripped, and remained seized, by a single event and its ramifications. In a very real sense, for statesmen and diplomats and soldiers, the war has never ended. For historians, it has only just begun.

Many books have been written about what most of the world calls the Six-Day War, or as the Arabs prefer, the June 1967 War. The literature is broad because the subject was thrilling—the lightning pace of the action, the stellar international cast, the battlefield held holy by millions. There were heroes and villains, behind-the-scenes machinations and daring tactical moves. There was the danger of nuclear war. No sooner had the shooting stopped than the first accounts—eyewitness, mostly—began appearing. Hundreds more would follow.

Some of these books were meant for a scholarly audience, while others addressed the general public. All, however, were based on similar sources: previously issued books, articles, and newspapers, together with a spattering of interviews, largely in English. Most of the books focused on the military phase of the war—examples include Trevor N. Dupuy's *Elusive Victory*, and *Swift Sword*, by S.L.A. Marshall—and dealt only superficially with its political and strategic facets. The authors, moreover, tended to be biased in favor of one of the combatants, either the Arabs or the Israelis. There was no one book that drew on all the sources, public as well as classified, and in all the relevant languages—Arabic, Hebrew, Russian. No single study of the war examined both its political and military aspects in a manner that strove for balance.

A change began to occur in the 1990s with the release of secret diplomatic documents, first in American archives and later in Great Britain and Israel. The fall of the Soviet Union and the easing of press restrictions in Egypt and Jordan also yielded some important texts that could not have been published earlier. Many of these new sources were incorporated into two superb academic works, Richard B. Parker's *The Politics of Miscalculation in the Middle East* and William B. Quandt's *Peace Process.* Readers were for the first time afforded a glimpse of the complex diplomacy surrounding the war and insights into international crisis management. Parker and Quandt also achieved a degree of neutrality and scholarly detachment unprecedented in the study of the 1967 war, a refreshing departure from the previous partisanship.

Still missing, however, was the comprehensive book about the war: a book that would draw on the thousands of documents declassified since Quandt and Parker wrote, on the wealth of foreign language materials now available, and on interviews in all the countries involved. Needed was the balanced study of the military and political facets of the war, the interplay between its international, regional, and domestic dimensions, a book intended for scholars but also accessible to a wider readership. This is the book I have set out to write.

The task would prove formidable, due not only to the vastness of the research involved, but also to the radically controversial nature of Arab-Israeli politics. Great wars *in* history invariably become great wars *of* history, and the Arab-Israeli wars are no exception. For decades now, historians have been battling over the interpretation of those wars, beginning with the War of Independence, or the Palestine War of 1948 and progressing to the 1956 Suez crisis. Most recently, a wave of revisionist writers, Israelis mostly, have sought to amplify Israel's guilt for those clashes and evince it in the debate over the borders, or even the legitimacy, of the Jewish state. That debate is now sharpening as historians begin to focus on 1967 and the conquest of Arab territories by Israel, some of which—the Golan, the West Bank—it still holds, and whose final disposition will affect the lives of millions.

I, too, have been part of the debate, and have my opinions. Yet, in writing history, I view these preconceptions as obstacles to be overcome rather than as convictions to confirm and indulge. Even if the truth can never fully be ascertained, I believe every effort must nevertheless be exerted in seeking it. And though the distance of over three decades affords invaluable historical perspectives, such viewpoints should never cloud our understanding of how the world appeared to the people of those tumultuous times. Employ hindsight but humbly, remembering that life and death decisions are made by leaders in real-time, and not by historians in retrospect.

My purpose is not to prove the justness of one party or another in the war, or to assign culpability for starting it. I want, simply, to understand how an event as immensely influential as this war came about—to show the context from which it sprang and the catalysts that precipitated it. I aspire to explore, using the 1967 example, the nature of international crises in general, and the manner in which human interaction can produce totally unforeseen, unintended, results. Mostly, I want to recreate the Middle East of the 1960s, to animate the extraordinary personalities that fashioned it, and to relive a period of history that profoundly impacts our own. Whether it is called the Six-Day or the June War, my goal is that it never be seen the same way again.

Jerusalem, 2002

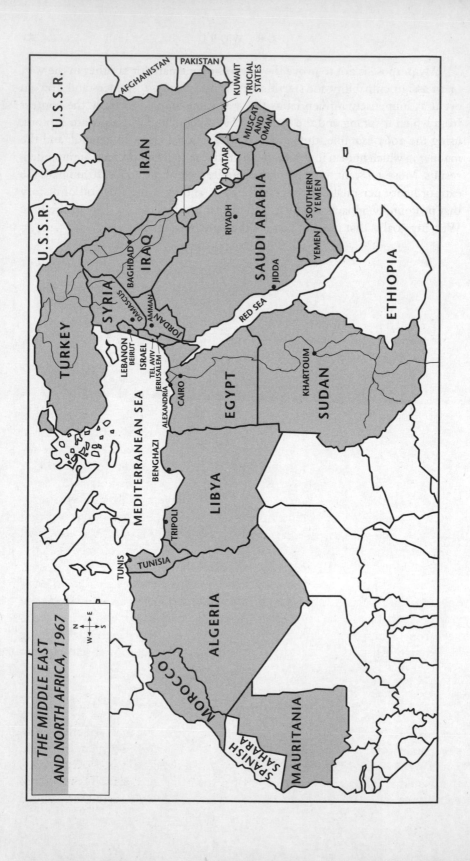

THE MIDDLE EAST AND NORTH AFRICA, 1967

THE CONTEXT

Arabs, Israelis, and the Great Powers, 1948 to 1966

NIGHTTIME, DECEMBER 31, 1964—A squad of Palestinian guerrillas crosses from Lebanon into northern Israel. Armed with Soviet-made explosives, their uniforms supplied by the Syrians, they advance toward their target: a pump for conveying Galilee water to the Negev desert. A modest objective, seemingly, yet the Palestinians' purpose is immense. Members of the militant al-Fatah (meaning, "The Conquest, " also a reverse acronym for the Movement for the Liberation of Palestine), they want to bring about the decisive showdown in the Middle East. Their action, they hope, will provoke an Israeli retaliation against one of its neighboring countries—Lebanon itself, or Jordan—igniting an all-Arab offensive to destroy the Zionist state.

This, al-Fatah's maiden operation, ends in fiasco. First the explosive charges fail to detonate. Then, exiting Israel, the guerrillas are arrested by Lebanese police. Nevertheless, the leader of al-Fatah, a thirty-five-year-old former engineer from Gaza named Yasser Arafat, issues a victorious communiqué extolling "the duty of Jihad (holy war) and . . . the dreams of revolutionary Arabs from the Atlantic Ocean to the Gulf."[1]

A singularly limber imagination would have been required that New Year's Eve night to conceive that this act of small-scale sabotage, even had it been successful, could have triggered a war involving masses of men and matériel— a war that would change the course of Middle Eastern history and, with it, much of the world's. Yet al-Fatah's operation contained many of the flashpoints that would set off precisely such a war in less than three years. There was, of course, the Palestinian dimension, a complex and volatile issue that plagued the Arab states as much as it did Israel. There was terror and Syrian support for it and Soviet support for Syria. And there was water. More than any other individual factor, the war would revolve around water.

Yet, to claim that that first al-Fatah operation, or any one of its subsequent attacks, brought about a general Middle East war, would be far too simplistic and determinist. "A beginning is an artifice," wrote Ian McEwan in his novel *Enduring Love*, "and what recommends one over another is how much sense it makes of what follows." The observation certainly applies to history, where attempts to identify prime causes are often at best arbitrary, at worst futile. One could just as easily begin with early Zionist settlement in Palestine, or with British policy there after World War I. Or with the rise of Arab nationalism, or with the Holocaust. The options are myriad and equally—potentially—valid.

While it may be useless to try to pinpoint the cause or causes of the Middle East war of 1967, one can describe the context in which that war became possible. Much like the hypothetical butterfly that, flapping its wings, gives rise to currents that eventually generate a storm, so, too, might small, seemingly insignificant events spark processes leading ultimately to cataclysm. And just as that butterfly needs a certain context—the earth's atmosphere, gravity, the laws of thermodynamics—to produce its tempest, so, too, did events prior to June 1967 require specific circumstances in order to precipitate war. The context was that of the Middle East in its postcolonial, revolutionary period—a region torn by bitter internecine feuds, by superpower encroachment, and by the constant irritant of what had come to be known as the Arab-Israeli conflict.

A Context Contrived

Even a discussion of a context must have a starting point—another arbitrary choice. Let us begin with Zionism, the Jewish people's movement to build an independent polity in their historical homeland. The introduction of Zionism into the maelstrom of Middle East politics galvanized what was already a highly unstable environment into a framework for regional war. Facile though it may sound, without Zionism there would have been no State of Israel and, without Israel, no context of comprehensive conflict.

What began as a mere idea in the mid-nineteenth century had, by the beginning of the twentieth, motivated thousands of European and Middle Eastern Jews to leave their homes and settle in unthinkably distant Palestine. The secret of Zionism lay in its wedding of modern nationalist notions to the Jewish people's mystical, millennial attachment to the Land of Israel (*Eretz Yisrael*). That power sustained the *Yishuv*, or Jewish community, in Palestine throughout the depredations of Ottoman rule and during World War I, when many Jewish leaders were expelled as enemy (mostly Russian) aliens. By war's end, the British had supplanted the Turks in Palestine and, under the Balfour Declaration, pledged to build a Jewish national home in the country.

Under the British Mandate, the *Yishuv* swelled with refugees from European anti-Semitism—first Polish, then German—and established social, economic, educational institutions that in a short time surpassed those furnished by Britain. By the 1940s, the *Yishuv* was a powerhouse in the making: dynamic, inventive, ideologically and politically pluralistic. Drawing on Western and Eastern European models, the Jews of Palestine created new vehicles for agrarian settlement (the communal *kibbutz* and cooperative *moshav*), a viable socialist economy with systems for national health, reforestation, and infrastructure development, a respectable university, and a symphony orchestra—and to defend them all, an underground citizens' army, the *Haganah*.[2] Though the British had steadily abandoned their support for a Jewish national home, that home was already a fact: an inchoate, burgeoning state.

This was precisely what the Arabs of Palestine resented. Centuries-established, representing the majority of the country's total population, the Palestinian Arabs regarded the *Yishuv* as a tool of Western imperialism, an alien culture inimical to their traditional way of life. Though the Jews had long been tolerated, albeit in an inferior status, by Islam, that protection in no sense entitled them to sovereignty over part of Islam's heartland or authority over Muslims. No less than their co-religionists straining under French rule in Syria and North Africa, or under the British in Iraq and Egypt, the Palestinian Arabs earnestly sought independence. They, too, had been promised a state by Britain, and demanded to see that promise fulfilled.[3] But independence under Jewish dominion could never be an option for the Arabs, only a more odious form of colonialism.

So it happened that every wave of Jewish immigration into Palestine—in 1920, 1921, and 1929—ignited ever more violent Arab reactions, culminating in the 1936 Arab revolt against both the Jews and the British. The insurrection lasted three years and resulted in the deportation of much of the Palestinian Arabs' leadership and the weakening of their economy. The *Yishuv*, conversely, grew strong. Yet victory was denied the Jews. Fearful of a backlash by Muslims throughout their empire, Britain issued a White Paper that effectively nullified the Balfour Declaration. Erupting shortly thereafter, World War II saw Zionist leader David Ben-Gurion declaring his movement's intention to "fight the White Paper as if there were no war and to fight the war as if there were no White Paper." By contrast, Hajj Amin al-Husayni, the British-appointed Mufti and self-proclaimed representative of the Palestinian Arabs, threw in his lot with Hitler.[4]

The Arab revolt of 1936–39 had another, even more fateful outcome. If previously the conflict had been between the Jews and Arabs in Palestine, it was now between Zionism and Arabs everywhere. Palestine's plight aroused a groundswell of sympathy throughout the surrounding Arab lands, where a new nationalist spirit was blossoming. Pan-Arabism, another outgrowth of modern European thought, proclaimed the existence of a single Arab people whose identity transcended race, religion, or family ties. That people was now called upon to avenge three centuries of humiliation by the West, and to erase the artificial borders (of Syria, Lebanon, Transjordan, Palestine, and Iraq) created by colonialism. Though the dream of a single, independent Arab state extending from the Taurus Mountains in the north and the Atlas in the west, from the Persian Gulf to the tip of the Arabian Peninsula, would remain just that—a dream— the emergence of an Arab world bound by sentiment and culture had become a political fact.[5] From the late 1930s onward, increasingly, incidents in Palestine could set off riots in Baghdad and Cairo, in Homs and Tunis and Casablanca.

Nobody understood this process better, or feared it more, than the Arab leaders of the time. Lacking any constitutional legitimacy, opposed to free expression, this assortment of prime ministers, princes, sultans, and emirs, were highly sensitive to outpourings of public opinion—the Arab "street." The leaders' task, then, lay in discerning which way the street was heading and maneuvering to stay ahead of it. The street was fulminating against Zionism. Responding to that rage, locked in bitter rivalries with one another, Arab regimes became deeply embroiled in Palestine. The conflict would never again be local.

The British, meanwhile, shrewdly took advantage of Zionism's neutralization during the war to placate Arab nationalism, fostering the creation of an Arab League whose members could display their unity and preserve their independence all at once.[6] But then, with victory in Europe assured, Zionism came back with a vengeance. Incensed by the continuation of the White Paper, inflamed by the Holocaust, many of whose six million victims might have lived had that document never existed, the Zionists declared war on the Mandate— first the right-wing *Irgun* militia of Menachem Begin, then the mainstream *Haganah*.

War-worn, hounded by an American president, Harry Truman, who was publicly committed to the Zionist cause, Britain by 1947 was ready to hand the entire Palestine issue over to the United Nations. The consequence came with the passage of UN General Assembly Resolution 181. This provided for the creation of two states, one Arab and the other Jewish, in Palestine, and an international regime for Jerusalem. The Zionists approved of the plan but the Arabs, having already rejected an earlier, more favorable (for them) partition offer from Britain, stood firm in their demand for sovereignty over Palestine in full.

On November 30, 1947, the day after the UN approved the partition resolution, Palestinian guerrillas attacked Jewish settlements throughout the country and blockaded the roads between them. The Zionists' response was restraint, lest the UN, shocked by the violence it wrought, deem partition unworkable. But Palestinian resistance proved too effective, and in April of 1948, the Jews went on the offensive. The operation succeeded in reopening the roads and saving the settlements, but it also expedited the large-scale flight of Palestinian civilians that had begun in November. Spurred by reports of massacres such as that which occurred at the village of Deir Yassin near Jerusalem, between 650,000 and 750,000 Palestinians either fled or were driven into neighboring countries. Most expected to return in the near future, after the combined Arab forces intervened and expelled the Zionist "usurpers."

Rigorous attempts would be made to prevent such intervention. Jewish leaders secretly sought a *modus vivendi* with 'Abdallah, Transjordan's Hashemite monarch, based on their common fear of Palestinian nationalism. The U.S State Department, never enamored of the Zionist dream and deeply opposed to partition, championed an international trusteeship plan for Palestine. Proposals were floated for a binational Arab-Jewish state or an Arab federation in which the Jews would enjoy local autonomy.[7] None of these initiatives succeeded, however, and when, on May 14, the British Mandate ended, the Jewish state was declared. Henceforth, the Jews were Israelis, while Palestine's Arabs became, simply, the Palestinians.

It was also that day that the civil strife burning since November exploded into a regional clash between Israel and the five nearest Arab countries. Always the most truculent of anti-zionists, Syria and Iraq led the invasion, followed by Lebanon and Transjordan. Egypt could not resist the momentum, and fearing the territorial expansion of other Arab states, hastened to join. Thousands of troops, fortified by bombers, fighter planes and tanks, swept forward in what was cavalierly described as a "police action."

That action succeeded in throwing the nascent state on the deep defensive as Arab armies penetrated through the Negev and Galilee, reaching the approaches to Tel Aviv, Israel's largest city. The 100,000 Jews of Jerusalem were subject to a brutal siege. Yet Ben-Gurion refused to despair. Short but imposing, a visionary with a pragmatist's appreciation of power, he exploited UN-mediated truces to refresh and rearm his forces. That advantage, together with the Arabs' egregious lack of command, dramatically turned the tide.

By the fall of 1948, the newly constituted Israel Defense Forces (IDF) had managed to bypass the Arab blockade of Jerusalem and to fight Transjordan's British-led Arab Legion, if not to victory, then at least to a stalemate. Also stymied were the Syrian advances in the north and Iraq's incursion into the country's center. But the brunt of the Israelis' armed might was aimed at Egypt, the largest Arab contingent. Egyptian troops were driven from the vicinity of Jerusalem and Tel Aviv and out of the entire Negev but for a small pocket of men. These held out until early 1949, when Cairo sued for an armistice.

The War of Independence, as the Israelis called it, had ended. The Jewish state had captured some 30 percent more territory than the UN had allotted it, and, by dint of the Palestinian exodus, a solid Jewish majority. Only the threat of forfeiting that majority and possibly inviting a war with Britain—Egypt's and Jordan's protector—deterred the IDF from conquering the West Bank and Gaza as well. In a final operation launched in March 1949, after the armistice with Jordan, Israeli troops took Umm al-Rashrash on the Red Sea, an area that had originally been partitioned to the Jews. Renamed Eilat, the port would serve as Israel's lifeline through the Gulf of Aqaba and the Straits of Tiran, to the markets of Africa and Asia.

Against what had seemed to them near-impossible odds, young commanders such as Yigal Allon and Yitzhak Rabin had won a prodigious military victory, but at an almost pyrrhic price. Six thousand Jews had been killed—1 percent of the population—and scores of villages bombed and decimated. Despite repeated assaults by IDF troops, the Old City of Jerusalem remained in Hashemite hands, as did the Latrun Corridor leading up to it. The Arab Legion also uprooted the Jewish settlements of the Etzion Bloc, outside Bethlehem, and occupied the West Bank of the Jordan River. Syria, too, retained possession of areas beyond the international frontier. All of Israel's major population and industrial centers were within easy artillery range of one or another Arab army. At its narrowest point, the country was a mere nine miles wide, easily bifurcated by a Jordanian or an Iraqi thrust from the East, with nowhere to fall back to but the sea.

The mixed bag of Israel's victory, added to the aggregate trauma of Jewish history, created an ambivalence within the Israelis: an overblown confidence in their invincibility alongside an equally inflated sense of doom. To the West, Israelis portrayed themselves as inadequately armed Davids struggling against Philistine giants, and to the Arabs, as Goliaths of incalculable strength. Visiting Washington prior to becoming IDF chief of staff in December 1953, Moshe Dayan told Pentagon officials that Israel faced mortal danger, and, in the same breath, that it could smash the combined Arab armies in weeks.[8]

No such antitheses plagued the Arabs, however. For them, the 1948 war was *al-Nakbah*, "the Disaster," and an unmitigated one at that. The victory parades held in Cairo and Damascus could not disguise the fact that the Arab states had failed in their first postcolonial test. The annexation of the West Bank by Transjordan (ensconced on both sides of the river now, the country would soon drop the "trans"), and Egypt's occupation of Gaza, only underscored the Palestinians' loss of a state that was to have included both territories. Defeat at the hands of the relatively small, formerly disparaged Jewish army only redoubled their humiliation.[9] That defeat could produce no heroes, only embittered soldiers such as Gamal Abdel Nasser, one of the young officers who had held out in that Negev pocket, who now sought revenge not only against Israel, but against the inept Arab rulers it had humbled.

The Impossible Peace

The General Armistice Agreements (GAA) signed between Israel and its four adjacent adversaries—Egypt, Jordan, Lebanon, and Syria, in that order—in the first half of 1949 deeply influenced Arab-Israeli relations over the next nineteen years. Under its ambiguous terms, one side, the Arab, claimed full belligerent rights, including the right to renew active hostilities at will, and denied the other side any form of legitimacy or recognition. As a diplomatic document, the GAA was *sui generis*. Intended as the basis "for a permanent peace in Palestine"—according to Ralph Bunche, the UN official who received the Nobel Peace Prize for mediating it—the Armistice in fact perpetuated the conflict and prepared the ground for war.

The Israelis had been duped. Thinking that they could retain the territories they had conquered beyond the Partition borders and keep the refugees out, Ben-Gurion and other Israeli leaders had spared Arab armies further punishment from the IDF. Attaining peace was only a matter of months, if not weeks, they believed. Yet no sooner had their forces withdrawn when the Arab governments declared the Armistice no more than a temporary truce under which Israeli goods could be boycotted and Israel shipping denied passage through the Straits of Tiran and the Suez Canal. There was no Israel, they claimed, only an Israeli army, and no Israeli borders but arbitrary Armistice lines pitted with Demilitarized Zones (DZ's) of questionable ownership.

So the agreement initially hailed as a trophy for Israel soon became its millstone. An attempt to challenge the Suez blockade in the Security Council in 1951 was promptly ignored by Egypt while, in the north, Syrian forces advanced further and occupied strategic hilltops over the Armistice line. The Mixed Armistice Commissions (MACs) created to handle day-to-day affairs became arenas for recriminations and counter-recriminations; most ceased functioning altogether. Efforts by a UN Palestine Conciliation Commission, by the U.S. and British governments, and by a procession of independent would-be mediators failed to move Israel and the Arab states substantially in the direction of peace.

Yet not all Arab leaders were opposed to peace, in principle at least, especially a peace that brought them territorial assets. While publicly clamoring for war, appeasing their "streets," some leaders sought secret agreements with the Zionists. Thus, Syrian dictator Husni Za'im clandestinely offered to resettle 300,000 refugees, but only in return for gaining control over half of the Sea of Galilee. 'Abdallah of Jordan wanted a corridor between his newly annexed West Bank and the Mediterranean, and Egypt's King Faruq demanded the entire Negev desert—62 percent of Israel's territory. Ben-Gurion, however, opposed any unilateral concessions of land, preferring to maintain the status quo in which Israel could develop its infrastructure, absorb immigrants, and gather strength. But the failure to make peace ultimately owed less to his obduracy than to the Arabs' inability to deal with Israel in any formal way. Thus, the Jordanian cabinet prevailed upon 'Abdallah to abandon his talks with the Israelis, and Egyptian emissaries explained that an agreement with the Zionists now or even in the foreseeable future would surely cost them their lives.[10]

The efforts of Arab rulers to pander to public opinion proved futile eventually, as one by one they fell. Husni Za'im was barely six months in power before being overthrown and executed, setting the pattern for another sixteen regimes that would rise and dissolve in Syria in almost as many years. Next was 'Abdallah, felled by a Palestinian bullet outside Jerusalem's Al-Aqsa mosque in July 1951, while his grandson and later successor, Hussein, looked on. Iraq's Hashemite king, Faisal, would be dismembered by a savage Baghdad mob in 1958, along with Prime Minister Nuri al-Sa'id, another vociferous anti-Zionist who had secretly contacted the Israelis.[11] Egypt's turn came in July 1952 with Faruq's ouster by a clique of self-styled Free Officers under General Muhammad Naguib.

Within a year, Naguib himself was deposed by the true strongman behind the regime, the inspired and purportedly moderate colonel: Gamal Abdel Nasser.

Here was a man with whom the Israelis thought they could do business. Egyptian and Israeli representatives again engaged in secret contacts, even producing a letter (unsigned) from Nasser to Israeli leaders. But the basic Egyptian position had not altered: Peace was unthinkable under current circumstances, and should those circumstances change, would become possible only once Israel ceded the entire Negev desert. By 1953, as Egypt began sponsoring raids by Palestinian guerrillas (fida'iyyun in Arabic: self-sacrificers) into Israel, and its propaganda renewed calls for a "second round," Ben-Gurion had come to view the contacts as a ploy, an attempt to anesthetize Israel before slaughtering it.

The following year, 1954, undistinguished elsewhere in the world, was a Middle Eastern watershed. That year, the Soviet Union, having supported Israel since its creation, having recognized and armed it, switched its allegiance to the other side. The USSR indeed had nothing more to gain from Zionism—the British empire was dying—and everything to gain in terms of placating the new, post-colonial governments, securing its vulnerable southern border, and threatening the West's oil supplies. "Deserving of condemnation [is] . . . the State of Israel, which from the first days of its existence began to threaten its neighbors," declared Communist party First Secretary Nikita Khrushchev, who further accused Israel of plotting with imperialism to "crudely ravage the natural treasures of the region." Short of destroying Israel, the USSR endorsed all and every means of realizing "Arab rights in Palestine." [12]

The cold war had come to the Middle East, and 1954 was also the year that the U.S. and Britain aspired to defend the region through an alliance of Northern Tier states (Iran, Turkey, Pakistan) and their Arab neighbors. Viewing the Arab-Israeli conflict as an obstacle to the bloc, Anglo-American planners sought to remove it with a secret peace initiative. Code-named Alpha, the plan was to coerce Israel into conceding large chunks of territory in return for an Arab pledge of nonbelligerency. The assumed key to the plan's success was Nasser, who was close to the Americans—the CIA had quietly assisted his coup—and who stood to gain substantially from his cooperation. Payment would include boatloads of American arms as well as Egypt's long-coveted land bridge across the Negev. [13]

The physical link between Egypt and the East was looming even more prominently in Nasser's thinking. The officer who had risen to power on the promise of reforms at home now discovered the world beyond. He declared Egypt an Arab country, a country nonaligned in the Cold War, and began speaking of concentric spheres of interest—the Arab and Islamic worlds, Africa—at the core of which lay Egypt and at the center of Egypt, Gamal Abdel Nasser.

His challenges set, Nasser lost no time in meeting them. He concluded an agreement for ending Britain's seventy-two-year occupation of the Canal Zone, then turned around and thwarted Britain's attempt to append Iraq to the Northern Tier—the so-called Baghdad Pact. Subtly at first, he adopted socialist ideas, blending them with both Arab and Egyptian nationalism. Islamic extremists consequently branded him a heretic and tried to take his life, but Nasser remained undeterred. Escaping from one assassination attempt, he reportedly exclaimed, "They can kill Nasser but another will take his place! The revolution will live on!"[14]

The drama around him mounted, and yet Nasser had all but ignored the most poignant of Arab issues: Palestine. While maintaining the blockade and a moderate level of guerrilla activity, the Egyptian leader downplayed the conflict with Israel, keeping it—as diplomats liked to say—"in the icebox." But the "street" demanded more. The mere existence of the Jewish state was abhorrent to Arabs, a reminder of Palestine's plundering and a bridgehead for imperialism's return. More pressing on Nasser was the fact that not only did Israel exist, but that it asserted its existence militantly.

In reprisal for guerrilla attacks, special IDF units launched punishing raids across the border. In one such action alone, in the West Bank town of Qibya in October 1953, Israeli commandos led by Major Ariel Sharon blew up dozens of houses, killing sixty-nine civilians—inadvertently, he claimed. To the Syrians' chagrin, Israel drained the Hula swamp in the northern Galilee, and cultivated the DZ's. Nor was Nasser spared this activism. In the summer of 1954, the Israeli ship *Bat Galim* sailed into the Suez Canal, where its seizure by Egyptian authorities caused an international scandal. Finally, in an ill-conceived scheme to thwart Britain's evacuation from the Canal, Israeli agents attempted to foment chaos in Egypt by vandalizing public institutions. Eleven Egyptians, Jews, were arrested and charged with treason.

Outraged and humiliated, Nasser intensified his support for the Palestinian guerrillas. He refused to release Israel's boat or to pardon the arsonists, two of whom were eventually hanged; the rest were sentenced to prison. Also rejected was the Alpha plan, in spite of its territorial enticements. Ben-Gurion's response was quick and exacting: the largest retaliation against regular Arab troops since 1948. The Gaza Raid, as it came to be called, on February 28, 1955 claimed the lives of fifty-one Egyptian soldiers and eight Israelis, and inaugurated the countdown to war.

So throughout 1955 the violence spiraled. Nasser went on the offensive against Israel with guerrilla operations and, politically, against the conservative Arab dynasties—the Hashemites of Jordan and Iraq, the Saudis—who opposed his intensifying radicalism. Then, in September, Nasser delivered a blow to Israel and Arab monarchs alike. Operating through Czech suppliers of Soviet arms, he purchased more tanks, guns and jets than those amassed by all the Middle East's armies combined. In one *coup de théâtre*, the USSR had leapfrogged the Northern Tier and landed at the crossroads of Asia and Africa, while Nasser soared to a status unprecedented in modern Arab history. Transcending the borders contrived by colonialism, Nasser now preached directly to Arab populations on the need for *wahda* and *karama*—unity and dignity—under his, and Egypt's, aegis.

Ben-Gurion observed Nasser's ascension with deepening anxiety. He had long prophesied the emergence of a strong and charismatic individual, another Ataturk, who could unite the Arab world for war. Suddenly that nightmare had materialized. It was only a matter of time, Ben-Gurion reasoned, before the Egyptian army absorbed its massive influx of arms and Nasser lost the excuse not to use them. His prediction proved accurate: the six months following the Czech arms deal witnessed large-scale border fighting, retaliations, and guerrilla attacks that took the lives of hundreds.[15]

By the spring of 1956, Ben-Gurion had decided on the need for a conclusive showdown with Egypt. Together with protégés Moshe Dayan, the IDF chief of staff, and Defense Ministry director Shimon Peres, he conceived of an operation to defeat the Egyptian army and deflate Nasser's prestige. All Israel required was a Great Power to provide it with arms and protection from Soviet intervention. Having rebuffed Israel's repeated requests for a defense treaty, the United States was out of the question, as was Great Britain, which had threatened to bomb Israel in reaction to its raids into Jordan. But finally an alliance was formed with France, which was also at war with Arab nationalism—in Algeria—and which shared Israel's socialist ideals.

Ben-Gurion prepared for war but Nasser had another confrontation in mind. On July 26, just weeks after negotiating a treaty with Britain and France over the future of the Suez Canal, he unilaterally nationalized the waterway. Following Nasser's threats to Britain's allies in Jordan and Iraq, and to French rule in Algeria, the Europeans were ready to employ force in compelling Nasser to "disgorge" the Canal. But just as Israel needed Great Power backing for its own action against Egypt, so, too, did Britain and France require the support of a superpower, the United States.

The Eisenhower administration was hardly enamored of Nasser, given his nonalignment policies and his arms deals with the USSR. The latest American disappointment came in the first half of 1956 with the advent of Gamma, another secret initiative to purchase Egyptian nonbelligerency with a swath of Israeli land. President Eisenhower sent a personal emissary, Robert B. Anderson, a Texas oilman and former Treasury secretary, to mediate the deal. He found Ben-Gurion closed to territorial concessions but willing to meet Nasser anywhere, anytime. But Nasser first made light of the mission—Why risk talking with Israel for the sake of the Baghdad Pact? he asked—then refused to receive Anderson at all. Thereafter, Eisenhower approved another top-secret project—Omega—geared to toppling Nasser by all methods except assassination.[16]

Washington indeed disliked Nasser, but it abhorred European colonialism even more. Though signatory with France and Britain to the 1950 Tripartite Declaration prohibiting any attempt to alter Middle East borders by force, the United States refused to regard the Canal's nationalization as such an attempt, or to sanction the use of force against Egypt. A succession of international initiatives followed, all aimed at resolving the crisis, all notable for their lack of teeth. Exasperated, the French finally turned to their Israeli allies, and convinced the British to do so as well. On October 24, in the Paris suburb of Sèvres, representatives from the three countries signed a top-secret protocol. Israeli forces would feign an assault on Suez, thus providing the Europeans with an excuse to occupy the Canal, ostensibly to protect it. In return, the Israelis would receive air and naval support as its forces destroyed Egypt's army in Sinai and opened the Straits of Tiran.[17]

The second Arab-Israeli war, known in Israel as the Sinai Campaign, and among the Arabs as the Tripartite Aggression, began in the afternoon of October 29th. Israeli paratroopers landed in the Mitla Pass, twenty-four miles east of the Canal. With the pretext established, the Powers issued their ultimatum which the Egyptians, as expected, rebuffed. Dayan's armored columns, meanwhile, broke through the Egyptian lines in central and southern Sinai and rolled through Egyptian-occupied Gaza. General Muhammad 'Abd al-Hakim 'Amer, the Egyptian commander-in-chief, panicked and ordered his troops to retreat. Israel's victory was swift—too swift, in fact, for Britain and France. The Anglo-French armada dallied at sea, while French and British leaders wavered under international pressure. Not until November 4 did the invasion commence, by which time the Egyptians could claim they had never been driven from Sinai but had rather retreated tactically in order to defend their homes.

Operation Musketeer, the invasion's codename, was a consummate military success. The Egyptian army was shattered and three-quarters of the Canal reoccupied. Politically, though, the results were disastrous. Cold war and cultural differences disappeared as the world community united in condemning the attack, and under the dual threat of American sanctions and Soviet missiles, the French and the British buckled. Their troops ignominiously withdrew and their flags lowered forever over the Middle East.

The Israelis, by contrast, controlling all of Sinai, Gaza, and the Straits of Tiran, were not so quick to retreat. Though also subject to enormous pressures from the U.S. and Russia, Israel still enjoyed international sympathy as the victim of blockades and terrorism, and Ben-Gurion had strong support at home. While bending to demands to pull his troops from Sinai, he dug in his heels over guarantees for free passage through the Straits of Tiran and for protection against border raids. The Armistice, under which Egypt had exercised belligerency against Israel, was dead, he declared.

Four months of breakneck diplomacy would follow, during which Abba Eban, Israel's highly articulate ambassador to Washington and the UN, strove to secure his country's irreducible interests. But the role of rescuer fell not to Eban or to any other Israeli but to Canada's Foreign Minister, Lester "Mike" Pearson. Uniquely trusted by all parties involved—Arabs, Israelis, Europeans— Pearson came up with the notion of creating a multi-national United Nations

Emergency Force (UNEF) to oversee the Anglo-French withdrawal from Egypt. He then applied that concept to Israeli forces in Sinai. The idea was to deploy UN troops from a consortium of countries along the Egyptian-Israeli border, in the Gaza Strip, and at Sharm al-Sheikh overlooking the Straits of Tiran. Nasser, predictably, resisted the idea, which struck him as a qualification of Egyptian sovereignty and a reward for Israeli aggression. Ben-Gurion, too, raised objections, noting that Nasser could evict the force whenever he saw fit.

The logjam was eventually broken by two "good faith" agreements—one between Nasser and UN Secretary General Dag Hammarskjold and the other between Secretary of State John Foster Dulles and Golda Meir, Israel's foreign minister. Hammarskjold promised Nasser that Egypt would have the right to remove UNEF, but only after the General Assembly had considered whether the peacekeepers had completed their mission. Dulles pledged that the U.S. would regard any Egyptian attempt to revive the Tiran blockade as an act of war to which Israel could respond in self-defense under Article 51 of the UN Charter. In such an event, Meir would undertake to inform the United States of Israel's intentions. Britain and France also acceded to this agreement, as did Canada and several other Western countries—Sweden, Belgium, Italy, and New Zealand. Several glitches ensued when Egyptian troops returned to Gaza and when Dulles reiterated his support for the Armistice, but by March 11, 1957, UNEF was in position and the last Israeli soldier left Sinai. [18]

Through it all, the Arab-Israeli conflict remained an immutable fixture of Middle Eastern life. From a local dispute in the 1920s and '30s, it had expanded in the 1940s to engulf the region and then, in the '50s, the world. The context of inter-Arab and Great Power rivalry, of Israeli fears and bravado, and of abiding bitterness on both sides, had coalesced. If a new status quo had been created, it was one of inherent instability, a situation so combustible that the slightest spark could ignite it.

Cold Wars/Hot Wars

The 1956 war, strangely, had benefited both sides. Buoyed by Egyptian propaganda, Nasser claimed political and military victory in the war; that he had single-handedly defeated the imperialists, and mobilized world opinion against Israel, which had not dared take on Egypt alone. The Suez Canal, now restored to its inalienable owner, would make Egypt a regional, if not an international, superpower.[19]

The Israelis believed that the war had brought them ten years of quiet at least, a solid decade of development. IDF arms had taught the West that Israel was an established fact and could not be divvied up piecemeal by the Powers. Gone were the Alphas and the Gammas. Instead there were close relations with a wide range of Asian and African countries, oil from Iran, and sophisticated jets—Ouragans, Mystères, and Mirages—from France. The French also helped construct what would become Israel's boldest and most controversial achievement in the security field: the nuclear reactor near the southern town of Dimona.

But along with these pluses, there was also the downside to 1956. If the Israelis' confidence in their military prowess had been reinforced, so too had the fear of international pressure. The Arabs possessed incontrovertible proof that the "Zionist entity"—"Israel" was too repugnant to pronounce—was an imperialist tool, aggressive but ideologically weak. If the second round had been more successful than the first, the third would prove triumphant, they believed. Nasser had only to wage it.[20]

Fortunately for Israel, Nasser did not fall victim to the Arabs' "Suez syndrome" or to the lure of his own propaganda. He knew that the Egyptian army had been bested by the IDF, and that another war, however heralded, had to be delayed as long as possible, until the Arabs were strong. He cooperated with UNEF and kept only token forces in Sinai; Israeli ships passed unmolested through Tiran. For all Nasser's belligerent rhetoric, the Palestine issue was once again, firmly, "in the icebox."

Instead, Nasser thrust his energies into a yet more radical blend of Arab socialism and nationalism—Nasserism—and a series of single-party movements to animate the masses and jump-start Egypt's economy. Few of these efforts bore fruit. Desperate for success, Nasser edged toward a closer alliance with the USSR and escalated his conflict with the Middle East monarchies—what one scholar termed the Arab Cold War.

A savage succession of coups, assassinations, and bombings ensued, culminating in the Iraqi revolution of 1958 and the attempted overthrow of the Lebanese and Jordanian governments. The latter was averted only through Western military intervention as President Eisenhower, having ousted Britain and France, sought to fill that void with the doctrine that bore his name. From now on, the United States would defend any Middle Eastern country threatened by communism or its allies, the most obvious of which was Egypt.[21]

Along with his setbacks of 1958, however, Nasser also registered a stunning achievement in Egypt's unification with Syria. There, the regime had also adopted an extreme socialist, pro-Soviet line, and the United Arab Republic, as the new entente was called, epitomized the radical Arab ideal. A year later, Nasser created an Entity in Gaza, a kind of government-in-exile which, though devoid of real authority, expressed his commitment to the Palestinian cause. His crowning accomplishment, however, came in 1960 with the Soviet-financed construction of the Aswan Dam, "the greatest engineering feat in the Middle East since the pyramids." The "street" was ecstatic. With the linking of the two halves of the Arab world, east and west, and the stranglehold around Israel tightened, expectations of a military effort to liberate Palestine rose. Nasser could not ignore them, especially when, in February 1960, Syria seemed threatened with war.[22]

It started with an Israeli attempt to cultivate the DZ's along the northern border. Syrian troops fired on the tractors and IDF guns blasted at Syrian positions on the overlooking Golan Heights. As friction heated, the Soviets stepped in and informed Nasser that Israel was planning to invade Syria, and even supplied a date for the attack: February 22, UAR day. Nasser had received similar warnings in the past, but in view of the sharp pitch of Arab opinion, he chose this time to act. Two Egyptian divisions, including the crack 4th Armored, were rushed into Sinai. The commanders of UNEF were told to be ready to evacuate the peninsula within twenty-four hours, should hostilities erupt.

It was a splendid display of muscle flexing that caught Israel, with only thirty tanks in the south, completely off-guard. Frantically, the army mobilized while Israeli diplomats scurried to assure foreign governments against any warlike designs on either Syria or Egypt. Tensions remained ultra-high until the beginning of March when, just as quietly as they entered, the Egyptian troops slipped out of Sinai.[23] Called Operation Retama, after the fragrant desert plant (*Rotem*, in Hebrew) by the IDF, the episode was a major trauma for Israel and no less a triumph for Nasser. Memories of it would still be fresh, and its lessons seemingly clear, in 1967.

But the Aswan Dam and Retama were merely exceptions in the otherwise rueful saga of the UAR. Under 'Abd al-Hakim 'Amer, whose administration of the joint government in Damascus was as inept as his generalship in 1956, the union began to unravel. Corruption and despotism reigned as unyielding state control was imposed on Syria's traditionally open economy. Syrian officers were also incensed, finding themselves outside the loops of power. In September 1961, a clique of these officers, among them Salah Jadid and Hafez al-Assad, staged a successful coup and declared Syria's departure from the union.[24] 'Amer and his staff were ingloriously herded onto a plane and whisked back to Cairo. Their sole memento of the United Arab Republic was the name itself, which Egypt unilaterally retained.

The period of "The Secession" (*infisal*) marked the downswing in the heretofore ascendant career of Abdel Nasser. Physically sick—he contracted diabetes that year—Nasser also suffered through a stormy relationship with Khrushchev, for whom the Egyptian was never quite radical enough. The country's economy was in free fall. The only illumination in this gloom came from the marked improvement in Egypt's relations with the United States, under the new administration of John F. Kennedy.

In contrast to the more confrontational Eisenhower, Kennedy believed that carrots would prove more effective than sticks in containing Soviet influence in the Middle East and keeping Nasser out of trouble. Using what one top Kennedy aide, Chester Bowles, called the "great unseen weapon," Washington offered Nasser semiannual shipments of wheat and other basic commodities, as an incentive "to forsake the microphone for the bulldozer." The policy worked for a time. Nasser appeared to withdraw from the farrago of inter-Arab politics and to focus more on domestic affairs. Though Egypt's support for militant liberation movements, particularly in Africa, and its championship of the non-aligned movement still irked the Americans, a door to dialogue had cracked open. Evidence of the change could be found in the warm correspondence between the two presidents ("differences will always remain between us," Nasser wrote, and Kennedy replied, quoting him, "but mutual understanding will keep those differences within limits not to be exceeded") and in expanding American aid, which, by 1962, was feeding 40 percent of Egypt's population. [25]

But other events in 1962 sowed the seeds of disaster in the American-Egyptian détente, and in Nasser's fortunes generally. The problem was Yemen. The Imam of the remote southern Arabian country, Badr, was overthrown in September by a group of Free Officers under a Gen. 'Abdallah al-Sallal. Badr fled to Riyadh, where he sought and secured Saudi backing for a counterinsurgency. Al-Sallal turned to Cairo.

Al-Sallal's appeal found Nasser still reeling from the UAR's dissolution and the collapse of his economic policies, and fearing for the loyalty of some of his senior army officers. The latter, by providing tactical support to al-Sallal's troops, presented Nasser with a fait accompli. He accepted it, though, deeming Yemen a good place for occupying the army's attention, as well as for drubbing his Saudi rivals and even for harassing Britain's colony in Aden. Khrushchev, eager to avenge his recent embarrassment in the Cuban missile crisis, also gave his blessing.[26]

Thus began an entanglement so futile and fierce that the imminent Vietnam War could have easily been dubbed America's Yemen.[27] Prisoners were routinely executed, bodies mutilated, entire villages wiped out. Egyptian forces bombed royalist depots in Saudi Arabia and, for the first time in the history of any Arab army, unleashed poison gas. Besides igniting the previously cold conflict between Arab "progressives" and "reactionaries," the war also soured the all-too-brief honeymoon between Egypt and the United States. In Nasser's intervention Kennedy perceived the beginnings of Soviet penetration of South Arabia, and through his special mediator, Elsworth Bunker, he hammered out an agreement whereby the Saudis stopped aiding Badr and Egypt withdrew its troops. But while Riyadh complied, Cairo broke faith, sending even larger forces to Yemen. "A breakdown of disengagement . . . could not but lead to a situation in which the US and the UAR, instead of moving closer together, would drift further apart," Kennedy warned on October 19, just over a month before his assassination.[28]

It seemed inconceivable that the Arabs' situation could have grown bleaker—and yet it did. The ruling regime in Iraq, whose relations with Egypt had hardly been cordial, fell violently in February 1963, when its leaders were shot by radicals of the Ba'th (Renaissance) party. Talk of a tripartite union—Egypt, Syria, and Iraq—resulted in the drafting of a joint constitution, but little else. A bloodbath ensued as Nasserist sympathizers were purged from the Iraqi army and then, as a result of an abortive coup in July, from the Syrian army as well. Hundreds were killed, executed, or caught in crossfires.

Such events, the deepening malaise of Egypt's foreign relations and of inter-Arab affairs in general, could not but gladden the Israelis. With the UAR disbanded and Nasser's army bogged down in Yemen, the danger of a third round of Arab-Israeli fighting seemed remote. Further assurance came from the momentous improvement in U.S.-Israel relations inaugurated by Kennedy. Unlike the Republicans, who did not enjoy the support of most American Jews and had little affection for Israel, the new Democratic president owed much of his narrow electoral victory to Jewish votes and spoke warmly of the Jewish state. "The United States has a special relationship with Israel comparable only to that which it has with Britain," he told Foreign Minister Meir; "I think it is quite clear that in the case of invasion the United States would come to the support of Israel." The commitment was concretized by the unprecedented sale of $75 million of U.S. weapons to Israel, a third of which was earmarked for Hawk ground-to-air missiles.[29]

Yet, U.S.-Israel relations were hardly friction-free. The Kennedy administration, no less than Eisenhower's, objected to Israel's retaliation policy, its attempts to divert the Jordan River, and its resistance to repatriating Palestinian refugees. Most galling for Kennedy, a committed nonproliferationist, was Israel's nuclear program. Israel's production of fissionable material, he feared, might prompt the Arabs to install Soviet missiles on their territory, or even to launch a preemptive strike. Nasser had already cited Israel's supposed capability as a pretext for initiating his own missile-making effort, one that employed German and ex-Nazi scientists rather than Russians. Israel's repeated pledges that nothing untoward was transpiring at Dimona, and that it would "not be the first [country] to introduce nuclear weapons to the Middle East," failed to appease the president. He insisted on semi-annual inspections of the reactor, threatened to review all of America's security commitments to Israel if Ben-Gurion refused to cooperate, and proffered the Hawks in the hope that he would. Ben-Gurion argued that Israel's nuclear projects were its own sovereign business, its best guarantee against a second Holocaust. The Hawks were deployed around Dimona.[30]

But for all his mettle, his rigid jaw, and defiant corona of hair, Ben-Gurion was no longer the dynamo of 1948 and 1956. In spite of its improving relations with America, its alliance with France and ties with Africa and Asia, Israel increasingly seemed to Ben-Gurion less a regional power than a ghetto, isolated and exposed. "The UAR is getting stronger and stronger thanks to Soviet arms," he told French President Charles de Gaulle in 1961, "Nasser believes that in another year or two he can launch a lightning attack, destroy our airfields and bomb our cities." When, in the July Revolution celebrations of 1962, Nasser paraded his new missiles through the streets of Cairo—"they can hit any target south of Beirut," he boasted—the prime minister nearly panicked, then nearly panicked again the following May, when Egypt, Syria and Iraq pledged to join forces to liberate Palestine. "We alone are threatened each day with destruction," he now warned America's ambassador in Tel Aviv, "Nasser is clamoring for war with Israel, and if he achieves a nuclear capability, we're done for." The fact that the missiles were little more than V-1 rockets, "a costly failure and . . . not operational for several years at least," according to U.S. intelligence sources, and that the new Arab alliance was a sham, had little impact on Ben-Gurion. Urgently, he pressed for a deal with the French Marcel Dassault corporation for the completion of surface-to-surface missiles several years hence, in 1966 or 1967.[31]

Not that Israel was without causes for concern, a country surrounded by 639 miles of hostile borders and some thirty Arab divisions. Potentially, Egypt could again blockade Israel's shipping through the Straits of Tiran, and Syria, in control of the Jordan River's origins, could shut off its water supply. The Arabs' combined outlay on arms—some $938 million annually—was nearly twice that of Israel in spite of a fivefold increase in its defense budget. Though "only" 189 civilians had been killed by hostile fire between 1957 and 1967, down from 486 during the years 1949 to 1956, the danger of ambushes and bombings was constant.

Israelis never forgot any of this, yet for many of them the early 1960s was not a time of overriding fear but rather of relative security, even prosperity. The country, its population trebled to 2.9 million, enjoyed an annual growth rate of 10 percent, equaled only by Japan, and the fifth highest proportion of university graduates per capita in the world. The arts flourished, and the press was active and free. And while prejudice and discrimination, particularly against the new North African immigrants, were rife, there persisted an all-embracing sense of national purpose, a uniquely Israeli élan. Basically conservative—the Beatles were barred from performing in the country, ostensibly on security grounds but really to shield Israel's youth—the society was grappling with new ideas, an incipient materialism, and the emergence of a new generation of leaders, all with considerable confidence.

Much of that confidence was grounded in the IDF, an army that had burgeoned to 25 brigades, 175 jets, and nearly 1,000 battle tanks. The latter, armed with an improved 105-mm gun, provided the "mailed fist" that would break through Arab lines and secure an early victory before Israel's vulnerable cities could be devastated. The air force was also geared to delivering a "knock-out punch" to Egypt, with the understanding that with Egypt neutralized, other Arab armies would crumble. But the IDF was more than a mere fighting force; it was an ethos. Undergirding it were deeply held notions of volunteerism, of officers leading their men into battle (with the cry *Aharai!*—"After me!"), and social responsibility. With women required to serve eighteen months of regular duty, and men at least two years, followed by weeks of annual reserve training through age fifty-two, Israeli civilians were more like permanent soldiers on temporary leave. Highly informal—saluting and marching were rare—the IDF placed its emphasis on speed, improvisation, and a flexibility of command in which even junior officers could make on-the-spot, far-reaching decisions. The assumption was always that Israel would have no choice but to fight yet another war of survival, a war in which the enemy would, in spite of the IDF's growth, grossly outnumber it.[32]

Political confidence and military might combined in June 1963, when Israelis felt sufficiently sanguine to let Ben-Gurion, the father of their country, resign. The immediate cause was the never-ending scandal surrounding the 1954 sabotage operation in Egypt and the question of who ordered it, a former minister or elements in the security establishment. Ben-Gurion insisted on setting up an independent legal board to investigate the charges, as opposed to the internal governmental panel that had already exonerated the minister, and staked his office on it. He lost. The majority of his Mapai (Israel Workers' Party) colleagues sided with the panel, and Ben-Gurion quit in protest. Such a changing of the guard—for that was really what lay behind the controversy, the desire of political parvenus such as Golda Meir and Yigal Allon, to advance—could not have been possible in truly perilous times. Nor would the state have been entrusted to the person chosen to replace its founder, an aging technocrat by the name of Eshkol.

They could not have been less alike, Ben-Gurion and Levi Eshkol. Colorless, seemingly artless as well, Eshkol, the former minister of agriculture and finance, knew much about finance and farming but little of matters of state. Few politicians expected him to hold out for long, assuming that Ben-Gurion would someday return. Eshkol, himself, at first described his post as "caretaker prime minister." But when it came to Israel's relations with the Arab world, their perspectives were almost indistinguishable. Eshkol also believed that the Arabs wanted war and that Israel was at once militarily invincible and mortally vulnerable—what he called (characteristically, in Yiddish) *Shimshon der nebechdikker*—Samson the nerd. Thus, within a single month in 1963, the new prime minister could tell an IDF airborne unit that "Perhaps the time will come when you, the paratroopers, will determine Israel's borders. Our neighbors should not delude themselves that weakness prevents us from spilling blood," and then turn around at the War College and warn, "The danger we face is one of complete destruction."[33]

The Context Redux

Paradoxically, Israel owed some measure of its success to the Arabs, to their hostility that helped galvanize an otherwise factious society. Yet that same hostility also united the Arabs in visceral ways that their leaders were eager to harness. Thus, the proposed union of Egypt, Syria, and Iraq was presented first and foremost as a coalition against Israel because, for all their ideological affinity, there was no other issue on which all three could agree. Egypt portrayed its intervention in Yemen as a "step in the process of getting rid of Zionism," while the Jordan-Saudi (Ta'if) pact opposing that intervention signified "a front against Jewish aggression."[34]

But Palestine was a current that pulled in antithetical directions, joining but also splintering the Arab world as its leaders marshaled the cause against their rivals. With the stillbirth of the tripartite union in 1963, for example,

Syrian dictator General Hafiz Amin accused Nasser of "going soft" on Israel and "selling out Palestine for a few bushels of American wheat." Nasser countered by assailing Syria for "stabbing Egypt in the back" and trying to drag the Arabs into war before they were unified. Wasfi al-Tall, Jordan's perennial prime minister, joined with his archenemies in Damascus and excoriated Nasser's failure to fight Israel, his willingness to "hide behind UNEF's skirts."[35] The continuing plight of a million Palestinian refugees, together with Israel's assertive foreign and defense policies, ensured that the conflict would continue to serve as an agent for unity and discord.

By the beginning of 1964, the current seemed to swing away from divisiveness and back to cooperation. The pretext was Israel's plans to channel Galilee water to the Negev. Irrigated, the Arabs feared, the desert would support an additional three million Jewish immigrants and strengthen Israel's grip on Palestine. The Syrians would capitalize on that fear in their own competition with Nasser. Citing the Algerians' recent victory over France—a victory that owed much to Nasser's support—they called for a "people's war" to destroy the Zionist plot. Jordan and Saudi Arabia weighed in on the side of Damascus, and suddenly Egypt found itself isolated, the strongest Arab state but seemingly unwilling to act.

Still, Nasser would not be outmaneuvered. He responded with a dramatic idea: a summit meeting of all the Arab states. "Palestine supersedes all differences of opinion," Egypt's president declared, "For the sake of Palestine, we are ready to meet with all those with whom we have disagreements."[36]

Behind this bombast lay Nasser's reluctance to cede Syria the initiative on Palestine, and behind that, his need to avert a war from which Egypt would be unable to abstain or emerge victorious. He explained as much in a speech in Port Said a week before the summit:

> We cannot use force today because our circumstances will not allow us; be patient with us, the battle of Palestine can continue and the battle of the Jordan is part of the battle of Palestine. For I would lead you to disaster if I were to proclaim that I would fight at a time when I was unable to do so. I would not lead my country to disaster and would not gamble with its destiny.[37]

Avoiding war and saving face were motives enough to convene the summit, yet Nasser had an even stronger incentive: the need to get out of Yemen. From a small contingent in 1962, Egyptian forces in Yemen had swelled to over 50,000, severely straining an economy already on the brink. 'Amer and his coterie may have been growing rich on the war, but it had cost the country some $9.2 billion—about $.5 million for every Egyptian village—and thousands of casualties. Withdrawal, however, required negotiating an agreement with the Saudis, as well as with other hated "reactionaries"—a price that a warweary Nasser was finally willing to pay.

The largest gathering of Arab leaders since the Palestine war convened in Cairo on January 14, 1964. Over the next three days, Nasser would bully his way to achieving most of his goals, controlling the loose-cannon revolutionaries and coopting the conservative monarchies. But it cost him. A $17.5 million Arab League plan was approved for diverting the Jordan at its sources—the Banias and Hatzbani rivers—and so drastically reduce the quantity and quality of Israel's water. Then, assuming that the Israelis would not watch passively while their country dried up, the conference also created a United Arab Command, both to protect the project and to prepare for an offensive campaign. With a ten-year $345 million budget, the UAC was charged with standardizing Arab arms and providing military aid to Jordan, Lebanon, and Syria. Plans were made for bolstering Lebanon's defense with Syrian troops and Jordan's with Iraqis, and for placing Iraq's fine air force at the UAC's service. Conditions were laid down for waging war: secrecy, unity, and total military preparedness.[38]

The summit, hailed as "the first in the history of the Arab peoples to be agreed upon by all the Arab leaders," spelled victory for Nasser. The UAC was placed under direct Egyptian authority, with Gen. 'Ali 'Ali 'Amer as its commander, and as its chief of staff, Gen. 'Abd al-Mun'im Riyad. Egypt had taken the initiative in the armed struggle against Israel but the showdown was to be delayed for two and a half years at least, until the UAC became operational, in 1967. With the Arab world now mobilized yet firmly under Nasser's control, his motto for the conference—"Unity of Action"—appeared to have been actualized.[39]

But the summit did not find an exit from the Yemen quagmire, nor did it palliate the Syrians. No sooner had Hafiz Amin returned home when his regime reiterated that "what we have to do is push the whole Arab people into entering the battle with all means . . . " and again accused Egypt of hiding behind UNEF's skirts.[40] The UAC was the means and Syria was anxious to exploit it. In his search for Arab unity and deferral of any conflict with Israel, Nasser had unwittingly created a framework for dissent and accelerated the momentum toward war.

These facts gradually dawned on Nasser over the course of two subsequent summits, in Alexandria that September and in Casablanca, Morocco, one year later. The delegates approved the establishment of the Palestine Liberation Organization under Ahmad al-Shuqayri, a stout and voluble lawyer widely seen as Nasser's stooge, and a Palestine Liberation Army to deploy along Israel's borders. More substantively, the UAC budget was expanded by nearly $600 million and plans were drafted for "the elimination of the Israeli aggression" sometime in 1967. Arab leaders agreed to cease interfering in one another's internal affairs, and to concentrate on Palestine's redemption, the paramount goal.[41]

But inter-Arab cooperation again remained largely on paper. Jordan opposed the stationing of PLA units on the West Bank or Iraqi and Saudi troops on any part of its territory. Lebanon was also loath to host foreign forces, and Iraq to lend its planes to the UAC. None of the Western-oriented armies wanted to standardize their arsenals with Soviet arms, and nobody wanted to take orders from Egyptian generals. Except in Egypt, Shuqayri was universally despised and the PLO in constant arrears, as the Arab states uniformly defaulted on their pledges.[42]

And these were only the beginning of Nasser's headaches. Deeper troubles would arise as Syria, taking advantage of Egypt's predicament in Yemen, in the spring of 1964 began unilaterally implementing the Arab diversion plan. As predicted, the Israelis did not sit idly but responded with withering bombardments that wrecked the Syrian earthworks. "Every soldier in our army feels that Israel must be wiped off of the map," retorted Syrian Chief of Staff Salah Jadid, and urged the Arab masses to "kindle the spark," of war with Israel and support Syria's efforts for liberation.[43]

The Saudis, meanwhile, taunted Nasser by reminding him that his entanglement in Yemen prevented him from rescuing Palestine. A peace agreement for Yemen negotiated by Nasser and the Saudis' King Faisal in August 1965 was ultimately ignored, and the former threatened to invade Saudi Arabia. As many as 70,000 troops, the cream of the Egyptian army, remained as bogged down as ever. Slipping, Nasser sought to rally by leading a boycott of West Germany after it recognized Israel—Saudi Arabia, Morocco, Libya, and Tunisia declined to join—and then of Tunisian president Habib Bourgiba, for heretically accepting the UN Partition plan.[44]

Nearly two years of Arab summitry had produced scarce benefits for Egypt or indeed for any Arab state. There was no end to the Yemen war, no end to inter-Arab bickering. Instead of a common front against Israel there were joint offensive plans almost certain to provoke it—in short, all of the liabilities and none of the advantages of unity. Even the sole accomplishment of note, the creation of the PLO, was deeply qualified, as no less than seven Palestinian guerrilla movements—al-Fatah among them—renounced the organization as impotent.

Still the Arabs' imbroglio worsened. U.S.-Egyptian relations, severely strained by the end of President Kennedy's administration, ruptured under that of his successor, Lyndon Baines Johnson. Along with Egypt's long-standing policies toward the wars in Vietnam and the Congo, toward Israel and Yemen and pro-Western Arab monarchies—all of them fundamentally at variance with Washington's—were now added attacks against Wheelus, America's strategically vital airbase in Libya.

The breaking point came in November 1964, in what U.S. ambassador in Cairo, Lucius Battle, called "a little series of horrors." First, rioters in the capital attacked the U.S. embassy, burning down its library, then Egyptian forces accidentally shot down a plane owned by John Mecom, a Texas businessman and personal friend of the president's. When Battle suggested that Nasser moderate his behavior to ensure his continued access to American wheat, the Egyptian leader let loose: "The American Ambassador says that our behavior is not acceptable. Well, let us tell them that those who do not accept our behavior can go and drink from the sea . . . We will cut the tongues of anybody who talks badly about us . . . We are not going to accept gangsterism by cowboys."[45]

So ended U.S. aid to Egypt. By 1965, Washington was working sedulously to undermine Cairo's efforts to reschedule its international debt and to gain credit in world monetary funds. The shipments of American wheat that accounted for 60 percent of all Egyptian bread were suspended. Nasser was convinced that Johnson was out to assassinate him. While some of its colossal loss was made up by the $277 million economic and military aid promised by Khrushchev during his May 1964 visit to Cairo, nothing could remedy the country's woefully chronic ills: a population of 29.5 million growing at 3.5 percent annually, poor (about $140 per capita per year, 40 percent inflation), unhealthy (average male life expectancy thirty-five years), and to a large extent (45 percent) illiterate. Brutal crackdown of dissidents, the arbitrary nationalization of property, a suffocating bureaucracy: This was Egypt in the mid-1960s, a police state. Even the High Dam at Aswan, Nasserism's grandest symbol, proved toxic, spreading the dreaded bilharzia disease throughout the countryside.[46]

This depressing picture was not Egypt's alone, however. Rampant population growth, dwindling employment opportunities, low levels of health care and education were endemic to most of the Arab world.[47] Patriarchal, capped by totalitarian regimes, Arab society was hardly ripe for progress. And even the basic goal of unity—retribution against the arrogant West and the noxious Jewish state it had forced upon them—continued to elude the Arabs.

Disappointment and frustration helped impel al-Fatah's marauders as they crossed into Israel on the first night of 1965. That action, though abortive, had a rippling effect throughout the region—scarcely perceptible at first but ultimately tectonic. Held in abeyance during much of the Arab Cold War, the Arab-Israeli conflict had resurfaced with a vengeance. The context was nearly complete.

Out of the Icebox

Failures though they seemed to the Arabs, to Israelis, the Arab summits of 1964–65 appeared nothing short of volcanic, the reification of their neighbors' desire to eradicate them. IDF intelligence, which had previously denied that the Arabs would go to war over the water issue, suddenly changed its tone. "This desire had always been abstract—until now," explained an IDF intelligence estimate from the period, "For the first time we know of a plan . . . with clear stages; a date has been set for the showdown. Thus, in 1967–8, we are liable to face a renewed Arab initiative. The practical expression of this may come in the form of another attempt to divert the Jordan, the encouragement of terrorist attacks . . . border incidents . . . closing the Straits of Tiran." To restore its deterrence power, Israel would have to strike on more than one front and at a time not of her choosing, enabling the Arabs to counterattack overwhelmingly, IDF intelligence warned.[48]

The downhill course toward war, from the Israeli perspective, was marked by Arab acts on the ground. The northern border erupted in November 1964 with Syria's unilateral efforts to divert the Jordan headwaters and then to prevent Israeli cultivation of the DZ's (see map, p. 285). The latter, it will be recalled, had been created by the Armistice Agreements in areas of Israel evacuated by the Syrian army. Divided into three main sectors totaling some 66.5 square miles, the DZ's contained archipelagos of irregularly shaped plots—each had a nickname: the Legume, for example, and De Gaulle's Nose—over which Israel claimed total sovereignty. Pressing this claim, the Israelis denied the Mixed Armistice Commission any jurisdiction over the DZ's (Syrian representatives sat on the MAC) and declared them off-limits to Syrian farmers. But the Syrians just as adamantly opposed Israeli attempts to control the plots, and, from their emplacements atop the Golan Heights, fired on any tractors plowing them.

At the epicenter of these tensions was the Sea of Galilee itself, which was wholly within Israeli sovereignty, but just barely. A 10-meter strip along the lake's northeastern bank technically belonged to Israel, but, falling directly under the Syrian guns, was virtually impossible to defend. Syrian snipers regularly fired at Israeli fishing boats while Israeli patrol craft just as frequently violated a 250-meter demilitarized zone extending from the eastern shore into the lake itself.

The two issues, land and water, were inextricably linked in the Israeli mind. By affirming their sovereignty over the DZ's, the Israelis sought to deter the Syrians from diverting the Jordan. "Without control over the water sources we cannot realize the Zionist dream," Eshkol had told the government, "Water is the basis for Jewish existence in the Land of Israel." Tactically, too, there was a connection, as Israel exploited DZ incidents as pretexts for bombing the diversion project. Increasingly proficient at hitting long-range targets, Israeli tanks could zero in on Syrian bulldozers miles behind the border. But then the Syrians upped the ante.

North of Tel Dan on November 13, near a DZ, an Israeli patrol came under Syrian fire. Israeli tanks, camouflaged nearby, opened up in return. Artillery atop the Golan Heights leveled a blanket of shells on Israeli settlements across the Hula Valley. With the enemy's cannons out of range, Israel's obvious riposte was to bombard them from the air, but Eshkol hesitated, fearful of starting a war and of jeopardizing Israel's attempts to purchase American aircraft. "Is it a question of just a few more holes in the roof or no roof and walls at all?" he asked Yitzhak Rabin, now the chief of staff.

Rabin favored hitting Syria and hitting it decisively. With the Arab world divided and the USSR unlikely to intervene, he explained, retaliatory action would not lead to war. The United States, moreover, busy as it was bombing North Vietnam, could hardly assail a similar strike against Syria. Convinced, Eshkol deferred to Rabin's reasoning, and the IAF took to the air.[49]

The ensuing three-hour battle resulted in four Israeli dead and nine wounded; settlements were seriously damaged. The Syrians' losses were also extensive—at least two tanks and several earth-moving machines—but their deepest wound was psychological. Syria's air force was simply no match for Israel's. Though work on the diversion would continue through the spring of 1965, five miles from the border and out of tank range, it could never be completed as long as Israel ruled the skies. Syria's answer was to procure more planes—some sixty Soviet MiG-21s—and fast, while embarking on a new and less risky endeavor.

Palestinian guerrilla raids, first used by Nasser in the 1950s, had proven a viable means of goring the Israelis while scoring points in Arab public opinion. Their operations were cheaply financed and, in face of charges of government collusion, plausibly denied, especially when mounted from neighboring countries. Nor was there any difficulty in recruiting fighters from the Palestinian organizations disgusted with Ahmad Shuqayri and his PLO sinecure. These rejectionist groups now shared Syria's interests in fomenting tensions with Israel. Over the course of 1965, The Storm (al-'Asifa), the armed wing of al-Fatah, received Syria's support in carrying out thirty-five attacks according to Israel's reckoning, 110 by Palestinian accounts.

These operations again embarrassed Nasser, upstaging his leadership on Palestine and renewing the danger of an Israeli reprisal to which Egypt, now committed to the UAC, would have to respond—in other words, war. The guerrillas' appearance came at the worst possible time, with Egypt's army stalled in Yemen and its economy plummeting. Saudi Arabia, Jordan, and Iran had banded in an Islamic League for the purpose of limiting Nasser's influence. Denouncing the league as a joint plot of the U.S. and the Muslim Brotherhood, Nasser canceled his participation at the next Arab summit, scheduled to be held in Algeria. "We could annihilate Israel in twelve days were the Arabs to form a united front," he strove to explain, "Israel can only be attacked from . . . Syria and Jordan." Then, declaring his intention to "liberate Palestine in a revolutionary and not a traditional manner," he quietly arrested all the al-Fatah activists in Egypt and in Gaza.[50]

Nasser was not the only Arab leader threatened by Syria-sponsored terror. More immediately imperiled was Jordan's King Hussein. Having successfully resisted the UAC's plans for stationing Saudi and Iraqi troops on his territory, certain the Israelis would use the move as a pretext for seizing the West Bank, Hussein now faced a similar situation as a result of the al-Fatah's raids. Over half of these originated in the West Bank, where Hussein had been resisting Shuqayri's influence and Shuqayri was now forced to rival al-Fatah by forming his own guerrilla groups. The Jordanian monarch went to considerable lengths to stifle these activities, but there was a limit, he knew, to suppressing legitimate Palestinian resistance, and a limit to Israel's restraint.[51]

The Israelis had told him as much. Since 1960, when Ben-Gurion congratulated him on surviving an Egyptian-orchestrated bomb attack ("Your Majesty will continue to defy with courage and success all treacherous attempts to subvert law and order"), Hussein had been in occasional contact with Israeli representatives. Another assassination attempt, also traced to Egypt, was foiled by the Mossad intelligence service two years later. Like his grandfather before him, Hussein proceeded cautiously with these talks, conducting them in London and under the strictest secrecy. Though unreceptive to Eshkol's offers of a full peace treaty, unwilling to break with the Arab consensus, he was open to practical measures, such as quiet cooperation on sharing the Jordan's waters. The contacts helped conciliate the Israelis—and the Americans, their common ally—during the period of the Arab summits when Jordan's anti-Zionist propaganda easily rivaled the Syrians'. But propaganda was one thing, terror another, and the Israelis warned Hussein that terrorism had to stop.[52] It did not, however, and in May 1965, after the killing of six Israelis, the IDF struck back.

Three reprisals followed, on Qalqilya, Shuna, and Jenin, in the West Bank. These were small-scale attacks by IDF standards, aimed at water installations, an ice factory, and a flour mill. Nevertheless, they provided the rhetorical ammunition Shuqayri needed to castigate the "colonialist rule" of the Hashemites and to demand its overthrow as the first step toward Palestinian liberation. Hussein, vowing to "sever any hand raised against this struggling country and to gouge out any eye that glances at us with hate," retorted by arresting some 200 "subversive" elements in Jordan and closing the PLO office. "The purpose of the PLO is the destruction of Jordan and everything we have achieved throughout these long years for our nation and for Palestine," the king wrote to Nasser, but Nasser remained unsympathetic, unwilling to defend a "reactionary" monarch against Palestinian freedom fighters. The Syrians condemned both Hussein and Nasser—Nasser because he had failed to come to the Palestinians' rescue, to cast off UNEF and initiate the "third round."[53] Al-Fatah's strategy had thus far worked: Having provoked Israel into retaliating against Arab states, the Arab states were gradually goading one another to war.

The Israelis observed this process unfolding with a growing sense of helplessness—in spite of their impressive victories in the North. Eshkol, for one, suspected that the Arabs would not wait until 1967 to strike. "Okay, okay," he protested when presented with optimistic intelligence estimates, "but what if intelligence is wrong?"

Haunted by the specter of an all-Arab assault, the IDF initiated Anvil (Hebrew: *Sadan*), a comprehensive defense plan designed to rebuff attacks on all fronts and then enable the army to take the offensive. But the plan would take another year, until July 1966, to implement, and meanwhile the country lay vulnerable. Horrified, Eshkol learned that the tank corps had only enough ammunition for three days' fighting—he ordered it doubled to six—and one-third the number of planes necessary to take on Egypt's air force alone. Adding to these anxieties was the capture in January 1965 of Eli Cohen, alias Kamal Amin Thabet, a Mossad agent who had insinuated himself into the upper ranks of Syria's military establishment. With Cohen's execution in May, Israel lost an irreplaceable source of information on Syria's deployment in the Golan Heights and its bounteous support for al-Fatah.[54]

An even greater cause of worry for the Israelis was the state of their alliance with France. This had cooled considerably since Ben-Gurion's ouster and the advent of de Gaulle, since the end of the Algerian war and the implication of certain pro-Israeli generals in anti-Gaullist coups. Though seventy-two Mirage III fighter jets had been supplied to Israel in 1961, further deliveries had lagged as France sought to put Suez in the past and rebuild its Middle Eastern bridges. By 1965, Egypt's General 'Amer was being welcomed as an honored guest in Paris.[55]

For Israel, then, the only answer to these concerns lay with the United States, and with its well-disposed president. "You have lost a very great friend. But you have found a better one," Johnson reportedly told an Israeli diplomat after Kennedy's assassination. That friendship was manifest in June 1964 when Levi Eshkol became the first Israeli prime minister to be officially received in the White House. "The United States is foursquare behind Israel on all matters that affect their vital security interests," the president assured his guest, "just as it is [behind] Southeast Asia . . ." The two, of a similar age and farming background, got along famously. Baring his trepidation, Eshkol replied, "We cannot afford to lose. This may be our last stand in history. The Jewish people have something to give to the world. I believe that if you look at our history and at all the difficulties we have survived, it means that history wants us to continue. We cannot survive if we experience again what happened to us under Hitler . . . I believe that you should understand us."[56]

Johnson understood and gave Israel $52 million in civilian aid, but military support was another story. American M-48 Patton tanks had been sold to Israel—albeit indirectly, through Germany, with a counterbalancing tank sale to Jordan—and forty-eight A-4 Skyhawk fighters, due for delivery in December 1967. But Germany succumbed to Arab pressure to stop selling Israel arms while Egypt's acquisition of long-range Soviet bombers meant Israel needed the planes at once. While American arms sales to the Middle East multiplied during the Johnson administration, from $44.2 to $995.3 million, Israel's share was negligible. "The United States had much good will for Israel and desired Israel to have an adequate deterrent," read a joint memorandum of February 1965, but Johnson refused to be Israel's primary arms' supplier.[57]

That refusal reflected America's traditional reluctance to identify itself totally with one side in the Arab-Israeli conflict or to get entrapped in a Middle East arms race. Beyond that, though, was Johnson's preoccupation with the Vietnam War and opposition to it at home, both of them escalating.[58] The U.S. simply could not commit itself in any other area of the globe, Johnson stressed, and to another confrontation with the Soviets. Appreciation of this fact brought meager solace to Eshkol, especially as the USSR seemed to have the wherewithal for supplying both the North Vietnamese *and* the Arabs.

The Israeli prime minister, moreover, had domestic problems of his own. Ben-Gurion, still reeling from his resignation from office, realized finally that Eshkol was no mere understudy. Together with acolytes Peres and Dayan, he formed his own breakaway party, Rafi (*Reshimat Poalei Yisrael*—Israel Workers' List), which performed poorly in the October 1965 elections. But if Rafi failed to take power, it succeeded in eroding Mapai's majority and exhausting its leader, literally giving him a heart attack. Eshkol recovered only to be hit by an economic depression caused by the falloff of immigration and the end of Holocaust reparations from Germany. Unemployment skyrocketed to 12.4 percent while annual growth contracted to a single percent. For the first time since the grim days of 1948, a sense of national listlessness set in, particularly among Israel's youth.[59]

All this occurred while the security situation went from worse to insufferable. Over the course of 1966, Israel recorded ninety-three border incidents—mines, shootings, sabotage—while the Syrians boasted seventy-five guerrilla attacks in the single month of February-March.[60] Those same months also brought a new government to power in Damascus—typically, through violence—as General Jadid and Air Force Commander Hafez al-Assad installed a Ba'thist regime even more radical than its predecessors. Comprised almost solely of Alawites, a heterodox sect abhorred by the Sunni majority, the regime was sorely lacking in popular support and obsessively afraid of Nasser. The panacea for these problems lay in manufacturing enemies such as Arab reaction and Western imperialism, though none more sinister than Zionism:

> The Palestine question [is] the main axis of our domestic, Arab, and international policies . . . The liberation battle can only be waged by progressive Arab forces through a popular war of liberation, which history has proved is the only course for victory against all aggressive forces . . . It will remain the final way for the liberation of the entire Arab homeland and for its comprehensive socialist popular unification.[61]

The latest Ba'thist coup brought to a climax the process that had begun in 1964 when, insecure at home and in fierce competition with Egypt and Jordan, Syria's rulers had tried to earn prestige by picking fights with Israel. The plan foundered, though, when the IDF thwarted Syria's diversion plan and its attempts to dominate the DZ's. Damascus then turned to the Palestinian raids that had the triple advantage of hurting Israel, shaming Nasser, and weakening Hussein. The possibility that the raids might confirm Israel's assessment of an Arab buildup to war was irrelevant to the Syrians, to whom war seemed a no-lose situation, resulting in either Israel's defeat or that of their Egyptian and Jordanian rivals. No harm, meanwhile, could come to Syria, protected by its unwavering alliance with the USSR.

The Soviets had indeed invested massively in the Middle East, about $2 billion in military aid alone—1,700 tanks, 2,400 artillery pieces, 500 jets, and 1,400 advisers—since 1956, some 43 percent of it to Egypt. Nasser, "a noncapitalist revolutionary democrat," in Soviet parlance, was seen as the Kremlin's main hope for defeating the West in the aftermath of the Cuban missile debacle. Moscow would not be disappointed. While warfare raged in Southeast Asia, NATO was

outflanked from the south and its oil supply threatened by pro-Soviet Arab regimes. In return for these services, Nasser and 'Amer were in 1964 both designated Heroes of the Soviet Union, an award never before granted to foreigners.

Yet the extent of Soviet largess in the region was also a source of dissent.
Party and army leaders disagreed in their assessment of the Arabs' qualities as
soldiers and their openness to Marxist ideas. Some observers even linked
Khrushchev's ouster in October 1964 to disenchantment with his overgenerosity
toward Egypt. His replacements, however—the triumvirate of Premier Alexei
Kosygin, President Nikolai Podgorny, and L. I. Brezhnev, the Communist party
secretary-general—proved no less giving. Invited to Moscow the following
month, 'Amer was told that "we will give you everything, even secret weapons," to which he reportedly replied, "and we will keep those secrets." [62]

Soviet philanthropy reached an unprecedented high following the Ba'th
revolution in Syria. In contrast to Egypt, where the Communist party was illegal and relations with Moscow accordingly complex, the new regime in Damascus included for the first time Syrian Communists. Aid poured in—$428
million in 1966 alone—refurbishing the country's infrastructure and financing
construction of a Euphrates River dam even costlier than Aswan's. Russian
became a second language taught in the schools. But Soviet-Syrian relations
rested on more than ideology. Third World policy, once an unmitigated success for the USSR, had suffered serious setbacks with the overthrow of Sukarno
in Indonesia and Ghana's Nkruma, and with the spread of Chinese influence in
Asia and Africa. Syria was compensation.[63]

Moscow and Damascus appeared to concur on all outstanding issues, with
the notable exception of Palestine. For all their invective against Zionism and
relentless condemnations of Israel, the Soviets had always stopped short of advocating violence. War in the Middle East, so close to their southern border,
and with the U.S. Sixth Fleet in the Eastern Mediterranean nearby, was not
among the Soviets' interests. Kremlin leaders had opposed Syria's attempts to
divert the Jordan and, instead, proposed peace talks on the basis of the Partition plan. Slowly, however, by mid-1966, this reluctance had begun to wane. A
joint communiqué issued after the visit of a high-level Syrian delegation to
Moscow described Israel as "a military arsenal and a base for aggression and
blackmail against the . . . Arab people," and pledged full Soviet backing for the
Arabs "in their just cause against colonialist Zionism."[64]

This shift in Soviet policy may have stemmed from internal struggles—
Marshal Andrei Antonovich Grechko, deputy defense minister, was making a
power play with Brezhnev's backing, and needed to flex military muscle—or a
desire to exploit America's immersion in Vietnam. The outcome, however,
was irrefutable that spring, as a fortified Syria expanded its support for guerrilla attacks against Israel. "We want a full-scale, popular war of liberation . . .
to destroy the Zionist base in Palestine," Dr. Nureddin al-Atassi, Syria's fig-
urehead president, told troops stationed on the Israeli border, "The time has
come to use these arms for the purpose for which they were created."[65]

Thus challenged, the Israelis might have been expected to retaliate directly against Damascus. They had the military capability certainly, and even tacit support from the United States. But overriding these advantages was the danger of sparking a much larger confrontation, playing into Syria's hands and provoking the Soviet Union. Like many of his generation, Eastern Europeans, Eshkol knew and feared the Russians. War with Syria was risky enough; with the USSR, it would be suicidal.[66]

The precariousness of Soviet-Israel relations was underscored on May 25, 1966, when the Soviet Foreign Ministry informed the Israeli ambassador, Katriel Katz, of a Zionist plot to invade Syria. IDF troops, "the secret weapon of imperialism and colonialism in the Near East," were massing on the northern border even as they spoke, he was told. Katz's vehement denials—and Eshkol's, to the Soviet ambassador, Chuvakhin, in Tel Aviv—could not dissuade the Soviets, nor could Israel's assurances of respect for Syria's territorial integrity. The crisis passed two days later with the Soviet news agency Tass trumpeting the "timeliness of the exposure . . . as proof of the Soviet Union's solidarity with the Arab countries in their struggle against . . . foreign powers and domestic reaction." But the message was also noted by the Israelis, who from that moment became particularly jittery about provoking the Syrians, even by so little as a reconnaissance flight.[67]

For Israel, then, the only viable target for retaliation remained the West Bank. The IDF struck twice there, both times in the Hebron area—eight civilians were killed—and traded shots with Jordanian soldiers. These actions may have served some purpose in mollifying Eshkol's critics, but they hardly deterred Damascus. Tank and artillery duels continued to rage along the border as the Syrians again moved their diversion work out of Israeli range, and intensified their shelling of Israeli settlements. Again, Rabin felt there was nothing to do but call in the IAF. Israeli planes went into action on July 7, downing a Syrian MiG.

The Syrian response was not long in coming. When, on August 15, an Israeli border patrol boat ran aground on the demilitarized eastern shore of the Sea of Galilee, Syria sent planes of its own. The attack, intended to "prove to the Arab people . . . the untruth of the Israeli claim of air superiority," according to Hafez al-Assad, backfired as two of the MiGs went down in flames. But Syrian gunmen nevertheless prevented IDF divers from dislodging the boat, which was extricated only with great difficulty at night.[68]

Yet the Palestinian raids continued, with credit now claimed by some twenty-six guerrilla groups with names like Youths of Revenge and Heroes of the Return. Israel's fury was once again directed at Jordan where, on April 30, IDF paratroopers blew up twenty-eight houses in the northern West Bank village of Rafat, killing eleven civilians. The reprisal failed to satisfy Rabin, however. He warned of the dangers of the weakening Hussein, and of the need to strike at the terrorists' source—Syria—on the model of the Sinai Campaign.

With the Egyptians in Yemen and the Arab world split, the timing would be ideal. "The reaction to Syrian acts, whether they be terrorism, diversion or aggression on the border, must be aimed at the perpetrators of that terrorism and at the regime that supports it," Rabin told *Bamahane*, the army's magazine, on September 9. "The problem with Syria is, therefore, essentially a clash with its leadership."

The remarks only angered Eshkol, who feared that such an assault on Syria would bring in the Soviets and unite the Arabs in full-scale war with Israel. The country's cities could be bombed, he warned, and even the Dimona reactor. He sharply reprimanded Rabin; Israel must not be seen to be meddling in internal Syrian affairs. Rather than attacking Syria head-on, the prime minister counseled an indirect route: extending compulsory army service for men an additional six months, and prosecuting Syria's crimes in the Security Council.

Both actions boomeranged, however. Rather than reinforcing public morale, the extended service further corroded it, while the Council's attempts to condemn the Syrians were repeatedly vetoed by the Soviets. In Damascus, the tone of Prime Minister Yusuf Zu'ayyin was unremittingly bellicose: "We are not resigned to holding back the Palestinian revolution . . . We shall set the area afire, and any Israeli movement will result in a final grave for Israel."[69]

Events were coming to a head, and not only for the Israelis. Egypt also looked with consternation at Syria's campaign to drag the region into war. "Nasser may well fulminate against Israel but we believe there is practically no possibility that he will attack or provoke the Israelis within the foreseeable future," read the State Department's assessment to President Johnson.[70] Improbable as it seemed, Israel and Egypt shared an interest in reining in the Syrians.

In recognition of this convergence, Nasser agreed to the renewal of secret contacts with Israel, the first since the Suez crisis. The connection ran through Mossad chief Meir Amit and General 'Azm al-Din Mahmud Khalil, head of Egypt's nonconventional weapons projects, who reported directly to both Nasser and 'Amer. Through an intermediary known only as "Steve," the two met clandestinely in Paris and discussed arrangements virtually identical to those proposed in the 1950s: Israeli assistance in procuring international aid for Egypt in return for a lessening of anti-Israeli propaganda in Egypt and an easing of the Suez Canal blockade. The Egyptians also offered to release the Jews accused of spying in 1954, upon receipt of a $30 million Israeli loan. Khalil went so far as to invite Amit to Cairo in June 1966, but Eshkol quashed the idea, unwilling to trust Nasser with the head of Israel's top-secret security force. Thereafter, the Egyptians, fearing that the contacts would be exposed and revealed to their Arab detractors, closed down the channel entirely. The Israelis would try to reopen it exactly one year later, in the throes of an even darker crisis.[71]

Secret diplomacy might help mollify the Israelis, but calming Syria meant dramatic démarches. What Nasser proposed was a mutual defense treaty which, while enhancing Syria's ability to lure Egypt into a conflict, would also enable

Egypt to limit Syria's maneuverability: the lesser of evils. Syria's leaders, moreover, seemed amenable to the idea. Shaken by the loss of their jets, they were further stunned in September by a coup attempt by one Major Salim Hatum, a Druze, and the subsequent purging of the officer corps. An agreement with the most powerful Arab country was far from the worst way of shoring up the regime.

The first move came in mid-October 1966 with an Egyptian military delegation to Damascus ("We are confident that we are making fast strides toward the realization of our common goal—the elimination of Israel and full unity," declared its head, General Sa'ad 'Ali 'Amer) and a reciprocal visit by Zu'ayyin to Cairo. There, on November 2, Nasser told the Syrian prime minister that Israel's technological edge and American aid made it almost invulnerable to Arab attack. Yet when Zu'ayyin protested that the Arabs would then have to wait 100 years, Nasser assured him: "You won't have to wait 100 or even 50, you just have to know that you can't achieve your goal except with a long-range gun."[72]

The Egyptian-Syrian defense treaty signed two days later restored all military and diplomatic ties between the two countries and committed them to come to one another's assistance in the event of battle. Secret codicils to the agreement provided for Egyptian strikes against Israeli targets in the South, should Israel attack in the North. The Egyptian and Syrian air forces, proclaimed Syrian Foreign Minister Ibrahim Makhous, "are now flying in one sky." The treaty also occasioned the breakup of the tacit alliance between Egypt and Jordan, founded as it was on common opposition to Syria. Damascus Radio and Cairo's Voice of the Arabs harmonized in vilifying Hussein as "reactionary" and "an agent and stooge of imperialism and Zionism," promising him "the same treatment given [assassinated Iraqi Premier] Nuri al-Sa'id."[73]

But if Nasser thought he could assuage the Syrians with talk of war in the not-too-distant future, events soon proved him mistaken. Eleven guerrilla attacks, most of them launched from Jordan, ensued in rapid succession—seven Israelis died and twelve were wounded. "The notepad is open and the hand is writing," Eshkol told the generals who demanded reprisals, assuring them that none of the murders were forgotten and would shortly be avenged. But he also implored the United States to intercede with Syria and Jordan. "There is a public to think about," he reminded Walworth (Wally) Barbour, the American ambassador. "I want you to know that the situation may lead to clashes. Sometimes we have to take action after rethinking more than once." The prime minister rejected the assessment of the Chief UN observer, a Norwegian general with the improbable name of Odd Bull, that Hussein was doing his utmost to prevent hostile infiltration. According to Israeli intelligence, the king was merely detaining the terrorists and releasing them days later.[74]

Then, on November 10, on the Israeli border opposite the West Bank city of Hebron, a paramilitary police vehicle struck a mine. Three policemen were killed, one wounded. Aware and wary of Israel's wrath, Hussein penned a personal condolence letter to Eshkol, along with a reaffirmation of his commitment to border security. He whisked it to the American embassy in Amman, which then cabled it to Barbour in Tel Aviv. Extremely tall, asthmatic, and portly, a lifelong bachelor with an unabashed affection for Israel—an affection fully reciprocated—Barbour had a reputation as a highly efficient ambassador. But this time he slipped. Instead of forwarding the letter at once to the prime minister's office, he laid it on his desk. It was Friday, and with no apparent rush, he believed, the message could wait until after the weekend.[75]

That weekend, Israel decided to strike. Not a limited attack, but a large-scale reprisal, mounted in broad daylight, with tanks and air cover. "In 1966, we can't carry out a 1955-style reprisal raid," averred IDF operations chief Ezer Weizman, arguing in favor of the raid. The usually pacific Abba Eban, now Israel's foreign minister, agreed, as did the majority of the government's ministers. Deterrence had to be restored, yet without provoking war. Explaining why the target would be the West Bank and not Syria, Eshkol told his cabinet that "we have reached the decision that responsibility for these acts rests not only on the relevant governments but also on the people providing shelter and aid for these gangs." He also expressed the hope that there would be no civilian casualties, and no clashes with the Jordanian army.[76]

Questions could later be raised whether Eshkol would have made the same decision had he received Hussein's apology in time, whether all subsequent events might have been averted had not Barbour so tragically procrastinated. Many "ifs" could be posited.

But the developments of the next six months cannot be traced to any individual person or incident. They arose, rather, from a context that by the end of 1966, had been fully forged. The conflict between the Arab countries and the Israelis, between Arab countries themselves and between the U.S. and the USSR—exacerbated by domestic tensions in each—had created an atmosphere of extreme flammability. In such an atmosphere, it would not take much—a terrorist attack, a reprisal raid—to unleash a process of unbridled escalation, a chain reaction of dare and counterdare, gamble and miscalculation, all leading inexorably to war.

THE CATALYSTS

Samu' to Sinai

T EN TANKS, FORTY HALF-TRACKS, and 400 men—the largest Israeli strike
force assembled since the 1956 war—crossed the West Bank border
before dawn, November 13, 1966. The operation aimed at punishing
Palestinian villages in the Hebron area that had aided and billeted al-Fatah
guerrillas. Those villages would then appeal to King Hussein to clamp down
on al-Fatah, or so the Israelis assumed. The prodigious display of firepower
would also impress upon the Jordanians the degree of retribution they might
expect in the future; the Syrians would be warned as well. It was to be a clean
attack, in and out, with little resistance expected, and no encounters with the
Jordanian army which, reportedly, was nowhere in the area.

Under the cover of IAF fighters, the Israeli column advanced to Rujm al-
Madfa', ten miles southwest of Hebron, and demolished its police station. The
next target was Samu', a village of 5,000 that Israel held to be a principal staging
ground for the terrorists. Most of these residents responded to orders to gather
in the town square, whereupon sappers from the 35th paratrooper brigade proceeded to dynamite a large number of houses in and around the village. All was
going according to plan when, at 7:30 A.M., the paratroops' reconnaissance unit
reported Jordanian soldiers approaching from the northwest.

There were roughly 100 of them, members of the Hittin Infantry Brigade
under the command of Brig. Gen. Bahjat al-Muhsin, riding in a convoy of
twenty vehicles. Al-Muhsin was leading his troops to Yata, another Hebron-
area village, where significant enemy activity had been reported. But the winding, rugged road to Yata passed through Samu' and there lay an Israeli ambush.

Three-quarters of the convoy went up in flames; fifteen soldiers were killed and fifty-four wounded. But the Jordanians fought back, wounding ten para-troopers and killing their battalion commander, Col. Yoav Shaham. Jordanian Hunter jets meanwhile scrambled, only to be driven off by the Israelis, with the loss of one aircraft. What had been intended as a swift and surgical strike had devolved into a pitched battle.[1]

Israel's leaders were stunned, and not only by the military losses. Three Arab civilians had also been killed, ninety-six wounded; and, while the IDF reported forty houses destroyed, the UN estimate was over three times that many. Then, instead of appealing to King Hussein for protection, the West Bank Palestinians demanded his overthrow. Riots raged throughout the area, from Hebron to Jerusalem to Nablus in the north, as demonstrators stoned government offices and burned pictures and effigies of the king. At least four Palestinians were killed and dozens wounded as the Jordanians were at last compelled to open fire.

Operation Shredder—so, aptly, it was named—had clearly backfired. The Security Council unanimously censured Israel for a "violation of the UN Charter and of the General Armistice Agreement between Israel and Jordan," and warned of adopting "effective steps . . . to ensure against the repetition of such acts."[2]

More troubling still for the Israelis was the bitter backlash from the United States, unprecedented in Johnson's tenure. The Americans were appalled at Israel's apparent recklessness, its willingness to undermine the only Arab leader with whom it enjoyed a *modus vivendi*, a pro-Western moderate struggling against a radical sea. Hussein, they pointed out, had agreed to Israel's demand to keep his newly purchased Patton tanks east of the Jordan, away from the border. But now, with the West Bank afire, he might have to rescind that pledge.

"You pushed him into a hell of a pot and . . . made life very difficult for the wrong fellow," Eban, visiting Washington, heard from Undersecretary of State Nicholas Katzenbach, "Now you have to take the consequences of what you did." Robert W. "Mad Bob" Komer, an old Israel hand at the National Security Council, assailed Eban for "opening up of a new source of disturbance in the Middle East," and for undermining "the whole [American] balance of power doctrine [that] rests upon the preservation of the status quo in Jordan and [its] insulation from a take-over by Egypt, Syria or the Palestinians." Why, Komer asked, had Israel attacked Jordan when "the only *Government* [emphasis in the original] which espoused the use of terrorism . . . was Syria and, therefore, it would have been understandable had you acted . . . against Syria." National Security Advisor Walt W. Rostow took the charge even further, insinuating that Israel

> for some machiavellian reason, wanted a leftist regime on the Left [*sic*] bank so that it could then have a polarized situation in which the Russians would be backing the Arabs and the U.S. would be backing Israel, and that Israel would not be in an embarrassing position where one of its friends among the Great Powers would also be a friend of an Arab country.[3]

Eban's attempts to explain the Samu' raid as an "overreaction" to Arab terror or as an "exercise in the controlled use of a limited force" frustrated by "intervening circumstances" failed to arouse any sympathy. Nor did Eshkol's letter to Johnson in which the prime minister admitted making an error but asked for appreciation of Israel's predicament. "It is important that friends should understand each other in their difficult hours, and this is a difficult hour for us." Johnson did not reply. Instead, he wrote Hussein expressing sadness for "lives needlessly destroyed" and support for Jordan's territorial integrity. The State Department, meanwhile, having failed to convey Hussein's condolence letter to Eshkol, now refused to pass on Eshkol's to Hussein.[4]

Back at home, Eshkol tried to put the best face on the situation. "After Samu' . . . the Arab countries will understand that we mean *business*," he told the Mapai Secretariat, using the English word. "They'll know that we meant what we said when we swore that we wouldn't consent to be killed in this country, not whole-sale and not retail, and not without reaction." Generals rose to assert that the raid had proven the Jordanian army's vulnerability, restoring Israel's deterrence power and calling the world's attention to the dangers of Arab terror.

Yet many Israelis, officials and government ministers, remained unimpressed with the operation. Among them was Col. Israel Lior, military aide to Eshkol and a shrewd observer of upper-echelon politics. "Obviously we had fallen into a trap of our own making," he noted in his diary, "We had consistently warned the Syrians, created an atmosphere of an impending response up north—and then struck Jordan." Rabin, himself, seemed to agree with this assessment, and offered to tender his resignation.[5]

Israeli and American interests were no doubt impaired by the Samu' raid, but none as grievously as Jordan's. Hussein ibn Talal ibn 'Abdallah, at 31, had survived no less than twelve coup and assassination attempts since assuming the throne as a teenager in 1953. Short, dapper, impishly smiling, the king had a refined demeanor that disguised an inner tenacity, enabling him to weather successive threats from Saudi Arabia, Iraq, Syria, and Egypt. The Israelis, he was convinced, had never abandoned their dream of territorial expansion at Jordan's expense. "They want the West Bank," he predicted to Findley Burns, Jr., the American ambassador. "They've been waiting for a chance to get it, and they're going to take advantage of us and they're going to attack."

All these perils seemed to converge in the Samu' attack. Cairo Radio, which had accused Hussein of leading a CIA plot to take over Syria and of colluding with Israel against Egypt, now denounced him for having refused to deploy Iraqi and Saudi troops in the West Bank, abandoning it to Israeli aggression. The Syrians were even more direct: Samu' was the result of the sinister cabal between "the reactionary Jordanian regime and imperialist Zionism."[6]

Hussein, who had seen his grandfather shot by a Palestinian assassin, had no illusions about these dangers. Though fervidly beloved by the East Bank Jordanians, a sizable majority of his subjects were Palestinians who, at best,

owed allegiance to Shuqayri, at worst to Nasser, Syria, and al-Fatah. After Samu',
the PLO leader publicly asserted that "Amman of 1948 is the Amman of 1966,
nothing has changed," and his propaganda broadcasts—from Cairo—called on
the Jordanian army to overthrow the monarchy. Nor could Hussein afford to
underestimate the vicious lengths to which Arab governments would go to unseat
him, recalling the deaths of eleven Jordanian officials, including Prime Minister Haza' al-Majali by an Egyptian bomb in 1960. Now, in the mercurial circumstances of 1966, the king could conceive of several scenarios in which Israel,
hungry for land but afraid of Egypt and Syria, would invade the West Bank.
The other Arab states would merely stand aside and watch, Hussein anticipated, while the Palestinians rose in revolt.[7]

"Hussein's weakness would be the cornerstone upon which the future Arab
alliance [against Israel] will be built," predicted Gen. Indar Jit Rikhye, commander of UNEF in Sinai, while briefing his officers on the impact of Samu'.
Hussein may indeed have been weak, but he refused to remain passive. Already
he had given shelter to Salim Hatum and other officers implicated in the recent
failed coup in Damascus. He had already closed the PLO office in Amman and
now outlawed the organization entirely, declaring martial law. Yet he also made
efforts to appear conciliatory. Guns were distributed to the West Bank villagers, and conscription was instituted for Palestinian men. Then, in a starkly
dramatic move, he published letters he had written secretly to Nasser after the
Casablanca summit. "Should we be a new scapegoat?" he asked the Egyptian
leader. "Should accusations be repeated against the country that can be the
springboard of action against the enemy? Should we let the 1948 disaster repeat itself? Why not let bygones be bygones and look forward to the future?
Put yourself in my place and tell me what you would do." Hussein even had
gestures for Damascus. "If Syria is directly attacked, we must offer all we can to
protect our brothers there," he told the *Christian Science Monitor*, and proposed
that the entirety of defense issues be discussed at another inter-Arab forum.[8]

That forum, the Arab League Defense Council, met in Cairo on December 15,
1966, and instantly turned anti-Jordanian. Amman's representatives found themselves vilified for failing to protect the Palestinians and fulfill their obligations
under the United Arab Command. Had Iraqi and Saudi troops been allowed
into the West Bank, Samu' would never have happened, the Syrians and the
Egyptians claimed. The reply that Israel viewed the entry of such troops as a
casus belli—neither Iraq nor Saudi Arabia had signed the Armistice—and that
instead of preventing a war, the move would start one, proved unconvincing.
Why didn't Egypt renew guerrilla attacks from its own territory, the Jordanians countered? Why didn't they remove UNEF and transfer troops from Yemen
to Sinai? And where was the touted Egyptian air force when the Israelis were
attacking Samu'—where was Syria's commitment to Arab defense?[9]

These questions—accusations, really—touched Nasser's rawest nerves. Just
over two weeks before, a pair of Egyptian MiG's had strayed over Israeli terri-

tory and were downed by the IAF. The incident followed a highly publicized speech in which Gen. Muhammad Sidqi Mahmud, commander of the Egyptian air force, boasted that "We possess the most powerful air weapon in the Middle East. Our bombers, armed with missiles, our modern fighters—are capable of destroying Israel's airfields and planes. We have no fear . . ."

In fact, not just the air force but the entire Egyptian army was in deplorable shape, drained by Yemen and by serious cutbacks in defense spending. The latter was necessitated by the country's economic crisis, so acute now that Nasser was forced to default on $1 billion in foreign loans. A campaign to "free Egypt from the taint of feudalism," turning over Egypt's fledgling industries to the workers, had failed miserably. The 5,000 employees of the El Nasr Automotive plant were now producing all of two vehicles per week. As public dissatisfaction in Egypt escalated, Western diplomats began to predict the regime's imminent demise—or worse. One representative, Britain's R. M. Tesh, observing that the "UAR policy adds up to the road to ruin," warned of a situation in which the military would try to restore Egypt's pride by plunging the region into war. "The scent of blood and distant noise of battle may start some hotheads wanting to fight—and damn the civilians."[10]

Such admonitions were all but muffled by the crescendo of militant rhetoric in the Arab world. Prime Minister al-Tall in Amman said he would "rather die" than allow UN troops on Jordanian territory, or engage in a "gentleman's agreement," as Nasser had with Ben-Gurion in 1956. UAC Commander Gen. 'Ali 'Ali 'Amer in turn claimed that al-Tall had waited four hours, long after Israeli troops had already withdrawn from Samu', to even call him. Next, the Egyptian press accused Hussein of embezzling Jordan's UAC defense allocation, and then headlined an interview with a Jordanian army defector, a Capt. Rashid al-Hamarsha, who confessed to masterminding subversion in Syria. Jordan dismissed al-Hamarsha as a Zionist spy, "in liaison with an Israeli belly dancer named Aurora Galili or Furora Jelli," and then produced its own deserter—Riyad Hajjaj, of Egyptian intelligence revealing plots against the Lebanese and Saudi governments. The climax came in a speech of February 22, 1967, in which Nasser, punning on the Arabic word for king ('ahil), called Hussein the "whore ('ahir) of Jordan."[11]

Relations between Hussein and Nasser had, according to one British memorandum, "reached the point of no return." Bristling from Nasser's speech, Hussein recalled his ambassador from Cairo, and for good measure, banished the Syrian consul from East Jerusalem as well. When the Arab League Defense Council next met on March 14, the Jordanian delegate walked out rather than sit with Shuqayri, "the spiller of military secrets and the spreader of lies." The meeting degenerated into a free-for-all, with the Egyptians and the Syrians accusing Hussein of collaborating with Israel's Jordan River diversion scheme and its purchase of U.S. arms. The Jordanians, along with the Saudis, the Tunisians, and the Moroccans, determined to boycott future sessions of the council.[12]

Hussein was furious, bitter, defamed, but above all disappointed. The tacit Egyptian-Jordanian alliance achieved during the period of the summit conferences, the implicit pact based on common opposition to making war on Israel before the Arabs were ready, had utterly collapsed. At fault were the Syrians, who, the king believed, had successfully lured Egypt into a trap in which war—and Egypt's defeat, Nasser's downfall—was inevitable. But Hussein reserved his deepest resentment for Nasser himself. "Every time he attacks us I hear people ask why we do not reply," he admitted to a Jericho gathering. "The answer is simple. If we have any feelings toward this person it is only pain because he did at one time have a unique opportunity to serve our nation."[13]

Athanasius Contra Mundum

"That person" had his own sources of pain—the economy, as we have seen, the Syrians, and the Muslim Brotherhood. Underlying these, though, was the enervating sense that the Free Officers revolution fifteen years earlier, the dream of Egypt's emergence from servitude to world ascendancy, had run out of steam. Gamal Abdel Nasser, *al-Ra'is* (president), *al-Za'im* (leader), had come to power at thirty-four, a determined and energetic figure. Dashingly handsome, possessed of a keen if unrefined intelligence, Nasser could enrapture audiences with his eloquence, his hypnotic blend of classical and colloquial Arabic. In just under five years, this son of an itinerant postal worker, scarred veteran of the Palestine war, had overthrown King Faruq and Gen. Naguib and become the first native-born Egyptian leader in 150 years. Within two years of taking power, he was legendary throughout the Middle East as the liberator of Egypt and the Arabs' defender against an ever-rapacious West—a modern-day Salah al-Din.

His early accomplishments were indeed astonishing. Single-handedly, it appeared, he had secured Britain's evacuation of the Canal Zone, acquired Soviet weapons, then nationalized the Canal; had fought off the Tripartite Aggression and made Arab unity a fact. Millions of Arabs revered him with a religious awe, and global leaders courted him as a spokesman for Third World nationalism, a champion, along with Nehru and Nkrumah, of nonalignment. A quiet man renowned for his attentiveness and humor, he lived frugally, faithfully with his wife and children, and, in a country notorious for graft, was by all accounts incorruptible.

But then, just as stunningly, the edifice crumbled. The breakup with Syria and the Arab monarchies, the nightmare of Yemen, and his estrangement from the United States—all followed in succession against the backdrop of unremitting domestic decline. Nasserism, the movement that bore his name, was effectively dead, the victim of a bizarre consortium of Syrians and Saudis, Jordanians and Palestinians. By 1967, Nasser was overweight and glassy-eyed—the result, perhaps, of his worsening diabetes—irascible and paranoid. "He knows how to start things, fine," Akram Hawrani, a Syrian leader, remarked of him, "but he doesn't know how to finish." The irrational element always present in Nasser's decision making, that had once passed for pluck, now predominated.

"His rule of government was that of the man who is not secure unless he acts through a secret apparatus," recalled Husayn Sabri, one of the original Free Officers, commenting on the massive police network (*al-Mukhabarat*) Nasser had constructed around himself. Egyptian literary critic Louis Awad put a finer point on it: "The law under the Nasser regime went on holiday." Reelected by a 99.99 percent majority, presiding over ministerial meetings in which he, alone, spoke and often ranted, Nasser had degenerated into a vindictive military dictator—an "Athanasius contra mundum," in one British diplomat's words—embittered against the world.[14]

What remained of Nasser was his pride, which, in an inverse process to his fortunes, had expanded monumentally. "It has to do again with a loss of face . . . with a sort of Messianic complex," Lucius Battle commented; "Nasser doesn't like to be proved wrong and can never admit to these wrongs."[15] That pride, already wounded by the Saudis and the Americans, had led to Egypt's deepened involvement in Yemen and a vendetta against President Johnson. Yet even graver affronts were being hurled from Jordan. Particularly biting were the charges, broadcast over Amman's powerful Marconi transmitters, of Nasser's fear of confronting the Israelis, his refusal to emerge from behind UNEF. The Egyptian leader, who had managed to hide UNEF's existence and Israeli traffic through the Straits from the vast majority of his countrymen, was mortified. Pride demanded that he retaliate, but how?

The answer was presently provided by Abd al-Hakim 'Amer. In Pakistan on a state visit on December 4, 'Amer wired Nasser with a proposal for ordering UNEF off Egyptian soil, concentrating Egypt's army in Sinai and reinstating the blockade in the Straits of Tiran. In addition to "taking the wind out of Hussein's sails," the action would deny Israel maneuverability in attacking either Jordan or Syria. Rather, the Israelis would eventually feel compelled to strike against Egypt, a battle that would last three to five days before the UN intervened and imposed a cease-fire. As in 1956, Israel would be condemned as the aggressor and forced to ignominiously withdraw, while Egypt appeared as the Arabs' savior.

The notion of ousting the peacekeepers was hardly new with 'Amer. A searing reminder that the 1956 war was not quite the "victory" he claimed, UNEF had always been a source of dishonor for the field marshal, a check on the military might he wielded. 'Amer had tendered a similar plan the previous year, during the rotation of Egyptian troops in Yemen, but then, as now, Nasser rejected it.

The reasons for that rejection were manifold. No less than 'Amer, Nasser felt the humiliation of UNEF and looked forward to its removal. "Both President Gamal Abdel Nasser and Marshal 'Amer made it clear to me before 1967 that they wanted to seize on any international or regional situation which would permit doing away with that force," recalled Gen. Muhammad Fawzi, Egypt's chief of staff. A CIA report of April 18, 1967, has Nasser telling a senior Egyptian diplomat of his desire to rid Sinai of UNEF and close the Straits of Tiran. But for Nasser there were also questions of timing, of preparedness. The elimination of UNEF meant Egypt's return to active belligerency against Israel; even if the Israelis did not act, Egypt would no longer have an excuse not to. Thus, in a 1965 speech to PLO delegates, he elaborated: "The Syrians say 'drive out UNEF.' But if we do, is it not essential that we have a plan? If Israeli aggression takes place against Syria, shall I attack Israel? Then Israel is the one which determines the battle for me . . . Is it conceivable that I should attack Israel while there are 50,000 Egyptian troops in Yemen?" [16]

Two years had passed and those same questions remained unanswered. Rather than ebbing, the war in Yemen had intensified, with Egyptian planes again bombing Saudi bases, carpeting them with poison gas. Egyptian officers, disgruntled, were reportedly on the brink of revolt. Yet the army would fight another twenty years if necessary, Cairo declared.

Between Arab leaders, meanwhile, coordination on security matters had all but disintegrated. Defense Council meetings in January and February 1967, both boycotted by Saudi Arabia and Jordan, again revealed the member states' failure to fulfill their pledges to the United Arab Command and the serious misuse of the few funds it had. "We just sat around and did nothing," recalled Gen. Yusuf Khawwash, Jordan's representative to the UAC General Staff. "But we did write some good studies." A report filed in March by 'Ali 'Ali 'Amer concluded that "the situation cannot facilitate the implementation of the task assigned [to the UAC], namely, the strengthening of Arab defense in order to ensure future freedom of action and to pave the way to the liberation of Palestine." Rather than the defeat of Israel, warned the UAC's commander, war at this time was liable to result in a substantial loss of Arab land.

These factors—Yemen, the absence of a viable military option against Israel—persuaded Nasser that the time was not yet right for the expulsion of UNEF. The Palestine issue would remain securely "in the icebox" until such time as Egypt and the Arab world could afford to have it thawed.[17] Yet there was another consideration in Nasser's decision, internal and highly personal. It related to the source of the recommendation itself, 'Abd al-Hakim 'Amer.

They could not have been closer friends, Nasser and 'Amer. They came from similar humble backgrounds; as young officers had served together in the Sudan, and together plotted the 1952 revolution. Nasser named his son 'Abd al-Hakim and 'Amer married Amal, his daughter, to Nasser's younger brother, Hussein. Their summerhouses in Alexandria were adjacent, and they called each other "brother"—*Akhi*—or by their nicknames: 'Jimmy' for Nasser, and 'Robinson' for 'Amer, who liked to travel. So deep was their intimacy that Nasser forgave 'Amer his pitiable showing in the Suez crisis, during which he reportedly suffered a nervous breakdown, and then his gross mismanagement of the union with Syria. He forgave, too, the bouts of alcohol and drug abuse to which 'Amer was prone, and 'Amer's secret marriage, unbeknownst to his wife, to Egyptian film star Berlinti 'Abd al-Hamid. Thin and swarthy, famously indolent and crude, 'Amer would seem an unlikely candidate for challenging Nasser's rule. Yet 'Amer was also a man of unbridled ambition, lavish toward those who supported him, ruthless with anyone opposed.

That ruthlessness finally dawned on Nasser in 1962, with the first reports of 'Amer's corruption in Yemen and his refusal to accept greater civilian control over the army. When Nasser tried to create a Presidential Council to oversee military activities, officers loyal to 'Amer threatened to revolt. Nasser backed down, and rather than circumscribing 'Amer's power, he ended up boosting it. Now 'Amer was first vice president in charge of the armed forces, a position he used to turn the army into his personal fiefdom, promoting officers on the basis of fealty rather than prowess, surrounding himself with a clique (*sila*) of *ahl al-thiqa*: yes-men. He promoted himself as well, to Mushir—field marshal—the highest rank in the Arab world.

And still his power grew. Five years later his titles included minister of science and chairman of the Egyptian Atomic Energy Commission, head of the Cairo Transportation Board and the Committee for Liquidating Feudalism, and even president of Egypt's scouts and football federations. He could appoint one-half of the seats on the Presidential Council, one-third of all ministerial and two-thirds of all ambassadorial posts. Nor was his influence confined to the domestic scene; Soviet communiqués of the period consistently emphasized his prominence, equating it with Nasser's. "The 'Mushir' . . . will have involved himself in nearly every phase of Egyptian life to a degree which seems to make him the undisputed heir apparent," reported America's embassy in Cairo, and Nasser would have certainly agreed. Yet when it came to 'Amer, the Egyptian president was either too fearful or too enamored—or both—to act. He put 'Amer under constant surveillance but refused to have him purged. "I would rather resign," he said. [18]

This profound ambivalence in Nasser's relationship with 'Amer would cast its shadow over the proposal to rid Egypt of UNEF. If Nasser, reluctant to give 'Amer credit for removing the force and restoring Egypt's army to Sinai, refused to approve the suggestion, neither did he reject it outright. Rather, he ordered the establishment of a committee to examine the eviction of UNEF in all its possible ramifications. Efforts were made to sound out the Soviets on the idea, and to seek the opinions of U Thant, the UN Secretary-General. [19]

But action on UNEF was still consigned to the future; Nasser had no immediate plans vis-à-vis Israel. In selecting a culprit for Egypt's woes, his preference remained the United States. In a February 22 speech that, Battle reported, "gathered up all the anti-American themes of the last few years and rolled them into one," Nasser linked "America" with "imperialism" no less than 100 times.

Underscoring this message was an eight-part series in *al-Ahram* by the paper's editor, Nasser's confidant, Mohamed Hassanein Heikal, which accused the U.S. of masterminding a "vast secret apparatus" designed to destroy Arab revolutionary regimes through "economic and psychological warfare [and] the hatching of plots and assassinations."

Battle, about to conclude his Cairo tour, speculated that Nasser's grim domestic situation would soon compel him toward some dramatic act abroad— in Yemen most probably, or in Africa. Battle's chargé d'affaires, David G. Nes, agreed, noting that Nasser had reached "a degree of irrationality bordering on madness, fed, of course, by the frustrations and fears generated by his failures domestic and foreign . . . [W]here will he strike next—Libya? Lebanon?" The possibility that Nasser's next target might be Israel scarcely occurred to the Americans.[20]

Israel indeed seemed to have dropped from Nasser's agenda. Hosting Iraq's new headman, 'Abd al-Rahman Muhammad 'Aref, Nasser admitted, "we cannot handle the Palestine question," which could only be solved, he claimed, through "continuous planning in a series of phases." Coming from the man who had once vowed "never to forget the rights of the Palestinian people" and someday to "recruit two to three million men in order to liberate Palestine," these were hardly fighting words. Nor did he need them to be, as long as there was quiet on the Syrian front.[21]

The Syrian Sphinx

Quiet on the Israel-Syrian border was always relative, of course. Since November and the signing of the Egyptian-Syrian treaty—since the Samu' operation and the failure of either Syria or Egypt to react to it—Damascus seemed eager to observe a tacit cease-fire. From then to the end of the year, few incidents of note were recorded. Then, starting in early January 1967, the area again began to simmer. Syrian tanks rained thirty-one shells on Kibbutz Almagor and wounded two members of Kibbutz Shamir with machine-gun fire. Clashes continued for a week before culminating in the death of one Israeli and the wounding of two others by an antipersonnel mine planted at Moshav Dishon. Al-Fatah took credit for the attack; the mine bore Syrian army markings. A candid Radio Damascus revealed on January 16 that "Syria has changed its strategy, moving from defense to attack . . . We will carry on operations until Israel has been eliminated."[22]

The reasons for this upsurge were obscure, as inscrutable as the Syrian regime itself. There was, still, the Ba'thist ideology that placed a premium on eliminating Israel, the "expanding pus which disseminates poisons of hatred and animosity," as a means of uniting the Arab world and ridding it of "reactionaries"—a process inverse to Nasser's, where unity was a precondition for warfare. "Our heroic people, singing songs of war, is longing to begin the final battle," declared the official daily *al-Ba'th* in a typical headline; "there is no way to remove occupation other than by smashing the enemy's bases and destroying his power." The day of action was imminent, said Col. Mustafa Tlas, the flashy and garrulous commander of the central front, because Arab conservatives were cowards and Syria could no longer wait.[23] War was much of what the Ba'th was about, a large part of its *raison d'être*.

Yet more than ideology lay behind Syria's border policy. Precisely at this juncture, in January, the regime was engaged in a protracted feud with the Iraq Petroleum Company. Dissatisfied with the payment received for permitting Iraqi oil to flow via pipeline over Syrian territory to the sea, Syria denounced the British-owned IPC as an agent of imperialism in the invidious pay of Israel. "The revolutionary flame emanating from the oil battle is the obvious cause for the Zionists' daily movements along our borders," Damascus radio explained. "Victory over the IPC," echoed *al-Ba'th*, is "just a first step . . . leading to the purification of Arab land from imperialism, reaction and Zionism." [24] In the peculiar logic of Damascus, the border situation and the oil negotiations were obverse sides of the same coin; showing stalwartness on one was sure to redound boldly on the other.

Then there were Syria's relations with Moscow, no less enigmatic. Soviet policy continued to pull in opposite directions, bolstering Syria politically and militarily, while also working to restrain its aggressive tendencies. This bifurcation seemed to reflect a continuing dissonance within the Kremlin itself. At the exact time when Foreign Minister Andre Gromyko was impressing upon the Politburo the need to avoid further conflicts with the United States, particularly in the Middle East, the Soviet fleet was rapidly building up in the eastern Mediterranean. In Damascus, Soviet diplomats were urging the regime to tone down its bellicose rhetoric, while in the field, Red Army advisers were spurring the Syrian army to activism. Ambitious to achieve its long-standing dream of isolating Turkey and controlling strategic waterways of the East, of neutralizing the threat posed by the U.S. Sixth Fleet, the Soviets were at the same time afraid of war, and afraid of the Arab radicalism that could trigger it.[25]

These contradictory impulses found expression in the repeated Soviet warnings of Israeli troops massing on the northern border—such warnings came in October and November 1966, and again in January 1967, each insistently denied by Israel—alongside expressions of support for Syria's shelling of Israeli settlements. Soviet schizophrenia was also in evidence during the state visit of Syrian strongman Salah Jadid on January 20. Noticeably snubbed by Kremlin leaders, Jadid nevertheless came away with pledges for large-scale military aid and backing for his stand against "aggressive Zionism." To both Israeli and American observers, the Soviets appeared to want to maintain a low boil in the Middle East, aiming for "tensions without explosions," for "small rather than big trouble."[26]

Emboldened by the Soviets, incited by their struggle with the IPC, Syrian leaders had another, personal, reason for increasing tensions with Israel. Despised by the general population, the ruling clique was also internally divided—officers against the civilian "doctors," President al-Atassi and Foreign Minister Makhous—and the officers amongst themselves. Hafez al-Assad, with the support of the air force, was pitted against the army and President Jadid, while both generals were opposed by Intelligence Chief 'Abd al-Karim al-Jundi. On January 17, three of al-Jundi's men reportedly tried to assassinate al-Assad, shooting at his car while the defense minister was en route to his physician. If true, the ambush was not an extraordinary event. Often the gray boredom of radically socialist Damascus was broken by explosions and the crackle of gunfire; soldiers surrounded the ministries. Ranking officers and even government ministers were routinely arrested, and death sentences handed down for a range of political crimes, from "spreading confessional bigotry" to "hindering the socialist order."[27]

Such internal conflicts greatly deepened the regime's insecurity and, to overcome it, the need to "out-Nasser Nasser"—the CIA's phrase—in confronting Israel. In a secret meeting with one Farid 'Awda, a businessman with close links to Britain, Hafez al-Assad tried to solicit money and guns for a "diversion on the southern [Israeli] front." This would allow him to oust both Jadid and Atassi and to avoid an imminent Egypt-led Sunni coup in Syria. The IPC controversy, Assad promised, could then be solved immediately.[28]

All these factors, foreign and domestic, impacted on the border, where violence steadily mounted throughout the early months of 1967. Fearing the outbreak of war, U Thant called on the parties to resolve their differences within the framework of the Israeli-Syrian Mixed Armistice Commission. Though it had received some 66,000 complaints over the years, most of them relating to the DZ's, the ISMAC had only intermittently functioned. Obstructing its work was Syria's demand for control over the DZ's, Israel's rejection of that demand, and the unmasked animosity between the delegates.

Animosity was indeed palpable from the moment the ISMAC reconvened on January 25. The Israelis suspected the Syrians of playing a double game: seeking a peaceful return of Arab farmers to the DZ's, while continuing the "popular war" against Israel. Moshe Sasson, the Israeli delegate, characterized the meeting as "extraordinary" and "informal," thus downplaying Damascus's role in the zones. The Syrians were no less dubious. They described their purpose as "putting an end to Zionist aggression against Arab land," and in no way guaranteeing the "security of the gang-state inside Palestine." The gap between the two sides proceeded to yawn as Sasson proposed a bilateral pledge "to abide faithfully by their non-aggression obligations and to refrain from all other acts of hostility against one another." Syria's representative, Capt. 'Abdallah, rejected this idea, and insisted instead on the adoption of practical measures to defuse the DZ conflict. Yet, when his turn came to table such suggestions, 'Abdallah launched into a prolonged tirade against Israel and its policies. Thereafter, Sasson and 'Abdallah could scarcely agree on an agenda, much less make progress toward resolutions.[29]

Border incidents, meanwhile, multiplied. On March 3, a member of Kibbutz Shamir was seriously injured when his tractor struck a Syrian mine. Similar mines were found three weeks later outside the Israeli villages of Kfar Szold and Zar'it. Far more turbulent than the Syrian border, however, was the frontier with Jordan. There, the first months of 1967 saw some 270 incidents—an increase, Israel acknowledged, of 100 percent. On March 12, for example, an Israeli train from Kiryat Gat to Kibbutz Lahav was halted by an explosion on the tracks; leaflets found nearby proclaimed "Death to the Zionist invaders—Victory to the heroic Palestinians." Four Palestinian saboteurs were arrested the following day, opposite the West Bank town of Qalqilya, carrying a load of explosives, and two were killed on March 26, trying to demolish a water pump east of Arad. Al-Fatah issued a series of thirty-four communiqués describing its actions in great detail and praising the courage of its martyrs.[30]

Without actually taking responsibility for these attacks, Syria exuberantly praised them. "Our known objective is the freeing of Palestine and the liquidation of the Zionist existence there," the regime reiterated on April 8, "Our army and our people will give our backing to every Arab fighter acting for the return of Palestine."[31]

This encomium, together with its resistance to UN mediation, led many Western observers to conclude that Syria was more than ever committed to war. Thus, the British embassy in Damascus, noting the threat to confront Israel "not defensively" but with a "massive offensive blow inside Occupied Palestine," reported that "there is every indication that the present mood of the Syrian Government and the Syrian armed forces means this threat will be carried out, whatever the cost." America's Ambassador Hugh H. Smythe descried Syria's "Stalinist" regime of "fear and frustration," and warned that "the paranoiac fear of plots and aggressions, with its constant provocations of Israel, could lead . . . to a military adventure which can only end in defeat."

Syria's sponsorship of Palestinian guerrilla attacks became so pronounced that American officials abandoned their long-standing opposition to Israeli retaliations. "The Syrians are sons of bitches," exclaimed Townsend Hoopes, a senior Defense Department official, during a visit to the Israeli Foreign Ministry in March, "Why the hell didn't you beat them over the head when it would have been the most natural thing to do?" Eugene Rostow put it more succinctly to Ephraim "Eppy" Evron, the minister at the Israeli embassy in Washington. "An attack *from* a state is an attack *by* a state," he said. [32]

Israel was indeed preparing the groundwork for a reprisal against Syria. As early as January 16, in a *note verbale*, Evron informed the White House that "the continuation of this aggressive [Syrian] policy will force Israel to take action in self-defense as is her international right and national duty." But the problem remained far more complicated than that, again due to the danger of Soviet intervention, as Eshkol was poignantly aware. Then, on April 1, Palestinian guerrillas blew up the water pump at Kibbutz Misgav Am on the Lebanese border. For Eshkol, the former farmer and water engineer, this was a final straw. "I believe that we have to punish the Syrians," he admitted in a private meeting with Rabin, "but I don't want war and I don't want fighting on the [Golan] ridge." Rabin, whom Lior described as suffering from a "Syrian syndrome" of abiding hatred for Damascus, agreed. At the next Syrian provocation, Israel would send armored tractors deep into the DZ's, wait for them to be fired on, and then strike back.[33]

Thirty Seconds over Damascus

The provocation was not long in coming. Palestinian guerrillas struck twice on March 31, planting charges under an irrigation pump and railroad tracks along the Jordanian border. As planned, the Israeli tractors advanced through the southern DZ, adjacent to the Ein Gev and Ha'on kibbutzim and, as anticipated, drew machine-gun and antitank fire from the Tawafiq position above them on the Golan. The IDF responded in kind. The exchanges were short, with little damage to either side. A similar clash seemed to be developing at nine o'clock on the morning of April 7, when two tractors entered the DZ near Tel Katzir, on the southern tip of the Sea of Galilee. This time the Syrians greeted them not with small arms but with 37-mm cannons. Almost instantly, both tractors were hit. Israeli tanks shot at the Syrian guns and the Syrian guns—81-mm and 120-mm mortars—bombed Israeli settlements.

What began as a skirmish rapidly escalated into a miniwar. Cannon and machine-gun fire raked the Golan and the flatlands beneath it. By 1:30 in the afternoon, according to UN observers, 247 shells had hit Kibbutz Gadot; several of its buildings were ablaze. The UN tried to arrange a cease-fire, which the Syrians accepted, but only on the condition that Israel stop all work in the DZ. Eshkol, in Jerusalem, but in constant contact with Rabin in his forward combat position, rejected these terms—fresh tractors would be sent in—but then balked at the chief of staff's suggestion that the IAF be activated to neutralize Syria's long-range artillery. An hour passed; the Syrian bombardment intensified. Finally, Eshkol relented. IAF Vatour bombers, covered by Mirages, were soon rocketing Syrian bunkers and villages—in one, Siqufiya, forty houses were destroyed and fourteen civilians reported killed. The Israelis had barely begun their sorties when they were engaged by Syrian MiG's.

Syria's air force had never fared well against Israel's, and this time was no exception. Two of the MiG's were downed over Quneitra, the Golan's largest city, and the remainder pursued back to Damascus. There, in a massive dogfight involving as many as 130 planes, another four MiG's were destroyed. In a mere thirty seconds, Israel had established supremacy over Syria's skies. The regime was at a loss to explain its predicament—"Citizens: we call your attention to the fact that enemy aircraft are flying in our airspace. Our air force is now engaging them"—and later claimed that "our heroic eagles" had shot down five Israeli planes. But the bitter truth could not be hidden; the entire capital had witnessed the clash. The Israeli Mirages indulged in a victory loop around Damascus, and cheers broke out in Rabin's post. Israel had regained the initiative, the chief of staff claimed. The Syrians had been humiliated while the Egyptians remained inert.

Rabin was not wrong: Like the Samu' raid before it, the events of April 7 underscored the impotence of the Syrian-Egyptian defense pact. "How many times have I pleaded with our Syrian brothers not to provoke Israel?" lamented UAC chief 'Ali 'Ali 'Amer in a private conversation with Shuqayri. "They know that we have not yet completed our military preparations . . . They know that we must choose the time and the place of the battle . . . We have begged them time and again and yet they continue shelling Israeli settlements, in sending al-Fatah cells to shoot up transport or to mine the roads, and all this hurts our military efforts." Lamely, Nasser claimed that Israel's aggression was an attempt to divert his attention from Yemen. The Golan, he explained, was out of Egypt's range. [34]

In a quick face-saving move, Nasser dispatched both his prime minister, Sidqi Suliman, and air force commander, Gen. Sidqi Mahmud, to Damascus. The two, the highest-ranking Egyptians to visit Syria since the UAR's breakup six years before, engaged in much rhetoric, denouncing the usual bugbears of Zionism, American imperialism, and Arab reaction. Behind the scenes, though, the Egyptians labored to persuade their hosts to desist from further support of al-Fatah. If it persisted and precipitated war, they warned, Syria would stand alone.

The Syrians remained noncommittal, however, and rejected their visitors' request to station Egyptian jets near Damascus. Instead, they again managed to extract a pledge for Egyptian assistance in the event of war. Code-named *Rashid*, the plan called for simultaneous air attacks against Israel, Syria hitting the north of the country and Egypt striking its southern and central regions. Syrian forces would also advance across the Galilee, aiming for Haifa. It was only here, in the area of ground activity, that the Egyptians drew the line. "All I told the Syrians," said Sidqi Mahmud upon his return to Nasser, "was that in the event of a concentration of Israeli troops on their border, I would raise the level of air activity inside Sinai and southern Israel in order to tie down the bulk of Israel's air force . . . We never talked about moving Egyptian troops into Sinai." [35]

The April 7 fighting also resembled Samu' in its impact on the inter-Arab struggle. Jordan was quick to exploit Nasser's discredit and claimed that Israeli planes had not only attacked Syria but had also buzzed airfields in Sinai, yet still the Egyptians recoiled. "Our enemy . . . unfortunately knows . . . how serious President Abdel Nasser is when he said in his recent speech that the

UAR would join the battle the moment Syria was attacked by Israel," Amman Radio chided. "All Arabs know that the recent Israeli aggression against fraternal Syria lasted several hours." Three of the downed Syrian planes had crashed in Jordan, the broadcast continued, and were found to be armed with wooden rockets; Assad was afraid to give them real ones. No less vituperatively, the Egyptians replied by accusing Hussein of colluding with Israel in the attack. "Jordan is becoming a garrison of imperialism, a camp for training mercenary gangs, a reactionary outpost for the protection of Israel," hounded Prime Minister Suliman. Like his grandfather, the king was in league with the Zionists—"born agents, raised on treason . . . Hussein works for the CIA"—Nasser harangued.[36]

From this violent tussle of words, Hussein no doubt came out the bloodier. His position, for one, was far more vulnerable than Nasser's. Alienated from Egypt, Syria, and Iraq, unprotected by Saudi Arabia and the other conservative states, Jordan was poised to drop out of the Arab League, where Shuqayri had indicted Hussein on thirty-three counts of treachery. Not a single Arab ally would help defend Jordan from Israel, which, as Samu' seemed to prove, would rather conquer the West Bank than take on Syria directly. Cornered, Hussein fought to break out of his deepening isolation. He effected the resignation of Wasfi al-Tall, his rabidly anti-Nasserist prime minister, and ordered a halt to anti-Egyptian propaganda.[37] Then, on April 28, he made the extraordinary move of inviting Egyptian Foreign Minister Mahmoud Riad, a long-standing acquaintance of his, to the royal palace. Taken aback by this sudden *volte face*, Nasser nevertheless consented; Riad flew off to Jordan.

The king's message was simple: Syria was laying a trap, heating up the border to the point where Egypt would have to intervene. A war was coming in which Nasser would fall and Jordan be destroyed. Riad's response was equally concise: Jordan must then allow Iraqi and Saudi troops to deploy on its soil, in accordance with the UAC plan. But Hussein said no, not before Nasser rid Egypt of UNEF and returned his army to Sinai. The meeting concluded thus with no change in either side's position. Four days later, Radio Amman was back in full vitriol, excoriating Nasser as "the only Arab leader . . . who lives in peace and tranquility with Israel. Not one shot has been fired from his direction against Israel . . . We hope he is satisfied with this . . . disgrace." Yemeni villages were certainly not "out of range," the broadcasts recalled, when they were bombed with poison gas.[38]

Relations between Arab rulers continued to deteriorate and so, too, did the situation along Israel's borders. Rather than reducing tensions, the events of April 7 further aggravated them. Over the next month al-Fatah undertook no less than fourteen operations. Mines and explosive charges were planted not only on the Israeli side of the Syrian and Jordanian borders, but across from Lebanon as well. Attacks from the latter peaked on May 5, when Palestinian gunmen launched a mortar barrage from Lebanese territory, shelling Kibbutz Manara. Israel, for its part, continued plowing the DZ's, and so invited Syrian bombardments. One such salvo, on April 11, sent 200 American tourists scrambling for the shelters of a kibbutz below the Golan Heights. But Syrian fire was not always a reaction to Israeli moves. At Kibbutz Gonen in the Hula Valley, farmers came under fire on April 12 while merely repairing a fence; one of them was shot in the head.[39]

The calculus of Syrian attacks, whether direct or through Palestinian guerrilla groups, had become overwhelming for the Israelis. Public opinion, particularly in the border areas, demanded that vengeance be exacted for the bloodshed and not from Jordan but from its actual perpetrator, Syria. The Americans and the British, whether for fear of Hussein's throne or out of genuine umbrage at Damascus, were pushing in the same direction. Abroad, Israeli diplomats were continuing to establish a case for retaliation. "Surely the Syrian government is under no illusion of being immune from Israeli attack should the terrorist incidents continue," Israeli Ambassador Avraham (Abe) Harman told Battle, now the Assistant Secretary of State for Near Eastern Affairs, in Washington. Even in public pronouncements, in Eban's complaint to the Security Council, the legitimacy of reprisal was stressed: "The Syrian assumption that there will be no reaction to provocation is fundamentally flawed. Every country with a healthy international conscience will identify with Israel's inability to reconcile itself to the dispatch of terrorists from Syria."[40]

A decision, however onerous, could no longer be avoided. Bearing its brunt were two men, radically different in age and background, yet complimentary in character. Compared to Nasser and 'Amer, with their ambivalent relationship and political machinations, Israel's prime minister and chief of staff made for a relatively simple, smooth running team.

Improbable Duo

Born near Kiev—the family's original name was Shkolnik—in 1895, when czarist pogroms were commonplace, Eshkol had grown up in a milieu of violence, religious fervor, and Zionism. At age nineteen, he moved to Palestine, to the first kibbutz, Degania, beside the Sea of Galilee. There he proved himself a robust worker, surviving bouts of malaria and attacks by marauding Bedouin. But while he loved the soil and always regarded himself as its tiller, Eshkol found his real forte in politics, first as a representative of the kibbutz movement and then of the leading labor union. In contrast to Ben-Gurion, the visionary, Eshkol was the pragmatist, the realist. His years of public service had yielded lasting accomplishments, among them building the country's infrastructure and freeing Israeli Arabs from the military administration imposed on them in 1948. His proudest feat, though, was the founding of *Mekorot* (Sources), the national water utility. It was Eshkol's dream to crisscross the country with irrigation pipes, "like the veins of a human body," and to see every inch of open land cultivated.

Like Nasser, Eshkol was a man of simple tastes. The only flamboyance in his life was his young and attractive third wife, Miriam (he divorced his first wife; a second died). But while Egypt's leader possessed a powerful charisma, Israel's prime minister was utterly devoid of it. With his lackluster, nondescript face, plain glasses, and monotonic delivery, he appeared the classic bureaucrat—a character from Kafka's *Castle*. Yet that gray exterior masked a warm and ebullient personality, a penchant for humorous aphorisms ("Want to make a small fortune in Israel?" he once asked, "Bring a big one"), and a passion for Yiddish. Ezer Weizman remembered him as "a lovable man, easy-going . . . Open, a grand conversationalist," and even a political rival such as Shimon Peres could praise him as "determined but not obstinate, flexible but not submissive; he knew that life without compromise is impossible." He was famous for his dexterity in avoiding commitments—"Sure I promised, but did I promise to keep my promise?" was one of his favorite sayings. But that same elusiveness often made him seem indecisive. One popular joke had Eshkol, asked by a waitress whether he wanted coffee or tea, hedging, "half of both."

On no point was Eshkol's reputation weakest than on military matters, a crippling flaw in a country in which the powers of prime minister and defense minister were traditionally wielded by one man. That man had been Ben-Gurion. From his bungalow on the desert kibbutz of Sde Boker, he harped on his successor's alleged inadequacy on defense, specifically his neglect of the Franco-Israeli alliance and his buckling to American strictures on Dimona. But such charges were largely unfair. Eshkol had been instrumental in building the IDF into a modern force based on tank power and jets. As prime minister, he rarely refrained from authorizing retaliation raids—though too rarely, for some pacific-minded Israelis. What Eshkol lacked, however, was combat experience, having served only briefly with the British in World War I. He was deeply stung by Ben-Gurion's criticism—"It was like a father throwing him out of Eden," Miriam recalled.[41]

The image of Eshkol as military lightweight nevertheless persisted, along with accusations that he was either too quick or too hesitant on the trigger. Eager to change that image, the prime minister lost no opportunity to don his signature beret and visit the troops in the field or, behind closed doors, to hold counsel with his chief of staff.

When it came to combat, Yitzhak Rabin was richly experienced. He had seen some of the heaviest fighting of the War of Independence, commanding elite troops in the battles in and around Jerusalem. Unlike most of his fellow officers, however, kibbutzniks and farmers, Rabin had grown up in Tel Aviv, the son of Labor Zionist activists who were often away from home. He was a native-born Israeli, soft-spoken and direct, but also surprisingly shy. He and Eshkol were practically mirror images of each other—the first attractive yet quiet, the second physically bland but personally vivid. For that reason, perhaps, and because they needed each other, the two men got along well. "Talkative, overflowing with simplicity and humor," Rabin's memoirs describe the prime minister, "a brilliant administrator, a pragmatist, and a master at assimilating every minute detail." Eshkol reciprocated by deed, in 1966 asking the IDF chief to remain for a second three-year term after his first was completed. Together, they embarked on a large-scale armament program that gave precedence to the air force and armor, and a defense strategy predicated on deterrence.[42]

Apart from occasional skids of friction—Rabin could be *too* popular for Eshkol's tastes, and Eshkol too intrusive in defense matters—the relationship between prime minister and chief of staff remained felicitous through the first months of 1967. But then that relationship had never been tested in a crisis. In early May, however, as Arab attacks mounted on the northern border, the Israeli Cabinet authorized the army to launch a limited retaliation against Syria. Rabin reiterated his demand for a large-scale raid to thoroughly discredit, if not topple, the Ba'th regime. But Eshkol again opposed the attack, fearful of a Soviet backlash. The Kremlin had again condemned Israel for plots against the Syrian government, this time with the collusion of Western oil companies. Israel was a "serious threat to peace" and a "puppet used by foreign elements, Soviet Deputy Foreign Minister Viktor Semyonov had scolded Ambassador Katz; if catastrophe ensued in the Middle East, the Zionists would be held responsible.[43]

Rebuffing Rabin's advice, Eshkol instead turned to Washington. He requested a public reaffirmation of America's commitment to Israeli security, specifically through the accelerated sale of Patton tanks and Skyhawk jets. "Eshkol really finds himself in a serious dilemma," Barbour wrote his superiors in support of the sale, "and would appreciate as much hand holding as possible." But congressional constraints on arms transfers, tightened in light of Vietnam, militated against such a deal, as did Israeli resistance to on-site American inspections of Dimona. Though Johnson was not averse to bolstering Israel verbally, weapons were out of the question.[44]

American resistance to military involvement with Israel was further illustrated when Eshkol told *U.S. News and World Report* that, in the event of war, Israel expected to receive help from the U.S. Sixth Fleet. The Arab world reacted acridly, canceling port-of-call visits for American ships in Beirut and Alexandria. An "imperialist base floating on the seas," Syria's al-Attasi had described the fleet, pledging that "the Arab seas and the fish in them will feed on their [the Americans'] rotting imperialist bodies." The State Department was quick to announce that there was no such commitment on the part of America's armed forces, intimating that in the event of fighting in the Middle East, the Sixth Fleet would remain neutral.[45]

A final effort to find an alternative to violence was directed not at the U.S. but at what was, for the Israelis, an unlikely address: the United Nations. Gideon Rafael, Israel's ambassador to the UN, appealed to secretary-general U Thant to speak out against Syrian support for terror. Though rarely known to criticize the

Arabs, U Thant could no longer ignore the evidence of Syrian implication in the guerrilla attacks. At a press conference on May 11, he denounced those attacks as "deplorable" and "insidious," as "menaces to peace" and "contrary to the letter and spirit of the Armistice." Noting that the raids "seem to indicate that the individuals who committed them have had more specialized training than has usually been evidenced in al-Fatah incidents in the past," he called on all the responsible "governments" to stop them.

Seemingly a victory for the Israelis, this unprecedented censure of an Arab state by the top UN official in fact came to nothing. A proposed Security Council debate on the issue never materialized due to Soviet foot dragging and the fact that a full third of the Council's members refused to recognize its current president, a Taiwanese. The Syrians roundly condemned U Thant's statement, their UN ambassador, George Tomeh, claiming that it had "condoned Israel's use of force."[46] With the Security Council paralyzed and the Arabs so incensed, the secretary-general refrained from taking his initiative any further. The matter was dropped.

Rabin, meanwhile, aware of Israel's failures in both the U.S. and the UN, resorted to defiant rhetoric, telling the IDF magazine *Bamahane* that "the [Israeli] response to Jordan and Lebanon is appropriate only for states that are not interested in terrorist attacks launched against their will. With Syria the problem is different, because the regime is sponsoring the terrorists. Therefore, the essence of the response to Syria must be different."

Eshkol, along with many cabinet members, thought that Rabin had gone too far in his threat, and again criticized him for it, but then the prime minister came out with exhortations of his own. "We have no choice," he told a Mapai party forum on May 12, "we may well have to act against the centers of aggression and those who encourage it by means no less serious than those we used on April 7." And the following day, on Israel Radio: "There will be no immunity for a state that encourages sabotage operations against us and Syria is the spearhead of such actions." Further inflammatory statements ensued, and not only from Eshkol and Rabin, but also from generals David Elazar, commander of the Northern Front, and IDF intelligence chief Aharon Yariv, many of which were picked up and amplified by the foreign press. Ezer Weizman, writing years later in his memoirs, recalled, "High-flown speeches (on second thought, they may have been too high-flown) were the order of the day."[47]

The Israelis' barbs caught the Syrians at a particularly sensitive juncture, when opposition from observant Muslims and middle-class merchants was increasingly threatening the Ba'th. Should Israel attack, President al-Atassi warned, "Syria will launch a popular liberation war in which all the Arab masses will take part." Ibrahim Makhous, the foreign minister, told Ambassador Smythe of an alleged "imperialist plot" against Damascus, and of the "probability of a large Israeli offensive in the near future." Zionist troops were already massing in the DZ's, he claimed. But when Smythe suggested that regime rein in the guerrillas, Makhous balked. "Syria refuses to take responsibility for Palestinians fighting for their despoiled homeland," he bristled. "Palestine is a sacred cause that will never die."

Rather than deterring Damascus from further aggression, remarks made by Eshkol and Rabin spurred it to redoubled support for al-Fatah. The organization struck again on May 9 and 13, with sabotage raids across the Syrian and Jordanian borders, respectively. A highly trained infiltrator, described as blond, Hebrew-speaking, and carrying a British passport, crossed the Sea of Galilee in a boat launched from a shore area under Syrian army control. Apprehended, he was found to possess a large amount of explosives and detonating devices to be used, he confessed, for assassinating Israeli leaders.[48]

Israel's efforts to forestall a major confrontation with Syria only succeeded in multiplying the chances for one. That same pattern would recur with another controversy brewing that May, surrounding Israel's Independence Day parade.

Held in various cities on a rotational basis, the 1967 parade was scheduled to take place in Israeli West Jerusalem on May 15, the first time in the country's nineteen-year history that the Hebrew and Gregorian dates of its independence coincided. The presence in the Holy City of so many Israeli troops, though not technically a violation of the Armistice, sparked protests throughout the Arab world and from Jordan in particular. The UN also objected to the parade, as did the Western Powers, which prohibited their ambassadors from attending.

Eshkol dismissed this opposition, noting that Jordan, which in violation of the Armistice denied Jews access to the Western Wall and the Mount of Olives, had no say in what Israel did on its own side of the city. Yet, in an effort to limit tensions, Eshkol excised several militant lines from a poem scheduled to be read at the event by Israeli laureate Natan Alterman, and agreed to refrain from introducing heavy weapons into Jerusalem.[49] Though Rabin bristled at these decisions, he ultimately complied. No tanks or artillery pieces would take part in the parade.

After a period of dissonance in their reactions to the Syrian threat, the prime minister and his chief of staff had together avoided a minor crisis in Jerusalem. Neither man was aware, however, of the degree to which that avoidance would trigger a far vaster, bloodier, upheaval.

Action and Reaction

Egyptian leaders were also unsuspecting of any imminent catastrophe. One of them, Anwar al-Sadat, left the country on April 29 on a mission that had nothing to do with the Arab-Israeli conflict. Sadat was merely to pay courtesy calls on political figures in Mongolia and North Korea, and return by way of Moscow. "We expect nothing significant to emerge from these visits," forecast the U.S. embassy in Cairo.

Much of the Americans' lack of expectations was due to Sadat himself, a unexceptionable figure who had never held any serious military post, serving innocuously as speaker of the National Assembly. But Sadat's anodyne exterior—tall, dark, taciturn—obscured a record that included two prison terms for pro-German activity during World War II and conspiracy to assassinate an Egyptian official loyal to Britain. A co-conspirator in the 1952 revolution, he later maintained ties with the Muslim Brotherhood and opposed Egypt's secret contacts with Israel. Perhaps because of this ideological stalwartness, his unflagging loyalty to the regime, Nasser trusted him. If nothing else, Sadat had the president's ear.

The Soviets understood this, and assured that Sadat's itinerary included meetings with Premier Kosygin and President Podgorny, with Foreign Minister Andrei Gromyko, and his deputy, Semyonov. The talks proved to be far more than a mere exchange of pleasantries. In portentous terms, the Soviet leaders informed Sadat of an imminent Israeli invasion of Syria aimed at toppling the Ba'th. Though the Kremlin had already given a stern warning to the Israeli ambassador, between ten and twelve brigades were now massed on the Syrian border, ready to advance sometime between May 16 and 22. Podogorny told him, "You must not be taken by surprise, the coming days will be fateful," and "Syria is facing a difficult situation and we will help Syria in that situation." To substantiate their information, the Soviets cited the absence of tanks and artillery from the impending Independence Day parade in Jerusalem—concrete evidence, they claimed, that the weapons had been moved up north.[50]

The reasons for the Russians' warning would remain obscure, leaving room for a gamut of theories as to why they had tendered it at that particular juncture and what they sought to gain. Some speculated that Moscow invented the crisis in order to bolster Nasser's stature and to cement the Soviet-Syrian alliance. Other hypotheses held that the Soviets sought to lure Nasser into a war with Israel, to destroy him and so clear the field for Syrian preeminence and the penetration of Communist cadres. The time was right to exploit America's distraction in Vietnam, many experts postulated, to curb rising Chinese influence in the region, and to deal a smashing blow to Zionism. Still others went so far as to suggest that the United States had leaked the information on Israel's attack plans in order to lessen Egypt's pressure on the Gulf countries, or that Israel, itself, was the source, seeking a war of territorial aggrandizement. Former Soviet officials would later blame the misinterpretation of intelligence received from well-placed KGB agents inside Israel regarding the probability of retaliatory action against Syria. "The information was unconfirmed and required further investigation," recalled Supreme Soviet member Karen Brutents, "But Semyonov couldn't control himself and passed it on to the Egyptians."[51]

Lost in this conjecturing is the fact that there was little new in the Soviet warning to Sadat, that reports of intended Israeli aggression against Syria had been issued repeatedly over the previous year. Those admonitions, it was noted, reflected deep rifts in the Kremlin leadership and differing perceptions of Soviet interests in the Middle East—a middle road between avoiding all clashes in the region and plunging it into war. Fully expecting an Israeli retaliation against Syria, the Soviets were keen to prevent a battle that was liable to result in Arab defeat and superpower confrontation. Yet, at the same time, they wanted to maintain a heightened level of tension in the area, a reminder of the Arabs' need for Soviet aid. Hence the stress on Egypt's role in deterring the Israelis; hence the specific mention of ten to twelve Israeli brigades allegedly massed on the border. The tendency of Communist decisionmakers to be influenced by their own propaganda on imperialist and Zionist perfidy—"ideological myopia," in the British Cabinet's phrase—also played a part, magnifying the threat Israel really posed to Syria. [52]

In the end, why, exactly, the Soviets acted as they did proved less important than the way the Egyptians reacted. Sadat returned to Cairo after midnight on May 14 and hastened to Nasser's house. There he found the president and Field Marshal 'Amer already discussing the Russian report. Further details of the Israeli mobilization had also been furnished to the Foreign Ministry by Soviet ambassador Dimitri Pojidaev, and to Egyptian intelligence chief Salah Nasir through a local agent of the KGB. Then a similar message—the first of many—had arrived from Damascus:

> We have learned from a dependable source that, one, Israel has mobilized most of its reserves and that, two, it has concentrated the bulk of its forces on the Syrian border. The estimate force strength is 15 brigades. Three, The Israelis are planning a large-scale attack on Syria, including paratrooper drops, to take place between the 15th and the 22nd of May.

'Amer also boasted of having seen aerial photographs that confirmed the Israeli concentrations.[53]

Syrian claims of impending invasions had become commonplace in recent months, and Nasser had summarily ignored them. But there could be no dismissing a warning of such specificity from so many Soviet sources, including the Kremlin itself. Viewed against the backdrop of the menacing statements of Eshkol and Rabin, and the absence of heavy weapons in Israel's parade, the intelligence had the ring of truth. Nasser and 'Amer spent much of the rest of the night discussing the possible ramifications of an Israeli attack on Syria and possible Egyptian responses, including the removal of UNEF. At 7:30 A.M. they resolved that the general staff would convene in another four hours and decide on the army's action.[54]

That decision was not to be taken cavalierly. Egypt's economic crisis had begun to take its toll on the army, whose ranks, in spite of budget cuts, had continued to swell. The deficit was felt in declining maintenance—eight pilots were now available for every functioning jet—and a halt to nearly all training exercises. But the military's fault lines were not merely financial. Senior positions were meted out on the basis of family or political ties, not merit, while subalterns were purposefully chosen for their incompetence, so as not to threaten their commanders. There was little loyalty among officers and even less between them and the common soldier. "I always felt sorry for the abandoned Egyptians in the Sinai when large numbers of their officers took off for long weekends in Cairo," recalled UNEF's Gen. Rikhye. On the structural level, no framework existed for cooperation or even communication between air, ground, and naval forces. Orders followed wildly circuitous routes before finally reaching troops in the field, where initiative was virtually unknown. Ideology, rather than performance, was the yardstick for success. "We had great stacks of books and brochures on the glories of the July 23rd Revolution," Gen. 'Abd al-Mun'im Khalil, commander of Egypt's paratroopers, complained. "The books, kept in perfect condition and inspected constantly, served as the basis for determining a unit's fighting ability. Officers joked about them, but took them to Yemen anyway to show their loyalty."[55]

The army's deficiencies had been brought to Nasser's attention and in ways certain to reinforce his long-standing opposition to any war with Israel. Though his rhetoric remained as fiery as ever—"We want to fight to liberate and regain Palestine," he assured Alexandria University law school students on May 10—Nasser took no concrete steps in response to the air battles of April 7. Egypt's ambassador to Washington, Mustafa Kamel, consistently told Americans of Nasser's commitment to keeping the Israel issue "in the icebox," to the point that the White House was willing to reconsider its Egyptian aid policy. "While no one likes the idea of paying off a bully," wrote Walt Rostow in an internal memorandum to the president, "Nasser is still the most powerful figure in the Middle East . . . and has restrained wilder Arabs who have pushed for a disastrous Arab-Israeli showdown."[56]

Unbeknownst to the Americans, however, was the existence of a countervailing force in the Egyptian military, one that assiduously pressed for war. Many generals believed that, shortcomings aside, the army had several times as many planes, tanks, and guns as the Israelis, and that numerical superiority alone would suffice to guarantee an Arab victory. Demoralized, economically depressed, Israel, they argued, was no longer the juggernaut the Egyptians once feared and should be struck before it launched its own attack against Syria or Jordan. Siqdi Mahmud gloated that Egypt's "warning system and air defense are capable of discovering and destroying any air attack by the enemy, no matter how many aircraft were involved, or from what direction they come." Under the umbrella of Russian missiles, Sidqi Mahmud believed, Egyptian armor could advance unimpeded. 'Amer was particularly bluff in his confidence. "Our armed forces are not only capable of repulsing Israel but of moving eastward," the field marshal reported to Nasser in early May, "Egypt can establish a position from which to impose its own political conditions and to force Israel to respect Arab and Palestinian rights."[57]

Such praise for Egypt's military did little to persuade Nasser, who constantly reminded his advisers that Egypt would be fighting not only Israel but also the United States. But the key question for him now was no longer whether the army could prevail over Israel but whether his rule could survive another failure to come to Syria's defense. The toppling of the Ba'th could generate the fall, domino-style, of "progressive" regimes throughout the region—beginning in Iraq and Yemen and ending possibly in Egypt itself. The Egyptian-Syrian defense pact would be proven useless and Egypt's stature in Soviet eyes vastly diminished. "The Eastern front could collapse," Nasser told Heikal over the direct, encoded line between their offices, "Egypt could find itself facing Israel alone." After Samu', after April 7, Nasser could no longer sit aside and watch.[58]

But neither could he let 'Amer take the lead. Tensions between the president and his field marshal remained as high-pitched as ever. Increasingly fearful of sedition, Nasser had attempted to employ retired officers as sources of information on 'Amer's influence in the army. 'Amer checked the move, then rejected Nasser's offer to appoint him prime minister in exchange for conceding his control over the military. Instead, 'Amer's power expanded, to the extent that Defense Minister Shams Badran and Air Force Chief Sidqi Mahmud, both of whom were his protégés, completely neutralized Chief of Staff Fawzi, a Nasser loyalist. Now, with crisis brewing in the north, 'Amer showed signs of wanting to exploit that situation to elevate his status yet higher, leading the army to a glorious victory.[59] Nasser sought to prevent this, to regain his prerogatives at home and the initiative in the region, all the while proving to the Arabs that he—not 'Amer, not Syria—was their best defense against Israel.

The Egyptian general staff convened at the Supreme Headquarters as planned, at 11:30, under 'Amer's aegis. Military intelligence chief Maj. Gen. Muhammad Ahmad Sadiq surveyed the information received from Soviet, Syrian, and Lebanese sources regarding the concentration of Israeli forces on the Syrian border and the probability of attack sometime between May 17 and 21. 'Amer then took control of the meeting, and ordered that all air and frontline troops be put on the highest alert, and the reserves called to active duty. Over the next forty-eight to seventy-two hours, the army would advance into Sinai and take up positions on the three lines of the Conqueror (*al-Qahir*) plan. The deployment would be defensive, but offensive operations would not be ruled out, 'Amer said. Gen. Fawzi, meanwhile, was to fly posthaste to Damascus and assure Syrian leaders that Egypt was ready to fight with every resource it had, "to destroy Israel's air force and occupy its territory."[60]

While the general staff deliberated, Nasser was in Tahrir Square, at the office of Dr. Mahmoud Fawzi, his chief adviser for foreign affairs. Like Sadat, Fawzi enjoyed unusual access to the president. The British Foreign Office described him as an *éminence gris*, "an able negotiator and [a] resourceful diplomat . . . a past-master at putting on the most moderate terms the policies of his hairier masters." The subject of their discussion was particularly delicate: the possible eviction of UNEF. Though 'Amer was adamant about removing the force entirely, Nasser was less categorical. Reluctant to take on the defense of Gaza—in the event of war, Israel's likeliest target—or to substitute the crisis in Syria with one in Sinai, Nasser was especially loath to return Egyptian troops to Sharm al-Sheikh. Once there, those soldiers could not simply watch as Israeli ships passed under their noses through Tiran. The straits would have to be closed again, and Israel would almost certainly strike back.

Fawzi was ready with a number of briefs affirming that Nasser had the sovereign authority to dismiss UNEF without prior review by either the General Assembly or the Security Council. Fawzi further suggested that Nasser could order UNEF to pull back from the border and to concentrate in Gaza and Sharm al-Sheikh, and that instructions to this effect could be given to Gen. Rikhye rather than to U Thant, thus emphasizing their practical, as opposed to legal, nature. Nasser was impressed with these arguments, and was confident of his chances for success. His previous contacts with India and Yugoslavia, contributors of two of UNEF's largest contingents, and with U Thant, had indicated that all would accede his request to relocate the force.[61]

While Fawzi drew up the letter to Rikhye, Nasser reviewed the decisions of the general staff and consulted with several senior officials, among them his vice president, Zakkariya Muhieddin. By mid-afternoon, the plan was in motion. A national emergency was declared; soldiers' and policemen's leaves were canceled and student visas revoked. Bridges and public buildings were placed under strict double guard. But these measures, justified by the "tense situation on the Syrian-Israeli armistice line, Israel's large military concentrations, its threats and its open demands for an attack on Damascus," were merely a sideshow for the army's procession through Cairo. Starting at 2:30 P.M., thousands of troops paraded through the city's center, past the American Embassy, under 'Amer's personal review. The field marshal had just issued top-secret instructions urging his commanders "to be vigilant to all developments, political and strategic, in order to determine the proper place and time to initiate successful military actions."

"Our forces, hastily gathered, marched toward the front," recalled Muhammad Ahmad Khamis, a communications officer with the 6th Division and decorated veteran of the Yemen War. "We moved without preparation, without the basic precautions for a military maneuver." Lt. General Anwar al-Qadi, chief of operations on the general staff, testified that "our headquarters knew nothing about the orders issued to the army directly by the senior commander ['Amer]. Egypt's political leaders sought to escalate the situation—we knew not why—while continuous and contradictory orders sent entire divisions into Sinai without planning or strategic objectives."[62] Packed onto two narrow roads, soaked by a late spring downpour, those divisions eventually reached the Suez Canal. There, the soldiers commandeered ferryboats used for supplying UNEF, crossed and fanned out into Sinai.

Had Egypt intended to attack Israel immediately, the army's advance into Sinai would have been conducted as quietly as possible, at night. Instead, by acting conspicuously, Nasser sent a double message to Israel: Egypt had no aggressive designs, but neither would it suffer any Israeli aggression against Syria. But that same message eluded Egyptian commanders, left without instructions as to what they were supposed to *do* in Sinai. Gen. Fawzi recalled that "our forces pulled out of Cairo and poured into Sinai to concentration areas that were never established. And then the question arose: what's our mission?" Similar questions were being asked at the Egyptian Foreign Ministry, where Mahmoud Riad knew even less than his military counterparts. There were no briefings, no appraisals, only what diplomats had read in the papers.

If aware of this chaos, Nasser seemed untroubled by it. The objective of demonstrating that Egypt, even with over 50,000 men in Yemen, was still a formidable power had been stunningly achieved. "The troops in Yemen were not particularly important," 'Ali Sabri, a powerful figure in Nasser's entourage, testified. "Our main armored units were all in Egypt, along with our air force." That army, marching in broad daylight, would deter the Israelis and restore Egypt's pride. Nasser would win the propaganda war but would not have to fire a shot.[63]

All this transpired without the Israelis having a clue. Absorbed in their Independence Day festivities, Eshkol and Rabin barely had time to deal with yet another Soviet claim of threats against Syria. The prime minister met with Chuvakhin and, as in the past, reassured him that the IDF was not planning the conquest of Damascus, and invited him to inspect the northern border himself. If twelve brigades were massing there—40,000 men, 3,000 vehicles—surely the ambassador would see them. The blond, barrel-chested Chuvakhin, bland and humorless, replied simply that his job was to communicate Soviet truths, not test them. The Soviet ambassador would be invited twice more to visit the north, and asked to intervene in restraining Syria, and each time his answer was no. Yet few Israelis sensed the immensity of the crisis approaching. When Chuvakhin, in a conversation with Arye Levavi, director-general of Israel's Foreign Ministry, predicted that "you will be punished for your alliance with imperialism, and you will lose your access to the Red Sea," no alarms were raised in Jerusalem. [64]

Nor did the Israelis pause to consider whether these same Soviet warnings were reaching Egypt and, if so, whether Nasser would act on them. By all reports Israel received from the Americans, and according to its own intelligence, Nasser had no interest in bloodshed and had not even closed the door to some future peace settlement. Further assumed were the Egyptian leader's continued support for UNEF and his imperviousness to Arab—Jordanian, especially—propaganda aimed at that support. Israel's assessment of Egypt's willingness to fight had brightened since the gloomy days of 1965 and the Arab summit meetings. With the Egyptian economy in a tailspin and Arab unity dashed, Nasser would have to be deranged to take on an Israel backed by France and the U.S. Sixth Fleet. War, according to the Israelis, could only come about if Nasser felt he had complete military superiority over the IDF, if Israel were caught up in a domestic crisis, and, most crucially, was isolated internationally—a most unlikely confluence.[65]

And yet Eshkol, for one, remained unsure. He was wary of the context of inter-Arab and superpower rivalries surrounding Israel, and reacted to it with that same blend of bravura and fear, temerity and timorousness, that had helped make that context explosive. Thus, in his speech on Israel's Memorial Day, May 13, he vaunted that "firm and persistent stand . . . [that] has strengthened the awareness among our neighbors that they will not be able to prevail against us in open combat. They recoil today from any frontal clash . . . and postpone the date of such a confrontation to the remote future." But then, in an address to the Mapai leadership, the same Eshkol could also warn: "We are surrounded by a serious encirclement of hostility and that which doesn't succeed today could well succeed tomorrow or the day after. We know that the Arab world is now divided in half . . . but things can always change."[66]

THE CRISIS

Two Weeks in May

I N THE FACE OF ARAB AND UN CONDEMNATIONS and boycotts by Western
ambassadors, Israel marked its independence. The parade had been pared
down to a mere twenty-six minutes, 1,600 soldiers and a few vehicles—"a
boy scouts march," Colonel Lior derided it. Eshkol's decision to put the lowest
possible profile on the celebrations elicited bitter criticism from his opponents,
most vocally Ben-Gurion, who accused him of kowtowing to international pressure. And yet some 200,000 spectators turned out for the event, gathering under an illuminated Star of David that shimmered from the top of Mt. Scopus.
Few of the celebrants were aware, however, of a more ominous presence gathering in the south, as thousands of Egyptian troops streamed into Sinai.

Reports of the buildup, culled from Western news agencies, had reached
Rabin the previous evening at the prime minister's office, while he and Eshkol
and their wives were preparing to attend a rally at the nearby Hebrew University stadium. Eshkol's initial reaction was restrained. He reminded Rabin that
Nasser was fond of exhibitions and that, at worst, this was a repeat of Operation Retama, Egypt's surprise remilitarization of Sinai in 1960. Rabin agreed,
and gave orders to prevent all potentially provocative movements along the
northern border, and to step up reconnaissance patrols in the south. The matter was then dropped. Rabin and Eshkol departed for the stadium, there to
hear the censored poem by Natan Alterman and a new song by composer Naomi
Shemer, "Jerusalem of Gold," soon to become an anthem.

But for all his outward composure, the prime minister was concerned. Dispatches on the situation in the south continued to arrive throughout the evening,

at a reception at the home of Venezuelan millionaire Miles Sherover. Egyptian forces were taking up positions according to the Conqueror plan, well known to the Israelis, and Gen. Fawzi had flown to Damascus. Though the IDF was deployed along the lines of Anvil, ready to stem Arab invasion from any front, the plan presupposed a prior warning of forty-eight hours—a period that Eshkol could not be sure he had. Asked by his wife, Miriam, why he seemed so preoccupied, Eshkol snapped, "Don't you realize that there's going to be a war?"

His anxieties would mount higher the following day. While waiting inside the King David Hotel for the parade to begin, Eshkol listened as Rabin recommended beefing up Israel's small armored units in the Negev, mining the border area, and calling up a brigade or two of reserves.

Rabin was aware of the situation's delicacy, and exceedingly wary of Nasser. He had actually met the man once, at the end of the 1948 war when Rabin helped negotiate the withdrawal of besieged Egyptian soldiers from the Negev. The future Egyptian president had told him, "Our main enemy is the British . . . We should be fighting the colonial power rather than you," and had impressed the young Israeli officer. Since achieving power, though, Nasser had proved himself an implacable and unpredictable opponent. Rabin had to prepare for the worst.

"Had we failed to react—giving the Egyptians the impression that we were either unaware of their moves or complacent about them—we might be inviting attack on grounds of vulnerability," Rabin later recorded. "On the other hand, an overreaction on our part might nourish the Arabs' fears that we had aggressive intentions and thus provoke a totally unwanted war." The latter scenario seemed the more treacherous, Eshkol felt. While he approved a first-level alert for the army, and the transfer of several tank companies southward, he refused to mobilize reserves.

Throughout the rest of that day, during a national Bible quiz and an Israel Air Force ball, news from Sinai continued to filter in. Two Egyptian divisions had moved into fortified areas of Jabal Libni and Bir Hasana, Rabin informed Eshkol; the advance was well planned and organized. The only good news was that the 4th Armored Division, Nasser's best, had yet to leave Cairo. Rabin was sure that Egypt's maneuvering was merely for show—Washington confirmed the assessment—and counseled caution. Eshkol agreed, but remained anxious. What if Nasser's action encouraged the Syrians to release more terrorists? he wondered. What if the Syrians pushed Nasser to close the Straits of Tiran?[1]

The prime minister pondered these questions while Israeli diplomats went into action. The State Department, the British Foreign Office—any channel to Nasser, even U Thant—was utilized in assuring Nasser that Israel had no warlike intentions and warning him of Syrian chicanery. Chief UN observer Odd Bull was invited to tour the north and verify the absence of IDF concentrations while, abroad, Israeli emissaries were instructed to impress upon their host governments the seriousness of Egypt's moves. Mossad head Meir Amit tried to renew communications with Gen. 'Azm al-Din Mahmud Khalil, his one-time Egyptian liaison. The Lebanese were also secretly contacted and told of the terrible explosion liable to erupt if the terrorist attacks continued.[2]

Yet none of these responses could substitute for activating at least some reserves, Rabin explained. As Egyptian infantry advanced in rapidly increasing numbers, Cairo Radio exulted, "our forces are in a complete state of readiness for war." Nasser, in a statement released on Palestine Day—a day of mourning throughout the Arab world, lamenting Israel's independence—exhorted, "Brothers, it is our duty to prepare for the final battle in Palestine." While Rabin did not believe that Nasser wanted war, a momentum was gathering that could seriously erode Israel's deterrence power, to the point where the Arabs felt free to attack.[3]

That danger seemed to skyrocket between the nights of May 15 and 16. Initial IDF estimates had put the size of the Egyptian buildup at one division, the 5th—this in addition to the 30,000 troops already stationed in Sinai and the 10,000 man Palestine Liberation Army division maintained in Gaza. But then the numbers jumped threefold. The 2nd and 7th Infantry Divisions had also crossed the Canal, and the 6th Armored was not far behind. Significantly, the 4th Division under the command of Maj. Gen. Sidqi al-Ghul had crossed the Canal and dug in at Bir al-Thamada. Each of these units comprised 15,000 men, close to 100 T-54 and T-55 tanks, 150 armored personnel carriers, and a range of Soviet artillery: howitzers, heavy mortars, Katyusha rockets, SU-100 anti-tank guns. Along with these forces came vast amounts of ammunition, MiG-17 and 21 fighters, and—IDF intelligence believed—canisters of poison gas.[4]

Rabin was baffled. The Egyptian deployment, though still defensive, with tanks and troops digging in, had surpassed the dimensions of a mere power display. With the 4th Division on the move and heavy bombers transferred to the forward base at Bir al-Thamada, the enemy could be preparing to invade the Negev or to bomb the Dimona reactor. Cairo's tenor was bellicose—"If Israel now tries to set the region on fire, then Israel itself will be completely destroyed in this fire, thus bringing about the end of this aggressive racist base"— and was duly echoed by Damascus: "The war of liberation will not end except by Israel's abolition." Syrian troops were also reportedly advancing, though Israel could not match their buildup without then justifying Egypt's. The IDF's hands were tied; al-Fatah could attack at will.

"Israel faces a new situation," Rabin told the general staff on May 17. "Nasser never initiates anything—he only reacts and then he gets himself into trouble as he did in Yemen." There was a need to transfer troops to the southern border, to bolster the air defenses around Dimona, but to do so quietly, under darkness if possible. Later, locating Eshkol at a reception for a visiting African dignitary, Rabin requested the call-up of at least two brigades, as many as 18,000 men. Eshkol agreed, reluctantly, and advised Rabin to refrain from provocative rhetoric. "This week has had its fill of threats and warnings," he said. For Col. Lior, writing in his diary, the moment was decisive. "It was clear to all of us that we had reached the point of no return," he recorded, "The lot had been cast."[5]

Egypt Deliberates

In their political struggle with Egypt, the Syrians threatened to make war on Israel. Then, when Israel responded by asserting itself in the DZ's, the Syrians unleashed guerrilla attacks that provoked the Israelis to plan a reprisal. This the Soviets told Nasser, meant invasion. Such was the strange concatenation that had brought Egypt's forces into Sinai. Yet that outcome would in turn launch another chain of events as Egyptian leaders deliberated over what to do with those forces, where to put them and how to command them, and whether they should be there at all.

Gen. Muhammad Fawzi, austere and by-the-book, had commanded the Egyptian Military Academy for seventeen years before being named chief of the general staff by his former academy classmate, Nasser. That appointment had far less to do with Fawzi's military prowess than his unwavering loyalty to the president, who saw in him a means—albeit frail—of limiting 'Amer's power.

That same trust had prompted Nasser to dispatch Fawzi to Damascus, where he arrived on May 14. He found the capital in a state of high agitation—not because of the Israelis, but because of an anti-Islamic article that had appeared in the official military magazine *Army of the People* (*Jaysh al-Sha'b*) dismissing Allah as an "embalmed toy in the museums of history." Though the regime quickly disclaimed the piece as an imperialist conspiracy and sentenced its author to life imprisonment, 20,000 protesters took to the streets. Exacerbating this upheaval were renewed tensions between rival factions in the junta, and the growing resentment of merchants whose businesses had been confiscated by the government. America's Ambassador Smythe observed wryly that "such machinations can go on while the country is allegedly facing serious external threat [is a] sign of [the] times in present day Syria."[6]

One thing Fawzi did not find was evidence of unusual Israeli troop movements. He conferred with Syrian Chief of Staff Ahmad Suweidani and closely studied aerial photographs of the border area taken the previous day. Then, in a private plane, he surveyed the border himself. There was no sign of IDF concentrations anywhere. The Syrian army was not even on a state of alert.

Fawzi reported his findings to Nasser. "There is nothing there. No massing of forces. Nothing." A similar assessment arrived from the chief of Egypt's military intelligence, Lt. Gen. Muhammad Ahmad Sadiq, who sent several Israeli Arabs to reconnoiter Northern Galilee. "There are no force concentrations," Sadiq deduced. "Nor is there justification, tactical or strategic, for such concentrations."

The U.S. embassy in Cairo corroborated these conclusions, as did the CIA. Alone among foreign observers, only Gen. Bull gave even the slightest credence to the charge that Israel was poised to invade. "We have no reports, thus far, of any buildup," he admitted, but then cautioned that "Israel does not have to concentrate her forces in any one area in order to mount an attack."[7]

Fawzi's report could only have meant that the Soviet alarm was false, and yet the Egyptian president preferred to overlook these repudiations and to proceed as if the Israelis were indeed about to attack.[8] The reasons were not difficult to fathom. A major share of the army was already in Sinai; to call it back now would be humiliating in the extreme at a time when Nasser could ill afford further humiliations. Continuing the buildup, on the other hand, could greatly enhance his status. Reactions to the move throughout the Arab world were enthusiastic, even ecstatic; years had passed since Nasser had been so hailed. Finally, the absence of a manifest threat to Syria was welcome news. Egypt could remilitarize Sinai, and reap the credit for it, without actually risking a war.

The situation seemed to be no-lose, and not only to Nasser; 'Amer was excited as well. Enlightened by Fawzi as to the true situation up north, 'Amer showed no reaction. "I began to believe that the question of Israeli concentrations, from his ['Amer's] point of view, was not the only or the chief reason for the mobilization and deployments we were undertaking so quickly," Fawzi wrote.

The reason was yet another opportunity to expand the field marshal's power. He swiftly exploited the situation by placing cronies in key operational jobs. First among these was fifty-nine-year-old Lt. Gen. 'Abd al-Muhsin Kamil Murtagi, chief of the Ground Forces Command, which 'Amer had created in 1964 to bypass Chief of Staff Fawzi. Murtagi, who had served as a political commissar in Yemen but had no operational experience, became head of all ground forces in Sinai. Under him, in command of the Eastern Front, 'Amer placed Gen. Ahmad Isma'il 'Ali and under him, twelve new division and brigade commanders. With Sidqi Mahmud and Adm. Suliman 'Izzat, the air force and navy chiefs since 1953, personally answerable to him, 'Amer completed his grip on the army. "You can be my chief of staff," he told Murtagi, "and we can have nothing more to do with Supreme Headquarters."[9]

Fulfilling 'Amer's political ends meant more than appointing yes-men, however; it also required erasing the 1956 disgrace and leading Egypt to victory. But the field marshal could not initiate offensive action against Israel as long as the army adhered to Conqueror. Devised by the Soviets in 1966, this plan provided for three deeply entrenched lines running on a north-south axis across Sinai. The first line, from Rafah to Abu 'Ageila, was to be lightly defended and to serve as bait for luring the Israelis into a frontal assault. Advancing, enemy forces would soon find themselves deep in the desert, cut off from supplies and facing the second line—the Curtain (*al-Sitar*)—massively fortified, stretching across a triangle inscribed by the bases at al-'Arish, Jabal Libni, and Bir Hassana. Having broken themselves on these defenses, Israeli armor and infantry would then be prey for a counterstrike from the second line together with forces from the third, in the Mitla and Giddi passes, protecting the approaches to the Canal. This "shield and sword" strategy culminated in a "comprehensive attack, drawing on tactical and strategic reserves, that will shift the battle onto enemy territory, hitting its vital areas."[10]

Construction of all the fortifications and infrastructure for Conqueror had yet to be completed by 1967, and many officers familiar with the plan had been replaced by others beholden to 'Amer. Moreover, Conqueror could not be implemented with so many of Egypt's frontline troops far away in Yemen, an army report of December 1966 warned. Repeatedly over the first half of 1967, the general staff complained of the lack of funds necessary to defend Sinai, and strongly recommended against any further military confrontations. "There can be no war with Israel," Gen. Fawzi declared, "the budget simply won't allow it."

Such admonitions failed to deter the field marshal, however. 'Amer not only believed the army capable of repulsing an Israeli first strike, but insisted on mounting an offensive. His plan was Operation Lion (*al-Asad*), in which combined infantry, armored, and commando units would penetrate Israel and cut across the Negev to the Jordanian border, detaching the entire Eilat salient. The Egyptian navy would blockade the port from the south and prevent any reinforcements from the sea. Other plans stipulated an armored thrust eastward along the Israeli coast—Operation Leopard (*Fahd*)—and Operation Arrow (*Sahm*), the aerial bombing of Israeli settlements opposite Gaza.[11]

As early as May 14, a battle order, number 67-5, was issued to forward air bases in Sinai. These cited specific targets—port facilities, power and radar stations—to be bombed over a sixteen-hour period upon receipt of the password "Lion." Also distributed were aerial photographs of the area, most of which had been taken in World War II. One pilot, Hashem Mustafa Husayn, described pressing his commander on whether the objective of the attack was merely to destroy Eilat or the Jewish state in general:

> A worried look came over the squadron commander's face. He said that we must carry out the assignment without asking questions, and that it was imperative that we trust the supreme commanders who have a clear operational plan, and that because of issues of security and confidentiality, he cannot divulge anything else.[12]

The acquisition of a Negev land bridge was a long-standing goal of Egypt, as was the elimination of Eilat. In his *al-Ahram* editorials, Heikal often called for the conquest of Eilat as a step toward Israel's destruction. But any attempt to seize parts of southern Israel would almost certainly be frustrated by UNEF. For that reason, 'Amer wanted the force disbanded completely, and not merely removed from the border, as Nasser preferred. He planned to put offensive forces in Gaza, and to position troops on the shores of Tiran as well. Accordingly, the field marshal ordered paratrooper commander Gen. 'Abd al-Mun'im Khalil to quietly fly his units into Sharm al-Sheikh and be ready to take control of the area by May 20. Senior generals—Fawzi, Murtagi, and Sidqi Mahmud—argued that such moves would force Egypt to close the Straits and incite the Israelis to war, but 'Amer ignored their advice. "The High command has already decided to occupy Sharm al-Sheikh," he insisted, "and it's the army's job to implement that decision."[13]

On the morning of May 16, as 'Amer inspected Egyptian armor rolling into Sinai, Dr. Mahmoud Fawzi presented his draft of what was to be Gen. Fawzi's letter to Rikhye:

> To your information, I gave my instructions to all UAR armed forces to be ready for action against Israel, the moment it might carry out any aggressive action against any Arab country. Due to these instructions our troops are already concentrating in Sinai along our eastern border. For the sake of complete security of all UN troops which install Observation Posts along our borders, I request that you give orders to withdraw all of these troops immediately.

According to Heikal, the president found discrepancies between the Arabic and English versions of the letter, and replaced the word "withdraw" with "redeploy" and crossed out the "all" before "these troops." His purpose, *al-Ahram's* editor explained, was to prevent any misunderstanding regarding the continued presence of UNEF in Gaza and in Sharm al-Sheikh. Nasser purportedly asked 'Amer to insert these changes into the final letter, only to be told that the letter was already being delivered, and that efforts would be made to intercept the courier. 'Amer's reply upset the president, though not unduly; ambiguities in the text could always be clarified with U Thant.[14]

Eviction

Occupying forty-one observation posts along the international border, in Sharm al-Sheikh and in Gaza, the United Nations Emergency Force numbered 4,500 men—Indians, Canadians, Yugoslavs, Swedes, Brazilians, Norwegians, and Danes—about half of its original contingent. Since 1957, UNEF had been subject to severe cutbacks in budget and personnel, together with skepticism from Western states disaffected by the UN's increasingly pro-Soviet stance. Following the failure of other peacekeeping efforts, most notably in the Congo, little faith attended UNEF's ability to prevent Egypt-Israeli hostilities, for indeed the force could only observe them once they broke out. Yet, for all its handicaps, the mere presence of UNEF had sufficed to deter warfare during periods of intense Arab-Israeli friction, to keep infiltrators from exiting Gaza and ensure free passage through the Straits of Tiran.[15]

That presence, however, hung on a legal fiction. The "good-faith agreement" forged by Dag Hammarskjold in 1957, according to which Egypt would consult with the General Assembly and the UNEF Advisory Council before altering the force's mandate, was in no way binding. The Egyptians could, in fact, dismiss UNEF whenever they chose. This prerogative could be qualified only by arguing that the state of belligerency that UNEF restrained had never ceased to exist. In the words of India's former UN ambassador, "a demand for withdrawal of the Force in order to battle effectively with the adversary was in

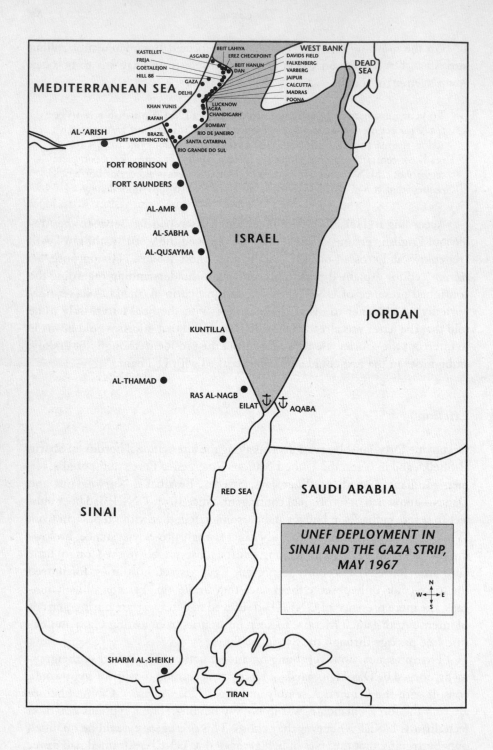

KASTELLET
FREJA
GOETALEJON
HILL 88
ASGARD
BEIT LAHIYA
EREZ CHECKPOINT
BEIT HANUN
DAN
GAZA
DELHI
KHAN YUNIS
RAFAH
BRAZIL
FORT WORTHINGTON
LUCKNOW
AGRA
CHANDIGARH
BOMBAY
RIO DE JANEIRO
SANTA CATARINA
RIO GRANDE DO SUL

WEST BANK
DAVIDS FIELD
FALKENBERG
VARBERG
JAIPUR
CALCUTTA
MADRAS
POONA

MEDITERRANEAN SEA

DEAD SEA

AL-'ARISH

FORT ROBINSON

FORT SAUNDERS

AL-AMR

AL-SABHA

AL-QUSAYMA

ISRAEL

JORDAN

KUNTILLA

AL-THAMAD

RAS AL-NAGB
EILAT
AQABA

RED SEA

SAUDI ARABIA

SINAI

UNEF DEPLOYMENT IN SINAI AND THE GAZA STRIP, MAY 1967

N
W E
S

SHARM AL-SHEIKH

TIRAN

direct opposition to . . . the creation of the Force and its deployment in the area." But even this reasoning was not expected to hold should Nasser decide on eviction. In his talks with both Egyptian and Israeli leaders, U Thant had been bluff: the option was solely Nasser's.[16]

This was the assumption when, at ten o'clock on the sultry night of May 16, Brig. Gen. Ibrahim Sharqawy, Egypt's military liaison to UNEF, informed Gen. Rikhye that a special courier had arrived from Cairo. Rikhye had already received reports of unusual troop movements over the Suez Canal, but had thought nothing of them. "It was the season for an exchange of verbal threats, demonstrations, parades . . . high tension." Entering, the visitor introduced himself as Brig. Gen. 'Izz al-Din Mukhtar, and promptly produced the letter drafted by Dr. Fawzi and signed by Gen. Fawzi. "I would like to have your reply at once," Mukhtar said, and explained that UN forces would have to evacuate al-Sabha, a vital junction on the Israeli border, as well as Sharm al-Sheikh, that very night. Egyptian troops were already en route to those destinations, he warned, and attempts by UNEF to stop them could result in "clashes."

Rikhye, forty-eight years old and from a Brahmin nationalist family in Lahore, had a rich and distinguished record of service with the British army in World War II and then with the UN in the Congo, New Guinea, and the Dominican Republic. He had also spent long periods in the Middle East, knew that UNEF's mandate was "flimsy at best," and that an Arab-Israeli war could erupt momentarily. Only weeks before, he had written U Thant a detailed memorandum urging him to undertake an emergency mediation mission. He never received an answer. Yet not even that snub was as shocking as Fawzi's letter, which Rikhye took as a personal and professional blow. He asked the Egyptian brigadiers if they were aware of the consequences of their act.

"Oh, yes, sir!" Sharqawy replied, beaming, "We have arrived at this decision after much deliberation and are prepared for anything. If there is war, we shall next meet in Tel Aviv."

Rikhye was also confused as to the exact nature of Egypt's demands; the letter made no mention of either al-Sabha or Sharm al-Sheikh. It appeared as though Egypt wanted UNEF to remain in Gaza while pulling away from the border and the Straits of Tiran. He decided to play for time, telling his guests that he had no authority to order UNEF's removal; it was not a military matter between generals, but a legal issue to be settled between Nasser and U Thant. UNEF's chief then telegraphed the letter to UN headquarters in New York, and phoned the commanders of the battalions in al-Sabha and Sharm al-Sheikh, ordering them to stay in their posts for as long as possible but to refrain from using force, even if evicted.[17]

With the delay and the change in time zones, Fawzi's letter reached U Thant's desk early in the evening. With him was Ralph Bunche, no longer the dynamic mediator of the 1940s, now ill with cancer and diabetes, but still the international organization's leading expert on Middle East diplomacy. His initial reaction to the crisis was optimism, assuring Goldberg that "there's a great deal of face and political maneuvering involved, but with careful handling we might yet preserve the situation and UNEF's role." But Bunche fully adhered to the secretary-general's position that Egypt had a sovereign right to dismiss UNEF, however imprudent that decision might be. Unfortunately for him, that consideration was not reciprocated by the Egyptians, who viewed Bunche as Washington's lackey—an "agent of imperialism," in Nasser's words.

At 6:45, U Thant and Bunche summoned the Egyptian ambassador to the secretary-general's office. "Dour and rigid," according to one observer, gaunt and bald, Mohammad Awad El Kony had been a diplomat for forty of his sixty years, and, since the Egyptian Revolution, a staunch supporter of Nasser. "A noble man from a noble family, of high character," Syria's ambassador Tomeh described his Egyptian colleague, "he hated the thought of war." But El Kony made no secret of his aversion to Bunche, and directed his attention to what U Thant, alone, had told him.

U Thant told him that Egypt had erred in treating UNEF as a military rather than a diplomatic issue; it was a matter to be settled between Nasser and the secretary-general. Nor could the force's mandate be summarily altered or whittled down.

"UNEF cannot be asked to stand aside in order to enable the two sides to resume fighting," he explained, "A request for the temporary withdrawal of UNEF would be considered tantamount to a request for the complete withdrawal of UNEF from Gaza and Sinai, since this would reduce UNEF to ineffectiveness."

The good-faith agreement was mentioned repeatedly, as were the dangers of dismantling the force. There was no evidence of any impending Israeli attack, U Thant stressed. Having listed all these caveats, the secretary-general then arrived at his crux: "If it was the intention of the Government of the UAR to withdraw the consent which it gave in 1956 for the stationing of UNEF on UAR territory and in Gaza it is, of course, entitled to do so."[18]

While insisting that it was not a good idea, the secretary-general had upheld Egypt's right to evict UNEF peremptorily, and Nasser was swift to exercise it. He communicated his decision to Marshal Tito of Yugoslavia and India's Indira Ghandi, both of whom, as predicted, agreed to pull their contingents from Sinai. At dawn the next morning, May 17, a troop of thirty Egyptian soldiers and three armored cars circumvented the Yugoslavian-manned observation post at al-Sabha and proceeded to the border. Rikhye protested this development to Sharqawy and in reply received another letter from Gen. Fawzi, advising him to remove all UN personnel from al-Sabha within twenty-four hours, and from Sharm al-Sheikh within forty-eight. And still the Egyptians came. By 1:00 that afternoon, the Egyptian contingent at al-Sabha had swelled to 100, with thirty vehicles, while a forward element had reportedly reached Kuntilla, in the south, as well.[19]

UNEF had been circumvented—at key points it was no longer observing the border but the Egyptian soldiers' backs—and then hamstrung by two of its main contributors. Appraised of these developments, U Thant was more than ever reluctant to resist Nasser's decision. He could not, he felt, go to the General Assembly, where the Communist and African-Asian blocs were certain to back Egypt, nor to the Security Council, paralyzed by Soviet and American vetoes. He feared that any attempt to hinder the Egyptian army could endanger the safety of UNEF personnel, and jeopardize future peacekeeping operations elsewhere. Though his own legal counsel firmly advised against taking the "radical action" of bending to Egypt's ultimatum before consulting the relevant UN bodies, U Thant's mind was made up. "It is inconceivable to me that once UAR consent for the presence of the Force was withdrawn, there could be any decision other than compliance with the request . . . " he later wrote, "In fact, the question of compliance was moot once the consent was terminated." Among the greatest obstacles to UNEF's survival, it seemed, was the secretary-general himself.[20]

In a meeting that afternoon with the UNEF Advisory Committee, while Western ambassadors argued strenuously for postponing a final decision, U Thant sided with the Pakistani and Indian delegates in upholding Egypt's right to dismiss the force unilaterally. "It was generally supposed [in 1957] that UNEF would be stationed there for only a few months," he told the committee, claiming that the "good-faith" agreement related only to removal of forces from Sinai—a goal long since achieved. "If the consent of the UAR ceases to exist, then UNEF has to be withdrawn; there is no alternative," he insisted. Similar reasoning would inform the *aide-mémoire* sent to Nasser that evening, in which the secretary-general reiterated his recognition of Egyptian rights, and a note reminding Rikhye that his troops were in Sinai at Egypt's discretion.[21]

Egypt had an unassailable right to evict UNEF, though by doing so it risked igniting regional, if not global, war—that was the paradoxical position of the man charged with maintaining world peace. "Emotionless and moon-faced . . . rather simple-minded," in the view of one of his closest advisers, the fifty-eight-year-old U Thant was a former high school headmaster turned journalist and government press secretary who, in 1957, became Burma's permanent representative to the UN. Notwithstanding a penchant for schoolboy jokes, he was a tense and quiet man—"a Buddhist in every sense of the word," said George Tomeh, "it was very difficult to anticipate his reactions"—and, apart from cheroots and spicy Burmese food, viceless. Four years later, after Hammarskjold's death in a plane crash in the Congo, U Thant, then chairman of the UN's Congo Conciliation Commission, was chosen to complete the late secretary-general's term of office. Reappointed by the Security Council in December 1966, he earned a reputation as a patient, if parochial, statesman.

"He had strong views of right and wrong," Brian Urquhart, a UN undersecretary, remembered, "[his] moral sense overrode his political sense and caused him to do what he believed right, even if it was politically disadvantageous to him." What he thought right, however, was often seen by American officials as anti-Western and, perforce, pro-Soviet. Thus, according to H. Eugenie Moore Anderson, an American UN representative, "he had . . . inherited the psychology of the Asian . . . and had sort of a built-in reaction against the white man."[22]

Though not ill disposed toward Zionism—Israel had supported the extension of his tenure as secretary-general—U Thant nevertheless exhibited ambivalent feelings toward the Jewish state, which did not quite fit in with the dichotomy of East and West, Asian or Caucasian. Egypt, on the other hand, did, though its opposition to UNEF was clearly worrisome. The consequent confusion wrought in U Thant's mind was apparent when, in a personal letter to U.S. Ambassador Goldberg, he reasoned, "Obviously it cannot be urged that because the Force has contributed so much to the maintenance of quiet in the arena for so long, which has been possible because of UAR cooperation, that Government should now be told that it cannot unilaterally seek the removal of the Force and thus be penalized for its long cooperation with the international community in the interest of peace." In other words, Egypt's past contributions to peace entitled it to threaten that peace in the future.[23]

Yet a simple solution to the UNEF conundrum existed, U Thant believed, and he presented it the next morning, May 18, to the Israeli ambassador. The UN force would cross the frontier and redeploy on Israeli territory. The idea was hardly new; Hammarskjold had tabled it at the time of UNEF's inception, with the United States's support. Israel had opposed it then on the grounds that Egypt, not Israel, had maintained a state of war, had sent guerrillas from Gaza and blockaded the Straits of Tiran. Incorporating contingents from countries hardly sympathetic to Israel, UNEF would be less likely to stop Egyptian aggression than to limit Israel's responses to it.

These arguments were well known to Gideon Rafael, Israel's UN ambassador. Though only recently appointed, the German-born Rafael, fifty-four, had been one of the founders of Israel's Foreign Ministry, and was present at the UN Partition Plan vote and at the marathon debates surrounding the Suez crisis. Now, under orders to prevent UNEF's eviction at all costs, he rejected the notion of peacekeepers on Israeli soil, and criticized the UN's passivity in the face of Egyptian troops—"Before shooting at them at least you could have shouted at them," he scolded U Thant. Rafael reminded the secretary-general of the pledges Israel had received from his predecessor, that any request to dismiss UNEF would first be brought to the General Assembly. U Thant professed ignorance of these promises—"bewildered . . . perplexed," Rafael described him—and assured the Israelis that he would soon make a compelling appeal to Nasser.[24]

Events in Sinai, meanwhile, were rapidly outpacing those in New York. UNEF aircraft were no longer allowed to land at al-'Arish airport, leaving food to rot in the fuselages and UN troops to languish without supplies. The Egyptians had entirely taken over the observation posts at al-Sabha and Kuntilla, and had fired artillery shells perilously close to those at al-Qusayma. In Sharm al-Sheikh, helicopter-borne paratroopers, supported by two gunboats offshore, had demanded the immediate evacuation of the thirty-one-man Yugoslav garrison. Yet the friction did not emanate from Egypt alone. The Caribou aircraft Gen. Rikhye was flying in close to the border was chased away, with warning shots, by Israeli Mystères.[25] Though Rabin later apologized for the incident, it reinforced Rikhye's sense that a crisis was close.

The vicissitudes of the day climaxed in a cable from Foreign Minister Riad to U Thant. This was the letter that the secretary-general had demanded of El Kony, and now he had it:

> The Government of the United Arab Republic has the honour to inform Your Excellency that it has decided to terminate the presence of the United Nations Emergency Forces from the territory of the United Arab Republic and Gaza Strip. Therefore, I request that the necessary steps be taken for the withdrawal of the force as soon as possible.

The text indicated a decisive shift in official Egyptian thinking. Throughout the previous two days, since Rikhye was first informed of Egypt's intentions, confusion had surrounded the question of whether UNEF was being ordered to leave certain areas in Sinai or leave the Middle East entirely. Gen. Fawzi's original letter could have been interpreted as a request to remove UNEF from along the border only, in accordance with Nasser's wishes. But it was 'Amer's wishes that appeared to be carried out by Gen. Mukhtar in his demand for the evacuation of Sharm al-Sheikh, and by the landing there of Egyptian troops. Now Riad had stated categorically: all of UNEF must go.

Bunche, Nasser suspected, had tried to trick him, threatening to dissolve UNEF if Egypt removed it from the border. Now the Egyptian president claimed that he had called that bluff and ousted the peacekeepers entirely. Though a debate would later arise over whether Nasser had truly sought to retain UNEF in Gaza and Sharm al-Sheikh—Bunche vigorously denied it— the distinction was irrelevant to U Thant. For him, a request for any change in the force's disposition was tantamount to a demand for total withdrawal. Believing that he had avoided Bunche's trap, Nasser had set one for himself.[26]

Fawzi's letter was received with resignation, if not regret, by the secretary-general. "I am proceeding to issue instructions without delay for the . . . orderly withdrawal of the force," he replied dryly, adding that, "I have serious misgivings that this . . . withdrawal may have grave implications for peace." He considered wiring a more personal appeal to Nasser, and asked Brian Urquhart to formulate a draft. El Kony, too, was inclined to advise prudence, certain that a General Assembly debate on UNEF could not be avoided. But Nasser would have none of it. His response, sent through Riad, was terse: "Advise him [U Thant] not to send any appeal regarding the emergency forces in order to avoid its being rejected by Cairo which would lead to an embarrassment for him,

something we do not want at all." The secretary-general needed no more prodding. The appeal was never sent.[27]

Copies of the correspondence between Riad and U Thant reached Gen.
Rikhye at 4:30 on the morning of May 19. He was bitterly disappointed—the
UN could have tried any number of delaying tactics, he believed, such as sending a fact-finding mission to the region—but not surprised. "I stood and told
my boys, pick it up, it's time to go," he remembered. One by one over the
course of the afternoon the observation points were taken over by Egyptians.
The safety of UNEF personnel in the area could no longer be guaranteed, they
said. At 5:00 P.M., units of the Palestinian Liberation Army manned the Erez
checkpoint, separating Gaza from Israel. Rikhye described the scene: "The guard
of honour presented arms, the band played a salute, and the United Nations
flag was lowered by a young Swedish soldier who folded and handed it over the
lieutenant, who in turn presented it to his commander. Colonel Lindskog walked
up to me heavily and with sadness written over his face, handed the flag to me."

Rikhye saw a different expression—"grinning from ear to ear"—on the
face of the Palestinian soldier now guarding the gate. The general saluted him,
thinking, "It is all yours now," and feeling sorry for him. He proceeded through
the barriers to the IDF liaison office, there to report that UNEF's evacuation
of Gaza was complete. By midnight, the Egyptians had informed the UN that
"the UAR has taken over all sovereign rights in Sinai. No UN personnel will
be allowed in Sinai until further notice." Nasser proposed decorating UNEF
for its services and for consenting to evacuate peaceably, but Rikhye politely
declined. The force's task had never been fulfilled, he believed, as was already
evident that evening, with the first exchange of rifle fire across the border.[28]

Reports on the UNEF decision were circulated to the General Assembly
and the Security Council on May 19. In these, U Thant sought to justify his
acquiescence to Nasser's dictates while expressing regret for the dangers those
dictates produced. He summarized the background to the current controversy—
the struggle over the northern DZ's, al-Fatah attacks, and the unsubstantiated
reports of concentrated Israeli forces. He was particularly critical of Israel for
the "inflammatory" statements of its officials and its refusal to recognize the
Mixed Armistice Commission in Gaza which might, he suggested, be a partial
substitute for UNEF. Of singular concern to the secretary-general was the fact
that UNEF's ouster was unrelated to its performance, which had been carried
out "with remarkable effectiveness and great distinction."

This was to be UNEF's epitaph. Critics of U Thant hastened to point out
that he had acted with regrettable—indeed, unprecedented—speed in acced-
ing to, and exceeding, Egypt's demands. Prior to making his decision, he never
consulted formally with the countries contributing troops to the force, certainly not with Israel, and never sent an appeal to Nasser. His action would be
widely denounced in the West—by *Newsweek* columnist Joseph Alsop as "pol-
troonery" and by *New York Times* editor C. L. Sulzberger as having "the objec-

tivity of a spurned lover and the dynamism of a noodle." Yet nothing more was done about it. Fearing Afro-Asian unity and the Soviet veto, the Western nations refrained from taking the issue to either the General Assembly or the Security Council. Nearly a month later, on June 17, when the last UN soldier left Sinai, the event was scarcely reported. But by then, Sinai, and indeed the entire Middle East, was a very different place.

For U Thant, the question now was not how to revive UNEF but rather how to prevent the outbreak of war. Abba Eban had proposed that the secretary-general, together with Urquhart and Bunche, embark on an immediate mediation mission to Cairo, Damascus, and Jerusalem. The proposal appealed to U Thant, but only in part. He would stop only in Cairo on what would be billed as "a regularly scheduled visit," and would not take Bunche or Urquhart, both of whom were unpalatable to the Egyptians. Nor would he leave at once, but wait another three days, when his horoscope said it was propitious for him to travel.[29]

Israel Waits

"Ha-Hamtana," Israelis came to call it: "the waiting." It described the period beginning on May 14, with the first reports of Egyptian troops entering Sinai, and the almost maddening ascent of tensions thereafter. These began on May 17, when a "top secret source" informed the Israelis of U Thant's decision on UNEF. "It is still unclear what diplomatic consideration or defect of character brought him to make this disastrous move," the Foreign Ministry cabled its representative in Rangoon. "If you can record any explanations that might shed light on his motivations, wire them immediately." Beyond its disappointment with the secretary-general, Israel had to grapple with the loss of its most concrete achievement from 1956, assuring free passage through Tiran and a quiet southern border. Suddenly, the decade of security afforded by UNEF had ended, supplanted by the specter of war and the question: What will Nasser do next?

The answer seemed to be furnished by the Egyptian air force which, at 4:00 on the afternoon of May 17, carried out the first-ever reconnaissance of the Dimona nuclear reactor. Two MiG-21 jets cut through Jordanian airspace, entered Israel from the east, and swooped low over the top-secret site. They were over the border and into Sinai before the IAF had even begun to react.

The incident touched on one of Israel's darkest concerns, that its pursuit of nuclear power would impel Egypt to launch a conventional attack while it still had the chance. Back in 1964, Nasser had warned the Americans that Israel's development of nuclear capabilities "would be a cause for war, no matter how suicidal." The U.S. assured Nasser that Israel was not developing strategic weapons, and he never renewed his threat, but the memory of it stuck with the Israelis. They never forgot the reactor's proximity to the border, its vulnerability to aerial bombardment. Thus, though Nasser never once cited Dimona as a motive for his decisions in May, Israeli commanders assumed it was and con-cluded that they had to strike first. Israel's fear for the reactor—rather than Egypt's *of* it—was the greater catalyst for war.[30]

No sooner had the MiG's flown off when the army's alert was elevated to the second level and the air force's to the highest. Operation Bluebird, upgrad-ing the protection of Israel's airfields and other strategic sites, was implemented. All at once, IDF analysts were compelled to revise their initial assessments.

Responsibility for this revision fell to a diminutive, delicately featured man, the chief of military intelligence, Gen. Aharon "Aharale" Yariv. At forty-seven, Yariv had held field commissions in the *Haganah*, the British army, and finally the IDF, before serving as Israel's military attaché in Washington. Returning to Israel, he was appointed chief of *Aman*—the intelligence branch—in 1964, at the time of the Arab summits and Nasser's plan for a phased buildup to war. While other general staff officers were charged with dealing with the almost daily flare-ups along the border, Yariv had the unenviable job of gauging when the Arab world would be in a position to wage a full multifront attack. That point, he concluded, would arrive sometime between 1967 and 1970, with the later date the likelier. But that estimation was predicated on the belief that Egypt would remain economically strapped and pinned down in Yemen—an assumption that had been suddenly and stunningly disproved. Now, as Egyptian troops and ar-mor continued to flood Sinai, Yariv was to suggest alternative scenarios.

"It's unclear whether Egypt's intention was from the start aimed at a mili-tary confrontation or at a limited gain of prestige," Yariv briefed his senior officers on May 19. "In any event, we are prepared for a confrontation, whether as a result of an intentional or unintentional provocation." He showed aerial photos of the Egyptian forces, now numbering 80,000 men, 550 tanks, and 1,000 guns, and surveyed their possible courses of action. The Egyptians might blockade or bomb the nuclear reactor, Yariv speculated, though his best guess had them simply building up strength in Sinai. As such, they could either keep Israel indefinitely mobilized, bleeding economically, or provoke an Israeli first-strike that the Arabs could turn into a rout.

Later, elaborating before the general staff, Yariv opined that Nasser no longer thought that Egypt was ill matched for Israel militarily, but was ready to gamble on short, focused assaults to conquer parts of the Negev or to smash the IDF among the Sinai dunes. "They'll strike you with something limited. You'll strike back and then they'll bomb Dimona . . . Their forces in Bir Hasana and Jabal Libni are ready to maneuver." He recommended activating most of Israel's 140,000 reserves, and telling them frankly that their call-up was in preparation for war. Israel's civilian population should be told the truth as well, advised Yariv.[31]

The army's analyses all assumed that Nasser operated according to a ratio-nal, quantifiable impetus—no mention was made, for example, of his turbulent relationship with 'Amer—and yet his next moves remained a mystery. "There won't be a fight as long as the Egyptians just sit in Sinai and don't budge,"

Eshkol assured his cabinet on the afternoon of the 19th, explaining that it was prestige Nasser wanted, not war. "When we reach that river, we'll look for a life preserver," he mollified Rabin when warned that Nasser would most likely close the Straits. That same night, however, the prime minister informed Mapai leaders that "things are worse than they appear," and warned Deputy Defense Minister Zvi Dinstein, "There's going to be a war, I'm telling you, there's going to be a war." Eshkol more than doubled the number of mobilized reserves, and brought the number of tanks in the south to 300. He asked that operational plans be drafted for reopening the Straits by force and for destroying Egyptian airfields if the enemy attacked Dimona.

Yet, for all his uncertainty, Eshkol continued to counsel prudence. He asked his ministers to refrain from making public statements on Israel's rights to free passage, and his diplomats to avoid a Security Council debate that, at best, would produce no results or, worse, call those rights into question. Whether it was restoring the *status quo* in Sinai or affirming Israel's right to self-defense, Israel's reaction to the crisis was to be low-key and focused on the most influential factor, the United States.[32]

But was American thinking on the crisis totally in line with that of Israel? In a meeting with Undersecretary of State Eugene Rostow on May 17, Ambassador Harman for the first time heard that Israel "will not stand alone," provided that it did not act alone militarily. The U.S. was willing to talk to the Russians, but its ability to influence the Egyptians was limited. After all, Rostow pointed out, Nasser was within his rights in placing troops on his own sovereign territory. A preemptive strike by Israel would, therefore, be "a very serious mistake."

Rostow's words had a disquieting resonance for any Israeli who remembered the Suez crisis, evoking threats of economic sanctions and relentless American pressure on Israel. That sense of *déjà vu* was reinforced later that afternoon by a personal letter Eshkol received from Johnson. While recognizing that Israel's patience had been "tried to the limits" by border attacks, the president expressly ruled out preemptive action. "I want to emphasize strongly that you have to abstain from every step that would increase tension and violence in the area," Johnson warned. "You will probably understand that the United States cannot accept any responsibility for situations that are liable to occur as a result of actions in which we were not consulted."[33]

The Israelis were willing to oblige, informing Washington that the call-up of reserves was for defensive purposes only, and asking it to convey that assurance to Cairo and Damascus. "There are no automatic switches open," Eban told Ambassador Barbour; no offensive action was planned as long as the Straits remained passable. But as a *quid pro quo* for its temperance, Israel also had a demand: American guarantees for its security. Israel, Eban explained, could "either shoot or shout, but it is politically impossible for it to be quiet about terrorism. If the United States believed that a tranquil Israel is worth preserving it should take steps to see that its commitment was believed."

The request was reflected in Eshkol's reply to Johnson. "I understand that you do not wish to be committed without consultation," the prime minister wrote. "But with a massive build-up on our southern frontier linked with a terrorist campaign from the north and Soviet support for the governments responsible for the tension, there is surely an urgent need to reaffirm the American commitment to Israel's security with a view to its implementation should the need arise." Israel had other requests as well, for jets and tanks and the dispatch of a U.S. destroyer for a port-of-call visit to Eilat.

None of these entreaties were met. While American officials promised to consider an aid package "that substantially meets Israel's requests," no arms were in fact cleared for delivery. "A propaganda horse for the Arabs to ride" was how Secretary of State Dean Rusk dismissed the port-of-call idea; "a red flag to Egypt." Barbour was even instructed to avoid direct discussions with Eshkol, for fear of creating the impression of collusion. Harman wrote of yet worse possibilities—that the U.S. would pressure Israel to accept UNEF on its territory and recognize the new *status quo* in Sinai. "These policies are fundamentally flawed and potentially disastrous," the ambassador emphasized to Eban. "A large share of the responsibility for the current crisis falls on the U.S. government. Only a bold, unilateral move by Washington will now bring results satisfactory to us both."[34]

Gravely disappointed in Johnson's response, Eshkol turned to De Gaulle. "An open expression of French support for Israel's security and integrity and for the preservation of peace in the Middle East will be a most important diplomatic and psychological asset in the delicate situation we now find ourselves in," the prime minister implored. A similar appeal was sent to the British government of Harold Wilson, though neither of Israel's erstwhile allies from 1956 was willing to make such a statement. Meanwhile, Soviet Ambassador Chuvakhin was again summoned to the Foreign Ministry and again assured by Eban of Israel's interest in peace. He replied by defending Egypt's right to evict UNEF and to denounce Israeli aggression, verbal and military, against Syria. Chuvakhin denied Syrian involvement in the terrorist attacks, which he ascribed to American agents. "You have been warned," he lectured Eban, "You are responsible. You are responding to provocation by the CIA."[35]

Israel sought assurances futilely, and the Egyptian buildup continued. A full six divisions had by May 20 taken up positions in Sinai, "from which they can deliver massive retaliation against Israeli aggression," reported 'Amer. An armada of Egyptian warships was rumored to have entered the Red Sea, en route to Eilat, and Egypt's ministry of religious affairs declared a state of holy war to liberate Palestine. The PLO's Shuqayri predicted Israel's "complete destruction" in the coming war, while in Damascus, Hafez al-Assad said it "was high time . . . to take the initiative in destroying the Zionist presence in the Arab homeland." Arab military delegations were suddenly on the move—Iraqis to Syria and Syrians to Egypt. "Our two brotherly countries have turned into one mobilized force," declared Syrian Foreign Minister Makhous upon returning from Cairo. "The withdrawal of the UN forces . . . means 'make way, our forces are on their way to battle.'"

Nasser's deeds had whipped the Arab "street" into a fervor unequaled since the heady 1950s. Conservative Arab leaders had no choice but to join that procession, even as Syria and Egypt continued to plot their overthrow. Thus, on May 21, after Syria expelled two Saudi diplomats for consorting with "reactionaries" and Egyptian planes again gassed Saudi bases, Riyadh called on all Arabs to unite around Cairo and Damascus. That same day, a Syrian car bomb exploded in the Jordanian border town of Ramtha, killing twenty-one. "We no longer knew who was less trustworthy: Israel, or our Arab allies!" wrote Hussein as he sent the Syrian ambassador packing, but his palace nevertheless declared its "readiness to stand by its sister Arab states against the common enemy with determination." An editorial in the moderate Lebanese newspaper *al-Zaman* summarized the situation best: "We are in the forefront of those who wish to see the Marxist-atheistic regime in Damascus collapse. But if bringing it down is to be by Israel's hands, then our wish is to see it become immortal."[36]

The intensity of this tumult could no longer be hidden from the Israeli public, nor could the call-up of what now amounted to 80,000 reservists. The price of the mobilization was staggering, and public opinion was gradually turning critical of the government's inability to take more definitive action. Ben-Gurion was quick to seize on this trend. He castigated Eshkol for his failure to obtain international guarantees for Israel's defense, as well as for his belligerent statements which, Ben-Gurion alleged, had merely antagonized the Soviets. So intense was the pressure on Eshkol that Lior began to fear that the prime minister would suffer either an emotional or a physical breakdown—or both.

Yet an even heavier strain was weighing on Rabin. By advancing into Sinai, the Egyptian army had snatched the initiative from Israel, and initiative was the cornerstone of Rabin's policy, essential for keeping the Arabs off-balance. By not meeting Nasser's challenge at once, Israel had sacrificed much of its deterrence power, Rabin feared. And though the enemy's deployment remained defensive, the situation was so volatile that a single sniper bullet could set off a full-scale war.

"It will be a terribly hard war with many casualties, but we can beat the Egyptian army," Rabin confided to Eshkol during a visit to Israeli troops in the south. The prime minister did not disagree, yet when Rabin inquired as to what steps Israel should take next, his only reply was, "We pursue our diplomatic options to the end."

Though used to working in tandem with Eshkol, Rabin had begun to sense a lack of leadership at the top, particularly with regard to preparing the army for war. Increasingly he felt he was being asked to formulate policy, rather than carry out the government's orders. "It's about time we realized that nobody is going to come to our rescue," the chief of staff told his generals on May 19, referring to Israel's isolation, both diplomatic and military. "The politicians are convinced that they can solve the problems through diplomacy. We have to enable them to exhaust every alternative to war, even though I see no way of returning things to the way they were. If the Egyptians blockade the Straits—there'll be no alternative to war. And if there's war—we'll have to fight on two fronts." He noted that Israel had no effective means of guarding its densely populated coast or of defending itself against chemical weapons.

Rabin was already thinking in terms of preemptive action, specifically a massive attack to destroy Egypt's air force. The IAF had been perfecting such a plan, code-named Focus (*Moked*), for several years, and Rabin was confident that it would work. Far less certainty surrounded the ground campaign, however. Queried by Rabin as to how long Israel would be able to fight before the Security Council stepped in and imposed a cease-fire, Eban estimated between twenty-four and seventy-two hours—not long enough to drive the Egyptian army from Sinai. "Give me time, time, time. We *need* time," Rabin implored. The state could not ask its citizens to die, he felt, for an objective it already knew was unobtainable.[37]

Not yet a week into the crisis, Rabin was smoking heavily and subsisting on black coffee. Reporters who interviewed him on May 21 found him stammering, almost incoherent, and visibly close to the edge. "Rabin's in a daze," Eban confided to Barbour. That day, the chief of staff was summoned to Ben-Gurion's bungalow at Sde Boker. There, Israel's founding father, 81 years old now and embittered, held court for his loyalists and plotted Eshkol's downfall. "When Ben-Gurion calls you, you go," Rabin later explained to Miriam Eshkol, and he went, but without informing Eshkol. He was hoping to receive Ben-Gurion's support and blessing; what he received instead was a tongue-lashing.

"We have been forced into a very difficult situation," Ben-Gurion assailed Rabin as soon as he walked in the door, "I very much doubt whether Nasser wanted to go to war, and now we are in serious trouble." He proceeded to take Rabin to task for his provocative statements to the press, for the massive call-up of reserves—all of which increased the chances of war while Israel remained utterly isolated. "You, or whoever gave you permission to mobilize so many reservists, made a mistake," he charged. Tackling Nasser without at least one Great Power ally would be ruinous at best for Israel, jeopardizing all its security accomplishments of the past twenty years, and possibly suicidal. Eshkol, of course, received special excoriation: "The prime minister and the Cabinet should take responsibility for deciding whether or not to go to war. That's not a matter for the army to decide. The government is not discharging its proper duties. This is no way to function."

The accusations, for Rabin, were devastating. Though disappointed by Ben-Gurion's failure to grasp the modern might of the IDF or the fact that Israel no longer needed the protection of a Britain or a France, he was deeply stung by the criticism from his former mentor. "You have led the state into a grave situation. We must not go to war. We are isolated. You bear the responsibility"—the words would ring in his ears long after he exited the bungalow with, according to one witness, "head down and shoulders drooped, a cigarette dangling from his lips."[38]

"The higher you climb, the higher the wall," an aide quoted Rabin as muttering as he drove from Sde Boker. Yet the IDF chief was en route to higher walls yet. He next met with Moshe Dayan.

Since resigning as agriculture minister in 1964, at the time of Ben-Gurion's final break with Mapai, the former chief of staff had been a steady critic of the Eshkol government, particularly in its policy toward the northern border. Thus, in October 1966, he told the Knesset that "there is no major wave of infiltration today. Just because several dozen bandits from al-Fatah cross the border, Israel does not have to get caught up in a frenzy of escalation. Arab states will join Syria in its political struggle, but they won't get involved in any military adventure it might initiate." He criticized the Samu' raid, the April 7 air battle with Syria, and Rabin's threats of retaliation. "This will end in war," he predicted, adding, "He who sends up smoke signals has to understand that the other side might think there's really a fire." The government's bungling, he claimed on May 17, would enable Nasser to win a bloodless political victory, to bomb Dimona or to close the Straits of Tiran.

What sort of support, then, could Rabin expect from Dayan? Ostensibly, the chief of staff wanted his predecessor's feedback on a new plan he had developed in the event that Nasser blockaded the Straits. Instead of merely defending the border, the IDF would conquer Gaza and trade it for renewed free passage. Rabin presented his idea, code-named *Atzmon*, to Dayan that evening, only to have it rebuffed. There were too many refugees in Gaza, Dayan averred, and Nasser would happily unload them on Israel. There was no territorial reply to closure, only military and psychological. Egypt's army would have to be destroyed and Nasser utterly humiliated.

Rabin had his response on *Atzmon*, but he clearly wanted more—a sympathetic ear for his complaints against the government. Incapable of making up its mind whether or not to make war, the Cabinet was forcing *him* to decide, placing him in an untenable position, Rabin said. He complained but his host offered nothing but silence. Rabin left that night, Dayan recalled, "unsure of himself, perplexed, nervously chain-smoking," hardly looking like a commander preparing for battle.[39]

Battle indeed seemed imminent if Nasser acted in Tiran. Few Israeli flag vessels in fact transversed the Straits, yet the narrow (seven mile) channel between Sinai and the Arabian Peninsula was nevertheless a lifeline for the Jewish state, the conduit for its quiet import of Iranian oil. Passage through the Straits also had symbolic value for Israelis, a testament to their 1956 triumph over Egypt. Having struggled to obtain international recognition of its right to act in self-defense if the Straits were ever blockaded, Israel could not now waive that right without forfeiting the last of its deterrence power.

Would Nasser close the Straits? The question divided Israeli leaders, even as Egyptian paratroopers landed at Sharm al-Sheikh. Meir Amit was positive that he would not. "Such an action would result in Nasser's annihilation," the Mossad chief explained, "It conflicted with all military and diplomatic logic." IDF intelligence agreed: to blockade the Straits meant certain war, and Nasser did not want war, only kudos. But Eshkol and Rabin disagreed. Addressing the Cabinet on May 21, the prime minister speculated that "the Egyptians plan to close the Straits or to bomb the atomic reactor in Dimona. A general attack will follow." A war would ensue in which "the first five minutes will be decisive. The question is who will attack the other's airfields first."

And yet, certain as he was of war, Eshkol refused to push Nasser's hand. He turned down a proposal for sending an Israeli flagship through the Straits, and saw to it that reservists were not stationed near the southern border. Journalists were requested not to report on ships departing and docking in Eilat. Through American and British channels, Eshkol also asked King Hussein to cease calling Nasser a coward for failing to reimpose the blockade. Speaking at the opening of the Knesset's summer session, just hours before U Thant's departure for Cairo, Eshkol denounced Palestinian terror and its Syrian sponsors, but only mildly rebuked Nasser for "clutching at mendacious rumors." He stressed the limited nature of Israel's mobilization and instead called for "reciprocal respect for the sovereignty, integrity, and international rights" of all Middle East nations. If Nasser were to be warned it would only be clandestinely, in a message to be conveyed by the secretary-general: "The freedom of passage in the Strait of Tiran is of supreme national interest and right, which Israel will assert and defend, whatever the sacrifice."[40]

Closure

If Nasser was displeased by the total—rather than the partial—pullout of UNEF, he never showed it. The same upsurge of Arab support that had so panicked the Israelis, now bore the once-great Egyptian leader on its crest. But while it was one thing to banish UNEF, it was dangerously another to renew the blockade of Tiran. The first had wrought a political victory; the second could lead to war. "It is here that Nasser's character comes into play," an Egypt expert at the British Foreign Office later commented, "you can respond to failure by cutting your loses or doubling your stakes; add to success by taking your profit, or by trying to double your winnings . . . Nasser has consistently been the gambler in failure and success."[41]

In this particular gamble, however, the stakes were exceptionally high. Though the average Egyptian was unaware that Israeli shipping had been plying the Straits since 1956—Nasser never admitted it publicly—or even where Tiran was located, the constant taunting of Jordan and Saudi Arabia was hateful to Egyptian leaders. It reminded them of their failure to fulfill the task

Egypt had taken upon itself in 1949 to "keep the Jews out of the Gulf" and preserve Aqaba as an Arab lake. That failure had led to the emergence of Eilat as a thriving port. Through its Red Sea terminus, Israel had established commercial footholds in Asia and Africa, two of Egypt's traditional spheres of interest, and had imported oil from the Shah of Iran, Nasser's personal rival. In the previous two years alone, some 54,000 tons of cargo had entered the port, and 207,000 had exited; over 500 ships had docked.

Retaliating for this insult, Egypt had refused to sign the 1958 Geneva Convention guaranteeing the international status of straits. The reason, Cairo argued, was that Israel had occupied Eilat illegally, after the signing of the Armistice, and had obtained free passage through a war of aggression. Israel had no right to ship war materials through Egyptian territory, nor could the UN protect Israel's ill-gotten gains.[42]

Nasser longed for the blockade, and as early as May 17, with UNEF still guarding the Straits, decided in principle to reinstate it. But implementing that decision was another matter entirely. Not forgotten were the memories of 1956, when the IDF broke through Egyptian lines in Sinai en route to Sharm al-Sheikh. Now, with military intelligence reporting that the Israeli mobilization was nearly complete, the threat of another invasion could not be overlooked. If the expulsion of UNEF had increased the chance of war to 20 percent, Nasser told a midnight meeting of his top military and civilian officials at his home on May 21, the closure of Tiran would raise it further, to over 50 percent. The question was whether the army was ready.

The answer, without hesitation, came from 'Amer. "*Bi raqbati,*" he volunteered, "on my neck, the army is prepared for the situation with both defensive and offensive plans." Since Israel would attack the Straits anyway, Egypt lost nothing by shutting them, the field marshal explained. Failure to blockade, on the other hand, was disgraceful. "How can my forces stationed there [Sharm al-Sheikh] simply watch the Israeli flag pass before them?" he berated Prime Minister Suliman, an engineer by training, who suggested that barring traffic through the Straits might not be in Egypt's best interests. Having sent those forces there, disregarding his staff's advice, 'Amer now argued that their presence necessitated closure. His power, if not his logic, was such that none of the officials present could oppose it.[43]

Nor did Nasser object, though he, alone, could have. No record has been found of any reservations the Egyptian leader might have raised regarding the blockade, not even in the writings of his apologist, Mohamed Heikal. Indeed, Heikal was present, along with 'Amer, Badran, and Muhieddin, the following day at the Abu Suweir air force base where Nasser greeted an ebullient group of pilots. He told them of receiving "accurate information" on Israel's pending invasion of Syria, and of his decision to oust UNEF, "a force serving neo-imperialism," from Sinai, "as an affirmation of our rights and sovereignty over the Aqaba Gulf." Then came the thrust:

The Aqaba Gulf constitutes our Egyptian territorial waters. Under no circumstances will we allow the Israeli flag to pass through the Aqaba Gulf. The
Jews threatened war. We tell them: *Ahlan Wa-sahlan* (You are welcome), we
are ready for war. Our armed forces and all our people are ready for war, but
under no circumstances will we abandon any of our rights. This water is ours.

No sooner had Nasser uttered these words than cables went out to Arab
governments informing them of Egypt's decision and requesting their help in
thwarting oil shipments to Israel. "Sea mines have been laid in certain areas
inside Egyptian territorial waters," Cairo Radio announced. The army went on
high alert. On 'Amer's order, the navy was instructed to send one destroyer
and a squadron of torpedo boats to bar the Straits to Israeli flagships or freighters carrying oil to Eilat. Two warning shots would be fired at these boats. "If
they fail to respond to the warnings," 'Amer wrote, "they will be damaged. If
they still fail to respond, they will be sunk."

"We were issued the order to close the Tiran Straits," Muhammad 'Abd al-
Hafiz, a paratrooper commander at Sharm al-Sheikh, remembered. "We were
joined by seven SU 100 motorized cannons and four heavy shore cannons . . . A
destroyer, six torpedo ships and a submarine were off shore [in addition to] the
MiG-21 squadron positioned at Hurghada . . . We were ordered to shoot warning shots at every [Israeli] ship sailing through the straits . . . and if it didn't stop,
to shoot at closer range, and so on." Hafiz, who never knew that UNEF had
stationed in the area or that Israel had enjoyed rights of passage, was elated by
the action. "Of course, the closing of the straits was a declaration of war . . . but at
that point we did not know this and we carried out orders without questioning."[44]

Similar elation was registered throughout the Arab world, where Nasser's
Ahlan Wa-sahlan reverberated. In Hebron and Jerusalem, in the streets of
Baghdad, Beirut, and Tripoli, mass demonstrations erupted in acclaim of Egypt's
action. The armed forces of Lebanon, Kuwait, and Saudi Arabia were activated; Iraqi armored columns were reportedly moving toward the Syrian and
Jordanian borders "to participate in the battle of honor." King Hussein donned
a military uniform and reviewed units of his army, among them American-
made tanks that were not supposed to cross the Jordan River, parading toward
the West Bank.[45]

U Thant did not partake of the Arabs' exultation. He learned of the closure order during a stopover in Paris, en route to Cairo. Deeply insulted, he
considered canceling his trip, but then determined to press on in the hope of
persuading Nasser to either rescind his decision or pledge that Egypt would
not be the first to fire.

The secretary-general's plane landed at Cairo International Airport on Tues-
day afternoon, May 23, exactly one week after Rikhye first received Egypt's
eviction order. Hundreds of people were on hand to greet him, cheering "Long
live Nasser!" and "We want war!" as he descended to the tarmac. Among them

was Mahmoud Riad, who was prepared to begin talks immediately. But U Thant, feeling tired, delayed his meeting with the foreign minister until 9:45 the following morning.

The morning was cool and clear as U Thant's limousine—license plate UNEF 1—crossed the Nile at University Bridge, passed the Soviet embassy, and arrived at the Semiramis Hotel, that temporarily housed the Foreign Ministry. Riad's disposition was anything but sunny, though. He rejected as worthless American assurances that there were no Israeli concentrations in the north, and insisted there was a plot to conquer southern Syria and impose UNEF there as well. The remilitarization of Sinai was aimed at making Israel "think twice" before mounting aggression, Riad said. But Egypt's action had served another purpose as well: "to pull the last curtain on the Israeli aggression of 1956." There would be no restoring that curtain, either, even at the cost of war. UNEF troops would be evicted from Egyptian soil "by force, if necessary," and Israeli ships prevented from sailing to Eilat. Riad left little latitude for diplomacy. While Egypt was willing to discuss the possibility of reviving the Armistice and its machinery, it rejected any measure—the marking of the border, for example—that granted Israel recognition or detracted from the state of belligerency.

A cigar-smoking Thant allowed Riad to finish before presenting his idea for a two-to-three week freeze in the situation: Egypt would not blockade the Straits, but neither would Israel try traversing them. This moratorium—"along the lines of the Cuban [missile] crisis"—would afford time for a specially appointed UN mediator to work out a peaceable solution. Riad reacted skeptically. The government could show no hesitation to its people, he asserted, and especially not to the army, which was determined to defend the Arab cause. The message U Thant brought from Eshkol, that Israel would act militarily to reopen the Straits, had no impact on the foreign minister.

U Thant next lunched at the Tahrir Club where his host, Dr. Mahmoud Fawzi, informed him that the meeting with Nasser would only take place late that evening, after dinner. If piqued by this delay, the secretary-general showed no inkling. He was fond of Nasser, had always found him "very simple, charming, polite . . . the real leader of his people," and never forgot their first encounter in Rangoon, where the Egyptian agreed to don traditional Burmese dress and to get soaked, while attending a water festival. That fondness was apparent when the talks began at the president's residence at ten o'clock. U Thant readily accepted Nasser's explanation that he had decided to announce the closure before, rather than after, the secretary-general's visit, in order to spare his guest undue embarrassment. Had U Thant asked him to refrain from blockading, he, Nasser, would have had to rebuff him.

Nasser reiterated much of what Riad had said earlier: that the Sinai buildup was necessitated by Israel's designs on Syria, and by the requisites of Arab dignity and honor. He admitted to having dreamt of seizing the initiative and of having asked his generals whether they were ready to take on Israel. Their reply, Nasser recalled, was, "We will never be in a better position than now. Our forces are well equipped and trained. We will have all the advantages of attacking first. We are sure of victory." Shrugging, Nasser asked U Thant, "My generals tell me we will win—what would you say to them?" but U Thant just smiled back.

Nasser then embarked on a long tirade against the United States, which he accused of waging a "war of starvation" against Egypt, of trying to topple him with the Islamic Pact, and of lying about Israeli troop concentrations. As for Israel, it had neither legal claim to Eilat nor any need for a Red Sea port; oil could be imported through Haifa. He realized that removing UNEF from the border meant evicting it from Sharm al-Sheikh as well—no mention was made of a request for a mere redeployment—and that this, in turn, meant war. Yet he repeatedly pledged not to fire the first shot. "We have no intention of attacking unless we are attacked, and then we will defend ourselves . . . We will not attack first." Further, he agreed to instruct his troops in Tiran to be "good boys" and observe the proposed moratorium, provided that Israel reciprocated.

The meeting ended curiously, with Nasser again offering UNEF Egypt's highest medal for distinguished service, and by asking for permission to purchase its surplus equipment. U Thant emerged puzzled by these requests, but optimistic nevertheless. He remarked to Rikhye, who had taken notes on the discussion, that "Nasser, his Foreign Minister, and other UAR leaders had reaffirmed their great respect for the office of the secretary-general, who enjoyed their high personal regard and immense popularity throughout the Arab world." His proposal for a "breathing space" had been accepted; now it was up to Israel to comply. But his hopefulness was not shared by Rikhye. The former UNEF commander had found Nasser strangely unfocused and weak, as if the army, and not the president, were sovereign. Asked for his impression of the meeting, Rikhye responded, "I think you're going to have a major Middle East war and I think we will still be sorting it out 50 years from now."[46]

Rabin Waits

Yitzhak Rabin emphatically agreed, at least about the prospects for war. News of the closure reached IDF intelligence at 2:30 A.M., on May 23, along with reports of Egyptian submarines passing through the Straits and the emplacement of heavy guns at Sharm al-Sheikh. On the Golan Heights, Syrian forces were at maximum strength and war footing; the movements of UN observers had been strictly curtailed. The chief of staff would recount that "the key piece of the Middle Eastern puzzle—Nasser's provision of a *casus belli*—had just fallen into place. In effect, the ball was now in our court . . . " At stake, he knew, was more than just the issue of free passage and the well-being of Eilat. "It is now a question of our national survival," he told his generals that night, "of to be or not to be."[47]

Still, Eshkol refused to approve a preemptive strike. Awakened before dawn by Col. Lior with the words, "Sir, the Egyptians have closed the Straits," the prime minister hurried to the Pit (Hebrew: *Bor*) deep beneath IDF headquarters in Tel Aviv. Waiting for him there were Rabin and the general staff and an atmosphere taut with expectation.

Intelligence chief Yariv began: "The post-Sinai Campaign period has come to an end . . . If Israel takes no action in response to the blockade of the Straits, she will lose her credibility and the IDF its deterrent capacity. The Arab states will interpret Israel's weakness as an excellent opportunity to threaten her security and her very existence." Next came Weizman: "We must strike now and swiftly . . . we must deal the enemy a serious blow, for if we don't, other forces will soon join him." Lastly, Rabin spoke: "The Syrian and Jordanian position depends on the success of Egypt's move," he said, telling Eshkol that the IDF could either take Gaza as a bargaining chip or else try to destroy the Egyptian army. Either way, the offensive would open with a surprise attack on Egypt's air force. "We have to admit the truth. First we'll strike Egypt, and then we'll fight Syria and Jordan as well."

Eshkol now understood that time was not on Israel's side and that the army advised preemption. But the prospect gravely disturbed him. While IAF planes struck at Egypt, northern Israel would be exposed to Syrian fire; entire settlements might be annihilated. More discomforting, however, was the knowledge that Johnson still opposed any resort to violence. Thus, after acknowledging the generals' recommendation, Eshkol again decided to wait. An oil tanker was due in Eilat in one week, he revealed, and could challenge the blockade if necessary. Meanwhile, another appeal would be made to Washington.[48]

Washington had, in fact, appealed to Eshkol. During the night, another letter from Johnson had arrived exhorting Israel to "manifest steady nerves" and recalling his and previous presidents' commitments to its security. Though U Thant's decision on UNEF was regrettable, Johnson wrote, the Soviets seemed cooperative, and the United States was working to peaceably resolve the crisis "in the United Nations or outside it." Until it did, the U.S. was willing to furnish a number of items—100 half-tracks, Patton tank and Hawk missile parts, food and economic aid totaling $47.3 million, plus a $20 million loan—to tide Israel over. The package came with a catch, however: Israel could not challenge the blockade with a test boat or under any circumstances precipitate war. "Any Israeli unilateral action could be justified only after all peaceful measures had been exhausted," Undersecretary Rostow warned Eppy Evron. "Such justification would have to be demonstrated before the people of the United States and the world."[49]

The letter only spotlighted Eshkol's bind: to convince the world that he had to act while convincing Israelis why he shouldn't. That dilemma was painfully apparent at the next meeting of the Ministerial Defense Committee. Since 1948, Israel's governments had always been coalitions, and Eshkol's was no exception. Alongside ministers from the socialist, centrist Mapai party—the largest—sat members of the radical socialist Mapam (the United Workers' party), the socialist but militant Ahdut ha-Avoda (Labor Union), and the ritually observant, politically moderate Mafdal (National Religious party). All these factions were represented on the Defense Committee, but in view of the crisis, opposition representatives were included as well—Menachem Begin from the Gahal right-wing party, along with Moshe Dayan and Shimon Peres, both of Rafi. A broad spectrum of opinions was thus present in the Cabinet, and the divisions within it ran deep.

Rabin opened the session. Somberly he informed the committee that the Straits would be officially closed as of 12:00 that day. With Israel's power of deterrence impaired, Nasser could now dictate the time and place of any confrontation, switching his forces' disposition from defensive to offensive in a matter of hours. Thus, if the IDF tried to seize the Straits, the Egyptians—the Syrians probably too, and perhaps Jordan—would strike into Israel proper. The situation was the reverse of that which had obtained in 1956: Then Egypt alone faced an Israel allied with Britain and France, while now an isolated Israel faced Egypt and numerous Arab states. The Soviets were liable to intervene as well. "We're not talking about a stroll through the park," Rabin concluded, but there appeared to be no choice. "We must destroy Egypt's air force with a surprise attack followed by the advance of our ground forces into Sinai."

Rapid-fire, the questions then flew at Rabin. Would Israel attack Syria and what damage could Syria cause while the IAF was bombing Egypt? How could Israel act alone, without a Great Power alliance? Education Minister Zalman Aran, from Mapai, raised the most frightening prospect: "Is it possible that the air force, without which this country is totally defenseless, will be obliterated?"

Rabin, frazzled, tried his best to answer. No, Israel would not attack Syria, though Syria could be expected to launch massive artillery bombardments, and yes, the damage would be extensive until the air force could turn its attention to the north. As for the fear that Israel's planes, instead of smashing Egypt's, would themselves be shot down, Rabin turned to Weizman. Though now IDF chief of operations, the forty-one-year-old former RAF pilot had commanded Israel's air force throughout most of its previous decade and was the main architect of the Focus plan. Raffish, swashbuckling, never known for his modesty, Weizman dismissed Aran's fears. "The IAF will lose 20 planes out of 600," he ventured, and then explained that no country could effectively seal off its sky; Israel's first wave would get through undetected.

Weizman's swagger failed to impress Haim Moshe Shapira, the interior minister. A representative of the National Religious party, sixty-five years old, Shapira was an outspoken dove who had often opposed Eshkol's activist defense policies toward the Syrians. He reminded Rabin how the army had once believed that Syria stood alone and could easily be taught a lesson, but now Syria was no longer alone and that lesson could lead to war. "I'm prepared to fight," Shapira declared, "but not to commit suicide."

Siding with the army were Transportation Minister Moshe Carmel and Israel Galili, a minister without portfolio. Both called for a declaration of war against Egypt. Begin, outspoken in his militant views, also expressed support for a preemptive strike, as did Shimon Peres.

Throughout this debate, Eshkol sat with a drawn, nervous expression, aware that his personal future, and quite possibly the country's, lay on the line—in Lior's view, "worried, worried, worried." Popular opinion had turned against him, with calls for his resignation as minister of defense, if not as prime minister as well, in favor of Ben-Gurion. Struggling to restore public confidence in him, Eshkol warned the Knesset that "any interference with freedom of passage in the Straits constitutes a gross violation of international law, a blow at the sovereign rights of other nations and an act of aggression against Israel." But behind this bluster, the thought of war still terrified him.

"What's to stop the Egyptians from taking the south? The Syrians from attacking our settlements?" he asked while reminding the cabinet that the Arabs outnumbered Israel three-to-one in tanks and aircraft. The prime minister seemed to have internalized the rifts in his government. He stressed the need to show the Arabs that "the Jews are not just standing here and bleating," but also to explore all diplomatic options. He professed reluctance either to provoke a clash or to rely on international pledges. "We don't want war, but if the Arabs bomb us—and it doesn't matter what they bomb—we must respond swiftly and massively," he stated, but then wondered if the retaliation could be put off until Israel acquired more weaponry.

Eshkol seemed steeped in his quandary, but then Abba Eban rose to extricate him. The foreign minister agreed that the issue was not Eilat, but deterrence. "A nation that could not protect its basic maritime interests would presumably find reason for not repelling other assaults on its rights," his memoirs affirmed. "Unless a stand was made here, nobody in the Arab world . . . would ever again believe in Israel's power to resist." Yet Eban opposed taking a military action that the United States was unlikely to support and the USSR would probably resist—a replay of the Suez crisis. He told the Cabinet of a request he had received from Washington: Israel would accept a forty-eight-hour consultation period during which the U.S. would consider mobilizing a multinational convoy to escort Israeli ships through Tiran. The plan went beyond Eisenhower's pledge to support Israel in defending itself, he pointed out. "The historical weight of this moment—and there won't be many like it in Jewish history—requires that we take this step," Eban, with his signature eloquence, concluded. "If not, then for generations to come, we will not be able to explain to ourselves and to others why we failed to put it [the closure] to the test."

The American proposal was to be put for a vote, but not before Dayan had his say. Still wearing the uniform he had donned for a tour of the southern front where military policemen had found him and escorted him back to Jerusalem, Dayan spoke bluntly. He was opposed to "banging on the doors of the

Powers" and granting the Egyptians additional time to dig in. "We're not England here, with its tradition of losing big battles first," he quipped. Nevertheless, he endorsed the forty-eight-hour delay, if only to placate the Americans, after which he recommended mounting an all-out air and ground attack against Egypt. "We should destroy hundreds of tanks in a two-to-three-day battle," he proposed, and be ready for counterattacks from Jordan and even from Israeli Arabs.

The meeting adjourned with a decision to postpone military action to give Eban time to garner support for Israel's position in Western capitals, above all Washington. In the interim, the government would work to downplay the crisis—no major Knesset debates, no cancellation of official ceremonies—while exploring the possibility of creating a national unity Cabinet with the opposition. Preparations would be made for Operation *Atzmon* (the capture of Gaza as bargaining chip for free passage), and 35,000 more reservists would be called up, but otherwise "the waiting" would continue. Only if Egypt attacked first, bombing Israeli airfields or strategic targets, would Israel strike back and strike with all its forces.[50]

Eshkol had steered a middle course between war and diplomacy, but his helmsmanship appeared to appease nobody. Several Mapai ministers, Aran among them, disapproved of Eshkol's choice of Eban as his emissary, believing him ineffective and untrustworthy. In the Pit, meanwhile, Israeli generals were complaining of government indecisiveness. Plans were completed for launching Focus, for advancing into Sinai and, if necessary, on other fronts as well—to the Jordan headwaters in the north and the Latrun corridor leading to Jerusalem. The success of all these operations hinged on gaining the element of surprise which, in turn, hung on the word of Eshkol, which the prime minister hesitated to give.

Rabin also had misgivings—deep misgivings. While he knew that Israel could not ignore a direct appeal from the American president, he also realized that far more than forty-eight hours would pass before Eban completed his mission. The news in the interim was frightful. Egypt's 4th Division had completed its deployment in Sinai and the Straits had been mined. Arab leaders were lining up to volunteer their armies to, in the words of a convocation of religious clerics in Egypt, "wash away with Muslim blood the 19 year-old Arab disgrace in Palestine."

The weight of decision making was becoming too great for Rabin. A few hours after the ministerial meeting, he woke Eshkol from his afternoon nap to tell him that he had changed his mind: Israel must go to war. "Is there any way out of this?" the prime minister asked. Rabin answered grimly, "We will suffer many losses, but we have no other choice." But Eshkol was still unconvinced. "The IDF will not attack before the political options have been exhausted," he responded, and permission to strike was withheld. Rabin's position was quickly becoming untenable. A new, morale-boosting song was making the rounds in Israel, with the refrain "Nasser waits for Rabin." The reality, however, was radically different, as Rabin's memoirs recalled: "If Nasser was waiting for Rabin, Rabin was waiting for Eshkol; Eshkol was waiting for his Cabinet; the Cabinet for Eban [and] Eban for President Johnson . . . "[51]

The pace of the following hours was frantic. "The tension rose and rose and rose," Lior recounted, "Messages poured in from around the world. Telephones rang incessantly . . . The clock raced." The combined mass of these pressures converged on Rabin, along with the onus of personal culpability first imposed on him by Ben-Gurion. "Egypt will be fighting on a single front, but we will have to fight on at least two, perhaps three," Haim Moshe Shapira reminded him. "Now we will be totally isolated, and we won't receive arms supplies if we run short during the fighting . . . Do you want to bear the responsibility for endangering Israel? I shall resist it as long as I breathe!"[52]

Whether it was Shapira's words or reports of the gathering Egyptian threat to Eilat, by the night of May 23 Rabin snapped. "I sunk into a profound crisis brought on by my guilt . . . that I had led the country into war under the most difficult circumstances," he later told an Israeli journalist. "Everything was on my shoulders, rightly or wrongly. I had eaten almost nothing for almost nine days, hadn't slept, was smoking non-stop, and was physically exhausted." His wife, Leah, seeing his condition, forbade him from embarking on a tour of the southern front. Instead, she called the army's chief physician, Dr. Eliyahu Gilon, who diagnosed a case of acute anxiety and administered a tranquilizer.

Rabin's collapse was kept secret from the Israeli public, and would only be disclosed many years later and then ascribed to "nicotine poisoning." That night, however, Weizman was summoned to the chief of staff's house where he found his commander "silent and still" and extremely depressed. "I endangered the state . . . my mistakes," Rabin stammered. "The biggest and most brutal war yet." In a report filed six months later, Weizman claimed that Rabin offered him his post. The operations chief declined, though, citing the need to maintain the nation's morale and to guide the government to a brave and inevitable decision. Rabin subsequently denied that the conversation ever took place, but the fact remained that the chief of staff was incapacitated, and his operations chief was de facto in charge.[53]

Free of Rabin's hesitations, Weizman expanded the army's attack plans. Now, in addition to destroying Egypt's air force and conquering Gaza, Israeli troops would advance westward to al-'Arish and, time permitting, beyond in the direction of the Canal. The Central and Northern Commands were also prepared for counteraction should Jordan or Syria intervene. Operation Axe (*Kardom*), as it was called, would be launched on May 26, at the latest. "By tomorrow, the Israel Defense Forces would be ready and prepared for war," Weizman told the general staff, and expressed complete confidence in the government's approval. Well before midnight of the 25th, Israeli armor was rolling toward the border.[54]

'Amer's "Dawn"

Weizman would be sorely disappointed, however, for Eshkol had no intention of approving Axe. Deeply disturbed by Rabin's breakdown, afraid of triggering a war in the middle of Eban's talks, the prime minister ordered a strict reduction of IDF activity in the south. He even restricted the number of reconnaissance flights over Sinai.

While Eshkol held back, in Egypt, the pressure for a showdown mounted. "The streets of Cairo looked more like a carnival rather than a city preparing for war," commented Mahmud al-Jiyyar, a high government official and close associate of Nasser. The city was now festooned with lurid posters showing Arab soldiers shooting, crushing, strangling, and dismembering bearded, hook-nosed Jews. Cairo Radio boasted, "The Gulf of Aqaba, by the dictum of history and the protection of our soldiers, is Arab, Arab, Arab," and targeted the United States: "Millions of Arabs are . . . preparing to blow up all of America's interests, all of America's installations, and your entire existence, America."

Caught up in this frenzy, encouraged by the lack of response, Israeli or American, to the closure of Tiran, Field Marshal 'Amer continued to plan his offensive. "This time we will be the ones to start the war," he confided to Gen. Murtagi during a tour of forward fortifications. Beyond air strikes at strategic targets and the detachment of Eilat, 'Amer now broadened his objectives to include the entire Negev. Orders for the new operation, code-named Dawn (*al-Fajr*) were to be issued directly from 'Amer's house, further circumventing Supreme Headquarters. Al-Jiyyar observed: "I now understood that the streets of Cairo reflected the concept that had seized the leadership, namely that the destruction of Israel was a child's game that only required the hooking up of a few telephone lines at the commander's house and the writing of victory slogans."[55]

'Amer's Dawn clearly violated Nasser's strategy of drawing Israel into starting the war. Why, then, did Nasser not veto it? Egyptian sources are divided over this question—indeed over the degree to which Nasser even knew about the plan. Loyalists like Heikal insist that Nasser wanted a blueprint for attack and, while not directly involved in its drafting, implicitly approved it. Writers critical of Nasser, however, assert that 'Amer, alone, devised the operation in blatant opposition to Nasser's will. The truth, no doubt, lay somewhere between: Nasser was apprised of Dawn but lacked the political strength to override 'Amer's order. Also, the preparation of an Egyptian invasion of Israel had certain advantages for Nasser, as will be seen.

In its initial phase, the only objections to Dawn were raised by senior officers, many of whom believed that the remilitarization of Sinai was merely an exercise, and who now realized that war was its intended outcome. Having already opposed the reoccupation of Sharm al-Sheikh as a needless provocation, Chief of Staff Fawzi considered Dawn disastrous. "Did the plan have any political objectives?" he asked in retrospect, and then answered himself: "How could it when the link between the military and the political echelons was missing?"[56]

The application of Dawn was also wreaking havoc on Conqueror, Egypt's triple-tiered defense strategy. Already lacking the troops necessary to man all the fortifications and trenchworks, the army was redirecting entire brigades to forward jump-off positions. The last-minute, contradictory orders only deepened the confusion created by the influx of tens of thousands of men—reservists, newly repatriated units from Yemen—many of whom arrived on cattle cars, without uniforms or guns, ragged and hungry. At the Qantara railroad junction, Gen. 'Abd al-Fattah Abu Fadel, deputy chief of Egyptian military intelligence, saw "a great heap of men and boys lost because of the negligence and recklessness of the armed forces leadership," and wondered, "Is this the status of our forces which will face our enemy Israel?"

An estimated 20 percent of Egypt's tanks, a quarter of its artillery pieces, and a third of its planes were unfit for action, and less than half of its troops reached their designated positions. Of these, many were now being ordered to undertake a mission they had never studied, into territory totally unfamiliar to them. "There were no provisions for communications, no directives for the artillery or for the administration [of the captured areas], no multi-staged plan," recalled Fawzi. Yet when he protested to 'Amer that "our forces know nothing of this plan," the field marshal barked back: "Then train them!"[57]

So vast was the chaos that even a hireling like Murtagi began to question the wisdom of Dawn. Like Fawzi, he, too, had thought the army's purpose was more political than strategic, and was shocked to hear of the intended offensive. He pointed out the shortage of manpower, the dearth of preparations. "He ['Amer] seemed surprised by my response," the general remembered, but the field marshal remained wedded to his plan. Sidqi Mahmud, too, cast doubts on his pilots' ability to carry out all the sorties assigned to them, complaining to 'Amer, "An attack on Eilat . . . an attack on the Dimona atomic reactor . . . on the Haifa oil refineries . . . Do you think that I'm the commander of the American air force? I can't plan an attack on Eilat and operation Leopard [bombing the Israeli coast] at the same time!"[58] The response he received was silence.

Still Nasser refused to intervene. The days after the closure decision were intensely busy for the Egyptian president. There were delegations to receive from Arab states—Syria's prime minister, Kuwait's foreign minister and the Iraqi vice president—and letters of support to answer from China, North Vietnam, and North Korea. There were daily meetings at Supreme Headquarters, and increasingly bombastic speeches to deliver. "We knew that closing the Gulf of Aqaba meant war with Israel," he revealed to a convention of Arab trade unionists, "If war comes it will be total and the objective will be Israel's destruction . . . This is Arab power." Nasser also harped on "American gangsterism" and what he regarded as America's obsession with Israel's rights. "What is Israel?" he asked rhetorically, then answered: "Israel today is the United States."[59]

Though hardly new, Nasser's reproofs of the U.S. had been sharpened by a speech President Johnson broadcast on May 23. This described the blockade as "illegal" and "potentially disastrous to the cause of peace." The United States considered Tiran an international waterway, Johnson said, and reiterated America's commitment to the "political independence and territorial integrity of all nations in the area." *Notes verbales* sent by the White House went further: Egypt had committed "aggression" in the Straits, harming vital U.S. interests, and would face "gravest international consequences" by initiating violence "overt or clandestine . . . by regular military forces or irregular groups." Rumors were circulating of an American plan to break the blockade by force, of Marines already training for an amphibious landing at Tiran. The 6th Fleet had gone on alert in the eastern Mediterranean.

Nasser's fear of U.S. military intervention would not be mitigated by a private letter he received from the White House in which Johnson denied harboring any animosity toward Egypt or to its president personally. "Your task and mine is not to look back, but to rescue the Middle East—and the whole human community—from a war I believe no one wants," Johnson wrote, and proposed sending Vice President Hubert H. Humphrey on a mediation mission to Cairo. Nasser was unimpressed. This was the same Hubert H. Humphrey who, that very week, had called Israel "a beacon to all peoples in the Middle East and elsewhere." Though Riad tried to allay his fears, noting Johnson's expressions of support for the Armistice Agreements and the absence of any ironbound U.S. commitment to Israel, Nasser remained distrustful of Washington's intentions, and fearful of U.S.-Israeli plots.[60]

Nasser's apprehensions were at least partly a reflection of the general state of U.S.-Egyptian relations, close to ruinous even before the crisis. The quiet diplomatic channels that had once helped siphon some of the venom from those relations in the past were now obstructed, the result of personnel changes in both Washington and Cairo. Egypt's veteran ambassador, Dr. Mustafa Kamel, a 58 year-old bachelor, former law professor, and ambassador to India, was due to retire within days. Urbane and philo-American, Kamel believed Egypt's future lay in economic development, not in ruling the Arab world. He labored to maintain open lines to the White House, assuring staff members that Nasser admired the United States and was determined to keep the Palestine issue "in the icebox." Even after the blockade of the Straits, Kamel went on insisting that the situation was not irreversible and that room for negotiation remained.

Kamel's departure from Washington was preceded by Lucius Battle's from Cairo in March. His replacement, Richard H. Nolte, arrived only on May 21, the day before Nasser closed the Straits. On paper, at least, Nolte was an ideal ambassador: a naval aviator in World War II, a Rhodes Scholar with degrees from Oxford and Yale, knowledgeable in Arabic, and the director of the Middle East Studies Association. He believed that Nasser had gained the upper hand in Sinai, enabling him to claim a moral victory or to label Israel as the aggressor if it attacked. Yet none of Nolte's training prepared him for the hands-on, high-caliber diplomacy the situation now required. When asked by reporters for his reaction to the crisis, Nolte responded, "What crisis?"[61]

In view of Nolte's inexperience, the State Department had decided to reinforce the Cairo embassy with Charles Yost, a former ambassador to Damascus and close acquaintance of Mahmoud Riad. Until Yost arrived, though, Nolte was on his own, and had not even presented his credentials. Riad was quick with him: Egypt would stop all Israel-bound ships and cargoes and defend itself against any force that tried to defend them. Nolte reported that Nasser had decided on a course of war with Israel, a war for which he was well prepared and confident, not entirely without reason, of winning. "[The] current state of [the] Arab mind seems to be that of early 1948 rather [than] 1956," he warned. "[The] Arab[s] believe [that] victory is no tentative possibility, but a reality."[62]

Nolte had realized what was already clear to many Western diplomats, that any doubts surrounding Egypt's ability to vanquish Israel had been vitiated by the West's refusal to defend Israel and the Israelis' reluctance to defend themselves. "An armed clash between the UAR and Israel is inevitable," wrote Heikal in *al-Ahram*, and explained how the blockade, by undermining Israel's deterrence power, would soon force it to fight. "Let Israel begin. Let our second blow then be ready. Let it be a knock-out."

Egyptian confidence was crescendoing, yet Nasser could not entirely free himself of the fear of military collaboration between the United States and Israel. Confiding to Dr. Fawzi, he described a scenario in which Israel sent a flagship through the Straits with an American escort, and the Egyptians at Sharm al-Sheikh opened fire. While the Arabs were preoccupied fighting the Americans, Israel would conquer Sinai. Fawzi had to admit that such a maneuver was possible. "America's behavior in the crisis is like an iceberg. Most of it is hidden beneath the surface."[63]

It was in grappling with his America dilemma that Nasser saw certain advantages in Dawn. If Johnson sent warships to the Straits, the Egyptian army would proceed with its planned invasion of southern Israel. The operation enabled Nasser to hedge his bets—to maintain a defensive posture while preparing an offensive option; to exhort the Arabs to war while quietly preventing its outbreak. Nasser boasted that the Straits had been mined and that Egypt stood fully behind Palestinian guerrilla raids. In reality, the waterway remained mine-free while Cairo acted strenuously to rein in al-Fatah. Through back channels, Nasser reminded the Americans of his continuing interest in peace. In a conversation with a Mr. Siddiqui of ALCO products on May 26, Nasser said that his only goal was to demonstrate his leadership of the Arab world; he had no intention of fighting anybody. Siddiqui reported to the State Department, "His urgent request is that the United States undertake no direct military action in the form of landings, shifting of the naval fleet or otherwise."[64]

The danger of American intervention was only half of Nasser's worries, though. The other half was how and whether the Soviet Union would react to that intervention.

Egyptian confidence in Soviet support had been strong, at least at the outset of the crisis. This had followed talks on strategic cooperation with Foreign
Minister Gromyko in Cairo in March and then, in April, a state visit by Premier Kosygin. Some $500 million in Soviet aid had been pledged for "strength-
ening the common anti-imperialist front" between the USSR and Egypt. 'Amer's
orders to his commanders on May 15 expressed certainty that the "Eastern
bloc will not stand detached from events and allow the Western imperialist
forces to act wantonly in Arab areas." The assumption appeared to be substan-
tiated, as both the remilitarization of Sinai and the removal of UNEF were
lauded by the Communist press. "Let no one have any doubts about the fact
that should anyone try to unleash aggression in the Near East, he would be met
not only with the united strength of the Arab countries but also with strong
opposition to aggression from the Soviet Union and all peace-loving peoples,"
Moscow's communiqué warned. Promises of economic aid were extended to
Egypt, while, in the UN, the Soviet delegation made it clear that no Security
Council interference in Sinai would be brooked.[65]

All that changed with the closure. Though Pojidaev, the Soviet ambassador, was informed of the decision before its announcement, the Kremlin's views
on the blockade had not been canvassed in advance. A curious silence settled
over Egyptian-Soviet relations, nearly as complete as that between Cairo and
Washington. Diplomatic sources reported that the Soviets were now changing
their tune; instead of warning the West not to interfere with Egypt's actions in
Sinai and emphasizing their backing of Nasser, they stressed the need for a
negotiated settlement and their willingness to help achieve one. Though Egyptian Ambassador Murad Ghaleb appealed repeatedly for indications of where,
precisely, Moscow stood in the event of war, his inquiries remained unanswered.

On the afternoon of May 23, a petulant Nasser again summoned Pojidaev
to his office, this time to upbraid him: "I want you to tell your bosses in Moscow that the USSR is the main factor influencing everything that is happening
now." Nasser reminded him that it was the Soviet warning about an Israeli
attack on Syria that had spurred Egypt into Sinai, the result being that Israeli
forces were now massed not in the north, but in the south, against Egypt. The
USSR could not leave Egypt in the lurch, but must supply it with additional
military equipment—air-to-surface rockets were especially lacking—and political backing against the United States. Pojidaev countered with a standard
response: "You and the rest of the Arab world must know that the USSR stands
decisively behind the independent Arab states, and if the situation develops
into aggression by imperialism and its 'straw child' Israel, we will take the necessary measures." But Nasser was not appeased. "I don't want you to send a
warning to Israel," he chided. "That gives her a form of recognition that it
doesn't deserve, and allows her to reap the benefits of the weak. Your warnings
have to be directed against the imperialist Power."[66]

The conversation convinced Nasser that irrespective of whether Egypt initiated the war or waited until the U.S. challenged the blockade, the Soviet

position had first to be clarified. To this end, a special delegation left for Moscow on May 25. At its head was Defense Minister Shams al-Din Badran, 'Amer's man, though Nasser made sure to include loyalists of his own as well, including Salah Bassiouny and Ahmad Hassan al-Feki, both of the Foreign Ministry. Billed by the Soviets as an effort "to obtain types of arms the UAR does not now have," the mission's real purpose was to ascertain how far Egypt could go and still have the USSR behind it.[67]

In spite of the disorder of the Egyptian buildup, and the uncertainty of American and Soviet intentions, preparations for Operation Dawn proceeded apace. Strike Force 1, a specially constituted division—9,000 men, 200 tanks and guns—under Gen. Sa'ad al-Din Shazli, along with the 14th Armored Brigade, had been moved up to Rafah, in preparation for invading the northern Negev. Battle orders 1 through 6 were issued specifying targets to be eliminated, including airfields, missile and radar sites, and desalination plants. The families of Egyptian officers were evacuated from Gaza while scores of civilian managers, engineers, and even doctors were transferred there in preparation for occupying the Negev. "I was fully confident of victory," recalled Amin Tantawi, a 4th Division company commander. "Nasser's speeches gave me that confidence. I believed that the day of liberation had arrived and that we would attack first and destroy Israel in a matter of hours. I had many ideas about what to do to Israel once we conquered and erased it."

All was ready by the morning of May 25. That day, Lt. Gen. Salah Muhsin, commander of Egypt's land forces, gathered his senior infantry officers and informed them that the army was now at full strength, outnumbering the enemy three-to-one in tanks, troops, and artillery. Those forces would begin their attack in two days' time exactly—fittingly, at first light.[68]

Every Delay a Gamble

The scope and intensity of Egypt's buildup, together with the mobilization of virtually every Arab army, was observed with near-panic in Israel. "We had seen photographs of the victims of Egyptian gas attacks in Yemen," recalled Lt. Yossi Peled, a Holocaust survivor and future general, of his weeks of waiting in the Negev. "We had already started thinking in terms of annihilation, both national and personal."

Gen. Yariv was now convinced that an Egyptian attack was only hours away. "There is reason to assume that Nasser no longer thinks that he has to wait," he informed Eshkol, "All evidence indicates that he will soon stage a provocation." He pointed to the continued advance of the 4th Division and the transfer of four brigades from Yemen to Sinai. Saudi troops were on the move, as were Iraqi forces, prepared to enter Syria. Intercepted communications between Arab embassies referred to a "sudden explosion" about to erupt. Hod, the IAF commander, envisaged a massive aerial assault against Israeli bases and cities, while the Mossad's Meir Amit reported on Egyptian designs on the Negev. Intelligence from the field held that the army's morale was plummeting. "We sit and we wait," Yoni Netanyahu, a platoon commander in the paratroopers, wrote to his girlfriend back home. "What are we waiting for?" His commanders fully agreed. Noting that each day without battle cost the country an estimated $20 million, while the Egyptians industriously dug in, the general staff determined that "every delay is a gamble with Israel's survival."[69]

Should Israel preempt the Egyptian attack and, if so, how? These were the questions on the table at the prime minister's office on the evening of May 25. Present were Yariv, Amit, Lior, and Weizman, along with the Foreign Ministry's Levavi and Dr. Ya'akov Herzog, the Director General of the Prime Minister's Office. But the most significant attendant was Yitzhak Rabin. After an absence of over thirty hours, the chief of staff had returned to active service. "He was not—how shall I say it?—in full form," another senior officer, Haim Bar-Lev, remembered. "Of course, he was briefed on all developments, but he lacked his usual strength." Indeed, Rabin's first act upon entering the room was to tender his resignation. Eshkol merely said, "Forget it," and waved him off. "Eshkol was a warm, wise man," Rabin wrote many years later. "Perhaps he had long known—and I had just then been forced to face—the frightening depths of a man's vulnerability."[70]

Vulnerability was, in fact, the topic—not Rabin's, but Israel's. Washington had been unwilling to make any commitment to Israeli security, either material or verbal, and was delaying the shipment of military goods already purchased by the IDF. Eshkol listened, already regretting his decision to accept the forty-eight hour delay. He heard proposals for recalling Eban before his meeting with Johnson, so that the Americans would not feel they had been "Pearl Harbored" by a sudden Israeli attack, and for sending an Israeli flagship through the Straits. He rejected them, afraid that they would broadcast Israel's intentions and so enable the Egyptians to strike first. The prime minister did, however, support calling up the rest of the reserves and positioning a phantom brigade opposite Kuntilla, to deter the Shazli Force. But still no decision could be reached on preemption.

"What would you have me tell the Cabinet?" a despairing Eshkol asked his chief of staff. If not yet recovered, Rabin replied brusquely: "We have reached the point of explosion. The only question is: why and until when should we wait? If the Americans agree to declare that any attack on us is tantamount to an attack on the United States, that could be a reason to wait. If not—no!"

Rabin's idea was quickly endorsed by most of the participants. Yariv proposed supplying the Americans with Israel's intelligence estimates, and Levavi suggested telling Johnson that Israel was about to be invaded by a combination of Arab armies. The goal of the letter would be threefold: to preclude American charges of bad faith if Israel launched a first strike; to create, if rejected, a moral basis for Israeli action; to prod the United States into intervening more vigorously in the crisis. To these motives Eshkol added the need to prevent Eban from agreeing to any measures that would tie Israel's hands. The sole reservation was raised by Dr. Herzog, son of the former chief rabbi of Ireland, considered a genius in foreign affairs. Voice cracking, he cautioned that "the President of the United States cannot issue the kind of declaration you want" because of congressional constraints. Yet, when requested, Herzog drafted the text of a message for Eban to present to American leaders. Rabin concluded the discussion: "I want it to be recorded for history that, before acting, we did everything we could to find a diplomatic solution."

The Israeli leadership had once more elected to wait, but that choice was again challenged at the next Ministerial Defense Committee meeting. The ministers heard briefings from Rabin and Yariv, who repeated the threats now facing Israel's security, if not its existence. The reaction, however, was different.

"Since we've already lost strategic surprise, what's so important about who strikes first?" asked Zorach Warhaftig, religious affairs minister, who, like his NRP colleagues, opposed any move toward war. Zalman Aran warned of the "cosmic power" of the Soviet Union, of the "wall of steel and fire" that could decimate Israel's cities. Haim Moshe Shapira added to this chorus by demanding Ben-Gurion's return as defense minister.

Eshkol had just begun replying to Shapira—"I won't form a government and go to war with a man who's called us liars and cheaters"—when word arrived of yet another overflight of Dimona. Soaring at 55,000 feet, four MiG-21s had passed over and photographed the reactor. Israeli pilots had scrambled and Hawk missiles were fired, but neither could intercept the MiGs.

"Egyptian fighters are flying over Dimona and here we're arguing over Ben-Gurion!" Eshkol shouted. He stormed out of the meeting to confer with Rabin and Weizman, asking them point-blank: "Am I to understand that you both want to attack today?"

"All the signs indicate that the Egyptians are ready to strike," Weizman said, "We have no option but to attack at once."

Rabin revealed that strange radio signals had been sent by the MiG's, perhaps to strategic bombers. The dangers were manifest, he said, but the diplomatic possibilities had yet to be exhausted. "We wait until after Eban's meeting with Johnson."[71]

Eban Abroad

To many outside observers, Israel's fate could not have been in better hands than those of its foreign minister. Cambridge-educated, polyglot, a prolix author and orator, Abba Eban was closely associated with the drama surrounding Israel's birth—at the UN, where he served as Israel's representative from 1947 to 1949, and in Washington, where he doubled as ambassador from 1950. Many *bons mots*, for example on the Arabs' post-1948 support for Partition ("Like the child who, after killing his parents, pleads for mercy as an orphan") or the demise of UNEF ("What is the use of a fire brigade which vanishes from the scene as soon as the first smoke and flames appear?"), were ascribed to him. In the United States, he was celebrated by public officials, widely quoted by the press, an icon for American Jewry. Returning to Israel in 1959, he ran for the Knesset, won, and almost immediately became a minister, first of education under Ben-Gurion and then deputy prime minister to Eshkol. Though only a year and a half into his term as foreign minister, his experience in international diplomacy was highly regarded, if not revered—again, outside of Israel.

For many within the country, though, he remained the ungainly Aubrey Solomon of Capetown, a foreigner hopelessly out of step with Israeli ways and mentality, long-winded and dull. "He doesn't live in reality," Eshkol once sniped; "he never gives the right solution, only the right speech." Privately, the prime minister referred to him, in Yiddish, as "der gelernter naar"—"the learned fool." But in addition to deriding him, Eban's detractors also distrusted him. Many believed that he had misled the government in 1956 by exaggerating the guarantees the U.S. and the UN were willing to give Israel in return for exiting Sharm al-Sheikh and Gaza. Now that the true frailty of those promises had been revealed, critics argued, and with the country's survival at stake, Eban was the last man to rely upon. Several Mapai ministers, among them Eshkol himself, preferred to send Golda Meir, the party's general secretary, to Washington—and would have, had not Meir taken ill.[72]

Eban chose a circuitous route to Washington, stopping first in Paris on the morning of May 24. Relations with the French had greatly compounded Israel's worries. Requests for reaffirmations of France's commitment to Israel's security, for intercession with the Soviets and a condemnation of Nasser's stance, had not even merited a response. While French munitions continued to reach the IDF—apparently without the government's knowledge—French diplomacy was pursuing a course directly inimical to Israel's.[73]

"Do not make war," de Gaulle instructed Eban after a perfunctory handshake. "Do not be the first to shoot." Taken aback by this curtness, as well as by the president's drawn and aged veneer, Eban rallied and stated that Nasser had in effect already fired the first shot by blockading the Straits, a blatant act of war. He further reminded his host that it was largely on the strength of French commitments to free passage that Israel had agreed to withdraw from Sharm al-Sheikh in 1957. "That was 1957," de Gaulle retorted. "This is 1967."

However tautological, the remark conveyed a clear message to Eban: France would no longer honor those commitments. At the height of his power, freed of colonial burdens, de Gaulle was at that juncture repositioning France as the mediator between East and West, communism and capitalism. He was also proud of the bridges he had built with the Arab world, and was not about to jeopardize them "merely because public opinion felt some superficial sympathy for Israel as a small country with an unhappy history." Rather, he would bring American, British, and Soviet leaders together to resolve the Straits issue "as in the Dardanelles." Eban recalled, "He spoke as if this were an institutional reality that I ought to know about."

Eban expressed doubt whether the Soviets would cooperate with the Four-Power proposal, or whether Israel would wait for an indefinite period of diplomacy. In carefully articulated French, he said, "If the choice lies between surrender and resistance, then we will resist. The decision has been taken . . . I do not believe that Israel will accept the new situation created by Nasser for any serious length of time."[74]

The conversation ended much as it began, with de Gaulle admonishing Eban, "Ne faites pas la guerre." Later, alone with his foreign minister, Maurice Couve de Murville, de Gaulle predicted that Israel would, after all, go to war. Later still, he told the press that "if Israel is attacked we shall not let her be destroyed, but if you [Israel] attack, we shall condemn your initiative." A spokesman for the president went a step further: Israel did not have to shoot first to be labeled the aggressor, but merely send a ship through Tiran.[75]

By comparison with Paris, Eban's reception in London was warm, almost fraternal. At 10 Downing Street, Eban sat at a table inhaling the smoke of Prime Minister Harold Wilson's "not very savory pipe" and gazing at Foreign Secretary George Brown—"incalculable, abrasive, monumentally tactless . . . an Arabist"—seated across from him. Eban was prepared for words more disheartening than those he had heard from de Gaulle, but quite the opposite happened.

Wilson was a long-time admirer of Israel, to which he would later dedicate a book, and where his son had volunteered on a kibbutz. Nasser's "coups," he believed, had radically altered the Middle East balance of power in the Soviets' favor, and not to respond to them would "be like 1938." He told Eban of his commitment to reopen the Straits through action "in or outside of the UN," and to that end, had sent Minister of State George Thompson for secret talks in Washington. Foreign Secretary Brown would travel to Moscow to sound out the Soviet view. Britain would do everything to fulfill its promises from 1957, Wilson said, and offered to expedite the delivery of tank ammunition and a surplus frigate—the HMS *Leviathan*—to Israel.

In fact, Wilson was wary of Britain "getting out in front" of any international convoy initiative and of possible clashes with Egypt. "We think it important that attention should be concentrated on free passage and not on the shore positions," he had told the Americans. The former Oxford economist had reason to fear the impact of an Arab oil embargo on his policy of fiscal reforms. Yet, curiously, Wilson offered Eban no advice—no warning, certainly—on whether Israel should or should not shoot first. The left-wing Laborite once quoted as saying, "Every dog is allowed one bite, but a different view is taken of a dog that goes on biting all the time," was silent on the question of war.[76]

The London talks should have lifted Eban's mood, but fatigued, aware of his responsibility for the 1957 guarantees ("Israelis were less likely to credit me with the decade of stability than to blame me for its termination"), he remained anxious about the meetings pending in Washington. "We have to be clear with the United States that Israel has decided not to make peace with the closure of the Straits," he cabled ahead to Harman, "We cannot be satisfied with an American declaration that leaves the Straits in Nasser's hands."

The task Eban set was more easily described than accomplished. Though Johnson had publicly denounced the blockade, he had yet to commit himself to combating it and, more disturbingly for Eban, to supporting Israel should it decide to. On the contrary, administration officials had shown an alarming willingness to abide by Nasser's provocations, first by embracing U Thant's idea for moving UNEF to Israel, then by denying that, until shots were fired, provocations had actually taken place. Under no circumstances, they said, was Israel to "go it alone."[77]

Yet only the threat of going it alone seemed effective in jarring the Americans out of apathy. Thus, Ambassador Barbour, when briefed by Israel's Foreign Ministry on the advanced state of Egypt's deployment in Sinai, asked, "Does this mean you people are going to jump the gun?" and received the stonewalling reply: "This is all we have been authorized to transmit." Israeli diplomats in America, meanwhile, lobbied both Houses of Congress, Democratic party activists, even the president's personal friends, in an effort to spur the administration to action. Harman rushed to Gettysburg, Pennsylvania, to urge Dwight Eisenhower to make public the pledges he and Dulles had made to Israel in 1957. The ailing ex-president agreed, adding that "I don't believe Israel will be left alone."

None of this seemed to sway the White House. Johnson, the Israelis were told, was all but hobbled by Vietnam and congressional constraints; he resented being pressured by Israel. "Any Israeli unilateral action could be justified only after all peaceful measures had been exhausted," Rostow reminded Evron, "Such justification would have to be demonstrated before the people of the United States and the world." Whatever steps Johnson might take in the Middle East would be subjected to both UN and constitutional scrutiny.[78]

This was the nebulous realm that Eban entered on Thursday morning, May 25, landing at New York's Kennedy Airport. Despite some initial flashes of brightness—eighty-seven Congressmen had called on Johnson to support Israel, reported Evron and Rafael, and progress had been made in Anglo-American planning for the maritime convoy—the news quickly turned glum. At his hotel, Ambassador Harman presented Eban with what he later termed "one of the severest shocks of my life."

Shocking was the message signed by Eshkol and warning of an imminent attack. "The Arabs are planning a large-scale offensive," the text began. "The question is no longer the Straits of Tiran but Israel's very existence." Mention was made of the six Egyptian divisions in Sinai, of missile boats entering the Gulf of Aqaba, and armored brigades transferred from Yemen. Syria and Iraq were poised for aggression as well. "The deterioration of the West's position is encouraging the Arabs and increasing their appetite by the hour. You must press Johnson to clarify which concrete measures—repeat concrete measures—he is willing to take to avert the impending explosion."

Eban was livid. Unconvinced that Nasser was either determined or even able to attack, he now saw Israelis inflating the Egyptian threat—and flaunting their weakness—in order to extract a pledge that the president, Congress-bound, could never make. "An act of momentous irresponsibility . . . eccentric . . . " were his words for the cable, which, he wrote, "lacked wisdom, veracity and tactical understanding. Nothing was right about it." Never a devotee of Rabin, resentful of amateur interference in the intricacies of U.S.-Israel relations, Eban would later attribute the initiative to the chief of staff's precarious state of mind. He nevertheless acknowledged his new instructions, and asked that his first meeting with the Americans be moved up two hours, to 3:30 P.M.[79]

The eye of the crisis now focused on those discussions, first at the State Department, then at the Pentagon, and finally at the White House. Forwarding his impressions of his conversation with Eban, Harold Wilson warned Johnson that Israel would almost certainly go to war unless its foreign minister received concrete commitments to its security. Wilson's assessment was fully confirmed by Wally Barbour in Tel Aviv: "Whether unilateral Israeli action is imminent in a matter of hours I suppose only history will reveal, but my impression is that it was and this has now been postponed for several days, although I am aware [that the] possibility of postponement is wishful thinking on my part."

Both Wilson and Barbour knew that Eban's report on his talks, scheduled to be presented to the Israel Cabinet that Sunday, would tip the scales for or against preemption. When asked by the ambassador, "What will happen if you receive sympathy rather than support for specific action?" Moshe Bitan, head of the Foreign Ministry's U.S. desk, replied: "Well, then, that's the end of the line for us."[80]

En Route to Regatta

Rarely in the annals of American foreign policy had an international crisis caught an entire administration so completely off-guard. The day Egyptian troops entered Sinai, the White House was considering sending Vice President Humphrey to Cairo to patch up the many rents in U.S.-Egyptian relations. Hope for the success of the mission derived from Nasser's continuing moderation on the Palestine issue. "Nowhere in the Arab world is there cooler calculation that now is not the time to take on Israel," wrote Harold Saunders, a National Security expert on the Middle East, on May 15. If any problems hung on the horizon, they emanated from Syria, specifically its support for Palestinian terror. The solution, suggested Saunders, was an "in-and-out [IDF] raid on Syria," telling the Israelis, "Do what you have to, but make sure it's quick and limited." The proposal was accepted by Walter Rostow, the national security adviser, who passed it on to the president: "We sympathize with Eshkol's need to stop these [Palestinian] raids and reluctantly admit that a limited attack [on Syria] may be his only answer." Apprised, finally, of the Egyptian buildup in Sinai, American officials at first dismissed it as symbolic; Nasser would never let the Syrians trick him into a war.[81]

Then came the demise of UNEF and U Thant's "weak-kneed"—Goldberg's word—response to Nasser. Suddenly, U.S. policy toward the Middle East was plucked out of insouciance and thrust into emergency mode. A Middle East Control Group was set up under the chairmanship of Eugene Rostow, composed of representatives from State, Defense, the NSA, and the CIA, along with such foreign affairs veterans as McGeorge Bundy and W. Averell Harriman. The goal, according to Walt Rostow's revised estimate, was to "(a) prevent Israel from being destroyed, (b) stop aggression, and (c) to keep U Thant out in front and stiffen his spine," all the while making no American commitments.

Suddenly, President Johnson was dispatching personal letters to Nasser and Atassi, urging them to exercise restraint, and to Kosygin, asking him to use his influence over the Arabs. "Your and our ties to nations of the area could bring us into difficulties which I am confident neither of us seeks," he cautioned the Soviet leader. Queries went out to Britain and France about the prospects of "breathing new life" into the Tripartite Declaration, and about assembling Western warships in the eastern Mediterranean. Questions were asked about the use of poison gas by Egypt.[82]

The most pressing issue, however, was Israel and how its leaders might react. The country over which the United States had the greatest influence in the crisis remained a source of deep uncertainty for Johnson officials. The danger was that Israel, unable to retaliate for Syrian support of terror without provoking a major attack from Egypt, would first strike preemptively in Sinai. The result would be a further blow to America's standing in the Arab world, if not worse: Soviet intervention and possibly global war. Asked to convey Israel's assurances against such an attack to Nasser, the State Department refused. If the Israelis *did* strike, officials argued, America would appear guilty of collusion.

The key to avoiding such catastrophes, according to Walt Rostow, lay in convincing Eshkol "not to put a match to this fuse." Better that Israel absorb the initial blow, denying the Soviets a moral basis for stepping in, and only then mount its offensive. Though the Israelis would incur greater casualties, they were almost certain to win, U.S. intelligence estimated. Washington's objective, then, became finding ways of delaying the Israeli response, of buying time through arms sales and economic aid. Yet even these palliatives were rendered ineffective on May 22, when Nasser closed the Straits.[83]

The announcement, first received from the Agence France Presse, again caught the administration unawares. Johnson was just then penning letters to Nasser and Eshkol on the need for further restraint. In a hastily convened meeting of the National Security Council, the president's advisers appeared to be in the dark as to the degree of Moscow's foreknowledge of Nasser's move or even the motivations behind it. "He [Nasser] either has more Soviet support than we know of or he's gone slightly insane," offered Lucius Battle. Pentagon officials expressed concern over the Sixth Fleet's ability to reopen the Straits militarily—it lacked landing forces and anti-submarine units—while Rusk reported on strong Senate opposition to any unilateral American moves. At the same time, White House and State Department archives were frantically searched for the text of the pledges Dulles had made to Golda Meir, as well as other U.S commitments to Israel; few were readily found. Virtually the only concrete action the government took was to order the evacuation of all nonvital personnel from its embassies in Tel Aviv, Cairo, and Damascus.[84]

As in France, 1957 in the United States was not 1967. With its forces mired in Vietnam, its campuses and urban ghettos ablaze, America could not risk another foreign war. The obvious answer was to preempt Israeli preemption by lifting the blockade and reestablishing the rights of passage. But how? The French were opposed to Tripartite action while the Americans resisted the Four-Power summit which, they feared, would only serve as a soapbox for Soviet propaganda. The Security Council was deadlocked. Yet, out of this void of possible solutions emerged the concept of an international convoy.

It was not a new concept; the Israelis had floated it during the Suez crisis as a means of reclaiming the Canal, only to have it shot down by Dulles. But then Britain's George Thompson, in Washington on May 24, revived the notion and the Americans responded enthusiastically.

Specifically, the plan called for a declaration of maritime nations asserting the right of free passage through the Straits. If Egypt rejected the declaration, an international convoy of freighters would sail for Eilat under the escort of Sixth Fleet destroyers bolstered by the British warships, the HMS *Hermes* and *Victorious*. This "probing force" would rebuff any Egyptian effort to block the convoy and, if necessary, call for reinforcements from a much larger "covering force" in the Mediterranean and Indian oceans. British and American bombers would neutralize airfields, bases, and other strategic targets in Egypt, and deter the Soviets from intervening. While the Israelis might participate in the convoy, any benefits they derived would be wholly "incidental," as the issue was free passage, not Israeli rights. The "marching orders" for the plan, according to Eugene Rostow, were to be worked out over a two week period, then personally approved by the president. Its code name was "Operation Red Sea Regatta," or simply, Regatta.[85]

The initial reactions to Regatta were encouraging. In Canada for a short visit on the 25th—the ostensible purpose was a tour of Expo 67—Johnson conferred with Prime Minister Pearson, the original architect of UNEF. "Mike is ready to join the party," Johnson reported to Wilson, adding that, "this track will keep the Israelis steady." Wilson's response was equally upbeat: "I believe that there are enough countries in the world with the sense to realize that world peace is more important even than trying to go on working through an impotent UN, and with the guts to stand up and be counted . . . Who knows, perhaps even France might agree?"

Support for the plan was even voiced, albeit clandestinely, by some Arabs. In a top-secret conversation with the CIA, Prince Muhammad, son of Saudi King Faisal, and 'Umar 'Azzam, son of a former Arab League secretary-general, described the convoy plan as the only means of saving the moderate Arab states. Though the leaders of those states would pay lip service to Nasser, they would welcome an international effort to belittle if not destroy him, Muhammad and 'Azzam said.

But then, less than forty-eight hours after its inception, the concept ran into difficulties. Initial contacts with the European allies showed no enthusiasm for an operation that was liable to jeopardize their Arab oil supplies, if not embroil them in a war. The Shah of Iran opposed spotlighting his own trade with Israel, and shipowners were reluctant to endanger their boats. Within Washington itself, in the State Department and the Pentagon, doubts were raised about the wisdom of "getting out in front" of Regatta, antagonizing the Arabs and assuming a logistics burden too heavy for wartime America. The signs also augured poorly for congressional approval of the plan—the absolute prerequisite for its execution.

None of this information would be passed on to the Israelis, though. On the contrary, in their discussions with Israeli representatives, White House officials consistently boasted of the progress in Regatta's preparations, of the numbers of countries willing to join it, and of the administration's commitment to see it through. The Israelis took these prognoses at face value—at least initially. "As long as the U.S. committed itself to definite action," Harman told Rostow, "the matter of *when* it acted is secondary."[86] But the cable that Eban received from Eshkol indicated that Regatta, irrespective of its timing and chances for success, was rapidly becoming irrelevant. Free passage, even if restored, could not guarantee Israel's survival.

Alone or Not Alone

Dean Rusk was no stranger to Middle East politics. As chief of the State Department's UN desk in 1947–48, he was personally involved in the *Sturm und Drang* surrounding the creation of Israel, which he strenuously opposed, preferring instead the establishment of a binational Jewish-Arab state. Thereafter, as president of the Rockefeller Foundation, he promoted several peace plans based on mutual recognition and the functional division of Jerusalem— all rejected by the Arabs. "Anyone who works for peace in the Middle East inevitably gets clobbered by both sides," he concluded. Yet that conclusion would not deter the man who had risen from rural poverty to a Rhodes Scholarship to distinguished service in China in World War II and who then became secretary of state under two presidents. At 58, reserved and vaguely elfin, Rusk had helped steer his country through monumental crises—Berlin, Cuba, Tonkin—some more successfully than others. In this latest flare-up in the Middle East, he was determined to counsel multilateralism, nonintervention, and, above all, prudence.

Nor was Rusk a stranger to Abba Eban. Though the latter would not number him "among the Americans whose powerful enthusiasms were aroused by Israel's statehood," Rusk shared a worldly sensibility with the foreign minister, a wavelength. Their previous meeting, at New York's Waldorf-Astoria hotel in October 1966, was a *tour d'horizon* of international affairs, spanning from the war in Vietnam to the situation in South Africa, from de Gaulle's megalomania ("We're not dealing with the Cross of Lorraine," said Rusk, "but with the spirit of Pétain in 1940") to the incompetence of U Thant (Rusk, facetiously: "There's no better man available"). Their repartee, the protocol shows, was droll:

Rusk: Do you have representation in Cambodia?
Eban: We are sending in a man next month.
Rusk: All I can say is that you should send in a good psychiatrist.
Eban: We're sending in a kibbutz member.
Rusk: How is your balance of payments?
Eban: We have reserves of some $600 million.
Rusk: Perhaps you could lend us some money.[87]

Humor, however, was not in evidence on Thursday, May 25, as Rusk and Eban again locked minds, this time at Foggy Bottom. The foreign minister defined his mission as "fateful," and Israel's mood, "apocalyptic." Since the beginning of the crisis, he said, "the reality has been consistently worse than the projections," and now "Israel could not take much more if it were a question of surrender or action." Either he returned with ironclad guarantees or Israel "would feel alone." Then, in a demeanor Rusk described as "relaxed," belying a sense of urgency, Eban quoted from the message from Jerusalem: "An all-out Egyptian-Syrian attack is imminent and could occur at any moment," he said, but then added that the request should not be taken too literally. Needed was an express American statement of "warning and deterrence" to Egypt.

The warning was not news for Rusk. Barbour had received a similar estimate earlier that morning from the Israel Foreign Ministry. "I am confident that Israeli apprehensions are to them genuine," Rusk's ambassador had reported, describing the information as "in large part the result of hard intelligence." Now, fixing drinks for himself and his guest, the secretary asked that Eban read the entire message aloud, slowly, and that Washington be given further time to verify its accuracy.

While Eban waited, American intelligence agencies "scrubbed down" the Israeli warning. The conclusion, confirmed both by British intelligence and by the UN, was that the Egyptian deployment remained defensive and that there was no sign of an imminent attack. Ambassador Nolte in Cairo speculated that Israel's warning was merely a smokescreen for its own impending offensive. Rusk was more reserved, telling CIA director Richard Helms, "If this is a mistake, then in the words of Fiorello LaGuardia, it's a beaut."

Nasser would have to be "irrational" to invade at this stage, Rusk explained when he next met with Eban. As for guarantees for Israel, the U.S. government could not issue "NATO-like language" along the lines of "an attack on you is an attack on us" without congressional approval. Forty-one Congressmen had come out against unilateral U.S. action in the Straits, Rusk revealed; many others were opposed to any military commitment in the Middle East while Americans were still fighting in Vietnam. Thus, Israel would be advised to trust in the UN and in Britain's proposal for a maritime convoy and declaration. The question of stationing UN troops on Israeli soil should also be reconsidered, the secretary intimated. Most vitally, Israel must not open hostilities. "I do not wish to assume that your information is meant to give us advance notice of a planned Israeli preemptive strike," Rusk admonished. "That would be a horrendous error."

The conversation continued at a desultory pace, with Eban expressing Israel's willingness to "harmonize" with any international initiative, and exhorting the White House to write Eshkol a letter with the words "we are going to open the Straits." Rusk concluded with concern for the "arm's length attitude" Israel had shown to the American embassy in Tel Aviv, and for a more open exchange of information. And that was it: no guarantees, no commitments, overt or confidential. Eban was unperturbed, though, sensing that Rusk had intuited the political dynamics behind Eshkol's warning, and knowing that the real discussion still lay ahead, with Johnson. Glibly he recalled that "I did not get the impression that the U.S. had ever decided to enter a new and complicated defense alliance between cocktails and the first course of a dinner party."[88]

The dinner party took place that evening, on the State Department's roof, hosted by Eugene Rostow. In contrast to his brother, the National Security adviser, who had assimilated fully into mainstream American life, the Undersecretary was fond of emphasizing his Jewish roots, spicing his private conversations with Yiddish. His warmth toward Israel was express. Yet, in opening the discussion, Rostow merely repeated what Rusk had said earlier: The president could not guarantee Israel's security without congressional approval, which, under the circumstances, he was highly unlikely to get. Instead, Israel should place its faith in a process beginning with a UN review of the Straits issue, followed by the maritime declaration and convoy.

Eban responded by summarizing Dulles's 1957 pledges to Israel and by stressing the need to conclude any UN discussions swiftly—four days at most. Otherwise, the blockade would become a reality and the Israeli people would lose faith in the maritime convoy idea. Apart from such emphases, there appeared to be no major gaps between the U.S. and Israeli positions.

Ben-Gurion (left) and Eshkol:
"Like a father banishing him
from Eden." (Fritz Cohen, Israel
Government Press Office)

Eshkol (left) and Johnson, 1964.
"Israel's friend in the true sense of
the word." (Israel State Archives)

Nasser and Arafat. (*al-ahram*)

Moshe Dayan: "Liar, braggart, schemer, prima donna—and object of deep admiration." (Fritz Cohen, Israel Government Press Office)

From left to right: Bar-Lev, Rabin, Weizman. (Israel Government Press Office)

(Facing page, top)
From left to right: Sharon, Begin, Yoffe. (Moshe Milner, Israel Government Press Office)

(Facing page, middle)
Exit UNEF. General Indar Jit Rikhye (first row, first on left). (Ilan Bruner, Israel Government Press Office)

(Facing page, bottom)
The Straits of Tiran: "How can my forces simply watch Israel's flag passing them?" asked 'Amer. (Israel Government Press Office)

"My generals tell me we will win," Nasser (right) informed U Thant. "What would you say to them?" (Associated Press)

"The Waiting": Israeli civilians digging trenches. (Ilan Bruner, Israel Government Press Office)

(Above) Eban (center) at the White House with Johnson (right): "Israel will not be alone unless it decides to." (LBJ Library Photo by Yoichi Okamoto)

(Right) Hussein ibn Talal ibn 'Abdallah, King of Jordan. (Suliman Marzug)

(Below) From left to right: Eshkol, Allon, Tal, and Gavish. (Israel Government Press Office)

Hussein soars over Eshkol
en route to Cairo.
(*Ma'ariv*, Israel)

Nasser crushes Eshkol in bed.
(*Ma'ariv*, Israel)

Eshkol picks petals "Yes" and "No." (*Ma'ariv*, Israel)

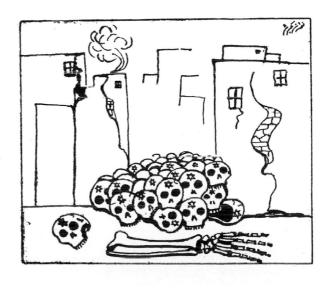

(*Top*) Israel pierced by
Egyptian, Syrian, Jordanian,
Lebanese tanks. (*al Hayat*,
Lebanon)

(*Middle*) Nasser, backed by
Arab states, kicks Israel into
the Gulf of Aqaba.
(*al-Jarida*, Lebanon)

(*Bottom*) Jewish skulls in
the ruins of Tel Aviv.
(*al Jundi al-'Arabi*, Syria)

Arab unity: Egyptian Prime Minister Sidqi Suliman (in sunglasses) greets a Syrian delegation of (from right to left) Security Chief Jundi, Chief of Staff Suweidani, Prime Minister Zu'ayyin, and Foreign Minister Makhous. (Courtesy of Prof. Itamar Rabinovitch)

Best of friends, bitter enemies: 'Amer (left) and Nasser. (*al-Ahram*, Egypt)

"I cannot forget the calm, matter-of-fact attitude in which the situation was analyzed while we sipped our wine," Moshe Raviv, Eban's assistant, recalled. The foreign minister, "not agitated . . . serious and moderate" described Washington's policy "as the best chance for peace if the [American] intelligence information about Egypt's intentions turned out to be not true." He then went further by asserting that of course he knew that the president lacked the powers to issue the guarantee Eshkol wanted, and that "the message would not have been phrased in that way if I had been in Tel Aviv." Told that the U.S. would in any case pass a "precautionary note" to its Cairo embassy, Eban, Rostow wrote, "seemed entirely satisfied with this step as a response to their [Israel's] request."[89]

In his effort to broadcast calm, to counterbalance the panic he detected in Eshkol's letter, Eban had inadvertently eased Washington's own sense of urgency. Rostow reported to British ambassador Patrick Dean that "we expected they would tell us they were going to strike but instead they merely requested clarification regarding the proposed maritime plan." Rusk, advising Johnson in preparation for his own meeting with Eban, proposed that the U.S. could either "unleash" Israel and let it fend for itself or "take a positive position, but without commitment," on the convoy idea. The secretary opted for the latter, which would enable the U.S. to delay an Israeli preemptive strike. The UN discussions could then run their course and the U.S. could then seek alternative measures, such as the stationing of UNEF in Israel. As for the demand for formal security guarantees for Israel, wrote Rusk, Eban was not expected to press them in his talk with the president.[90]

A more exact reflection of Israeli thinking might have been obtained from Harman, who was also present at the Rostow dinner and came away from it furious. In a heated cable to Jerusalem, the former Oxford-trained lawyer, and ambassador since 1959, charged the administration with giving Israel "unsaleable merchandise" and acting in bad faith:

> For the past 12 days the US has undertaken the responsibility of restraining us from the protection of our rights and our security . . . They [the Americans] held us back by giving us the impression that they were involved with us and would stand by us. They knew that we would ultimately have to fight to protect that vital interest, but as a result of their intervention and their assurances, we would now have to fight in very different military circumstances . . . In fact, what they had told Eban this evening contained nothing definite and precise, contained no specific and binding time-table and, above all, contained no definite commitment in that the US assumed a binding responsibility in regard to Aqaba.

The impact in Jerusalem was seismic. If Johnson was unwilling to commit to Israel on any level, then clearly Eban had not carried out his terms of reference. These were promptly restated and in language incontrovertible even to the foreign minister:

> Israel faces grave danger of general attack by Egypt and Syria. In this situation, implementation of the American commitment is vital—in declaration

and action—immediately, repeat, immediately, meaning a declaration by the U.S. government that any attack on Israel is equivalent to an attack on the United States. The concrete expression of this declaration will be specific orders to U.S. forces in the region that they are to combine operations with the IDF against any possible Arab attack on Israel. Whatever reply you get from the United States, limit yourself to stating that you will report to your government. In view of the gravity of the situation, this notification is to be delivered without delay to the highest American authority. In the absence of the president, deliver to Secretary of State Rusk . . . We stress the top secrecy of all dealings arising from this cable. Under no circumstances are you to phone us on this matter.[91]

The keen displeasure and lack of trust manifest in these orders could not have been lost on Eban. He irascibly cabled Jerusalem demanding details of the alleged Egyptian preparations. But flustered as he was by his own government, he was also losing patience with the Americans. When Rusk next called and asked to postpone his meeting with the president—he wanted time to read the just-issued report on U Thant's talks with Nasser—Eban bristled. Warning of the "catastrophic psychological effects" of delaying his return, he told Rusk that on Sunday the Israeli Cabinet would hold "perhaps the most crucial . . . meeting in our history," and he could not miss it. "I tell you frankly that I think we are in for hostilities next week. This is an act of blockade which must be resisted. I doubt if anything at this stage can change that outlook. The only thing that might have an effect would be an affirmation by your president that he has decided unreservedly to get the Straits open." Rusk, "audibly flurried," merely replied, "I get it," and hung up.

Yet, at his next round of talks, with Defense Secretary Robert McNamara and Gen. Earle G. Wheeler, chairman of the Joint Chiefs of Staff, Eban again played down his government's instructions. "I felt that I had done my duty in having this 'idea' passed to the president and that I need not waste time in hypochondriac frivolities anymore." Instead of stressing the dangers Israel faced, he listened as Wheeler and McNamara explained how the IDF would win a war in two weeks even if attacked on three fronts simultaneously—one week if Israel shot first. In training, motivation, and communications, Israel was vastly superior to its foes, and therefore had nothing to fear. If Israeli intelligence had information on Egyptian attack plans, it had better reveal its sources, the Americans said, otherwise it had no basis for preemptive action.[92]

The Americans were perplexed, and understandably so. While the Israeli government forecast war, U.S., British, and UN sources agreed that there was no change in Egypt's disposition, and even Eban seemed to disavow the claim. Yet the White House was unwilling to take chances.

In one of his last acts in office, Mustafa Kamel appeared before Walt Rostow. The atmosphere was cordial but tense. The national security advisor was irked by the latest Egyptian propaganda, especially charges alleging the existence of a secret CIA-Mossad plot to overthrow the Ba'th in Damascus and install UNEF on Syrian territory. "Your adversaries believe that a surprise attack by Egypt and Syria is imminent," Rostow informed Egypt's ambassador. "We know this is unthinkable. We cannot believe the government of the UAR would be so reckless. Such a course would obviously have the most serious possible consequences." Rostow, concluding, sought to temper his warning by describing it as "friendly," and by noting that Israel had been similarly admonished. Kamel's only response was to deny the truth of the rumor—perhaps the evacuation of American nationals from the area had triggered it, he suggested—and to cite Egyptian reports of Israeli war plans. "Nasser will cooperate to the fullest with the United Nations," he pledged.[93]

As a further precaution that night, the White House cabled the essence of Israel's warning to Moscow. Johnson was frank in informing Soviet leaders that he could not verify the warning, yet he expected the Kremlin to check it out with the Egyptians and to discourage any warlike acts. Egypt and the USSR had thus been put on notice—America would not countenance war. But what of the Israelis? The portentous messages from Jerusalem seemed incompatible with that proffered by Eban: a readiness to strike and an openness to diplomacy. The task of deciphering which of these was more accurate, and deciding the crucial course the United States would take, now fell to one man, the last of Eban's interlocutors.

He has been described so disparately as to appear almost two different men. To those, like Richard Helms, who worked closest with him, he was "a fine man to work for, a man of his word . . . a man of great understanding of human problems." Walt Rostow recalled that "he was always for the underdog," and his brother, Eugene, that "he was a wonderful person of tremendous heart." His warmth and compassion found expression in his advocacy of civil rights, in his War Against Poverty, and his vision of the Great Society. But other observers saw different sides to him: unscrupulous, power-hungry, manipulative. These flaws, together with his tragic entanglement in Vietnam, led more than one biographer to denounce him as a narcissist with dubious scruples, a tyrant driven by "a hunger so fierce and consuming that no consideration of morality and ethics, no cost to himself – or to anyone else – could stand before it."[94]

Duality also characterized Lyndon Johnson's attitude toward Jews and the State of Israel. He had intimate ties with Jewish activists in the Democratic party, in particular its chairman, Hollywood mogul Arthur Krim and his wife, Matilde, a former Israeli, and with Abe Feinberg, his informal liaison with the Jewish community. Unusual for a man hailing from Texas's rural Hill Country, Johnson chose Jews—the Rostow brothers, speechwriter Ben Wattenberg, and domestic affairs aide Larry Levinson—as his top advisers, appointed Supreme Court Justice Arthur Goldberg as ambassador to the UN, and was exceptionally close with another Jewish Justice, Abe Fortas. White House Counsel Harry C. McPherson, Jr., was openly disposed toward Israel, as was presidential aide John P. Roche, who once admitted, "I look at the Israelis as Texans, and Nasser as Santa Ana." Critical of the Eisenhower administration's handling of the Suez crisis, a proponent for massive foreign aid to Israel, Johnson's ability to attract the Jewish vote was purportedly one of the reasons for his selection as Kennedy's running mate in 1960.

Then came Vietnam and the disproportionate role Jews played in the antiwar movement. One 1967 poll showed that nearly half of American Jewry opposed Johnson's Vietnam policy; a popular button read, "You don't have to be Jewish to be against the war." When Feinberg assured him that America's defense of Saigon was proof that it would also protect Israel, Johnson exclaimed, "Then why the hell don't the Jews of America believe that!" American Jews were, to his mind, ungrateful for his advocacy of Israel and hypocritical for not supporting a war against an enemy—the Vietcong—not unlike the Palestinian guerrillas. His anger turned on Israel as well, for its refusal to come out publicly in favor of the war and to press its American friends to back his Asian policies. Such grudges only hardened his resentment of Israel's retaliation policy and its resistance to American inspections of Dimona. "Israel gets more than it's willing to give," he once complained to Feinberg, "It's a one-way street."[95]

Nevertheless, Johnson remained staunchly pro-Israel, "a friend," as he once told Eban, "in the true sense of the word." Though closely allied with oil companies, he never sought to ingratiate himself with the Arabs. Routinely, he overruled the objections of both the State Department and the Pentagon in personally approving aid packages for Israel.[96]

That ambivalence—both resentment of and admiration for Israel—was present in the Oval Office on Friday, May 26. "I will see Eban, as I feel I must," Johnson had written Harold Wilson. He had before him the file of presidential pledges for Israel's security that the State Department—with Evron's help—had finally managed to assemble. There was an affidavit from Eisenhower, secured by Walt Rostow, who also traveled to Gettysburg, regarding the 1957 commitments. These obligations weighed heavily on him, as did the intelligence estimates of a swift Israeli victory; he had seen similar estimates of America's ability in Vietnam. He was determined not to let Israel be destroyed. But then LBJ was also angry, "fed up with being pushed around" by American Jews who had bombarded the White House with telegrams and delegations demanding his intervention on Israel's behalf. What kind of impression would be created if he received the foreign minister and Israel went to war the next day?[97]

"What should I tell Eban?" the president asked a 1:30 P.M. gathering of his most senior officials. "Around sundown I'm going to have to bell this cat. I need to know what I'm going to say." Lucius Battle summarized America's position *vis-à-vis* the Arabs: "Whatever we do we're in trouble. If we fail to stand by Israel, the radical Arabs will paint us as a paper tiger. If we stand by Israel, we will damage ourselves seriously with all the Arabs." Joe Sisco of the State Department said that the Israelis feared the UN would come up with some "gimmick" to legitimize the status quo. "Israel's existence is at stake," added Vice President Humphrey, citing the Egyptian overflights of Dimona. Gen. Wheeler outlined the Regatta plan, but McNamara was against promising Eban anything concrete. Judge Fortas stated, "the United States cannot let Israel stand alone," but Rusk disagreed: "If Israel fires first, it'll have to forget the U.S." The meeting thus ended inconclusively. Instead of answers, Johnson's advisers had left him with little but questions: "If you were in Eban's place and we told you we were relying on the UN and a group of maritime powers, would that be enough to satisfy you? Will I regret on Monday not giving Eban more today?"[98]

There seemed no solution for Johnson other than to play for time. Using the long Memorial Day weekend as an excuse, he hoped to put off Eban for a day or more, trusting that the Israeli government would not make a decision in his absence. This would give the White House time to review its options while the intense press coverage surrounding Eban's visit—Israeli-engineered, Johnson suspected—waned. He had all but decided to put Eban off, indefinitely perhaps, when Eppy Evron interceded.

"I've heard good things about you from my friends Harry McPherson and Abe Feinberg," Johnson had told Evron when Matilde Krim first introduced him, one year before. Since then a unique friendship had blossomed between the president and Israel's minister plenipotentiary, so close that letters from Evron would be hand-delivered to Johnson the same day. Whether or not Johnson's amity was, as Harman suspected, a ploy to curry American Jewish favor, everyone acquainted with Evron agreed that the former union and government bureaucrat had an unusual capacity for networking. "He could get senior officials to meet him at 2:00 A.M.," recalled a former colleague, Mordechai Gazit.[99]

It was 5:30 in the evening when Evron, upset by Johnson's refusal to set a time for his talk with Eban, rushed to the White House. He demanded to see Walt Rostow and bluntly told him that failure to hold the meeting, with the press corps already gathered outside, would broadcast a serious rift in U.S.-Israel relations. Obvious conclusions would be reached by both the Arabs and the Soviets. Rostow had begun explaining how the president needed time to study the issues, how he resented Israel's pressure tactics, when a message arrived from the Oval Office. Evron was to enter.

Johnson, looking agitated, greeted him: "I understand the seriousness of Israel's situation, but I can't promise to do more than Rusk and Rostow already told you." He would pursue the convoy plan, he said, claiming that Canada, Italy, and Argentina had already expressed support for the idea, but only once certain conditions had been fulfilled. Though the UN was "a zero," and the U.S. owed nothing to U Thant, the administration had to exhaust all efforts by the international organization to find a peaceful solution. Once the UN failed— and it would, Johnson was certain—he would seek congressional approval for concerted action in the Gulf. "Without it, I'm just a six-foot-four Texan friend of Israel," he claimed, recalling how Congress had never forgiven Truman for Korea. He assured Evron that the U.S would keep its promises on free passage, but that it could not risk war with the Soviets simply because Israel had set Sunday as its ultimatum. And if Israel went to war it would do so on its own and at great risk. "Israel is not a satellite of the United States nor is the United States a satellite of Israel." Johnson spoke for over an hour while Evron was mute, but at the end the president agreed to meet Eban after all. His one condition: There would be no more leaks to the press.[100]

An interlude of confusion followed, during which Evron went off to find Eban, and the foreign minister together with Harman, entered the White House by a side entrance. "Some guy out here by the name of Eban says he's supposed to see the president," one of the guards reported, and the press was on hand to report it as well, concluding that Johnson had let the Israelis "cool their heels" before admitting them.

The Yellow Oval Office looked for all purposes like a war room. There, in addition to LBJ, sat McNamara and Wheeler, the Rostows and Sisco, along with presidential press secretary George Christian. Yet the floor was first given to Eban, and he seized it theatrically: "We are on a footing of grave and anxious expectancy." He summarized the history of U.S. commitments to Israel's security, and quoted from the latest telegrams from Jerusalem, casting doubt not only on the state's welfare but on its very existence. The United States had to issue a statement saying that it was coordinating its military strategy with Israel and would retaliate for any Arab attack. "The question to which I have to bring the answer is, do you have the will and determination to open the Straits?" Eban asked, "Do we fight alone or are you with us?"

Johnson hesitated a moment before answering, leaning close to Eban, who believed he detected "a tormented look in his eye." Then, emphatically, the president spoke: "You are the victims of aggression." In "robust terms," he described precisely what he thought of U Thant and his decision to withdraw UNEF from Sinai, but also his need to first exhaust all UN venues. "I am not a king in this country and I am no good to you or to your prime minister if all I can lead is myself . . . I know that your blood and lives are at stake. Our blood and lives are at stake in many places and may be in others . . . I do not have one vote and one dollar for taking action before thrashing this matter out in the UN."

Only then, Johnson averred, could the convoy be launched, roughly within two weeks. "I'm not a feeble mouse or a coward and we're going to try. What we need is a group [of maritime states], five or four or less or if we can't do that then on our own. What you can tell your Cabinet is that the president, the Congress and the country will support a plan to use any or all measures to open the straits." Preliminary talks with certain senators had revealed guarded support for the plan, the president said, but Israel could contribute as well, exploiting its connections abroad. "You in Israel have the best intelligence and the best embassies so put them to work to line up all those who are concerned about keeping this waterway open."

Johnson at last moved to the thorniest issue of all: the danger of an Israeli first strike. Citing the conclusions reached by all of America's intelligence branches—"there is no Egyptian intention to . . . attack, and if there were, Israel would win"—Johnson warned of the dangers Israel faced through unilateral moves:

> If your Cabinet decides to do that they will have to do it on their own. I am not retreating, not backtracking, and I am not forgetting anything I have said . . . I think it is a necessity that Israel should never make itself seem responsible in the eyes of America and the world for making war. *Israel will not be alone unless it decides to go it alone* (Emphasis in the original).

He repeated the last line three times, and then presented Eban with a handwritten note from Rusk—"I must emphasize the necessity for Israel not to make itself responsible for the initiation of hostilities . . . We cannot imagine that Israel will take that decision"—further emphasizing his position. "Our Cabinet knows your *policy*," said Johnson, "What they want to know is your *disposition to take action*."

Eban did not supply an answer. He merely cautioned against getting bogged down in a prolonged UN debate, and proposed the creation of a U.S.-Israel military liaison to prepare for possible hostilities. On cue from the president, McNamara agreed to look into the matter provided it remained top-secret.[101]

On that equivocal note, the meeting on which much of the world's attention was riveted, that represented the high-water mark in efforts to avert a third Arab-Israeli war, ended. Before exiting, Eban asked one more time: "I would not be wrong if I told the prime minister that your disposition is to make every possible effort to assure that the Straits and the Gulf will remain open to free and innocent passage?" Johnson responded yes, sealing it with a shake of his hand so strong that Eban doubted "that I would ever regain the use of it." The president then followed his guest down the hall to remind him, yet again, that "Israel will not be alone unless it decides to go it alone."

Versions differ as to Johnson's perception of the talk. The president's diary has him exclaiming, "They came loaded for bear, but so was I! . . . McNamara said he just wanted to throw his cap in the air, and George Christian said it was the best meeting of the kind he had ever sat in on." But another source has Johnson slumping into his chair and sighing, "I failed. They're going to go." Yet another, John P. Roche, recalled Johnson chatting with Walt Rostow, drinking a Diet Dr. Pepper and imitating Eban, "a miniature Winston Churchill." He then asked Rostow what he thought the Israelis would do, to which the national security advisor allegedly replied, "they're going to hit." LBJ agreed. "Yes, they're going to hit. And there's nothing we can do about it."[102]

Eban came away from the encounter stunned by Johnson's "rhetoric of impotence," by the image of a "paralyzed president" speaking in "defeatist terms." While he felt that the Americans had gone beyond their 1957 commitment to free passage, the absence of a joint communiqué seriously undermined that pledge. Eban's impressions were reinforced in New York the next day,

when Goldberg warned him about relying too heavily on the "rather impetu-
ous" remarks of the Rostows and other advisers. The ambassador, convinced
that no other country would join the Regatta plan, was blunt in his advice:
"You owe it to your government, because lives are going to be lost and your
security is involved, to tell your Cabinet that the president's statement means a
joint resolution of Congress, and the president can't get such a resolution because of the Vietnam War."

Yet Eban remained undiscouraged. Riding to the airport with Gideon
Rafael, he mused that since the United States was willing to "take any or all
measures in its power to open the Straits," it could hardly fault Israel for "taking all measures in *its* power." The pledge would prove priceless when the time
finally came—and it would, Eban believed, soon—for Israel to act alone.[103]

Enter Kosygin

At approximately the same time that Eban deplaned at Kennedy, the Egyptian
defense minister arrived for his talks at the Kremlin. The issue was remarkably
similar and no less crucial: What position would the superpower take in the
event of war? Like Eban, Shams Badran sought a definitive answer to this question, yet the Soviet responses—much as the Americans' to Israel—would prove
elusive.

"Since Moscow appears to define the threshold of danger in the Middle East
as a higher level than we, Soviet policy has always smacked of brinkmanship,"
submitted one Kremlin-watcher at the State Department. But what appeared to
outside observers as daring was more than likely an attempt to cover up divisions
within Soviet leadership over how to handle the Middle East.

Those schisms were evident in the conflicting signals emanating from Moscow. While the official press continued to expose Israeli plots to conquer Syria—
in tandem with America's bombing of Hanoi—Soviet diplomats stressed their
commitment to averting violence. Thus, the Soviet chargé d'affaires in Washington, Tcharniakov, assured Walt Rostow that the USSR had no desire for a
confrontation in the Middle East and was urging restraint on the Arabs. "We can
stop Egypt from shooting," Mikhail Frolov, the Soviet commercial attaché in
Tel Aviv offered his American counterpart; "Can you stop the Israelis from running a ship [through the Straits of Tiran]?" Ambassador Anatoly Dobrynin, on
home leave from Washington, told America's ambassador in Moscow, Llewellyn
Thompson, that "I think we can match you in doing the utmost to avoid war."
The USSR was "the last country on earth to want war in the Middle East," swore
Nikolai Trofimovich Federenko, the Soviets' UN ambassador, to Goldberg.[104]

In practice, though, the USSR had not urged caution on either Egypt or
Syria, while articles in *Pravda* and other paragons of the state-controlled press
appeared to goad them on. "Unless it is accompanied by private warnings and

counsels of restraint," Thompson wrote, "[these] statements can easily be read by Arab leaders as justification if not support for the course they are following." He concluded by noting that the Soviets were content to let America tackle the crisis alone and so assume the Arabs' wrath, secure in knowing that, irrespective of the outcome, they would emerge victorious. "Even if the Israelis should clobber their Arab neighbors, the Soviets might calculate that the hatred this would engender for the West would enable them to reestablish their position in the Arab world."[105]

The crisis indeed seemed to be playing deftly into the Kremlin's hands until May 22 and Nasser's announcement of the blockade. The Soviets had received no forewarning of the move, and distinctly avoided praising it. Impugning the right of another nation to free passage was problematic for the Russians who, for centuries, had struggled to obtain that same right in the Dardanelles, and who were signatory to the 1958 Geneva Convention on international straits. But while the closure sparked no joy in Moscow—"it was not permissible to start a war simply because a few ships were unable to sail from Aqaba to the Red Sea," one Soviet scholar observed—neither could Nasser be condemned. The only answer was to support the Arabs in a general sense, without getting down to particulars. Thus, Chuvakhin, in his conversations with Israeli leaders, distinguished between the "principle" of free passage and Egypt's unassailable sovereignty in Tiran. Thus, *Pravda* warned, "Should anyone try to unleash aggression in the Near East, he would be met not only with the united strength of the Arab countries but also with strong opposition from the Soviet Union and all peace-loving peoples."

The very vagueness of the threat left it open to interpretation. Did it mean, as many Arabs understood, that the USSR would come to Egypt's aid if attacked? Or was it rather, as the Americans thought, that the Soviets were reluctant to commit to any specific course of action and had distanced themselves from Nasser?[106]

These were the questions that Badran and his ten-man entourage sought to answer. Their principal host was Kosygin, the sixty-three-year-old premier, a former Leningrad technocrat promoted after Khrushchev's ouster to a position second only to Brezhnev's. Regarded by colleagues as a highly intelligent, if colorless leader, Kosygin had always counseled prudence, never quite convinced of the Arabs' real value as allies. Nor was he certain that the Americans would watch passively if Israel were attacked. With their conventional forces tied up in Vietnam, the U.S. might react to a threat in the Middle East with their only remaining means—nuclear.

Brushing aside Badran's claim that the Egyptian army was ready and able to defeat Israel, the premier warned of British and American intervention in the Straits and advised his guest to compromise. "We are going to back you, but you have made your point and won a political victory," he opened. "It is better to sit at the negotiating table than to wage a battle by the sword." He agreed to fill Egypt's standing weapons orders, but only after three months, and would only "consider" additional requests. Arms for the PLO were out of the question. "We don't want any part of the PLO or its army. You are free to give them what you want, but think carefully about what you're doing lest they lead you into a war," Kosygin said.[107]

Kosygin's line—essentially, "quit while you're ahead"—was echoed by the Foreign Ministry, by Alexei Schiborin, head of the Middle East department, and by Deputy Foreign Minister Semyonov. At an all-night discussion held at Semyonov's dacha, the Egyptians were told that "the Soviet Union was neither ready nor willing to enter into any confrontations. [They] had had enough suffering during World War II and . . . it was time for Egypt to de-escalate."

But a sharp distinction emerged between the stand espoused by Kosygin and the diplomats and that proffered by the generals, protégés of Brezhnev. Defense Minister Grechko, a veteran of World War II battles in the Caucasus, viewed the Middle East as a supreme strategic interest. He professed admiration for Egypt's military preparedness, which, he claimed, had all but paralyzed the West. Though he stopped short of advising Egypt to start a war, he expressed total confidence in its ability to win one, even if attacked. Grechko described the *Pravda* statement as but the first of many that would establish Moscow's fidelity to Nasser and his cause. "There should be no doubt about the Soviet Union's commitment to give political and material aid to the Arabs . . . even to support them spiritually."

Grechko's remarks left a striking impression on Badran who, though a brigadier, had never commanded a squad. At the relatively young age of thirty-eight, unimposingly round-faced, lanky, and bespectacled, Badran had achieved immense power solely from his service to 'Amer, assuring his control over the army. Badran was determined to extract from the Soviets precisely what the field marshal wanted to hear, a paraphrase of the same pledge Eban had sought from the U.S.—namely, that war with Egypt was tantamount to war with the USSR. Grechko's remarks seemed to approximate that equation, and Badran was inclined to ingest them while ignoring Kosygin's. "From a military point of view the trip was a failure," Badran remembered a decade later. "But politically, I achieved the propaganda effect sought." Wary of precisely such a success, Undersecretary of State al-Feki and Ambassador Ghaleb mailed a copy of the discussions' protocol directly to Nasser. It would arrive on June 13, too late to have any impact.[108]

Badran was still in Moscow when, in the first hours of May 27, a cable arrived from Washington and in it, the Israelis' warning of an imminent Arab attack. For Kosygin, the message confirmed what Badran had intimated, that Egypt was preparing a first strike. More shocking was the realization that the Israelis had learned of Egypt's plans and were no doubt intending to preempt them. The premier fired off telegrams to Johnson and Wilson warning that "Israel is actively engaged in military preparations and evidently intends to carry out armed aggression against neighboring Arab states." Such an attack, he alleged, could not be launched without Anglo-American backing ("There can be no two opinions on this"), and he threatened to intervene to stop it. "If Israel commits aggression and military action begins then we would render assistance to the countries which would be the victims of aggression." Most astringent were the words Kosygin reserved for Eshkol: "It is easy to light a fire, but to put out a conflagration may not be at all as easy as those who are pushing Israel beyond the brink of war may be thinking."[109]

But Kosygin did not rest with written representations. Instructions were also sent to his ambassadors in Cairo and Tel Aviv to contact their host leaders at once, wake them if necessary, and warn them of the danger of war.

Thus, at 2:15 on Saturday morning, Chuvakhin rushed to Tel Aviv's Dan Hotel where Eshkol was spending the night, and there convinced the guards to disturb him. He read Kosygin's letter out loud and demanded to know whether Israel intended to fire the first shot. Eshkol, in his pajamas, replied only that, "The Egyptians, sir, have already fired the first shot in this war." He poured the ambassador some warm orange juice left over from a previous meeting into a bathroom glass. Then he chaffed: "Although we're not a developed country with historic rights like Syria, mightn't a senior emissary come to hear our point of view? Mightn't I be invited to Moscow?" The ambassador kept asking questions about Israel's plans while Eshkol kept avoiding them. "It's acceptable in the world when ambassadors present their credentials to the president they commit themselves to keeping the peace—and how have you kept that promise?" he assailed Chuvakhin. "Now we have not just the first shot, but shells and mines all over the place." The ambassador suggested that an equitable solution might still be worked out, at which point Eshkol exploded: "Please! Please! Give us a straw to clutch at. One way, one suggestion, tell me. Just as long as there's peace and quiet!"[110]

A flustered Chuvakhin left the Dan at 4:00 A.M., convinced that his mission had gained nothing. The same could not be said by Dmitri Pojidaev in Cairo, however, when, that same night, he knocked on Nasser's door.

Sunset on Dawn

"One hour ago, President Johnson informed me that Egyptian forces are preparing an attack on Israeli positions and that this attack is about to be launched. If such a thing happens, then the United States will consider itself freed from the commitments it gave to the USSR to exercise restraint." Pojidaev read Kosygin's text to Nasser, adding only that a tougher warning had already been sent to Eshkol. Nasser's reaction was composed: "It's essential that everybody know that Egypt does not want war and is not heading in that direction, but will defend itself if attacked."

But what Nasser knew, and the Soviet ambassador did not, was that Operation Dawn was already set to be launched in only a few hours' time, at sunrise. Final orders had been issued to the elements involved—air squadrons, ground and naval forces—which were ostensibly prepared to begin the offensive against Israel. 'Amer had been bragging about the overflight of Dimona, of how, with only handheld cameras, the MiG's had sent all of Israel into a panic. Surely the Zionists would flee at the first shot.

Whether or not Nasser participated in this exultation is not known, only that his mood soured precipitously with the receipt of Kosygin's message. For him, the crux of the cable was not that the Soviets might fail to aid Egypt, nor even that the Americans might intervene. Rather, it was the proof that Israel had accessed Egyptian secrets and compromised them.[111]

Nasser hurried to Supreme Headquarters to an emergency meeting with 'Amer. The president informed him of the exposure of Dawn and of the need to cancel the operation immediately. 'Amer resisted, protesting, "By waiting, Egypt loses even before the war starts." But Nasser, rather than simply giving him an order, attempted to explain why he had changed his mind about launching the first strike, why it was better for Egypt to hold back. "What action can we take now that wouldn't give Johnson and Israel another opportunity that they're looking for?" he asked. Though the world regarded the massing of Israeli troops as routine, the Egyptians were seen as aggressors, especially after their decisions on UNEF and Tiran. "Many countries would find justice in Johnson's giving the order to the Sixth Fleet to start operations against us [if Egypt attacked first]." Though he still thought war very probable, he believed that a diplomatic solution might still be found, perhaps through the offices of U Thant.

Nasser's *volte face* on Dawn undoubtedly stemmed from security concerns, from the fear of American intervention at a time when the Soviet position was yet unknown, and from his sensitivity to world opinion. But behind these considerations lay the byzantine relationship between the president and his field marshal—a relationship in which Nasser could not impose his decision on 'Amer, and in which 'Amer could delay his response to Nasser's request, saying only that he would "think about it."

He did, retreating to his private headquarters at home, where he dispatched a cable to Badran in Moscow—"Shams, it seems there is a leak"—and then to Sidqi Mahmud. "When can you implement the Eilat plan?" 'Amer asked.

The forty-three-year-old air force commander had eagerly awaited the attack signal. Israel, he believed, would never permit the blockade of its southern port, and would certainly strike first—unless Egypt did. Now, he ebulliently replied, "One hour at the most and we'll be ready."

Orders immediately went out and pilots took to their planes, awaiting the final go-ahead. But then, forty-five minutes later, Sidqi Mahmud received another call: "Cancel the plan."

The commander was despondent. "Why? Don't we trust that Allah will aid us?"

"That's not the point," 'Amer interrupted, and then spoke of the pressure from Russia. It brought little consolation to Sidqi Mahmud. "When I spoke to the pilots I thought they'd jump with happiness," he complained. "They want to do something."

The Egyptian offensive was all but dead, struck down by a chance intervention just short of H-hour. The coup de grâce came later that morning with the capture of five Egyptian officers, all believed to be privy to the plan, who stumbled over the Israeli border. Soon reports from Sinai claimed that a force of 500 Israeli vehicles was observed passing through Eilat, heading west. Their objective seemed to be the desert opposite the Egyptian stronghold of Kuntilla—precisely where the IDF had broken through in 1956. 'Amer quickly ordered massive reinforcements to meet the Israeli threat. As evening fell, Gen. Shazli's tanks pulled out of Rafah for the grueling journey to Kuntilla, burying in their dust the vestiges of Operation Dawn.[112]

Reprieve

Shazli pulled out and Abba Eban landed, also at night, and was whisked from the airport to an emergency meeting of the Cabinet. The mood there was petulant, almost explosive. Many ministers were incredulous of the optimistic reports Eban had filed on his talks in London, Paris, and Washington. The headline in the semi-official *Davar* daily read: "U.S. Did Not Propose Effective Action to Open the Straits." Notably, no protocol had been sent of the fateful White House discussion. Eban insisted on conveying its contents in person.

Thus kept in the dark, Israeli officials plied Wally Barbour for any information he may have received from the State Department. The American ambassador, alarmed by their desperation, urged Washington to approve Israel's request for a military liaison, if for no other reason than to dispel the pressure for war. "Eban may be able to provide a voice of reason on his arrival, but I am convinced that the Israel Government's situation is so closely balanced that this additional exercise is worth the effort." But no liaison arrived, only Eban, who now faced eighteen ministers in what Col. Lior called "the longest night."

The meeting took place against the darkening backdrop of threats from the National Religious party to quit the government were it to vote for war and the army's warnings of disaster if it failed to. In the street outside Eshkol's Tel Aviv office, the mothers and wives of mobilized soldiers demonstrated in favor of appointing Dayan as defense minister. Nasser's speech to the trade unionists had been widely reported in Israel, as was Heikal's editorial welcoming war. That very day, Cairo Radio blared, "We challenge you, Eshkol, to try all your weapons. Put them to the test; they will spell Israel's death and annihilation." Tanks and troops of Iraq's 1st and 8th Mechanized Brigades were heading for Damascus, while the armies of Jordan, Lebanon, and even distant Kuwait, all went on combat footing.[113]

The Cabinet discussion began with briefings by Yariv and Weizman on the state of the Arabs' war preparations and the dangers of imminent attack. Rabin revealed his concern for the army's deteriorating morale and for the possibility that the U.S. would soon start placating Nasser. "The noose is closing around our necks," he was saying just as Eban, jet-lagged and unshaven, walked in.

Eban first addressed the cables that had been sent to him in Washington, denouncing them as a "cheap trick" designed to justify an Israeli attack and, in the process, implicating Johnson. He did not dwell on his resentment, though, but turned quickly to the American plan. He described its stages—UN "proceedings," maritime declaration, then the convoy—and the benefits Israel stood to reap through involvement in an international initiative. Johnson was "firm as a rock" on the right of free passage, and would secure it with the 6th Fleet if necessary, but he would never support preemption. If Israel attacked first, Eban warned, it would do so on its own.

A tempestuous discussion followed during which the Eban-Johnson protocol was subject to near-Talmudic scrutiny. "Advising Israel not to act alone was not the same as ordering Israel not to act at all," one minister pointed out, while another noted the absence of any threat of sanctions, as in 1956. Could it be that Washington was merely signaling an inability to help Israel defend itself without explicitly denying it that right?

Eban cautioned against reading too deeply into Johnson's words. He did not mention Goldberg's caveat to him, that the president's promise was conditional on Capitol Hill, but only that the convoy would be ready to launch in a "few weeks." That period was not too long to wait if the army remained mobilized and Israel stayed focused on its fundamental issues, rather than its prestige. "There are no widows and orphans from prestige," he said.

Leading the opposition to Eban was Yigal Allon, the Labor Minister, who previously had been away on a state visit to the Soviet Union. There he had done his best to convince Kremlin officials of Israel's sincerity in exercising restraint, but now, back in Tel Aviv, he asked, "Does anyone around this table really think that we should let the enemy strike first just to prove to the world that they started it?" Allon predicted the renewal of Syrian terror now that Israel's hands were tied, and that Egypt would strike Dimona the moment America challenged the blockade. "Nasser could portray himself as the hero who saved the Middle East from nuclear weapons." Israel sought no territorial gain, Allon stressed, only enough to trade for free passage and "to break the enemy's bones." He expressed total faith in the IDF's ability to beat the Egyptians—"The [Galilee] settlers will go down into the shelters, and later we'll take care of the Syrians, too"—and the respect Israel would gain internationally once it did.

A succession of ministers then seconded Allon's position. Haim Givati, in charge of agriculture, warned of the danger of Israel becoming an American protectorate, of the damage to the nation's morale. Zvi Dinstein and Israel

Galili spoke of the Emperor's New Clothes factor—Nasser's exposure of Israel's unwillingness to fight—and of the potential fall of Jordan. "Israel can only be saved by destroying Egypt's power," averred Moshe Carmel. "Anyone who says we can't stand alone is saying that we can't exist here." The generals, Rabin and Weizman, also threw their weight behind Allon. Weizman protested the lack of faith in the IDF, taking it as a personal affront. "We'll beat the Arabs simply because we're better," he vaunted. Rabin was more subdued: "If the State of Israel thinks that its existence hangs on an American commitment and not on its own power—I have nothing more to say."

Yet, for every naysayer another minister rose in support of Eban. There was, as in the past, Haim Moshe Shapira declaring, "I have more confidence in the American promises than I do in the IDF's ability to break the Egyptian army," and Aran and Warhaftig expressing their faith in LBJ. Yisrael Barzilai, from the left-wing Mapam party, worried that America's backing of Israel was less than that of the USSR for the Arabs, while Moshe Kol, the tourism minister, warned of the hazards of alienating Washington. Finance Minister Pinchas Sapir, unexpectedly, expressed doubts whether Israel could sustain casualties as well as the Arabs. He concluded, "It's hard to create a state but easy to lose one."

Caught between these two camps, once again torn, was Levi Eshkol. The prime minister reviewed the pros and cons of the situation—the loss of Israel's deterrence power versus time to raise additional arms and money; his reluctance to trust Johnson as opposed to Israel's need to "show we're the good guys." The American plan, he knew, offered no solution to the Egyptian military threat or to Palestinian terror, and greatly limited Israel's maneuverability. Yet the prospect of defying the world's only sympathetic superpower was daunting.

The schisms in Eshkol's thoughts were reflective of those dividing the Cabinet. At 4:00 A.M., "weary and dejected," according to Rabin, Eshkol called a recess to give the ministers several hours' sleep before voting. "We must decide in whose hands we will place this generation," he exhorted them, "into fate's, America's, or Chuvakhin's." The meeting adjourned while, over the next few hours, two top-secret telegrams arrived from Washington.

The first of these shored up Eban's credibility by reconfirming Johnson's support for the Regatta plan and his willingness to pursue "any and all measures in his power" to reopen the Straits. An addendum from Rusk further indicated that Canada and the Netherlands were inclined to join the operation. The second cable, hand-delivered by Barbour, contained the president's reaction to Moscow's assertion that Israel, and not Egypt, was preparing to strike. "It is essential that Israel not take any preemptive military action and thereby make itself responsible for the initiation of hostilities," Johnson wrote, and warned of the possibility of direct Soviet intervention. "Preemptive action by Israel would make it impossible for the friends of Israel to stand at your side."

The communications served to tilt the balance in the Cabinet when it reconvened early on Sunday afternoon. Instead of a slight majority in favor of war, a straw poll revealed a deadlock. Nine ministers (from the NRP and Mapam, mostly, with one Independent Liberal and two members of Mapai) were opposed to a preemption, and nine, including the prime minister, supported it. With the exception of Carmel, all present recommended continued talks with the Americans.

The government concluded its session by resolving to wait as long as three weeks for the U.S. to act on its promise, and to utilize that time to garner international sympathy, raise money, and purchase arms. In the interim, no further demand would be made for reconstituting UNEF, nor would Israel consider reviving the Armistice until the status quo was restored in Sinai and Egypt ceased all forms of blockade. A communiqué would be issued affirming that Israel "views the closure of the Straits of Tiran as an act of belligerency and will defend itself against it, at the appropriate time, in exercising its rights to self-defense as all states have."

Rabin was sorely disappointed. "I'm certain that in another three weeks we'll find ourselves facing the same problem but under harder conditions," he ventured. "Now the IDF faces its biggest challenge: to remain mobilized without acting." Allon also thought that Israel had "missed the boat militarily and politically," but half the Cabinet thought otherwise. Zalman Aran seemed to speak for that half when he told Mapai members that, "I wasn't sure that it [diplomacy] would prevent any war—I had no illusions. But if there was one chance—we must find it. The war would not run away and diplomatic activity would continue. Nasser is not the only one who can exploit time."[114]

By the thinnest margins, war had been averted—a war that, whether started by Israel or Egypt, at that stage would have radically altered the subsequent history of the Middle East. With Nasser's decision not to launch a first strike, followed closely by Israel's, the crisis appeared to have crested. To varying degrees, both sides had committed themselves to explore nonviolent solutions.

A step toward such a solution was set out in U Thant's long-awaited report on May 27. Though over half the text was devoted to justifying his actions on UNEF ("I had very good reasons to be convinced of the earnestness and the determination of the UAR in requesting the withdrawal"), and much emphasis was placed on reviving the Armistice machinery, the secretary-general did manage to set out his moratorium concept. He called on all parties to "exercise special restraint [and] forgo belligerence," and referred to "possible steps . . . to help reduce tension," by which he meant the appointment of a UN mediator. In Israel, Eshkol decided to demobilize as many as 40,000 reservists. Nasser concluded that he now had a "breathing spell" of two weeks at least in which to consider his options.[115]

But the impression of de-escalation was deceiving. Disgruntled with the Cabinet's decision to delay a preemptive strike, incredulous of America's commitment to help Israel, IDF leaders ignored Eshkol's orders and continued to call up the reserves. Within the army's senior ranks the conviction spread that the government was incapable of handling the emergency, and had to be prodded out of its stupor. The prime minister's position, already shaky, was further undermined when, in preparing to inform the Knesset of Eban's talks, Eshkol received a warning from Washington. His remarks were to make no mention of the convoy proposal, no reference to America's "unambiguous attitude" and "forceful determination" to reopen the Straits. Even the request for an Israeli liaison with the U.S. army failed to receive approval.[116]

Shams Badran, on the other hand, returned triumphantly from Moscow. Just prior to departing, Marshal Grechko had pulled Egypt's defense minister aside and told him that "if America enters the war we will enter it on your side." The USSR, he said, had sent destroyers and submarines to the waters near Egypt, some armed with missiles and "secret weapons." "I want to confirm to you that if something happens and you need us, just send us a signal. We will come to your aid immediately in Port Said or elsewhere." This pronouncement—"only normal Russian expressions while tossing back vodka and bidding Badran farewell," thought the diplomat Salah Bassiouny—was richly embellished by Cairo Radio, in a broadcast that Moscow did nothing to disavow:

> The USSR, its government and its army, will stand by the Arabs and will continue to support and encourage them. We are your loyal friends and shall remain so. We the armed forces will continue to aid you for this is the policy of the Soviet people and their party. In the name of the Ministry of Defense and in the name of the Soviet People we wish you success and victory against imperialist Zionism. We are with you and are willing to help you at every moment.

Badran, who had hindered other delegation members from reporting Kosygin's urgings of caution, was convinced that Egypt was now invincible. "If the Sixth Fleet intervenes in our struggle with Israel, our bombers together with our missile boats can destroy its largest carriers," he boasted to several government ministers. "We have the power to turn it into a can of sardines." Confirmation of his estimates came from Syria's President Atassi who had just returned from his own visit to Moscow. Though he, too, had been told by Soviet leaders to exercise restraint and to halt al-Fatah raids into Israel, Atassi declared that "the USSR pledged to stand firm against any aggression to which the Arab people are exposed by Israel."

Nasser needed no more persuasion. Confidently, he told his Free Officer colleagues that "the message from Kosygin is that the Soviet Union supports us in this battle and will not allow any power to intervene until matters are returned to what they were in 1956."[117]

Egypt's confidence in Soviet support was further bolstered by events in the UN Security Council. The Soviet delegate, Federenko, described by colleagues as "brilliant" and a "fiery orator," a Manchurian-born Far East expert with a penchant for bow-ties and pipes, received strict orders to prevent the acceptance of any resolutions inimical to Egypt. Previously, he had blocked Danish and Canadian attempts to initiate a UN debate on the Middle East, exploiting the opportunity to lash out at the Security Council's Taiwanese president, Liu Chieh. He also drew sweeping comparisons between Israel and Nazi Germany.

Council members were accustomed to such brimstone from Federenko. But nothing prepared them for his rejection of U Thant's moratorium idea. The entire crisis, he explained, was a fabrication intended to malign the Arabs and justify aggression. "The USSR does not see sufficient grounds for such a hasty convening of the Security Council and the artificially dramatic climate fostered by the Western Powers." Federenko evinced a similar rationale in rejecting France's Four-Power summit proposal, which Britain and the United States had begrudgingly approved. Starting on May 28, he made himself "unavailable" for consultation.[118]

The moratorium would be beset from other quarters as well—from Israel, which viewed it as UN approval for a blatant act of war, and then from the United States, which, while supporting the suspension of Israeli flagships through the Straits, rejected any ban on "contraband cargoes," such as oil. Finally, even the Egyptians balked. A hysterical Mohammad El Kony rushed to U Thant's office with word that Nasser would never agree to the passage of oil and other "strategic materials" to Israel, even on foreign vessels. The secretary-general had just finished giving Gideon Rafael a memorandum asking Eshkol to verify that "no ship flying the flag of Israel is likely to seek passage through the Straits of Tiran in the coming two weeks." Apprised of the Egyptian position, though, he instructed Bunche to retrieve the cable from Rafael. No explanation was offered.[119]

Thus, rather than representing the ebb of tensions, the events of the last days of May were merely a reprieve. Far from culminating, the crisis was in fact only beginning, as would soon be evident in Jordan, the country around which it had erupted but which had scarcely been heard from since.

COUNTDOWN

May 31 to June 4

HIS POSITION WAS UTTERLY UNTENABLE. Hunted by Arab radicals, unable to call on Arab moderates for help, King Hussein faced a crisis in which every party seemed backed by powerful allies. Only Jordan stood alone. If it came, war could cost him half his kingdom, his crown, and, not inconceivably, his life.

Since the Samu' incident, Hussein had worked hard to avoid further clashes, and secretly exchanged intelligence with Tel Aviv on suspected West Bank terrorists. He hoped to focus Israel's wrath where it belonged—on Damascus—yet when reports circulated of an impending Israeli invasion of Syria, the king remained incredulous. Jordan's powerful radar station at 'Ajlun had picked up no signs of any IDF buildup in the north. Nevertheless, when Eshkol requested that Jordan cease needling Nasser as "the only Arab leader . . . to live in peace with Israel," Hussein readily complied. The situation, he could see, was rapidly getting out of control. Not only the West Bank but also the East was seething with praise for Nasser and calls for Israel's demise.[1]

"It [Israel] could attack Jordan with impunity, calculating that Egypt and Syria would not come to Jordan's assistance," Foreign Minister Ahmad Touqan explained to Ambassador Burns. But now Jordan faced a potentially greater threat: an Egyptian first strike. If the offensive were repulsed, Nasser would use Jordan as his scapegoat. The Palestinians would revolt, perhaps the army as well, toppling the government and replacing it with the PLO. On the other hand, if Egypt succeeded, its forces could then cut across the Negev and continue onward to Amman. Indeed, Hussein was convinced that the Ramtha bombing on May 21 was a device to draw Jordanian soldiers to the Syrian border, leaving the West Bank exposed. Either way, Jordan would lose. The predicament, as defined by royal confidant Zayd al-Rifaʻi, was mind-boggling: "Even if Jordan did not participate directly in a war . . . it would be blamed for the loss of the war and our turn would be next. If we were isolated from the mainstream of Arab politics, we would be an easy target."[2]

Navigating through the Egyptian Scylla and Israel's Charybdis—this was Hussein's challenge, but the prospects for succeeding seemed meager. Repeatedly, he appealed to Washington for an open statement assuring Jordan's territorial integrity in the event of a war. He asked Cairo to revive the mutual-defense clauses of the United Arab Command. But none of these efforts bore fruit. The Americans reaffirmed their commitment to Jordan's independence but, pleading congressional constraints, refused to guarantee it publicly. In Egypt, Gen. ʻAmer Khammash, Jordan's chief of staff, was told that the UAC was dead, that Jordan should mind its own defense and not "rock the boat." Even Saudi Arabia and Iraq, which had once volunteered to help defend Jordan, now retracted their offer and extended it instead to Syria.

Hussein's only answer, then, was to try to stay out of a war between Syria and Israel, and if Egypt became involved, to participate only indirectly and symbolically, by sending a few regiments to Sinai. In either event, Israel was likely to seek vengeance against Jordan—or so the king told an emergency meeting of his ministers and general staff on May 22. Burns observed that Hussein was "prepared for brinkmanship," and that he would "react like Samson in the temple . . . risking possible annihilation by the Israelis rather than the high probability of internal revolt."[3] Later that day, the monarch donned a military uniform and watched as his two armored brigades, the 40th and the 60th, paraded through the streets of Amman. The purpose was to make a show of force in the hope of not having to use it. Yet even that goal was denied Hussein by Nasser's decision on Tiran.

"I was stunned," Hussein admitted. "For such a measure, lacking in thought and consideration, would only lead to disaster because the Arabs were not ready for war. There was no coordination, no co-operation, no common plan amongst them." Nasser, he complained to Western diplomats, was "acting like a madman," "incomprehensible and extremely dangerous" and "playing for keeps," with untold Soviet backing. But sharp as they were, the king's reservations did not prevent his spokesman from praising the blockade and pledging Jordan's categorical support for it. No protest could be raised when the USS *Green Island*, loaded with vital ammunition for the Jordanian army, turned back short of the Straits. The ship's owners feared that the waters were mined.

Hussein was furious at Nasser, but also bitter towards the White House, which, he claimed, was run by the "Zionist" Rostows, and the Regatta plan, which he saw as a ruse to fortify Israel. "Nasser's objectives are not a military war with Israel but a political war with the United States," he warned

Burns, and suggested that the president step back and let Israel attack Tiran, so that he could later play the peacemaker. "It would be a great pity if the United States sacrificed its Arab friends, and, indeed, the free world's influence in the Middle East, for a limitation on Israeli navigational rights."

Yet, as Washington adhered to what the Arabs perceived as a pro-Israeli line, as Egypt remained in Syria's grip and rapidly gearing for war, Hussein had no choice but to close ranks with Nasser. He had to convince the Arabs that he was not a puppet of the West, and his own population—"two-thirds Palestinian," by his own count—that he was willing to fight for their homeland. "It would not be surprising if the Jordanian Government decides to make some moves in the weeks ahead to reduce what the regime sees as its vulnerability," Burns predicted, and suggested that Saudi and Iraqi troops would be welcomed on Jordanian territory.[4]

Hussein, indeed, lost no time in making those moves. He ordered the 40th brigade and its 100 Patton tanks to cross the Jordan River near Jericho, thus violating limits placed on their deployment by the Americans. Next, in a placating gesture to Nasser, he removed Wasfi al-Tall, Chief of the Royal Court, from the limelight. "We will watch him like a hawk and sit on him when he goes into orbit," Touqan confided to Burns. Chief of Staff Khammash, meanwhile, was sent to Cairo, there to confer with UAC Commander 'Ali 'Ali 'Amer—Nasser refused to receive him—on Jordan's role in the coming conflict.

But even as he went on a war footing, Hussein assured the Americans that Jordan had no aggressive intentions toward Israel, and asked them to assure the Israelis as well. But he also warned Washington of the dangers facing Arab moderates should it ally too closely with Israel: "Once Nasser has succeeded in identifying the United States with Israel in this crisis, the United States will be fully compromised," he said in an oral message to Johnson. "Nasser is clearly striving for this objective and is very close to achieving it."[5]

Hussein's attempts to win Nasser's favor were not conducted unopposed, however. Several of his closest advisers, led by Tal, tried to warn him of the disastrous consequences of such a course, but their counsel went unheeded. The king was determined to forge an alliance. Hearing that Damascus was still branding him a traitor, he swore to his assistants, "The Syrians will soon find out just who is loyal to the Arab cause and who is a traitor to it."[6]

The first to find out, however, was not a Syrian but 'Uthman Nuri, Egypt's ambassador to Amman. Invited to Prime Minister Sa'd Jum'a's house on the morning of May 28, Nuri was shocked to discover the king there and to hear his desire to make a top-secret visit to Cairo within the next forty-eight hours. The ambassador rushed to communicate this request to his superiors, and returned after midnight with the answer. If Hussein would pledge to resist any Israeli attempt to attack Syria through Jordan's territory, and if Iraqi troops were allowed into the West Bank; if Amman would recognize Shuqayri and the PLO as the Palestinians' representatives and comply with the Arab boycott of

West Germany, then Hussein was welcome. The terms were steep but Hussein accepted them. He would fly to Egypt the following dawn, May 30.

Waiting on the tarmac that day were Touqan and Jum'a, Khammash and Royal Air Force Commander Brig. Salah al-Kurdi. Hussein was in uniform still, bearing the rank of field marshal and toting a .357 Magnum pistol. Running late, he barely had time to sign his powers over to his younger brother, Hassan, before personally piloting his Caravel plane to Al-Maza military airfield near Cairo. There to receive him were no less than four Egyptian vice presidents, Foreign Minister Riad, UAC Chief of Staff Gen. 'Abd al-Mun'im Riyad, and the secretary-general of the president's office, 'Abd al-Majid Farid. Heading this august party was Nasser himself, who, taking the Jordanian's hand, asked, "Since your visit is a secret, what would happen if we arrested you?" Hussein, unfazed, merely smiled. "The possibility never crossed my mind."

The entourage proceeded to the Qubbah palace, where it was joined by 'Amer. Then, the president, the king, and the field marshal adjourned to a separate room for a meeting that went on far longer than planned, through lunch and into the afternoon. "I feel that our nation is facing a fateful responsibility," Hussein opened, "and that my feelings toward this responsibility are those of every Arab. I know that Jordan is in danger, and know that war with Israel is inevitable." He blamed the state of Egypt-Jordanian relations on Syria, but said that his forces were ready to defend the Syrians as part of an all-Arab effort that would also protect Jordan. Nasser's response was broad: "It is necessary to reach a political and military position that will make everyone understand that the Arab nation is capable of uniting in the face of crisis . . . My original estimate was that we had three or four years before war broke out with Israel, but events have overtaken us."

But Hussein had not come for general statements; he wanted to close a deal. He told Nasser that he was willing to sign an exact copy of the Egyptian-Syrian defense treaty, and to admit all Arab contingents—Iraqi, Saudi, Syrian, and even Egyptian—to his territory. Nasser did not argue. He instructed Foreign Minister Riad to leave at once for Syria and Iraq to negotiate the rapid dispatch of these forces, including jet fighters to help guard Jordan's skies. Calls were put in to President 'Aref in Baghdad, asking for his cooperation, and to Gaza, with instructions to send Shuqayri to Cairo at once. But all these gestures, Hussein would soon learn, came at a considerable price, costlier than that he had already paid coming to Cairo. Now, in addition to reopening the PLO offices in Amman, he would have to place his army—Jordan's pride—under the command of Gen. Riyad, who was answerable directly to 'Amer.

The treaty, under which Egypt and Jordan agreed to consider "any armed attack on either state or its forces as an attack on both" and to "take all measure . . . at their disposal . . . to repulse that attack," was signed in the early afternoon. The rest of the day passed pleasantly enough, with tours of airstrips and the new army headquarters at Heliopolis. Maps were perused and briefings heard on the current military situation. Hussein warned his hosts of the perils of a surprise Israeli air attack, but Nasser showed no sign of concern, insisting that the Jews were incapable of mounting such an operation. The combined Arab armies would be victorious in a matter of days, he foresaw, adding that, "if the Americans intervene, I will be quite prepared to ask for Soviet assistance."

Finally, just before the king's departure, Ahmad al-Shuqayri was ushered in wearing a rumpled Mao-style uniform and looking disoriented. The PLO Chairman who had recently pledged to lead an army into Amman and "to take no account of Hussein," now strode up to the monarch, declared him "head of the Palestinians," and expressed his desire to visit Jordan in the near future. "You're not going in the near future," Nasser laughed. "You're leaving right away!" Then he turned to Hussein: "If he gives you any trouble, throw him into one of your towers and rid me of him!"[7]

Having, as he told Burns, "shifted the burden of the 'Palestinian problem' off his shoulders and onto Nasser's," Hussein returned to his kingdom. His reception was tumultuous. The supposedly secret summit with Nasser had been broadcast throughout the region—"The world will know that the Arabs are girded for battle as the fateful hour approaches," Cairo Radio blared—and greeted with rapturous applause. The car carrying Hussein and Shuqayri was literally lifted into the air. The king was exhausted, spent, "yet never have I seen him so happy and beaming as he was at that hour," recalled Jum'a. In Cairo, Hussein believed that he had purchased "political and military insurance" for Jordan at a time when the U.S. had refused to guarantee its territory and was instead arming Israel. He also believed that Egypt, while not backing down from its blockade, would not start a war but would wait for the Israelis to strike first and then destroy them. At the very least he had denied Nasser the ability to blame Jordan for failing to join the Arab alliance, irrespective of its fortunes in battle.[8]

But not all Jordanians celebrated Hussein's coup. Wasfi al-Tall again came out against the king's policy, telling him that "I'm ready to kill 2,000 rebels to prevent you from losing the West Bank." Even among the Palestinians, leaders such as East Jerusalem mayor Anwar al-Khatib and his colleague in Hebron, Muhammad 'Ali al-Ja'bari, feared that Egypt would drag Jordan into a war in which Israel would surely expand eastward. Critics of the treaty were quick to point out that while strategic decisions were supposed to be decided by a joint defense council until actual war broke out, in reality the Jordanian army was already under Egyptian command. The army did not even have a liaison in Cairo. The treaty also effectively nullified the secret agreement—code name: College Run—through which the United States supplied Jordan with twelve F-104 fighters, anti-aircraft guns, recoilless rifles, and ammunition. Fearing that the weapons would now find their way into Egyptian hands, the U.S. ceased arms shipments to Amman; the planes were removed to Turkey. Findley Burns, observing that "the king has opened a Pandora's box wider than he probably anticipated," noted how events in Jordan "are alarmingly reminiscent of August 1914."[9]

That fact was brought home on June 1 when Gen. Riyad landed in Amman and immediately began inspection of the West Bank's defenses. His objective was not only to prepare the area for the possibility of Israeli invasion, but to draw the maximum number of enemy troops away from the south, relieving some of the pressure on Egypt. Further help would come from two Egyptian commando battalions, the 53rd and the 33rd, that would be transferred to Jordan with orders to infiltrate and destroy a range of strategic targets in Israel.

The arrival of Riyad and his commandos further inflamed public passions in Jordan, particularly among the Palestinians—passions that Shuqayri was anxious to exploit. Ignoring Hussein's orders not to leave Amman, he traveled to Jerusalem and there delivered a fiery Friday sermon. The PLO, he pledged, was "prepared to take its place in advance positions on the Jordanian front so it can stand face to face with the Zionist gangs"; that it now possessed ultra-modern weapons that he, himself, would direct. Frenzy erupted in the crowds that gathered to hear him; rioters attacked Western consulates and clashed with soldiers trying to quell them. Still Shuqayri fumed on: "We shall destroy Israel and its inhabitants and as for the survivors—if there are any—the boats are ready to deport them!"[10]

Eshkol's Eclipse

Hussein's alliance with Nasser, a result of Israel's decision to wait and not to go to war, would increase the pressures on Israel to fight. That pressure was already bursting the evening of May 28, when, after the Cabinet meeting, Eshkol prepared to meet with the general staff. En route to that engagement, however, he made a brief stop at Israel Radio's studio to address his anxious nation.

Eshkol's purpose was to tell the country that the government, though ready to repel Arab aggression, was working with the United States to resolve the crisis peaceably. He was desperately short on sleep, had a nagging chest cold and an artificial lens in one eye—the result of recent cataract surgery—that kept shifting. Compounding his physical state was the condition of the script that he received only upon entering the studio, finding it crisscrossed with corrections and last-minute additions, which he now had to deliver live. The outcome was a stuttering, rambling, barely intelligible reading that listeners interpreted as a sign of exhaustion and panic. It was not only Eshkol's delivery that confounded Israelis, but also the news that Israel had placed its fate in the hands of another country rather than rely on its own resources. "It's amazing how a people who suffered a Holocaust is willing to believe and endanger itself once again," wrote Ze'ev Schiff, columnist for the daily *Ha'aretz*. Soldiers huddled around transistors in the Negev were said to have burst into tears.[11]

For Eshkol, though, the evening's disasters were hardly concluded. Awaiting him in the Pit were generals waiting to hear the results of the Cabinet's deliberations. Ever since the closure of the Straits, IDF intelligence had been predicting a surprise Egyptian attack on Dimona and Israeli airfields, an onslaught of missiles, poison gas, and even primitive radioactive devices. Syria was certain to join in the assault, and probably Jordan. The Americans would not intervene, the IDF believed, nor were they serious about Regatta. Consequently, the army revived and adapted a number of contingency plans to eliminate the Egyptian army and to seize the initiative on other fronts as well. Only needed was the government's go-ahead, but instead Israeli forces were placed on indefinite hold. In the Negev, a chaos ensued mirroring that in Sinai. "Units . . . were moving here and there crossing each other's paths and taking up positions, only to move back from them a day later and take up different ones," recalled Gen. Ariel "Arik" Sharon, the former paratroop officer who was now a divisional commander in the south. "The army did not look as if it knew what it was doing."

Relief from that confusion was expected to come with Eban's return to Israel and the government's decision to act. Now, unable to bring himself to tell the generals that this was not the case, Rabin asked Eshkol to do it.

Escorted by Allon, Eshkol entered the Pit and, without an introduction, addressed his senior officers. He reviewed the events of the past few days—the letters from Johnson and Kosygin, the plan for a maritime convoy. "It is not politically, diplomatically and perhaps even morally logical to start a war," he said. "We now have to restrain ourselves and to maintain our forces for a week or two or even longer." He expressed confidence in Washington's commitment to reopen the Straits, urged the generals to think in terms of the loss of equipment, of foreign aid, and of human lives that Israel would suffer in war. "I understand you commanders are disappointed, but maturity mandates that we stand up to this test." Even if the Egyptian army were totally destroyed, he ended, it would only arise anew. "In fifteen years perhaps another generation of Arabs will come and kiss us, but not now."

The commanders listened, and then they lunged. "In two weeks the Straits will still be closed and we will be in a worse situation," began Yeshayahu "Shaike" Gavish, chief of the Southern Command. "More of our men will die." His counterpart on the Central Front, Uzi Narkiss, concurred. "The problem lies not with us but with the younger generation that will never understand why the IDF didn't attack." The threat of Russian intervention was a bluff, he said, and as for the Arab forces, "They're soap bubbles—one pin will burst them." Divisional commander Avraham Yoffe weighed in with "Egypt with the help of the USSR, has created an army whose single purpose is the destruction of Israel. The IDF was created to defend the state, but the government is not letting the army carry out its mission—a mission that the people want."

The fusillade continued. Deputy Operations Chief Rehavam Ze'evi (dark and skinny, popularly known as "Ghandi"), later in life to become a leader of Israel's extreme right, and Quartermaster Gen. Mattityahu Peled, later head of the far left, agreed that the Egyptian threat had to be eliminated at once if

Israel were to survive. "Israel cannot expect anybody else to do its dirty work," declared Gen. Yariv, "We, alone, can break the stranglehold tightening around us." But the most compelling remarks were delivered by Sharon:

> Today we have removed with our own hand our most powerful weapon—the enemy's fear of us. We have the power to destroy the Egyptian army, but if we give in on the free passage issue, we have opened the door to Israel's destruction. We will have to pay a far higher price in the future for something that we in any case had to do now . . . The people of Israel are ready to wage a just war, to fight, and to pay the price. The question isn't free passage but the existence of the people of Israel.

Eshkol did his best to deflect these barbs. The IDF was not established to conduct wars of choice, he asserted, and its ability to make war could not be justification for waging one. The mere presence of the Egyptian army in Sinai was not grounds for launching a preemptive attack. "Deterrence means having patience," he said, "endurance." These arguments had no impact on the generals, though, whose contumely might have continued if not for Allon, who finally stepped in and ended the discussion. Neither he nor Rabin had defended their prime minister. Hurt and enfeebled, Eshkol fled the Pit.

"It was a real putsch," recalled Miriam Eshkol. "Everyone was worried and nobody cared about democratic processes." The split in the Israeli self-image between invincibility and weakness had come to the fore, bitterly dividing Israel's leadership. Rafael Eitan, a commander in the paratroopers, explained that "the honor of the army of Israel had been sullied and trampled, and the generals who led that army, who had made it their life's work, could no longer contain their wrath." Yet, however angry, those generals made no serious attempt to oust Eshkol, never threatened the rule of law. Rather, after the prime minister exited, they remained in the Pit discussing ways to lift the soldiers' morale, including the release of 30,000 reservists.[12]

The public, however, was not so forgiving. The papers the next day were brimming with reports of Eshkol's fumbled speech and its rueful impact. *Ha'aretz* claimed that "the government in its present composition cannot lead the nation in its time of danger," and called on Eshkol to step down in favor of Ben-Gurion and Dayan, and to focus exclusively on "civilian matters." A paid advertisement from the Citizens for Eshkol, formed during the 1965 elections, advocated the creation of a national unity government composed of all the mainstream parties. "It seemed to us that Eshkol's hesitation about attacking derived from weakness, not wisdom," Teddy Kollek, the mayor of West Jerusalem, wrote, dismissing as "nonsense" the notion of an international convoy. "Even after the American or British ships would have gone through, the Straits could have been closed again."[13]

The activity behind the scenes was no less feverish. "As long as Eshkol's in office we will plummet into the abyss," Ben-Gurion inscribed in his diary. And yet Menachem Begin, his old political rival, had persuaded him to return as head of a special War Cabinet with Eshkol as his deputy. Eshkol rejected the idea, quipping, "These two horses cannot be hitched to the same wagon." Whereupon Golda Meir met with Begin and the Rafi party's Shimon Peres and proposed that Dayan take on the newly created post of deputy prime minister for defense matters. Dayan refused to even consider the offer, however, and insisted on receiving the defense portfolio. Once he had it, he added, he would not merely sit in his office but would personally direct the war.

Without lobbying, cleverly letting other politicians argue his case, Dayan had surpassed Yigal Allon as the preferred candidate for defense minister. The former chief of staff, always a hero in the public's eye, popular particularly among Israeli women, was cheered wherever he went. The timely publication of his *Diary of the Sinai Campaign*, extolling his achievement of "freedom of shipping . . . in the Gulf of Aqaba; the end to the Fedayeen, and a neutralization of . . . the joint Egyptian-Syrian-Jordanian military command," further enhanced his prestige. To neutralize Dayan, Eshkol began floating the notion of enlisting him into active service. Rabin was willing to offer him the chief of staff position, but Dayan declined. He wanted only one post: head of the Southern Command.[14]

As public and political turmoil mounted, upheaval struck the army as well. Hoping to relieve some of the burdens from his shoulders, Rabin recruited Gen. Haim Bar-Lev as his deputy. Sarajevo-born, Columbia-educated, Bar-Lev had risen from the ranks to command infantry and armored units in 1948 and 1956, and was studying tactics in France when the call from Rabin arrived. The appointment, a popular one in the general staff, infuriated Weizman who saw himself, and not Bar-Lev, as Rabin's successor. "My status was undermined," his memoirs relate. "To them [Rabin, Eshkol] I was a wild man . . . who claimed that we have the right to Hebron and Nablus and all of Jerusalem, and that we must implement that right by force of arms . . . a 'national desperado.'"

Now, in the throes of national trauma, Weizman threatened to resign. He stomped into the prime minister's office, interrupted a lunch with Finance Minister Pinchas Sapir, and bellowed, "The State is being destroyed, Eshkol. Why waste your time with Moshe Dayan? Who needs Yigal Allon? Give the order and we will win . . . and you'll be the prime minister of victory!" He then tore the insignia off his epaulette, purportedly cast it on Eshkol's desk, and stormed out again.

For the mass of Israelis not involved in these power plays, however, the ordeal was all-consuming. Throughout the country, thousands were hurrying to dig trenches, build shelters, and fill sandbags. In Jerusalem, in particular, schools were refitted as bomb shelters, and air raid drills were practiced daily. Most buses and virtually all taxis were mobilized, and an emergency blood drive launched. An urgent request for surgeons—"in view of the tough conditions they must be physically fit and experienced"—was submitted to the Red Cross, and extra units of plasma ordered from abroad. Special committees were placed in charge of gathering essential foodstuffs, for replacing workers called to the front, and for evacuating children to Europe. Upward of 14,000 hospital beds were readied and antidotes stockpiled for poison gas victims, expected to arrive in waves of 200. Some 10,000 graves were dug.[15]

The sole bright spot in these otherwise morbid preparations was the un-precedented outpouring of sympathy from around the Jewish world. Volun-teers arrived in numbers greater than Israel could absorb—preference was given to young, skilled, Jewish bachelors—and donations exceeded all forecasts. Mass demonstrations were held in New York and London, and emergency fund drives launched globally. "For the first time in history, European Jewry is acting as one for Israel. All moral, political, and economic support is being mobilized," French Jewish leader Edmund de Rothschild wrote Sapir. From Paris, Israeli ambassa-dor Walter Eytan reported on a "total revolution," with French Jews willing to give blood, house evacuated children, even sell their artworks to raise money for Israel. Contributions poured in from non-Jews as well. Particularly welcome were some 20,000 American gas masks, supplied, ironically, by Germany.[16]

Yet these gestures did little to relieve the sense of approaching catastro-phe, of the Jews' abandonment to yet another Holocaust. "What are you wait-ing for?" Hanna Zemer, deputy editor of the daily *Davar*, accosted Eshkol. He retorted with a description of Israel's international isolation, of the massive casualties it would suffer. "Blut vet sich giessen vie vasser," he concluded in Yiddish: "Blood will run like water." Rabin wrote later of the mood: "The days dragged on with their burden of nerve-racking meetings and consultations . . . Time and time again, we assessed the situation, foresaw options, stationed units, formulated plans—while our political leaders remained captive to their illusory hopes that war might be averted." There was talk of the widespread bombing of Israeli cities, of an entire generation of soldiers being wiped out. A popular joke told of a sign hung at Lod International Airport, exhorting the last person out of the country to kindly turn off the light.[17]

The apocalypse appeared to have arrived when, for the first time, fire was exchanged on the Sinai border. An Egyptian patrol, entering Israeli territory near Kibbutz Be'eri southeast of Gaza, was ambushed by Israeli paratroopers. Egyptian artillery shells then rained on Be'eri and nearby Nahal Oz, setting crops ablaze. Though the paratroopers were pinned down for hours, Gen. Is-rael Tal, the local divisional commander, hesitated to send in reinforcements. The slightest escalation, he knew, could set off a war. The incident passed, however, only to be overshadowed by another, as Egyptian MiG's again pen-etrated Israeli airspace and reconnoitered IDF positions. The Arabs were get-ting restless, gaining confidence, military analysts concluded. "Colonel Nasser has created a position in which there is a danger of war," Eshkol told the Knesset on May 29. "A conflagration is liable to break out."[18]

Never had conflagration appeared closer, though, as when Hussein journeyed to Cairo. "All of the Arab armies now surround Israel," the king declared upon his return, "The UAR, Iraq, Syria, Jordan, Yemen, Lebanon, Algeria, Sudan, and Kuwait . . . There is no difference between one Arab people and another, no difference between one Arab army and another." Gen. Khammash had flown to Baghdad to request four Iraqi brigades, plus eighteen fighter aircraft to join Jordan's twenty-four Hawker Hunters. Together with Jordan's eleven brigades—56,000 men, 270 modern tanks, Centurions and Pattons—these forces would threaten Israel at its narrowest point, nine miles between the West Bank and the sea. On the Golan Heights, some 50,000 Syrian soldiers with 260 tanks and as many field guns were now in position, and were soon to be reinforced by Iraqi tanks as well. All these armies were now coordinated with Egypt's 130,000 men, 900 tanks, and 1,100 guns for what Nasser called "the operation that will surprise the world."[19]

The signing of the Egyptian-Jordanian treaty all but erased Eshkol's hope for retaining the Defense Ministry. In a last, desperate effort, he acted on Dayan's request for the Southern Command. Rabin summoned Gavish to the Pit and there informed him of the decision, offering him the position of deputy commander.

Gavish, sinewy and rugged, had recovered from a severe leg wound suffered in 1948 to serve as an operation chief in 1956, and was now, at forty-two, a full general. Indefatigably, over the past two weeks he had labored to prepare his men for what he believed was an inevitable showdown with Egypt. Under Operation Red Tongue (*Lashon Aduma*), using a few tanks and jeeps and many yards of camouflage netting, Gavish had created a phantom division—the 49th—and positioned it between Kuntilla and al-Qusayma, scene of Israel's breakthrough in 1956. Fooled by this ruse, Gen. Shazli's force had been shifted southward from Rafah, and the 4th Division moved to its reserve, further exposing Sinai's northern defenses to Israeli armor. The reward was now to be Gavish's removal. Crushed by Eshkol's decision, disappointed with Rabin for abiding it, Gavish tendered his resignation. "I salute Dayan," he said, "but I won't remain another minute."

Dayan seemed amenable to the appointment: "As a soldier, I'm ready to drive a half-track," he regaled the press. But political currents converged to drive him elsewhere. The NRP was ready to bolt the government if national unity were not achieved, but Rafi and Gahal refused to join without Dayan. Golda Meir wanted Allon as defense minister—Dayan could replace Eban, Allon suggested—but the motion was rejected by Mapai. And so the machinations continued, while the nation's patience wore thin. A mass rally demanding a unity government was planned for Saturday, June 3.

"Let me understand," an exasperated Eshkol asked Haim Moshe Shapira, "you want Dayan and you *don't* want war?" But Eshkol knew the answer: The Cabinet had lost faith in his competence as defense minister. That same lack of confidence had led Menachem Begin to support Ben-Gurion, in spite of his opposition to war. There was no longer an alternative to surrender. "Too many ministers, too many members of Knesset, too many generals, and the street, always the street, supported Dayan," Col. Lior lamented. "From that moment on until the time of his death, he wasn't the same Levi Eshkol."[20]

At 4:30 in the afternoon of June 1, in Tel Aviv, Dayan was finally sworn in. The restrictions on his office were draconian. At Eshkol's insistence, Dayan agreed not to order any attack without the prime minister's approval, nor to sanction any operation that strayed from the general war plan. No Arab cities were to be bombed unless Israeli cities were bombed first. As a further check on Dayan's powers, Eshkol brought in Yigal Yadin, an eminent archeologist and Israel's second chief of staff, as his special adviser on defense.

Rabin, too, was ambivalent about the appointment. "He wasn't enthusiastic about it, but he knew how to accept facts," recalled Rehavam Ze'evi. "He appreciated Dayan's contribution to the nation's morale, and realized that it was better to go to war with Dayan, rather than Eshkol, as defense minister. But unable to foresee the results of that war, Rabin also wanted to share some of its onus." Upon meeting his new superior, a man whose military reputation even exceeded his own, Rabin asked, "Are you ready to submit to my authority in operational matters?" Dayan assured him that he would respect the chief of staff the same as Gen. Maxwell Taylor, commander of American forces in Vietnam, respected the Joint Chiefs of Staff. With this, the new defense minister proceeded immediately to the Pit, there to insult the generals present by brazenly telling them, "Show me your plan—that is if you've even got one. I've got mine."[21]

Later that evening, Aharale Yariv stopped in at the British embassy for a "long late night drink" with the ambassador, Michael Hadow. In his cups, Yariv complained of Eshkol's inability to make a decision, of his fear of the Russians and culpability for Samu' ("a terrible blunder"). Eban, he claimed, had disobeyed orders and made the blockade, not Israel's security, the focus of his talks in Washington. The upshot was that Israel was now saddled with Dayan— "unpleasant and self-centered"—and would have to fight a three-front war in two days, winning it but only with monstrous casualties. Hadow, an expert on Israel and Middle East affairs since the early 1950s, was unruffled. He had been watching the situation in Tiran "like a terrier at a rat hole," and did not believe that war was inevitable. "It pays for Israel to make our flesh creep a bit from time to time," he wrote. He assured "little Yariv" that he had nothing to worry about, told him to trust that "the international community would not let Israel fight two hours, never mind 48," and to trust in the United States.[22]

Hadow's advice would have diminishing reverberations in Israel, however, as the crisis entered its third and most critical week. No sooner had Johnson promised to use "every possible effort" to reopen the Straits and not to abandon Israel, it seemed, than he was already backtracking. The White House continued to delay responding to Israel's requests for arms—the list, now including 100 Hawk missiles, 140 Patton tanks, and 24 Skyhawk jets, had lengthened—and for a liaison with U.S. forces. "If war breaks out, we would have no telephone number to call, no code for plane recognition, and no way to get in touch with the Sixth Fleet," Gene Rostow heard Harman complain. An Israeli proposal for mutual force reductions in Sinai and the Negev, to be mediated by the U.S. and the USSR, was similarly overlooked. At most, the administration was willing to exert economic pressure against Egypt—so it informed the Israelis.

This lack of decisive action prompted another ardent letter from Eshkol to Johnson. Reminding the president that his promise to use "all and every measures to open the Straits" had dissuaded his government from voting for war, Eshkol warned that Israel was "approaching a point at which counsels of restraint would lack any moral or logical basis." The only course was to compel U Thant to work for the restoration of the status quo ante in Sinai, to agree to a U.S.-Israel military liaison, and to launch the convoy "within a week or two." Eshkol concluded by emphasizing that Israel was "experiencing some of the heaviest days in its history," but his letter wrought no change in America's position. Instead, Johnson denied that he had even said "all and every measures," but only every measure within his constitutional powers. Walt Rostow was instructed to make that point perfectly clear to the Israelis at once.[23]

"Am I wrong in assessing the president's personal determination as I did?" was Ephraim Evron's response. Rostow replied obscurely, "You have known President Johnson for a long time and have a right to make your own assessment." With tears in his eyes he said, "So much hinges on that man." Evron rushed to report on the talk, his summary hitting Jerusalem "like a slap in the face," according to Rabin. "There was no way of misinterpreting the cable: we could not expect any action on the part of the United States . . . [It] had the look and feel of the proverbial last straw."

Another crisis, this one of credibility, was brewing between the United States and Israel. Asked by Rostow how long the Israelis would now wait, Evron speculated "about ten days." Ambassador Barbour predicted an even briefer span: "If major terrorism is mounted from Sinai or the Gaza Strip, Israel will have to do it eventually. They [the Israelis] feel they can finish Nasser off and if [there is] no other way to stop terrorism, they will have to do it." Yet Eshkol, though "thunderstruck" by Evron's report, was willing to make one last effort. He would dispatch Meir Amit to Washington, there to succeed where Eban had failed in ascertaining whether the administration truly intended to act with Israel and, if not, whether Israel *could* act alone.[74]

Every Possible Effort

What seemed to Israelis like backtracking, though, was for Americans the product of galling frustrations. "From the moment Eisenhower made clear that a commitment had been made," attested Walt Rostow, "Johnson had no doubt that he had to reopen the Straits." He had advocated adopting a strong public position on the crisis, warning Johnson that its policy was too much "for the record" and not enough "we mean business." But in grappling with the Middle East, the president faced a battery of obstacles. Opposition to the Regatta plan had stiffened within the defense establishment, in the CIA, and in the Joint Chiefs of Staff, which doubted whether the U.S. had sufficient forces to implement it. "Threats of force will only sustain him [Nasser] in his present course," concluded a Middle East Control Group analysis, "An appeal to vanity, and avarice, is needed." Asked by Battle what would happen if a U.S. warship, sent to Tiran, was fired upon, Gen. Wheeler slammed his fist down and bellowed, "Luke, it means war."

The military's objections to Regatta paled, however, compared to those raised by Congress when senior White House officials—Rusk, McNamara, Humphrey—took their case to the Hill.

They came with the draft of a joint resolution authorizing the president "to take appropriate action, including use of the Armed Forces of the United States, to secure effective observance of this right [of free passage] in concert with other nations." Congress was not impressed. The Senate Foreign Relations Committee, deeply afflicted with what Rusk called "Tonkin Gulfitis," showed no sympathy whatsoever for Regatta. Senators Mike Mansfield, William J. Fulbright, and Albert Gore were particularly adamant that the administration not lead the nation into a second Vietnam, and that the Middle East crisis be resolved solely within the UN framework. Even the most pro-Israel senators—Robert Kennedy and Jacob Javits—expressed reservations about the convoy idea. After canvassing nearly ninety congressmen, a dispirited Rusk and McNamara reported to the president: "While it is true that Congressional Vietnam doves may be in the process of conversion to [Israeli] hawks . . . an effort to get a meaningful resolution from the Congress runs the risk of becoming bogged down in acrimonious dispute."[25]

But obtaining congressional approval was only one of Regatta's problems; the other was getting additional countries to join. Johnson had assumed that at least fourteen of the eighteen nations approached would join the initiative, but only four—Iceland, New Zealand, Australia, and the Netherlands—would sign the declaration in support of free passage through Tiran, and only the Australians and the Dutch agreed to send ships. Italy, Germany, and Brazil balked at any commitment, however vague, to military action. The French still insisted on the Four-Power summit, and the Argentineans denied they were a maritime country at all. "The Belgians," wrote one U.S. diplomat, "are waffling." The keenest disappointment was Canada, one of the original sponsors of Regatta. Fearing an Arab backlash—their UNEF contingent, accused of pro-Israeli bias, was given forty-eight hours to leave Sinai—the Canadians abandoned the convoy idea in favor of reviving the Armistice Agreement and transplanting UNEF in Israel.

"The Canadians and the Europeans will not accept responsibility," the president recorded in his diary, "They say it's not their trouble, and they shouldn't get into the Middle East right now." Particularly intimidating was Nasser's threat to fire on any ship attempting to break the blockade, and to suspend the flow of Arab oil to its owners. In a memo to Walt Rostow, Saunders raised the possibility that the United States would launch Regatta and that no one else would follow.[26]

"We may not succeed; probably we shall not. But our public opinion will not, I believe, understand or support what we may have to do hereafter if we cannot show convincingly that we have tried." So Prime Minister Wilson tried to encourage an increasingly skeptical LBJ. The Anglo-American alliance, nearly shattered during the 1956 crisis, had held firm through the current one, as the U.S and Britain divided up the countries solicited about Regatta. But under the twin pressures of domestic and international opinion, even that relationship began to fray. "International action [on the Straits] will be perceived as a thinly disguised Anglo-US action," claimed a policy paper prepared for the British Cabinet, "At best can get the active support of one or two European countries, possibly of few more, and hostility from rest of the world." The Cabinet's conclusions agreed:

> The military disposition by the Arab countries and particularly by the UAR represented a permanent change in the balance of power in the Middle East to the disadvantage of Israel, which both she and the Western Powers would have to accept . . . It was doubtful whether we should seek to enforce in respect of the Gulf of Aqaba rights which we had failed to assert in respect of the [Suez] Canal over so long a period. Nor was it essential to British interests to restore the right of innocent passage in the Straits of the Gulf.

Britain, too, was "going soft" on Regatta, and "digging in its heels" in favor of restoring some symbolic UN force in the Straits which would remain under Egyptian army control. All "strategic cargoes" to Israel, except oil, would be impounded. Efforts meanwhile would be made to deter Israel from going to war and embroiling the world in a superpower showdown. Rankled over America's attempts to portray the convoy as a "British initiative" and to associate it with Israeli—not universal—interests, Wilson had begun to suspect that Johnson had promised Eban more than he admitted. The prime minister refused to host the signing of the declaration, and restricted British involvement in joint naval planning.[27]

Yet naval planning continued, albeit quietly so as not to arouse congressional suspicions. Briefs were compiled examining America's status in the murky legal waters of Tiran, and estimates made of the potential damage of implementing Regatta—$1 billion in foreign exchange, billions more in capital assets. A schedule was set for the operation. It would begin with an Israeli-owned vessel flying a foreign flag and carrying nonstrategic cargoes, followed by a similar ship bearing oil. If either of these were impeded in the Straits, two U.S. destroyers and a tactical command ship would then challenge the blockade. And if the squadron were attacked—an unlikely scenario, according to military planners—a Mediterranean-based task force would "neutralize enemy air capabilities" and, if necessary, conduct an amphibious landing. Finally, if war broke out between Egypt and Israel, food, humanitarian aid, and ammunition would be offered to Israel, irrespective of which side struck first.[28]

Contingency planning for Regatta was supposed to conclude on June 5, though mounting the operation could take a month or more—time that Johnson did not have. Acting on the assumption that the Israelis would delay their attack no longer than the two weeks cited in Eshkol's letter, the Joint Chiefs of Staff began moving some sixty-five naval ships into the eastern Mediterranean. The *Intrepid*, returning from Vietnam and successfully traversing the Suez Canal, joined its Sixth Fleet sister carriers, *America* and *Saratoga*. The armada remained "outside an arc whose radius is 240 miles from Port Said"—far enough not to provoke the Egyptians, but well within striking range.[29]

Not listed among these vessels, but instructed to proceed from the Ivory Coast to Rota, Spain, was the 455-foot, 294-man Auxiliary General Technical Research Ship (AGTR), the USS *Liberty*. Though armed only with .50-caliber machine guns, the ship was equipped with cutting-edge listening and decoding devices, and among its crew were members of the highly classified Naval Security Group. The *Liberty* was a spy ship, code-named Rockstar and operating at the behest of the National Security Agency. In Rota, the vessel picked up three Marine Corps Arabic translators, who joined three Russian experts already aboard, and after undergoing repairs set sail again on June 2. Overriding orders from U.S. Naval Command in Europe to remain in Rota "until directed otherwise," the *Liberty* made "best speed" to the Middle East, there to assume a patrolling pattern just beyond the territorial waters of Egypt and Israel.[30] Its exact mission, unknown even to the skipper, Commander William L. McGonagle, was probably to track the movements of Egyptian troops and their Soviet advisers in Sinai.

Johnson was committed to Regatta, yet that commitment did not prevent him from resorting to alternative types of diplomacy. The need for such options was brought home not only by the opposition of Congress and the maritime states, but by the bleak prophesies of American diplomats in the Middle East.

Ambassador Porter in Beirut reported that no one in the Arab world believed that the issue was really the Straits—"Would the United States be as concerned over the issue if it were Jordan's port of Aqaba?"—and warned against falling into a Soviet trap. "On the scales we have Israel, an unviable client state whose value to the U.S. is primarily emotional, balanced with [the] full range [of] vital strategic, political, commercial/economic interests represented by Arab states," wrote Hugh Smythe from Damascus. Citing national security exigencies, Burns in Amman recommended that the U.S. "not honor" its commitments to Israel. "In the event that Israel does go to hostilities," he explained, "we will never be able to convince the Arabs we have not encouraged her to do so. This will wreck every interest we have in North Africa and the Middle East

. . . for years to come." Finally, from Cairo, Nolte recalled that Nasser had simply done to Israel what Israel had done to Egypt in 1956—"tit for tat"—and the U.S. had no obligation to rescue the Jewish state, a nation "established by force." He further warned that the Egyptians would indeed open fire on the convoy. "It is inconceivable to us that [the] UAR with full Soviet backing would not, repeat not, militarily confront any naval or other force which attempts to enforce 'free passage.'"[31]

These exhortations—punctuated by bomb explosions at the Beirut and Jidda embassies—had a powerful impact on Rusk. Though still determined to go "full steam ahead" on Regatta, he had lost any delusions about its price. "Unless we show the Israelis that we are prepared in the last analysis to use force to keep the Straits open, we are not likely to dissuade them from taking the law into their own hands," he confided to Foreign Minister Harmel of Belgium. "On the other hand, to commit ourselves in this way now would not only reduce our flexibility in seeking a peaceful solution but could bring us into direct military confrontation with Nasser."

Rusk consequently redoubled diplomatic efforts in the Security Council, promoting a Danish resolution in support of U Thant's moratorium idea. Goldberg lobbied hard for the initiative, and appeared to be making headway when Egypt submitted its own draft denouncing "Israeli aggression" and calling for a revival of the Armistice. The sole chance for a breakthrough lay in reaching a tacit understanding with the Soviets. Privately, Federenko indeed expressed an interest in preventing hostilities; Soviet ships in the Mediterranean were merely "a military parade," he said. His speeches remained virulent, however, assailing Americans for denying Egypt the right to blockade while they, themselves, blockaded Cuba and "drowned Vietnam in blood."[32]

Stymied at the UN, the administration went above Federenko's head and directly to his bosses in the Kremlin. In letters to Kosygin and Gromyko, Johnson and Rusk, respectively, stressed their common interests in assuring free passage and averting war, but also Nasser's culpability in blockading the Straits and the dangers facing world peace. Using as their stick the threat of Israeli preemption—"We do not believe that Israel will back down . . . nor that she should be asked to"—the Americans proffered their carrot: agreement on the moratorium followed by a superpower summit in either New York or Moscow.[33] The White House was still waiting for an answer to this invitation when, after a session described as "more notable for heat than light," the Security Council finally adjourned. It would not reconvene for forty-eight hours, until Monday, June 5.

However vigorously pursued, diplomacy in the UN and with the Soviets was of limited value compared to direct talks with the antagonists themselves. Far greater benefits could be gained by restoring direct channels with Egypt. A first attempt in this direction was made on June 1 by Charles Yost, the State Department Middle East expert who arrived in Cairo to help Nolte. Yost made contact with his old acquaintance, Mahmoud Riad, who agreed to meet him at his home.

The foreign minister spoke for over ninety minutes, with "intense and uncharacteristic emotion and bitterness," excoriating U.S. policy ("hopelessly pro-Israel") and then Israel itself: "The Zionists' treatment of the [Palestinian] refugees is taught to every school child and the issue will not die." Nasser, he explained, could not lose face by backing down on the blockade, and would fight "anyone" attempting to break it. Though his generals were pressuring him to attack, he preferred to wait for the Israelis to strike first and then to destroy them in the desert. A short war, followed by a UN-engineered cease-fire, just might break the impasse, Riad mused. Then the parties could proceed to a "realistic settlement" in which the refugees would be repatriated and Israel could find alternative sources of oil. "The problem is not economic but purely psychological," he said.

The conversation did not augur well for continued dialogue with Cairo. Yost reported that there was no sign of Arab "battle fatigue" or a readiness to compromise on Tiran. "As long as the prospect either of Israeli attack or Western use of force in the Straits seems imminent, Arab excitement and unity will probably mount rather than decline," he wrote, warning that the Egyptians would defend their blockade with force. As such, Yost proposed that the United States accustom itself to Nasser's new status. Israel would learn to live without Eilat, as it did before 1957.[34]

But Yost's meeting with Riad was only the beginning of Washington's efforts to reach Nasser. These were redoubled on a different, clandestine plane, through Robert B. Anderson—the same Robert B. Anderson who had tried to mediate a secret Egypt-Israeli peace in 1956. The Texas oilman had been in direct phone contact with the president since the outset of the crisis. During a farewell meeting with Ambassador Kamel on May 24, Johnson proposed that Anderson undertake a secret junket to Cairo. The answer was positive, and Anderson embarked, confident in the belief that the crisis was largely the result of Egypt's financial problems, to be solved by inviting 'Amer to the United States. An agreement could be reached in which American wheat would be traded for Egyptian moderation.

Anderson arrived in Cairo on the evening of May 30 to find Nasser relaxed and confident, buoyed by King Hussein's visit. He insisted that Israel had massed thirteen brigades on the Syrian border and would eventually attack, but that Egypt had "elaborate plans" for a counterstrike. His main fear was that Syria, disgruntled by Egypt's new treaty with Jordan, or one of the Palestinian organizations would start a war in which Egypt would have to intervene. Complimented by Anderson about the fact that intellectuals throughout the Arab world were as committed to him as they were opposed to the notion of peace, Nasser quipped, "I am impressed more by the quality of the people who made these assertions than by the fact that they were made."

The discussion at last got down to defusing the present crisis. Nasser belittled the chances for successful arbitration by either the UN or the International Court of Justice, and rejected American mediation outright. He suggested, instead, a neutral negotiator, but declined to specify whom. As for inviting 'Amer to Washington, Nasser expressed a preference for sending his vice president, Zakkariya Muhieddin, who had just been named commander of the Peoples Resistance Forces. Anderson agreed, and proposed a reciprocal visit of Vice president Humphrey to Egypt.

The talk produced a letter in which Nasser finally responded to Johnson's appeal of eleven days before. The tone was anything but temperate as the Egyptian leader again accused Israel of plotting to invade Syria, of consistently violating UN resolutions, and committing aggression. By contrast, the measures taken by Egypt in the Straits were "only logical," and it was "unthinkable" that Israeli cargoes could pass. Yet, for all its obstinacy, the cable concluded by accepting Muhieddin's invitation to Washington and welcoming the American vice president to Cairo. This was precisely the opening the White House had sought. The Middle East Control Group went promptly into high gear preparing for the Muhieddin-Johnson meeting, including ideas for a comprehensive Arab-Israeli settlement and "certain Levantine touches" for Nasser's ego. Reservations were made for the advance Egyptian party's arrival on June 5.[35]

American policy was registering progress—in planning for Regatta, in spurring the Security Council and renewing ties with Nasser, in spite of still-formidable obstacles. Yet on one issue, and arguably the most crucial—Israel—as many questions as answers remained.

The swearing in of Moshe Dayan as defense minister was greeted ambivalently in Washington. While not "unduly optimistic," Barbour thought that the former general's appointment would bolster his country's sense of security: "If we are able to keep up the diplomatic momentum . . . our chances of success with the Israelis are better now than they have been heretofore." Rusk, more cautious, pointed out that, politically, Dayan was obliged neither to Eshkol nor to Ben-Gurion, and could be expected to strike an independent path. "There are no—repeat no—new indications [that an] outbreak of hostilities is imminent in the period of diplomatic maneuvering ahead," he advised his ambassadors. But others were less sanguine. Lucius Battle predicted, "This [Dayan's] appointment increases the likelihood of an eventual decision to resort to military action."

The salient question remained: How long would the Israelis wait? Would they hang fire for the month Regatta's planners deemed necessary to mount the operation or, as U.S. intelligence believed, start the war in two weeks?

While retaining a gut sense that the Israelis would, in the end, "go it alone," Johnson was determined to gain as much time as possible for diplomacy. As a counterpoint to Muhieddin's visit to Washington, the president instructed White House counsel Harry McPherson, then in Vietnam, to stop over in Israel on June 5. He also authorized high-level, candid meetings with Eshkol's personal emissary, Meir Amit.[36]

Compact, energetic (thirty-five years later, he would still be heading Israel's satellite program), the forty-four-year-old Amit had served with the *Haganah* and as operations chief in 1956, only later switching from the field to espionage.

In 1961, after earning his degree at Columbia Business School, he was appointed head of IDF Intelligence, and two years later took on the directorship of the Mossad. He guided the organization away from Nazi-hunting to tracking Egypt's missile program, ran—and lost—Eli Cohen as a spy, and scored his boldest achievement in August 1966 with the defection of an Iraqi MiG-21 pilot together with his plane. He had also established ties with Egyptian Gen. 'Azm al-Din Mahmud Khalil—ties that Amit tried to reestablish in the hope of easing the crisis in Sinai, only to receive no response. Since then he had helped Rabin and Ya'akov Herzog draft the warnings to Eban in Washington, convinced that Israel had to act immediately and that once it did, it would win. Confidently he assured Eshkol, "If he [Nasser] strikes first, he's finished."

Amit was well known in Washington, where his reputation was strictly no-nonsense. "A born Israeli . . . he is so much more natural and relaxed than Harman and Eban who must constantly prove their authenticity," Walt Rostow briefed the president, adding, "These boys are going to be hard to hold about a week from now." Particularly extensive were his contacts in the CIA, and especially with John Hadden, chief of the agency's Tel Aviv desk. Earlier in the crisis, Hadden had wakened Amit at 2:30 A.M. just to warn him, "if you fire the first shot, you're on your own."

Confirming whether that warning still held was Amit's first task. His second, no less critical, was to convince the Americans that, "had Israel been allowed to do the dirty work ten days ago, there would have been no danger of U.S. involvement, but now if Israel doesn't act, the United States will have to in order to save what's left of the Middle East." The Israelis did not want Americans fighting for them—"It's not Vietnam here," Amit would say—but only to check any Soviet intervention, provide political support in the UN, and expedite arms deliveries. Eshkol tried to make light of Amit's mission, dismissing it as *fantoflach* (Yiddish for "house slippers"), but the message it bore was grave: "Israel's blood is on America's conscience."

Leaving Israel incognito on May 31, Amit was distressed to see several prominent Israelis on board his plane, apparently fleeing the country. In Washington, he was met by James Jesus Angleton, the Americans' long-standing liaison with the Mossad, which dubbed him "the greatest Zionist in the CIA." Angleton, to Amit, sounded more bellicose than most Israeli generals, insisting that the Soviets had been planning this crisis for years and that Johnson would secretly welcome an Israeli initiative to thwart them. Regatta, he claimed, "will never get off the ground." Similar opinions were expressed by Richard Helms, another acquaintance of Amit's, who added, however, that the final word would have to come from Johnson, Rusk, or McNamara.

There was one more meeting at CIA headquarters, with thirty Middle East experts who "opened the books" on their estimates of Arab forces and found that they agreed entirely with Israel's. "The atmosphere was highly explosive, but also filled with good will," Amit commented, quoting Jack Smith, the department head, telling him, "You've been preaching to the converted." The key discussion, however, still lay ahead, with McNamara.

The former Harvard Business professor and Ford company president, the architect of much of America's involvement in Vietnam, McNamara was known for his cold, methodical demeanor. Yet, tieless and in his shirtsleeves, he greeted Amit warmly. He sent regards to Moshe Dayan—"I admire that man"—and asked some pointed questions: If a war broke out, how long would it last? How many casualties would Israel sustain? Amit answered succinctly. The war would be over in two days; Israeli casualties would be high, but less than they were in 1948. He presented Israel's requests for American political and military support, and then, in an effort to draw his host out on the question of a preemptive strike, Amit said that he was returning with a recommendation for war. "I read you loud and clear," McNamara replied simply: "this was very helpful."

Amit's records show that Johnson called twice during the meeting and was fully apprised of its substance. The Mossad chief thus concluded that the president, like his defense secretary, was not telling Israel explicitly *not* to go to war. McNamara would later object to that conclusion: "I cannot believe that he thought that. We were absolutely opposed to preemption. We were afraid that preemption, by provoking the Soviets to intervene, would necessitate American intervention to save Israel." But Amit had discerned the internal divisions over Regatta in the White House and, apart from supplying some gas masks and medicines, its refusal to aid Israel militarily. If Johnson's purpose in accommodating Amit had been to allay Israel's fears and buy more time for diplomacy, the goal had been emphatically missed. Amit would fly home more than ever convinced that Israel gained nothing by waiting, except compounding its losses. [37]

It was the same conclusion reached by Abe Harman, most reluctantly, after nearly three weeks of intensive efforts to achieve a modus operandi with the United States. The ambassador was set to return for consultations in Jerusalem, to submit his opinion alongside Amit's. Before departing, however, he petitioned Rusk one last time for concrete assurances for action. The secretary apologized, saying that he could not provide guarantees beyond what Israel had already received, and cautioned once again about striking preemptively. He also used the opportunity to announce the fact of Muhieddin's coming visit to Washington, and pledged to keep Israel "in the picture." Harman was crestfallen. The administration would now open prolonged negotiations with Egypt; the convoy would be indefinitely delayed. "Does Israel have to tolerate 10,000 casualties before the United States conceded that aggression had occurred?" he asked. Should Egypt attack first, "Israel has had it," he said.[38]

Dayan ex Machina

Amit would return to a country substantially different from the one he had left forty-eight hours before. The atmosphere of panic had begun to dissipate, to be replaced by a growing sense of equanimity, if not confidence. In the army, the

generals had begun to regard *ha-Hamtana*—the waiting period—as a mixed blessing, permitting the Egyptians to dig in but in increasingly forward lines which,
once penetrated, would leave much of Sinai defenseless. A large portion of Egypt's
air force had also been advanced eastward, to well within range of Israeli jets.
The IDF, meanwhile, had used the time to perfect its offensive strategies, to
train and position its men. The willy-nilly transfer of troops that Gen. Sharon
had complained about was over. "The army was bolted and locked," recalled
Shlomo Merom, a senior intelligence officer. "We had only to pull the trigger."

Politically, also, the situation in Israel had stabilized. The enervating wheel-
ing and dealing of the previous weeks was past, having produced a National
Unity Government including the major opposition parties. This held its first
meeting on Thursday night, June 1. Menachem Begin, now minister without
portfolio, delivered a characteristically purplish peroration on the destiny of
the Jewish nation and the harsh trials awaiting it, to which Eshkol responded,
"Amen. Amen."[39] Then, in its first concrete act, the Cabinet decided on a joint
session of the general staff and the Ministerial Defense Committee, to be held
at 9:25 A.M. the following morning, in the Pit.

These transformations were the result of many factors—public pressure,
improved logistics, the strangely calming realization that Israel indeed stood
alone. None was so pivotal, however, as the ascendance of one individual, the
new defense minister, Moshe Dayan.

"It is rather like arguing with an Irishman," wrote Michael Hadow of his
many conversations with Dayan. "He enjoys knocking down ideas just for the
sake of argument and one will find him arguing in completely opposite directions on consecutive days." Indeed, Dayan was a classic man of contradictions:
famed as a warrior, he professed deep respect for the Arabs, including those
who attacked his village, Nahalal, in the early 1930s, and who once beat him
and left him for dead. A poet, a writer of children's stories, he admitted publicly that he regretted having children, and was a renowned philanderer as well.
A lover of the land who made a hobby of plundering it, he had amassed a huge
personal collection of antiquities. A stickler for military discipline, he was prone
to show contempt for the law. As one former classmate remembered, "He was
a liar, a braggart, a schemer, and a prima donna—and in spite of that, the object
of deep admiration."

Equally contrasting were the opinions about him. Devotees such as Meir
Amit found him "original, daring, substantive, focused," a commander who
"radiated authority and leadership [with] . . . outstanding instincts that always
hit the mark." But many others, among them Gideon Rafael, saw another side
of him: "Rocking the boat is his favorite tactic, not to overturn it, but to sway it
sufficiently for the helmsman to lose his grip or for some of its unwanted passengers to fall overboard." In private, Eshkol referred to Dayan as Abu Jildi, a
scurrilous one-eyed Arab bandit.

But whether fans or detractors, no one could impugn the richness of his
experience. It began with his service under Britain's legendary guerrilla leader,

Orde Wingate, and then as a commander in the *Haganah*, an occupation that earned him two years in a British prison. Released in 1941, Dayan served as scout for the Allied assault against the Vichy French in Syria and Lebanon, losing his left eye in the engagement and acquiring his trademark black patch. Next, in the 1948 war, he commanded front-line units in Lod, Jerusalem, and the Jordan Valley. Along with his military talents, his political acumen was recognized early, and after the war he became a delegate to the Armistice talks on Rhodes. Four years later, at age thirty-eight, Dayan was chief of staff, pursuing a retaliation policy denounced by most of the world but which made him exceedingly popular in Israel—a popularity only enhanced by his stellar performance in the Suez campaign. Thereafter, as a member first of Mapai and then of Rafi, Dayan was a shrewd, inscrutable politician—close but not beholden to Ben-Gurion, opposed but not implacably to Eshkol. He was "a solo performer," wrote Rafael, "partly respected, partly feared for his political stunts."[40]

Dayan's return to public office had the unique result of assuaging both the military and the citizenry, and of galvanizing the Cabinet for the paramount decisions ahead. "Dayan's appointment was a breath of fresh air," recalled Gedalia Gal, a deputy commander of a paratrooper battalion, "He symbolized a change . . . People were anxious not because we didn't go to war, but because of the government's apparent fear of war."

This impact of this *Dayan ex Machina* was apparent at the new coalition's first meeting, Friday night, which the minister of defense dominated. Israel had two choices, he explained: either accept the blockade as a fait accompli and dig in for permanent defense—not a viable option—or strike the Egyptians at once. He stressed that the country's "one chance for winning this war is in taking the initiative and fighting according to our own designs," sounding optimistic. "If we open with an attack and break through with our tanks to Sinai, they have to fight our war. What's more, we have the chance of maintaining our other fronts with limited forces." His tone then dropped, turning baleful: "God help us though if they hit us first. Not only do we lose our first strike capability . . . but we'll have to fight the war according to their plan...and on territory vital to us."[41]

Dayan spoke as if war were a foregone conclusion, but Eshkol had yet to be convinced. Even if there were no diplomatic solution, Israel still had much to fear from the Soviets, he believed. An Israeli expert on Moscow's foreign policy, Berger Barzilai, a veteran Communist who had been exiled by Stalin to Siberia, had recently told IDF intelligence that the USSR would muster all its influence and power to maintain its Middle East position. Asked pointedly if the Soviets would intervene in a war, Berger replied, "of course." Berger's appraisal seemed to be confirmed by yet another cable from Kosygin to Eshkol, another warning that "if the Israel Government insists on taking upon itself the responsibility for the outbreak of armed confrontation then it will pay the full price of such an action."

Eshkol's hopes still focused on the Americans, on their willingness, if not to challenge the blockade themselves, then to back Israel's effort to break it. In an attempt to verify such willingness, Eshkol again turned to military intelligence, requesting that it document any sign that the White House might support unilateral Israeli action—the so-called "green light." Among the evidence collected were remarks by *Newsweek* columnist Joseph Alsop and the Defense Department's Townsend Hoopes denying any serious U.S. intent to reopen the Straits and urging Israel to do it alone. According to Abe Feinberg, Goldberg had already convinced Johnson that an Israeli preemptive strike was the only possible course. Also included in the file were intercepted communications showing that Arab leaders no longer regarded the convoy idea as a serious threat. After Muhieddin's visit to Washington, intelligence warned, the U.S. would probably support reviving the Armistice regime and stationing UN troops on Israeli territory.

These data spurred yet another, quieter Israeli initiative in Washington. In a private conversation with Walt Rostow, Evron sounded out the administration on a scenario in which an Israeli freighter would test the blockade. Egyptian troops would open fire on the ship and Israel would respond by attacking Sharm al-Sheikh, most likely precipitating war. Would the United States stand by its 1957 commitments to Israel, Evron asked; would it "stand off" the Soviets? The minister suggested that such a plan might better serve U.S. interests *vis-à-vis* both the Arabs and the Russians, while fulfilling Israel's as well. If, as both U.S. and Israeli intelligence predicted, Egypt did not fire at the international convoy, the issue of the blockade would never be decided. To Evron's— and Eshkol's—surprise, Rostow did not reject the suggestion, but passed it on to the president along with a personal caveat: "Whoever is the bigger winner [in the crisis], we are the sure loser."[42]

These developments strengthened Eshkol's determination to coordinate Israel's moves as closely as possible with the United States. "What do we have to do so that they [the Americans] won't say, 'but you promised to wait?" he asked Dayan and Eban late Thursday night. The foreign minister no longer had an answer, admitting that he, too, was despairing of diplomatic options. Asked by reporters that day how long Israel would now wait, Eban had replied, "You can eliminate years and months from your vocabulary . . . Israel will open the Straits alone if we must, with others if we can." Now he told Dayan that "there are two clocks ticking, one in Washington on the convoy and one in Israel on war, neither of them in sync." The observation brought no argument from Dayan, who had long distinguished between the political issue of reopening the Straits and the strategic necessity of assuring Israel's defense. The only question, he emphasized, was: "What does the U.S. intend to do about the Arab military threat?"

That same question faced members of the general staff and the Ministerial Defense Committee the next morning in the Pit. Yariv opened with "This is Egypt's greatest hour," predicting that the combined Arab armies could push

Israel back to the UN Partition lines, or further. His main topic, though, was the Americans. "Our view is that the United States does not intend to open the Tiran blockade forcibly or to take concrete steps in the near future in order to solve the problem between Egypt and Israel. Yet we do think that the U.S. understands our need to act, and we believe that we must act."

Rabin picked up the cue. "We have entered a situation of no retreat. Our objective is to give Nasser a knockout punch. That, I believe, will change the entire order of the Middle East. What's more, if we do it alone—not that I think anybody will help us—it will have a different impact than 1956." He explained that nobody in the general staff wanted war, but destroying Nasser was Israel's only option for survival.

The generals then rushed to present their war plans, beginning with air force commander Motti Hod. He claimed that the IAF knew the location of all Egypt's jets, and would destroy most of them on the ground, flying as many as 1,000 sorties per day. But he also called attention to the enemy's reconnaissance flights over Israel, and warned of the dangers of tarrying. "We're ready to go into operation immediately," Hod concluded, "there's no need to wait, not even 24 hours."

Shaike Gavish followed with maps of the Egyptian deployment in Sinai, traced the buildup from two divisions to six, all squarely dug in. "If we'd attacked Sharm [al-Sheikh] right after the closure, it would have been a picnic," he said.

"The army is ready as never before to repel an Egyptian attack and . . . to wipe out the Egyptian army," declared Arik Sharon. "A generation will pass before Egypt threatens us again."

The briefings ended; now it was the ministers' turn. "What about the bombing of our cities?" Haim Moshe Shapira demanded to know, and Zalman Aran joined him: "What about the loss of our planes?" If the Egyptian forces were already in Sinai, several ministers wondered, why not wait another week or two?

"The best defense for our cities is the destruction of the Egyptian air force," countered Hod, and assured the ministers that "America's [jet] losses in Vietnam are 14 percent—ours will be lower."

More questions were raised and then duly answered—all but one. When Health Minister Yisrael Barzilai asked, "But what if the first strike is so successful that it forces the USSR to intervene?" Hod stood speechless. Rabin tried to rescue him, telling Barzilai that the Soviets were unlikely to get involved militarily, but rather would seek to work with the U.S. on obtaining a cease-fire.

The atmosphere in the Pit—hot, cramped, smoke-laden—was rapidly becoming insufferable, and the generals' patience was strained. Avraham Yoffe leaped to his feet, shouting, "I've been sitting in the Negev with the reserves for 14 days and the feeling all along the line is of our failure to take the initiative. Nasser is getting stronger and we just sit there and do nothing. We have to grab the initiative from Nasser!"

On his heels came Matti Peled, the quartermaster, even more fervent: "The enemy is digging in and getting stronger while our economy weakens and all for a purpose which no one has yet explained!" Then Ariel Sharon: "All this fawning to the Powers, begging for help, undermines our case. If we want to survive here, we have to stand up for our rights."

A veritable melee ensued, a "war of attrition," according to Col. Lior, who was convinced that the generals had planned it all in advance. "They continued pounding on the ministers' heads. I wondered whether the object was to bring them to their knees or to get them to burst out crying."

Into this fray stepped Eshkol. Worn-out, relentlessly harried at home and at every turn disappointed by the Americans, the prime minister had all but reconciled himself to the outbreak of war within forty-eight hours. Still, on the chance that Washington might yet authorize the convoy or at least give Israel its "green light," Eshkol would argue for time. "We will still need Johnson's help and support," he lectured the generals. "I hope we won't need it during the fighting, but we shall certainly need it if we are victorious, in order to protect our gains. I want to make it clear to the president, beyond a shadow of a doubt, that we have not misled him; that we've given the necessary time for any political action designed to prevent the war. Two days more or less won't sway the outcome!"

Eshkol went on, angry now, reminding Sharon that "all the fawning to the Powers" had yielded the arms with which Israel could now defend himself, and Peled, of the need for friends once the fighting had stopped. "We have to ask ourselves whether we, a country of two million, can afford to go to war every ten years, can afford to thumb its nose at the United States and the world." He concluded, finally, on a typically somber note: "Nothing will be settled by a military victory. The Arabs will still be here."[43]

Conspicuously silent throughout the fracas was Moshe Dayan. Brooding, he resented what he viewed as the government's interference in his exclusive purview as defense minister, informing Lior that "I oppose decisions made on majority vote on matters of security." Yet, no sooner had the Pit meeting concluded then he conferred separately with Eshkol, Eban, and Allon; later, Rabin and Herzog joined them as well. The Cabinet should meet tomorrow, Sunday, Dayan told them, and authorize the army to act. The war would begin the next day at sunrise. Allon proposed taking the Suez Canal and using it as a bargaining chip in the negotiations over Tiran, but Dayan objected. Important foreign interests were vested in the Canal, and Israel could not afford to alienate them. He similarly rejected Allon's suggestion that Israel conquer Gaza. The 20-mile Strip would surrender without a shot, Dayan predicted, the minute Sinai fell.

Eshkol no longer resisted Dayan's dictate, and even Eban seemed willing to bend. The change in the foreign minister's heart had been gradual, wrought first by reports of Johnson's inability to mount the Regatta scheme, and then by indications that Washington no longer looked unfavorably on Israeli preemption. Much meaning was read into an off-the-cuff remark made by Secretary of State Rusk who, when asked whether the U.S. would continue restraining Israel, replied, "I don't think it's our business to restrain anyone." Then, through a confidential source, Eban received a message from Abe Fortas. The justice, furious with Rusk for "fiddling while Israel burned," appeared to be giving a go-ahead:

> If Israel had acted alone without exhausting political factors, it would have made a catastrophic error. It would then have been almost impossible for the United States to help Israel and the ensuing relationship would have been tense. The war might be long and costly if it breaks out. But Israel should not criticize Eshkol and Eban. The Israelis should realize that their restraint and well-considered procedures would now have a decisive influence when the United States comes to consider the measure of its involvement.

Even "greener" was the light that Arthur Goldberg seemed to be giving Israel. "You must understand that you stand alone and you have to know the consequences," he imparted to Gideon Rafael, explaining that Regatta was dead and that only Israel could meet the existential threat Nasser now posed. American and world opinion would favor Israel, Goldberg concluded, especially if the Arabs were to fire first. "I understand that if you do act alone you will know how to act."[44]

Such signals had a decisive impact on Eban; Dayan, however, had little time for them. He was already deep into the strategy of the war itself, conferring with the generals. "We'll have no longer than 72 hours in which to act," he told them Saturday night in the Pit. "Our success, therefore, will be judged not on the number of Egyptian tanks we destroy in that time, but on the size of the territory we'll seize." That territory would include all of the Sinai Peninsula, short of Gaza and the Canal. Rabin was also against taking Sharm al-Sheikh—the objective was too far away, too complicated logistically—but Dayan insisted it be included. Like Gaza, the Straits of Tiran would also fall to Israeli control, he reckoned, once Egypt's army collapsed. The myth of 1956—that the Egyptian army had not been defeated but had merely withdrawn from the field—would be smashed.

The invasion of Sinai, to begin shortly after the air offensive, would follow three axes: a thrust into northern Sinai, in the Rafah area, and two in the peninsula's center. In preparation for that launch, the army would engage in various acts of deception. The IAF would make several deep reconnaissance probes down the Gulf of Aqaba, and the navy would haul a number of landing craft overland from the Mediterranean to Eilat, leading Egypt to believe that the Israeli attack would come in the south of Sinai, rather than in the north and the center. Formations of armor and men would be pulled back from the border—later to return, surreptitiously—and photographs published of thousands of reservists on leave. The beaches, confirmed British Ambassador Michael Hadow, were "crowded as

Blackpool in the holiday season." Rather devilishly, Dayan told reporters that day that he was open to a negotiated solution, that peace should be given every chance. "The day of the firebrand in the Israeli Defense Forces is over," Hadow added. "They are now preparing for the long haul."[45]

No effort would be spared to ensure the success of the operation, but that success hinged not only on Egypt's front, but also on Syria and Jordan's. "If the Jordanians attack Eilat, in Jerusalem or in the Tel Aviv area, all of our plans will be undermined," Dayan warned the generals, "We cannot reach al-'Arish when we're battling in Jerusalem." Israel would adopt a position of "total passivity" on both the eastern and northern fronts, even if its border settlements were shelled.

No fighting with Syria and Jordan—this was the message that Dayan impressed on his commanders as he left the general staff for a tour of the field. "Get used to the idea, this is a war against Egypt," he told David "Dado" Elazar, chief of the Northern Command.

Both men were observing the Syrian front from Kibbutz Dan, eighteen miles from Kfar HaNassi, where two Israelis and a Palestinian guerrilla had been killed in a clash the previous day. IDF intelligence had warned of worse: Within an hour of any Israeli attack on Egypt, the Syrians would respond with infantry and armored thrusts into northern Galilee and the shelling of Israeli settlements and cities. To this end, Syrian forces had reportedly massed in an offensive deposition atop the Golan. Immense cargoes of Soviet ammunition had been spied arriving in Syrian ports.

Elazar had an array of contingency plans for dealing with Syria, from a limited assault on the Golan ridge—Operation Marmalade (*Merkahat*)—to Operation Pincers (*Melkahayim*) for conquering the entire Heights. Operation Hammer (*Makevet*) represented a compromise between the two. Feigning an attack in the Golan center, Israeli columns would scale the northern and southern ends of the Heights, capture the Jordan headwaters, and destroy Syria's army.

Hammer would be launched simultaneously with Focus in order to preempt the Syrian attack and further deter the Jordanians—so Elazar advised. "If there's a war against Egypt, there'll be war here as well," he reasoned. "Syria will leap in five or six hours after the fighting starts. We won't have to provoke them." Rabin approved the plan in principle, but refused to earmark the forces necessary to implement it, particularly helicopters, virtually all of which were reserved for the south. He also rejected Elazar's analysis of Syria's determination to fight under any circumstances. If Egypt were swiftly defeated, Rabin believed, Syria would soon retire.

Elazar's remaining hope was Dayan. "We must ensure that, if war breaks out, it doesn't end on the Green [Armistice] Line," he told the defense minister during his visit to Dan. "If we defend ourselves from the valley below, our situation will be terrible." He pointed at the fortified Syrian village of Za'ura, explaining how its capture would serve as a buffer between the Golan and the settlements, as well as a springboard for penetrating the Heights.

But Dayan's response was categorically negative. "You people up here have to sit tight and hold out," he ordered Elazar. While willing to approve a quick advance of troops into the DZ's, up to the international border, Dayan rejected any operation that would precipitate war with Syria.

The scene was reenacted at Central Command, with Gen. Uzi Narkiss. Like many soldiers of his generation, Narkiss regretted Israel's inability to seize the West Bank and Jerusalem in 1948. Rehavam Ze'evi, a friend and contemporary of Narkiss, recalled how "we all dreamed of completing the War of Independence and freeing the Land of Israel to the East. Only by seizing the highlands held by Jordan could we guarantee the survival of the western plains. That dream guided all of us, including Rabin, throughout our military planning."

Central Command had "drawers full" of such plans. Most called for counterattacks against Arab attempts to drive across Israel at its narrowest and cut the country in two, or to isolate West Jerusalem. The best known of the contingencies, code-named Whip (*Pargol*), involved a forty-eight-hour operation to knock out Jordanian artillery concentrations on the West Bank and lay siege to East Jerusalem. Rabin assigned Whip an almost paramount priority. "Even if it means the fall of northern settlements, we must defend ourselves against [attack from] the West Bank," he said.

Yet, when Narkiss met Dayan in the Jerusalem hills, neither Whip, nor even less ambitious plans received approval. "You must not do anything to entangle Israel with the Jordanians," Dayan ordered. "You mustn't bother the general staff with requests for help."

"And if the Jordanians attack us without provocation and take Mount Scopus?"

"In that case, bite your lip and hold the line," came Dayan's reply. "Within a week we'll get to the Canal and to Sharm al-Sheikh, then the whole IDF will come here and get you out of trouble."[46]

That Saturday had been long and arduous for Dayan, yet the day was far from over. Still ahead was another conference with Eshkol at his private apartment in Jerusalem.

The prime minister had just been informed that the IDF was only six jets short of the optimal number, but in all other areas—tanks, guns, half-tracks—was fully equipped for war. The report brought him only limited solace, though, as dismal news arrived from Paris. De Gaulle, who had earlier threatened to boycott arms sales to whichever country began hostilities in the Middle East, had banned all weapons for Israel. "You have condemned us as if we had already fired the first shot," Ambassador Eytan had remonstrated. "How can you levy an embargo on Israel without knowing in advance who will start the war?" But his protests were useless. Doubtful of Israel's ability to defeat the Arabs, eager to restore France's historic links with the Muslim world, De Gaulle had made up his mind, and brusquely rebuffed Eytan: "My dear sir, I know only one thing—that you also don't know what your government will decide."[47]

Now, at his home late on Saturday night, Eshkol waited for the entry of Dayan and Eban, of Levavi, Herzog, and Yadin—all gathered to hear the last word from Amit and Harman, freshly returned from Washington. "Perhaps the *jungermen* ('young men' in Yiddish) will bring back some unexpected news?" Eshkol wondered aloud to his wife, Miriam. "It's important that the world knows that we waited long enough. I'm sure that we'll win, but it will be a costly war. How long will they let us fight? If it goes well for us, the Russians will surely put the pressure on, and de Gaulle and others will demand a cease-fire."

"The tension was unbearable," wrote Col. Lior, who was also invited to record the meeting. If Amit and Harman recommended war, then no other considerations—not the French boycott, not the Soviet warnings—would stop Israel from acting. The two came in at close to midnight and delivered a uniform message. The United States could not mount the convoy operation—it was a nonstarter—nor would it cooperate with Israel militarily. "If we start a war and win—everyone will be with us. If we don't win, it's going to be tough," Amit admonished, but quickly added: "It is my impression that the Americans will bless any action that succeeds in sticking it to Nasser." Both he and Harman appeared to be advocating immediate preemption, but they then surprised their listeners by suggesting that Israel wait another week and then send a ship through Tiran. They had in mind the *Dolphin*, an Israeli freighter docked in Masawa, Ethiopia, and filled with $9 million worth of oil.

Dayan, silent until now, suddenly exploded. "The minute we send a ship through the Straits the Egyptians will know that we're about to attack. They'll shoot us first . . . and we'll loose the Land of Israel. It's total lunacy to wait!"

Dumbstruck by this outburst, Amit and Harman retracted their proposal. From that moment until the meeting's end near dawn, Dayan steered the conversation where he wanted it, toward the Cabinet session to be held later that morning, and to the offensive he was sure would be approved. "In one or two hours the air force will have achieved its major objectives, as will the land forces on the first day," he estimated. "By the second day we'll be on our way to the Canal. Egypt won't have an air force for at least a half a year."[48]

Within two days of joining the government, Dayan had seized control over much of Israel's decision making, guiding it ineluctably toward war. The defense minister was mistaken, though, if he thought that the Cabinet would rubberstamp his conclusions. Gathering at 8:15 on Sunday morning, the ministers first heard a drawn-out analysis of the diplomatic situation from Abba Eban. This noted the softening of Johnson's opposition to a military solution, but also stressed the president's insistence that Nasser fire the first shot, preferably at an Israeli boat. Absent that, the administration was pressing forward with the convoy project, in spite of disappointing reactions from congressmen and the maritime states.

Eban had scarcely finished his survey of American policy when another letter arrived from Johnson. This, too, underscored America's commitment to

Israel's security and to freedom of the seas—problems with the convoy notwithstanding. He noted that "We have completely and fully exchanged views with Gen. Amit," intimating an openness to preemptive action. But that impression was quickly erased by Johnson's conclusion: "I must emphasize the necessity for Israel not to make itself responsible for the initiation of hostilities. Israel will not be alone unless it decides to go it alone. We cannot imagine that it will make this decision."

It fell to Yariv, then, to convince the ministers that Israel had to act and act at once, in spite of Johnson's cautions. The picture he painted of Israel's security situation was the most lurid and terrifying yet: Jordanian forces poised at Jerusalem and at Israel's wasplike waist; Egyptian formations deployed to take Eilat, massively fortified at Rafah, and now stationed in the West Bank as well; the Syrians dug in on the Heights and actively preparing to descend them. Troops and tanks and planes from around the Arab world were converging for a united assault against Israel's existence, secure in Soviet support.

Dayan spoke next, emphasizing the need to move at once, before the combined Arab forces grew stronger yet, while there was still a semblance of surprise. "Nasser must fulfill the process he started," he stated, "We must do what he wants us to do." He predicted the destruction of hundreds of enemy planes— "It's our only chance to win, to wage this war our way"—followed by a bitter diplomatic battle.

Then came Eshkol's turn. The man who had resisted immeasurable pressures over the past three weeks, who had been lambasted and isolated and scorned, at last had the final word. "I'm convinced that today we must give the order to the IDF to choose the time and the manner to act."

Still, objections were raised. Haim Moshe Shapira quoted Ben-Gurion saying that Israel could never go to war without an ally. "Then let Ben-Gurion go and find us an ally," Dayan cut him off. "I'm not sure we'll still be alive!" To Shapira's defense came the religious affairs minister, Zorach Warhaftig. Short, almost dwarfish, he was endowed with a towering legal mind and a moral conviction that transcended his concern for his three sons serving in the army. Warhaftig demanded that Israel send a ship through the Straits to establish a *casus belli*. "Better that one or two of our sailors get killed than that Israel get blamed for starting the war," he later explained. "I had no doubts about victory. It was the day after victory that worried me."

But the threat of international condemnation failed to impress what had become the majority of ministers. Yigal Allon seemed to speak to them when he brushed aside Warhaftig's fears. "They will condemn us," he predicted, "and we will survive."

There remained only to take a vote. Twelve were in favor of war now, and only two opposed. The decision, drafted by Dayan, was short, understated, and devoid of any sentiment:

After hearing reports on the military and diplomatic situation from the prime minister, the defense minister, the chief of staff and the head of IDF intelligence, the Government has determined that the armies of Egypt, Syria, and Jordan are deployed for a multi-front attack that threatens Israel's existence. It is therefore decided to launch a military strike aimed at liberating Israel from encirclement and preventing the impending assault by the United Arab Command. [49]

The timing of the operation was to be left to Dayan and Rabin. Both were eager to begin as soon as possible, before Iraqi troops entered Jordan and Egyptian commandos crossed the West Bank. H-hour was thus set for the following morning, between 7:00 and 7:30, Monday, June 5, 1967.

Arab World Resurgent

"We must expect the enemy to strike a blow within 48 to 72 hours, by June 5 at the latest." So Nasser told the officers gathered at Supreme Headquarters on June 2. The meeting had first been addressed by Military Intelligence Chief Sadiq, who showed that the IDF had completed its mobilization and deployment. Dayan's appointment as defense minister, coupled with reports of Israeli aircraft carrying out deep reconnaissance flights over Sinai, indicated a new activism. Israel, it was pointed out, had two choices: either accept the new status quo or attack. The latter option seemed likelier as Iraqi troops prepared to enter Jordan. Israel had always regarded the presence of such troops as a *casus belli*, and would surely act at once. Should Egypt, then, strike first?

A debate, at times stentorian, broke out between Sadiq and Sidqi Mahmud, the former recommending that Egyptian planes be pulled back from forward bases in Sinai, vulnerable to surprise attack. The air commander balked at the idea, shouting, "I know my business, Sadiq! Abandoning the forward bases will ruin the pilots' morale!" He still opposed waiting for Israel to land the first blow. "We will lose between 15 and 20 percent of our planes," he forecast. "We will be crippled." Now it was Nasser's turn to object, stepping in to explain that Egypt could not risk alienating world opinion by assaulting Israel, or jeopardize its newfound rapport with France. There were also the beginnings of a dialogue with the United States, and Muhieddin's scheduled visit to Washington. Israel had suffered a serious strategic defeat, but that, too, would be forfeited if Egypt started the war, Nasser reasoned. "You will still have 80 to 90 percent of your planes," he reassured Sidqi Mahmud. "With those, how many losses can you cause the enemy?" The commander replied: "Sixty or 70 percent."[50]

Nasser seemed to be of two irreconcilable minds on the crisis. The first held that, backed into a corner, Israel had to lash out in a matter of days, striking Egypt's air force or oil refineries at Suez. But then he also sensed that war might be averted and diplomatic solution achieved, with Egypt its main beneficiary. Recognition would be obtained for the new status quo in Sinai, and substantial financial aid from the U.S. and the Arab states. Asked by his former Free Officer colleagues when Israel would attack, Nasser cavalierly replied "six to eight months," if at all. The Israelis would never move without permission from the Americans, he claimed, and the Americans had been stymied by the Soviets. The two minds would find expression in separate interviews Nasser granted to the British press on June 3. In one, he claimed that war was imminent, and in the other, that the crisis had already passed.[51]

Yet Nasser was not alone in believing that Israel had already been beaten and a bloodless victory won. "Few diplomatic observers seem to appreciate that there is the danger of a desperate Israeli attack or to watch or understand what is happening inside Israel," R. M. Tesh, Canada's ambassador in Cairo, related. "It is accepted that Nasser has brought off a very clever coup and the Russians cancel out the Americans." Though blackouts and air raid drills continued to be conducted, hospital beds reserved and military youth clubs formed, Egypt's mood was steadily returning to normal. Emergency regulations were eased along with restrictions on internal travel. Even tourism appeared to be up. Ambassador El Kony at the UN may have protested "colonial policies of 19th century warship diplomacy" and threatened to "take all necessary measures to stop aggression against Egypt's territorial waters," but the USS *Intrepid* sailed unimpeded through the Suez Canal, escorted by Egyptian ships and greeted by thousands of villagers. "If we have been able to restore conditions to what they were before 1956, God will surely help us to restore them to what they were in 1948," Nasser exulted before the National Assembly. "We are now ready to confront Israel . . . The issue now at hand is not the Gulf of Aqaba, the Straits of Tiran or the withdrawal of UNEF, but the . . . aggression which took place in Palestine . . . with the collaboration of Britain and the United States."[52]

Was a war still pending or was it already won? The emergence of that question deepened the confusion already rampant on the Sinai front. Thousands of reservists continued to arrive without equipment or food or a sense of either place or purpose. A report prepared by the army's planning wing concluded that Egypt needed another six months at least to shore up its Sinai defenses for battle, but the recommendation went unheeded and perhaps even unread. Instead, chaos reigned. Gen. Tawfiq 'Abd al-Nabi, formerly the Egyptian military attaché in Karachi, arrived in Sinai to take command of an antitank brigade only to find that he had no artillery, no mortars, and only seven tanks borrowed from another unit. His soldiers, moreover, knew nothing of antitank warfare.

Dozens of units had been exhausted, their vehicles worn out, transferring back and forth across the desert. Tanks and troops were first moved to Kuntilla, there to reinforce Shazli's unit, and then to Gaza, on Nasser's personal order. The more experienced generals viewed these peregrinations with horror. Not only was the army's strength being wasted, but the deployment based on the Conqueror plan had all but unraveled. The sole voice of protest, though, was 'Amer's. "This is a substantive departure from our plan," he reminded Nasser.

"Gaza has supreme political and propaganda value," the president replied. "What will the Arabs say about me if I promise them to restore Palestine and then I lose Gaza and al-'Arish?"

But 'Amer demurred. "And what will they say if we lose the war entirely?" he retorted, and purportedly marched off in a huff.[53]

If Nasser was divided over whether Israel would or would not attack, 'Amer remained committed to an Egyptian offensive along the lines of the Lion plan. He still hoped to launch an air and ground offensive in the Negev, and entrusted the Shazli Force with blocking any Israeli countermove into Sinai. "Between me and Moshe Dayan there is a feud going back to the Tripartite War," he told Gen. Murtagi, "This is my opportunity to teach him a lesson he won't forget and to destroy the Israeli army." To Sidqi Mahmud he declared, "Forget your 20 percent [losses] and fight Israel!" Preparing for that fight, 'Amer continued to shift troops around—the 124th and 125th reserve brigades, for example, moved four times in ten days—and to ignore intelligence reports showing Israeli forces concentrating in northern and central Sinai, and not in the south, as assumed.[54]

But 'Amer was too fixed in his plans for the coming fight, and absorbed in the effort to expand his power yet further. Throughout the first days in June, he assiduously altered the army's structure in Sinai, dividing the peninsula into an Eastern and Western Command, a Canal Command, a Forward and a Field Command. Orders from Supreme Headquarters had to pass through the hands of no less than six senior officers before reaching the field. These positions were again filled with 'Amer's cronies, military bureaucrats with little if any combat experience and responsible directly to him. Observing these changes, the Israelis were thrilled. "He created five new layers of command and with people who'd never fought," Shaike Gavish remembered. "We'd be halfway to Suez before they'd even get an order approved."

But 'Amer seemed oblivious to these pitfalls. He remained confident in his army and particularly in his air force. "Maybe this war will be the Jews' chance, for Israel and Rabin, to try their might against ours and discover that all they wrote on 1956 and the conquest of Sinai was nothing more than a collection of nonsense," he told a briefing of pilots in Sinai. In a phone conversation with Shuqayri on June 4, he expressed the hope "that soon we'll be able to take the initiative and rid ourselves of Israel once and for all."

The following day, the field marshal planned to personally inspect his forward positions in Sinai, and in preparation for that review, issued his second war order. Summarized were the week's events—the Egypt-Jordanian pact, the dispatch of Iraqi forces to Jordan, Israel's efforts, thwarted by the Soviets, to obtain American support for aggression. Pressured by the exorbitant cost of mobilization, facing intolerable threats to its eastern front, Israel would attack in two weeks, 'Amer had determined, and had issued his orders accordingly. "Our goal is the destruction of the enemy's main armed forces. Our army can accomplish that with the immense capabilities at its disposal." He called on the army to show discipline and bravery, "to fight with the utmost aggressiveness." The battle, he concluded, was not just for Egypt but for the entire Arab nation. "In your hands is the honor of the armed forces and of the Arab nation. I am assured and confident of victory. Allah strengthen your hand and preserve you."[55]

Neither 'Amer nor Nasser had any doubt now about the army's ability to defend the country against Israel. Defeating it, however, required an all-Arab effort. As much as Dayan's strategy rested on keeping Syria and Jordan out of the war, Egypt's was contingent on enlisting them.

The prospects for Jordan seemed sanguine. There, as in Egypt, life continued at a normal pace in spite of emergency blood drives, Nasserist demonstrations, and the army's frenetic preparations for war. Gen. 'Abd al-Mun'im Riyad, now the commander of the Jordanian army and the Egyptian commandos in Jordan, worked quickly to complete his survey of the West Bank's defenses. These were dictated not only by the vulnerability of the 300-mile border with Israel, but also by the political need of assuaging the Palestinians. "The loss of a single Palestinian village to the Israelis would have serious and violent repercussions," noted an official history of the Hashemite army, "not only in Jordan, but throughout the Arab World." Thus, instead of concentrating forces in key strategic areas, nine of Jordan's eleven brigades were spread out in villages and towns where the people could see them. Once war came, the dispersed units would converge on vital axes to parry any Israeli thrusts or, failing that, fall back to the high ground overlooking the Jordan Valley.

Hussein personally approved Riyad's plans, and the army's generals raised no objection. The lone voice of dissent came from Brig. Gen. 'Atif al-Majali, the senior and widely venerated chief of operations, who urged that all of Jordan's forces be deployed in Jerusalem. "He who controls Jerusalem, controls the West Bank," al-Majali said, but Riyad overrode him. Only one infantry brigade, the Imam 'Ali, was moved up to Jerusalem, reinforcing the 27th king Talal Brigade already there, with ammunition to last for a month. The 40th and the 60th Armored Brigades, meanwhile, took up positions in the Jordan Valley, from which they could advance into either the West Bank or Jerusalem, as combat needs determined. With its superior command and training, the army was expected to hold the line, at least, until reinforcements arrived from other Arab countries, principally Iraq.[56]

But the army was not content with merely holding its line. Anticipating victory, military planners revived Operation Tariq (after the famed eighth-century Arab General, Tariq ibn Ziyad, for whom Gibraltar is named), an old plan for cutting off Jewish Jerusalem and using it as leverage against any Israeli conquests in the West Bank. With the opening of battle, a four-pronged assault would be launched on Israeli positions north and south of Jerusalem—on

Mount Scopus, Government House ridge, and around the Latrun corridor. Jordanian forces were to "destroy all buildings and kill everyone present" in these areas, including civilians. Jordanian planes and artillery would bomb Israeli airports as well.

Not even Hussein, better known for his temperance, resisted the fervor. On June 4, after receiving word from Nasser that Israel was liable to strike within forty-eight hours, the king summoned non-Arab ambassadors and warned them against becoming involved in the fighting. "Leave us alone with the Israelis," he said. "Those who stand by us we will never forget. Those who stand with Israel are our enemies and they can forget any friendship they ever had here."[57]

While Egypt and Jordan cooperated closely in preparing for war, Syria pursued its own inscrutable path. Ignoring their defense treaty with Egypt, Syrian leaders refused to coordinate their policies with Cairo. They agreed to host Iraqi forces—the first contingent, fifty tanks, arrived in Aleppo on June 1—but declined an offer of Egyptian planes. The frosty state of Syrian-Egyptian relations was then further chilled by the thawing of those between Nasser and Hussein. "We shall not change our attitude towards Jordan and its King Hussein so long as he takes his salary from his masters in Washington," declared Gen. Mustafa Tlas. The official newspaper *Al-Ba'th* featured photographs of Hussein, Nasser, and Shuqayri, and under them the banner, "The Three Treasonous Agents." First Mahmoud Riad and then Zakkariya Muhieddin were dispatched to Damascus on appeasing missions, but neither proved successful. 'Amer complained to his staff that "Syria's present position is not encouraging, and that has been made clear by the treaty with Jordan . . . They received Muhieddin poorly, and have turned down our military requests."[58]

In contrast to Egypt and Jordan, Syria looked very much like a country on the brink of war. Emergency regulations were enacted and strictly enforced; heavily armed detachments guarded every bridge and utility, and militiamen roamed the streets. The vigilance was more than just a show. The army was readying to move the minute either side, the Egyptians or the Israelis, attacked. Shelving its plans for the defense of the Golan Heights—Operation Holy War (*Jihad*)—the Syrians prepared to implement Victory (*Nasr*), an offensive operation. As designed by the Soviets, Victory called for a forty-mile blitzkrieg by three expanded divisions. After breaking through the Israeli defenses at Kibbutz Mishmar HaYarden, these forces would take the cities of Tiberias and Safad, together with the settlements of the Dan region, then regroup for the conquest of Afula, Haifa, and Nazareth.

The units designated to take part in Victory began assembling on the night of May 24. Troops from the 35th Division reinforced the positions at Banias and Tel 'Azzaziat, above the Golan escarpment. In Quneitra, the largest city on the Golan, the requisite units began assembling—three infantry, two artillery, and two tank brigades. Leading the attack would be two crack brigades, the 123rd and the 80th. Finally, on June 3, Syrian infantrymen began digging forward trenches for the breakthrough. Antipersonnel obstacles were removed along the sources of the Jordan, and rubber boats moved up to facilitate the crossing. The operation was to be concluded in six days.[59]

Whether the army was capable of carrying out such an operation was a question never asked. The officer corps had been repeatedly purged, those ousted replaced by some 2,000 Ba'thist-indoctrinated 'educators.' "I worked as a teacher in the staff college," remembered Ibrahim Isma'il Khahya who, in 1966, became commander of the 8th Infantry Brigade. "My officers were mostly teachers, too. They weren't ready for war." The head of intelligence for the Golan district, Col. Nash'at Habash, had been kicked out and replaced by a mere captain, brother of a high-ranking Ba'th official. Ahmad Suweidani, the former military attaché in Beijing, had been boosted from colonel to lieutenant general and chief of staff. Though Syria's 250 tanks and 250 artillery pieces were generally of more recent vintage than Israel's, their maintenance was minimal. Supply, too, could be erratic; deprived of food, front-line troops had been known to desert their posts. The air force was particularly substandard. An internal army report rated only 45 percent of Syria's pilots as "good," 32 percent as "average,'" and the remainder "below average." Only thirty-four of the forty-two jets at the Dmair and Saiqal airfields were operational.

Yet, within the ranks, morale had never been higher. Capt. Muhammad 'Ammar, an infantry officer serving in the fortress of Tel Fakhr, recalled: "We thought we were stronger, that we could cling to our land, and that the Golan was impenetrable. We were especially heartened by the unity between Syria, Egypt, and Jordan." Another captain, Marwan Hamdan al-Khuli, heard that "we were much stronger and would defeat the enemy easily. We awaited the day of liberation." Members of the general staff were no less confident. "If hostilities break out," Tlas calculated, "the UAR and Syria can destroy Israel in four days at most."[60]

In spite of the bitter differences between them, the divisions of opinion in each, Arab nations were united as at no time in their postcolonial history. There could now be no doubt: An Arab world existed and could act. This was the moment that so many in that world had yearned for since well before 1948. Retribution would be exacted not only from Israel but from the West that had created it to perpetuate a centuries-old oppression. Algerian Prime Minister Houari Boumedienne boasted: "The freedom of the homeland will be completed by the destruction of the Zionist entity and the expulsion of the Americans and the British from the region." Yemen's Foreign Minister Salam agreed: "We want war. War is the only way to settle the problem of Israel. The Arabs are ready." Even the most outspoken moderates had been radicalized. "You must be mad," Prime Minister Jum'a told Burns in Amman, "not a single Arab, no matter how much he might secretly want to see Nasser's decline, wants to see it caused by the Straits of Tiran." Rashid Karame, a nationalist Lebanese leader, told Porter how "the Arabs can no longer bear the shame of Israel and have developed total unity on the issue . . . In the end, the Arabs will triumph."

Converging on Sinai were military contingents from countries that only days before had regarded Egypt as a mortal enemy, from Morocco and Libya, Saudi Arabia and Tunisia. Even the Syrians finally relented and agreed to send a brigade to fight alongside the Iraqis in Jordan. Combined, the Arab armies could field 900 combat aircraft, over 5,000 tanks, and a half million men. Added to this was immense political might. Arab oil producers had agreed to boycott any countries that assisted Israel, to nationalize their refineries and even destroy their pipelines. The Suez Canal, warned Nasser, could be blocked. Arabs across North Africa, throughout the Fertile Crescent and the Gulf, felt bound by a single, exalted effort, as expressed by President 'Aref of Iraq: "Our goal is clear—to wipe Israel off the face of the map. We shall, God willing, meet in Tel Aviv and Haifa."[61]

The Shortest Night

The night of June 3–4, found the president of the United States in New York, attending a Democratic party fundraiser. Hounded by Robert Kennedy for the party's leadership, Johnson was preoccupied with domestic politics and had spent much of the previous week at his Texas ranch conferring with senior advisers. But not even the question of his own long-term political fate could obscure the international calamity looming directly ahead.

The chances for averting that calamity now seemed exceedingly remote. Two days before, in a meeting with senior British officials in Washington, Rusk and McNamara had virtually admitted that Regatta was dead. Congress's "passionate aversion" to the concept, coupled with the maritime nations' refusal to join, militated against any launch in the near future, they said. Contingency planning had ground to a halt, for fear of leaks. And even if the United States issued the declaration, there was no way of "putting teeth in it." According to CIA estimates, the Egyptians were almost certain to fire on any American ship attempting to ply the Straits, while the Joint Chiefs of Staff reported that the U.S. forces east of Suez lacked the firepower necessary to repel a major Egyptian attack. Such conclusions appeared particularly grim in light of the passage of ten Soviet warships through the Dardanelles and into the eastern Mediterranean. Soviet vessels were now shadowing the 6th Fleet, waiting to appear as Nasser's savior from a vile and warlike West.[62]

Yet, in spite of what Saunders called the "parade of horribles" surrounding Regatta, key officials still supported the plan, the Rostows in particular. Walter continued to view free passage as a "naked principle" which the United States was duty-bound to uphold, while Eugene believed that the convoy could work, "provided we are prepared to show some muscle," that Nasser could be vanquished "by a show of diplomatic strength and a hint of steel." They were anxious to keep pressing the maritime nations to sign the declaration, watering down its text to expunge any connection between the Straits issue and Israel. They speculated whether oil might still be shipped to Israel under foreign flags or whether the blockade applied to the entire Straits or only to its main—the so-called Enterprise—channel.

While the Rostows speculated, Johnson was slowly moving away from the convoy concept. He focused instead on the possibility of unilateral Israeli action of the sort described in the "Evron scenario." Officials in the Defense Department strongly favored the option of "putting Israel out front," as they called it, confident that the Israelis would beat Nasser and save America a direct confrontation with both the Arabs and the Soviets. The scenario in any case appeared imminent. The CIA had learned of the Israeli freighter *Dolphin*, berthed in Masawa but ready to sail within seventy-two hours with its cargo of oil and its crew of disguised IDF personnel. Passing through the Straits, the ship was sure to be fired upon, providing the Israelis with the pretext they needed to strike. The chances that Israel would require American assistance in the ensuing combat were, according to agency estimates, slim.[63]

The dangers of such a gamble were manifest, but no less so than its benefits. "If Israel won its own battle, the Africans and Asians who sympathize with Israel . . . would simply conclude that Nasser had overreached himself," intelligence sources surmised. "But in a joint Western action, their sympathies would be offset by resentment at European powers again deciding the fate of other states." The USSR, moreover, was seen as less likely to intervene if Israel acted alone than if the U.S. stepped in on Israel's behalf. Harold Saunders at the NSC pointed out that "holding Israel back" entailed making a long-lasting commitment to Israeli security, while forcing the blockade meant reversing twenty years of American evenhandedness, fully identifying with Zionism and abandoning Arab moderates to Nasser. "The only other choice is to let the Israelis do this job themselves," he concluded. "We ought to consider admitting that we have failed and allow fighting to ensue."

Israel, Johnson believed, would move in two to three days, and complete the war in ten, at the very most. While the U.S. might back Israel diplomatically, there would be no collusion such as that between Israel and the Anglo-French expedition in Suez, no major military aid for the Jewish state. Rather, as Walt Rostow phrased it, Israel would move "like a sheriff in High Noon," alone, employing the force "necessary to achieve not merely self-respect but respect in the region." Johnson had already recommended that his staff start thinking of the postwar settlement. Thought should be given as to whether Nasser was "a Hitler . . . determined to crush Israel once and for all . . . or a shrewd operator trying to strike a deal"—again, Rostow's words—and whether a compromise could be reached on borders and refugee resettlement.

With a deeper sense of defeat, and less optimism, Dean Rusk had reached the same conclusions. The Israelis, he suspected, knew that Regatta had failed— "If any other country ever penetrated the American government the way they did, we would probably break relations with them"—and had resolved to act themselves. "It will do no good to ask Israel simply to accept the present status quo in the Straits because Israel will fight and we could not restrain her," he admitted to his ambassadors in Arab capitals. At the same time, he wrote, "We cannot throw up our hands and say let them fight while we try to remain neutral." The secretary of state summarized the history of America's Middle East policy—its support for the territorial integrity and independence of every state in the region, its protection of Egypt from Israel, Britain, and France, and its protection of the pro-Western Arab states from Egypt. The impossibility of sustaining this balancing act, though, had now been brutally exposed. "The 'Holy War' psychology of the Arab world is matched by the apocalyptic psychology within Israel . . . Each side appears to look with relative equanimity upon the prospect of major hostilities and each side apparently is confident of success . . . [S]omeone is making a major miscalculation."

Fears of that miscalculation—and its outcome—no doubt accompanied Johnson to his reception in New York. An earnest desire to help Israel in its plight, to aid America's allies in the Arab world, and to prevent a war that could well snowball into global dimensions had been frustrated by another war in Southeast Asia and a Western world unwilling to act. Given his constraints, Johnson felt that he had done his best, exhausting all possible options. With sadness more than surprise, he received the information whispered to him during dinner by Abe Feinberg, "Mr. President, it can't be held any longer. It's going to happen within the next twenty-four hours." [64]

In Cairo, Nasser spoke at a ceremony marking Iraq's accession to the Egypt-Jordan defense treaty—an event that, according to Rusk, "livened up an otherwise quiet Sunday." Enthusiasm was indeed generated when the president took the opportunity to restate Egypt's claim to Tiran. He rejected any attempt to declare the Straits international, and swore to use force against any ship or ships that dared to challenge the blockade.

Gen. Murtagi meanwhile made a note to meet with 'Amer the next morning to discuss the still-critical shortages of supplies and officers. The general had just issued his own order to Egypt's fighters, exhorting them to "reconquer the stolen land with . . . the strength of your arms and your united faith," and reminding them that "the eyes of the whole world are on you in your glorious war against Israeli aggression." But Murtagi himself was on vacation in Isma'iliya that evening, while 'Amer attended an all-night party in Cairo. Nasser's whereabouts were unknown. Sidqi Mahmud was at his daughter's wedding; at dawn, he would join 'Amer and a high-ranking Iraqi delegation for an inspection of the front. Much of the general staff had traveled to Bir al-Thamada airfield, there to await the field marshal's landing.

"The commander of the [Sinai] front wasn't in place and the army's commander wasn't in place, and neither were their subordinates," Maj. Gen. 'Abd al-Hamid al-Dugheidi, chief of the air force in Sinai, bemoaned. "It was the first war of its kind, where all the commanders were far from their commands." No commander, certainly, was present after midnight when the first reports arrived of intensified Israeli activity around Gaza and Rafah, and of tanks converging on the central sector.[65]

Gen. Rikhye, by contrast, was convinced that war would break out the next day. In Cairo arranging the evacuation of UNEF, he had read Murtagi's order—"a clarion call for attack"—and immediately ordered a plane back to Gaza. Beneath him, he spotted countless troops and tanks deployed "in a manner usually resorted to for a last ditch stand." He reported the situation to New York, attesting that the "large-scale deployment of UAR army, including tanks and artillery, cannot be for anything but an offensive. There is no suitable defensible position between these points . . . Implications of Mortaga's [sic] message are evident." Rikhye intended to send the wire in the morning, though U Thant would not be present at UN headquarters to receive it. The secretary-general was scheduled to undergo oral surgery at that time, on a tooth that had become infected during his recent visit to Egypt.[66]

King Hussein had a similar premonition. The Turkish ambassador had come to him with information that the war would begin the following day, with an Israeli air strike against Egyptian bases. Later, Hussein would claim that he warned the Egyptians of the probability of an Israeli attack the following day. He put his own air force on highest alert, spoke with his generals, and went to bed at 1:00 A.M. for a short and fitful sleep.[67]

Katriel Katz was again called to the Kremlin, where Gromyko again reproved him for the "war frenzy" in Israel. Only this time, the Israeli ambassador lost his temper. "In Cairo and Damascus they're calling for the destruction of a neighboring country, Arab leaders are demanding genocide, and I'm summoned to the foreign ministry of a peace-loving nation to be delivered a warning for Israel?" Gromyko listened expressionless, then explained that Israel could not expect the Arabs to forget 1956—"they have emotions too"—nor that the Soviet Union would abide by Zionist aggression. "The surest way to jeopardize your future is to choose the way of war," the foreign minister said, then repeated several times, "Do not let your emotions get the better of you."[68]

"The IDF was wound up like a mighty spring," Yitzhak Rabin recalled of the night before the war. "Over the weeks of waiting, they [our operational plans] had undergone repeated revision as the circumstances shifted on the southern front. We had gone through Operation Fork and Operation Hoe—what seemed like a whole farmyard of plans—on paper, on maps, with sticks in the sand. Now we would make our way through the final plan with tanks, half-tracks and trucks."

Rabin, on tour of the Southern Command, was summoned back to Tel Aviv to hear Dayan's final briefing. It was short, a series of directives. The forces around Jerusalem would be bolstered, but without bringing tanks into the city. There would be no action against Jordan, not even minor land grabs, unless the Jordanians attacked first. The same order held for the northern front: no war with Syria if the Syrians sat out the war. In the south, Dayan surveyed Operation Nachshon 1 (after the biblical Nachshon ben Aminadav, the first Hebrew to set foot in the freshly split Red Sea) for "the conquest of the Sinai front up to the al-'Arish–Jabal Libni line, the opening of the Abu 'Ageila – Rafah–al-'Arish axes, and the destruction of the Egyptian army in this sector." Israeli forces would advance as rapidly as possible, never pausing. Though Sharm al-Sheikh was not included in the objectives—too much time was needed to reach it—captured territory in Sinai could later be traded for free passage through Tiran. Lastly, Dayan spoke about Focus, the all-out effort to annihilate Egypt's air force before any ground fighting began. This would take place at 7:45 Monday morning, at which point the password Red Sheet (*Sadin Adom*) would be sounded, and the ground war would commence.

The 275,000 men, 1,100 tanks, and 200 planes of the Israel Defense Forces were ready to embark on the largest offensive in Middle East history. Only now, in the few remaining hours before dawn, did Dayan finally find time for reflection. "I was conscious at all times of the heavy burden that had become mine," he subsequently wrote. In spite of his conviction in Israel's ultimate survival, he also was aware of the crushing price it might have to pay. "I could not dismiss lightly the words of Ben-Gurion, who had warned against embarking on this war. Nor could I ignore the stand taken by de Gaulle, the cautionary advice of Dean Rusk, and particularly the threats of the Russians." The Soviets, he reckoned, would be slow to react if Israel's victory were swift. If progress lagged, however, or even stalled, the danger of intervention would multiply.

Similar fears were experienced that night by Ben-Gurion, whom Dayan had updated during the day. "My heart is troubled by tomorrow's action . . . " he wrote in his diary, "I'm very worried about the step we're about to take . . . The haste involved here is beyond my understanding. Would it not really be wiser to consult [with American leaders] first?"

Yitzhak Rabin was also haunted by the lack of full coordination with the Americans. "The government and the general staff had brought the State of Israel to war under the worst possible strategic circumstances," he recalled. Yet the fact of having made that decision, finally, after so much wavering, was a source of solace for the chief of staff. He left the briefing and hurried home for what he later described as "my first night's rest in weeks."

Grabbing a last short sleep was also the goal of Col. Lior when, well after midnight, he left the prime minister's office. The previous three weeks, since the entry of Egyptian troops into Sinai, seemed to Eshkol's aide "like a story taken from another planet." Now he was scared, uncertain whether Israel could withstand a combined Arab onslaught if the preemptive strike failed. Hurrying home, Lior slipped into bed next to his wife, Zuhara, and set the alarm for 6:00 A.M. He would wake her then, and ask her to descend to the shelter.

One man did not sleep, however. Alone at his desk sat Levi Eshkol, composing a brace of letters. The first was to Kosygin, essentially a plea for non-intervention by Soviet forces against Israel. "Surrounded on all sides by hostile armies, we are engaged in a life or death struggle to defend our existence and to prevent Nasser from fulfilling his goal of repeating the crimes perpetrated by Hitler against the Jewish people. We are certain that the Soviet Union's role in history will again be determined by understanding and brotherhood toward the Jewish people at the time of its great trial."

The second letter, no less ardent, was destined for Johnson. Earlier that evening, a tense debate had emerged over whether Israel should claim that Egypt had started the war. Dayan was opposed, but Allon, backed by Eban and Herzog, believed that Israel had nothing to lose, and perhaps something to gain, by pinning the immediate blame on Nasser. Thus, Eshkol wrote that the Egyptian guns had opened fire on Israeli settlements, and that formations of Egyptian aircraft had been observed flying toward the border. He then went on to describe the chain of events that had led to the present confrontation: Nasser's call for Israel's demise, the eviction of UNEF and the closing of Tiran, the alliances between Egypt and Syria, between Egypt and Jordan, and the reckless prevarication of the Soviets.

Implicit in this summary was an understanding that the Middle East morass had sprung from a context, an environment in which the Arab-Israeli conflict could be inflamed by inter-Arab and superpower rivalries, and by the internal politics of every country involved. Primed by catalysts—terrorist attacks, border clashes, reprisal raids—that context then produced a crisis that, once ignited, burned irreversibly toward war.

"The struggle before us has not ended," wrote Eshkol, and asked for the "energetic support" of Israel's "largest friend," particularly in checking the Soviets. As for the goals of the war, the prime minister remained modest. There was no thought of altering that context fundamentally, of eliminating the possibility of similar wars erupting in the future. Rather, all Israel strove for was an end to the immediate threat, and for an indefinite period of quiet thereafter. "We want nothing but to live peacefully in our territory and to enjoy our legitimate maritime rights."[69]

THE WAR: DAY ONE, JUNE 5

Israel's air force strikes.
The ground war begins.
Jordan and Syria counterattack.

IT STARTED AT 7:10 IN THE MORNING, Israel time, when sixteen Magister Fouga jets—French-manufactured, 1950s-era trainers, newly outfitted with rockets—took off from the airfield at Hatzor. The Fougas were transmitting on frequencies used by Mystère and Mirage jets, and, simulating those craft, they flew in a routine patrol pattern. Four minutes later, the real fighters—Ouragan bombers—left Hatzor airfield, followed five minutes after that by a squadron of Mirages from Ramat David and fifteen twin-engine Vatours from Hatzerim. By 7:30, close to 200 planes were aloft. With them went the orders issued that morning by Air Force Commander Motti Hod: "The spirit of Israel's heroes accompany us to battle . . . From Joshua Bin-Nun, King David, the Maccabees and the fighters of 1948 and 1956, we shall draw the strength and courage to strike the Egyptians who threaten our safety, our independence, and our future. Fly, soar at the enemy, destroy him and scatter him throughout the desert so that Israel may live, secure in its land, for generations."

They flew low, often no more than fifteen meters, to avoid detection by any of Egypt's eighty-two radar sites. Most of the planes turned west, toward the Mediterranean, before banking back in the direction of Egypt. Others raced down the Red Sea toward targets deep in the Egyptian interior. Radio silence was strictly observed. Communication would be limited to hand signals, even as flight paths crossed. "The name of the game is reaching the Egyptian coast without being spotted," Col. Rafi Harlev, chief of IAF operations, had lectured his pilots. In the event of mechanical trouble, there could be no calls for assistance, he warned them. They would have to crash in the sea.

But those pilots also had major advantages. They were better trained than their Egyptian adversaries, had more flying time, and almost all of their 250 planes (65 Mirages, 35 Super Mystères, 35 Mystère Mark IV's, 50 Ouragans, 20 Vatour light bombers, and 45 Fougas) were operational. These had repeatedly practiced Focus, carrying it out on mock-ups of Egyptian airfields, under circumstances of near-total secrecy. Only a few ministers knew of the plan, while members of the general staff received no more than a single-page summary. On the other hand, a great deal was known about Israel's targets—the location of each Egyptian jet, together with the name and rank and even the voice of its pilot.

Most of this information had been obtained through electronic means, but some was the product of espionage. Wolfgang Lotz, a German-born Israeli spy posing as a former SS officer, obtained vital details from the Egyptian military leaders he befriended until his capture in 1964. Other high-placed sources, among them an intelligence officer named Anwar Ifrim and 'Ali al-'Alfi, Nasser's personal masseur, contributed to what Hod later called "Israel's real-time intelligence" on Egypt's aircraft. The Egyptians, for their part, did little to shield their planes. These were concentrated by type—MiG's, Ilyushins, Topolovs—each to its own base, allowing the Israelis to prioritize their targets. Though proposals for constructing concrete hangars had been submitted by the air force and approved, none had ever been implemented. Egypt's jets were parked on open-air aprons, without so much as sandbags surrounding them. "A fighter jet is the deadliest weapon in existence—in the sky," Hod was fond of saying, "but on the ground it is utterly defenseless."[1]

Almost all of Egypt's planes were on the ground at that moment, their pilots eating breakfast. Assuming that any Israeli attack would begin at dawn, the MiG's had already flown their sunrise patrols, and had returned to base at 8:15 Egypt time, an hour ahead of Israel's. Only four training flights were in the air, none of them armed. Taking off from al-Maza base, however, were two Ilyushin-14 transports. In one, bound for the Bir al-Thamada base, flew Field Marshal 'Amer and Air Commander Sidqi Mahmud; in the other, Internal Intelligence Chief Husayn al-Shaf'i, the Iraqi prime minister, and a senior Soviet adviser, headed for Abu Suweir. All of the army's commanders were either seated in those two planes or waiting for them to land. Noting the Ilyushins on their radar screens, the Israelis were concerned that the planes would detect their approaching squadrons. Such an alarm was indeed sounded, though not by the bombers, which calmly climbed to cruising altitude. The warning, rather, came from 'Ajlun.

Supplied by Britain, Jordan's radar facility at 'Ajlun, near Jerash, was one of the most sophisticated in the Middle East. At 8:15 A.M., the station's screens were suddenly studded with blips. Though the Jordanians had grown accustomed to large numbers of Israeli aircraft heading out to sea, the density of the concentration was unprecedented. The officer on duty radioed in Grape—'*Inab*, in Arabic, the prearranged code word for war—to Gen. Riyad's headquarters in Amman.

Riyad, in turn, relayed the information to Defense Minister Shams Badran in Cairo, and there it remained, indecipherable. The Egyptians had changed their encoding frequencies the previous day, but without updating the Jordanians. The Israelis had also altered their frequencies, leaving 'Ajlun's observers to wonder whether the blips were IAF planes or foreign aircraft—British or American— launched from carriers at sea. They watched as the radar suddenly showed a diversion eastward, toward Sinai, and then cabled the code word repeatedly.

But even if those messages could have been read, Badran was not present to read them. The defense minister had gone to bed only a few hours before, leaving strict orders not to be disturbed. Similarly absent were Col. Mas'ud al-Junaydi, in charge of decoding, and Air Operations Chief General Gamal 'Afifi. At his subsequent trial for incompetence, 'Afifi claimed, "I was out of the army for ten years before that, and less than six months in that job. Thank God I wasn't there, for the man who was at least knew who to call and what to do. Had I been there, the situation would have been much worse." Air force intelligence also reported extensively on the Israeli attack, but the officers at Supreme Headquarters, devoted to 'Amer and distrustful of Nasser loyalists in the air force, ignored them.[2]

For the Israelis, those minutes were pivotal. "The suspense was incredible," Ezer Weizman recounted. He had not resigned in the end, swallowing his pride and remaining chief of operations. But Weizman cared little about ground battles; his main concern was the air force and the Focus plan he had helped originate. "For five years I had been talking of this operation, explaining it, hatching it, dreaming of it, manufacturing it link by link, training men to carry it out. Now, in another quarter of an hour, we would know if it was only a dream, or whether it would come true."

The plan, requiring dozens of squadrons from different bases to rendezvous silently over eleven targets between twenty and forty-five minutes' flying time away, was labyrinthine in its complexity, and exceedingly hazardous. All but twelve of the country's jets were thrown into the attack—American football fans would call it a Hail Mary—leaving the country's skies virtually defenseless. Innumerable practice runs had convinced IAF commanders that the Egyptian air force could be destroyed, even if it managed to get off the runways, in as little as three hours. Yet Rabin continued to entertain doubts, and even ordered commando units to prepare for nocturnal attacks on enemy airstrips in the event that Focus failed.[3]

Now Rabin, along with Dayan, waited in IAF headquarters with Weizman and the anxious commander of Israel's air force. "The first forty-five minutes felt like a day," said Hod, on whose shoulders fell the immediate responsibility for the attack. A lean, taciturn former kibbutznik, Hod had smuggled Holocaust survivors into Palestine after World War II and then, prior to the War of Independence, smuggled in a British Spitfire as well. Throughout the battles of 1948 and 1956, he had earned a reputation as a skilled and cool-headed pilot,

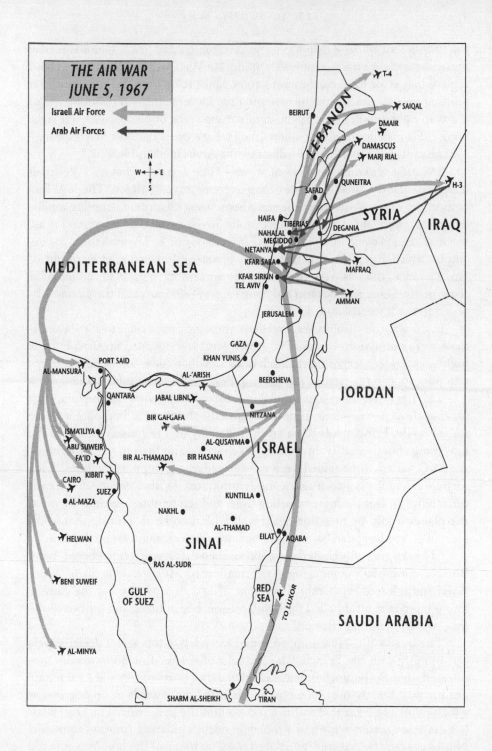

THE AIR WAR
JUNE 5, 1967

Israeli Air Force
Arab Air Forces

N
W E
S

T-4

SAIQAL

DMAIR

DAMASCUS
MARJ RIAL

BEIRUT

LEBANON

QUNEITRA

H-3

SAFAD

SYRIA

IRAQ

HAIFA
TIBERIAS
NAHALAL
MEGIDDO
NETANYA
KFAR SABA

DEGANIA

MAFRAQ

KFAR SIRKIN
TEL AVIV

AMMAN

MEDITERRANEAN SEA

JERUSALEM

GAZA

KHAN YUNIS

AL-MANSURA

PORT SAID

AL-'ARISH

BEERSHEVA

JORDAN

QANTARA

JABAL LIBNI

BIR GAFGAFA

NITZANA

ISMA'ILIYA
ABU SUWEIR
FA'ID

AL-QUSAYMA

ISRAEL

BIR AL-THAMADA
BIR HASANA

CAIRO
KIBRIT
SUEZ

AL-MAZA

KUNTILLA

NAKHL

HELWAN

AL-THAMAD

EILAT
AQABA

SINAI

RAS AL-SUDR

BENI SUWEIF

GULF
OF SUEZ

RED
SEA

TO LUXOR

SAUDI ARABIA

AL-MINYA

SHARM AL-SHEIKH

TIRAN

less known for brilliance than for his resourcefulness and grit. Cincinnatus-like, his strongest desire was to return to farming, but Weizman had insisted that Hod replace him as air force chief early in 1966. Since then, he had concentrated on refining Focus, reducing the turnaround time for refueling and rearming jets to less than eight minutes. The Egyptian turnaround rate, by comparison, was eight hours. "He may not be able to quote [the Hebrew poet] Bialik or Shakespeare," Weizman said of Hod, "but he will screw the Arabs in plain Hebrew."

Sweating, guzzling pitchers of water—"like a giant radiator," Weizman observed—Hod waited for news of the opening wave of attack. The lead formations had now passed over the sea where, using electronic jamming equipment, they were able to elude detection by Soviet vessels. At 7:30 Israel time, the first targets came into view. In the huge bases of Fa'id and Kibrit, for example, which Egyptian intelligence had erroneously concluded were out of Israel's range, the jets were parked on the aprons, in rows or in semicircular revetments. Many airfields had only one runway—block it and the planes supposed to use it were doomed.[4]

In the sky, the visibility was excellent, the wind factor close to zero. Conditions were optimal for attack. The Israeli jets now swooped up sharply to as high as 9,000 feet, exposing themselves to Egyptian radar and sending Egyptian pilots out to the tarmac, scrambling. Few would reach their planes.

The jets dove. They approached in foursomes and attacked in pairs, each making three passes—four, if time permitted—the first for bombing and the rest to strafe. Priority was to be given to destroying the runways, then to the long-range bombers that threatened Israeli cities, and then to the jet fighters, the MiG's. Last to be raided were missile, radar, and support facilities. Each sortie was to take between seven and ten minutes. With a twenty-minute return flight, an eight-minute refueling time, and ten minutes' rest for the pilot, the planes would be in action again well within an hour. During that hour, moreover, the Egyptian bases would be under almost uninterrupted attack.

"The sky gradually cleared as we approached the target," remembered Avihu Bin-Nun, a captain commanding a formation of Mystères over Fa'id. "As I dived and released my bombs, I saw four MiG-21's at the end of the runway lining up to take off. I pulled the bomb release, began firing and hit two of the four, which went up in flames."

The bombs Bin-Nun dropped were Durendals, a top-secret device developed jointly with the French, who had named it after Roland's sword. Once released, the 180-pound bomb was stabilized by a retro-rocket and a parachute until it was directly over its target and pointed downwards at 60 degrees, at which point a booster rocket drove it deep into the pavement. The Durendals left craters 5 meters wide and 1.6 meters deep, rendering runways unusable. Nor could they be repaired, as delayed fuses on many of the bombs continued exploding. Over one hundred of the devices were dropped on Abu Suweir alone, in less than one hour. Bin-Nun continued, "We destroyed sixteen of the forty

MiG's scattered around the field, and paralyzed a SAM-2 battery on our way back. We could see all the other Egyptian airfields in flames."

Below, the Egyptian pilots were in a state of shock, incredulous of Israel's ability to penetrate their defenses, to catch them so totally off-guard. "I stood on the runway, at exactly 9:00 A.M., ready to leave with the training sortie," recalled Brig. Gen. Tahsin Zaki, commander of the Malis base. "I heard the noise of jet planes, at the very same moment, and I looked toward the direction of the noise and saw two gray Super Mystère planes. They dropped two bombs at the beginning of the runway. Two additional planes were behind them, and they dropped two bombs in the middle of the runway, and the last two planes dropped two bombs at the end of the runway. After a couple of minutes, the whole runway was bombed. It was a complete surprise." [5]

The Egyptian planes were inextricably trapped, easy prey for the 30-mm cannons and heat-seeking rockets that next raked them. At the Beni Suweif and Luxor airfields west of the Canal, colossal Topolov-16 bombers and their ten-ton payloads exploded with such force that one of the attacking jets was literally blown out of the sky. In Sinai, mixed formations of Mirage and Mystère fighters hit the forward bases at Jabal Libni, Bir al-Thamada, and Bir Gafgafa, strafing the scores of parked MiG's and incinerating the few that attempted to take off. Only at al-'Arish was the runway spared, in the assumption that it would soon be serving Israeli transports.

By the end of that first wave, 8:00 Israel time, an average of twenty-five sorties had been carried out against Cairo West, Fa'id, and Abu Suweir bases. Four airfields in Sinai and two in Egypt had been entirely knocked out. The main communication cable linking Egyptian forces in Sinai with Supreme Headquarters had been severed. The most devastating damage, though, was done to the air force itself. In little over half an hour, the Egyptians had lost 204 planes—half of their air force—all but nine of them on the ground.

The Israelis were stunned. No one had ever imagined that a single squadron could neutralize an entire air base, and that Focus's kill ratio would exceed expectations by almost 100 percent. Those expectations had taken into account the possibility that Egyptians would soon overcome their initial shock and rally, shooting down as many as a quarter of their attackers' planes. Indeed, Israeli pilots were ordered to reserve five minutes of their combat fuel and a third of their ammunition for dogfights. None occurred, however, nor was there significant ground fire. All of Egypt's 100 anti-aircraft batteries, its 27 SAM-2 missiles sites, had been issued no-fire orders by 'Amer, who feared they might mistake his plane for one of Israel's. Only in Cairo did the anti-aircraft units try to repel the planes, shooting wildly at the delta-wing aircraft overhead. "We were on high alert, with more than enough ammunition, but we received no orders to shoot," attested Sa'id Ahmad Rabi', the major commanding the guns. "Finally, I opened fire myself, and thought I'd be courtmartialed for it. But instead I received a medal for valor, and have kept my job ever since."

Rabi' claimed to have downed several Israeli jets. In all, the IAF lost eight aircraft in the first wave, and five pilots. One of the planes, damaged but unable to break radio silence, was destroyed by Israeli Hawk missiles after it strayed over Dimona.

Only now, with the first strike completed, were the results made known to headquarters. These seemed too fantastic to believe, and it was not until Hod had personally debriefed his pilots that he could confirm their remarkable success. "A stone—just one, but of agonizing weight—rolled off the heart," Dayan wrote. Yet that same stone would remain on the Israeli public. The extent of the IAF's success would be kept secret for as long as possible, delaying a UN-imposed cease-fire while Israeli tanks rolled into Sinai. At 8:15, Dayan issued the Red Sheet password. The ground war was about to begin.

The second wave of fighters, meanwhile, reached its destinations: fourteen enemy bases, nearly half of them west of the Canal, and all of Egypt's radar sites. Though the Israelis no longer enjoyed the element of surprise, and no longer observed radio silence, resistance from these facilities was moderate and largely confined to anti-aircraft fire. The IAF carried out 164 sorties in just over 100 minutes and destroyed another 107 planes, while suffering only nine losses. Of the 420 combat aircraft in Egypt's arsenal that morning, 286 were destroyed—30 Tupolev-16's, 27 Ilyushin-28 medium bombers, 12 Sukhoi-7 fighter-bombers, 90 MiG-21 interceptors, 20 MiG-19's, 75 MiG-17's, 32 transport planes and helicopters—and almost a third of their pilots killed. Thirteen bases were rendered inoperable, along with twenty-three radar stations and anti-aircraft sites. At 10:35, Hod turned to Rabin and reported, "The Egyptian air force has ceased to exist."[6]

As the picture of the battlefield became clear in Israel, in Egypt and the rest of the Arab world it grew deeply obfuscated. Officers at the ravaged air bases were aware that a terrible tragedy had transpired. The pilot Hashem Mustafa Husayn, stationed at Bir al-Thamada, described the feeling:

> Some 30 seconds from the end of the [first] attack, a second wave of planes arrived . . . We ran about the desert, looking for cover, but the planes didn't shoot. They merely circled, their pilots surprised that the base was completely destroyed and that no targets remained. We were the only targets . . . weak humans scurrying in the desert with handguns as our only means of self-defense. It was a sad comedy . . . pilots of the newest and best-equipped jets fighting with handguns. Five minutes after the beginning of the attack the [Israeli] planes disappeared and a silence prevailed that encompassed the desert and the noise of the fire that destroyed our planes and the airbase and the squadron. They completed their assignment in the best way possible, with a ratio of losses–100 percent for us, 0 percent for them.

Brig. Zaki had a similar experience. Helplessly he had watched as Husayn al-Shaf'i's plane, having barely managed to land on a secondary airstrip, was strafed by enemy Mirages. The crew and passengers managed to escape, but those in an accompanying craft proved less fortunate; all died on the runway. "Israel spent years preparing for this war, whereas we prepared for parades," he testified later. "The drills for the annual Revolution Day parade went on for weeks . . . but there were no preparations for war."

Surrounded by what Sidqi Mahmud called "a forest of Israelis jets," 'Amer's plane could not land at all. It circled from base to burning base for nearly ninety minutes before touching down at Cairo's International Airport. There, Col. Muhammad Ayyub, 'Amer's air force liaison officer, was waiting with a drawn pistol, convinced that a coup had been staged against his boss. "You want to murder him, you dogs!" Ayyub shouted as the other officers present also pulled out their guns. Sidqi Mahmud stepped between them, though, averting a firefight. "Fools," he scolded them, "put your guns away! Israel is attacking us!"

Lacking military transportation, 'Amer took a taxi to Supreme Headquarters. Only thirty-seven of his MiG's were still flightworthy and he had nearly been shot out of the sky, but 'Amer was nevertheless elated. The war had finally begun. He promptly commanded Sidqi Mahmud to provide air cover for the conquest of Israel's coast (Operation Leopard) and to deploy Egypt's newest Sukhoi jets, if necessary with their Russian instructors. 'Amer then called Damascus and Baghdad and requested that they execute Operation Rashid—the bombing of Israeli airfields—at once. The Iraqis consented, but then complained of "technical delays." The Syrians claimed that their planes were presently engaged in a training exercise.

Such disappointments did little to dampen the mood in Egypt's Supreme Headquarters which seemed to the Soviet attaché S. Tarasenko, "tranquil, almost indifferent, the officers merely listening to the radio and drinking coffee." Throughout the capital, however, the citizenry was celebrating. "The streets were overflowing with demonstrators," remembered Eric Rouleau, Middle East correspondent for *Le Monde*. "Anti-aircraft guns were firing. Hundreds of thousands of people were chanting, 'Down with Israel! We will win the war!'" But Rouleau, together with other foreign journalists, was not allowed near the front. All international phone lines were cut. The sole source of information was the government's communiqué: "With an aerial strike against Cairo and across the UAR, Israel began its attack today at 9:00. Our planes scrambled and held off the attack."

The accounts of that counterstrike were promising. A total of eighty-six enemy planes were reportedly shot down, including an American bomber. Egypt's losses were put at two. "There is a good deal [of] effervescence and clapping at this news," American ambassador Nolte reported. "The radio [is] playing patriotic songs interspersed with calls for a return to Palestine and rendezvous in Tel Aviv." 'Amer wired Gen. Riyad in Amman with the news that, in spite of their initial surprise, the Israelis had lost 75 percent of their air power. The Egyptian army was hitting back and mounting an offensive from Sinai.[7]

Not present at Supreme Headquarters when the news of the Israeli air strikes arrived, Nasser also welcomed the opening of hostilities and believed the tide would soon turn. Nevertheless, by 10:00—the height of the second wave—when the air force claimed to have downed 161 Israeli bombers, Nasser became suspicious. He tried contacting 'Amer, but received no reply; Sidqi Mahmud was also unreachable. One of the few men who would have told him the truth, Anwar Sadat, had secluded himself at home. Entering headquarters at 11:00, Sadat heard from Soviet ambassador Pojidaev and from other senior officers of the full extent of Egypt's disaster. "I just went home and stayed in for days," he wrote, unable to watch the "crowds . . . chanting, dancing, and applauding the faked-up victory reports which our mass media put out hourly."

But Nasser remained in the dark, not the least because no one in the army or the government dared enlighten him. All went along with the version, broadcast on Cairo Radio, that "our airplanes and our missiles are at this moment shelling all Israel's towns and villages," that called on "every Arab to avenge the dignity lost in 1948, to advance across the Armistice line to the den of the gang itself, to Tel Aviv." [8]

Red Sheet over Sinai

Secretly advanced during the night, camouflaged, and observing radio silence, Israeli forces on the Egyptian border had watched as successive waves of Israeli planes soared overhead. Then, at 7:50 A.M., the Red Sheet password arrived and the columns moved out. Gen. Tal's *Ugdah*—an IDF division expanded for specific tasks—composed of 250 tanks, 50 guns, a paratrooper brigade, and a reconnaissance unit, crossed the border at two points, opposite Nahal Oz and south of Khan Yunis. They proceeded swiftly, holding their fire to prolong the element of surprise. Ahead lay the Rafah Gap, a seven-mile stretch containing the shortest of the three main routes through Sinai to Qantara and the Suez Canal. For this reason, Egypt positioned a full four divisions in the area, reinforcing a warren of minefields, pillboxes, underground bunkers, hidden gun emplacements, and trenchworks. For the attacking Israelis, there was little choice but to break through these defenses; the terrain on either side of the road, sand and ravines, was impassable.

Yet that was precisely the Israeli plan, to hit the enemy at selected key points and with a "mailed fist" of concentrated armor. A hardened veteran of World War II and the two previous Arab-Israeli wars, Tal had commanded the armored corps since 1964, turning it into a highly disciplined and mobile force. Tested in earlier skirmishes with the Syrians—Tal, himself, had been wounded— the corps was to crack Egypt's strongest defenses, sowing confusion and demoralization, precipitating a domino-like retreat. Upon completing his prebattle briefing, Tal had reminded his officers that wars were rarely fought according to plan. They only had to follow one principle: "Everyone attacks, everyone penetrates, without looking sideways or back." The armored corps had broken through the same area in 1956 in just over thirty-six hours. This time they had twenty-four.[9]

For Tal's division, the going at first was easy. Leading the thrust was Israel's finest armored brigade, the 7th, under Col. Shmuel Gonen. Swinging south of Gaza, Gonen's column was greeted by Egyptian soldiers who mistook its tanks for their own. Similarly, the commanders of Egypt's 11th Brigade, equipped with Stalin tanks—the Middle East's biggest—allowed Israeli paratroopers of the 35th Brigade to slog relatively unmolested through the dunes as they made their frontal assault. "Apparently someone in heaven was watching over us," remarked the commander, Rafael (Raful) Eytan, after the war, "Every unintended action they took and every unintended action we took always turned out to our advantage." But Israeli advances were more than a product of luck. Egyptian intelligence had concluded that enemy movements in the sector were merely diversions for the main axis of attack, opposite Rafah and Khan Yunis.

Gonen (Gorodish), 37, an upholsterer's son who left his religious studies at age thirteen to join the *Haganah*, was a prepossessing officer, staunch and bullish. The day before he had assured his men that "we will thrash them [the Egyptians] as we did in 1948 and 1956," that the Israelis would "wash their feet in the Canal" and topple Nasser in Cairo. But he also reminded them that "if we do not win, we will have nowhere to come back to," and cautioned them to conserve ammunition. The goal was not to attack Rafah directly—that was left to the paratroopers—but to outflank it from Khan Yunis in the north. An axis was chosen farthest from the Egyptian guns and downwind of the sea, to avoid poison gas. From the south, 60th Brigade, under Col. Menachem Aviram with eighty-six Sherman and AMX tanks, would enclose Khan Yunis in an iron vise.

Though he fielded a formidable arsenal, including fifty-eight Centurions and sixty-six Pattons, Gonen entrusted the breakthrough at Khan Yunis to a single tank battalion. This advanced on the town, encountering only scant opposition. Then, "suddenly all hell opened up," recalled Ori Orr, an officer in the reconnaissance unit, half of whose men became casualties. "Artillery shells, machine guns, anti-tank guns—everything fired at us . . . Along the whole area, Egyptian T-34 tanks took their positions and fired. An [Israeli] half-track was hit by a shell before it could get off the road. All eight soldiers inside were killed." Another tank battalion was brought up and this, too, was pummeled. Some of the fiercest resistance came from the 20th Palestinian Division, not considered a first-rate unit, under the command of Gen. Muhammad 'Abd al-Mun'im Husni, Gaza's military governor.

Gonen's six lead tanks were quickly knocked out and thirty-five of his officers killed. Aviram's force became bogged down in the sand, while the dunes created a navigational nightmare for the paratroopers.

"This is a battle for life and death," Tal had told his men, "We will attack all the time, no matter what the cost in casualties." The Israelis' casualties were indeed high as they fought their way through antitank ditches, roadside pill-boxes, and stone terraces that forced them off the main axes and into a maze of alleys. And yet their progress was remarkable. In little over four hours, Gonen's brigade reached the Khan Yunis railway junction and then covered, in twin columns, the nine remaining miles to Rafah.

Rafah, with its sprawling military camps, was in fact to be circumvented, the main target being the Egyptian defenses at Sheikh Zuweid, eight miles to the southwest. These were held by two brigades of the 7th Division, a unit created three weeks before in anticipation of Operation Dawn and Egypt's conquest of the Negev. Led by the commandant of the army's infantry school, Maj. Gen. 'Abd al-'Aziz Suliman, most of the division's officers were also instructors and, as such, ill prepared for the Israelis' unconventional approach from the sea and through the sands. Nor, with their twenty guns and sixty-six largely antiquated tanks, were the Egyptians a match for the larger Israeli force of more modern Centurions and Pattons. "We were exposed to a heavy armor attack on several axes, with the sea to our backs in the north, and constant aerial and artillery bombardment," recalled battalion commander 'Izzat 'Arafa. "We had almost no communications with other headquarters in the sector, and no knowledge of what was happening on the battlefield."

Yet, deeply entrenched and camouflaged, the defenders exacted a painful price. "The [Egyptian] artillery positions were dug in low," Gonen later told reporters. "They fired ten rounds at a time and with each volley a tank went up in flames. We left many of our dead soldiers at Rafah, and many burnt-out tanks." Heavy artillery and air strikes had to be called in to enable the lead Israeli elements to break through. Suliman and several of his staff were killed. Leaderless, many Egyptian troops abandoned their positions, leaving behind forty tanks and some 2,000 dead and wounded.

The battle turned into a rout, complete except for Aviram's battalion which, having misjudged the enemy's flank, found itself pinned between strongholds. Extricating the force took several hours, yet by nightfall, the Israelis had finished mopping up. Thousands of Egyptian soldiers, hundreds of jeeps and trucks, streamed past the attackers as they regrouped on the road to al-'Arish.

That road was now open to the IDF. Already by late afternoon, elements of the IDF's 79th Armored Battalion had charged through the seven-mile-long Jiradi defile, a narrow pass through shifting dunes. Its well-emplaced defenders, troops of the 112th Infantry Brigade, mistook the Israeli tanks for their own. The effect, later described by an IDF internal report, was eerie:

> On both sides of the road were dug-in tanks, antitank guns, mortar pits and machine-gun nests all linked by trenches and surrounded with mines. The longest distance between any two positions was 50 meters. The Egyptians were so surprised [by the Israeli column] that they did not shoot. The [Israeli]

commander thought the Egyptians had fled and so told his men to hold their fire. Only when the column reached the midway point was it revealed that the Egyptians had not fled.

The pass changed hands several times before the Israelis finally cleared it and emerged at its western end, having advanced over twenty miles in a single afternoon. Just beyond lay the outskirts of al-'Arish, a town of 40,000 and the administrative hub of Egypt's army in Sinai. "We reached our objective at 10:00 in the evening, in the pitch darkness," wrote Lt. Yossi Peled, "Egyptian tanks were burning for as far as we could see, and Egyptian soldiers lying between them. But many of our tanks were also ablaze, and the Israelis lying beside them were no longer alive." In all, the Israelis lost twenty-eight tanks; ninety-three men were wounded and sixty-six killed.[10]

However costly, Israel's offensive was proceeding well ahead of schedule—so much so that a combined sea and airborne assault on al-'Arish planned for the next day was canceled, and the paratroopers preparing for it were diverted to Jerusalem. Though the war was far from decided, a crucial battle had been won and under circumstances in which the antagonists were generally well matched and in which air power—Focus still preoccupied the IAF—played only a minor role.

A similar balance prevailed farther to the south, in the heavily fortified area, six miles deep and two wide, of Umm Qatef. This was the first line of Egypt's Conqueror strategy, and its defenses were a microcosm of Sinai's: three 'linear dispositions'—trench systems, minefields, antitank and machine-gun positions, 80 guns, 90 tanks, and 16,000 men—between which the enemy could be crushed. Guarding the vital Abu 'Ageila junction leading into the peninsula's interior, to the Mitla Pass and Isma'iliya, the stronghold had withstood repeated Israeli onslaughts in 1956, surrendering only when its supplies were exhausted. Since then, Umm Qatef had been further buttressed by powerful redoubts at Ruwafa Dam and at nearby al-Qusayma. Manning these positions were troops of the 2nd Infantry Division who, though battle-ready, were commanded by Maj. Gen. Sa'di Nagib, a political appointee best known as one of 'Amer's drinking mates.

Facing Nagib was Arik Sharon. At 39, Sharon cut a dashing, if controversial, figure who had earned both censure and encomium for his role in the retaliation raids of the 1950s and the bloody Mitla Pass battle in the Sinai campaign. In his previous position as IDF director of training, Sharon had thoroughly studied Umm Qatef's defenses, and was determined not to repeat Israel's mistakes of the previous war. Sharon's plan was to cross the sand wastes deemed impassable by the Egyptians and to deliver an armored thrust from the north. Simultaneously, from the west, his tanks would engage the Egyptian bastions on the Umm Qatef ridge, and block any reinforcements they might receive from Jabal Libni or al-'Arish. Israeli infantrymen would clear the three 3,000-yard trenches while, a mile behind them, heliborne paratroopers would silence the Egyptians' artillery park. Lastly, an armored diversion would be made at al-Qusayma, preoccupying and isolating its garrison. All this would be accomplished, Sharon hoped, in time for the three brigades of his 38th Division to join Gen. Yoffe's 31st Division in assaulting the second Egyptian defense line—Jabal Libni, Bir Lahfan, and Bir Hasana—in central Sinai.

At 8:15 A.M., the lead Centurion tanks of Col. Natan "Natke" Nir left Nitzana and crossed the border at al-'Awja, passing its abandoned UNEF posts. The Egyptians, though, staged successful delaying actions at Tarat Umm, Umm Tarfa, and Hill 181. An Israeli jet, swooping low, was downed by anti-aircraft fire. Then the guns at Umm Qatef opened up. Under heavy shellfire, struggling through dunes and mines, Israeli forces made their approaches from the north and the west. Casualties were high, and visibility confounded by a dust storm. Yet Nir's tanks managed to penetrate the northern flank of Abu 'Ageila—'Oakland,' in the IDF's code—and by dusk all units were in position. Over ninety guns had been moved up to rain a punishing barrage on Umm Qatef, and civilian buses had brought the infantry reservists under Col. Yekutiel "Kuti" Adam to within marching distance of the enemy trenches. The helicopters also arrived to ferry Col. Dani Matt's paratroopers. These movements went totally unobserved by the Egyptians. Preoccupied with enemy probes against their perimeter, they waited in vain for Supreme Headquarters' order to counterattack, without which they would not move.[11]

As night fell, the Israeli assault troops lit their flashlights, each battalion a different color, to prevent friendly fire exchanges. But before the final signal could be given, Sharon received a phone call from Gavish. The Southern Command chief recommended that the attack be postponed for twenty-four hours to allow the air force, now free for ground support, to soften up the target. Sharon disagreed, but his response was garbled by electrical interference. The conversation was cut off, but then another call came for Gavish. The air force was rescinding its offer of assistance; its planes were needed elsewhere. A second front had suddenly opened, with Jordan.

The "Whip" Cracks

"It is always possible, if hostilities do occur, that Jerusalem will be spared," surmised Evan Wilson, America's consul-general in the city, before the outbreak of war. Seemingly shielded from the upheaval engulfing the region, Jerusalem's mood remained relatively calm. Along the two-mile line separating the Jewish from the Arab sectors, Israeli and Jordanian soldiers faced each other with the same methodical vigilance they had maintained for the last nineteen years. The bifurcation of the city was complete, effected by high firewalls, barbed wire, and mines. In some cases, even houses were divided, where property fell within the width of the pencil used to draw the armistice map in 1949. And while bunkers and observation posts were often only meters apart, those man-ning them rarely came within visual, much less physical, contact.

The night of June 5 augured no change in this strange *modus vivendi*. Though small-arms fire occasionally burst from Jordanian positions, the Israe-lis were under strict orders to ignore them. The IDF also cancelled the bi-weekly convoy to Mount Scopus, together with a number of training exercises. "Standing guard, we even took the magazines out of our Uzis," Yoram Galon, a reservist serving in Jerusalem, remembered. "Just in case a bullet went off accidently and ignited the front." The Israelis could not afford to fight. Much of Central Command's ammunition had been transferred southward to the Egyptian border, leaving a total of 50 vintage Sherman tanks, 36 cannons, and 27 mortars to defend the greater Tel Aviv area. Within the capital, many re-servists had been sent home; a mere seventy-one men held the line facing the Jordanian army. "It seemed as if the security [of the central sector] was indeed based on miracles," Gen. Narkiss told an IDF review board after the war. "We wanted to believe that the enemy would never attack."[12]

And yet Narkiss did not share that belief. Hussein, in his eyes, was "unre-liable," had signed a treaty with Nasser, and had allowed Egyptian commandos onto his territory. If the Jordanians did strike, there was a good chance that Israel would lose several border areas, including the Lakhish settlements and the Jerusalem suburb of Mevasseret Zion. Narkiss's greatest fear, however, cen-tered on the small (one-mile-square) enclave of Mount Scopus. Dominating Jerusalem's highest hill, enclosing the buildings of the Hadassah hospital and Hebrew University that had stood dormant since 1948, Mount Scopus was defended by a UN-monitored garrison of eighty-five policemen and thirty-three civilians. Though Israel had succeeded in smuggling some heavy arms into the enclave, it remained exceedingly susceptible to attack, both from the Mount of Olives to the east and to the north, from the West Bank city of Ramallah. The fall of Mount Scopus would not only deal a tremendous blow to Israeli prestige—"No conquest in Sinai could make up for it," Narkiss warned—but would enable the Jordanians, by linking up with their forces in south Jerusalem, to isolate the city's 197,000 Jews.[13]

Little better was Israel's situation along the West Bank border. Though IDF contingency plans called for augmenting Israel's defenses along the east-ern front in time of war, none of the designated forces were available on June 5. Remaining were five reserve brigades, two in the north to guard the Jezreel Valley, and one each to protect Jerusalem, Lod airport, and the approaches to Tel Aviv. While Israeli commanders often talked of grabbing land around Latrun—*hap*, they called the maneuver, in Yiddish—they knew that there could be no offensive action without those fifty Shermans. But the tanks of the 10th Harel Brigade were being kept as a strategic reserve in Tel Aviv, to block any Egyptian attack from the south. "Our mission wasn't clear," recounted Narkiss, who, in the Independence War, had fought with that same Harel brigade in its abortive attempt to seize Jerusalem's Old City. "There was no order to conquer the West Bank or the Jordan Valley. Yet I was certain that war would come, and certain that it would end in Jerusalem."[14]

Narkiss was not surprised when, at 7:55 A.M., the air raid sirens began wailing in Israel's capital. Many other Israelis, however, soldiers and civilians, believed it was a mistake, even when the 8:00 news carried the (fabricated) report of Egyptian tanks and planes moving toward the Israeli border. Nevertheless, emergency preparations were accelerated in the city. Hospitals went on high alert and museum exhibitions, among them the Dead Sea scrolls, were placed in secure storage. Broadcasting call-up codes, the radio directed reservists to their units.

The government still hoped that Jordan would fire off a few shells—"a salutatory salvo to fulfill its obligations to inter-Arab unity," Narkiss put it— but would otherwise remain passive. To further ensure that passivity, personal appeals would be sent to Hussein, urging him to show restraint. Dayan opposed the idea. "Doesn't Hussein know he's not supposed to attack us?" he asked. Allon, however, insisted that the monarch be warned. Three channels were selected: the U.S. State Department, British Foreign Office, and Gen. Odd Bull in Jerusalem. Thus, at 8:30, Bull was summoned by Arthur Lourie, a veteran UN specialist at the Foreign Ministry, who told him:

> At 8:10 Egyptian planes were spotted crossing into our airspace, and our planes and armor have commenced action against them. In the name of the foreign minister, Lourie asked that Bull urgently convey to King Hussein that Israel will not, repeat not, attack Jordan if Jordan maintains the quiet. But if Jordan opens hostilities, Israel will respond with all of its might.

Bull, lanky and severe-looking, a former fighter pilot with nearly ten years' experience observing for the UN in the Middle East, was not impressed with the gesture. Ill-disposed toward Israel—he would dedicate his memoirs to redressing Norway's pro-Israel bias—he rejected the claim that Egypt had started the fighting, and resented the tone of the text. "This was a threat, pure and simple, and it is not the normal practice of the UN to pass on threats from one government to another," he responded. He wanted two hours to consult New York, but Lourie insisted that the message be conveyed immediately. By all appearances, Jordan was preparing for war.[15]

Such preparations had indeed been accelerated over the past twenty-four hours as Jordanian troops were informed that the time had come to fight. "The reserve ammunition was dispersed," attested Gen. Ma'an Abu Nawwar, commander of the positions abutting Mount Scopus. "All the machinegun belts were loaded, the shells primed." King Hussein showed no consternation when, at 8:50, his aide-de-camp, Col. Ghazi, interrupted his breakfast with the announcement, "Your Majesty, the Israeli offensive has begun in Egypt." Calling his headquarters, Hussein learned of 'Amer's claim of crippling Israeli casualties and of Egypt's swift counterattack. 'Ajlun reported hundreds of aircraft flying from the direction of Sinai—actually returning Israeli jets, though the Jordanians assumed they were Egyptian. This information went a long way toward allaying the king's fears of Israeli attempts to conquer East Jerusalem and its 80,000 Arabs, or all or part of the West Bank. Jordan could go on the offensive.

The extent of that offensive, however, had yet to be determined by Hussein. He entered headquarters just after 9:00, and found that Riyad had already ordered a number of far-reaching actions, including the destruction of Israeli airfields by a combination of artillery fire, jet bombing, and commando attacks. Requests had gone out from ten Syrian brigades to descend from the Golan to the Jordan Valley, where they would meet with 150 Iraqi tanks and cross the Jordan on assault bridges that Riyad requisitioned from Egypt and Saudi Arabia. He also instructed the 2nd Imam 'Ali Brigade to seize Government Hill ridge in south Jerusalem. These operations aimed at covering the flank of the Egyptian column that Riyad believed would soon roll north from Beersheva and Bethlehem. To prevent any outflanking maneuver—an Israeli thrust into the West Bank from the Negev—Riyad further shifted Jordan's tank brigades southward. The 60th descended to the Jerusalem-Jericho road, and the 40th to Hebron.

Once implemented, these instructions would embroil Jordan fully in the war with Israel. Though well liked by the Jordanians—"one of the best Arab officers, not only in the Arab world, but anywhere," one infantry Col. 'Awad Bashir Khalidi, extolled—Riyad had not had time to fully study the defense of the area. Nor did he understand the mentality of the Jordanian army, where command structure closely paralleled family ties. "He didn't know our terrain," said Shafiq 'Ujeilat, an intelligence officer. "He didn't know how we talked to one another or how we fight." By giving priority to Egypt's immediate needs of neutralizing enemy airfields and supporting its supposed offensive, he ignored Jordan's concern for safeguarding the West Bank and East Jerusalem. This fact was pointed out by several general staff members, most vociferously 'Atif al-Majali, who stressed that neither artillery nor armor was available to support an assault on Government House ridge. Better to take Mount Scopus immediately, he argued, and implement Operation Tariq. Harsh words were exchanged—al-Majali stormed out—but in the end Riyad's word proved final. Hussein, who alone had the power to rescind or alter the orders, said nothing.[16]

Rather, speaking on Radio Amman at 9:30, Hussein informed his people that Jordan had been attacked and that "the hour of revenge had come." He had just received a brief telephone call from Nasser in which the Egyptian president had confirmed 'Amer's earlier claim of staggering Israeli losses and the destruction of its airfields. "Quickly take possession of the largest possible amount of land in order to get ahead of the UN's cease-fire," Nasser urged him, anticipating that the Security Council would meet that night. The Iraqis assured Hussein—falsely—that their airplanes were already in action against Israel.

Hussein was clearly excited by this news, and distrustful of Israel's motives in asking for restraint. He may still have believed that limited shelling of bases and the capture of Government Hill ridge—a UN area—would not provoke a full-scale Israeli counterattack. Ultimately, though, there was no choice but to comply with Riyad's decisions; to survive politically, physically, Hussein had to fight. Thus, when Ambassador Burns found him in a forward observation position and handed him Lourie's note, the king responded matter-of-factly. "They started the battle," he said, "Well, they are receiving their reply by air. The lot has been cast."[17]

The shelling of Israel from Jordan had already begun an hour earlier, at 10:00 A.M. Two batteries of the American-made 155-mm 'Long Tom' guns went into action, one zeroing in on the suburbs of Tel Aviv and the other on Ramat David, northern Israel's largest airfield. The commanders of these units were instructed to lay a two-hour barrage "on all enemy positions cited on your lists," which included military bases and even civilian settlements situated in Israel's narrow midland. Harry McPherson, billeted at Barbour's house north of Tel Aviv, was awakened by the crump of explosions. Tanks soon joined in the fusillade, and then planes. At 11:50 A.M., sixteen of Jordan's serviceable Hawker Hunter fighters performed sorties near the towns of Netanya, Kfar Sirkin, and Kfar Saba. Though the attacks failed to inflict major damage—one civilian was killed and seven injured, and one transport plane destroyed—their psychological impact was weighty. Greeting Ambassador Burns outside Hussein's palace, the Soviet ambassador to Jordan remarked, "Our estimate is that if the Israelis do not receive arms, we think the Arabs will win the war if they are allowed to fight it to the finish."

One result of Jordan's offensive was to draw both the Syrian and Iraqi air forces into the war. Syria activated Operation Rashid for the bombing of northern Israel, and by noon, twelve of its MiG's were striking Galilee settlements, including Kibbutz Degania, home to both Eshkol and Hod. Three of the planes were shot down and the rest driven off by Israeli fighters. Meanwhile, three Iraqi Hunters strafed settlements in the Jezreel Valley, including Dayan's village of Nahalal. A Tupolev-16 bomber, also from Iraq, attacked the Lower Galilee town of Afula before being shot down near the Megiddo airfield. Again, the material damage was minimal—several chicken coops and a senior citizens' home were hit—but sixteen Israeli soldiers were killed, most of them when the Tupolev crashed. Damascus Radio quickly trumpeted that, "The Syrian air force has begun to bomb Israeli cities and to destroy its positions." The war had come to Israel's eastern front, and would soon engulf Jerusalem as well.[18]

Intermittent machine-gun exchanges had been raging in the city since 9:30. The Jordanians gradually escalated the fighting, however, introducing 3-inch mortars and 106-mm recoilless rifles. Gen. Narkiss ordered his men to respond with small arms only, firing in a flat trajectory to avoid hitting civilians and Holy Places in the Old City. "They'd start shooting . . . and we would take pains not to answer," attested Col. Eliezer Amitai, commander of the 16th Jerusalem (Etzioni) Brigade, a reserve unit comprised mostly of city residents. Like

Narkiss, Amitai had fought in Jerusalem in 1948, as a platoon commander with Harel. "Tanks couldn't fire, recoilless rifles couldn't move around for fear of provoking the Jordanians. We wanted them to be quiet." Though increasingly anxious about Mount Scopus, Narkiss adhered strictly to Dayan's instructions to avoid any provocation of Jordan. Even when, at 10:30, Jordan Radio announced that Jordanian forces had taken Government Hill ridge—a false claim, it turned out—the Israelis refrained from responding.

So far, the Jordanians had reacted much as Israeli leaders had predicted, demonstrating their Arab solidarity but in a limited way, short of all-out war. But then, at 11:15, that situation changed. Jordanian army howitzers launched the first of 6,000 shells on Jewish Jerusalem, beginning with Kibbutz Ramat Rachel in the south and Mount Scopus in the north, before ranging into the city center and outlying neighborhoods. Military installations were targeted, along with the Knesset and the prime minister's house, but the firing was also indiscriminate. Over 900 buildings would be damaged, among them the new Hadassah hospital in Ein Kerem, where stained glass windows by artist Marc Chagall were shattered. The roof of Mount Zion's Church of the Dormition was also set on fire. Over a thousand civilians were wounded, 150 seriously; 20 of them died. "Very heavy machine and mortar fire, probably cannon, continuous in Jerusalem," reported the British consul-general at around 11:30. "It looks as though Jordanians were pouring a lot into the New City. Jerusalem totally engulfed in war. Bullets have already hit the consulate, one narrowly missing Her Majesty's Consul."[19]

Coming in the wake of their swift gains against Egypt, the sharp deterioration of the Jordanian border was the Israelis' first major setback in the war. Dayan had wanted to avoid opening a second front at least until the south was secured. Also, France had declared an arms embargo of the Middle East—French weapons would continue to reach Israel but secretly and at a slower rate—and there was new need to conserve ammunition. While he rejected repeated requests by Narkiss to mount an infantry breakthrough to Mount Scopus, Dayan sanctioned a number of actions in response to a new eastern threat. The air forces of Jordan, Syria, and Iraq would be neutralized, along with the radar facility at 'Ajlun. The enemy's frontline positions around the Old City would also be reduced. The 10th Harel Brigade, along with several units from the Northern Command, would be activated for the possible implementation of Operation Whip against Jordan.[20]

Shortly before 12:30, the IAF conducted a lightning strike against the airfields of Mafraq and Amman. Before the war, Weizman had favored eliminating the Jordanian air force even without provocation, as a preventive measure, but Rabin had vetoed the idea. Now, after the Hawker attacks on Netanya, Weizman had his pretext. The Hawkers were on the ground refueling when the Israelis struck. Within nine minutes, both bases were rendered inoperable, the runways cratered, their control towers knocked out. The second Israeli wave came at 1:10 P.M. and completed the task by destroying all twenty of Jordan's Hawkers. Eight other aircraft went up in flames, along with Gen. Bull's private plane. A sole C-130 Hercules managed to take off with fourteen pilots for the H-3 airfield in western Iraq, there to continue the battle. Israel lost a single Mystère, to ground fire.

Hussein watched the attack from his yard, where his young sons, 'Abdallah and Faisal, thrilled to the thud of the bombs. He witnessed the death of his friend, Maj. Firas 'Ajluni, as he tried to take off in his jet. The king's presence at home, he would later claim, saved his life, for his office at the Basman Palace was riddled with Israeli cannon and rocket fire.

Another observer of the slaughter was Wasfi al-Tall, the royal adviser who had opposed Jordan's alliance with Egypt. Tall slapped his hands over his eyes and wept, "We've lost everything our Majesty built over the entire course of his rule!" He then turned to Shuqayri, berating him as if he were Nasser: "And where is the Egyptian air force? Where are your MiG's, your missiles?"[21]

For Jordan, the destruction of the air force was only the beginning of Israel's retribution. The IAF also attacked the 40th Brigade as it moved south from the Damiya Bridge. Maj. Arye Ben-Or, commander of the Fouga squadron that rocketed the Jordanians, recalled that "it was an extraordinary experience flying over Bethlehem, Hebron, and Jericho . . . The feeling was that this time we're fighting on our historic homeland." The Fougas destroyed dozens of tanks and set alight an ammunition convoy of twenty-six trucks. "I didn't know that the fighting there would release such powerful emotions hidden inside me," admitted Ben-Or, who would die on a similar sortie five days later, up north.

In Jerusalem, Israel responded to the Jordanian bombardment by unleashing a secret weapon, code-named L after its inventor, Col. David Laskov of the IDF engineering branch. Hidden in all the forward bunkers and pre-sighted on enemy positions opposite, the L was a coffin-shaped ground-to-ground missile that hit with devastating impact. "People, sandbags, stones flew into the air," one eyewitness remembered. "Thick clouds of smoke enshrouded all the [Jordanian] bunkers. Pieces of buildings fell down on them, and telephone poles." One Jordanian soldier, surrendering, was convinced that Israel had dropped an atomic bomb.[22]

Yet, even as Israel took a more aggressive stand against Jordan, it continued to seek ways of containing, if not ending, the battle. An 11:40 attempt by Gen. Bull to arrange a cease-fire was accepted by the Israelis. Their representative to the IJMAC, Col. Jerry Bieberman, met with Jordan's Col. Stanowi and informed him, "on the basis of reliable sources," that "the Egyptian air force has been annihilated" and therefore Jordan should agree to a cease-fire immediately. The initiative made no impression, however. In a radio address, Prime Minister Jum'a told listeners: "We are today living the holiest hours of our life, united with all the other armies of the Arab nation, we are fighting the war of heroism and honor against our common enemy. We have waited years for this battle to erase the stain of the past." Loudspeakers atop the Dome of the Rock mosque exhorted the faithful "to take up your weapons and take back your country stolen by the Jews."[23] Thus entreated, the Jordanians began their attack.

At 12:45, Maj. Badi 'Awad, commander of the 27th 'Isam bin Zayt Battalion, had been listening to radio reports of Egyptian victories and of Jordan's capture of Government House, when he received the password "Way of Happiness" (*Sabil al-Sa'ada*). Sent directly from Riyad's office, this was the go-ahead for 'Awad and two companies to proceed up the ridge. 'Awad, stocky and tough, a veteran of the Jerusalem battle of 1948, was certain that the Israelis would counterattack with tanks. Yet he was confident of his ability to defend the position with his 400 men, his four recoilless rifles, plus some heavy machine-guns and mortars, from behind the walls of the compound.

Known in Hebrew as *Armon ha-Natziv* (High Commissioner's Palace) and in Arabic as *Jabal al-Mukabbar* (the Exalted Hill), the Government House compound had served as headquarters for the British Mandate and then, after 1948, for UN observers. The building occupied the easternmost point of a ridge dominating the vital axis to Bethlehem and Hebron, and could be used as a staging ground for cutting off either Arab or Jewish Jerusalem. As such, both the Israelis and the Jordanians had contingency plans for seizing the ridge in wartime. Though demilitarized under the Armistice, the area was flanked on the south and southeast by a string of fortified Jordanian emplacements, and on the West by an Israeli experimental farm and the Allenby Base. The IDF also maintained a secret lookout post on the northern slope of the ridge—the so-called isolated house—to provide advance warning of any Jordanian movements there. Yet, in contrast to Mount Scopus and the DZ's with Syria, the ridge had rarely been a source of Jordan-Israel friction. Minor run-ins did, however, occur between Israel and the UN, such as that on May 11, when Bull complained that the UN flag had been stolen from atop Government House and replaced by a powder-blue pajama bottom of Israeli manufacture.[24]

Major 'Awad's men dug in around the wooded perimeter of Government House, from where they directed mortar and recoilless rifle fire at Ramat Rachel, Allenby, and the Jewish section of the mixed neighborhood of Abu Tor. Bull ran out to them, furious. "I don't remember ever having been so angry in my life," his memoirs relate. He insisted that 'Awad reconfirm his orders from Riyad, and the major promptly obliged, suggesting that all civilians be evacuated from the area. Bull refused, and instead barricaded himself and his workers inside the compound. From there, he tried to contact the Israeli Foreign Ministry, hoping to avert a counterattack.

The time was 1:35 P.M. 'Awad sent an advance patrol to scout out Israeli strength at the western end of the ridge. Approaching the experimental farm, these soldiers came under fire from Rachel Kaufman, the wife of the farm's director, and three workers armed with old Czechoslovakian guns. Reports from the farm, as well as from the "isolated house," had corroborated Jordan's

offensive. Word had also spread to East Jerusalem where *Life* magazine correspondent George de Carvalo witnessed Arab residents celebrating the fall of
Government House ridge and cheering, "tomorrow we shall take Tel Aviv."

Already alarmed by these events, the Israelis were then dumbfounded when,
at 2:00, Amman Radio proclaimed the fall of Mount Scopus. Remembering
how the announcement of the seizure of Government House had preceded the
actual attack, Narkiss concluded that Israel's enclave was next. "It was a sign
that the Jordanians had a plan," he later testified, "a plan revealed by their
over-zealousness and their sense that their problem was at last solved." His
estimate was that hundreds of Jordan's Patton tanks would ascend the Jordan
Valley to Ramallah, and attack Mount Scopus from the rear. The journey would
take eight hours.[25]

Circumstances, for the Israelis, had turned critical. From Government
House ridge, Jordanian forces could fan out through Jerusalem's southern
neighborhoods—Talpiot, Katamon, San Simon—and link up with troops and
tanks descending Mount Scopus in the north. The entire city could be lost.
In the West Bank, meanwhile, Iraq's 8th Mechanized Brigade, reinforced by
a Palestinian battalion, was proceeding to the Damiya Bridge, taking up positions formerly held by the 40th Armored Brigade. Together with the seven
Jordanian brigades in the area, the Iraqis could spearhead an effort to sever
Israel in half.

These events necessitated a major reevaluation of Israel's strategy in the
east. Convening with Eshkol, Rabin and Yariv in the Pit, Dayan spoke of the
need to silence the long-range guns that had already caused serious damage to
Ramat David. Israeli tanks would have to attack the batteries near the West
Bank city of Jenin, preferably without entering the city itself. The shelling in
Jerusalem would also have to be stopped, and any Jordanian advances reversed.
Most crucially, Mount Scopus would have to be relieved. In preparation for
that effort, Dayan was willing to consider the capture of the Latrun Corridor,
but no additional conquests. "Our purpose was to strike Egypt and no one
else," he said, "I suggest we don't get caught up in two wars."

Eshkol went along with this plan, but then Rabin objected: "We're pounding their [Jordan's] air force, why do we have to conquer their territory at this
stage?" Yariv agreed: "Hussein has to act against us, but what we're doing now
is providing him with the basis for acting." The defense minister registered
this advice, and asked that further attempts be made to convince the Jordanians
to stop firing. But to Col. Lior, also present at the meeting, Dayan appeared to
be contradicting himself, saying he wanted to avoid war with Jordan while opening offensives against it. "The man said one thing for posterity and protocol,
and in the field did something else entirely," he wrote. "Damn it, what did
Moshe Dayan really want?"

In the field, though, Dayan's directives bore no such ambiguity. He gave
the green light to the Northern Command to release two armored brigades to

begin the assault on Jenin, and then instructed Rehavum Ze'evi, the deputy chief of operations, to draw up an attack plan for Jerusalem. The Harel Brigade's tanks were to advance along the Jordanian-held ridge that dominated the Jerusalem-Tel Aviv highway, block any enemy armor descending from the north, and relieve the garrison at Mount Scopus. Simultaneously, infantry would breach the fortified Jordanian positions at the enclave's southern foot. Government House and its ridge were to be retaken immediately.[26]

The latter task fell to Lt. Col. Asher Dreizin, thirty-four, commander of reserve Battalion 161 of the Jerusalem Brigade. Shortly before the outbreak of hostilities, Rabin had told the unit that "I fought here in '48. I hope if we have to fight here in this war, that you will complete what we were unable to finish." Dreizen shared that sentiment. Like many of the brigade's regular officers, he was anxious to avoid war but also to smash the myth of the Jordanian army's invincibility. He had already prepared a plan for regaining Government House, but when the order to attack arrived, he had time only to draw a map in the dirt and curtly brief his men. "Because of the swiftness of everything, I had a feeling that we would surprise the Jordanians," he later told fellow officers, "Still, the operation was complicated. Confused."

Dreizin's force, setting out from Allenby at 2:24, consisted of two infantry companies and eight Sherman tanks. Of the latter, several broke down en route or got stuck in the mud of the experimental farm; three tanks remained for the assault. Resistance was determined. Ensconced behind the compound's walls, 'Awad's men succeeded in knocking out two of the Shermans, killing one Israeli—a company commander—and wounding seven others, among them Dreizin. But superior in firepower and numbers, the attackers eventually broke through the building's western gate and began clearing the compound with grenades. Bull raced about frantically, shouting at the Israelis to hold their fire, that the Jordanians had already fled. Dreizin consented, and just in time: A grenade had been readied for a room found later to contain thirty UN workers, together with their wives and children.

Relations between Israel and the UN, never ideal, were hardly enhanced by the action. The Israelis had not spared ammunition in their charge, damaging much of the compound and destroying Bull's car. The UN chief wanted the building evacuated but the Israelis, angry that the Jordanians had so easily gained entrance to it, refused. Dreizin did not have time to argue, though. The battle was continuing, first on the high ground behind Government House— Antenna Hill—and then in the series of bunkers to the west and the south, each nicknamed for its shape: the Bell, the Sausage. Beyond lay the Arab villages of Sur Baher and Jabal al-Mukabbar.

The fighting, often hand-to-hand, raged for nearly four hours. 'Awad and his surviving men fell back to trenches held by troops of the Hittin Brigade, and called for reinforcements from the armored brigades in the Jordan Valley. None came, and the Jordanians were steadily overwhelmed. By 6:30 P.M., they had retired to Bethlehem, leaving close to 100 dead and wounded. Dreizin, twice more wounded and down to ten men and scant ammunition, was hardly in better shape. Yet the Israelis who dug in that evening on Government Hill ridge, expecting a counterattack, had indeed shattered the Jordanian army's myth of invincibility. They also controlled south Jerusalem.[27]

The Jordanian attack on Government House had not come as a surprise to Uzi Narkiss, nor was the Central Command chief disappointed. Jewish Jerusalem was being shelled and now he had the grounds for responding. At the height of that battle, at 3:10, Narkiss was offered the service of the 55th Paratrooper Brigade under Col. Mordechai "Motta" Gur. Their original assignment, a combined parachute drop and amphibious assault on al-'Arish, had been obviated by the quick pace of the Sinai offensive; the paratroopers were packed onto buses and rushed to Jerusalem.

"The 55th dropped on us from heaven," Narkiss regaled his staff after the war. "The south's heaven didn't want them." Though Dayan refused to entertain even the suggestion of capturing the Old City, Narkiss was set on that goal. Here, finally, was the opportunity to rectify Israel's failure in 1948, a miraculous second chance. "However it [fighting] started in Jerusalem, I knew it would end up in the Old City," he later admitted to his staff. No sooner had Gur arrived at Central Command than Narkiss told him, "Take whatever you can while there's still light." The colonel, the country's youngest brigade commander, had fought only briefly in 1948 and only in the Negev. Nevertheless, he had been born in the Old City and shared Narkiss's vision of its capture. He promptly positioned his paratroopers to move on both Mount Scopus and the Old City. "We will free Jerusalem!" Gur exclaimed.

But the task would not be that simple. Gur and his officers knew little of the lay of the city. They had rarely trained for urban combat and lacked maps and aerial photographs of the battleground, many of which were destroyed in the Jordanian shelling. Now, with much of their heavy weapons and communications equipment still packed for the airdrop, the paratroopers had only five hours to formulate a plan. "Our objective was to transform the brigade into a force that would be ready to fight in Jerusalem by midnight," recalled Col. Arik Akhmon, the 55th's intelligence officer. "The problem was not how to do it right, but how to avoid doing it terribly."

Merely assembling the paratroopers proved to be a major obstacle, as the Jordanian bombardment forced the buses onto unpaved detours that were already jammed with the Harel Brigade's vehicles. Like the paratroopers, the brigade was also a stranger to the area—all its maneuvers had been in the Negev—and ill equipped to deal with the dense minefields and rocky hillsides so inimical to tanks. "We faced two enemies—the Jordanians and the terrain," said Col. Aharon Gal, a battalion commander, after the battle. "I couldn't tell you which was worse."

To its advantage, the 10th had as its senior commander Uri Ben-Ari, a colorful, captious figure whose father had won the Iron Cross fighting for Germany in World War I, only to die in Dachau. Escaping to Palestine, Ben-Ari—born Banner—fought with the Harel Brigade in 1948, and in 1956, commanded the lead tank into Sinai. Though a financial scandal ended his military career, he continued to study German Panzer tactics, and even affected a riding crop. Of the first day of the war, he recalled, "We were all sorry about being in the Central Command . . . The war, we were told, started at 8:00, and by 10:30 we were still sitting around. We sat like pregnant women—we knew something was going to be born but didn't know what."[28]

The orders finally came in the afternoon. As stipulated by Dayan, the brigade was to attack northward into the hills overlooking the Jerusalem-Tel Aviv highway, penetrating at three points, and then proceed east for eleven miles, through the fortified villages of Bidu, Nabi Samwil, Beit Iksa, and Sheikh 'Abd al-'Aziz. The goal was to reach the Ramallah-Jerusalem highway near Beit Hanina, take the Arab neighborhood of Shu'afat, and link up with the paratroopers at Mount Scopus. By 4:00 P.M., the bulk of the forces were in place. Facing them was Jordan's al-Hashimi Brigade, infantrymen, and two battalions of Egyptian commandos.

Though they possessed considerable intelligence on their enemy, the Israelis were unprepared for the difficulty of the terrain and the complexities of their objectives. Two miles north of the Armistice Line, they encountered Radar Hill, a former British-built radar station, scored with bunkers and surrounded by 300 meters of mines. Col. Gal recounted: "The tanks that were supposed to cover our advance hit mines. Our forces were scattered. With no other choice, the infantry had to attack without tank cover . . . under a heavy Jordanian bombardment, leaping from stone to stone to avoid the mines. The battle was brutal, with knives and bayonets." The worst problem was the mines, which, according to Ben-Ari, "were both old and new and totally unpredictable. We didn't have equipment for clearing them . . . dozens of legs were lost."[29]

Two Israelis had been killed, and seven Shermans destroyed. Jordanian casualties were also relatively light: eight killed. But by midnight, the al-Hashimi Brigade was falling back to positions to the north of the road to Ramallah, leaving it open to Israeli tanks. Mount Scopus could be relieved and Arab Jerusalem severed from the northern West Bank, which itself was under attack.

As shelling from the Jordanian Long Toms between the villages of Burqin and Ya'bad intensified in the late afternoon, an *Ugdah* under Brig. Gen. Elad Peled moved into position. His forces, deployed for action against Syria, had to be hastily repositioned toward Jordan, regrouping in transit. Peled was a soldier's soldier, having served first, as a teenager, as a *Haganah* scout and then in a series of infantry and armored commands, culminating in his appointment as assistant to the IDF chief of operations. The terrain he entered, less mountainous than that around Jerusalem and replete with roads, was ideal for tanks. Rolling from Israel's Jezreel Valley—site of the legendary Armageddon—into Jordan's Dothan Valley, Elad planned to surround Jenin and compel its surrender. His force consisted of two armored brigades on loan from Northern

Command, and from Central Command, a mechanized brigade of infantry. "We crossed the border at 17:00 hours and penetrated deep into enemy territory," Peled recounted, "At the front there were batteries of anti-tank guns, but our tanks passed right through them. Only then did the [Jordanian] gunners wake up and open fire with light arms."

Charged with stopping Elad were three Jordanian infantry brigades and one armored brigade, along with a half-dozen supporting battalions. Part of this force had been drawn off by an Israeli feint in the northern Jordan Valley, near Beit Shean, while the rest was spread across the countryside. The stretching of Jordan's defenses over a thirty-mile front led Col. 'Awad Bashir Khalidi, commander of the 25th Khalid bin Walid Infantry Brigade, to protest directly to Hussein, "I appreciate your political problem in abandoning villages, but you cannot have politics and the military at the same time." But to his advantage, Khalidi had the trenchworks and bunkers around Jenin, and thorough knowledge of the terrain. He also could count on strong reinforcements from the 40th Armored Brigade.

The youngest brigade in the Jordanian army, commanded by Brig. Gen. Rukun al-Ghazi, the 40th boasted M-47 and M-48 Patton tanks and an infantry battalion equipped with M-113 Armored Personnel Carriers. The force had been positioned to reach Jenin area within twelve hours but then, with the outbreak of war, had been shifted south toward Jerusalem and bloodied by the IAF. Now, as the Israeli threat to Jenin materialized, Riyad ordered the brigade north again, in daylight, fully exposing it to Israel's aerial might. Dozens of vehicles were obliterated. Also hit was Iraq's 8th Mechanized Brigade, en route from Mafraq to replace the 40th at Damiya.[30]

The Israeli offensive began at 4:00 P.M. and involved a pincer of the armored brigades under Col. Uri Ram and Lt. Col. Moshe Bar Kokhva (Brill) swinging south and southwest, respectively, of Jenin, while the infantry of Col. Aharon Avnon descended from the north. The two axes to these destinations—the Megiddo-Jenin and Afula-Jenin roads—were both covered by Khalidi's 25th Brigade. No sooner had the Israelis crossed the border than the Jordanians greeted them with a storm of artillery, tank, and mortar fire.

"We thought we were the only people being attacked," Khalidi concluded, his troops coming under heavy bombardment from both the ground and the air. His men, well concealed and armed with antitank weapons and some thirty tanks, nevertheless put up a savage resistance, at one point enveloping the lead Israeli force until they, in turn, were enveloped. At close range, the Israeli Shermans were able to penetrate the armor of the Jordanians' more modern Pattons, and to ignite their external fuel tanks. Israeli reconnaissance companies meanwhile took the strategic 'Arabe junction, blocking the enemy's reinforcements.

Yet still the Jordanians battled. Khalidi called for air cover; his request passed from Riyad in Amman to Cairo, where Fawzi conveyed it to the Syrians. With Jordan beleaguered and Egyptian tanks crossing the Negev, now was no time to hang fire, the general said. Fawzi's reply came at 9:30 that night: Syrian planes would attack Israeli forces in the Jenin area at first light tomorrow.[31]

In fact, Syria had little air force left. Two-thirds of it—2 Ilyushin-28 bombers, 32 MiG-21's, 23 MiG-17's and 3 helicopters—had been eliminated in eighty-two midday sorties conducted by the IDF against the air bases of Dmair, Damascus, Saiqal, Marj Rial, and T-4. The Iraqi base at H-3 was also hit and ten of its planes destroyed. Shorn of the element of surprise, the Israelis lost ten planes as well, most of them to ground fire. Six pilots were killed, two of whom managed to bail out, only to be butchered by Syrian villagers.[32]

"Our forces carried out a heavy bombing of the enemy throughout the northern sector," declared Hafez al-Assad. "The enemy has lost most of its air power." The Syrians claimed that they, and not Israel, had started the war, that sixty-one Israeli planes had been downed, and Haifa's oil refinery razed. "We have decided that this battle will be one for the final liberation from imperialism and Zionism . . . We shall meet in Tel Aviv," proclaimed President Atassi.

The Syrians' sword-rattling merely hid their shock at the devastating blow just dealt them. Central front commander Mustafa Tlas, having narrowly escaped his tent as Israeli jets peppered it with cannon fire, quickly moved his headquarters to the rear. "Major Tawfiq al-Jahani offered me a cigarette to calm my nerves, but I refused it and swore off smoking from that moment on." But not all of Syria's officers were numbed. "We must attack before Israel preempts and surprises us with a combined armored and infantry assault," Assad urged at a meeting of the junta that afternoon. Atassi raised the possibility of striking Israel through Lebanon to lessen the danger of a counterattack on Syrian territory. But the Lebanese proved resistant to the idea, and orders were instead issued to begin Operation Victory at 5:45 the next morning. In preparation for the offensive, Syrian artillery was to open fire on Israeli settlements— Rosh Pina, Ayelet HaShachar, and Mishmar HaYarden were singled out—along the thirty-mile front.[33]

The shelling commenced at 2:30 P.M. and intensified throughout the afternoon. Residents of the settlements furiously lobbied the government to invade the Golan and so free them once and for all from the Syrian threat. Yariv warned of a Syrian offensive forming in the central Golan sector, opposite Kibbutz Gadot, and reported that Russian communications had been intercepted in the area. Rabin requested permission to strike preemptively, at least across the DZ's, but Dayan would not be persuaded. With Israeli forces already fighting on two fronts, they hardly needed to face a third, the defense minister reasoned. Reluctantly, he allowed IDF artillery and planes to return Syria's fire, but warned them to avoid hitting civilian villages. As long as Damascus refrained from land operations, Dayan decided, there would be no war in the north.[34]

Dayan's efforts to limit the conflict—earnest or, as Lior believed, disingenuous—could not diminish the fact that tens of thousands of men, Arabs and Israelis, were already engaged in combat. Though the course of the fighting, particularly in the air, had gone in Israel's favor, there was no way of predicting the directions it would ultimately take. The same chaos that had characterized political events of the preceding months continued to hold sway in the war. But the context also remained salient—a context comprised not only of the actions of Israel and the Arab states, but of the United States, the Soviet Union, and the UN.

Diplomacy Stumbles

The phone in the presidential bedroom started ringing at 4:35 A.M. On the other end was Walt Rostow, reporting that war in the Middle East had commenced. Rostow had spent the previous two hours in the Situation Room, listening to the first reports of military activity. Only once these were verified did he put through his call. Johnson said, "thank you," calmly, then made several calls of his own—to Rusk, McNamara, and Goldberg. Then, after a quick breakfast, the president joined Rostow, Richard Helms, and Earle Wheeler in the Situation Room where, the log recorded, "all HELL broke loose."

The problem was basic intelligence. The Americans knew only that several Sinai airfields had been rendered unserviceable, and that a ground war was now under way. Egyptian sources claimed that Israel had initiated hostilities with an attempt to bomb Cairo and block the Suez Canal, losing 158 planes in the process. But Israeli officials—Eban and Evron—swore that Egypt had fired first, dispatching waves of jets in the direction of the border and penetrating the Negev with tanks. U.S. intelligence sources nevertheless concluded that Egyptian estimates were "probably highly inflated," and should be "reduced by a coefficient of ten." Israel, rather, had acted preemptively and had quickly gained the upper hand in both its air and ground maneuvers.

Such news brought little joy to the administration, however. "There was no relief at the early indications of Israeli successes," McNamara remembered, "We had no idea how things would work out, whether we might not have to get involved directly ourselves." Rusk, though relieved that the Israelis were not "being driven onto the beaches," remained "angry as hell" at them for undermining Regatta and the Muhieddin visit, which he still believed might have yielded results. Johnson also felt saddened by the failure of his diplomatic efforts—later he wrote, "I have never concealed my regret that Israel decided to move when it did"—and apprehensive about the future course of the war.[35]

The deepest of those fears concerned the Soviets and their willingness to intervene. At 7:47, a general on duty at the Pentagon's War Room called McNamara and told him that, "Premier Kosygin is on the 'hot line' and asks to speak to the president." The hot line, locally known as Mo(scow)link, had been installed in the Pentagon after the Cuban missile affair and used subsequently for conveying holiday greetings, but never during a bona fide crisis. The defense secretary had the hot line patched into the White House Situation room.

"What should we say?" McNamara asked.

"My God," was Johnson's reply. "What *should* we say?"

Kosygin waited for acknowledgment that Johnson was indeed present before dispatching his message. "It is the duty of all great powers to achieve the immediate cessation of the military conflict. The Soviet Government has acted and will act in this direction. We hope that the Government of the United States will also act in the same manner and will exert the appropriate influence on . . . Israel."

The reply came half an hour later, when Rusk conveyed to Gromyko his "dismay" at reports of the fighting, and assured him of Washington's efforts to prevent it. "We feel it is very important that the United Nations Security Council succeed in bringing this fighting to an end as quickly as possible and are ready to cooperate with all members . . . to that end." Finally, the president himself wrote, opening his cable with "Dear Comrade Kosygin"—in the Kremlin, some people thought it was a joke—agreeing with the Soviet concept of great power duties and reiterating Rusk's request for swift action in the Security Council. "You may be assured we will exercise all our influence to bring hostilities to an end," Johnson pledged.

The "constructive and friendly" nature of these exchanges—seventeen more would follow—went far toward assuaging American anxieties regarding the Soviets' state of mind. Yet Johnson was loath to take any chances. To avoid the impression of collusion with Israel, he ordered the 6th Fleet, including the carriers *America* and *Saratoga*, to remain near Crete, and a marine landing team to continue its leave on Malta. An embargo of all U.S. arms shipments was also levied on the entire Middle East. The sole communication with Levi Eshkol was indirect, conveyed by Harry McPherson as he arrived in Israel, and very brief. "May God give us strength to protect the right," wrote Johnson.[36]

Presciently, even while addressing urgent strategic matters, Johnson was already thinking of a possible postwar settlement in the Middle East. The notion that war might facilitate, rather than void, such a breakthrough was not new to American thinking. As early as May 15, Harold Saunders had suggested that the White House consider whether, "if fighting starts, there is some gain in delaying our response long enough to allow a clear Israeli military victory (presuming they're able) . . . [and] whether there's anything to be gained from a blowup in the form of settling borders and, maybe even refugees." Two weeks later, Eugene Rostow empowered a Middle East Task Force of senior military and civilian officials to submit their "brightest ideas" on a peaceful resolution of the Arab-Israeli conflict. "Let us not forget that a crisis is also an opportunity," he reminded the Force. "Many patterns become loosened, and doors open. Let your minds rove over the horizon."

Now, as the first day of the war drew to a close, Walt Rostow wrote the president recommending "we should begin . . . talking with the Russians and, if possible, with others about the terms of a settlement." This would be achieved by trading Israel's newly acquired territories for Arab concessions. "A cease-fire will not answer the fundamental questions in the minds of Israelis until they have acquired so much real estate and destroyed so many Egyptian planes and tanks that they are absolutely sure of their bargaining position." As a first step in this direction, European ambassadors in Washington were alerted to the fact that "the military events of the next few days will determine the possibility for diplomacy to solve the wider problems." The Israelis were also asked to put forth their ideas about a postwar arrangement.[37]

The pitfalls of that diplomacy, however, were painfully evident already in the opening phase of the war. Regatta was effectively dead, a fact confirmed that morning by the refusal, even before they learned of the fighting, of Japan, Nigeria, Ethiopia, and Portugal to join the operation. The Muhieddin visit, though not formally canceled, was indefinitely postponed. Arab ambassadors in Washington rejected American affirmations of neutrality in the conflict, and accused the U.S. of willfully misleading Egypt by encouraging Israel to attack. Beginning in Beirut, U.S. embassies and consulates throughout the Arab world were assaulted by angry mobs. Nor was the situation calm domestically. When State Department spokesman Robert McCloskey said, "our position [on the war] is neutral in thought, word, and deed," American Jews protested vehemently. An embarrassed Rusk was compelled to explain that "neutral, a great concept in international law, is not an expression of indifference." Thus constrained, the administration had little choice but to react multilaterally, through the UN, as indicated by its first communiqué on the conflict:

> We are deeply distressed to learn that large scale fighting has broken out in the Middle East, an eventuality we had sought to prevent . . . The United States will devote all of its energies to bring about an end to the fighting and a new beginning of . . . peace and development of the area. We call upon all the parties to support the Security Council in bringing about an immediate cease-fire.[38]

Johnson's assumption was that the Security Council, once confronted with an actual war, would work swiftly and effectively to end it. Word of the fighting first reached UN headquarters at 2:40 A.M. from Gen. Rikhye, who reported that Israeli planes had bombed Egyptian positions in Gaza and strafed a UNEF column, killing three Indian soldiers. Bunche then called the secretary-general's residence, awakening him with the words, "war has broken out!" Forty-five minutes later, forgoing his quotidian morning meditation, U Thant was en route to UN headquarters. At virtually the same time, Gideon Rafael phoned Danish ambassador Hans Tabor, Security Council president for the month of June, and informed him that Israel was responding to "a cowardly and treacherous" attack from Egypt. Rafael had been instructed to read a statement to that effect to the Council, but by 6:30 those instructions had changed. Receiving an envelope marked "Your Eyes Only," Rafael learned of the destruction of Egypt's air force. His orders were now to delay the adoption of a cease-fire resolution by any means and for as long as possible.

A similar delay, paradoxically, was being sought by Mohammad El Kony, Egypt's ambassador. He, too, had complained of "a treacherous premeditated aggression," against Gaza, Sinai, and Egyptian airports, and announced that "Egypt has decided to defend itself by all means in accordance with the UN Charter." But El Kony had also spoken at length with Cairo and believed that an immense counterattack was now under way. He and the other Arab ambassadors—Tomeh of Syria and Jordan's al-Farra—were in a jubilant mood, listening to radio reports of Arab victories and receiving congratulations from Communist and other friendly delegations. "We deceived the Israelis," El Kony boasted to Federenko, insisting that the only planes Egypt lost were plywood models. "We shall see who wins this war."[39]

Convened at 9:30 A.M. by the USSR and the British—the French representative, Roger Seydoux, "wondered whether the meeting was necessary"—the Council quickly foundered. Arab delegates objected to the very notion of a cease-fire, while Gideon Rafael declared that Israel would take a "frigid view" of any attempt to order its forces back to the border. Federenko denounced Israeli "adventurism . . . encouraged by covert and overt actions of certain imperialist circles," and threatened to veto any resolution that failed to condemn Israel expressly. Stalemated, the Council recessed for "urgent consultations," but among the delegates only Goldberg seemed committed to pursuing such talks. Federenko shut himself up, incommunicado, inside his embassy, the Arabs were triumphant, and the Israelis mum. Circumstances seemed unpropitious for launching the peace process Washington had in mind.

And yet Goldberg persisted in viewing the war as a long-awaited opportunity, both diplomatically and personally. The youngest of eight children whose father, a Chicago greengrocer, died when he was three, Goldberg had worked his way up from urban poverty to become a nationally known labor lawyer. Appointed labor secretary by Kennedy, he later gave up a seat on the Supreme Court to accept the president's offer to name him America's ambassador to the UN—a decision he quickly came to regret. Long-winded and dry, he was overshadowed by his eloquent predecessor, Adlai Stevenson, and despite his daily contact with Johnson, cut off from the decision-making process he had hoped to influence. Increasingly opposed to the war in Vietnam, Goldberg seriously considered resigning.

All that changed with the Middle East crisis. Goldberg, an outspoken Zionist whose support for Israel had often caused friction between him and the State Department, could now capitalize on his close ties with both Tel Aviv and the White House to act as a primary go-between. When, on May 15, Goldberg was entertaining fellow UN ambassadors aboard the Circle Line ferry around Manhattan, Johnson dispatched a Coast Guard cutter to retrieve him with the news that the Egyptian army had entered Sinai.

Now, at 4:40 A.M. on June 5, Goldberg was on the phone first with the Situation Room and then with Bunche, coordinating the emergency session of the Security Council. His idea was to secure a simple cease-fire in place. At midday, he asked Rafael what Israel wanted. Rafael's reply was, simply, "time."[40]

Time was already dwindling, however, as rumors of Israeli victories reached New York. At 6:30 P.M., India insisted that the Security Council reconvene to restore the *status quo ante bellum* of June 4. The draft, implicitly legitimizing both the blockade and the eviction of UNEF, was fundamentally unacceptable to Goldberg. Coordinating closely with Johnson and Walt Rostow, he joined with Britain's ambassador, Lord Caradon (the former Hugh Foot, the last British governor of Cyprus and a one-time official under the Palestine Mandate), in tabling an alternative resolution. This called upon the warring parties to cease firing immediately, to "insure [the] disengagement of forces," and to "refrain from acts of force regardless of their nature and to reduce tension in the area." The language was designed to compel Egypt to reopen Tiran and to remove its troops from Sinai.

Goldberg's view, he later attested, was that "we would have to act quickly before the situation congealed if we were to have a chance of restoring peace." Federenko also appeared to be awakening to that fact, having learned of the situation in the field. But he still balked at approving a resolution that did not provide for the withdrawal of Israeli troops and recognition of Egypt's rights in Tiran. He proposed postponing further discussion until the following morning, and advised Goldberg in the interim to consult with El Kony. "The Arabs always seem to accept yesterday's formulations too late," Goldberg reminded the Egyptian ambassador, with whom he enjoyed cordial relations. But cordiality did not count; El Kony refused to consider the American draft.[41]

American efforts to transform the third Arab-Israeli war into a permanent peace—to change the context—had begun inauspiciously. Neither the Arabs nor the Soviets as yet were interested in stopping the fighting, much less in reaching a settlement. The Israelis, for their part, were resolved to prevent a cease-fire for forty-eight hours at least, and to link any cessation of hostilities to an Arab declaration of nonbelligerency. In his latest delaying tactic, Rafael announced that Abba Eban was flying to New York and would address the Council the following day. The foreign minister was hoping that no decisions could be reached before he arrived and pressed Israel's case. "In going to battle we did not determine our objectives," he wrote his UN ambassador, "but we did know what our goals were in terms of more secure and stable existence and for getting us closer to peace."[42]

"The First Day's Turkey Shoot"

The very notion of peace, for Arab and Israeli soldiers, could not have seemed more distant. By that evening, the opposing armies were pitted in desperate battles that would soon determine the course of the war—indeed, of the entire Middle East.

In Sinai, at 10:00 P.M., six battalions of 105-mm and 155 mm guns fired the largest barrage in Israeli military history, leveling 6,000 shells in less than twenty minutes on Umm Qatef. "Let everything tremble," Sharon purportedly announced. While Israeli tanks continued to pound the northernmost Egyptian defenses, IDF infantrymen poured into the triple line of trenches in the east, and paratroopers neutralized Egypt's artillery to the west. This was the implementation of what Sharon called "a continuous unfolding of surprises" —striking the enemy from multiple and unexpected directions, simultaneously, at night. One Egyptian officer, taken prisoner, agreed: "It was like watching a snake of fire uncoiling."

The Egyptians were devastated. Throughout the day, they had heard ecstatic news reports of Arab victories. "We heard about the war from the radio," recalled Hasan Bahgat, a senior intelligence officer positioned behind Umm Qatef. "The whole world thought that our forces were at the outskirts of Tel Aviv." Military Order 4, released by 'Amer's headquarters at 11:45 A.M., reported that "a ground clash occurred along the border, with the enemy attempting to break through our front line defenses in Sinai. The attack failed." This was followed by Military Orders 12 and 13, at 4:30 and 6:00, which claimed that the Israeli forces attacking Kuntilla and Umm Qatef had been either driven off or destroyed. Gen. Murtagi, who had never anticipated a direct Israeli assault on Umm Qatef, ordered counterattacks from his forces at Jabal Libni and Bir Lahfan. Neither succeeded, blocked by Israeli lodgments on the roads and relentlessly bombed from the air. Despairing of reinforcements, Egyptian commanders in Umm Qatef ordered artillery barrages onto their own positions.[43]

Not all went smoothly for the Israelis, though. Half the helicopters transporting Dani Matt's paratroopers got lost and never found the battlefield; others could not land because of mortar fire. An entire armored brigade under Col. Mordechai Zippori, attacking the front, was stalled for want of a single mine-clearing tank, while Col. Nir, having broken through the rear defenses at Ruwafa Dam, was hit by a tank shell and severely injured in both legs. Yet the overall plan was largely maintained and in some respects exceeded. At a cost of 40 killed and 140 wounded, the Israelis had broken through the Egyptian defenses and were poised to attack Umm Qatef.

A similar fate was met by virtually all of Egypt's first-defense line in Sinai. Further south, the 8th Armored Brigade under Col. Avraham (Albert) Mendler, initially positioned as a ruse to draw off Egyptian forces from the real invasion routes, struck and captured the fortified bunkers at Kuntilla. In an action later lionized by Egyptian military history, reconnaissance troops put up a valiant fight. "The battalion placed ambushes for the advancing enemy forces which outnumbered us in quantity and firing capacity," one recon officer, Yahya Sa'ad Basha, recalled. "They confronted them fearlessly and hit a number of Israeli tanks. Only three Egyptian tanks remained and one of these was damaged. Most of the officers and soldiers were killed. I watched my battalion disintegrate . . . I saw the bodies of soldiers after the Israeli tanks had run them over . . . I saw the wounded lying on the ground and was utterly unable to help them." By night-fall, Mendler's men had achieved a strategically valuable position, able to pre-vent Shazli Force from aiding Umm Qatef and also to join Sharon's next major engagement, at Nakhl.

In the north, Tal's division consolidated its hold on Rafah and Khan Yunis, and reached the outskirts of al-'Arish. "Clearing the city was hard fighting," according to the IDF record. "The Egyptians fired from the rooftops, from balconies and windows. They dropped grenades into our half-tracks and blocked the streets with trucks. Our men threw the grenades back and crushed the trucks with their tanks."

Between Tal and Sharon's forces, close to midnight and with lights blaz-ing, passed the third of Israel's southern divisions—Gen. Yoffe's—en route to Bir Lahfan and Jabal Libni. Skirting Abu 'Ageila to the north, threading through Sharon's battlefield and exchanging friendly fire with some of his tanks, the lead Centurions of Col. Elhanan Sela advanced and turned southwest. Farther to the north, in the sandy wastes of Wadi Haridin, inched the 200th Brigade of Col. Yissachar "Yiska" Shadmi. Believed impassable by the Egyptians, the wadi had been studied by IDF paratroopers in 1956 and found suitable for tanks. Bedeviled by mines and artillery bombardments, Sela and Shadmi nevertheless managed to cut off all the major road junctions—to Jabal Libni, Abu 'Ageila, and al-'Arish—and to stop two Egyptian armored brigades attempting to en-circle Sharon.

Less success attended the Israelis' advance in a battle they had hoped to avoid, in Gaza. Dayan had expressly forbade entry into the twenty-five-mile Strip, explaining that Israel did not need to saddle itself with 250,000 Palestin-ian refugees and complicated inner-city fighting. Yet, shortly after issuance of the Red Sheet order, Palestinian positions in Gaza opened fire on nearby Is-raeli settlements of Nirim and Kisufim. Rabin overruled Dayan's orders and instructed a reinforced mechanized brigade, the 11th, under Col. Yehuda Reshef, to enter the Strip. The force promptly met withering artillery fire and spirited opposition from Palestinian soldiers and remnants of the 7th Division from Rafah. "The Egyptian soldier, by his nature, is better at static than mobile defense," Rafael Eitan, the paratrooper commander, observed. "The Palestin-ian soldiers, by contrast, were more willing to make sacrifices."

Seventy Israelis would be killed in some of the war's heaviest fighting. Also killed were Ben Oyserman of the CBC, *Life* magazine's Paul Schutzer, whose final photographs would appear in a special edition on the war, and twelve more members of UNEF. By sunset, IDF forces had taken the strategically vital 'Ali Muntar ridge, overlooking Gaza city, but were beaten back from the city itself.[44]

Other unanticipated battles continued to rage along the eastern front, where the resistance offered the Israelis was no less dogged. Around Jenin, the Jordanians'

12th Armored Battalion held off repeated attempts by Bar Kokhva's column—a far larger force—to break through Burqin woods, close by the Kabatiya cross-roads. The deputy battalion commander, Maj. Muhammad Sa'id al-'Ajluni, ordered the woods held "to the last man and shell," and claimed to have destroyed eighteen Israeli tanks. "Confused and panicky, the Israelis were running around their blazing vehicles like frightened ants," 'Ajluni's commander, Maj. Salah 'Alayyan, recorded. But relentless IAF air strikes began to take their toll on the Jordanians. Their M-48 Pattons, equipped with external fuel tanks, proved vulnerable at short distances, even to Israel's older Shermans. Twelve of 'Ajluni's tanks were destroyed, and only six remained operative. Then, just after dusk, 'Ajluni spotted lights approaching from the south that he believed belonged to reinforcements from the 40th Armored Brigade. In fact, they were the lights of yet more Israeli tanks which, once within range, immediately opened fire.

"The Jordanians fought bravely and effectively," conceded an official Israeli history of the battle, "Their tanks and antitank weapons had to be destroyed before the [Peled's] *Ugdah* could proceed to higher ground and the enemy's infantry positions." Ephraim Reiner, commander of the IDF's 37th Armored Brigade, described how his forces were unable to advance without first waiting for supporting artillery fire and air strikes against the enemy. "One plane swung around and dove right onto the Jordanian commander's tank, wounding him and killing his radio operator and intelligence officer. Only then did I inform the division that I was attacking . . . a classic night attack, very nice." Wounded, 'Ajluni ordered his surviving tanks to fall back to Jenin where, together with the remnants of Khalidi's 25th Infantry Brigade, they found themselves effectively surrounded.[45]

The IDF's breakthrough in the northern West Bank was mirrored in the Jerusalem area, where Ben-Ari's 10th Brigade was approaching Bidu and the crucial Beit Iksa-Beit Hanina junction. Another Brigade, the 4th, under Col. Moshe Yotvat, had been thrown together from sundry infantry units and sent to open the Latrun Corridor. The Jordanian police fort at the corridor's western entrance—*Bab al-Wad* in Arabic, and in Hebrew, *Sha'ar HaGai*—had withstood successive Israeli forays in 1948, but it fell with surprisingly little resistance in the early evening of June 5. So, too, did the adjacent villages of Yalu, Imwas, and Beit Nuba.

Billeted within those villages were commandos of Egypt's 33rd and 53rd "Thunderbolt" battalions, prepared to attack Israeli airfields. "The patrols, each led by Jordanian intelligence scouts, moved out toward Ramla and Hatzor at 7:00 P.M.," confirmed commando officer 'Ali 'Abd al-Mun'im Marsi. "We started infiltrating through Israeli settlements . . . We had no clear idea of our assignment, only a palm-sized photograph of one of the bases." Marsi's men were soon detected, however, and sought shelter in nearby fields, which the Israelis then set on fire. Of the original force of 600 commandos, only 150 survived and fled to Jordan.

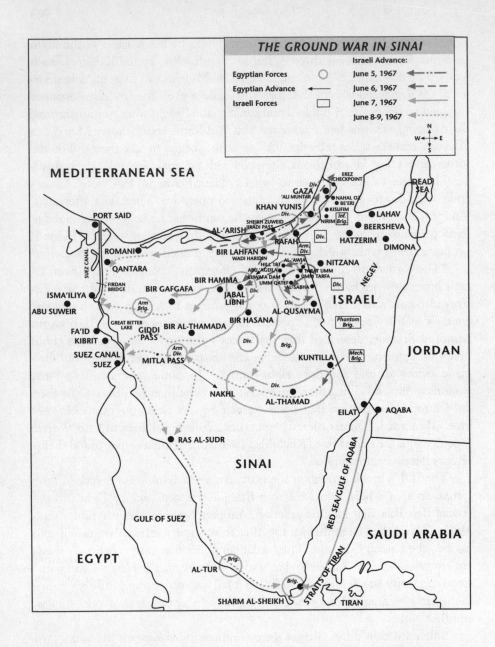

THE GROUND WAR IN SINAI

Israeli Advance:

Egyptian Forces

Egyptian Advance

Israeli Forces

June 5, 1967
June 6, 1967
June 7, 1967
June 8–9, 1967

MEDITERRANEAN SEA

EREZ CHECKPOINT

DEAD SEA

GAZA
'ALI MUNTAR

KHAN YUNIS

NAHAL OZ
BE'ERI
KISUFIM
NIRIM

LAHAV

PORT SAID

AL-'ARISH

SHEIKH ZUWEID
JIRADI PASS

BEERSHEVA

RAFAH

Div.

HATZERIM

DIMONA

ROMANI

BIR LAHFAN

QANTARA

WADI HARIDIN
HILL 181
ABU 'AGEILA
RUWAFA DAM
UMM QATEF

AL-'AWJA
TARAT UMM
UMM TARFA
AL-SABHA

NITZANA

SUEZ CANAL

FIRDAN BRIDGE

BIR HAMMA

BIR GAFGAFA

JABAL LIBNI

Div.

AL-QUSAYMA

NEGEV

ISRAEL

ISMA'ILIYA

Arm Brig.

Div.

Phantom Brig.

ABU SUWEIR

GREAT BITTER LAKE

BIR AL-THAMADA

BIR HASANA

Div.

Brig.

FA'ID
KIBRIT

GIDDI PASS

JORDAN

SUEZ CANAL
SUEZ

MITLA PASS

Arm Div.

KUNTILLA

Mech. Brig.

NAKHL

Div.

AL-THAMAD

EILAT

AQABA

RAS AL-SUDR

SINAI

RED SEA/GULF OF AQABA

SAUDI ARABIA

GULF OF SUEZ

EGYPT

AL-TUR

Brig.

SHARM AL-SHEIKH

Brig.

STRAITS OF TIRAN

TIRAN

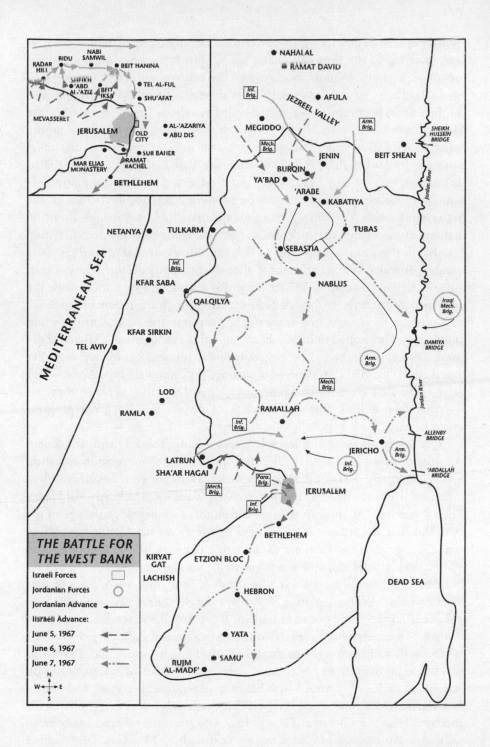

THE BATTLE FOR THE WEST BANK

Israeli Forces
Jordanian Forces
Jordanian Advance
Israeli Advance:

June 5, 1967
June 6, 1967
June 7, 1967

N
W E
S

Inset (upper left):

RADAR HILL
RIDU
NABI SAMWIL
BEIT HANINA
SHEIKH 'ABD AL-'AZIZ
BEIT IKSA
TEL AL-FUL
SHU'AFAT
MEVASSERET
JERUSALEM
OLD CITY
AL-'AZARIYA
ABU DIS
SUR BAHER
MAR ELIAS MONASTERY
RAMAT RACHEL
BETHLEHEM

Main map:

NAHALAL
RAMAT DAVID
Inf. Brig.
JEZREEL VALLEY
AFULA
Arm. Brig.
SHEIKH HUSSEIN BRIDGE
MEGIDDO
Mech. Brig.
JENIN
BEIT SHEAN
BURQIN
YA'BAD
'ARABE
KABATIYA
TUBAS
NETANYA
TULKARM
SEBASTIA
Jordan River
Inf. Brig.
KFAR SABA
NABLUS
QALQILYA
Iraqi Mech. Brig.
DAMIYA BRIDGE
KFAR SIRKIN
TEL AVIV
Arm. Brig.
Mech. Brig.
LOD
RAMLA
RAMALLAH
Inf. Brig.
ALLENBY BRIDGE
LATRUN
SHA'AR HAGAI
JERICHO
Inf. Brig.
Arm. Brig.
'ABDALLAH BRIDGE
Para. Brig.
Mech. Brig.
JERUSALEM
Inf. Brig.
BETHLEHEM
KIRYAT GAT
ETZION BLOC
LACHISH
DEAD SEA
HEBRON
YATA
RUJM AL-MADF'
SAMU'

MEDITERRANEAN SEA

"They'll be in the city within two hours," Deputy Chief of Staff Haim Bar-Lev, referring to the Harel Brigade's tanks, blithely reported to the government that evening. Within the city, too, the confrontation was coming to a head. Starting at 7:45 P.M., salvos of Israeli mortar and artillery shells saturated the Jordanian positions along the so-called northern line leading from the Mandelbaum Gate up to Mount Scopus. Flares and search beams lit up the night. Israeli infantrymen stationed along that line received their first relief from the Jordanian shell and small-arms fire that had continued unabated throughout the day. For Motta Gur's paratroopers, though, the countermeasures were merely preparations for the pending effort to burst through the Arab neighborhood of Sheikh Jarrah and link up with Mount Scopus. Resisting that assault was a dense network of obstacles—bunkers, barbed wire, and mines.

Rabin tried to persuade Gur to delay his attack until dawn, when cover could be provided by the IAF, but the offer was promptly declined. Jets were of little use in the close, street-by-street fighting ahead, Gur explained, while the paratroopers preferred to fight in darkness. Also, if fighting intensified in Sinai, or broke out with Syria, the army might postpone the Jerusalem operation indefinitely. Gur hoped to move out at midnight, but logistical difficulties delayed H-hour until 2:15 A.M., leaving only ninety minutes before daybreak. Yet the colonel remained confident, later writing, "We knew that the Arabs would defend Jerusalem from its fixed positions . . . [and] that they never constructed a second defense line. Once we broke through [the first line], our progress would be easy."[46]

Jordan's brigades in the Jerusalem area—King Talal, Hittin, and Imam 'Ali—were indeed immobile, with little coordination or even communication between them. By the late afternoon, however, as the Israeli attacks intensified, command over the city was entrusted to King Talal's general, 'Ata 'Ali Haza'. The 44-year-old 'Ali, mild-mannered and slight, a soldier since the age of fifteen, had been decorated for gallantry in fighting near the Mandelbaum Gate in 1948. A graduate of England's Camberley College, he was a no-nonsense officer, deeply patriotic, and averse to Arab radicals. "Before 1967, I had no fear that Israel would start a war," he attested, "but since 1956, I feared that Nasser would." While deploring Jordan's entanglement in "Nasser's war," he was determined to hold out in Jerusalem, at least until a cease-fire.

'Ata 'Ali ordered his forces consolidated in a line extending from Abu Tor in the south and northward to the Old City, Sheikh Jarrah, and Tel al-Ful astride Mount Scopus. At his disposal were 5,000 Jordanian troops and 1,000 Palestinian militiamen, armed with heavy mortars, machine-guns, and howitzers. But he had no tanks, and believed that the Israeli forces outnumbered his own by at least three-to-one. Though his own transmitter was seriously damaged, 'Ata 'Ali managed to get a message through to Maj. Gen. Muhammad Ahmad Salim, commander of the Western Front, urging him to send tanks and troops immediately.

Salim obliged and dispatched a Patton battalion from the 60th Armored Brigade. Like the 40th, the 60th Brigade was a *corps d'élite*, commanded by King Hussein's cousin, Brig. Sharif Zayd bin Shaker, a graduate of the U.S. Army Staff College. His original orders were to repel Israeli forces from the Latrun Corridor, but in view of the worsening situation in Jerusalem itself, the brigade was now to proceed to the city's Arab suburbs and from there attack Mount Scopus. Inching forward in the dark, the tanks climbed the twenty-mile, 2,700-foot ascent from Jericho. Parallel to them, struggling up a mountain track from Wadi Qelt to 'Isawiya, came infantrymen from Imam 'Ali Brigade. Well before they reached their destinations, though, both forces were spotted by Israeli planes and, subjected to rocket and cannon fire, virtually decimated.

At 9:00 that night, just as the Israelis completed their capture of southern Jerusalem and prepared to assault the northern line, 'Ata 'Ali saw the sky light up over the Mount of Olives. Instinctively, he knew what had happened. Further appeals to send troops from Ramallah and Hebron were rejected; both cities were braced for attack. Jerusalem would receive no reinforcements.[47]

The worsening plight of the Jordanians was closely monitored by Israeli leaders. For them, the question now was not whether the IDF would win in Jerusalem, but whether capture of the city's eastern half was politically prudent. Several members of the government, most notably Menachem Begin and Yigal Allon, emphatically thought so, and throughout the day had pressed Eshkol to approve a Jerusalem offensive. "*Sis Agedank,*" Eshkol sardonically replied—in Yiddish, slapping a hand to his forehead—"That's an idea." The prime minister was once again torn between total confidence in Israel's fighting ability and fear for its future safety. Now, in addition to Soviet intervention, Israelis faced the danger of censure and even embargo by the Christian world should they capture the Old City and its Holy Places.

Eshkol was not alone; other ministers, most notably those from the National Religious party, shared his fear of an international backlash. But countervailing pressures were also at work, beginning with those from Jordan. Despite repeated Israeli requests, conveyed through diplomatic channels, for a cease-fire, the shelling of outer Tel Aviv and downtown Jerusalem had continued. Dayan, arriving at the Knesset for his own swearing-in ceremony as defense minister, found the building deserted and returned to Tel Aviv. It was not until the early evening that the other ministers managed to get through and, at Begin's request, convene in an underground shelter.

Begin's purpose was to discuss the Old City—whether Israeli forces should enter it and what Israel's policy would be if they did. In addition to the military requisites of forcing Hussein to stop the shelling and of defending Mount Scopus, the ministers were seized by the millennial vision of a united Jewish capital. "Perhaps the most important Cabinet meeting Jerusalem ever held," Col. Lior wrote, mindful of his own elated state: "As the son of an observant family exterminated in the concentration camps, as the scion of the Jewish people and a citizen of the State of Israel, I could not hold back my soaring emotions."[48]

Emotions indeed flared as the ministers, speaking above the *basso continuo* of incoming shells, spoke their minds. "This is the hour of our political test," Begin opened. "We must attack the Old City in response both to the unheeded warnings we sent Hussein as well as to the Jordanian shelling." Allon concurred: "We all want to see the Old City as an indivisible part of Israel—or that Israelis at least have access to the Holy Places." But Eshkol advised caution. "We have to weigh the diplomatic ramifications of conquering the Old City," he said, "Even if we take the West Bank and the Old City, we will eventually be forced to leave them." The NRP's Haim Moshe Shapira supported Eshkol, declaring, "I assume that there will be pressure to internationalize the city, and I, for one, won't oppose the idea." The debate broke down less on ideological than on visceral lines, with Mapai's Zalman Aran seconding Shapira and Mordechai Bentov, of the left-wing Mapam, siding with Begin. Abba Eban expressed concern for possible damage to the Holy Places.

In the end, the ministers agreed not to agree, accepting a compromise formula proposed by Eshkol: "In view of the situation created in Jerusalem by the Jordanian bombardment, and after warnings were sent to Hussein, an opportunity has perhaps been created to capture the Old City." The immediate task, however, was to silence the Jordanian guns.

Dayan was already wrestling with that question, deep in the Pit with his generals—Rabin, Weizman, Bar-Lev. "I know what you want," he told them. "You want to take Jenin." None of them raised an objection, nor did Dayan demur. Thus, laconically, the first step was authorized for Israel's entry into the West Bank. As for Jerusalem, Dayan ordered another message sent to Hussein, this one threatening to bomb Amman if his forces persisted in bombarding Israel. In the interim, the IDF could press its attacks to the north and south of the Old City, surrounding it. "The Old City can be in our hands by tomorrow," Dayan responded when Eshkol informed him of the Cabinet's discussion. But the defense minister was determined to delay that action even longer, until the conquest of Sinai was complete.[49]

The Egyptian and Jordanian fronts remained intrinsically related. Jordan's bombing of Israel came in reaction to Israel's attack on Egypt, the early success of which enabled Israel to strike back at Jordan. Another nexus existed in the fact that neither Nasser nor Hussein was aware of the perilous state of their armies. Nasser's officers were afraid to enlighten him while Hussein's, lacking communications with the field, were clueless. Neither would easily believe that Egypt's air force, the linchpin of the Arab war effort, had been eliminated in a matter of hours, or that Israeli tanks were advancing on two fronts while the Syrians remained inert. Egypt's propaganda organs, radio and press, continued to boast of extraordinary victories, while according to Jordanian communiqués, Israeli forces had been repulsed from Jerusalem and Jenin and thirty-one Israeli planes shot down.[50] Such ignorance could not withstand the mounting evidence of disaster, however, as the first day of fighting waned.

The truth became known to Nasser at 4:00 P.M. when, for the first time that day, he entered Supreme Headquarters and encountered bedlam. 'Amer, either drunk or drugged or both, had gone from a state of extreme excitement to one of profound depression. Screaming into the phone, he told Murtagi first to move his forces at al-'Arish to Umm Qatef, and then changed his mind and ordered a retreat to Jabal Libni and the second line of defense. He spoke with Sidqi Mahmud and declared that U.S., and not Israeli, planes had performed the attack against Egypt, and that one of his pilots—Husni Mubarak—had seen the American jets. 'Amer refused to take other calls, whether from the Soviet ambassador or from the Foreign Ministry, all of them anxious for information. Nor could they get through to Shams Badran. The defense minister had a bed moved into his office, then sequestered himself inside. "To think that's our highest security official," scoffed 'Abd al-Latif al-Baghdadi who, along with Kamel Hassan and Hassan Ibrahim—all former Free Officers—had volunteered their services at headquarters. "That's our equivalent to Dayan."

Nasser tried to talk with his field marshal but found him inconsolable and practically incoherent. The exact substance of their conversation remains unknown, but its outcome was indisputable. Orders went out to Gen. Salah Muhsin, commander of the 14th Armored Brigade at al-'Arish, to counterattack at dawn, even without air cover. A decision was also made to inform Algeria of the air force's destruction and to request that it loan Egypt a large number of its MiG's. Lastly and most fatefully, Nasser and 'Amer agreed to maintain the fiction of direct Anglo-American involvement in the war, both to minimize Egypt's dishonor and to prod the Soviets to intervene. Ambassador Ghaleb in Moscow was instructed to request an immediate audience with Kosygin to inform him of the collusion. Arab oil producers, beginning with Iraq and Kuwait, answered Nasser's call to suspend all shipments to the U.S. and Great Britain. At 6:05 P.M., listeners to Cairo's Voice of the Arabs learned that "the United States is the enemy. The United States is the hostile force behind Israel. The United States, oh Arabs, is the enemy of all peoples, the killer of life, the shedder of blood, that is preventing you from liquidating Israel."[51]

Rumors, traditionally a vehicle for disseminating information in the Middle East, had begun to spread. Sixteen hours after the first Israeli jet dropped its bombs on an Egyptian runway, the results of that operation were being whispered in the streets of Lebanon and Syria, in Iraq and Saudi Arabia. Jordanian Military Intelligence Chief Brig. Gen. Ibrahim Ayyub summoned his staff at 7:00 P.M. and told them that, "I have just received information that 90 percent of the Egyptian air force has been destroyed on the ground."

One of the few populations in the region to remain totally ignorant of the course of the battle was, strangely enough, Israel's. Air raid sirens had sounded throughout the day, but no signal of "all clear" had followed. Egyptian tanks, for all Israelis knew, were rumbling into the Negev, while other Arab armies prepared to invade as well. Speaking on national radio, Eshkol described the "cruel and bloody campaign" his fellow citizens faced, warning them that "the distinction between front and rear may become blunted . . . all of Israel is a front line." In spite of the grave insecurity these pronouncements instilled, Dayan insisted on maintaining absolute press silence about the IDF's achievements. His purpose was to delay as long as possible international pressure for a cease-fire and the danger of Soviet meddling.[52]

This did not prevent the Israelis from updating the Americans, however. Meir Amit briefed McPherson and Barbour, stressing the existential threat Israel had faced and its intention to "press all the buttons" now that the shooting had started. The battle, he declared, was not only for Israel's security but also for the survival of all pro-Western forces in the Middle East. Subsequently, a general depiction of the IDF's successes in Sinai, Jerusalem, and the West Bank was forwarded from Tel Aviv to Washington, along with a report on the 400 Arab aircraft destroyed and Israel's 19 losses. The updates were reviewed by Walt Rostow, who then passed them on to the president. "Herewith the account, with a map," Rostow's memo began, "of the first day's turkey shoot."[53]

THE WAR: DAY TWO, JUNE 6

Israeli advances and Arab retreats.
America on war and peace.
"Big Lies" and cease-fires.

THOUGH FIFTY-THREE YEARS OLD AND PAUNCHY, the director of Israel's Nature Protection Society, Avraham Yoffe, was a seasoned fighter in Sinai. In 1956, he had led an infantry column down the peninsula's eastern coast to capture Sharm al-Sheikh. Later, as head of the Southern Command, he developed contingency plans for moving tanks over desert wastes that were widely believed insurmountable. Summoned a few weeks before the war by Gen. Gavish, Yoffe had arrived at camp in civilian clothes, thinking he was making a courtesy call. He returned in a brigadier general's uniform and took charge of the 31st *Ugdah* with its two reserve brigades, each with 100 tanks. His assignment was to penetrate Sinai south of Tal's forces and north of Sharon's, dividing the two fronts and preventing enemy reinforcements from reaching either. Then, dashing eastward, he would attack Egypt's second line of defense while its first was still busy fighting.

Yoffe's initial objective, taking the vital road junctions of Abu 'Ageila, Bir Lahfan, and al-'Arish, had already been accomplished before midnight. "We received information that two Egyptian armored brigades were approaching," Yissachar Shadmi, commanding twenty-four Centurions, later related. "They had turned off all their lights, and my forward observer reported, 'I can't see them!' I told him, 'shoot blindly,' and our first barrage blew up seven vehicles. The Egyptians then spread out in the dunes and a bitter battle ensued, lasting from 11 P.M. to 10 A.M. the next morning." Israeli planes completed the work begun by Shadmi, and by midday, the desert was strewn with burning wrecks. The Egyptians fled westward, toward Jabal Libni, which the Israelis regrouped to attack.

The thrust to Egypt's center enabled Tal and Sharon to complete the unfinished business of the previous day—conquering the Jiradi Defile, Khan Yunis, and the bastions at Umm Qatef. Each of these battles was savage. Having pressed a frontal attack through Abu 'Ageila, Sharon's Centurions launched their main thrust against Umm Qatef, the main Egyptian redoubt, only to find the approaches thickly mined and cratered. When IDF engineers finally cleared a path, at 4:00 A.M., Israeli and Egyptian tanks engaged in intense combat, at ranges as close as ten yards. Forty Egyptian and nineteen Israeli tanks were left side by side, smoldering. Kuti Adam's infantry, meanwhile, completed its clearance of the triple-tier trenches. Israeli casualties were 14 dead and 41 wounded, as opposed to the 300 Egyptians killed and 100 taken prisoner.

Sharon's men passed the morning cleaning up around Umm Qatef and preparing to seize al-Qusayma in the southeast. Meanwhile, to the north, Col. Gonen's tanks managed to smash through the Jiradi Pass—again—to link up with forward elements stranded on its western side. These, however, had not waited for relief, but had advanced to the outskirts of al-'Arish. Gonen rushed to reunite with them and, after receiving supplies via airdrop, proceeded to al-'Arish airport, which he captured at 7:50. Yet the battle was far from finished. "We entered the city at 8:00 A.M., intending to cross it and reach the coast road. Al-'Arish was totally quiet, desolate," recounted company commander Yossi Peled. "Suddenly the city turned into a madhouse. Shots came at us from every alley, every corner, every window and house."

While detailing several units to clear out al-'Arish, Gonen split his force three ways. A column of tanks, engineers, and artillery under the command of Col. Yisrael Granit continued down the Mediterranean coast toward the Canal, while a second force led by Gonen himself turned south to Bir Lahfan and Jabal Libni. Col. Eytan and the paratroopers of the 35th brigade were detailed for the conquest of Gaza. Much as Dayan had feared, the fighting in the area, from Khan Yunis to 'Ali Muntar ridge, was brutal, accounting for nearly half of all Israel casualties on the southern front. But Dayan's prediction that Gaza, once severed from Sinai, would quickly fall proved correct. By mid-morning the Israelis had already captured the Egyptian headquarters in the city, and had begun mopping-up operations.[1]

For the Egyptians on the front lines, the Israeli offensive was devastating. The 2nd Division had been badly mauled and isolated, while the 7th and 20th Divisions had essentially ceased to exist. Thousands of vehicles had been destroyed—their flaming hulls lined the roads, illuminating them at night—and hundreds immobilized by mechanical failures as Soviet-made engines proved unsuitable to desert conditions. At least 1,500 soldiers had been killed. Reconnaissance Officer 'Adel Mahjub, having fled from Umm Qatef, reached Bir Hasana before dawn, only to find it "burning and totally destroyed. Those soldiers still alive were left without food. There was no petrol for the vehicles and no ammunition for the weapons. It was like a journey to hell." At Jabal

Libni, Reconnaissance Officer Hasan Bahgat watched as Egyptian artillery opened fire on thousands of soldiers advancing toward him from the east. "An hour later, one of those soldiers reached us and we found out that he was Egyptian. Our guns had destroyed Egyptian soldiers retreating from Abu 'Ageila."

Harassed by enemy artillery, the Egyptians were hounded throughout the day by continuing air strikes. 'Azzam Shirahi, a security officer at the Bir Gafgafa airfield, recalled how, "on the second day, Field Marshal 'Amer spoke with the base commander and asked him to repair the runway quickly so that new planes could be sent. We all went down to try and repair the runway but the bombings continued. The anti-aircraft guns fired at the Israeli planes without respite, fired until their barrels melted, but with no effect. Many of the pilots were killed along with many aerial defense soldiers and officers. After that, no new planes arrived and no one opposed the Israelis." The few Egyptian jets that did manage to get airborne, such as the two Sukhoi's that strafed Gonen's supply trucks that morning, were swiftly set upon by Israeli squadrons.[2]

Yet, for all this destruction, the Egyptian army in Sinai was far from vanquished. Over half of Nasser's forces were still intact, and important elements—the 3rd and 6th Divisions, and the Shazli Force—had yet to fire a shot. Hundreds of pilots were available to fly once new planes were secured. And forty-eight Algerian MiG's were already en route to Egypt, along with volunteer forces from Morocco, Tunisia, and Sudan. Expressions of support also poured in from Egypt's sympathizers around the world. "We are highly indignant at the action of Israeli reactionary agents of the United States and British imperialists," wrote Vietnamese Communist leader Ho Chi Minh in a personal wire to Nasser. "They are doomed to ignominious defeat." An official Soviet statement proclaimed "resolute support" and "complete confidence" in the Arabs' "just struggle against imperialism and Zionism." The Egyptian people, listening to Cairo Radio, were informed that their army had "wiped out" the enemy attacks on Kuntilla and Khan Yunis, and was penetrating enemy territory.[3]

These circumstances contrasted sharply with Israel's. Unlike the majority of Egyptian soldiers, the bulk of the Israeli invasion force and planes had been in almost constant combat for over twenty-four hours; they were tired and low on ammunition and fuel. Politically, both Britain and the United States had declared their neutrality in the conflict, and France embargoed further arms shipments to Israel. Though morale improved after Rabin, in a 1:00 A.M. radio broadcast, finally informed the Israeli public of the IDF's successes in the air and on the ground, that admission increased the chances of an internationally imposed cease-fire. Preparing for that contingency, Rabin acknowledged that Israel would have no choice but to honor the UN's decision, albeit mostly in the breech until minimal objectives could to be achieved, especially in Sharm al-Shcikh.

"We'll find the war coming to an end before we get our hands on its cause!" Dayan exclaimed to his generals. His orders to Rabin, issued at 7:45 A.M., were precise: "Complete the conquest of Gaza. Clear the al-'Arish axis. Advance west but remain four miles at least from the Canal. Prepare to attack southward toward al-Qusayma." He considered sending Mendler's column in a race from Kuntilla down the Red Sea coast, but in the end settled on a combined airborne and naval assault. This would be launched no later than the following night, June 7. As for the 6th, the southern front would continue to occupy Israel's main attention, the entire day dedicated to "the thorough treatment of Egyptian armor."[4]

Ironically, the Egyptians did not share the Israelis' assessment of the situation—ironically, because both Nasser and 'Amer saw it as far more desperate than it really was. Rather than calling for an immediate halt to the fighting and focusing international pressure on Israel, Cairo continued to claim victories for its forces advancing through the Negev. Rather than rallying their still-extensive forces, digging in during the day and counterattacking at night when the IAF's edge was blunted, Egypt's leaders ordered a wholesale and wildly disorganized retreat.

The question of who, exactly, issued that order would divide Egyptians for many years to come. Apologists for Nasser, among them Hassanein Heikal and Anwar Sadat, insist that the initiative was solely 'Amer's, that the president learned of it only belatedly and then tried to rescind it. 'Amer's defenders admit that he gave the instructions, but assert that Nasser was fully informed of them and concurred. Both sides agree, however, in tracing the order to 5:50 on the morning of June 6, when Gen. Fawzi received a copy of a wireless message from 'Amer directing the garrison at Sharm al-Sheikh to prepare to withdraw westward. Shortly before noon, the field marshal began calling for a fallback to the second line of defense, but at 5:00 P.M., he summoned Chief of Staff Fawzi and gave him twenty minutes to draw up plans for a general retreat. Fawzi was convinced that 'Amer had acted on his own, but 'Amer and Badran later testified that Nasser personally approved the order.[5]

Fawzi, in any event, was crushed. In spite of the deep psychological blow dealt the army, he believed that the Conqueror plan was still operational. Israeli forces, bloodied by the first line of Egypt's defense, could still be drawn into the second line at Jabal Libni and Bir al-Thamada and crushed. Fawzi was not alone; virtually the whole general staff agreed. Earlier that morning, when 'Amer had phoned Murtagi, inquiring in a quavering voice, "how fare our forces?" the Sinai commander had replied optimistically. Only four brigades had been lost out of fourteen, he assured 'Amer, and three of them were still holding out at Umm Qatef. Additional troops—the Soviet Union's or, as in 1956, the UN's—were sure to intervene soon. "Sir, if you reinforce the northern axis, we can hold out until foreign forces come to secure the Canal." He never suspected that 'Amer was thinking retreat.

Yet retreat was precisely his intention, as Fawzi presently found out. He and Operations Chief al-Qadi drafted a plan for a gradual rollback to the Giddi and Mitla passes and a concentrated defense of the Canal. "The withdrawal was supposed to have taken three days," Murtagi remembered. "The 4th Division was to have remained at the Straits. The next night, that division's place would be taken by the 6th Division, and on the third night, the 6th would pull out and be replaced by a reserve brigade." The strategy appeared workable, given the circumstances, yet 'Amer rejected it on the spot. "I gave you an order to withdraw!" he shouted. "Period!"

No longer waiting for a written plan, the field marshal telephoned his cronies in Sinai. "Make sure that all the planes you have left are ready and waiting by 13:00," he instructed Sidqi Mahmud, "You are to undertake no missions other than providing aerial cover for the 4th Division, until it gets west of the Canal." Other protégés he merely advised to evacuate, by whatever means and as quickly as they could. Maj. Gen. 'Uthman Nassar, for example, commander of the 3rd Infantry Division, told his officers that he had an urgent meeting in headquarters, packed up, and left. He was later seen frequenting cafés in Cairo. But most officers would learn of the order only by hearsay. The direct lines between them and Fawzi's headquarters had all been severed before the war, on 'Amer's explicit instructions.

'Amer would later justify his decision by citing the collapse of Egypt's air power and the fall of the first line of defense: "Withdrawal was the only way I could prevent the army from total destruction and captivity." But the results of the order were precisely that, as a massive army assembled over twenty-four days attempted in as many hours to retreat.

"The Battalion Commander summoned us and told us that we had to pull back," remembered Muhammad Ahmad Khamis, a communications officer with the 4th Division. "It came as a total surprise. My soldiers' morale was high, in preparation for the attack—how was I to face them?" Telling them nothing, Khamis had his men drive through the night. "Suddenly, as dawn rose, my driver looked out and saw the Canal. 'We have retreated! We have retreated!' he started screaming, weeping with astonishment and fear." Other units were less fortunate. Jammed on roads with thousands of vehicles, tens of thousands of men, many Egyptians became easy prey for marauding Israeli jets. The aerial cover ordered by 'Amer never materialized.[6]

The arcane and convoluted relationship between Nasser and 'Amer had finally translated into anarchy in the field. Their honor irrevocably tarnished by the loss of their air force, of Gaza and northern Sinai, neither man had the will or the presence of mind to effect damage control. Neither had the skill to execute an organized retreat, always the most difficult of military maneuvers. Perhaps they believed that the face-saving myth of 1956 would repeat itself, and that the retreat could be spun as a tactical maneuver necessitated by overwhelming, imperialist odds. Maybe they hoped that so dramatic a setback to Soviet arms would impel the Russians to intercede. Ultimately, though, the question of why the order was given and who, Nasser or 'Amer, issued it, became moot. The Egyptian army was running.

Watching that flight from Bir Lafhan, Col. Arvraham 'Bren' Adan, Yoffe's second-in-command and a veteran of the two previous campaigns in Sinai, was stupefied. "You ride past burnt-out vehicles and suddenly you see this immense army, too numerous to count, spread out of a vast area as far as your eyes can see," he told IDF debriefers after the war. "It was not a pleasant feeling, seeing that gigantic enemy and realizing that you're only a single battalion of tanks." Dayan, tracking the course of the war from the Pit, was no less puzzled. "Though Israel had gained command of the skies, Egypt's cities were not bombed, and the Egyptian armored units at the front could have fought even without air support."[7]

Intelligence Chief Yariv, reporting to the general staff that afternoon, revealed the radical change that had transpired in Sinai. "Our pilots report that the Egyptian army is in bad shape, retreating en masse on roads partially blocked by our earlier airstrikes." Haim Bar-Lev stressed the need to press on with the destruction of Egypt's army. But with the enemy fleeing faster than the IDF could follow, how was this to be done?

"There was no planning before the war about what the army would do beyond the al-'Arish-Jabal Libni axis, not even a discussion," Gen. Yoffe recalled. "Nobody believed that we could have accomplished more or that the [Egyptian] collapse would be so swift. Nobody believed we would have four uninterrupted days of combat—we were thinking in terms of a surgical operation." The questions of where to lead the army, how far, and with what objectives, were all addressed by Shaike Gavish at dusk when he convened his three *Ugdah* commanders—Sharon, Tal, and Yoffe—at Jabal Libni.

Gavish's strategy was to prevent the Egyptians from stabilizing their second defense line and mounting a possible counterattack on al-'Arish. He wanted to hit them hard and then beat them to the passes, destroying what remained of their tanks. Accordingly, Tal's forces were to overwhelm the Egyptian positions to the west of Jabal Libni, to attack Egypt's 3rd Division east of Bir al-Thamada and the 4th Division at Bir Gafgafa. Yoffe, striking south through Bir Hasana and the remnants of the 3rd Division, would divide his force into two columns, one each to the Giddi and Mitla passes. Farther south, Sharon would block Shazli's retreat at Nakhl before driving the rest of Egypt's army into Tal and Yoffe's ambushes. Col. Granit's column, meanwhile, would continue to advance along the Mediterranean coast, through Romani en route to Qantara. But there would be no conquest of the Canal itself, at least not yet, for political reasons. "Once Gavish gave us our orders," Yoffe recounted, "the course of the rest of the war became obvious. Though some unexpected turns might occur—the 4th Division might be waiting for us, or worse—we were essentially in a pursuing operation. The battle was already decided."[8]

Egyptian leaders appeared to agree, at least with regard to the military struggle. In the wake of the retreat, Egypt's emphasis swerved from tanks and guns to political propaganda, specifically the charge of U.S. and British intervention for Israel. Here, at least, the coordination between Nasser and 'Amer was complete. Both held conversations with Soviet ambassador Pojidaev, evincing the collusion claim as a means of securing direct Soviet support. 'Amer, unable to furnish proof of U.S. and British attacks, accused the USSR of supplying faulty weapons to Egypt. "I'm no expert on weaponry," Pojidaev replied, "but I do know that the arms we've given the Vietnamese have certainly proved superior to the Americans'." But Nasser left little room for debate. He simply dictated a direct letter to Kosygin informing him that the 6th Fleet, together with U.S. bases in the region, was actively aiding the Israelis. The Jews now stood to reap a great victory unless Moscow extended similar help to Egypt, which was desperately in need of planes.[9]

The myth snowballed rapidly as the day progressed, reaching all corners of the Arab world. "British bombers, taking off in endless waves from Cyprus, are aiding and supplying the Israelis," Damascus Radio declared. "Canberra bombers are striking our forward positions." Radio Amman claimed that three American aircraft carriers were operating off Israel's coast. American warships were reportedly sighted off Port Said, in Haifa harbor, and blocking the entrance to the Canal. Other sources spoke of Israelis piloting American planes with CIA-supplied maps of Egypt and of American pilots flying incognito for Israel. Captured Israeli pilots purportedly "confessed" to collaborating with the U.S. Israel, which had attacked Egypt with 1,200 jets, could not possibly have acted alone— so the argument ran. In a widely distributed communiqué, Nasser called on "the Arab masses to destroy all imperialist interests."

Within hours of the broadcast, mobs attacked American embassies and consulates throughout the Middle East. In Baghdad and Basra, Aleppo, Alexandria, and Algiers, even in congenial cities such as Tunis and Benghazi, American diplomats barricaded themselves in their compounds and prepared for the worst. Oil facilities were shut in Iraq and Libya, while Saudi Arabia, Kuwait, and Bahrein banned oil shipments to the United States and Britain. "America is now the number 1 enemy of the Arabs," proclaimed Algiers Radio, "the American presence . . . must be exterminated from the Arab homeland." Americans in Egypt, many of them long-time residents, were given minutes to pack and then, at gunpoint, searched and summarily deported. "This is how people felt on their way to Auschwitz," wrote Thomas Thompson, a *Life* correspondent, who was among the hundreds banished. In Cairo, Richard Nolte watched as an angry crowd gathered outside his office. "We are burning all—repeat all—classified papers and preparing for demonstration and attempt to enter building," he wired. Yet, at the height of this tension, Nolte was summoned and escorted to the Egyptian Foreign Ministry, there to be told the "facts" of the Anglo-American conspiracy with Israel.

"You say you are against aggression, but when you have aggression of Israel against Egypt you do nothing," Mahmoud Riad excoriated Nolte. "You say you don't know who is the aggressor. It is perfectly clear who is the aggressor and there are 90 or at least 80 ambassadors in Cairo who know this to be true."

The ambassador's only reply was to stress the international sympathy Egypt could reap by accepting a cease-fire resolution that would specifically label Israel as the aggressor. Muhieddin could then come to Washington as planned, and a diplomatic solution could then be found for the Straits. But his words failed to impress the foreign minister, who continued in a similar vein: "If Egypt had been the aggressor, the Sixth Fleet would now be on its shores!"[10]

Convinced though he was of America's complicity in Israel's attack, Riad opposed any rupture of relations with Washington, with which Egypt would have to conduct the postwar negotiations. Nasser, however, dissented. He recalled Egypt's embassy staff from Washington and announced the severance of all diplomatic ties with the United States. Six additional Arab states—Syria, Sudan, Algeria, Iraq, Mauritania, and Yemen—quickly followed suit, and ten Arab oil-producing states banned exports to the U.S. and Britain. In Damascus, Ambassador Smythe was given forty-eight hours to leave the country, and until then, was confined to his residence. Nolte wrote, "Thus endeth my meteoric mission to Cairo."

Politically, at least, Nasser was succeeding where militarily he had capitulated, rallying the Arab world around his leadership. And yet that victory remained incomplete as long as one Arab state, Jordan, failed to follow Egypt's lead. Once reviled as an imperialist tool, Hussein had become for Nasser "our heroic and nationalist brother" and "the brave little king."[11] Enlisting the monarch in the charge of Anglo-American collusion would have powerful repercussions in the area, especially among Arab allies of the West. Nasser needed Hussein's cooperation, but Hussein had concerns of his own.

The Charnel House

"That night was hell," Hussein recounted in his memoirs. "It was clear as day. The sky and the earth glowed with the light of the rockets and the constant explosions of the bombs pouring from Israeli planes." In the darkness, the king shuttled between his headquarters in Amman and his still-secure positions at the front. The latter were dwindling steadily.

In Jenin, where Col. Khalidi's infantry and Maj. 'Ajluni's three surviving tanks were holding off substantially superior Israeli forces advancing from both the north and the south, relief arrived unexpectedly at 4:00 A.M. in the form of two battalions from the 40th Armored Brigade. Having slipped through undetected by the Israelis, the 4th Armored Battalion reinforced Khalidi in defending the city, while the 2nd Battalion blocked the Israelis at 'Arabe, to the east. At the cry of "Fight for Allah!," Brig. al-Ghazi's Pattons charged with every gun blazing. A mechanized battalion—the Amir 'Abdallah—equipped with M-113 armored personnel carriers also joined the fray. One after another, Israeli vehicles burst into flames, and the tide began to shift. "The enemy allowed our forces to get within close range and fought us bravely and stubbornly," remembered Moshe Bar Kokhva, the Israeli brigade commander. Al-Ghazi was already thinking of moving from a defensive to an offensive strategy, consolidating the remainder of the 40th's Pattons and driving the Israelis back across the border.

Then the sun rose, and the Jordanians were again exposed to the sky. Israeli jets and artillery dropped a two-hour barrage on al-Ghazi's men, killing 10 and wounding 250, many of whom had to be left on the field. Only seven tanks—two without gas—and sixteen APC's remained to limp eastward to the Tubas road and then south, toward Nablus. Bar-Kokhva's armored forces, together with Avnon's infantry, meanwhile blasted their way into Jenin. Resistance proved obstinate, especially around the city's police fort, where Bar Kokhva himself was wounded. Not until noon could the Israelis claim functional control over the city, the key to the northern West Bank.[12]

The Jordanians were losing ground in the Jerusalem theater as well, in the hills west of the city. Though one of Harel's column ran into strong opposition outside Bidu—one Israeli and twenty Jordanians were killed—and another lost most of its tracked vehicles to boulders, five Shermans reached Nabi Samwil at 2:55 A.M. Waiting for them there was a company of Jordanian Pattons which, after a fifteen-minute battle, were driven off with their external fuel tanks aflame. The road was now open to Beit Hanina, a suburb of East Jerusalem situated only 500 meters from the Ramallah-Jerusalem highway.[13] Mount Scopus was virtually secured.

Gen. Narkiss, however, could not afford to believe that. He was convinced that the 60th Brigade still posed an imminent threat to Jewish Jerusalem—soldiers on Mount Scopus reported hearing tanks approaching—and had begged for additional air strikes. Bar-Lev at first declined the request, explaining that Israel's pilots were exhausted, having flown five missions in less than twenty-four hours, but Narkiss could not be put off. Without air support, he argued, Jerusalem would be lost—"tired or not, they have to knock out that armor." Yet, even after the IAF wrought havoc among Brig. bin Shaker's tanks, the Central Command chief remained skeptical. Unsure how many enemy vehicles survived, he refused to take any chances with the fate of Mount Scopus. The garrison would be relieved, as planned, by the paratroopers.

Blocking that effort were the strongest fortifications in Jerusalem, a ganglia of trenches, bunkers, minefields, and concrete obstacles known since World War I, when Gen. Allenby stored his ordnance there, as Ammunition Hill. The Israelis perceived the bastion as a direct threat to Mount Scopus and the western half of the city, while for the Jordanians, it represented a first line defense against any Israeli assault on the east. The soldiers on both sides of that line, Israelis and Jordanians, had been under continuous shellfire for many hours. Yet their morale remained commensurately high and their vital supplies undiminished. The scene was set for a grueling battle when, at 1:25 A.M., Motta Gur's paratroopers moved quietly into position.

Gur's men were to divide into three forces. The first would cross the no-man's land near the Mandelbaum Gate, the UN checkpoint between the two sectors of the city, and assault the Police Academy that guarded the southern approaches to Ammunition Hill. The second group would proceed east through the neighborhoods of Sheikh Jarrah and the American Colony to reach the Rockefeller Museum, while the third followed the ravine of Wadi Joz up to the Augusta Victoria Hospital, on the ridge midway between Mount Scopus and the Mount of Olives. At battle's end, it was hoped, Israel would not only be free of any Jordanian threat but also be poised to enter the Old City. "Jerusalem is not al-'Arish," Narkiss told the paratroopers just prior to the attack. "Let's hope this time we'll atone for the sin of '48."[14]

At 2:10 in the morning the Jerusalem sky was again illuminated, this time by intense Israeli artillery, tank, and mortar fire to soften up the enemy line. Giant searchlights placed atop the Labor Federation building—West Jerusalem's highest—further exposed the Jordanians and effectively blinded them. Thus heralded, Battalion 66 under Maj. Yosef "Yossi" Yoffe, a farmer in civilian life and a veteran of the 1950s retaliation raids, crept up to the first line of barbed wire and blasted their way through. But beyond that row lay another, and four more after that, none of which appeared on the IDF's maps. The attackers were caught in no-man's land, in a blistering crossfire and under a rising moon. "We made our way, Bangalore [torpedo] after Bangalore, fence by fence, squad by squad," Arik Akhmon, the paratroop intelligence officer, remembered. "And the most difficult battle had yet to begin. Before us lay Ammunition Hill." Seven Israelis were killed and over a dozen wounded before the last of the wires were cut. Only at 3:10 did Gur, anxious about the approaching dawn, receive the signal that Yoffe's men had broken through to the Police Academy. Gur replied, "I could kiss you."

Built by the British during Mandate times and later passed to the UN, the Police Academy was believed by the Israelis to house 'Ata 'Ali's main headquarters and was therefore heavily defended. In fact, the area was manned by a single company, 140 men, of the 2nd al-Husseini Battalion under Capt. Suliman Salayta. With the covering fire from two Shermans borrowed from the Jerusalem Brigade, Israeli engineers cleared a path for the assault units which, over the next two hours, destroyed some thirty-four bunkers and machine-gun nests. Still, the Jordanians fought, stalling the Israeli charge just fifteen meters from Salayta's position. The captain, with seventeen killed and forty-two wounded, ordered an artillery barrage on his own position, and with those of his men still able, fell back to nearby Ammunition Hill.

The battle for the Police Academy also proved costly for the Israelis, only a squad of whom remained fit for further fighting. Reinforcements arrived, however, and the paratroopers proceeded to Ammunition Hill, attacking it from three directions: west, east, and center.

"Sir, the enemy has succeeded in penetrating the area to the left of the Police Academy," Pvt. Farhan Haman reported to Maj. Mansur Kranshur, in

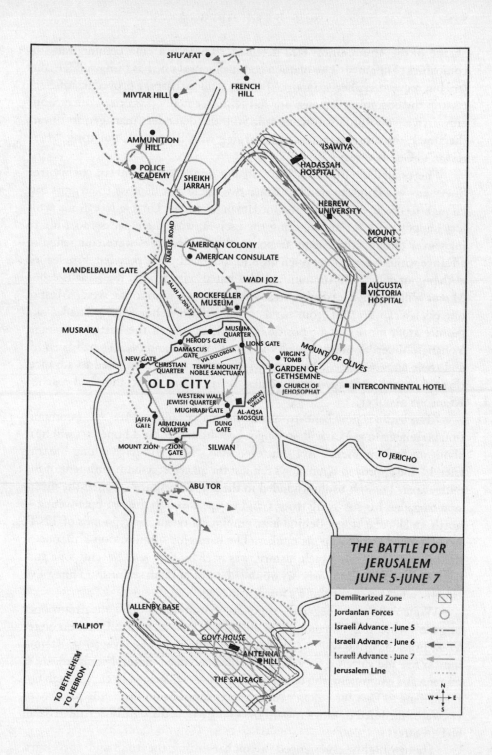

SHU'AFAT

FRENCH
HILL

MIVTAR HILL

AMMUNITION
HILL

POLICE
ACADEMY

SHEIKH
JARRAH

'ISAWIYA

HADASSAH
HOSPITAL

HEBREW
UNIVERSITY

MOUNT
SCOPUS

MANDELBAUM GATE

AMERICAN COLONY

AMERICAN CONSULATE

WADI JOZ

ROCKEFELLER
MUSEUM

AUGUSTA
VICTORIA
HOSPITAL

NABLUS ROAD

SALAH AL-DIN ST

MUSRARA

MUSLIM
QUARTER

HEROD'S GATE

DAMASCUS
GATE

NEW GATE

CHRISTIAN
QUARTER

VIA DOLOROSA

LIONS GATE

VIRGIN'S
TOMB

MOUNT OF OLIVES

TEMPLE MOUNT/
NOBLE SANCTUARY

GARDEN OF
GETHSEMNE

OLD CITY

WESTERN WALL

JEWISH QUARTER

MUGHRABI GATE

KIDRON
VALLEY

CHURCH OF
JEHOSOPHAT

INTERCONTINENTAL HOTEL

JAFFA
GATE

ARMENIAN
QUARTER

AL-AQSA
MOSQUE

DUNG
GATE

MOUNT ZION

ZION
GATE

SILWAN

TO JERICHO

ABU TOR

THE BATTLE FOR
JERUSALEM
JUNE 5-JUNE 7

ALLENBY BASE

TALPIOT

GOVT HOUSE

ANTENNA
HILL

THE SAUSAGE

TO BETHLEHEM
TO HEBRON

Demilitarized Zone

Jordanian Forces

Israeli Advance - June 5

Israeli Advance - June 6

Israeli Advance - June 7

Jerusalem Line

N
W E
S

charge of the Ammunition Hill defenses. "There is a tank column and two companies of infantry. The platoon commander says he has things under control but requests artillery support." But the artillery barrage proved insufficient to stop the oncoming Israelis; nor did reinforcements from the Police Academy arrive, only Jordanian wounded. Still, the defenders managed to thwart the attack, throwing grenades and charging with Bren guns, hollering "*Allah Akbar*"—God Is Great.

The point Israeli squads were all but annihilated. One of their three Shermans was knocked out; the other two could not depress their guns low enough to fire at the submerged Jordanian positions. Unable to call for artillery support without endangering themselves, with their packs too wide to maneuver through the enemy trenches, the paratroopers were compelled to advance without cover over open ground, and one by one they fell. Fire leaped at them not only from Ammunition Hill but also from what the Israelis called Mivtar Hill, another Jordanian stronghold, across a wadi to the west. "Most of our casualties were not from hand-to-hand fighting but from grenades and gunfire from more distant positions," testified one of the battle's veterans, Yohanan Miller. Soon, nearly all the Israeli officers and NCO's had been hit and their units scattered. Yet improvised attack teams continued to advance, through trenches clogged with bodies. By 4:30, first light, they had reached Kranshur's bunker.

"The battle is now hand-to-hand," the major radioed 'Ata 'Ali, "ammunition is running low. You will no longer hear from me, but I hope you will hear about me and my men." 'Ata 'Ali responded, "May you have a long life, my friend," and approved Kranshur's request for an artillery bombardment of the entire area. Though badly wounded in the leg, Kranshur exploited the diversion to gather his surviving troops, and escape through the last open venue— north, to Shu'afat ridge. Behind him, employing twenty-one pounds of TNT, Israeli engineers blew up his bunker. The battle for Ammunition Hill, one of the bloodiest in Arab-Israeli history, was over by 5:15 A.M. Seventy-one Jordanians were killed and forty-six wounded, most of them seriously. Thirty-five Israelis, a full fourth of Yoffe's force, also died.[15]

While Yoffe's men began the conquest of Ammunition Hill, the paratrooper brigade's remaining battalions crossed the city line. The 28th Battalion under Yossi Fradkin, while waiting for the sign to advance, was ravaged by 81-mm mortar fire and suffered sixty-four wounded and dead. Severely delayed, short on men and equipment, the battalion nevertheless managed to cut through no-man's-land to East Jerusalem's American Colony. From there, the paratroopers were scheduled to move toward the Old City via the lightly defended Salah al-Din Street.

Though highly experienced in combat during the 1948 and 1956 wars, Fradkin had never fought in Jerusalem. "Our soldiers almost never knew what was expected of them," he told fellow officers after the war. "They didn't know where we were taking them. They didn't know the place." Instead of heading down Salah al-Din Street, he made a wrong turn onto Nablus Road, where the Jordanians were waiting in force. Having spotted the Israelis' advance from Ammunition Hill, Maj. Kranshur called Cap. Nabi Shkhimat, commander of the Nablus Road sector. "The enemy's tanks are coming in your direction," Kranshur warned him, "be prepared to fight on a large front, house to house, to the last man and bullet."

Shkhimat made ready, beefing up his bazooka and antitank gun crews in the triple-tiered bunkers facing Nablus Road. The Israelis blundered into a maelstrom. The tanks fired point-blank down the street, wave after wave of paratroopers charged, but the Jordanians held their ground. "They were like drunkards, exhausted and lost," Mahmud Abu Faris, a company commander in the 2nd al-Husseini Battalion, described his assailants. "We fought out of faith, not on orders." One Israeli officer, he claimed, tried to tackle him, but Abu Faris cut off his ear, then shot him with his pistol.

However robust, Jordanian resistance gradually gave way to Israeli firepower and momentum. Platoon commander Ghazi Isma'il Ruba'iyya remembered trying to raise the morale of his five remaining men: "I failed. I looked into their faces and saw what a soldier sees before death." Ruba'iyya radioed battalion headquarters but got no answer. Shkhimat had ordered his men to withdraw to Musrara, a neighborhood abutting the Old City, leaving 45 dead and 142 wounded.

The scene was no less hellish for the Israelis. "Suddenly the street turned into a slaughterhouse," Yigal Nir, a paratrooper, averred. "In seconds, everyone around me was hit. Having not felt fear before, the transformation was drastic. I felt abandoned suddenly and hopeless." Only thirty men—half the original force—crossed the 600 meters from the American consulate to the YMCA—*Simtat ha-Mavet*, they dubbed it, the Alley of Death.

More fortunate was the 71st Battalion, which succeeded in breaching the wire and minefields and emerged near Wadi Joz at the base of Mount Scopus. Its commander, Maj. Uzi Eilam, a Chicago-trained engineer and another veteran of the retaliation raids, had been disappointed about his unit's transfer from Sinai. "When they told us we were going up to Jerusalem, I felt a keen disappointment," he confided after the war. "Clearly, we were not going to parachute there, that we would merely guard the border . . . But then, when the shelling started . . . we realized that this was something serious. That there was going to be war."

From Wadi Joz, the Israelis could cut off the Old City from Jericho and East Jerusalem from Ramallah. The one remaining route to the West Bank—eastward through the suburb of al-'Azariya—was zeroed in by IDF artillery. Israeli shellfire also deterred the Jordanians from counterattacking against Eilam from their still-formidable positions around Augusta Victoria. Confident, a detachment from the 28th Battalion ventured toward the Rockefeller Archaeological Museum, a gleaming castlelike structure on the Old City's northwestern corner, which it took at 7:27 A.M., after a brief skirmish.

This, Gur believed, was the ideal jumping-off site for the final assault on the Old City, to be effected through the nearby Herod's (Flower) Gate. Along with three Hebrew University archeologists anxious to protect the museum's relics, the paratrooper commander moved his forward headquarters to Rockefeller. He found that the area was still dominated by Jordanian snipers and that his brigade was seriously depleted. Nevertheless, he asked Narkiss's permission to penetrate the gate immediately. The answer was negative; the Cabinet had yet to make a decision on Jerusalem. Gur, furious, contemplated ignoring the government—"By obeying my orders not to enter the Old City, would I not reap sorrow for generations and shame on the IDF which was arrayed just outside the walls?" But Narkiss managed to assuage him. "Our goal is to surround the city and force its surrender," he explained. "Conversely, surrounding the city will be a staging ground for capturing it." The paratroopers were to regroup at Rockefeller and prepare to take Augusta Victoria ridge later that afternoon.[16]

While Gur's men rested at Rockefeller, Uri Ben Ari and the 10th Brigade broke through to the Ramallah-Jerusalem road. At Tel al-Ful, a rocky knoll on which construction had begun for Hussein's newest palace, the Israeli Shermans fought a vehement, running battle with as many as thirty Jordanian Pattons under Capts. Dib Suliman and 'Awad Sa'ud 'Eid. The Jordanians succeeded in thwarting the enemy advance and in destroying a number of half-tracks, but ultimately a combination of Israeli air power and the vulnerability of the Pattons' external fuel tanks proved decisive. Leaving half their tanks smoldering, Suliman and 'Eid withdrew toward Jericho.

Thereafter, the 10th Brigade joined with the 4th and descended through the Arab neighborhoods of Shu'afat and French Hill, through the Jordanian defenses at Mivtar, to emerge at Ammunition Hill. So swift was their thrust that forces in the Israeli side of the city, mistaking them for Jordanians, shot at them. Confusion ensued as tanks and their crews wandered the streets, looking for a battle. "We didn't know what had been captured and what wasn't," recalled the paratroopers' deputy commander, Col. Moshe Peles. "We knew nothing."

Israeli historians would later question whether the struggle for Ammunition Hill was truly necessary, whether the tanks' prompt arrival had rendered superfluous the sacrifice of so many lives. Such second-guessing comes easily in the clarity of a classroom, but viewed from Narkiss's perspective, through the fog of battle and the belief that Jordanian Pattons were still approaching, the assault on Ammunition Hill appeared the best means of rescuing Mount Scopus. The maneuver further established a double encirclement of Jerusalem—infantry on the inside, surrounded by an outer armored ring. By midday on June 6, a Jordanian army dispatch reported that "the enemy has conquered all of Jerusalem except for the Old City."[17]

The news came as no surprise to Hussein. "If we don't decide within the next 24 hours, you can kiss your army and all of Jordan good-bye!" Gen. Riyad had warned the monarch just before dawn. "We are on the verge of losing the West Bank; all our forces will be isolated or destroyed." The Egyptian commander of Jordan's armed forces had posed two possibilities: either accept a cease-fire at once or order a general retreat. Both options were drastic, but perhaps unwarranted. Jordanian troops remained in control of the Old City and most of East Jerusalem; Israeli advances in the West Bank were confined to Latrun and the Jenin area. Even without air cover, the army could have conceivably held out until a cease-fire was arranged, assuring that most of the West Bank remained Jordan's. The situation, as such, was analogous to Egypt's in Sinai, and as in Egypt, passions obfuscated reality. No sooner had he heard the general's advice when Hussein summoned the ambassadors of the U.S., the USSR, Britain, and France, and told them that his regime would "not survive one hour" without an "an immediate end to violent attacks."

Hussein was once again caught between clashing rocks. Acceptance of a formal cease-fire would be tantamount to a declaration of surrender at a time when Egypt was still fighting. The Palestinians would riot and even the army might revolt. Yet retreat was no less perilous, as Nasser could use it as a pretext for withdrawing his own troops and blaming Jordan for the collapse of the Arab war effort. "Jordan could have more difficulty maintaining law and order after a cease-fire than in the absence of one," was Burns's assessment, "What if Nasser calls for Hussein's overthrow so that Jordan can continue the battle?"

Hussein's solution was to seek a secret understanding with Israel on halting the fighting or, better yet, an internationally imposed cease-fire. Phoning Burns in a state of near-hysteria, he claimed to have only fifteen minutes to make a decision on whether to evacuate the West Bank. "If we do not withdraw tonight, we will be chewed up. Tomorrow will leave only the choice of ordering the destruction of our equipment and leaving every soldier to look out for himself." Asserting that Nasser had blundered terribly—"No one anticipated that the conflict would escalate so far and so fast"—and that Riyad was "pretty much running the show" in Jordan, Hussein assumed none of the blame for the situation, and denied that his troops had fired first on civilian targets. His sole concern was in obtaining an "an immediate end to the violence"—he avoided the term *cease-fire*—without which his regime would fall.

Over the course of the night, Hussein conveyed no less than four requests for a de facto cease-fire, but each time the response was negative. "I believe it is probably too late to arouse any interest in Israel for the preservation of Hussein and his regime," Barbour explained from Tel Aviv. Citing the continuing battles in both the Jerusalem and Nablus sectors, the Israelis claimed that Hussein had either lost control of his troops or was trying to deceive them into canceling their attack. While it supported a halt to the fighting, Washington's reply to Hussein was no warmer: Either take personal charge of your army or else remain a target.

Gravely disappointed, desperate, the king retorted with a warning of his own. If the fighting continued, Jordan would have no option but to corroborate Nasser's charge of Anglo-American conspiracy.[18]

It was not an idle threat, as Hussein proved a half-hour later, when a phone call arrived from Cairo. "Will we say that the U.S. and Britain [are attacking] or just the United States?" asked Nasser, inquiring whether the British even had aircraft carriers. Hussein responded, "United States and England," and agreed to issue a statement to that effect immediately. Nasser was heartened. "By God," he exclaimed, "I will make an announcement and you will make an announcement and we will see to it that the Syrians will make an announcement that American and British airplanes are taking part against us from aircraft carriers. We will stress the matter. And we will drive the point home." The discussion ended with the Egyptian president urging the king "not to give up," though the fighting was indeed hard. "We are with you with all our hearts and we are flying our planes over Israel today. Our planes have been striking at Israel's airfields since morning."[19]

Made on an unscrambled civilian line—the UAC's sophisticated communications equipment had never been installed—the conversation was recorded by Israeli intelligence and widely distributed. Hussein, in any case, never denied the call, and Egypt's *al-Ahram* confirmed it publicly: "The King and the president agreed between them that the entire Arab nation must be informed of this important development and to adapt its position accordingly." Jordan had received special dispensation from Nasser to maintain its relations with the United States, but that exception had come with a price. Hussein had become party to what Johnson would dub the "Big Lie."

The claim of a Western conspiracy to aid Israel helped Hussein mollify the Palestinians and preserve Jordan's alliance with Egypt. Militarily, though, his position continued to deteriorate. Despite repeated requests for assistance from Syria and Saudi Arabia, and repeated assurances that both had sent forces to Jordan, no such assistance arrived. Syria's 17th Mechanized Brigade got as far as the border but refused to move farther, its commander first claiming that he needed to reconnoiter the area and then that he lacked instructions from Damascus. The absence of orders was also the excuse proffered by Saudi forces, which similarly stopped at the border. An Egyptian military doctor attached to the Saudis, Dr. Munir Zaki Mustafa, bitterly recalled, "We hoped that one Israeli plane would attack us, so that we could say that we participated in the war and we fired our guns—but for naught."

Only Iraq's 8th Brigade tried to engage in combat and to cross the Damiya Bridge, but there it was bombarded by Israeli planes and decimated. The IAF also destroyed a PLO battalion and attacked the H-3 air base in western Iraq—Hussein's last hope for air cover. Though two of their Mirages were shot down, the Israelis left behind rows of smoking MiG's and Hawker Hunters.

By noon, a despondent Hussein asked Riyad to inform Field Marshal 'Amer of the truth. "The situation on the West Bank is becoming desperate," the general wrote, "the Israelis are attacking on all fronts. We are bombed day and night by the Israeli air force and can offer no resistance . . . the Jordanian, Syrian, and Iraqi air forces have been virtually destroyed." Riyad concluded by reiterating his belief that, in the absence of a UN-imposed cease-fire, Jordan would have to withdraw its forces from the West Bank or suffer total defeat. Hussein had reconciled himself to this realization as well when, at 12:30, he sent a follow-up cable to Nasser:

> In addition to our very heavy losses in men and equipment, for lack of air protection our tanks are being disabled at a rate of one every ten minutes. And the bulk of the enemy forces are concentrated against the Jordanian army . . . To this situation, if it continues, there can be only one outcome: you and the Arab nation will lose this bastion, together with all its forces, after glorious combat that will be inscribed by history in blood.[20]

In spite of his reluctance to accept either an open cease-fire or sanction retreat, the king was ready to relinquish his prerogatives and let Nasser decide. Yet, as the afternoon waned, no such decision arrived. In the interim, Israel's offensive thundered on. Gen. Peled's tanks around Jenin were now preparing to continue south to Nablus, as another Israeli column advanced on the city from Qalqilya to the west. Just outside Jerusalem, the 10th and 4th Brigades occupied Ramallah with its 50,000 inhabitants. In Jerusalem itself, the 163rd Infantry Battalion under Lt. Col. Michael Peikas attacked Abu Tor, a heavily fortified Arab neighborhood overlooking the Old City's southern wall. The fighting was vicious: seventeen Israelis were killed, Peikas among them, and fifty-four wounded. But the IDF secured the area, thus severing the Old City from Bethlehem and Hebron to the south, while Israeli forces descending from Ramallah would soon cut the last open road to Jericho.

By the late afternoon of June 6, the bulk of Jordan's army was in danger of being stranded on the West Bank. Riyad, usually calm and even-tempered—he never missed his afternoon nap, even during the fighting—now argued loudly with Hussein over the king's refusal to approve evacuation. "My hardest job has been to play U Thant to you," the general carped.

Exasperated, the king bolted out of his headquarters, commandeered a jeep, and raced down to the Jordan Valley. There he encountered the remnants of the 25th Infantry and 40th Armored Brigades, retreating from Jenin. "I will never forget the hallucinating sight of that defeat," he later recorded. "Roads clogged with trucks, jeeps, and all kinds of vehicles twisted, disemboweled, dented, still smoking, giving off that particular smell of metal and paint burned by exploding bombs—a stink that only powder can make. In the midst of this charnel house were men. In groups of thirty or two, wounded, exhausted, they were trying to clear a path under the monstrous coup de grâce being dealt them by a horde of Israeli Mirages screaming in a cloudless blue sky seared with sun." Hussein thought to inquire about 'Ali ibn 'Ali, a cousin serving with the 40th, but loath to exploit his station, the monarch kept silent.[21]

While their sovereign fretted, Hussein's troops continued fighting. Behind the Old City walls, 'Ata 'Ali was determined to hold out. Though he had only two heavy mortars left, there were rations and ammunition to last him and his men for two weeks. He set up headquarters in the Armenian Quarter, placed fifty soldiers at each of Jerusalem's seven gates, and waited for the Israeli attack.

It came just after 7:00 that night, though the Israelis' target was not yet the Old City but, yet again, Augusta Victoria ridge. Fradkin's 28th Battalion, aiming to reach the ridge via Wadi Joz, took a wrong turn and found itself under the parapets of the Lions (St. Stephen's) Gate. Murderous fire rained down on the attackers. Four Sherman tanks, caught on the narrow bridge linking the Garden of Gethsemane with the Church of Jehosophat, were hit as they tried to turn, as were three jeeps from the paratroopers' recon company. In all, five Israelis were killed and twenty-five wounded, while survivors huddled for cover in the depressed yard of the Virgin's Tomb. Observers on Mount Scopus, meanwhile, reported sighting a convoy of forty Pattons advancing through al-'Azariya, en route to the Mount of Olives. Gur, fearing that the entire force would be caught in open ground with their backs literally to the wall, ordered Fradkin's men back to Rockefeller. Israel's attempt to completely surround the Old City and force its garrison to surrender had failed. For the Jordanians, valuable time had been bought.[22]

The inability of the Israelis to reach Augusta Victoria should have provided a fillip to Hussein, strengthening his aversion to retreat. That action, though, had far less impact on Jordan than on Israel, where military and civilian leaders were deep in debate over the pros and cons of conquering the Old City. At stake were crucial considerations of time and world opinion, of Israel's relations with the UN and the United States. Equally pressing was the apparent kindling of yet another flashpoint, not in Sinai or in the West Bank, but on the northern border with Syria.

Damascus and Jerusalem

The Syrian shelling of Israel's northern settlements, unabated since the previous day, went largely unanswered. Residents of those settlements, comprising the country's largest lobbying group, continued to pressure the government to act, their cause championed by Labor Minister Yigal Allon. Oxford alumnus, elite forces' commander, and hero of the 1948 campaign against Egypt, the forty-nine-year-old Allon had promised the farmers that the war would not end with Syria's guns still trained on them.

In promoting an operation to eliminate those guns, Allon could count on at least implicit support from Eshkol. The former Galilee farmer and water expert, Eshkol had deep sympathy for the northern settlers—and an abiding interest in the Jordan headwaters. "From the moment war broke out, Eshkol showed special apprehension regarding the north," recollected Col. Lior, "In every consultation and every discussion . . . he would ask three or four times, 'what's happening up north?' I think he went a little crazy with it . . . constantly bothering people about the Banias (one of the Jordan River sources). Twelve times a day, he'd ask: 'What about the Banias?'"

But not all Eshkol's ministers shared his Golan obsession. Zalman Aran and Haim Moshe Shapira, among others, still feared the opening of yet another front and possible intervention by the Soviets, and in this they had a powerful ally in Dayan.

The defense minister also expressed anxiety about the Russians, and doubted whether the Northern Command, already committed on the West Bank, had the troops necessary to take the Golan. In conversations with the Cabinet ministers, he dismissed the strategic threat posed by Syria. "We're afraid of the Egyptians, even though they're far away, because they're very strong, and we're afraid of the Jordanians, though they're weak, because they're very close. But the Syrians are weak *and* far away—there's no immediate need to attack them."

But along with strategic considerations, Dayan was also guided by a political interest in safeguarding his exclusivity over all military decisions. "Don't interfere with security matters," he warned Allon and the other ministers—Galili, Carmel—in favor of capturing the Golan. "In security matters there's no democracy. If you try to interfere, I'll quit." Dayan would sanction only minimal action in the north: occupation of the Demilitarized Zones and, possibly, of the Banias springs. Yet he told Ben-Gurion confidentially that the Syrians' "recklessness" was insufferable. Once the other fronts were decided, he said, Syria's turn would come.[23]

Dayan's position was predicated on maintaining an acceptable level of violence in the north, but at 2:00 A.M. on the morning of June 6, that assumption was substantively challenged. A massive artillery barrage fell from Kibbutz Dan and Kfar Szold at the tip of the Hula Valley to Ein Gev on the southern shores of Galilee. As many as 265 guns rained an estimated forty-five tons of ordnance per minute on the settlements; nearly a thousand shells pummeled the town of Rosh Pina alone. In an effort to deflect the Syrian fire, IDF engineers ignited barrels of smoke along the border, but the tactic proved only partially effective. Some 205 houses, 14 public buildings, and 45 vehicles were damaged; 16 people were injured and 2 killed.

Launching the salvos were two Syrian battalions—the 129th and the 168th—of 130-mm guns, in addition to four companies of heavy mortars and antitank weapons. "The enemy appears to have suffered heavy losses and is retreating," reported Capt. Ibrahim Aktum, observation officer in Syria's 11th Brigade, positioned atop Tel 'Azzaziat. "At this crucial and historical hour our forces have begun to fight and to bomb the enemy's position along the entire front," declared Defense Minister al-Assad. "These are just the first shots in the war of liberation."

After the enemy's air attacks of the previous day, Syria's confidence was restored by the Israelis' failure to respond to the shelling. Close to midnight, general headquarters in Damascus received a top-secret wire from its counterpart in Cairo: "Our forces are striking Israel and its army fiercely. We have destroyed most of the Israeli planes and our army is now advancing toward Tel Aviv . . . Report to us at once on the situation on the northern front and the enemy's disposition." Suweidani quickly called a meeting of the general staff and ordered Operation Victory—the conquest of northern Israel—implemented.

The offensive was to begin with a feigned thrust into the tip of the Hula Valley. The main incursion would follow in the south, close to the Sea of Galilee, with three full brigades.

The feint began at 7:00, when troops of the 243rd Infantry Battalion, accompanied by two companies of T-34 tanks, descended from the Banias toward Kibbutz Dan. The settlement's inhabitants were nowhere in sight, and the Syrians believed the Israelis had deserted. In fact, they were merely in bomb shelters, and when the alarm sounded, they ran to defend the perimeter. "I came out and suddenly saw six tanks swooping down on us firing explosive shells straight at us, and then smoke and phosphorous," recalled one kibbutz member, identified in the record as Yossi. "That was the signal for the infantry charge . . . I heard shouting and saw 70 soldiers lined up and charging us from 350 meters away . . . I fired everything I had point-blank and saw how they began to fall."

Similar assaults were attempted on other Israeli targets, on Tel Dan and the IDF bunker at Ashmora, each with identical results. Seven Syrian tanks were destroyed, and twenty troops killed. An Israeli commander, Col. Yitzhak Halfon, also lost his life.[24]

The probe was repulsed while the main Syrian thrust never materialized. Unfamiliar with the terrain, the commanders of three brigades failed to arrive at the launching site. The bridges over the Jordan were found to be too narrow for the wide-bodied Soviet tanks, and the tanks lacked radio contact with the infantry. Other units simply remained in their camps near Quneitra, ignoring orders to move out. The failure of the attack effectively dissuaded Damascus from pursuing Victory further. Any lingering doubts were dispelled by the pounding of Syrian positions by Israeli artillery and jets. "The situation at the Syrian front was bad," concluded an internal army report. "Our forces did not go on the offensive either because they did not arrive or were not wholly prepared or because they could not find shelter from the enemy's planes. The reserves could not withstand the air attacks; they dispersed after their morale plummeted. By the evening of June 6, a large part of the reserves had wandered without orders back to base."

Thereafter, citing "the most severe conditions—continuous aerial bombardment of every sort of ordnance, including napalm—and losses of 20 percent," the Syrians revived their defensive plan, Operation Holy War. The decision did not deter them from mounting a virtual offensive, however. Damascus Radio claimed that Sh'ar Yishuv had been occupied (it was not even attacked) and five Israeli jets shot down. The Jews were fleeing toward Haifa, it said. Nor was the truth told to the Egyptians. "Our forces are conquering the Hula Valley and advancing swiftly toward Rosh Pina and Safad," general headquarters relayed to Cairo. "By day's end we shall surely be in Nazareth."[25]

The shelling of Israeli settlements escalated meanwhile, reaching various levels of lethality throughout the day. Rabin was not impressed with the display, dismissing it as an attempt to refute the allegation, already gaining currency in the Arab world, that "Syria is willing to fight to the last Egyptian." He favored several small operations to occupy the DZ's and Banias headwaters and to capture POW's later to be exchanged for Israeli pilots shot down over Syria. But the IDF's priorities were still in the West Bank, Rabin concluded, and not on the Golan Heights.

That conclusion was hardly to the liking of David Elazar, the Northern Command chief. Born in Sarajevo, where he and Bar-Lev had been childhood friends, "Dado" had moved to Palestine at age sixteen and made the army his home. As an armored corps commander in 1956, he had earned a reputation for gallantry and aggressiveness. Handsome, charismatic, he had gained the affection of Israeli settlers throughout the north and, reciprocating that warmth, sought to protect them permanently from Syria.

According to Dado, the bombardment of Galilee and the attack on Kibbutz Dan were merely preludes to a much larger, deadlier, offensive. Though many of his units were engaged in the West Bank, he felt he had sufficient forces to take the northern Golan, at least. Elazar had scheduled his attack for the morning of June 8—hazy skies were forecast for the 7th, complicating air cover—and was certain that the government would approve it.[26]

But while Dado planned, Dayan continued to oppose fighting on a third front and risking further provocation of the Soviets. Rabin stressed the need to eliminate the guns shelling Jewish settlements and to capture the Jordan headwaters; Meir Amit insisted that the Americans would support the campaign. But the minister of defense remained unshakable: Elazar and his Hammer operation would not get a green light.

Dayan's clemency toward Syria did not, however, extend to Jordan. Angered by Hussein's rejection of Israel's earlier appeals for quiet, Dayan had little patience for the king's latest requests for a tacit cease-fire. "First we finish the work he imposed on us," he told Rabin, "then we'll send him an appropriate reply." The "work" he had in mind was the complete conquest of the West Bank high ground overlooking the Jordan Valley. IDF elements might also descend to Jericho and the Jordan River crossings, once the enemy's armor was eliminated. Only in Jerusalem did Dayan continue to counsel restraint, rebuffing all suggestions that Israel capture the Old City.

He would reiterate his position that noon when he and Weizman joined Uzi Narkiss in visiting the newly relieved Mount Scopus. "What a divine view!"

Dayan exclaimed, enjoying the stunning scene of the Old City with its golden dome and church towers. But Narkiss, anxious to receive permission to penetrate those walls, was in no mood for sight-seeing. Recalling how, two thousand years before, the Roman general Titus had tried and failed to destroy the Jewish connection to Jerusalem, Narkiss requested immediate permission to occupy the Old City. "Under no circumstances," was Dayan's reply. The army could mine the area around the city, surround it, and prompt it to surrender on its own. Breaking through the walls, however, would spark an international backlash that Israel could hardly afford. "I want none of that Vatican," said Moshe Dayan.[27]

The allusion to Rome was not unintentional, word having reached Israel of a papal proposal to declare Jerusalem an open city, inviolate from attacks by either side. The plan swiftly received blessings from Washington, which began to exert pressure on the Israelis to accept a cease-fire with Jordan and desist from entering the Old City. To do so now meant not only angering Christians worldwide but antagonizing the Americans as well.

But the army's encirclement of the Old City had presented the government with a fait accompli. How could victorious Jewish soldiers gathered just meters away from Judaism's holiest site not try to reach it? This question was weighing on the Ministerial Defense Committee when it next met at 2:00 that afternoon.

Eshkol, after much hesitation, arrived at an answer. Israeli forces would take the Old City, whereupon the government would convene the leaders of all the main churches and guarantee its respect for their shrines. Begin, recalling efforts to reach a cease-fire at the UN, warned, "we're liable to remain outside the walls of Jerusalem as we did in 1948." He proposed that the country's leaders, military and civilian, march to the Western Wall and offer a prayer for the city's sanctity. Yigal Allon agreed: Take the city and be done with it. Haim Moshe Shapira's idea was that Israel would appeal to Christian and Muslim leaders to quietly persuade Hussein to surrender the city without further bloodshed. Most ministers reacted cynically to these suggestions; Galili, for example, demanded that the city be taken immediately, without fanfare, before international pressure could mount.

It was Dayan's word, however, that again proved decisive, and Dayan still opposed breaking into the Old City. Since the IDF controlled the area militarily anyway, he reasoned, it would wait until the Sinai fighting was completed before committing itself to another urban battle. In a private conversation with Ben-Gurion, however, the defense minister offered another explanation: Israel should not seize the holy places only to have to give them up later under the threat of international sanctions. Having been sworn by Eshkol not to authorize unnecessary offensives, Dayan had more often than not served as a brake on Israeli activism. Yet his true thinking on Jerusalem and other battles remained a mystery. As one senior defense official, not without raillery, remarked to an American diplomat, "General Dayan will turn a blind eye on any attempt to interrupt the course of events."[28]

Battling for Cease-Fire

Whether to capture the Old City, attack Syria, or occupy Sharm al-Sheikh immediately or wait an additional day—all such questions were subject to the all-important time factor. The war, the Israelis understood, would be decided not only on the battlefield, but 6,000 miles away in Washington and New York.

That understanding lay behind Abba Eban's early morning departure from Tel Aviv, his assignment to forestall the adoption of a UN cease-fire resolution. Eban intended to present the Council with a comprehensive peace plan confident that the Arabs would reject it and so grant Israel additional hours, if not days, of fighting. But Eban was also looking beyond the end of the war, to the period of intensive diplomacy certain to follow. He was determined to avoid what he termed the "nightmare" and "political trauma" of 1956, in which a triumphant Israel was forced to concede its gains without exacting peace. "Here we were again breaking out of the closing circle of Arab aggression and here again plans would be laid to see that our neck was restored to the . . . noose."

Eshkol, however, was hesitant. While he, too, hoped that a military victory could alter the context of Arab-Israeli relations existing since 1948, he found the mere mention of peace at this stage too risky. "We ask that you do not put forward diplomatic plans or peace proposals at this stage," Dr. Ya'akov Herzog, Cabinet secretary, instructed Eban. "We must complete the military phase, and promoting far-reaching diplomatic trends may only increase pressure to stem the advance of our forces. Furthermore, by making such proposals to the UN, we are liable to hinder the chances for realizing them through direct contacts in the field . . . or through whatever bilateral channel may open during the talks."[29]

Sleepless for nearly two days, Eban embarked on a tortuous journey. First, a hunk of Jordanian shrapnel narrowly missed him crossing his own front lawn, then military traffic delayed him for hours reaching his plane, a twin-engine domestic aircraft; all others had been mobilized. Flying at extremely low altitudes to avoid enemy radar, Eban landed at Athens and began searching for a connecting flight. Another stopover in Amsterdam followed before a visibly drained foreign minister finally landed in New York. He received no rest, but rather was whisked immediately to the Security Council.

Waiting for him anxiously was Gideon Rafael. The Israeli ambassador had spent the last twenty-four hours struggling hard against a cease-fire resolution, specifically one that restored the *status quo ante bellum* but without ending the *status belli*. "Nasser should never again reap a political victory from a military defeat," he wrote Arthur Goldberg, "This is vital not only for Israel but also for the Western position in the Middle East." Eban, arriving, insisted that the resolution contain no reference to the Armistice regime, and treated Goldberg to a prolonged lecture on the damage such allusion could cause to later peace-making efforts. "Abba . . . don't worry," Goldberg, finally getting a word in, reassured him, "It's finished, draft resolution and everything . . . Send Gideon over; I'll give him the draft."

But Eban had no time for text-viewing. Moments later he was called to address the Council where, reading from handwritten notes jotted in transit, he delivered a tour de force.

Declaring that Israel had "passed from serious danger to successful and glorious resistance," Eban went on to chronicle the origins of the crisis, beginning with remilitarization of Sinai, the removal of UNEF, and Nasser's blockade of Tiran. Rich in metaphor—"Israel . . . is breathing with a single lung," he said, referring to the blockade, and then to UNEF: "an umbrella that is taken away as soon as it begins to rain"—his remarks were also high on drama. "Look around this table and imagine," he asked with a glance at each ambassador present, "a foreign power forcibly closing New York or Montreal, Boston or Marseilles, Toulon or Copenhagen, Rio or Tokyo or Bombay Harbor. How would *your* government react? What would *you* do? How long would *you* wait?" Finally, all but ignoring Herzog's caveat, he evinced Israel's "instinct for peace" and called for a comprehensive peace plan for the Middle East. "Let us build a new system of relationships from the wreckage of the old! Let us discern across the darkness the vision of a brighter and gentler dawn!"[30]

Whatever the risks Eban incurred by again exceeding his instructions were more than offset by his genius at oratory. Broadcast throughout the world, hailed by the *New York Times* for his "mastery of phrase-making," and the *Chicago Tribune* for delivering "one of the great diplomatic speeches of all time," Eban profoundly impacted public opinion. This was already running markedly in Israel's favor. Of the 17,445 letters received by the White House in the first forty-eight hours of the war, 96 percent were pro-Israel, 3 percent isolationist, and only 1 percent in support of the Arabs. A Harris poll showed that over half of all Americans believed that the Soviets had engineered the Middle East war as a means of strengthening the Communist position in Vietnam. The press, generally evenhanded on Middle East issues, could barely contain its excitement over Israel's advances.

These developments did not escape the attention of Lyndon Johnson, a man acutely attuned to public sentiment. Ensconced in the Situation Room where Lady Bird, his wife, served him breakfast, together with Rusk, McNamara, and the Rostows, the president continued to scrutinize the war. He was thoroughly disgusted with the Soviet role in the crisis and with the Arabs' Big Lie. The upsurge in pro-Israeli feeling throughout the United States also engaged Johnson, as did the requisites of the approaching election year. His inclination was to permit Israel to keep its conquests in Sinai at least, and use them as a bargaining chip in future negotiations. Clearly, Rusk asserted, "we can't make Israel accept a puny settlement." Walt Rostow put a finer point on it, questioning "whether the settlement of this war shall be on the basis of armistice agreements, which leave the Arabs in the posture of hostilities towards Israel, keeping alive the Israeli issue in Arab political life as a unifying force, and affording the Soviet Union a handle on the Arab world; or whether a settlement emerges in which Israel is accepted as a Middle Eastern state with rights of passage through the Suez Canal."

The Israelis were, of course, amenable. In a secret message passed from Israeli Supreme Court Chief Justice Shimon Agranat to Goldberg, and from Goldberg to Johnson, Eshkol assured the president that he understood America's difficulties in relieving the Tiran blockade and the threat to Israel's security. He asked only that America help delay attempts to impose a Security Council cease-fire, that it support Israel's demand for peace in return for evacuating captured Arab territory, and, most crucially, that it deter the Soviets from intervening. Other than that, Eshkol wrote, "We are prepared to handle the matter ourselves." The administration seemed ready to honor that request, Israeli officials believed. "It turns out that Eban did not relate Johnson's message accurately," Ben-Gurion, drawing on his own sources within the government, concluded. "America wants us to finish off Nasser quickly."[31]

But if Johnson was willing to let Israel win the war, he was also eager to minimize damage to America's Middle East interests and avert a clash with the USSR. "We continue to believe that the fighting in the Near East should be stopped as soon as possible," the president wired Kosygin at 10:03 A.M. Urging the Soviets to refute Nasser's charge of U.S.-Israeli collusion, and reminding them of America's commitment to free passage in the Straits, Johnson sought cooperation in the Security Council. Specifically, he asked Kosygin to support a cease-fire resolution that called for troop withdrawals "behind the Armistice Lines," but "without prejudice to the respective rights, claims or positions of anyone," and also for an end to "acts of force regardless of their nature."

No answer was forthcoming from Kosgyin, while in the UN, efforts to obtain a cease-fire remained stalemated. In express terms, Goldberg told Federenko that the American draft was intended to terminate the blockade and initiate direct talks on the separation of forces and certain "territorial changes." The Israelis, who sought to trade their gains for Arab recognition and peace, would not be happy with the resolution, Goldberg explained, but Washington would support it if Moscow did. "It's a package deal," he concluded. "Take it or leave it."

For all his anti-American fustian, Federenko was fond of Goldberg—"a slick Jew who could fool the devil himself," he called him—and admired his creativity. But the American draft went far beyond the Russian's terms of reference, which still linked a cease-fire with an immediate and unconditional withdrawal. Later that day, however, the Soviet ambassador received an extraordinary phone call from Deputy Foreign Minister Semyonov in Moscow. Speaking in Gromyko's name, Semyonov instructed him to accept a simple cease-fire, even without a pullback. "You must do that, even if the Arab countries do not agree. I repeat, do not agree."

American officials, shocked by this sudden turn of Soviet policy, wondered if Federenko had exceeded his instructions or if communications between him and Moscow had collapsed. Confusion deepened with the receipt of another hot line cable from Kosygin—a full eight hours after the last—acknowledging his support for a cease-fire plus withdrawal. A debate ensued at the White House over whether to respond to Federenko's position or Kosygin's. "Our two Ambassadors in the Security Council have been in close consultation throughout the day," Johnson answered finally. "We understand that our Ambassadors agreed to a very short resolution calling for a cease-fire as a first step."

The Americans were delighted with this development but, as Goldberg anticipated, not so the Israelis. They greeted with skepticism Goldberg's claim that the withdrawal from occupied lands would take "four months at least," leaving ample room for diplomacy, and bristled at the very mention of the Armistice. And yet, having claimed to be waging a defensive war, they could not reject a cease-fire on the grounds that they needed more territory for trading. Hiding this dilemma behind a display of overexuberance, Eban told the Council, "We welcome, we favor, we support, we accept" the cease-fire.

Seven minutes later, at 4:30 P.M., the resolution passed. The cease-fire would go into effect that evening at 10:00 GMT. Johnson lost no time in appearing on national television and announcing "the necessary first step . . . forward to what we all must hope will be a new time of settled peace and progress for all the people of the Middle East."[32]

But Johnson's appearance proved premature; the Arab delegates had yet to register their reaction. The Jordanian ambassador, Dr. Muhammad al-Farra, a Khan Yunis-born, American-educated diplomat who had once refused a position on the UN Secretariat for fear that he might have to shake an Israeli's hand, was the first to respond. Al-Farra had just received a phone call from Ahmad Touqan, his foreign minister, who informed him of the extent of Jordan's defeat. The assessment was confirmed by U Thant who, still smarting from the obloquy of his decision on UNEF, had kept a low profile since the war's eruption. "My friend, the picture is very gloomy," the secretary-general said, and al-Farra burst out in tears. His trauma was now compounded as he rose to accept the cease-fire, aware that without Egyptian support, the resolution was essentially worthless.

The keys to ending the fighting, to preserving the Egyptian army, Jerusalem's Old City, and the rest of the West Bank, were now in the hands of Mohammad El Kony. Earlier in the debate, Goldberg had approached the Egyptian delegate and informed him that Nasser's air force had been destroyed and his troops set to flight. He promised to work for an Israeli withdrawal, but only if Egypt supported the cease-fire resolution. El Kony, bewildered, requested instructions from Cairo. Those he received were categorical. El Kony was to reject any resolution that did not order the unconditional withdrawal of Israeli troops. Anything short of that provision was unworkable, Foreign Minister Riad explained, adding—apparently without irony—that "Israeli forces in Sinai have become intermingled with Egyptian troops and there are no UN emergency forces to determine or identify the positions of either party."

Thus, taking the microphone, El Kony rejected the Goldberg-Federenko compromise, and further denounced the United States and Britain for conspiring with the aggressors. In quick succession came George Tomeh—a radical Ba'thist, squat and bespectacled—asserting Syria's unity with Egypt's position, and Iraqi ambassador Adnan Pachachi, who deplored the resolution as "surrender to Israel."

Goldberg's efforts had been vitiated. Denying the Big Lie, offering to open the 6th Fleet to UN observers, the American ambassador made a last-ditch attempt to establish a mechanism for verifying the cease-fire. This, too, failed to gain ground and, stymied, the Council finally recessed. It would not reconvene for nearly twenty-four hours.[33]

Day Two: Denouement

The stillbirth of the first cease-fire resolution in New York was not regretted in Tel Aviv. "Unwittingly," Rabin recorded, "Nasser was beginning to act more like an ally than an enemy." As the Security Council reached an impasse, the IDF general staff completed its preparations for Operation Nachshon 2—the second phase of the war.

The plan continued to give priority to the Egyptian front, to eradicating Nasser's army and gaining control over the Mitla and Giddi passes. Special concern was again expressed about Sharm al-Sheikh, where the size of the Egyptian force remained uncertain. Dayan and Rabin authorized Operation Lights (*Urim*), involving a naval probe of the area and an assault by paratroopers approaching from either the Red Sea or the Gulf of Suez coast. In Gaza, the installation of a full military government was approved and charged with preventing looting and restoring normal life. But all action was again postponed on the Syrian front where, apart from preparing for limited land grabs, the army's sole task was to block any further enemy incursions. If Lebanon entered the war—two Lebanese Hawkers had strafed positions in Galilee that afternoon; one was shot down—the IDF would be permitted to cross that border as well, conquering up to the Litani River. Finally, in Jerusalem, Israel would accept the surrender of the Old City, but for the time do nothing to force it. Military governors would meanwhile be appointed to administer the major cities of the West Bank, where the Arab population would be respected. As for those residents who wanted to flee to Jordan, Dayan pointed out, Israel would not stand in their way.

The future of the West Bank, Gaza, and Jerusalem preoccupied the Cabinet as well when it met late that night in the prime minister's office. After hearing a briefing by Gen. Bar-Lev on the first forty hours of the war, Israeli leaders listed the issues to be addressed once the fighting concluded, among them water sources, the Demilitarized Zones, and the Palestinian refugee problem. From Washington, Abe Harman submitted a proposal for creating a West

Bank Palestinian state federated with Israel, and for sending "symbolic units" of friendly Palestinians to fight on the Egyptian and Syrian front. Eshkol was more concerned that Arab civilians and POWs be treated humanely, though the notion of a permanent settlement had sparked his imagination as well. "We have to consider new definitions of diplomatic and strategic concepts," he exhorted his ministers. "We must devise a program that will ensure Israel's proper place in the Middle East within the context of a permanent peace and secure borders."[34]

Thirty-eight miles away, in Amman, a message arrived at the army's headquarters. The time was 11:15 P.M., over ten hours after Hussein had requested a directive from Nasser, and only now he received his answer. "My dear brother, King Hussein," Nasser's cable began. "We find ourselves face to face with one of those critical moments that nations are sometimes called upon to endure . . . We are fully aware of your difficult situation as at this very moment our front is crumbling too. Yesterday, our enemy's air force inflicted a mortal blow on us. Since then, our land army has been stripped of all air support and compelled to withstand the power of superior forces . . . I think that our only choice now is to evacuate the West Bank of the Jordan tonight, and hope that the Security Council will order a cease-fire."

So, tersely, Nasser finally admitted what Hussein already knew: that the Egyptian air force was nonexistent and its army in full retreat. Permission had been granted to withdraw the Jordanian army to the East Bank without fear of repercussions from Egypt or other radical regimes. At the price of the West Bank and Jerusalem, Hussein had gained legitimacy. Nasser concluded: "I want to tell you how much I appreciate your heroic behavior, your strong and gallant will, and the bravery shown by the Jordanian people and their army. Peace be upon you, and the mercy of God."

There was little Hussein could do. The Israelis had turned down his requests for an implicit cease-fire. Soon their troops would drive through the rest of the West Bank—through Nablus and Qalqilya, Bethlehem and Hebron—seize the Old City and descend to the Jordan Valley and Jericho. Though many of its units had yet to see combat, the army was thoroughly demoralized. Faced with these ineluctable facts, depressed and fatigued, Hussein approved Riyad's evacuation proposal. At 11:30 P.M., Jordanian commanders received orders to retreat, essentially every man for himself, over the Jordan River. Floridly, in a letter to president 'Aref of Iraq, he composed a final tribute to himself and the battle his forces had waged:

> The painful events of the past two days demonstrated to us that Arab brotherhood, Arab understanding and pure ethics expressed in the desire and longing for paradise—these in time shall remain . . . [Our] blood . . . has mixed in the green expanses, on the hills and the walls and within the immaculate earth.[35]

Then, seemingly miraculously, events began to shift. In New York, seven hours behind Jordan time, the U.S. and the USSR reached their agreement on a cease-fire. The Jordanians, together with the Israelis, accepted the resolution. But unlike the Israelis, who were counting on Egypt's rejection of the cease-fire to enable them to keep advancing, Hussein believed the resolution could rescue him from defeat. Fortifying this impression were sanguine reports from field commanders—al-Ghazi and Brig. Turki in Nablus—assuring him that there was mettle in their units yet, that the army could still fight on.

Thus, less than two hours after issuing the evacuation order, the king prepared to rescind it. The cease-fire would go into effect at dawn, and until that time all units that had fled to the East Bank were instructed to cross the Jordan River again and to try to hold their ground. The Prince Hasan bin Talal Brigade, reinforced with Iraqi commandos, was ordered to hold the approaches to Jericho and the Jordan bridges, while the remains of the 40th Brigade regrouped east of Nablus. If these positions could be defended for twenty-four hours, Hussein believed, much of the West Bank and the Old City of Jerusalem would be saved.[36]

THE WAR: DAY THREE, JUNE 7

The fateful battle for Jerusalem.
Egypt's "Curtain" torn.
Soviet threats and American brainstorming.

"I HAVE ORDERED ALL OUR TROOPS on the West Bank of the Jordan and all other fronts to hold onto their positions. With God's help may victory come to you as well as us." Thus King Hussein informed Nasser of his decision not to evacuate his army to the East Bank. The dispatch to his soldiers took a more bellicose tone, entreating them "to kill the enemy wherever you find them with your arms, hands, nails and teeth," and reminding them—incongruously, perhaps—to respect the cease-fire if Israel did.

The new instructions reached 'Ata 'Ali after 2:20 in the morning of June 7, just as Israeli loudspeakers outside the Old City were encouraging him and his men to lay down their arms and surrender. The Jordanian commander had given his troops the choice of remaining in their positions or retreating by any route possible. Maj. Badi 'Awad, with no ammunition left and little fuel, drove his jeep up the Mount of Olives and from there through the desert to Jericho. Others were not so fortunate. Under fire and desperately hungry, Lt. Ghazi Isma'il Raba'iyya led his 120-man platoon from house to house, begging for shelter, only to be turned away. "When you're losing, nobody respects you," he recounted. Three more days would pass before, ragged and emaciated, he managed to reach the Dead Sea.[1]

For King Hussein, having told his army to stand firm at a time when Egypt's was fleeing, the situation was no less perilous. Nasser was sure to be irate. Shortly after issuing his new instructions, Hussein received another cable from Cairo confirming that "the High Command of our Armed Forces deduced that beyond a shadow of a doubt, the United States and Great Britain were aiding

Israel." The king responded obliquely, asserting that he had no choice but to accept the cease-fire, and ascribing the decision to his "Oriental fatalism." The danger from Egypt could not be discounted, though. Pro-Nasserite demonstrations had already broken out in Amman, the protestors demanding Jordan's realignment away from the West and toward the USSR. Even more destabilizing was the flight of tens of thousands of Palestinians from the West to the East Bank. Adding their numbers to the disgruntled refugees from 1948—the majority of Jordan's population—this new wave of displaced Palestinians threatened to scuttle Hashemite rule.

Yet, mortal as they were, the Egyptian and Palestinian threats to Hussein paled beside those posed by Israel. Just before dawn, the tank brigades of Uri Ram and Moshe Bar Kokhva set out from Jenin in the direction of Nablus. Advancing from 'Arabe to Tubas to attack the city in an unconventional eastern thrust, Ram's tanks destroyed thirty-five of al-Ghazi's tanks and blocked any reinforcements from reaching them. While infantry and recon units paired off to chase stragglers over the Damiya Bridge—only five Pattons managed to cross—armored formations took Sebastia, the capital of ancient Samaria. Waiting for the Israelis at Nablus were twenty-five tanks, all that remained of the 40th Armored Division, with instructions to hold their ground. "We were on full alert, ready to meet the enemy," Capt. Muhammad al-Darubi, a company commander, remembered. "At 6:30 we spotted a column of enemy tanks approaching. Another column came by way of the main road from 'Arabe. These presented excellent targets, and we rained shells down on them. But our fire exposed our positions, and we knew it was only a matter of time before the enemy's air force appeared."

Within Jerusalem, only token Jordanian forces held on to resist Israel's impending assault. All but one hundred of the Old City's defenders had withdrawn and far less than that remained on Augusta Victoria ridge. Among the last to believe that the Arabs could lose were Palestinian notables led by Jerusalem mayor Ruhi al-Khatib and Anwar al-Khatib, the district governor. Confident of Nasser's invincibility and of Israel's imminent defeat, East Jerusalem had made no provisions for war. No emergency medical supplies had been stockpiled, no bomb shelters built. Since the fighting started, Palestinian officials had persuaded themselves that the planes circling overhead and the tanks on Mount Scopus were Jordanian or even Iraqi. By the morning of the 7th, though, with the Star of David flying over the Rockefeller Museum and 'Ata 'Ali's troops retreating, the notables could no longer deny reality. They beseeched Hussein to declare Jerusalem an open city and so spare its Muslim shrines from destruction.[2]

Hussein was not insensitive to these concerns. On the contrary, as scion to a family that had already lost Islam's two holiest places—Mecca and Medina—to the Saudis, he was determined to preserve the third. He urged the Palestinians to trust in God and not to abandon hope. For his part, he rescinded his previous call for a de facto "end to the violence" and now expressed his readiness for a formal cease-fire. He had only to convince the Israelis.

With redoubled gravity, Prime Minister Jum'a appealed to the UN and to Ambassador Burns to persuade Israel to refrain from seizing the Old City and to stop its advance on Nablus. Failure to do so, he warned, would result in the collapse of the Hashemite regime. As proof of Jordan's sincerity, Jum'a pointed out its defiance of Nasser's evacuation proposal and its refusal of further aerial support from Iraq. General Khammash also lobbied Burns, beseeching him to end the "meaningless massacre" and to save the monarchy from collapse. The American ambassador quickly relayed these messages, along with warnings of his own regarding the safety of the 1,200 U.S. citizens in Jordan and the dangers of Soviet intervention should Israel press its attack. Time was exceedingly short, Burns emphasized; the president must speak with Eshkol directly.

When it came to making that call, however, the White House hesitated. The advent of the Big Lie had made administration officials wary of suggesting any military move to Israel, lest it be seen as collusion. At most, Rusk was willing to communicate Hussein's cease-fire offer to Tel Aviv, and to advise the Israeli government to "take care of its own interests in the Arab world." Hussein had always exerted a moderating influence on the region, the secretary recalled, and there were long-term dangers to toppling him.[3]

Rusk's cable reached Jerusalem at 7:00 A.M., following two intense hours of activity, political and military, which began when Dayan informed Eshkol that the Jordanian army was no longer retreating but returning to its former positions. The Jordanians would try to hold their ground until a cease-fire came into effect. Though the IDF had yet to encircle the Old City, Dayan averred, it had better move swiftly to breach it. Eshkol agreed, and Dayan, supplied with an attack plan by Rabin, assigned Haim Bar-Lev to oversee the operation. His orders were brief: reach the Jewish Holy Places as quickly as possible and refrain from using heavy weapons.

Bar-Lev promptly contacted Narkiss: "There's a danger that the Security Council will decide on a cease-fire. You have to break into the Old City immediately. But proceed carefully—use your head." Narkiss, in turn, radioed Gur at the Rockefeller Museum, and ordered him to take Augusta Victoria ridge at once and move his men from Herod's Gate east to the Lions Gate ("Vietnam," in IDF code), the closest to the Western Wall. The Central Command chief was anxious to get started. "My experience fighting in Jerusalem in 1948 had scarred me deeply," he admitted to his staff after the war, "In Jerusalem, I knew, what you don't finish today you may not be able to finish tomorrow."

Narkiss's fears were shared by Menachem Begin. Having heard of the impending cease-fire on the 4:00 A.M. BBC news, Begin phoned Dayan. "The Security Council's decision changes the whole situation," he stressed, "We must not wait a second more." Dayan peevishly replied—"I don't need any more advice . . . I've given the order to enter the city even if it's not surrounded"—

and advised Begin to consult with Eshkol. Begin proceeded to call the prime minister's office and, after apologizing for disturbing him, to convince Eshkol to convene an emergency Cabinet meeting for no later than 7:00. Dayan, meanwhile, approved the limited use of tanks and planes to help facilitate the breakthrough. The order came with a strict caveat against hitting the Dome of the Rock, the al-Aqsa Mosque, or the Holy Sepulchre, damage to any of which could ignite yet another international crisis.

Israeli guns opened fire on the Muslim Quarter at 6:00 A.M. Two hours later, IDF artillery laid a heavy barrage on the area around Augusta Victoria, followed by jets dropping napalm. The trenches around the hospital, built by Kaiser Wilhelm in 1909 and named for his wife, became deathtraps. "I found one of my soldiers shriveled to the size of my hand," claimed company commander Mahmud Abu Faris. The few surviving Jordanians fled, and the paratroopers who soon arrived—the 71st Battalion from Mount Scopus and the 66th from Wadi Joz— found the once-contested ridge deserted. Most of the Israeli casualties were in fact self-inflicted: nine dead and eleven wounded by errant artillery rounds.

The paratroopers proceeded southward, seizing the Intercontinental Hotel, built atop the Mount of Olives and the world's oldest Jewish cemetery, and then Abu Dis, completing the encirclement of the city. From there, they descended to the Garden of Gethsemane, scene of Jesus' arrest and of the previous night's disastrous battle with the Jordanians. Before them stood the Old City and the gate erected by the Mamluk Sultan Baybars in 1320 and still decorated with his leonine coat of arms. Gripped with anticipation, Gur sent a message to his battalion commanders (see book jacket photo): "We occupy the heights overlooking the Old City. In a little while we will enter it. The ancient city of Jerusalem which for generations we have dreamt of and striven for—we will be the first to enter it. The Jewish nation is awaiting our victory. Israel awaits this historic hour. Be proud. Good luck."[4]

The anticipation was not the army's alone, however. The civilian population was also hanging on edge. The song "Jerusalem of Gold," first sung on Independence Day, blared from every transistor. Teddy Kollek had not slept for sixty hours, but it did not hinder him from rushing to the formerly Jordanian Ambassador Hotel and setting up a provisional municipality for the soon-to-be-reunited city. There, the Vienna-born Kollek, a close protégé of Ben-Gurion, ran into Chaim Herzog, brother of Ya'akov, a Cambridge-educated lawyer who had twice headed IDF intelligence. Since the start of the crisis, Herzog had been broadcasting regularly on the radio, calming his listeners with his sober analyses of the situation. Now, too excited to sit in his studio, he also hurried toward the Old City.

En route, Herzog encountered Rabbi Shlomo Goren, the IDF's chief chaplain. Scholar and paratrooper, the bearded firebrand had just arrived from Sinai, where the half-track he was riding in received a direct hit and its driver killed. Armed with a Torah scroll and a ram's horn—*shofar*—Goren had found Gur at the Rockefeller Museum and warned him, "history will never forgive you if you sit here and fail to enter [the Old City]." With Herzog, however, he was more magnanimous, promising him a place in the hereafter if he convinced the government to liberate Jerusalem.[5]

But the government had yet to be convinced, having just received Rusk's telegram recommending that Israel accept the cease-fire.

"*Nu?* So what do we say to Hussein?" Eshkol asked an impromptu meeting of leading ministers and advisers. Before him now was not only Rusk's cable but a similar message from Harold Wilson asking that Israel observe the cease-fire with Jordan. From New York, Eban reported an appeal from Goldberg saying, in the president's name, that continuing the war with Jordan was liable to embroil Israel in "serious international complications." There was little choice but to comply with the resolution, Eban added, and hope that somehow the Arabs would violate it.

"Every word we say is only liable to complicate matters," Dayan counseled. "We have to be very careful." He proposed inviting the king to a secret meeting, but beyond that making no promises. Ya'akov Herzog suggested that Israel complete its conquests on the eastern front and only then begin a dialogue with Hussein, while Arye Levavi insisted that Hussein first expel Riyad and other Egyptian officers as the precondition for any deal. "That'll be the king's death," observed Yigal Allon. Eshkol wondered whether Israel's agreement to the cease-fire might be linked to immediate peace talks with Hussein. "Maybe we'll just ask him who's the boss in Jordan?" he mused.

In the end, Eshkol's question became Israel's reply to Rusk: Was Hussein really in control of his troops and, if so, could he confirm that fact? Claiming that West Jerusalem was still being shelled, the Israelis insisted on knowing the precise moment when that bombardment would stop, and where Jordanian and Israeli representatives could meet to discuss the cease-fire and a "permanent peace."

The chances that Hussein might respond favorably to these demands were minuscule, the Israelis knew. Still, with their troops literally only yards from entering the Old City, the ultimatum was a gamble. If the monarch accepted its terms, even theoretically, the opportunity to regain the Western Wall and other sacred sites—to realize a two-thousand-year-old Jewish aspiration—might be lost.

Jordan's rejoinder was equivocal, though, evasive and indirect. Chief of staff Khammash told Burns that the army had no contact whatsoever with Jerusalem, and no way of knowing whether its cannons were still shelling enemy positions. Prime Minister Jum'a called in Western ambassadors and complained of repeated Israeli violations of the cease-fire. "Jordan has reached the limits of its patience!" he exclaimed, and warned of a massive counterattack.[6] Other than that, silence. For the second time since the start of the war, Hussein had ignored a personal appeal from Eshkol. The ultimatum was effectively defied.

At 9:45 A.M., Sherman tanks fired point-blank at the twelve-meter-high Lions Gate, destroying a bus that had been positioned to block it, and blasted open the door. Then, led by a half-track commanded by Capt. Yoram Zammush, an observant Jew whom Gur had promised would be the first to reach the Western Wall, the Israelis charged. Jordanian gunners shot from the walls and from rooftops around the square inside the gate, but the assault was overwhelming. Tanks lumbered forward, only to get wedged in the narrow alleyways. Half-tracks, one of which bore Motta Gur and his staff, edged by Zammush's vehicle and headed for the Via Dolorossa, with its Stations of the Cross sacred to Christians. Other units fanned out toward the Damascus and the Jaffa Gates, through the Muslim and Christian Quarters, respectively.

Simultaneously, a company of the Jerusalem Brigade under Captain Eli Kedar climbed Mount Zion on the Old City's southeastern corner, heading for the Zion Gate, the scene of Israel's abortive breakthrough attempts in 1948. Kedar had fallen prisoner in that battle at age fifteen, but now, returning, he crawled through a hatch in the gate's door and emerged into the Armenian Quarter. Fifty men followed and marched downhill to the former Jewish Quarter, which had been sacked and resettled by Muslims, and found its dwellings draped with surrender flags. Encountering only scattered small-arms fire, Kedar led his force toward the Dung Gate—in Herodian times, a conduit for garbage disposal—and a rendezvous with the 71st paratroopers, who had approached the city from the Kidron Valley in the east.

Gur and his men, meanwhile, stepped into the tranquil, tree-lined plaza known to Muslims as the Noble Sanctuary (*al-Haram al-Sharif*) and to Jews as the Temple Mount (*Har ha-Bayit*). The site of both the First and Second Temples, believed to be the scene of Isaac's binding and of Muhammad's ascent to heaven, it was a Holy Place par excellence, revered by millions. Arik Akhmon, the intelligence officer, described the moment: "There you are on a half-track after two days of fighting, with shots still filling the air, and suddenly you enter this wide open space that everyone has seen before in pictures, and though I'm not religious, I don't think there was a man who wasn't overwhelmed with emotion. Something special had happened." After a brief skirmish with Jordanian riflemen, Gur radioed Narkiss the three words—seven in English—that would resonate for decades afterward. "*Har ha-Bayit be-Yadenu*"—"The Temple Mount is in our hands."

Gur received a delegation of Arab notables who proffered him the city's surrender, along with arms that had been stored in the mosques. To their surprise, the general released them and allowed them to return to their homes. But neither he nor any of his staff knew how to get to the Western Wall, and were forced to ask an old Arab man for directions. He guided Gur through the Mughrabi Gate, exiting just south of the Wall. A retaining structure of giant ashlars erected by King Herod, the wall was the only remnant of the Second Temple destroyed by the Romans in the year 70, Jews had not had access to the shrine, their holiest, for nineteen years.

As Gur descended, men from both the Jerusalem Brigade and the 71st paratroopers converged on the wall, ecstatic and all but oblivious to the persistent sniper fire. Rabbi Goren broke free of the three soldiers Gur had designated to restrain him, and ran headlong to the wall. He said *Kaddish*—the mourner's prayer—blew his *shofar*, and proclaimed, "I, General Shlomo Goren, chief rabbi of the Israeli Defense Forces, have come to this place never to leave it again." Crammed into the narrow space between the stones and the ramshackle dwellings of the Mughrabi Quarter, the soldiers broke into spontaneous songs and prayers. Above them, the Star of David was hoisted.[7]

Eshkol wasted no time in placing the Holy Places under the jurisdiction of their relevant clergy—rabbis, Muslim clerics, the Catholic Church. His intention was to visit the Old City himself, but in view of continuing sniper fire, he was advised against it by the army. To his chagrin, at 2:30 P.M., Eshkol learned that his defense minister had ignored his advice. Accompanied by Rabin and Narkiss, in a procession that he took pains to have photographed, Dayan marched triumphantly to the Temple Mount. There he suggested to Narkiss that part of the Old City walls be pulled down—an ancient practice symbolizing conquest. Rabbi Goren also had an idea: In preparation for the imminent Messianic era, the IDF should utilize the explosives it had on hand and demolish the Temple Mount's mosques. Narkiss ignored both proposals. His concern was maintaining order and achieving the security needed to establish Israeli governance of the city. "The thought that it was my destiny to be the vehicle of that mission," he wrote, "overwhelmed me."

Arriving at the Western Wall, Dayan observed the tradition of writing a prayer on a note—rumor had it that he wished for peace—and inserting it between the stones. Then, with his usual ambiguity, at once militant and magnanimous, he declared: "We have reunited the city, the capital of Israel, never to part it again. To our Arab neighbors we offer even now . . . our hand in peace."

Rabin listened to Dayan's words and watched with awe the scene of hundreds of soldiers, joined by Ultra-Orthodox Jews, dancing. "This was the peak of my life," he recalled. "For years I had secretly harbored the dream that I might play a role . . . in restoring the Western Wall to the Jewish people . . . Now that dream had come true, and suddenly I wondered why I, of all men, should be so privileged." His words at the wall sounded less like a soldier's than a prophet's:

> The sacrifices of our comrades have not been in vain . . . The countless generations of Jews murdered, martyred and massacred for the sake of Jerusalem say to you, 'Comfort yet, our people; console the mothers and the fathers whose sacrifices have brought about redemption.'[8]

Jubilation had also gripped the government. Begin was demanding that the Jewish Quarter be reconstructed at once and resettled with several thousand Israelis. Eban, hearing about the victory in New York, wrote of "a flood of historic emotion [that] burst the dams of restraint and set minds and hearts in movement far beyond the limits of our land." Among the most strenuous opponents of the war, Religious Affairs Minister Zorach Warhaftig recalled how "my heart was filled with gladness," as he rushed to kiss the Western Wall and embrace both Dayan and Rabin. Yigal Yadin, the prime minister's special military adviser, was already thinking of the next objective—Hebron. "We have a long history with Hebron, going back to Abraham," he reminded Eshkol who, alone among the ministers, remained subdued. Dispirited by the deaths of 97 paratroopers in the battle, and the 430 wounded, he was also wary of occupying a large and hostile Palestinian population. "Have you already thought about how we can live with so many Arabs?" he asked. Yadin's retort was brash: "Truth is, your honor, once our forces arrive they [the Palestinians] will flee to the desert."[9]

The momentum of the Israeli advance indeed appeared unstoppable. At the same moment that Motta Gur's paratroopers claimed the Western Wall, Ben-Ari's tanks reached the outskirts of Jericho. The first of several heavy battles had broken out west of Nablus while, south of Jerusalem, Israeli infantry over-ran the defenses around the Mar Elias monastery. Beyond that lay Bethlehem and Hebron. Jordanian forces were in total disarray, abandoning vehicles in their rush to reach the East Bank and safety. Amid the ruins of the Etzion Bloc, a cluster of Israeli settlements outside Jerusalem destroyed in 1948, the attack-ers found twenty Patton tanks in pristine condition. A similar number was left stuck in the mud of Jericho. The strength of the Jordanian army had been reduced by 80 percent, Prime Minister Jum'a complained to Burns, and claimed that the Israelis were determined to destroy the rest. The evacuation proceeded at an ever-diminishing pace, as the roads became clogged with refugees.

Early that afternoon, Hussein appeared before his general staff. He spoke of the need to rally the country's remaining forces to defend the East Bank, and of his continuing hope for reinforcements. The only Arab ruler to have come anywhere near the actual fighting, having gone two and a half days without food or sleep, the king looked to one witness "stunned, depressed, and humili-ated." He had just lost one-half of his kingdom, along with its principal sources of revenue—tourism and agriculture. His army lay in ruins. Under such cir-cumstances, Hussein could scarcely be consoled by the latest cable to arrive from Cairo. This revealed that Nasser had approved the king's evacuation or-der and that, in view of the need for international pressure to save Jerusalem, had exempted Jordan from breaking relations with the West.[10]

"The Curtain" Falls

Hussein's willingness to accept the cease-fire—if not yet to eject the Egyp-tians—alerted Israeli leaders to the fact that the war's end was in sight. "The sand in the political hourglass was beginning to run out," Rabin noted, and in view of that fact, he ordered the immediate launching of Operation Lights—the conquest of Sharm al-Sheikh—originally scheduled for that evening.

The operation began, as planned, with a naval probe of the Egyptian defenses. These were assumed to include two infantry battalions, artillery and anti-aircraft units, and, offshore, a large naval contingent—six torpedo boats, a destroyer, and a submarine. An aerial reconnaissance conducted at 4:00 A.M., however, showed that the area was practically deserted. Still, Rabin refused to be lulled, and half an hour later, a formation of three Israeli missile boats opened fire on the enemy's shore batteries. Paratroopers and commandos meanwhile prepared to board Nortatlas cargo planes and helicopters for Al-Tur, on the Gulf of Suez, and the overland assault on Tiran.

But the Israelis were unaware that few of the 1,600 Egyptian soldiers initially stationed in the Straits in fact remained at their posts. At 'Amer's insistence, the Sharm al-Sheikh garrison had had no contact with the army's headquarters in Sinai, receiving its encoded orders directly from Cairo. "We knew nothing about the war except what we heard on the radio," the local commander, Gen. 'Abd al-Mun'im Khalil, recalled. "But then, on June 6, I received instructions from 'Amer to retreat. The instructions were carried out." Khalil's officers were appalled. One of them, Mahmud 'Abd al-Hafiz, said that, "We were in a state of shock. The radio continued to broadcast victory songs and announcements about the destruction of the Israeli air force and that our troops were at the gates of Tel Aviv." Lacking sufficient fuel for the 180-mile trip up the Gulf of Suez, 'Abd al-Hafiz and his men covered most of the distance on foot. "I cannot describe to you what we felt during the retreat from Sharm al-Sheikh. We nearly cried, for we could not believe what was happening. We never saw one Israeli soldier."

News that Sharm al-Sheikh had effectively been abandoned reached Murtagi just after midnight. Confused, he instructed elements of the 4th Armored Division to reinforce the position immediately. But the 4th had been one of the first divisions to cross the Canal from Sinai; some of the units were already approaching Cairo. Its commander, Maj. Gen. Sidqi al-Ghul, had received his orders personally from 'Amer, and later claimed ignorance of Murtagi's.

Reports from both the air force and the navy finally convinced Rabin that most of the Egyptians had fled. Instead of landing at Al-Tur, the paratroopers were ferried directly to Sharm al-Sheikh where, in a pitched battle, they killed twenty Egyptians and took another eighty prisoner. At 12:15 P.M., Dayan declared that the Straits of Tiran constituted an international waterway open to all ships without restriction. The Israeli freighter *Dolphin*, still anchored in Masawa, immediately set sail for Eilat, while two ships departed Eilat for Africa.

The Red Sea was again open to Israeli shipping, but not so the Suez Canal. Dayan did not care. When he learned that an IDF scout patrol had probed toward the waterway, he immediately ordered it withdrawn. With the trauma of 1956 still vivid in his mind, the defense minister continued to oppose any action that might result in the closure of the Canal, again angering its maritime users.[11] Accordingly, he instructed Israeli troops not to venture beyond the Mitla and

Giddi passes, which dominated the main access routes into central Sinai, and offered an ideal defense line against any counterattack. But the momentum of the war in the south was rolling far faster than even Dayan could anticipate.

Pursuing the plan worked out with Gen. Gavish at Jabal Libni the night before, all three *Ugdah*s were on the move. Forces under Gen. Tal continued to advance in two directions—south to Bir Lahfan with Gonen's 7th Armored Brigade and along the coast with Granit's mechanized unit. Gonen broke out of the Jabal Libni redoubt to hit the densely fortified rear of the Egyptian 3rd Division at Bir Hamma, and then struck forty miles west to Bir Gafgafa. His objective was to cut off the 4th Division's main escape route, via the Firdan Bridge, over the Suez Canal. Also plowing through the 3rd Division's ranks was Yoffe's *Ugdah*, swinging south through Bir Hasana and Bir al-Thamada. Yoffe's goal, however, was not Firdan but the entrance to the Passes and the retreating Second Division. Farthest south, Ariel Sharon crossed the desert to Nakhl in the hope of trapping Shazli Force before it, too, could reach the passes.

The Israelis hurried, but were impeded by the retreating Egyptians. Fleeing vehicles and burning wrecks jammed the roads, making progress slow and at times impossible. Apart from officers and NCO's, the Israelis were no longer taking prisoners, but encouraging Egyptian enlisted men to run toward the Canal or, shoeless, into the desert. On the roads to Bir Gafgafa and Bir al-Thamada, Israeli tanks had to wind their way through Egyptian columns in order to cut them off and destroy them. One witness to the debacle, Mahmud al-Suwarqa, a driver with the 6th Division, remembered:

> We were waiting to carry out our orders and advance on Eilat when suddenly, on June 7th, both the company and battalion commanders disappeared. Later I found out that they fled over the Canal. I abandoned my jeep and joined a column retreating to Nakhl, where we were exposed to aerial attack. Then, at the Mitla Pass, we ran into Israelis who appeared to be coming from Suez. They fired shells and machine-guns at us, and after that I felt nothing. I awoke in an Israeli vehicle soaked in my own blood.

Still, scattered Egyptian units continued to show initiative and resilience. Egyptian T-55 tanks, entrenched around the sprawling military facilities at Bir Gafgafa, held their ground in the face of Tal's advancing tanks. As many as twelve T-55's and fifty armored personnel carriers were lost, but the Egyptians stalled the Israelis long enough for most of the 4th Division to escape across the Canal. Sharon's *Ugdah*, while bogged down in a muddy riverbed, was hammered by missile fire that forced it to change direction—straight into a "friendly fire" duel with tanks from Yoffe's *Ugdah*. The delay enabled Shazli's Force to slip out of the trap Sharon was planning; the defenders of the al-Qusayma redoubt similarly managed to flee. Meanwhile, the Egyptian air force, though vastly reduced, continued to stage sorties, exploiting the proximity of their bases to the front. "Three cheers for our air force," one Israeli officer, a doctor identified in the record as Asher, remembered thinking. He had mistaken MiG's for Mirages:

The planes get nearer, they seem to be diving toward us. For some reason we're over-confident. We feel sure that today, the third day of the war, there just can't be a single Egyptian plane left intact. Anyway, this plane opens fire and an officer yells, "MiG's! Spread out quickly!" We run like mad among the sand dunes. The plane circles over us and fires. It was just like it is in the films—you hear *pap, pap, pap*. We look up and see more of their planes, three more MiG's getting into formation ready to strike. We . . . throw ourselves down on the sand about sixty meters off the road. The plane that just shot at us joins the other three who are waiting for him and then they all begin to strafe us.

Ilyushin-28 bombers struck the Granit Force west of Romani; Rafael Eytan, the paratrooper commander, was seriously injured. Such sorties had little impact, however, and Egypt lost another fourteen planes in what amounted to suicide attacks against overwhelming forces.[12]

Rearguard actions could no longer stem the tide of Egypt's retreat, much less reverse it. "The fleeing Egyptian forces were in a state of utter confusion," recalled security officer 'Azzam Shirahi. As the Israelis approached, Shirahi was instructed to dynamite all the remaining structures in Bir Gafgafa. "I simply broke down destroying my own base. The only thing I couldn't blow up was the mosque." "Everyone lost their heads," recalled Dr. 'Abd al-Fattah al-Tarki, a humanities student and a reserve officer with the 2nd Armored Brigade. "We were told to withdraw to Bir al-Thamada, but we arrived to find the positions there already in flames. The army on the roads was in a state of complete collapse. It was a massacre, a disaster. Israel never would have achieved a quarter of its victory if not for the confusion and chaos."[13]

The second line of Egypt's defense—the much-touted 'Curtain'—had collapsed. Though several generals, such as Salah Muhsin, the 14th Armored Brigade commander, tried to organize the withdrawal, most senior officers fled well in advance of their men. The brigade's operations officer, Al-Shirbini Sa'id Hamada, remembered, "though they had surrounded us, the Israelis had yet to break through our lines. But then came the order to retreat—why we didn't know—and the situation turned to bedlam."

Among the last commanders to leave the front was Murtagi himself. Moving his headquarters westward to avoid enemy air strikes, the head of Egypt's ground forces had nevertheless remained at the front. At 2:30 P.M., though, Murtagi was located by Maj. Gen. Sa'ad 'Abd al-Krim, chief of military police, who advised him to evacuate at once or risk becoming a prisoner of war. "Most ridiculously, the Eastern Front was now receiving Supreme Headquarters orders from lower staff officers," one Arab historian later commented.[14] Ridiculous or not, Murtagi carried out his instructions. The once highly structured Egyptian army was now left entirely structureless.

But then, later that afternoon, a development occurred that purported to change the situation radically, saving Egypt from debacle and threatening Israel with defeat. The Arabs' principal ally, so vociferous before the war but conspicuously silent ever since, suddenly rallied to their cause.

"Where's the war?" Soviet ambassador Chubakhin had inquired at Israel's Foreign Ministry on the morning of June 5. Caught utterly unawares by the outbreak of the battles, the USSR had struggled mightily over the next twenty-four hours to monitor them. Only when their course was ascertained and shown to be irrevocably in Israel's favor did Federenko receive a green light to seek a cease-fire. But by then a major dislocation had emerged in Soviet-Arab relations. While Moscow wanted a speedy end to the fighting, the Egyptians and the Syrians, counting on substantive Soviet help, insisted that it proceed.

Massive aid for the Arabs had indeed been intimated by official Soviet organs. *Pravda*, for example, declared that "the Soviet Government remains loyal to its pledge to assist the victims of aggression . . . and reserves the right to take all measures required by the situation." Federenko employed the same wording exactly in qualifying his Security Council vote on June 6. But the Arabs were hardly pleased that "all measures" amounted to Soviet acceptance of a cease-fire they did not want and which permitted Israel to retain conquered Arab land. "This same action cost the USSR something in the Arab world," concluded a CIA intelligence report, "the partial Soviet abandonment of the Arabs at the UN will have to many the appearance of at least a partial sell-out."

Avoiding that appearance, or at least mitigating it, grew increasingly difficult for the Soviets as the full scope of the Arabs' defeat became apparent. Nasser was expecting an emergency airlift of arms and ammunition, if not direct Soviet military action against Israel. But the Kremlin was loath to do either. "The war has shown that the Arabs are incapable of unity even when their vital interests are at stake," one Soviet official complained to an American diplomat in Moscow. Embarrassed by the poor showing of their weaponry, outgunned by the 6th Fleet, the Russians wanted to end the war before it tarnished their reputation irreparably, and before Syria fell victim to it, too.

Thus, while Soviet propaganda accused the 6th Fleet of "aiming" its weapons at the Arab states, it fell short of claiming those weapons had fired. On the contrary: Kosygin summoned Murad Ghaleb, Egypt's ambassador, and bluntly told him that no evidence had been found to substantiate the charge of Anglo-American collaboration. President Johnson had personally warranted against such interference, and Soviet cruisers shadowing American carriers in the Eastern Mediterranean had reported no unusual activity. The Soviets agreed to ship new planes, but only to Algeria—Iraq was too far away, they explained, and Libya too close to Wheelus—where they could be reassembled for transfer to Egypt. Ghaleb protested that the process would take weeks, but failed to arouse any sympathy.

The Big Lie had boomeranged. Instead of prodding the Soviets to come to the Arabs' assistance, it impelled them to pursue a cease-fire. The Arabs, in turn, were incensed. By the third day of the war, Nasser was not only talking in terms of Western collaboration with Israel, but of an implicit Soviet-American understanding not to come to blows in the Middle East. For the Soviets, the only way out of this vicious circle was to ignore the Arab dimension for now, and focus their attention on Israel.[15]

The Soviet premier undoubtedly remembered how his predecessor, Bulganin, had threatened to rain missiles on Tel Aviv. That admonition, as much as the Americans' willingness to impose economic sanctions on Israel, had ended the 1956 war and forced the Israelis from Sinai. But faced with an America disposed toward, rather than at odds with, the Jewish state, Kosygin refrained from specific prescriptions for violence. After the first day of fighting, he cautioned Eshkol, "Should the Government of Israel not follow the voice of reason and should it not stop the blood bath, it will bear the responsibility for the outbreak of war and for all its possible results." But the very obtuseness of the message undermined its effectiveness; the Israelis merely ignored it. Far stronger and less equivocal language was required to make the caveat credible.

Thus, on the afternoon of June 7, tired and pale-looking Chuvakhin called on Arye Levavi at the Foreign Ministry. The ambassador brought a message for Eshkol. It read: "The Soviet Union has warned the Israeli government but Israeli leaders refuse to listen to reason. If Israel does not comply immediately with the Security Council Resolution, the USSR will review its relations with Israel [and] will choose and implement other necessary steps which stem from the aggressive policy of Israel." Similar warnings were delivered to Western leaders, with the understanding that they would add their weight in pressuring Israel.[16]

Moscow's resurgent combativeness had an immediate impact on the war, albeit not on Israel's side of it. "Beware of the armed forces," 'Amer exclaimed when Gen. Fawzi found him that afternoon at Supreme Headquarters. The field marshal appeared to be in a greatly uplifted mood, jabbering incoherently, enraptured by what he perceived as the imminence of Soviet intervention. "Listen to me, Fawzi, beware of the armed forces," he repeated, exuberantly. But then his manner shifted, grew suddenly sedate. He instructed his chief of staff to order the 4th Division to turn around, to recross the Canal and stop the enemy at the passes. "It's a political decision. The president has given the order and it must be carried out."

Unsure whether his commander had been overwhelmed by the Soviet pledge or was simply unbalanced, Fawzi nevertheless flew at once to Isma'iliya, on the western shore of the Canal. He found Murtagi, Muhsin, and other high-ranking officers, and showed them the change of orders. "It's a suicide mission!" Murtagi protested. "I can't send them back without air cover, and all the roads are jammed with soldiers and wrecked vehicles." The other officers registered similar objections, but at 4:00 A.M. the order went out to the 4th: "Remain in the Passes until you are otherwise instructed to withdraw." Though the Curtain may have permanently fallen, the third and last defense line might still be held.[17]

Brave New Worlds

Just as the Egyptian effort to spur the Soviets to intervene effectively pushed them to promote a cease-fire, so, too, did the Soviet attempt to deter the Israelis drive them to accelerate their attack.

On the heels of his government's démarche, Federenko ran to the Security Council and demanded immediate implementation of the cease-fire resolution of the previous day. Abba Eban again accepted the motion, and El Kony rejected it. Observing these developments from Jerusalem, Dayan told the Ministerial Defense Committee: "I don't dismiss the Soviet warning but neither am I intimidated by it. Israel is not far from fulfilling the objectives it set out for itself and we can accept the cease-fire while achieving them fully." Still, in light of the mounting pressures to end the fighting, the defense minister instructed the IDF to make every effort to reach the passes by nightfall. Col. Lior glibly recorded, "We might even go on to take Moscow."

In addition to moving up Israel's military timetable, Kosygin's warning had another effect that neither the Russians nor the Arabs sought, namely, spotlighting the question of peace. "This is an historic opportunity. We can get comprehensive peace or separate treaties," explained Yigal Allon, addressing yet another gathering of ministers and political advisers. "First we'll talk peace with Jordan, Lebanon, and Morocco. And if Hussein can't sign a treaty, he can escape with his family to England." Meir Amit asked, "We have to decide what we want to do with the West Bank. Do we want to annex it or do we have other plans?" Eshkol suggested separating the East Bank from the West, installing in the latter a system of local autonomy. "If not, we will face two million Arabs, armed and hostile to us. If one Egyptian general remains there, he could well insist that they fight to the last." The prime minister had no solution for Gaza, though—"a bone stuck in our throats"—nor was he certain how to proceed with Egypt. "I believe that we have reached the point where we can bring down the Egyptian regime entirely and make peace with the new one," proposed Joseph Tekoah, head of the Foreign Ministry's UN desk. "We have to convince the Americans to think in terms of peace."[18]

Yet the Americans were already thinking of peace, more systematically and in greater detail than the Israelis. With the Security Council paralyzed and the Soviets for the moment contained, Johnson and his advisers were free to spend most of June 7 investigating a future Middle East settlement. As told to the National Security Council, the president's goal was to "develop as few heroes and as few heels as possible," maintaining an evenhanded approach in mediation. A solution would be found for free passage through the Straits, for arms control, and for the refugee problem. Yet Johnson was also aware of the complexities and pitfalls ahead—"By the time we get through with all the festering problems we are going to wish the war had not happened"—and solicited his advisers' ideas on possible solutions.

The issue, Walt Rostow responded, "was whether the settlement of this war shall be on the basis of armistice agreements, which leave the Arabs in the posture of hostilities towards Israel, keeping alive the Israeli issue in Arab political life as a unifying force, and affording the Soviet Union a handle on the Arab world; or whether a settlement emerges in which Israel is accepted as a

Middle Eastern state." Rostow proposed that the administration move as swiftly as possible in formulating a comprehensive peace plan that would be mediated by the United States under a loose UN rubric.

Similar logic was evinced by McGeorge Bundy in the Middle East Control Group. The former National Security chief and Ford Foundation director waxed Polonius-like in lending advice to the president: "Make clear that we have now seen a historical event which necessarily changes the landscape. Project a positive picture of our hope for a strong and secure Israel in a prosperous and stable Middle East. Make clear the U.S. view that this time there must be a peace and not simply a set of fragmentary armistice agreements. Put us on record in favor of a real attack on the refugee problem . . . This is good LBJ doctrine and good Israeli doctrine."

The search for a peace program also led the White House beyond its own staff, to two Harvard professors with expertise in international and Middle East affairs, Nadav Safran and Stanley Hoffman. Both described the war as the first real opportunity for peace since the Armistice Agreements, especially now that the USSR had been humiliated and Egyptian power curtailed. Direct talks should be initiated on a country-by-country basis, the professors submitted, emphasizing: *"We must avoid like all hell putting all the Arab countries together on one side of the table and Israel on the other side."*[19]

Underlying these prescriptions was the assumption that the American and Israeli positions dovetailed on the question of peace. With the exception of certain "cosmetic" border changes, the Israelis were expected to forfeit all their conquests in return for face-to-face negotiations culminating in treaties. The impression was reinforced by the initial statements of Eshkol and Eban disavowing any territorial ambitions in the war, as well as by roseate reports from Tel Aviv:

> It is quite clear that the current success of the Israeli military effort has had the fundamental and lasting effect of convincing Israelis of all walks of life that this is the opportunity for them to move from the restricted status of semi and temporary acceptance which has characterized the first 19 years of Israel's existence to a condition of complete and entire nationhood enjoying all the attributes of other independent states . . . They will insist on moving from a cease-fire direction to the conclusion of final peace treaties with their neighbors.

Ambassador Barbour wrote glowingly of the IDF's "stunning military success" and the "brave new world" it opened for both the U.S. and Israel.

By the evening of June 7, however, the first cracks in the presumed U.S.-Israel consensus had emerged. Israeli officials were no longer eschewing all claims on their new acquisitions, but suggesting the need for some permanent IDF presence in Gaza and Sharm al-Sheikh, and for broadening the country's narrow waist opposite Jordan. Dayan was already floating the idea of an autonomous Palestinian state in the West Bank, federally linked to Israel. Most contentiously, Israeli rulers appeared united in declaring the "liberation" of

Jerusalem irreversible. "As a Jew and as a citizen of Israel, it is clear to me that Jerusalem belongs entirely to Israel," stated Israel's ambassador to Rome, Ehud Avriel, to Cardinal Dellacava of the Holy See, "that fact was determined a thousand years before Christianity and 2000 before Islam, and the Vatican had better find a way of reconciling itself to it." The Bank of Israel moved to establish a $50 million fund for West Bank development, and raised the idea of purchasing the Sinai Peninsula, much as the United States had purchased Alaska and Louisiana.[20]

Intimations of these changes invariably reached the White House, where they aroused the concern of Dean Rusk. "If we do not make ourselves attorneys for Israel, we cannot recoup our losses in the Arab world," he told a meeting of the NSC. Specifically, he was willing to represent Israel's demands for full peace treaties with the Arab states, as well as American ideas for arms controls agreements and a solution to the refugee problem. But in return for such advocacy, the secretary insisted on Israeli agreement to withdraw from all the occupied Arab territories. He informed his ambassadors that "we wish to convey the conviction that the territorial integrity and political independence of the Arab states are just as important to all of us as the security of Israel."

The potential for friction between the U.S. and Israel was still far from the president's focus, however. More immediate was the need to counter the Big Lie—disseminating reports on Egypt's use of poison gas in Yemen was one method considered—and to take precautions against any Arab oil boycott. Johnson was also eager to exploit his support for Israel's war aims to convince American Jews ("Doves for War," one aide called them) to support his own in Vietnam. Most pressing, though, was the need to watch the Soviets' reactions and not be lulled into passiveness. "I can't believe the USSR is just going to walk away from this," the commander in chief admitted to the NSC. "I'm not sure we're out of our troubles."[21]

While American policy makers planned for a new world of peace in the Middle East, the old world concluded its third day of war. At dusk, Israeli troops entered Bethlehem after hardly firing a shot. In Manger Square, they were greeted by cheering and shopkeepers rushing to sell them souvenirs. "We broke into the police station and prepared to get some sleep," Rafi Benvenisti, the Jerusalem Brigade officer, reminisced. "Suddenly, an old man was brought in and told me, 'the elders and notables of the city are waiting to receive the conqueror of Bethlehem." Benvenisti was taken to the Church of Nativity—one of the few buildings damaged, four shells having hit its roof—and into a candle lit chamber where churchmen and family heads waited. "I assured them that they had nothing to fear, that we had come in peace. They were in shock and so was I. Then everybody simply went home."

A less hospitable reception awaited Uri Ram's men as they entered Nablus, a city of 80,000—the biblical capital of the Samaritans. Ram recalled how "thousands of people stood applauding and waving white handkerchiefs, and we, in all innocence, responded to them with smiles . . . There was perfect order in the city; no signs of panic at all." That is until one of the Israeli soldiers tried to disarm a member of the local National Guard. Only then did the onlookers realize that the troops were not Iraqi, as they had originally thought, but Israelis. "In an instant the streets were empty and the sniping began."

From the Nablus area, forces of the Peled *Ugdah* turned east and then south to meet up with elements of the Harel Brigade, heading north. By midnight, all four bridges across the Jordan River had been occupied. Dayan ordered that they be demolished, demonstrating that the West Bank had been *physically* severed from the East.[22]

The battles in the West Bank were winding to a close, but those in Sinai were just reaching their climax. The task force under Yisrael Granit, proceeding virtually unopposed from al-'Arish, reached Romani, the Egyptian village closest to the Canal. Other elements of Tal's *Ugdah* meanwhile raced for the passes, which the Egyptians, in contrast to their abandonment of the coastal road, had resolved to defend with the returning 4th Division. Near midnight, advanced elements of the 4th—sixty T-55's—collided with thirty of Tal's AMX tanks west of Bir Gafgafa. Three of the far lighter AMX's burst instantly into flames along with eight half-tracks, one of which was laden with ammunition. Twenty Israelis were killed, including a company commander, Maj. Shamai Kaplan, before the rest of the column retired.

Yet, even as the Egyptians made a bold stand against Tal, Yoffe's tanks were approaching the entrance to the Mitla Pass. A detachment of nine Centurions, perilously low on fuel—four had to be towed by the others—and their crews exhausted, reached the entrance to the pass before sunset. There they arranged wrecks of Egyptian vehicles in such a way as to channel the retreating army directly into their guns.[23] Though vastly outnumbered, this tiny force controlled the single escape route through which three Egyptian divisions—300 tanks and over 30,000 men—were soon to stumble.

THE WAR: DAY FOUR, JUNE 8

Israeli coups de grâce.
A fatal accident.
Nasser capitulates and the Syrians wait.

THE FOURTH DAY OF THE THIRD ARAB-ISRAELI WAR began with a series of explosions in the Jordan Valley. Packing them with captured Jordanian mortar shells—explosives were in short supply—the Israelis destroyed the bridges over the Jordan River. Providing cover for the IDF engineers, elements of the Harel Brigade crossed to the East Bank and set off a new burst of panic in Amman. "For God's sake, get them to stop!" Hussein implored Findley Burns. Thirty Israeli tanks were tearing through the northern part of the country, the king claimed; they were already shelling Ramtha.

A similar plea was made to the British but, disgusted by Hussein's continuing support for the Big Lie, neither they nor the Americans were eager to rush to his aid. The king was forced to fall back on his own resources, meager as these had become. Of the eleven brigades fielded at the beginning of the war, only four were still functional. The remnants of Jordan's army—elements of the Yarmuk and al-Husseini Brigades, the Royal Guard, and the five surviving tanks of the 60th Brigade—joined with Iraqi units to protect the western approaches of Amman and the Golan's southern slopes. There seemed little chance of their success, though, or even their survival, if the Israeli juggernaut advanced.[1]

But there was no Israeli attack, no armored thrust, even feinted, toward Amman. On the contrary, IDF forces along the Jordan had deployed in a defensive alignment in anticipation of a Jordanian counteroffensive. "And so at the end of four days' fighting," Uzi Narkiss, at a postwar briefing, concluded, "Central Command fulfilled its natural aspirations and established Israel's border on the Jordan." The sense of accomplishment was tempered by an appreciation of the price: 200 Israelis killed, 144 of them paratroopers. If unimpressed with the inability of Jordanian commanders to adapt to changing circumstances, Israelis retained their respect for the Jordanians. An internal IDF report concluded that the enemy "demonstrated courage and determination, especially in Jerusalem, where he fought to the last in isolated bunkers." The marker placed by Israel over the grave of those Jordanians killed at Ammunition Hill extolled their singular bravery.

The consolidation of Israel's position on the West Bank—rather than its expansion into the East—soon became evident to the Jordanians as well. While Amman remained unscathed, Israeli troops invested Hebron, site of the biblical Cave of the Patriarchs. The Arab residents, fearful the Israelis would exact revenge for the 1929 massacre of the city's Jewish community, were quick to hang white sheets from their windows and to voluntarily surrender their weapons. The war on the West Bank was over. Writing from the Jordanian perspective, historian Samir Mutawi defined the moment: "By midday on 8 June, Jordan was once again the Transjordan of [King] Abdullah, while Israel completed the total occupation of historical Palestine."[2]

The question of not only when the war would stop but where had also become predominant on the southern front. Fighting had reached full intensity by dawn as thousands of Egyptians rushed toward the Mitla and Giddi Passes in the hope of reaching the Suez Canal. "Thirty-six enemy planes have attacked us in succession," Maj. Gen. al-Ghul, the 4th Division commander, reported to 'Amer. "Our tanks, artillery, and anti-aircraft guns are burnt. Communications with the rear headquarters have been cut, and those with armored brigade as well. We're under attack right now!" Murtagi also called in: "I believe that we must destroy the passes at once, after our forces have crossed the Canal." 'Amer asked both Fawzi and Land Forces Commander Lt. Gen. Muhsin where to draw the final defense line, west or east of the Canal. Both agreed with Murtagi. 'Amer issued the order, one of his last of the war: "All forces to defend the Canal from the west. The passes leading to the Canal are to be demolished, though not the Canal itself, pending further instructions. The air force will cover our forces' retreat during the night of June 8-9."

Neither task, destroying the passes or fording the Canal, would prove easy, however. Aided by an unremitting IAF, a few Israeli tanks continued to block the entrances to the canyons, turning them into deadly culs-de-sac. "All tanks, trucks, guns and equipment east of the passes were demolished, and 10,000 men lost their lives on that day alone," wrote Mahmoud Riad. "Many others died of hunger and thirst." Forward Israeli spotters worked feverishly to pick out enemy from friendly forces, so completely were the two intermixed. The slaughter continued until mid-morning, when Israeli pilots were ordered to cease destroying Egyptian vehicles so that they might be captured undamaged.

At least 100 Egyptian tanks had been destroyed at the passes, and another 60 east of Nakhl, along with 400 guns and innumerable vehicles. An entire

SAM-2 missile battery was taken, intact. No longer able to provide for prisoners, however, the Israelis directed capitulating Egyptians toward the Canal. "There were crowds of Egyptians with weapons running about wildly," Col. Jackie Even, a tank commander, later testified. "I told myself, 'hold on, there's going to be a massacre here, with both sides shooting. So I ordered everyone, 'no killing soldiers. Try to catch them and then let them go so that they'll spread the word that the Israelis won't kill them, just send them home." Only officers were taken into custody, to be traded for Israeli pilots shot down behind enemy lines. Among the hundreds of high-ranking commanders captured was Maj. Gen. Salah Yaqut, chief of Egyptian artillery, who surrendered to a disabled Israeli tank.

Such scenes repeated themselves far to the east, in the wastes between Nakhl and al-Thamad, where Col. Mendler's column drove elements of the Shazli Force and the Egyptian 6th Division straight into an ambush laid by Arik Sharon.

"We're on their heels," Aharon Yariv, the IDF intelligence chief, reported to Harry McPherson, adding that Egypt had lost as much as 70 percent of its armored force. But with the destruction of the Egyptian army now irrefutable, the issue arose of just how far the IDF would pursue its remnants. Rabin informed the cabinet that the IDF "had no problem reaching the Canal," and merely needed the approval of the defense minister. But while the defense minister was eager to complete Nasser's downfall—he proposed bombing Cairo airport as a further means of hastening it—he was just as anxious to keep clear of Suez. "I will personally court-martial any Israeli commander who touches the banks of the Canal," he threatened. Yet the pace of battle would soon outstrip even those who ostensibly controlled it, including Moshe Dayan.[3]

Yoffe's tanks, having effectively blocked the passes, were now chasing those Egyptian forces that had managed to slip through. To the north, Col. Gonen and the 7th Brigade overwhelmed al-Ghul's advance guard of T-55 tanks, destroying forty of them. Having lost over 50 percent of its equipment, the Egyptian 4th Division was again retreating toward the Firdan Bridge, with Gonen's men in close pursuit. Also racing for the bridge was Col. Granit's column, which had turned inland from the coast on the road to Qantara.

Israeli forces were closing in on the Canal, in spite of standing orders to remain at least twelve miles distant from it. Ostensibly, the reason was pursuit—the need to complete the destruction of Egypt's army and to prevent it from regrouping—but another, more visceral, motivation was involved. Spectacular though they were, the battles in Sinai had been overshadowed by the millennial liberation of Jerusalem. "The Temple Mount is in our hands," Gen. Gavish purportedly bemoaned to his officers, "We've lost the glory." Some of that glory could now be regained, however, along the banks of the Suez Canal.

Whether in the West Bank or in Sinai, Israeli offensives had been determined less by design than by expediency. The old army adage "When in the field, improvise," had been applied in the extreme, luring IDF forces farther than either military planners or civilian officials foresaw. "The Israeli government never set specific goals for the war," recalled Rehavam Ze'evi, the deputy operations chief. "The objectives rose from the bottom up, from the military to the political echelon. Only after the war did the government draw circles around our accomplishments and declare that these were its original goals."[4] Ze'evi's observation may have held for the fighting on the southern and eastern fronts, but in one theater the government was determined to exercise control. The Cabinet, not the army, would decide when, and whether, to strike Syria.

The Golan Looms

"[The] Syrian shelling of kibbutzim and settlements in Israel has been continuous and incessant," Barbour cabled the National Security Council on the morning of June 8. "Some kibbutzim have been completely leveled above ground." He stressed the Syrians' ongoing preparations for war—"[They] have made no, repeat no, reply to call for a cease-fire"—and predicted that the IDF would once again act preemptively, penetrating Syria to a depth of twelve miles. "In the circumstances, I would not—repeat not—be surprised if the reported Israeli attack does take place or has already done so."

Barbour's assessment was only partially correct, however. Syrian guns *were* maintaining their bombardment of Galilee farms—forty-eight of them were hit—and Damascus Radio continued to proclaim far-reaching victories in the north, including the liberation of Acre and Nazareth. The Syrians had condemned the abandonment of the West Bank, blaming it on "Jordanian reactionaries," and were pressuring Lebanese President Charles Helou and Prime Minister Rashid Karame to actively enter the war. But while Lebanese generals successfully resisted this pressure, the Syrian army itself remained hunkered down in its bases. Its official record read: "The Ground Forces Headquarters could not take any decision regarding a general or local offensive because of the complicated situation at the front and because of the unwillingness of the reserve brigades to fight. Therefore, it decided to keep low on the ground, and concentrate its artillery fire, to use anti-aircraft fire to the maximum and watch closely the enemy's movements." Incessantly bombarded, intimidated by rumors of Israeli invasions, Suweidani and other senior officers retired to Damascus. Yasser Arafat, leading a guerrilla group to the Golan front, found the roads entirely empty. Syria, he later concluded, had signed a secret pact with Israel.[5]

The Syrians had no intention of invading but neither, officially, did Israel. Though public opinion strongly supported a Golan offensive—"The time has come to settle accounts with those who started it all," the daily *Ha'aretz* clamored, "to finish the job"—the government still resisted it. The decisive victories on the Egyptian and Jordanian fronts seemed only to harden that opposition as the Ministerial Defense Committee again met on Israel's northern question.

"It [attacking Syria] will bring down the whole world on our heads," contended Zalman Aran. "I'm against accepting the cease-fire just to violate it later." Supporting him were the National Religious representatives, Haim Moshe Shapira and Zorach Warhaftig, while Yigal Allon was, as usual, opposed. Arguing that capturing the Heights was the only way of eliminating the Syrian threat, Allon suggested that Israel need not occupy the area, but could give it to the local Druze as an independent state. The army weighed in with Allon, as Bar-Lev later attested, "If the Syrians got away unscathed, the general staff believed, they would continue their policies and would not be deterred by our victories in the south and the east."

Between those in favor and those opposed to attacking Syria, the prime minister tread a middle path. No less eager to acquire the Banias and to silence the Syrian guns, Eshkol was also aware of the dangers. "I'm sorry that Syria received so little, but I know that this issue could entangle us with Russia." The deciding vote fell once again to Dayan.

The defense minister showed none of Eshkol's ambivalence and continued to oppose warfare with Syria. He evinced the usual arguments—the threat of Soviet intervention, the difficulties of conquering the Heights before a cease-fire took effect—adding that Israel had already conquered enough Arab land and did not need any more.

Guided by Dayan, the committee determined to "postpone for one to two days further decision regarding operations on the Syrian Golan and to order the chief of staff to submit an operations plan for approval by the Defense Committee." During these two days, the government added, nothing should be done to overtly provoke the Syrians.[6]

The news came as a bitter shock to David Elazar in the Northern Command. Having postponed his planned attack of the previous day because of bad weather, Dado now learned that the entire operation had been canceled. "Those hours were some of the worst I'd ever experienced," he recounted, "To feel that an historic opportunity had been lost and all because of my own over-cautiousness." At most, his troops were authorized to take Tel 'Azzaziat, just over the border. Exasperated, he phoned Rabin. "The IDF has defeated our enemies and saved Israel from a nightmare in the south and the east while we'll stay cannon fodder for the Syrian Heights?"

"Do you want to attack or not?" Rabin responded.

"I do not!" Elazar barked. "Attacking Tel 'Azzaziat means paying the maximum price without getting anything at all in return. It's the same price that the *entire breakthrough* would cost us, and what do I get for it?" He slammed down the receiver and canceled all preparations for combat. "Everyone is to return to the staging area. And get me a helicopter. I'm flying to Tel Aviv!"

Rabin agreed with Elazar's assessment: Why climb the Golan escarpment, risking hundreds of lives, just to take a single bunker? He received his Northern Command chief in the Pit, and escorted him to a meeting with Allon and Eshkol.

"What can you do?" the prime minister asked. Elazar spread out a map and pointed to Za'ura, noting that from there to Damascus the road was open. "I don't need additional forces. I don't need anything. I can get up there today, capture positions and advance. Of course we'll have casualties, but it won't be a slaughter. We can do it."

"The government must authorize the conquest of the Golan," urged Allon.

A call then came through from yet another spokesman of the settlers, Haim Ber. "We're being shelled nonstop!" he shouted into Eshkol's telephone. "We demand that the government free us from this nightmare!"

The prime minister was deeply perplexed. "Why, then, is the defense minister opposed?" he asked Elazar, but the general just shrugged: "I have no idea what his reasons are, but they can't be operational or tactical."

Exiting the office, Elazar ran into Eshkol's wife, Miriam. "I have a birthday coming up and I want the Banias," she told him.

"I'll do everything I can to get it for you," the general promised her, "but you have to do your part too."[7]

Elazar was arguing his case in Tel Aviv while, up north, the army proceeded with its preparations for Operation Hammer. No sooner had the last of the Jordan bridges been destroyed when Elad Peled's *Ugdah* swung out of the West Bank, heading north. Albert Mendler's 8th Armored Brigade and the 80th Paratroopers of Dani Matt were also transferred from Sinai. The streets of Israel's major cities were clogged with tanks, trucks, and troops; the highways were hopelessly jammed. On the Golan itself, the Israeli air force, unaware that Hammer had been canceled, leveled an intense barrage on Syrian bunkers and tank emplacements in what American sources characterized as "an apparent prelude to a large-scale attack in an effort to seize the Heights overlooking border kibbutzim."

Diplomatically, too, the Israelis appeared to be laying the groundwork for the offensive. "There still remains the Syrian problem, and perhaps it will be necessary to give Syria a blow as well," Yariv confided to McPherson. Though no action had taken place on the Golan yet—"unfortunately," Yariv said—Israel was likely to undertake it "to get more elbow room." In a conversation with Eban, McGeorge Bundy intimated that it seemed strange that Syria, having started the war and caused much Arab suffering, had gone unpunished and was free to start the "whole deadly sequence again." Though Rusk warned Barbour against any further Israeli initiative—"such a development, following on the heels of Israeli acceptance of the cease-fire resolution, would cast on Israeli intentions and create gravest problems for U.S. representatives in Arab countries"—Eban concluded that the White House would welcome Syria's defeat.[8]

Anatomy of an Accident

Washington spent the morning of June 8 much as it had the previous day, monitoring the war from a safe distance. Close track was kept on the fate of beleaguered U.S. embassies and consulates in the region and on evacuating endangered American citizens. The Middle East Control Group at the White House gave special consideration to Israel's appeal for forty-eight A-4 jets, noting Russia's resupply of Egypt's military through Algeria. The question was whether the administration could respond to Israel's requests but ignore others that might arrive from Saudi Arabia or Jordan. "If we don't suspend aid to all of them, we're going to have another McCloskey," recommended Bundy, recalling the State Department's 'neutral in thought, word, and deed' gaff. Most attention, however, remained focused on the Big Lie and American efforts to refute it. To verify that no U.S. forces were participating in the war, Libyan officials were invited to visit the Wheelus base. Rusk sent the Saudis' King Faisal his "own solemn assurances" that Nasser's allegations were false, and further pledged to "steer an even-handed course" in opposing "efforts to change frontiers or to resolve problems by force of arms."[9]

Virtually removed from Johnson's concerns was the possibility of direct American involvement in the fighting. Communications with the Kremlin had been frank and constructive, while at the UN, Federenko refused to cooperate with Goldberg. Though the war had spun off in unanticipated directions, there was little reason to fear that it would reach 6th Fleet vessels stationed at least 240 miles away.

But one boat was significantly closer. Just before dawn, the USS *Liberty* came within thirteen nautical miles of the Sinai coast, just outside Egypt's territorial waters. The ship began plying between al-'Arish and Port Said, in a lane rarely used by commercial traffic and which had been declared off-limits to neutral shipping by Egypt. The vestiges of fighting were clearly visible on the shore. Anxious about these factors, Commander McGonagle, the ship's skipper, asked the 6th Fleet for a destroyer escort. His request was denied. The *Liberty*, wrote Vice Admiral William Martin, "is a clearly marked United States ship in international waters and not a reasonable subject for attack by any nation."

But neither Martin nor McGonagle had received the five cables sent by the Joint Chiefs of Staff the previous night ordering the *Liberty* to withdraw as far as 100 miles from the front. The navy's overloaded, overly complex communication system had routed the orders as far east as the Philippines before relaying them back to the *Liberty*.[10] The cables would arrive the following day, by which time they would no longer be relevant.

That same morning, at 5:55 A.M., Israeli naval observer Major Uri Meretz was flying a reconnaissance run seventy miles west of the Gaza coast. Below, he noted what he believed to be an American supply vessel, designated GRT 5. At Israeli naval headquarters in Haifa, staff officers fixed the location of the ship with a red marker, indicating "unidentified," on their control board. Research in *Jane's Fighting Ships*, however, established the vessel's identity as "the electromagnetic audio-surveillance ship of the United States, the *Liberty*." The marker was changed to green, for "neutral." Another sighting of the ship—

"gray, bulky, with its bridge amidships"—was made by an Israeli fighter aircraft at 9:00 A.M., twenty miles north of al-'Arish. Neither of these reports made mention of the five-by-eight-foot American flag which, according to the testimony of the *Liberty*'s crewmen, was streaming from its starboard halyard. The crew also claimed that Israeli aircraft continued to fly over the ship, giving them ample opportunity to identify it. But Israeli pilots were not looking for the *Liberty*, but rather for Egyptian submarines, which had just been spotted off the coast.[11]

That coast, home to 90 percent of Israel's population and industry, was woefully vulnerable. Egypt's fleet alone outnumbered Israel's by more than four to one in warships, including the new Osa and Komar-class guided missile boats, and could call on support from some seventy Soviet vessels in the area. In stark contrast to its air and ground forces, Israel's navy had performed desultorily in the war. Combined naval and commando attacks on Syrian and Egyptian ports failed to inflict serious damage—six Israeli frogmen fell captive in Alexandria— while IAF jets nearly shot at Israeli torpedo boats off the coast of Tel Aviv. Though the U.S. 6th Fleet remained in the eastern Mediterranean as a counterweight to the Soviets, the Israelis had no way of contacting it directly. Their repeated requests for a naval liaison with the Americans went ignored.

Beset by these factors, Rabin summoned Comdr. Ernest Carl Castle, the U.S. naval attaché in Tel Aviv, and told him that Israel would defend its coast with every means at its disposal. The United States should either acknowledge its ships in the area or remove them, Rabin advised. All unidentified vessels sailing at over twenty knots—a speed attainable only by gunboats—would be sunk.[12]

At 11:00 A.M., while Israeli warships hunted for Egyptian submarines, the duty officer at IDF Naval Headquarters, Capt. Avraham Lunz, concluded his shift. In accordance with procedures, he removed the green "neutral" marker from the control board on the grounds that it was already five hours old and no longer accurate. As far as the Israeli navy was concerned, the *Liberty* had sailed away.

Twenty-four minutes later, a terrific explosion rocked the beaches of al-'Arish. Though the blast was caused by an ammunition dump igniting, Israeli observers noted two naval vessels offshore and concluded that the Egyptians were shelling them from the sea. Such a bombardment had indeed taken place the previous day, according to both Israeli and Egyptian reports.[13]

Shortly after the explosion at al-'Arish, the *Liberty* reached the eastern limit of its patrol and turned 238 degrees back in the direction of Port Said. In the Pit, meanwhile, news of the purported shelling unsettled Rabin, who had been warned of a possible Egyptian amphibious landing near Gaza. He reiterated the standing order to sink any unidentified ships in the war area, but also advised caution: Soviet vessels were reportedly operating nearby. Since no fighter planes were available, the navy was asked to intercede, with the assumption that air cover would be provided later. More than half an hour passed without any response from naval headquarters in Haifa. The general staff finally issued a rebuke: "The coast is being shelled and you—the navy—have done nothing."

Capt. Izzy Rahav, who had replaced Lunz in the operations room, needed no more prodding. He dispatched three torpedo boats of the 914th squadron, code-named Pagoda, to find the enemy vessel responsible for the bombardment and destroy it. The time was 12:05 P.M.

At 1:41 P.M., Ensign Aharon Yifrah, combat information officer aboard the flagship of these torpedo boats, T-204, informed its captain, Comdr. Moshe Oren, that an unidentified ship had been sighted northeast of al-'Arish at a range of twenty-two miles. Yifrah twice measured the ship's speed and estimated it to be thirty knots. This information, added to the fact that the ship was streaming in the direction of Egypt, led Oren to conclude that this was an enemy vessel fleeing to its home port after shelling Israeli positions.

The torpedo boats gave chase, but even at their maximum speed of thirty-six knots, they did not expect to overtake their target before it reached Egypt. Rahav therefore alerted the air force, and two Mirages were diverted from a routine patrol over Sinai. The squadron's commander, Capt. Yiftah Spector, was warned of the presence of Israeli torpedo boats in the area, and instructed to ascertain whether the suspect ship was Israeli. If not, the planes were cleared to attack.

At this point—1:54—one of the IAF controllers, Lazar Karni, whose function was to listen to ground-to-air communications and make occasional suggestions, blurted out, "What's this? Americans?" He later told Israeli investigators that his question arose from a gut feeling, his sense that the Egyptians were unlikely to send a lone boat to shell al-'Arish. Yet, when another controller on the line retorted, "Americans, where?" Karni did not respond. "An attack was underway on an enemy vessel," he testified, "and I didn't think it was my place to press what was merely a hunch."

Spector, meanwhile, located the ship and made an identification pass at 3,000 feet. He saw "a military vessel, battleship gray with four gun mounts, with its bow pointed toward Port Said . . . [and] one mast and one smokestack." Apart from some "black letters" on the hull, the ship had no other markings. Its deck had not been painted with the blue-and-white cross that distinguished all Israeli vessels. The pilot concluded that this was a "Z," or Hunt-class destroyer, and since his plane was armed only with cannons, he requested additional jets loaded with iron bombs.

The *Liberty* sailors would later deny that the Israelis made any reconnaissance runs, but immediately dove. The Americans would also reject Israel's claim that inquiries about the *Liberty*'s whereabouts were submitted to Comdr. Castle, though Castle, in fact, knew nothing about the ship. On one point, however, both versions dovetail: At 1:57 P.M., the Mirages began their attack.[14]

The first salvos caught the *Liberty*'s crew in "stand-down" mode, helmets and life vests removed. McGonagle and several officers had been sunning themselves on the deck. Suddenly, 30-mm cannon shells stitched the ship from bow to stern, severing the antennas and setting oil drums on fire. Nine men were killed instantly and several times that number wounded, among them McGonagle, seriously injured in both legs. He refused to be evacuated, though—he would later be awarded the Congressional Medal of Honor—but ordered the ship to turn full right, out to sea. Urgently he cabled the 6th Fleet, "Under attack by unidentified jet aircraft, require immediate assistance."

The Mirages made three strafing runs from the *Liberty*'s stern to bow; over 800 holes would later be counted in its hull. "We've hit her a lot," Spector reported, "I think she's putting out smoke on purpose, it's coming out of the smokestack." The chief IAF controller, Shmuel Kislev, twice asked whether the ship was responding with anti-aircraft fire, but the pilots seemed too engaged to answer. Three and half minutes into the attack, with their ammunition expended, the Mirages flew off and were replaced by a squadron of Mystères. These had just returned from bombing Egyptian infantry, and for the task were armed with napalm. While this, too, was an ordnance ill suited for naval warfare, the Mystères managed to swoop in low and deliver their payloads. Seconds later, much of the bridge and the deck were aflame, and the entire ship was enshrouded by smoke.

The Mystères were readying to strike again when the navy, alerted by the absence of return fire from the ship, warned Kislev that the target might in fact be Israeli. "If there is a doubt [about identification], don't attack," Kislev told the pilots. The navy quickly contacted its vessels in the area—none were under fire—and signaled the air force to continue. "You may attack," said Kislev. "You can sink it."

Yet Kislev was still disturbed by the lack of any response from the vessel— "This is easier than [shooting down] MiG's," another controller commented— but also concerned lest the navy get the credit for the kill. "If you had a two-plane formation with [500-pound iron] bombs . . . it would be a blessing," Capt. Yossi Zuk, the Mystères' commander, said. "Otherwise the navy will be here in ten minutes." Then, in the thick of these countervailing pressures, Kislev requested one last attempt to identify the ship. "Look for a flag if they [the pilots] can see one. See if they can identify it [the ship] with a flag."

Still flying at a low altitude, still strafing, Zuk responded that "there's no flag on her," but noticed what he thought was the letter "P." He then corrected himself: "Pay attention, the ship's markings are Charlie-Tango-Romeo-five."

"Leave her!" Kislev cried, aware that Egyptian warships were almost invariably marked in Arabic, rather than Latin, letters. His own guess was that the assaulted ship was American.

The news terrified Israeli officers in the Pit. Rabin feared that the ship was Soviet, not American, and that Israel had just given Moscow pretext to intervene. With Dayan away visiting Hebron, and Motti Hod en route from a briefing, the chief of staff took personal command of the situation. He sent two IAF helicopters to look for the survivors whom the jet pilots thought they had seen jumping overboard. Rabin also ordered that the torpedo boats, still in pursuit, remain at a safe distance from the ship.

The scene on the *Liberty* meanwhile was hellish. Men with ghastly napalm burns, their bodies torn by shrapnel, streamed into the petty officers' lounge that had been converted into an emergency hospital. In the communications room, radiomen sent out uncoded distress signals. Other able-bodied sailors frantically burned classified papers and flew up a large holiday American flag, to replace the original naval ensign that had been shot away. None of them had a clue as to who, exactly, their assailants were. Most thought they were Egyptian MiG's.

The same smoke that obscured the Israeli jets from the *Liberty*'s view now hid the *Liberty* from Capt. Oren. The Pagoda squadron arrived on the scene at 2:44, twenty-four minutes after Rabin ordered to it to hold back. But while that order appeared in T-204's logbook, Oren later claimed that he never received it. He paused, nevertheless, at 6,000 meters and scrutinized the ship. In spite of the smoke, he could see that the vessel was not the destroyer that had presumably shelled al-'Arish, but most likely a freighter that had either serviced that destroyer or evacuated enemy soldiers from the beach. He consulted his intelligence manual, and found that the ship's silhouette resembled that of the Egyptian supply ship *El Quseir*; the captains of the other two torpedo boats reached the same conclusion independently. Moreover, when he tried to signal the ship, asking for its identity, he received no explicit response. Oren ordered his squadron into battle formation.

As Pagoda neared the *Liberty*, the *Liberty*'s distress signals finally reached the USS *America*. "Help is on the way," came the reply. The carrier was in the middle of strategic exercises; the planes on its deck were armed with nuclear payloads, and there was no time to replace them with conventional ordnance. A detachment of eight F-4s took off in the direction of the Sinai coast, only to be recalled minutes later by Vice Admiral Martin. If Rabin feared that the ship was Russian, Martin suspected that its attackers were, and, without authorization from the highest level, would not risk starting a nuclear war.

Help never arrived from the *America*, but the Israelis came within range. McGonagle, who had tried to return their signal with a hand-held Aldis lamp—the searchlights had all been smashed—ordered his men not to fire at the approaching torpedo boats. One of the sailors, though, failed to hear the command, and opened up with one of the ship's four machine guns. Another machine gun also fired, triggered by exploding ammunition. Oren was now being shot at by a ship he assumed was Egyptian. He radioed Izzy Rahav at naval headquarters and requested permission to return the fire. After some hesitation, Rahav at last relented.

Of the five torpedoes fired at the *Liberty* only one found its mark, a direct hit on the starboard side, killing twenty-five men, almost all of them from the intelligence section.

"Kislev, it's an Egyptian supply boat," reported the IAF's liaison with the navy. "I won't have anyone telling me again that the air force has a problem with identification." Momentarily vindicated, Kislev instructed the helicopters to continue their rescue mission but to exercise caution. The command went out: "Tell the helicopters that they aren't Americans, they're Egyptians . . . Tell them [Israeli forces] at al-'Arish, that Egyptian sailors are arriving from the sea, from a boat that they [the navy] sank."

The navy had yet to sink the craft, however. Rather, the torpedo boats closed in with cannons and machine-guns, raking the *Liberty*'s hull—its life rafts as well, according to the crew. One of those rafts, picked up by T-203, was found to bear U.S. Navy markings. Oren began to suspect that the ship might not be Egyptian. Then, circling the badly listing craft, he confronted the designation, GRT-5. But Oren's attempts to contact the crew via megaphone went unanswered, and another half-hour would pass before the ship's identity was established. Thirty-five thousand feet above the area, an American EC121M spy plane picked up the torpedo boats' signals. "Hey Chief," Mike Prostinak, a Hebrew linguist, alerted his commander, Petty Officer Marvin E. Norwicki, "I've got some really odd activity on UHF. They mentioned an American flag."

Word of the ship's American nationality arrived as the IDF general staff considered the possibility of Soviet reprisals. "I must admit I had mixed feelings about the news—profound regret at having attacked our friends and a tremendous sense of relief [that the boat was not Soviet]," Rabin recalled. An apology was immediately sent to Castle who in turn informed the 6th Fleet. Another wing of jets, these armed with conventional bombs, had just been launched from the *Saratoga*. The pilots, though warned not to fly too near the coast or to pursue attacking aircraft, were authorized to "use whatever force is necessary to protect the USS *Liberty*."

Martin called back these planes as well, and the only aircraft to reach the *Liberty* were the two IAF Super Frelon helicopters. Realizing finally the identity of his attackers, gesturing coarsely, McGonagle waved them away. Another Israeli chopper carrying Castle—he dropped his business card onto the deck, inserted inside an orange—was unable to land because of darkness. By 5:05 P.M., the Israelis had broken off contact, and the *Liberty*, navigating virtually without systems, with 34 dead and 171 wounded aboard, staggered out to sea.[15]

Nearly two hours later, Johnson received a cable informing him that the *Liberty*, "located 60-100 miles north of Egypt," had been torpedoed by an unknown vessel. The president immediately assumed that the Soviets were involved. To forestall further escalation, he hot-lined the Kremlin with news of the attack and of the dispatch of jets from the *Saratoga*. Kosygin confirmed the receipt of this information, and promised to pass it on to Nasser.[16] Still the question remained: Who had tried to sink the *Liberty?*

Another two hours passed before the Israeli embassy in Washington confirmed what it termed the "mistaken action." An official letter of apology promptly followed from Harman. Johnson's initial reaction, like Rabin's before, was relief that the Soviets had not been involved. While "strong dismay" was conveyed to Harman, so too were the administration's thanks for the candor of Israel's notification. "Please accept my profound condolences and convey my sympathy to all the bereaved families," Eshkol hastened to wire, followed by Eban: "I am deeply mortified and grieved by the tragic accident involving the lives and safety of Americans." In a personal note to the president, Evron wrote, "I grieve with you over the lives that were lost, and share in the sorrow of the parents, wives and children of the men who died in this cruel twist of fate." Within forty-eight hours, the Israeli government offered to compensate the casualties; $12 million was ultimately paid.

These offers of restitution and regret at first seemed to satisfy the administration, eager to downplay the affair. "Its [the *Liberty's*] proximity to the scene of the conflict could feed Arab suspicions of U.S.-Israeli collusion," warned Barbour in Tel Aviv, while from Cairo, Nolte urged, "We had better get our story on the torpedoing of USS *Liberty* out fast and it had better be good." There may also have been fear that the incident would draw attention to the presence of U.S. submarines—codenamed Frontlet 615—operating in Egyptian waters. The Defense Department issued an official release acknowledging that "a U.S. Navy technical research ship" assigned to "provide information regarding the evacuation of American citizens from the Middle East" had been attacked in international waters "15 miles north of the Sinai Peninsula." Israel had admitted responsibility for the attack, the communiqué said, and had apologized. Otherwise, a total media clampdown was placed on the incident.[17]

Presently, though, American officials began caring less about the way the incident looked and more about why it had happened. A great many questions arose: Why did the Israelis attack a neutral ship on the high seas, without the slightest provocation? How had they failed to see the *Liberty's* flag or the freshly painted markings on its hull? How could they confuse the *Liberty* with the *El Quseir*, a far slower, smaller boat, with no distinctive antennae? And finally, how could a ship sailing at five knots, whose maximum speed was eighteen, be gauged at thirty?

"Beyond comprehension," fumed Rusk: "we cannot accept such a situation." Clark Clifford, a staunchly pro-Israel adviser to Truman and Kennedy, head of the Foreign Intelligence Advisory Board under Johnson, described the attack as "inexcusable . . . a flagrant act of gross negligence for which the Israeli Government should be held completely responsible." He recommended that the incident be handled "as if the Arabs or the USSR had done it." While no official could explain what motivation Israel might have had for assaulting an American vessel, neither did the facts seem to square. Either the Israelis had exhibited rank incompetence—in the midst of their faultless victory—or they had struck the *Liberty* on purpose. Indeed, many in the administration had already concluded that the attack was intentional and that Israel's explanations were entirely disingenuous.[18] The charge of criminal negligence gradually gave way to one of premeditated murder.

The Israelis moved to dispel these accusations with three internal reports, the last of which was a full inquiry under military jurist Col. Yeshayahu Yerushalmi. All three admitted the IDF's culpability in erroneously reporting a naval barrage on al-'Arish, in miscalculating the *Liberty*'s speed, and in confusing the ship with the *El Quseir*. They pointed out the faulty communications between various branches of the army, the pilots' exhaustion after four days of uninterrupted combat, and the navy's eagerness to compensate for its previous failures in the war. Yet all three studies concluded that the attack was an "innocent mistake," with no malice or gross negligence involved. "For all my regret that our forces were involved in an incident with a vessel belonging to a friendly state," Yerushalmi wrote, "I have not discovered any deviation from the standard of reasonable conduct which would justify a court martial."[19]

"This makes no goddamned sense at all," Eugene Rostow grumbled upon reviewing these findings. The attack, wrote Rusk, was "quite literally incomprehensible . . . an act of military recklessness reflecting wanton disregard for human life." Umbrage was taken at the Israelis' suggestion that the *Liberty* had no business being where it was, had failed to inform Israel of its presence, and had failed to use all means (semaphores, flares, flags) to identify itself. Evron's assurances that IDF officers would be "severely punished" for negligence proved groundless. The White House now demanded that Israel not only pay compensation but admit wrongdoing and try those responsible for the attack "in accordance with international law."

That demand, however, did not reflect a willingness on the part of the United States to investigate the incident thoroughly. A navy court of inquiry, convened in Malta by Rear Adm. Isaac C. Kidd, Jr., shortly after the attack, posited that, for lack of sufficient wind, the *Liberty*'s flag might not have been visible to Israeli pilots, and that the attack appeared to be "a case of mistaken identity." Further reviews were conducted by the CIA, Joint Chiefs of Staff, the House Appropriations Committee, and the NSA.[20] But at no time were answers sought to the questions of who sent the *Liberty*, lightly armed and incognito, into the middle of somebody else's war zone, and for what purpose. Never was it suggested, much less charged, that the *Liberty*'s mission was an egregious mistake.

The absence of such answers would later give rise to a mélange of conspiracy theories purporting to explain the incident. Israel was said to have launched the attack to prevent the *Liberty* from reporting on its gains in Sinai, its alleged execution of Egyptian prisoners, or its interception of messages between Cairo and King Hussein. The most widespread of the charges held that Israel—Dayan, in particular—wanted the *Liberty* destroyed in order to conceal preparations for the coming thrust into Syria.

None of the theories withstood historical scrutiny, however, or even made much sense. Israel did little to hide from the Americans either its progress in Sinai or its intentions *vis-à-vis* the Golan. Jordan was already *hors de combat* by

June 8. No evidence was found that Israel conducted mass executions of POW's or that it sought to disguise that act by killing Americans. Indeed, with their obsessive concern for U.S. opinion and their ingrained fear of the Soviets, the Israelis would have been loath to antagonize, much less make war against, their sole superpower protector. And while the IDF could have easily sunk the *Liberty*, the fact remained that it did not; it ceased firing the instant the mistake was realized, and offered to assist the ship. The logic of these arguments would be employed by Arab and Soviet commentators—ironically—who asserted that the *Liberty* had been spying for Israel during the war and was only erroneously attacked.[21]

A Four-Day War?

The *Liberty* incident, with its faulty identifications and close brushes between American and Soviet forces, spotlighted the ease with which the superpowers might inadvertently come to blows in the Middle East. "Israel must be careful not to push its advantage too far," Goldberg advised Eban, noting how the Arabs' wholesale defeat had increased the danger of Soviet intervention. Citing a secret Soviet source, the CIA had reported on the growing likelihood of direct Soviet involvement in the war—"we have no other choice," the source explained. Kosygin, too, seemed to be threatening a more aggressive Soviet role. "Israel's actions have placed the Arab States in such a situation they cannot but conduct a lawful defensive war against the aggressor," the premier wrote in his next hot line message to Washington. "Until complete withdrawal of Israeli troops [is obtained] . . . the reestablishment of peace in the Near East cannot be ensured."

The best hope for preventing superpower clashes lay in the Security Council, which reconvened at 2:00 P.M. after a hiatus of nearly twenty-four hours. The atmosphere had hardly improved. Now, in addition to the vast gap separating the U.S. and Soviet positions, discrepancies also emerged between the U.S. and Israeli positions. Eban opposed any linkage between the cease-fire and the return of Israeli forces to the June 4th line. He wanted no reference to the Armistice Agreements by the Council, no mention of the word *withdrawal*. Goldberg, in turn, reminded Eban of the requisites of public opinion. "It is necessary . . . that Israel should not emerge from the current situation as a power with designs to infringe on the territorial integrity of other countries." Rather patronizingly, he invited Eban to consult McGeorge Bundy "on how peace might be best brought about and the rancor and humiliation felt by the Arabs overcome."

American-Israeli differences, though sharpening, were minuscule compared to those between Israel and the Soviets. "Israel's military hordes [are] following in the bloody footsteps of Hitler's executioners," ranted Federenko, and

Gideon Rafael responded in kind: "Neither Israel nor the Jewish people concluded a pact with Hitler's Germany, a pact which encouraged Nazi Germany to unleash its aggression against the world." The Soviets proceeded to propose a resolution condemning Israel and demanding its complete withdrawal from Arab lands. The Americans countered with an artless draft of their own, calling for "discussions . . . among the parties concerned" to separate the battling troops, renounce the use of force and maintain international rights, and to establish "a stable and durable peace in the Middle East." Neither of the texts stood a chance of receiving the Council's approval; neither was seriously debated.

The question of whether Israel would or would not evacuate remained moot, however, so long as Egypt refused to accept the cease-fire. Countervailing pressures were at work on El Kony, the Soviets exhorting him to show flexibility, while members of the Asia-African bloc—Nigeria, Pakistan, Cyprus, Indonesia—urged him to stand firm. Rumors circulated the hall purporting that Soviet bombers were en route to the front, that the Egyptian army would soon regroup and stage a massive counterattack. Even if El Kony adhered to the cease-fire, the scuttlebutt went, Cairo would repudiate it. Confusion deepened when the Agence France Presse reported that Nasser had publicly welcomed the end of hostilities. The Egyptian ambassador rushed to confirm the claim, only to find it false. Thereafter, he sat removed from the Council chamber, in the observers' gallery, waiting for guidance from Nasser.[22]

But no one had seen or even heard from Nasser in almost three days. Locked up in his house, purportedly broken over his army's defeat, the president had shunned all contact with the outside world and with military leaders in particular. Repeatedly, Sadat had sought audiences with him, urging him to fire 'Amer and to take direct command of the military, but in vain. Nasser would not come out. Then, suddenly at midday on June 8, Egypt's leader emerged. Smiling broadly, he entered Supreme Headquarters and announced that he had just spoken with Soviet and Algerian leaders, and that 200 new MiG's were on their way. Egyptian forces would regroup, he predicted; they would hold the passes first, then rally for a massive attack. When asked by an old associate, 'Abd al-Latif al-Baghdadi, why Egypt had not coordinated its policies with Moscow and accepted the cease-fire, Nasser snapped: "It doesn't matter if we accept it or not. The Jews will keep fighting until they've achieved their objectives!"

Nasser next summoned Mahmoud Riad and showed him a telegram he had received from Moscow urging him to approve a cease-fire. Riad was to reply that since Soviet intelligence had impelled the Egyptian army to enter Sinai, the USSR should not now join with Washington in demanding that Egypt cease defending itself. Egypt, Riad would state, was determined to fight until the Israelis were driven from its territory—a fight the Russians were expected to back.

Riad was also optimistic, buoyed by reports that Egyptian anti-aircraft had driven off Israel's planes, that enemy paratroopers had been decimated in the Mitla Pass and an armored column halted at Romani. In addition to rejecting

Moscow's request, he personally phoned each of the permanent representatives to the Security Council to remind them that there would be no cease-fire without total and immediate evacuation. Radio Cairo again assured its listeners that fierce resistance was continuing on all fronts in Sinai, and the government had no intention of agreeing to a cease-fire.

The chances for obtaining a resolution appeared to be fading, diminished by the Egyptians' delusions of possible victory and their horror of public disgrace. In a conversation with Nolte, Secret Service Chief Salah Nasir discounted claims of Israeli triumphs and expressed confidence that Egypt would return to the prewar Armistice lines and perhaps even maintain the blockade. But Egypt could never agree to a cease-fire, he explained: "What would we tell the people?"[23]

Those delusions could not, however, dissemble the image of utter devastation sprawling along the Suez Canal. An estimated 11,000 soldiers had crossed the waterway, while another 20,000 were stranded in Sinai and in desperate need of water. Gen. Fawzi, observing the rout from Isma'iliya, saw entire tank companies abandoning their vehicles, their personal weapons, and swimming across the Canal. Mindless of these men and their plight, 'Amer ordered Gen. 'Abd al-Mun'im Khalil to dynamite the bridges spanning the Canal. "These were the last words that I heard from him," Khalil attested, "his last disgraceful command."

"It was a horrible sight," recalled Muhammad Ahmad Khamis, the 6th Division's communications officer, who had returned to Sinai amid rumors of Algerian air cover. "The broken pieces of the army strewn over the sand . . . burnt out tanks . . . destroyed vehicles . . . charred bodies that looked like statues . . . Suddenly, I saw senior officers in an army jeep and they asked me to turn back once again . . . They told me that there were no more [Egyptian] forces inside [Sinai], that it was all over." Reconnaissance officer Yahya Sa'ad Basha had also escaped the passes only to find himself trapped. "I reached the banks of the Canal and saw that the bridges had been blown. I sprawled on the ground and slept a deep sleep from exhaustion and sadness . . . and from the bitterness I felt at the defeat which we didn't understand."

In the Giddi Pass, Gen. al-Ghul found himself virtually alone with his 4th Division staff, with no artillery and only one tank left. "Our communications had been completely jammed by the American ship, *Liberty*," he later claimed. Fearing capture, al-Ghul gave his second and final order to retreat.

Witnessing that flight was British war correspondent David Pryce-Jones. Having reported on the fall of Abu 'Ageila, he had fallen back with Egyptian forces to Qantara, where ferryboats hauled Egyptian soldiers, fifty at a time, from Sinai:

> Supervising, a doctor was obliging them to sign a register, and one by one they pressed their thumb on to a purple ink-pad and then on to the floppy pages of a book. These were conscripts, and illiterate. On the other bank,

under the sun, waited mothers in immobile and resigned lines, assembled
from all over the country to learn the fate of their sons. Behind the serried
mothers ran the barbed-wire fencing of an officers' enclosure in the barracks
and four or five officers were reclining in striped deck chairs, scrutinizing the
masses through field glasses.

Foreign dispatches, rumors from the front, had finally bypassed Egypt's military censors. Cairo, so recently the scene of jubilation over Israel's reported
defeat, was now steeped in uneasy silence. Nolte warned of a "clear and present
danger of increased rioting and demonstrations" in the city, leading to "a serious breakdown in public order."[24]

By the late afternoon, Nasser had met with senior officers, who apprised him
of the irreversible situation in Sinai. The last of these was 'Amer. The field
marshal was conferring with al-Baghdadi and Kamal Hassan, when their president walked in. The former Free Officers rose, crying, and exited the room,
leaving the two leaders alone. A fierce argument ensued, the details of which
were unclear to Mahmud al-Jiyyar, Nasser's old-time associate, listening outside. A short while later, though, Nasser came out, hunched and downcast.
"Imagine, Jiyyar, everything's over and we're agreeing to a cease-fire." 'Amer
was quick to follow. "Enough, Jiyyar," he uttered, "we're capitulating."

Nasser recalled Riad, and in a choking voice told him that Egypt could no
longer continue the fight; El Kony had to be informed. Riad dreaded making the
call. In his memoirs, he confessed that, "During the past few days I had been
feeding him [El Kony] the exuberant military reports I had received, which he
accepted, discrediting the accounts of the collapse of the army conveyed to him
by his fellow ambassadors as malicious and inaccurate. For several moments we
were silent. In one dismal moment the great illusion we were living crumbled."
The foreign minister got through to the New York embassy at 9:00 P.M.

El Kony was shaken to the core. "It cannot be!" he cried. The ambassador
had prepared a different speech entirely, again rejecting the cease-fire. Sus-
pecting an Israeli trick, he immediately phoned Nasser's office and demanded
to speak personally with the president. "You did well by calling, Muhammad,"
Nasser assured him, "but yes, you are to accept the cease-fire."

Broken, openly weeping, El Kony descended to the Security Council chamber at 9:35 P.M. "I have the honor to convey, upon instructions of my government, the decision to accept the call for a cease-fire provided that the other
side ceases firing as well." Witnessing this, several nonpermanent delegates to
the Council persisted in believing that El Kony's speech was merely a tactic,
that Nasser would never have given in without some guarantee of Israeli withdrawal. Such speculation was soon erased, however, by a communiqué issued
by Supreme Headquarters in Cairo. This confirmed Egypt's adherence to the
cease-fire following battles "unprecedented in their ferocity and intensity against
the combined air forces of Israel, the United States and Great Britain." The
fighting would continue on other fronts, though, the announcement warned:

"100 million Arabs are consumed with avenging hatred for . . . the Chicago and Texas gangs."[25]

El Kony's words in the Security Council reverberated loudly in Jerusalem, in the debate over where to end the war. Along with news of an impending cease-fire came rumors that the United States would press for a mutual six-mile pull-back of Israeli and Egyptian troops. Eager to establish the passes as Israel's new line of defense, Dayan reversed his earlier opposition to advancing beyond them. Yoffe now divided his *Ugdah* into three columns. Two were to proceed south of the Great Bitter Lake. The third column would strike for Ras al-Sudr on the Gulf of Suez coast, there to link up with the paratroopers heading north from Sharm al-Sheikh. Tal was to continue his two-pronged thrust—from Bir Gafgafa and Qantara—toward the Firdan Bridge. The cease-fire, when it came into effect, would find the IDF firmly astride the Canal.

The war appeared to be coming to an end, a four-day war in which Israel con-quered all of Sinai and the West Bank. With Syria's announcement accepting the cease-fire expected momentarily, the question of whether Israel would or would not attack the Golan Heights became moot. The Soviets, moreover, appeared more than ever determined to protect their only Middle East allies—the Syrians—who as of yet remained unscathed.

Thus, early in the afternoon of June 8, a drawn-looking Ambassador Chuvakhin had presented the Foreign Ministry with a message. This denounced Israel's failure to fulfill the cease-fire resolution and its blatant violation of international norms of behavior. "If the Government of Israel does not abide by the decisions of the Security Council," the Kremlin warned, "the Soviet Union will review its diplomatic relations with Israel [and] . . . will consider additional steps necessitated by Israel's aggressive policies." Emerging from the meeting, the Soviet ambassador was quoted warning, "If Israelis become drunk with success and pursue their aggression further, the future of this little country will be a very sad one indeed."

The thrust of the Soviets' meaning was unmistakable, yet there remained influential voices in the Israeli leadership, Eshkol's among them, that continued to press for a last-minute offensive against Syria. At 7:10 that night, Eshkol recon-vened the Ministerial Defense Committee in his Tel Aviv office. His plan was to mobilize support for seizing at least part of the Golan—"like a bulldog breaking its chain," he told the settlers in Yiddish—and surmounting Dayan's opposition.

Rabin opened the session with a report on the continued shelling of north-ern Galilee. The IDF now had sufficient forces to remove the Syrian guns, he said, if time permitted before the cease-fire. Next, in an unprecedented move, representatives of the settlers' lobby were invited to address the ministers. "If the State of Israel is incapable of defending us, we're entitled to know it!" ex-claimed Ya'akov Eshkoli of Kibbutz Kfar Giladi. "We should be told outright that we are not part of this state, not entitled to the protection of the IDF. We should be told to leave our homes and flee from this nightmare!"

Yigal Allon was quick in seconding Eshkoli. "Assuming that as a result of our taking the Syrian ridge the USSR severs relations with us—I don't believe that will happen—I prefer the Syrian ridge without the Soviets to the Syrians remaining on that ridge and our retaining our ties with the Soviets."

His logic held sway with at least one of the ministers formerly opposed to the operation. "For 4,000 years we have spoken about the sacrifice of Isaac," affirmed Zalman Aran. "In those settlements, men, women, and children are threatened with sacrifice. The situation is insufferable."

Other ministers, though, remained impervious to these arguments, and opposed to provoking Syria. "I'm no coward," declared Zorach Warhaftig, "but a break with the USSR means breaking with ten other countries, and perhaps Asian and African nations as well. It could lead to our expulsion from the UN . . . We are drunk and not on wine . . . Without a clear breach of the cease-fire by Syria, we must not be dragged into a new war with them." Haim Moshe Shapira maintained the NRP front, agreeing, "We should wait another day . . . We shouldn't drag them [the Syrians] into battle."

Then, finally, came Dayan's turn to speak. He reminded the ministers of the great victory Israel had already accomplished, and of the fierce diplomatic battle it yet had to fight. "I am willing to be a minimalist—what we attained we attained and enough. Why, in the throes of this struggle, would we want to take on yet another state with different international borders? That is a little too much . . . The Syrians will never reconcile themselves to that, not today and not in years to come."

Continuing, Dayan stressed the danger not only of Soviet intervention, but of the total alienation from France, the supplier of Israel's jets. "The air force is not in good shape," he claimed. "We have not purchased new jets since 1962, and most of our planes were hit on the first day [June 5]." He spoke of the lack of sufficient forces in the Northern Command, of possible American opposition to the move. He denied that Syria posed a threat to Israel, but then turned around and exclaimed, "I fear a joint Syrian-Iraqi air attack. I fear that all of the Arab states, except perhaps Jordan, will continue fighting."

The defense minister again denounced government interference in what he regarded as his exclusive purview ("In military matters, I'm against making decisions on the basis of majority decisions") and then landed a bombshell. "I prefer to move the settlements ten or twenty miles from the Syrian artillery rather than get caught up in a third front leading to a clash with the Soviets. Thousands of Arabs were relocated as a result of this war; we can relocate several dozen Israelis."

The suggestion that settlements be uprooted rather than Syrian guns removed, sparked angry reactions from many ministers. "We must never consider moving farms," Allon shouted; "it's exactly like conceding parts of Israel." Eshkol affirmed, "There could be no greater victory for the Syrians."

And yet, when it came time to make a decision, Eshkol proved less than decisive. He merely proposed that, Dayan, Rabin, and he would approve a Golan operation when and if they saw fit. "It'd be a pity if the Syrians got away free," he added, suggesting that the Golan could be used as a bargaining chip in future border negotiations. "Of course we don't want a centimeter of Syrian territory."[26]

Close to midnight, Dayan called Gen. Elazar with the news of the Cabinet's latest decision. Egypt had not implemented the cease-fire, he explained, and Israel, which had already suffered enough casualties, could not afford another front. The Soviets' disposition, moreover, remained uncertain. Dado tried assuring Dayan that Israeli losses scaling the Heights would not be prohibitive—"it won't be that bad"—and that the USSR was more bark than bite. "If we don't do something on this border now," cried the Northern Command chief, "it will be a curse for generations to come." Dayan was sympathetic but stern: "I know you and understand you and what you want, but I also know that you're disciplined and won't do anything that runs contrary to what we have decided."

Dayan passed the phone to Rabin, who listened as the Northern Command chief vented his frustration. "What has happened to this country? How will we ever be able to face ourselves, the people, the settlements? After all the trouble they [the Syrians] caused, after the shellings and harassment, are those arrogant bastards going to be left on top of the hills riding on our backs?" Elazar expressed regret over having put off the operation because of the weather. "If I'd known that yesterday's postponement would become cancellation today, I would have attacked even without air cover. It would have cost us dearly, but the Heights we would have conquered."

Elazar, who had previously resisted the settlers' request to evacuate noncombatants from the border area, now asked Rabin for permission to do just that, and to allow his troops to stand down. But Rabin would agree only to the withdrawal of children, and insisted that the Northern Command remain in full battle formation. He told Elazar not to give up hope, that "something may still happen," and for a moment seemed to contradict Dayan. But the defense minister surprisingly concurred. "Though it was decided not to attack for the time being," he intimated to Dado, "the possibility exists that the decision will yet be changed."[27]

THE WAR: DAY FIVE, JUNE 9

Showdown atop the Golan.
Nasser attempts to resign.
The UN resurgent and the Soviets riled.
Israel's constitutional crisis.

IT WAS JUST AFTER MIDNIGHT when, direct from the Cabinet meeting, Dayan arrived at the Pit. Over the next three hours, he learned that the Egyptians had indeed accepted the cease-fire and that Syrian approval was soon to follow. Suddenly, in a remark that baffled Rabin, Dayan said that there was no sense in merely capturing Tel 'Azzaziat—a limited attack might be seen by the Arabs as a lack of Israeli will—when the Golan was effectively empty. He told his chief of staff, "If the Syrians sit quietly, I won't approve any action against them, but if in spite of all our restraint they continue shelling, I will recommend to the Cabinet that we take the entire Heights."

Rabin, always in favor of punishing Syria, did not raise any objections. But neither did he issue new orders to Northern Command. He left the Pit for the first visit home in four days ("I was asleep before my head touched the pillow"), unsure of whether the defense minister, having already reversed himself on conquering Jerusalem and reaching the Suez Canal, might yet change his mind again.[1]

Dayan remained in the Pit, and continued to monitor the situation. Bar-Lev arrived and tried to persuade him that the Cabinet really favored the attack—Eshkol, too—but could not find the right pretext for launching it. There were additional intelligence estimates, one alleging that the Soviets had lowered their tone, were no longer threatening intervention. At 3:10, Radio Damascus announced that Syria would respect the cease-fire if Israel did—"the battle cannot be swift, but will require long and patient preparations"—and at 4:45 A.M., Gen. Gavish phoned from Sinai to say that the Israeli forces were now digging in on the Canal. The war indeed appeared to be over.

That, at least, was the conclusion of IDF intelligence. Major Eli Halahmi, in charge of researching the Syrian army, had already reconciled himself to what he termed "the lost opportunity" to punish Damascus, and had requested leave to visit the Western Wall. But then, just before midnight, he received a fresh batch of aerial photos from the north. What they showed shocked him. The army camps around Quneitra, previously thick with armored, artillery, and commando units, appeared to have been deserted. "Our estimate is that the Syrian disposition on the Golan Heights is possibly collapsing," Halahmi reported, adding unconventionally, "It is not clear whether this situation will again present itself."

"What can we do?" shrugged Aharale Yariv when he read the report. "There's going to be a cease-fire."

Halahmi pressed him: "Sir, we must not let them [the Syrians] get off without a scratch. If they do, they'll continue to spit at us and to boast that they beat us and they, alone, scared us into inaction."

Still skeptical, Yariv nevertheless submitted the report which, at dawn, reached the hands of Moshe Dayan. So, too, did a cable recently intercepted from Cairo. "I am certain that Israel is about to concentrate all of its forces against Syria in order to eliminate the Syrian army," Nasser warned President Atassi. "For your own benefit allow me to advise you to accept the cease-fire immediately and inform U Thant of that fact. This is the only way of saving the valiant Syrian army. We have lost this battle. God help us in the future."

If Dayan was leaning toward yet another about-face of policy, the cable, together with Halahmi's report, impelled him. He scribbled a note to Eshkol:

1. In my opinion, this cable compels us to take the maximum lines.
2. Last night I had no idea that the leadership of Egypt and Syria would crumble like this and give up the battle. In any event, we must exploit this opportunity to the utmost. A great day.[2]

David Elazar meanwhile was having what he called "the worst night in my life." In a last-ditch effort to persuade Dayan to approve the Golan offensive, the Northern Command chief had sent one of his reserve officers, Uzi Finerman, a Rafi party member and personal friend of the defense minister's, to Tel Aviv. At 2:00, having heard no response from Finerman, Elazar gave up and went to bed. Four hours later, the phone rang.

"Can you attack?" Dayan asked.

However dazed, Elazar replied unhesitatingly. "I can—and right now."

"Then attack."

Dayan began to explain the reasons for his *volte face*—Egypt's adherence to the cease-fire, the Syrian army's collapse. But Dado cut him off. "Collapse or no collapse—I don't know. Nor does it matter to me. We're attacking. Thank you very much. Shalom. Shalom."

Dayan next asked his aide de camp, Col. Yitzhak Nissiyahu, to contact Col. Lior at the prime minister's office. "I couldn't believe my ears," Lior remarked.

"The previous day had been devoted to Dayan's opposition to conquering the Syrian Golan . . . The announcement fell like thunder on a clear day."

Eshkol's shock was no less total. "That's despicable. That's despicable," he kept mumbling when informed by Lior. Though he fully favored an operation to capture the Banias, at least, the prime minister was livid over Dayan's impudence, his contempt for democratic norms. "Can I cancel the order now? It's illogical!" he groaned. "If he thinks he can do whatever he wants, let him do it."

Lior next called the headquarters of the chief of staff. Though Rabin's reaction was not recorded, he immediately ordered a helicopter to take him to Northern Command. There, landing at 8:00, he rushed to find Dado. "The Syrian army is nowhere near collapse," Rabin admonished him. "You must assume that it will fight obstinately and will fight with all of its strength!"[3]

Between Hammer and Pincer

Now with more planes than targets, firing rockets salvaged from captured Egyptian stocks, the air force went to work. Beginning at 9:40 A.M., Israeli jets carried out dozens of sorties and dropped hundreds of tons of bombs on Syrian positions from Mount Hermon to Tawafiq. Artillery batteries and storehouses were knocked out, and transport columns driven from the roads. But the bombs could scarcely scratch the bunkers and trench systems overlooking Israeli territory and covering every route up the face of the Golan. Elazar nevertheless redoubled the barrage to provide time to clear paths through the mile-thick minefields, and to break the Syrians' morale.

If not broken, Syria's morale had at least been seriously cracked. Convinced that the Israelis were tired and intimidated by the shelling of their settlements, the Syrians were unprepared for the ferocity of the IAF's bombardment. Col. Ahmad al-Mir, commander of the central sector, reported 163 enemy sorties in just over three hours; 52 of his soldiers were killed and 80 wounded. The impact was psychological as well, as a number of senior officers deserted, to be followed by many of their troops. Instructed to reinforce the frontline positions, Maj. Gen. 'Awad Baha, the operations chief, pointed to the lack of air cover and dismissed the order as "suicidal." A similar response came from the 70th Armored Brigade stationed outside Quneitra. Its commander, Col. 'Izzat Jadid, refused to counterattack, even at night, and instead led his tanks back to Damascus. Though Syrian radio described the air strikes as an Anglo-American effort "to save the Israelis from destruction," there could be no dissembling the damage.

Nevertheless, the bulk of Syrian forces remained in their bunkers, ready to fight. The greatest concentration was in the central sector, where three brigades and 144 artillery pieces were aimed at the so-called Customs House road—the straightest axis to Quneitra and thus the most likely to be taken by invaders. The army was ordered to block that route at all costs, to hunker down and conserve its ammunition. "Avoid opening fire," Chief of Staff Suweidani told his commanders. "We have requested United Nations intervention. We are awaiting a response any moment."[4]

Contrary to Syrian expectations, the Israelis were not planning to take the Customs House road, at least not in the initial attack. The Hammer plan called for a swift smashing of the enemy's frontline defense where the enemy least expected it—in the north, near Kfar Szold, and south of the Sea of Galilee. But massive traffic jams caused by forces moving north from the West Bank and Sinai indefinitely delayed the southern assault. Instead, Israel's secondary thrust would be made in the central sector, between the fortresses of Darbashiya and Jalabina. Elazar expected the opening assault to be bloody, almost prohibitively so. Climbing extremely steep (2,000 feet), rocky terrain, in the daylight—the original attack was supposed to have been staged at night—the first wave would be totally exposed to Syrian fire. It would have to move swiftly, reaching the patrol roads that linked all of Syria's fortifications and then capturing the fortifications as well, which were strategically positioned to provide covering fire for one another. They were girded by mines and barbed wire, and bristling with concrete bunkers and pillboxes.

"If this is the plan, know that it's suicide," Avraham Mendler told Elazar, when informed of his assignment. The Shermans of his 8th Armored Brigade—Israel's only tanks on the front—were worn from the heavy fighting in Sinai and their crews exhausted. Now they were being asked to crack Syria's most formidable defenses, in broad daylight, over almost impassable terrain. Indeed, no sooner had it moved out at 11:40 A.M. and began scaling the escarpment than Mendler's column came under raking fire from dug-in Syrian tanks.

"At first, we weren't afraid at all," said Ya'akov Horesh, member of a tank crew in the 8th Brigade's 129th Battalion. "Bulldozers ran in front of us, clearing the wire and mines. But then the sky opened up. The bulldozers were knocked out . . . half-tracks were blown into the air. Suddenly, we were hit! . . . I went up to the turret hatch and saw that the tank was ablaze and that I was burning with it. I heard shots, heard someone on the radio calling for air cover. I decided it was better to be shot than burned to death, and I threw myself from the turret . . . They [Israeli soldiers] picked me up and put me on the deck of another tank. I was still on fire."

Five of the eight bulldozers were struck immediately, their burning hulls battered aside by other, still-advancing vehicles. The Shermans, their maneuverability sharply reduced by the terrain, moved slowly toward the fortified village of Sir al-Dib, aiming for the major fortress at Qala'. Casualties mounted, including the battalion commander, thirty-nine-year-old Arye Biro. Reconnaissance officer Maj. Rafael Mokady, in civilian life a university lecturer, assumed Biro's place, only to be killed ten minutes later. Then, with the situation already critical, part of the attacking force lost its way and emerged opposite another redoubt, Za'ura, manned by reservists from Syria's 244th Battalion. "If we could hold Za'ura," Mendler later testified, "I believed that we could turn the tide of the battle." Improvising, he ordered the attacks on Za'ura and Qala' to proceed simultaneously.

The fighting was intense and confused as Israeli and Syrian tanks struggled around obstacles, firing at extremely short range. Mendler recalled how "the Syrians fought well and bloodied us. We beat them only by crushing them under our treads and by blasting them with our cannons at very short range, from 100 to 500 meters." The first three Shermans to enter Qala' were halted by a Syrian bazooka team. Behind it, a relief column of seven T-54s rushed to repel the attackers. Mokady's replacement, Capt. Nataniel Horowitz, remembered how, "we took heavy fire from the houses but we couldn't turn back because forces behind us were pushing us forward. We were on a narrow path with mines on either side." Suffering from a head wound—blood shorted his helmet's intercom—and with his maps destroyed, Horowitz signaled his remaining vehicles to press forward, and called for an air strike on the enemy's armor. Mendler turned him down, saying there were simply no planes available. "Sir," the captain replied, "if we don't receive air support at once, it's good-bye, for I don't think we'll see each other again." A pair of jets materialized and disabled two of the T-54's; the remainder withdrew. The surviving defenders of Qala' also retreated, after their commander, Maj. Muhammad Sa'id, was killed.

By 6:00 P.M., both Qala' and Za'ura had fallen, along with a third fort, 'Ein Fit. The most accessible road to Quneitra lay open to the Israelis, but their victory had been largely pyrrhic. Dozens of Israelis had been killed and wounded, and of their original twenty-six tanks, only two remained battle-worthy.[5]

Similar carnage occurred throughout the central sector—in the battles for the strongholds of Dardara and Tel Hilal, which left twenty-one members of Israel's 181st Battalion dead and thirty-six wounded. Desperate fighting also broke out along Hammer's northern axis, where the 12th Barak ("Lightning") Battalion of the Golani Infantry Brigade was assigned to clear some thirteen positions, including Tel Fakhr—an imposing, horseshoe-shaped bastion three miles inside Syrian territory. All had been subjected to prolonged air attack in the hope of reducing their defenses or inducing their garrisons to flee.

But here, too, the Israelis underestimated the bunkers' ability to withstand massive bombing, while navigational errors again placed them directly under the Syrians' guns. One by one, the battalion's nine tanks and nineteen half-tracks were picked off, their passengers wounded or killed. Reuven Dangor, driver of one of those tanks, found himself targeted by multiple artillery pieces. "No sooner had we passed the southern part of the *tel* than I felt a violent jolt . . . The driver's compartment filled with smoke and then, when I finally recovered from the shock, we caught another blast, harder and deadlier than the first, in the turret. I escaped through the emergency hatch and looked for the crewmembers who'd been sitting in the turret. The turret, though, was empty."

The Israelis had been stopped, but the forces who stopped them had also taken a beating. The internal Syrian army report of the battle provided a stark record of fear, chaos, and desertion:

With the enemy just 700 meters away, under heavy shelling, the platoon in the front trench prepared for battle. The platoon commander sent Private Jalil 'Issa to the company commander to request permission to take cover, but 'Issa could not find him. The platoon commander sent another runner who returned with Private Fajjar Hamdu Karnazi who reported on the company commander's disappearance. When the enemy reached 600 meters, Sgt. Muhammad Yusuf Ibrahim fired a 10-inch anti-tank gun and knocked out the lead tank. But then he and his squad commander were killed. The enemy column advanced. First Sergeant Anwar Barbar, in charge of the second 10-inch gun, could not be found. The platoon commander searched for him but unsuccessfully . . . Private Hajj al-Din, who was killed just minutes later, took the gun and fired it alone, knocking out two tanks and forcing the column to retreat. But when the platoon commander tried to radio the information to headquarters, nobody answered.

On the road, meanwhile, the Israeli battalion commander, Moshe "Musa" Klein, ordered his twenty-five remaining men to dismount their vehicles, to divide into two groups, and to charge the northern and southern flanks of Tel Fakhr. The southern approach was densely braced with bunkers, trenches, and a double row of wire. Behind them, a company of the 187th Infantry Battalion under Capt. Ahmad Ibrahim Khalili waited with an arsenal of antitank guns, machine-guns, and 82-mm mortars. "It was one of our most fortified positions," he remembered. "It placed them [the Israelis] directly in our crosshairs."

The fighting that ensued was reminiscent of that at Jerusalem's Ammunition Hill, waged at extremely close quarters, often hand-to-hand. The first Israelis to reach the perimeter laid bodily down on the barbed wire so that the rest of their squads could vault over them. From there they dashed to the Syrian trenches.

Captain Diko Takum, the commander of Tel Fakhr's northern flank, ordered his men not to fire until the Israelis had reached the wire. "We'll catch them in a sure-kill zone," he said. Minutes later, Takum's deputy, Lieutenant Hatim Haliq, reported that "the Jews are already inside! I've taken heavy casualties!" Takum called for reinforcements, but when no answer came, he issued instructions to hold all positions indefinitely. "Nobody moves. Do not let them advance. We will all stand here or we'll all die here."

The Israelis charged. Shlomo Ben Basat, a Golani enlisted man, testified:

> I ran to the left with Kalman, my NCO. We ran through the trenches, clearing out bunkers, until suddenly we saw an alcove with beds and boxes in it. Kalman told me, "'I'll go in and you wait outside." But no sooner had he entered [the alcove] when he was hit by burst of fire from a wounded Syrian inside. Kalman managed to stumble out—he fell and died. Then the Syrian came out. He saw me and immediately started pleading to me for his life. He stood there with his gun still smoking from the bullets that killed Kalman. I avenged his blood.

Ten of the thirteen Israelis who assaulted the northern flank became casualties, while only one of the twelve on the southern flank, Corp. Yitzhak Hamawi, remained standing. "We ran, Musa (Klein) and I, through the trenches," he remembered. "Whenever a helmet popped up, we couldn't tell if it was one of ours or not. Suddenly in front of us stood a soldier whom we couldn't identify. The battalion commander shouted the password and when the soldier didn't answer, he fired a burst at him but missed. We jumped out of the trench, ran five meters, and then Musa fell on his face . . . killed by the Syrian soldier he'd missed. Our radio man waited for him to leap up again, then shot him."

The man who killed Klein was identified in Syrian records as 'Ali 'Issa Hafez. Dying immediately after him was Sgt. Jamil Musa, commander of the last trench to hold out in Tel Fakhr. Only eight of its defenders remained, under Corp. Mustafa Suliman, and these retreated when a detachment of Golani scouts breached the fort from an unmarked trail in the rear. A single Syrian officer, 2nd Lt. Ahmad 'Ali, and two privates, surrendered. In the seven-hour struggle, the Israelis had thirty-one dead and eighty-two wounded. Sixty-two Syrians were killed and twenty taken prisoner.

Tel Fakhr fell, as did Tel 'Azzaziat, taken by the Golani Brigade's 51st Battalion, and Darbashiya. Though Israeli forces had achieved most of their objectives and well ahead of schedule, they had penetrated no deeper than eight miles into Syrian territory. A five-mile-wide bridgehead between Za'ura and Qala' had been established and armed probes effected at five other points on the Syrian front. These were the minimal goals of Hammer, but Elazar and the general staff aspired to much more than that—to Operation Pincers and the conquest of the entire Golan. Accomplishing that, Rabin estimated, would take two more days of fighting, at least.[6]

Beyond its shattered first line, Syria's defenses were largely intact. Mount Hermon and the Banias in the north and the entire southern sector between Tawafiq and the Customs House road remained in Syrian hands. Meeting early that night, Syrian leaders decided to reinforce those dispositions as quickly as possible, and to maintain a steady barrage on the Israeli settlements. The 17th Mechanized Battalion, having advanced to northern Jordan at Gen. Riyad's insistence, was summarily moved back to defend Damascus. In a nationally broadcast speech, al-Assad swore to carry on the battle against "Zionist imperialist aggression," irrespective of the cost. "The enemy's objective is to break the people's morale, thus forcing it to retreat from its heroic stand in the battle against the enemies of the Arab nation." Arab ambassadors to Damascus were summoned to the Foreign Ministry and asked what their governments would do to assist Syria militarily. A special appeal was made to Egypt, Syria's ally by treaty.[7]

Curtain Call

The Egyptians could offer no help, of course, but were themselves in need of assistance urgently. Whether out of bitterness toward Damascus for failing to

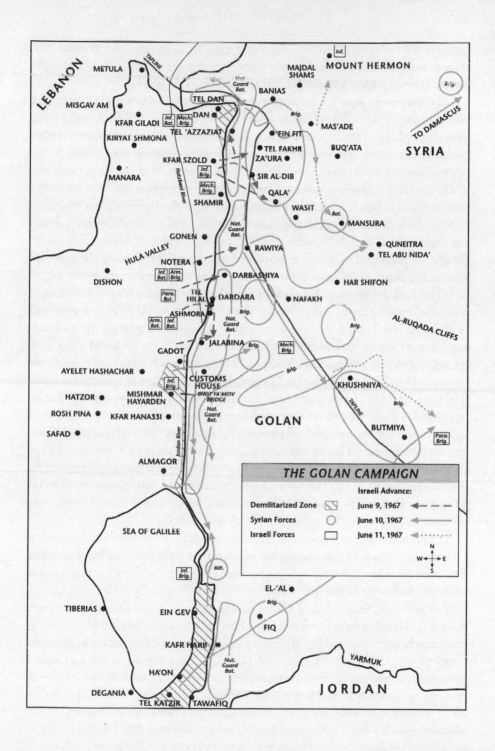

LEBANON

METULA

MISGAV AM

KFAR GILADI

KIRYAT SHMONA

MANARA

DISHON

AYELET HASHACHAR

HATZOR

ROSH PINA

SAFAD

TIBERIAS

TAPLINE

TEL DAN

DAN

TEL 'AZZAZIAT

KFAR SZOLD

SHAMIR

GONEN

NOTERA

TEL HILAL

ASHMORA

GADOT

MISHMAR HAYARDEN

KFAR HANASSI

ALMAGOR

EIN GEV

KAFR HARB

HA'ON

DEGANIA

TEL KATZIR

Nat. Guard Bat.

Inf. Bat.

Mech. Brig.

Inf. Brig.

Mech. Brig.

DARBASHIYA

Nat. Guard Bat.

RAWIYA

Inf. Bat. *Arm. Brig.*

Para. Bat.

DARDARA

Arm. Bat. *Inf. Bat.*

Nat. Guard Bat.

JALABINA

Mech. Brig.

CUSTOMS HOUSE

Inf. Brig.

BNOT YA'AKOV BRIDGE

Nat. Guard Bat.

HULA VALLEY

Hatzbani River

Jordan River

Inf. Brig.

Bat.

SEA OF GALILEE

TAWAFIQ

MAJDAL SHAMS

Inf.

MOUNT HERMON

BANIAS

'EIN FIT

TEL FAKHR

ZA'URA

SIR AL-DIB

QALA'

WASIT

Bat.

Brig.

MAS'ADE

BUQ'ATA

MANSURA

QUNEITRA

TEL ABU NIDA'

HAR SHIFON

NAFAKH

Brig.

Brig.

AL-RUQADA CLIFFS

KHUSHNIYA

Brig.

TAPLINE

BUTMIYA

Para. Brig.

GOLAN

EL-'AL

Brig.

FIQ

Nat. Guard Bat.

YARMUK

JORDAN

SYRIA

TO DAMASCUS

Brig.

THE GOLAN CAMPAIGN

Israeli Advance:

Demilitarized Zone	▨	June 9, 1967
Syrian Forces	◯	June 10, 1967
Israeli Forces	▢	June 11, 1967

N
W E
S

come to Egypt's rescue earlier in the war, or a need to recoil from the death-trap of inter-Arab politics, Cairo all but ignored the battle unfolding in the north. Its sole concern was Sinai and Israel's coup de grâce.

By noontime, June 9, the Israelis had completed the peninsula's conquest. Two columns from Yoffe's *Ugdah*—one heading south from Suez and the other west from Mitla—met up with paratroopers who landed by helicopter at Ras al-Sudr. The entire eastern bank of the Gulf of Suez was now in their hands. In the north, Gonen's 7th Armored Brigade reached the shore of the Great Bitter Lake, while the Granit Force, bypassing Qantara, took up position opposite Isma'iliya and Firdan. Though scattered skirmishes continued—the Egyptians lost fifty more tanks—the fighting had effectively ceased. The Egyptians scuttled ships to block the Suez Canal, but the Israelis, perhaps out of a sense of overconfidence or simply fatigue, failed to occupy its northern terminus. That port—Fu'ad—would soon serve as the main conduit for the massive Soviet rearmament of Egypt.

The first deliveries of Russian arms had in fact already landed near Cairo, and would total nearly 50,000 tons by the end of the month. Yet, not even this impressive effort could hide the scenes of thousands of Egyptian troops limp-ing back to the capital. Humiliated, many of these men removed their uni-forms, lest they be identified with defeat. "There were only four hundred soldiers between Isma'iliya and my house," Nasser later told Sudanese leader Mohamed Mahjoub. "Israeli troops could have entered Cairo if they wanted to." British intelligence sources reported that "defenses apparent along [the] approaches to Cairo consist of several sand barricades and trenches that could scarcely pose any serious problems for an advancing army except perhaps a dissident Egyp-tian one." Rumors spread of an impending revolt by disaffected officers or by pro-Soviet agents led by 'Ali Sabri. Intelligence Chief Salah Nasir went so far as to risk a secret meeting with Nolte, warning him of a Communist coup unless the United States embraced "pro-Arab" policies.

Gone were the mass demonstrations in praise of Arab victories, the reports of Israel's demise. The economy lay in shambles. "By the time the cease-fire had been arranged the UAR was approximately $448.5 million per year poorer than she had been before the war started," one British diplomat, tallying the loss of tourism, Sinai oil, and Canal revenues, calculated. Deeply depressed, Anwar Sadat still refused to come out of his villa near the pyramids. "I . . . was completely overwhelmed by our defeat. It sank into the very fabric of my con-sciousness so that I relived it day and night . . . trying, with all the fortitude I possessed, to weather the fierce campaign of denigration launched by both friend and foe against our armed forces." *Le Monde*'s Eric Rouleau recalled how "an air of mourning seized Cairo," and how secretly its citizens were calling Nasser *al-wahsh*—"The Beast." Nor was the disenchantment confined to Egypt. Riot-ers in Algiers chanted "Nasser traitor!" and attacked the Egyptian embassy; in Tunis they burned down the Egyptian cultural center. The Arab world had been shamed and angered, and desperately needed a scapegoat.[8]

Nasser seemed willing to play that scapegoat. The once-unflappable leader was suffering from severe depression, complaining of leg pains, and sleeping with a gun under his pillow. Repeatedly he phoned Gen. Fawzi, questioning him on the state of his troops. "I'm sitting here waiting for the army to come and take me," he told Madkur Abu al-'Izz, the governor of Aswan, whom Nasser would soon name to rebuild the air force. The president was sitting in the dark—a blackout was still enforced—a single candle lighting his face. "My personal guard is at the front, along the Canal. But I need nothing except for my pistol. It is here, in my pocket, ready." The implication was that Nasser would take his own life rather than fall victim to a military coup. And yet, shortly after midnight, when reports reached him that 'Amer had already attempted suicide, Nasser rushed to Supreme Headquarters.

There he found the field marshal heavily intoxicated, ranting about conspiracies, and demanding large doses of sleeping pills. Nasser managed to calm him down, and in doing so, to restore some clarity to his own thinking. "A regime which is unable to defend the borders of its homeland loses its legitimacy," the president told his best friend and fiercest political rival. "As sad as we may be right now, we have to know that our rule has ended in tragedy." 'Amer offered no argument, but instead proposed passing the reins of government to Shams Badran, his hand-picked defense minister. Nasser preferred his vice president, Zakkariya Muhieddin.

At 7:00 that morning, Nasser received a visit from his protégé, Mohamed Hassanein Heikal. The *Al-Ahram* editor was shocked: The president had aged ten years in half as many days. Nasser said that he accepted complete responsibility for the debacle and would face a firing squad, if the people so determined. He could not, however, continue in office, if for no other reason than that Egypt's leader would now have to work closely with the United States—a task for which he was far too bitter. Rather, he would announce his resignation that evening; senior military commanders would also forfeit their posts. With that, Nasser rose to leave, but before he could, the phone rang. 'Amer, crying hysterically, had called to say that the Israelis had crossed the Canal and were now racing toward Cairo. "He's completely lost his nerve," sighed Nasser, hanging up. "And that's how he lost his army."[9]

Nasser's announcement was broadcast live at 6:30 that evening, shortly after Cairo Radio informed its listeners that "calm now prevails on the front and all operations have been halted in accordance with the cease-fire decision." The president's tone was subdued, his voice uncharacteristically frail. Citing Israel's intention to invade Syria, he defended his decisions to remilitarize Sinai, oust UNEF, and blockade the Tiran Straits, and stressed the pressure that both the U.S. and the USSR had levied on Egypt not to fire first. He credited Israel with a surprise attack—"We expected the enemy to come from the east and the north, but instead he came from the west"—but assigned its success to the open assistance afforded Israel by U.S. and British aircraft. To reverse the "setback" (*al-naksa*), as Nasser called it, the Arabs would have to unite against Israel and maintain their faith in eventual victory. Then, as anticipated, Nasser accepted full responsibility for his actions; he tendered his resignation and announced Muhieddin as his successor. His concluding words seemed to evoke an earlier Nasser, the author of *The Philosophy of the Revolution*:

> The forces of imperialism imagine that Abdel Nasser is their enemy. I want it to be clear to them that it is the entire Arab nation and not Gamal Abdel Nasser . . . for the hope of Arab unity began before Gamal Abdel Nasser and it will remain after Gamal Abdel Nasser. It is the nation which survives. Whatever Nasser's contribution to the causes of his homeland, he is but an expression of a popular will and is not the creator of that will.

No sooner had Nasser uttered these words when planes were heard in the Cairo sky; anti-aircraft batteries began firing. Suddenly, as if on cue, the streets filled with people. Hundreds of thousands of people—children, women, university students—flooded down Manshiet al-Bakri avenue. Tearing their hair, their clothing, beating their heads, the demonstrators cried, "Nasser, don't leave us!" Eric Rouleau described hearing "a roaring, like the sea," and witnessing "a great black mass" proceeding toward the city center. "All of a sudden I found myself wading through multitudes of people," recounted Mahmoud Riad. "Angry people and highly incensed, clamoring that Nasser must stay . . . [and that] honor and dignity be avenged."

Similar outpourings of devotion for Nasser occurred in Alexandria and in cities throughout the Middle East, from Rabat to Baghdad. "I urge you to respond to the nation's wishes and stay on," King Hussein wrote Nasser in a cable broadcast over Radio Amman. "The battle is only beginning." Prominent Egyptian intellectuals, National Assembly representatives, and union officials, rushed to declare their allegiance to the president. Muhieddin publicly declined to assume his place. The TV anchorman covering the speech broke into tears, sobbing, "Let bombs fall and let the Sixth Fleet come to our shore, but we want you to stay!" Nasser's photograph promptly filled the screen.

Many Westerners were incredulous about the spontaneity of these events, dismissing them as "a deliberate ploy by Nasser to strengthen his sagging position with renewed popular mandate." R. M. Tesh, the Canadian ambassador, called the speech "a superlative stroke with all the weird and wonderful qualities of which Nasser is master . . . [that] quickly turned the tables of outrageous defeat to victory." *Life* magazine correspondent Thomas Thompson asked rhetorically, "Is Nasser putting on a show?" and then answered himself: "It would seem so. The resignation, the ack-ack, the blackout, the momentary panic, the hysterical mobs, all of it builds to the inescapable conclusion that only Nasser could keep the country together." Rouleau, virtually alone, rejected such skepticism. "You don't organize millions of people in a few hours," he explained. "People despised Nasser for leading them to disaster, but they also loved him as a father. They didn't want him to desert them, and they had nobody else to trust. After all, who was Muhieddin?"

Whether impromptu or not, the outpouring of support proved irresistible. Nasser accepted the resignations of 'Amer and Badran and of virtually all his general staff—the army's command went to Muhammad Fawzi—but quickly rescinded his own. A statement pledged that the president would discuss his position with the National Assembly, but en route to the session, his motorcade was allegedly blocked by celebrating citizens. The next communiqué revealed that Nasser "could not ignore the voice of the people," and would remain in office until "the traces of Israel's aggression were eradicated." [10]

"Imperialist Pressures"

Even as Nasser pledged to restore conquered Arab lands, the extent of Israel's conquests was expanding. Unsuccessful in their bid to recruit Arab assistance, fearful of an Israeli drive on Damascus itself, the Syrians had little choice but to appeal to the United Nations.

At 5:30 A.M. in New York, as the Israelis were pressing their attack beyond the Golan escarpment, George Tomeh called Hans Tabor, the Security Council president, and demanded an emergency session. "In spite of our observance of the cease-fire," Syria's formal protest read, "we are now being subjected to an Israeli attack on the whole length of the armistice demarcation line and against our towns and villages." Verbally, Tomeh went further, charging that Israeli planes were bombing Damascus and Israeli paratroopers landing in Quncitra.

Israel's response was reserved and evasive. Official sources had yet to announce that an offensive was even taking place—Israel Radio made no mention of it—only that the Syrian shelling of northern Galilee was continuing. Wally Barbour, reporting on a conversation with Eban, assured the State Department that the operation would soon be over and that "should make the cease fire with Syria effective not only *de jure* but *de facto*." At the UN, Gideon Rafael claimed that sixteen settlements were being shelled, and dismissed Syria's acceptance of the cease-fire as "nothing but camouflage for a premeditated . . . attack against Israel."

So began what the Israeli ambassador later described as a debate "unsurpassed in vehemence." Mohammad El Kony added to Tomeh's charges by reporting that the Israelis were also bombing Cairo. Rafael, incensed, dismissed the claim as "a malicious fabrication," adding that, "the spreading of irresponsible and false charges of this kind only aggravates the already tense situation in the Middle East." Federenko demanded that Israel be "severely punished" for its actions, and warned that "non-compliance [with the cease-fire] will have the gravest consequences for the Israeli State."

While the Soviets sparred, the Syrians were willing to settle for simple cease-fire resolution—anything to stop the Israeli advance. Before it could be voted on, however, Federenko suddenly insisted on appending articles condemning Israel and ordering it back to the Armistice lines. Goldberg countered by accusing the Russians of playing politics at the cost of human lives. Federenko asked in reply, "why then is it that Washington, which has sufficient means to do something, has not lifted one finger to stop the aggressive forces of Israel?"

Federenko's grandstanding had cost the Syrians dearly. At 12:30, Tabor called an end to the debate and read out a "lowest common denominator" statement confirming the Council's interest in a cease-fire and instructing the secretary-general to confer with the warring parties. Thereafter, Undersecretary General Aleksei Nesterenko, a beefy Russian, literally hauled both Tomeh and Rafael into his office—"into two opposite corners like prize-fighters," the Israeli delegate wrote, "positioning himself like a referee in the middle of the ring"—but made no progress. Rafael claimed that he was still awaiting instructions from Jerusalem. Reminding Nesterenko that "So far it has been the practice that governments instruct their ambassadors and not the Secretariat of the United Nations, and we had better continue to abide by this principle." He nodded at his Syrian counterpart, and exited.[11]

Through a combination of Soviet obduracy and their own stonewalling, the Israelis had gained valuable time for their offensive. The Council was not set to reconvene until 6:30 that night. But while demands to end the fighting waned in the international forum, in Washington they mounted sharply.

The opening of a third Arab-Israeli front fully exposed the fundamental contradiction in American policy toward the war. While welcoming Israeli gains that could be traded in a future peace settlement, and eager to see Syria's provocations punished, the administration was also anxious to uphold the cease-fire and avoid any clash with the Soviets. A confrontation with the USSR appeared conceivable when, shortly after news of Israel's offensive reached Moscow, the Kremlin pledged to "render them [Egypt and Syria] assistance in order to repel the aggression and defend their national independence."

The Soviets' statement strengthened the hands of Rusk and State Department officials who had always resisted armed action by the Israelis, and weakened those of Walt Rostow, Bundy, and Saunders, who had seen its possible advantages. The scales were further tipped by what many in the White House viewed as growing Israeli hubris. In an interview with UPI that day, Eshkol intimated that the U.S. had not lived up to its obligations before the war, thus forcing Israel to act alone. Though the prime minister had been egregiously misquoted—he had actually praised America's commitment to Israel—Johnson was piqued. "I had a firm commitment from Eshkol [honoring the cease-fire] and he blew it," the president scribbled on his notepad during a National Security Council meeting. "That old coot isn't going to pay any attention to any imperialist pressures"—pressures, that is, from both the U.S. and the USSR.[12]

Rusk wasted no time in calling the Israelis to task. "Deeply disturbed" by UN reports of Israeli attacks, disinclined to believe that Syria's guns posed a serious threat to Galilee, he instructed Barbour to find Abba Eban at once. He was to tell the foreign minister that the situation in the Security Council was "deteriorating rapidly"; that the United States expected Israel to observe the cease-fire "at all costs" and shoot only in clear-cut cases of self-defense. "We consider it very important that Israel demonstrate by actions on the ground that it. . . means what it says."

The deteriorating situation in the Security Council, the burgeoning Soviet threat and expressions of American displeasure, the alarmingly high casualty rate—all weighed on the Ministerial Defense Committee when it met at 8:00 that evening. The atmosphere was severely strained. Several members, most vocally the NRP's Haim Moshe Shapira and Yisrael Barzilai of Mapam, were opposed to continuing the Golan offensive, and furious with Dayan for sanctioning it.

The defense minister had, in fact, just approved the opening of Operation Hammer south. Israeli forces were to conquer Tawafiq, the Syrian fortress overlooking the southern tip of the Sea of Galilee, provided the resistance there proved light. Upon returning from the northern front, however, Dayan found himself on the defensive, forced to explain why he had suddenly reversed his previous opposition to attacking Syria. He cited the sudden move by Egypt and Syria to accept the cease-fire, and Nasser's telegram to Damascus. Just as the decisions to attack the West Bank and enter the Old City of Jerusalem had been taken on the spur of the moment, in reaction to altered circumstances, so, too, had the approval for the Golan offensive come in response to a new situation. "These notices gave us the possibility of thinking that maybe we had the ability to change the international border between us and Syria," Dayan attested, intimating—disingenuously—that Eshkol had fully approved the attack.

The prime minister came close to refuting this claim—"I cannot say that I was asked [by Dayan]"—but however hefty, his reservations about the defense minister could not outweigh his enmity toward Syria. He kept his response oblique: "All day yesterday we were walking on coals . . . I was really in favor [of the operation] and sorry that it was postponed, though it was truly decided that . . . if there's quiet [in the north]—that would oblige us to shut up as well. How can we stop now that we're in the middle of the operation—I cannot say."

But Shapira was less ambiguous. "Why are we now violating the cease-fire in front of the whole world?" he shouted. "I demand to know who's responsible for violating our [the Defense Committee's] decision!"

"The defense minister has a right to change his mind, but the substantive argument has changed from end to end," seconded Barzilai; "this forum should have reconvened in the middle of the night and made a proper decision."

Shapira insisted that the offensive be canceled immediately, and was once again opposed by Allon. "Even if Syria and Egypt had accepted the cease-fire before this meeting, I will still have approved the operation." Galili agreed: "I would have opposed [halting the attack] even if the cease-fire were mutual." Menachem Begin said that, while there may have been an "aesthetic" violation of the committee's decision, Dayan and Eshkol had legitimately exercised their prerogatives. "In the days of Maria Theresa there was a law that said that if a soldier broke discipline but performed an act of bravery, he'd get both a demerit and a medal."

Last to address the ministers was Dr. Herzog, the prime minister's foreign policy adviser, who stated that it was better to risk Israel's relations with Moscow than to allow Syria to retain the Golan. "The Syrians cannot be allowed to parade in victory," declared Eshkol finally, "Israel cannot have overturned all the Arab countries and not Syria."[13]

The meeting concluded with approval for continuing the campaign until the following morning, Saturday. Israel lacked both the military wherewithal and diplomatic latitude to pursue fighting further, Dayan argued. "The Syrians are battling like lions," he reported to yet another gathering of ministers and senior advisers later that night. "We cannot remain in combat during the daylight hours while the Syrians are trying to mount a counter-attack." He spoke of the need to rush additional troops, together with recently captured armaments, to the Golan, and to possibly bomb Damascus, should the shelling of Galilee continue. Though Eshkol was, for once, more optimistic, suggesting that "if the people at the front feel they can finish the task tonight and tomorrow—let them. In any case they'll condemn us in the UN." The goal of conquering the entire Golan seemed well out of Israel's grasp.

But events in the field once again outstripped discussions in government. While Dayan explained the reasons why Israel could no longer advance, David Elazar was planning to do just that. In addition to Tawafiq, he had authorized the capture of a wide swath of Golan territory, from Butmiya to Quneitra, following an oil petroleum pipe and its parallel service road, the so-called TAP Line. Farther north, the Banias would also be taken, and the approaches to Mount Hermon.

Contrary to Dayan's estimate, Elazar felt he had the forces necessary to complete the job. The traffic jams in the southern sector had finally unraveled, and thousands of reinforcements were reaching the front. Those tanks and half-tracks that had survived the day's fighting were refueled and replenished with ammunition. Morale, boosted by the evacuation of the wounded, was high. By dawn, a full eight brigades could be thrown against Syria's second-line defense, irrespective of the government's hesitations. When, near midnight, Rabin called and canceled orders directing the paratroopers to take the southern Golan, Elazar merely apologized. "Following your previous order, they began to move out," he replied coyly "I can't stop them."

The Syrians, meanwhile, continued to brace themselves for the onslaught. Convinced that Israel would strike Damascus through Lebanon—IDF troops had staged a feint at the Lebanese border—Suweidani ordered three brigades (the 42nd and 44th Armored and the 35th Infantry) to fall back to protect the capital. Three other brigades (the 11th and the 132nd Infantry and the 7th National Guard Armored Brigade) were ordered to dig in along the second defense line. A message was broadcast to them that night by Hafez al-Assad. "Oh soldiers, 300,000 fighters of the People's Army are with you in your battle, and behind them, 100 million Arabs," the defense minister declared. "The cream of our troops stand at the front. Strike the enemy's settlements, turn them into dust, pave the Arab roads with the skulls of Jews. Strike them without mercy."[14] The fight, Damascus held, was not over.

THE WAR: DAY SIX, JUNE 10

The Golan vanquished.
Furtive maneuvers at the UN.
Superpower saber-rattling.
Visions of impending peace.

T HE TASK, in David Elazar's view, was simple. "We must push inland, gentlemen," he told his officers, "as deep and as fast as we can, at least to the Quneitra junction in the north and Butmiya junction in the south. And we have to do all this before the telephone starts ringing." That call, Elazar knew, would inform him that Israel had undertaken to observe the cease-fire, and that the offensive in the north—the war—was over.

Operating against this inexorable clock, expecting the Syrians to counterattack, Israeli forces fought obstinately throughout the night. And the Syrians just as resolutely fought back. At the fortified village of Jalabina, a garrison of reserve infantrymen from Syria's 132nd Brigade, leveling their anti-aircraft guns, held off Israel's 65th Paratroop Battalion. "Twice I got up to charge the village and twice nobody followed me," recalled Uzi Finkelstein, an Israeli company commander whose men, exhausted and shell-shocked, had collapsed between the boulders. Four hours passed before Finkelstein and a small detachment managed to penetrate the village and knock out its heavy guns.

Mendler's tanks meanwhile rolled south from Qala', advancing six miles under heavy artillery and tank bombardment to Wasit. At the Banias, in the north, Syrian mortar batteries waited while Golani Brigade engineers cleared a path through a minefield and only then opened fire. Sixteen Israelis were killed in the action, and four wounded.

Though the anticipated counterattack had never materialized, the Syrian opposition was so keen—and the attackers' progress so slowed by it—that by daybreak Elazar had all but given up on the hope of taking Quneitra. Disappointed, convinced that Israel had missed its historic chance, the general went to sleep.

Half an hour later he was awakened by a phone call from Rabin requesting an update on the offensive. "Yitzhak, I've almost finished clearing out the front lines," Elazar informed him, "though as far as I'm concerned it's not yet cleaned."

Rabin then surprised him. The government was prepared to give the IDF additional time to "straighten out its lines." Though nothing was said about reaching Quneitra, the operation could proceed. "It seems we have some more time," the chief of staff said. "We haven't committed ourselves yet to the cease-fire."

"If so," Dado excitedly replied, "I'm pressing my attack immediately."[1]

The Israeli attack continued, but not so Syrian resistance. When Mendler reached Mansura, a village five miles distant from Wasit, he was surprised to encounter negligible opposition. "We couldn't make contact with the retreating enemy," he later testified. "We fired at a number of tanks and they turned out to have been abandoned. All around us was an immense amount of equipment, including tanks and radios, in perfect working condition." A similar scene greeted the Golani troops after their breakthrough into the fortified Banias village. Apart from several Syrian soldiers found chained to their positions, the trenches were deserted. The assault was completed in less than fifteen minutes.

At 8:30 A.M., a series of terrific explosions rocked the Golan. The Syrians were blowing up their own bunkers, burning documents, and retreating en masse. With their forward communications cut, unwilling to take charge at the front, Syrian commanders had lost all control over the battlefield. Yet even they were nonplused when Radio Damascus broadcast that Quneitra, a mere forty-five miles southwest of the Syrian capital, had fallen. "We swear to crush the Zionist viper's head in Quneitra and to leave its dead tail in Tel Aviv," it said.[2]

Crisis and Credibility

Despairing of receiving help from elsewhere in the Arab world, from the UN, or, most critically, from the Soviet Union, the Syrians had finally snapped. The premature announcement of Quneitra's fall provided a pretext for the regime to withdraw its forces from the front and to consolidate them around Damascus. The international community might also be spurred to act.[3]

The international community was, in fact, acting, as the Security Council reconvened at 4:30 A.M., at Syria's request. Tomeh alleged that Israeli forces had already occupied Quneitra and from there, were pressing on to Damascus. Federenko accused Israel of "openly misleading the Council, [of] playing for time," and labeled Rafael a liar. He and the Syrian ambassador pressed Tabor, the Council president, to demand a statement on the exact position of Israeli forces. Rafael refused, however, arguing that the Council had no right to force the representative of any sovereign state to speak, but the pressure on him was growing insufferable. Repeatedly, he fled the Council chamber to phone Eban in Jerusalem and beg him for a clear declaration of policy. "Not only is Israel's credibility at stake but we are in danger of being condemned by the Security Council, including [by] the United States." Aware of the postwar diplomatic struggle soon to begin, he warned of the erosion of Israel's moral position by the refusal to state Israeli goals on the Golan Heights.

A further pall on Israel's candor was cast early that morning when UN observers submitted that Israeli jets were bombing Damascus. Rafael strenuously denied the assertion, and noted that the observers had also seen smoke rising from Israeli settlements. But subsequent observer reports all confirmed that IDF planes had been spotted in the capital's skies. Israel's Foreign Ministry was compelled to issue its first acknowledgment, albeit oblique, of the battle: IAF jets were not striking Damascus, but providing cover for Israeli land forces. The admission did little to ameliorate the tension, however. Though Goldberg and Caradon called for a resolution ordering both sides to respect the cease-fire, Federenko insisted that Israel, alone, be condemned. "The circle is complete!" he bellowed. "The perpetration of the crime is proved!"[4]

Federenko's rancor was merely a reflection of the Kremlin's internal malaise. "[These have] been bad . . . weeks for the Soviet Union," Britain's Foreign Office observed. "The outstanding impression must be one of high hopes collapsed, confidence crumbled and a heavy bill to repair delapidations." Egypt's ignominious defeat, and the Soviets' impassivity in the face of it, had exposed the schism between those Politburo members in favor and those opposed to confronting America in the Middle East—between Kosygin and his technocrats and security officials close to Brezhnev.

That quarrel, together with the slow pace of Soviet decision making—the government met only once weekly, on Thursdays—had all but paralyzed Soviet diplomacy in the first days of the crisis. Former Soviet leader Khrushchev, observing the crisis from the side, bewailed the failure to rein in Nasser, or to correctly gauge Israel's strength. "From the beginning our country made mistakes—the mistake of allowing this war to happen, of allowing Nasser to provoke Israel, to gamble on everything." Israel and the U.S. had benefited from that gamble, as had the Chinese, their propaganda swiftly maligning Moscow's reliability. The Arabs were thoroughly disappointed. "The Soviet Union was ready to supply weapons to some Arab countries, to train their armies . . . to give them economic aid, but it was not prepared to risk military confrontation with the United States in the region," wrote Arkady Schevchenko, the deputy head of the Soviets' UN mission. The war, he added, had "demonstrated the USSR's willingness to turn away from these countries in a critical moment after having encouraged the passions which precipitated the showdown."[5]

Not only the Arabs were disillusioned with Moscow, but also its allies in Eastern Europe. They were exasperated with Soviet mishandling of the crisis and, to the degree that they could, told them so at a summit of Warsaw Pact countries on June 10. Prior to that date, few measures had been taken to restore Russia's tarnished reputation through military means. While air force, paratroopers, and naval vessels in the Mediterranean area had been on high alert since the outset of the war, there had been no major shift in the Soviet army's disposition. Assistance to the Arabs had been limited to the resupply of war materials, particularly of MiG's, to Egypt and Iraq.

But then the IDF broke through on the Golan Heights. Quneitra's fall was announced and shortly thereafter Israeli planes were reportedly bombing Damascus. Soviet propaganda organs immediately began charging Israel with "genocide" and plots to achieve world domination. Within the Soviet fleet in the Mediterranean, rumors circulated of imminent military intervention, including a possible landing at Haifa. Desperate to avoid any clash, Gromyko proposed a strong but nonviolent response: severing relations with Israel. The decision, according to one former Soviet official, "was more a move in the domestic policy game than a gesture in favor of the Arabs . . . It was a sop to pacify our hawks." Yet, with the capital of a major Middle East ally seemingly about to fall, those hawks were not so easily pacified.[6]

At 7:30 A.M., the hot line teletype at the White House again began ticking. "Mr. Kosygin wants the president to come to the equipment as soon as possible," Johnson was informed. Israeli troops were driving on Damascus, the Soviet leader wrote; the consequences were potentially grave:

> A very crucial moment has now arrived which forces us, if military actions are not stopped in the next few hours, to adopt an independent position. We are ready to do this. However, these actions may bring us into a clash which will lead to a grave catastrophe . . . We propose that you demand from Israel that it unconditionally cease military action . . . We propose to warn Israel that if this is not fulfilled, necessary actions will be taken, including military.

Further evidence of the Soviets' seriousness rapidly streamed in. Boris N. Sedov, second secretary and senior KGB official at the Soviet embassy in Washington, approached the State Department's Raymond Garthoff and informed him of Moscow's readiness to violate Turkish, Iranian, and Greek air space in order to fly troops into the region. "Four hundred Soviet advisors in Syria have already been authorized to fight," he said. The British Foreign Office also received a message from the ten Warsaw Pact countries pledging to "do all that is necessary to help the peoples of the Arab countries to give a determined rebuff to the aggressor . . . [and] to guard their lawful rights . . . The just struggle of the Arab peoples will triumph."

In the White House Situation Room "the atmosphere was tense," according to CIA director Richard Helms, with Johnson and his advisors speaking "in the lowest voices I've ever heard." Ambassador Llewellyn Thompson, who translated Kosygin's text and rechecked it to ensure that the term "including military" was indeed there, recalled "a time of great concern and utmost gravity."

Another cable from the Kremlin arrived at 10:00 reiterating the charge of Is-raeli designs on Damascus and advising Johnson to confirm that fact with America's ambassador there—as though Soviets had no knowledge of his ouster. Moscow's mood had clearly grown impulsive.

An hour passed while Johnson reviewed his options. Thompson expressed surprise at Kosygin's commitment to Syria, as compared to Egypt, and won-dered if he indeed believed the West wanted the Ba'th overthrown. Helms thought the Israelis were in fact aiming at Damascus, and asked for confirmation from the field. Yet the focus of the debate was whether the Soviets were serious about intervening or were merely testing America's resolve. As Thompson put it: "If our replies were polite, we might look as if we were backing down under a threat."

Ultimately, the president refrained from making any counterthreat, re-sponding cordially but tersely. He assured Kosygin that the U.S. had done its utmost to restrain the Israelis, and urged him to do the same *vis-à-vis* Syria. "Peace would be served," he added, if the Kremlin publicly and categorically eschewed Nasser's Big Lie.

Only later, after Johnson left the room, did McNamara turn to Thompson and ask, "Don't you think it might be useful if . . . we make it clear to them [the Soviets] that we don't intend to take this lying down? Wouldn't it be a good idea to simply turn the Sixth Fleet and head those two aircraft carriers and their accompanying ships to the Eastern Mediterranean!?"

Thompson said yes, it would be useful, and Helms agreed, recalling that Soviet ships were closely tracking the fleet. "The message is going to get back to Moscow in a hurry."

Johnson accepted his advisers' counsel. "Find out exactly where the Sixth Fleet is," he instructed McNamara, "and tell it to turn around."

The defense secretary went to the phone and immediately gave the order. The fleet, formerly sailing west of Cyprus between Crete and Rhodes, was instructed to steam eastward to within a hundred miles of Israel's coast.[7]

Along with checking possible Soviet moves, the Americans were also prepared to pressure Israel. Eban had been playing for time, assuring Barbour that Israel had "no intention of going to Damascus" and that it was willing to accept a cease-fire in place the minute Syria stopped shelling the northern settlements. Formerly amenable to these arguments, the American ambassador was now instructed to reject them. The reported fall of Quneitra, he replied, hardly accorded with the need to silence Syria's guns. "Israel must prove its accep-tance of the cease-fire on the ground before the Security Council meets this afternoon, otherwise it will jeopardize its gains on all other fronts," Barbour warned. In addition to condemnation in the UN and possibly Congress, Israel could find itself facing the Soviets alone.

At the UN, Goldberg invited Rafael to the delegates' lounge and urged him to make a statement on Israel's intention to stop the fighting. If not, he intimated, Federenko would soon declare that "the Soviet government is prepared to use every available means to make Israel respect the cease-fire resolution." Speaking, he said, on the president's express instructions, Goldberg confided that "the United States government does not want the war to end as the result of a Soviet ultimatum. This would be disastrous for the future not only of Israel, but of us all. It is your responsibility to act now."

In case Goldberg's point was missed, Eugene Rostow and Nicolas Katzenbach arranged an emergency meeting with Abe Harman and Eppy Evron. "In the most emphatic words" the Israelis were told that they, alone, bore responsibility for the continuing hostilities with Syria. World opinion was turning against them, while the Congress "had had its full of the failure to stop the fighting." Moreover, with the Soviets "busy saber-rattling," it was crucial that Washington be able to assure them that Israel would honor the cease-fire. The undersecretaries were adamant: "Our credibility with the Russians is at stake."[8]

These messages reached Jerusalem just as Eshkol received a cable from Moscow. This noted Israel's "criminal" violation of UN cease-fire resolutions, its "treasonous" invasion of Syrian territory and advance on Damascus. "If Israel does not cease its action immediately, then the USSR, together with other peace-loving nations, will take sanctions with all the implications thereof," the Soviets warned.

To back up their threat, Chuvakhin stormed into Eban's office and, his voice trembling, announced that, "in light of the continued aggression by Israel against the Arab states, and the flagrant breach of the Security Council's resolutions, the USSR government has decided to break diplomatic relations with Israel." Eban, improvising his response, acknowledged the bitter differences between Israel and the Soviets, but reasoned that such differences necessitated a strengthening—rather than severing—of ties. "If there was complete harmony," he said. "it would only be a question of cocktail parties."

Chuvakhin lowered his tone and replied, "What Your Excellency is saying is logical, but I haven't been sent here to be logical. I have come here to tell you about the rupture of relations." Then, to the foreign minister's astonishment, the Soviet ambassador burst into tears.

A scapegoat for the Soviets' failure in the Middle East, Chuvakhin would soon be ousted from the foreign service and exiled to Siberia. Yet not only the USSR, but nine other Communist bloc countries—Romania was the sole exception—recalled their representatives from Israel. The immediate response of the Israelis was to appeal to Washington for military assistance in the event of direct Soviet involvement in the war. The White House withheld its response.[9] Isolated suddenly, facing condemnation in the Security Council and possible clashes with Soviet troops, Israeli leaders had no choice but to pause and reconsider their decisions on attacking Syria, whether it was still worth the risk.

Playing for the Brink

"I advise, I think, I believe, that we must and can reach Quneitra and Butmiya," Elazar stated. "There will be no Syrian counter-attack. Syrian forces are about to collapse."

The time was 10 A.M. and the Northern Command chief was addressing an ad hoc meeting of Eshkol, Dayan, Weizman, and Haim Bar-Lev. Over the previous hour, Israel Radio's Arabic channel had been re-broadcasting Syria's claim of the fall of Quneitra—a claim the Israelis knew to be false but one that they hoped would expedite the enemy's collapse. Now, in view of the Syrian retreat, the question was: would Israel have the time to exploit it.

"We must finish quickly. We're under heavy pressure from the UN," Eshkol stressed. The prime minister was also resisting demands from Cabinet ministers whose opposition to the offensive had stiffened with the strain in Israel's relations with the United States, and the rupture of those with Moscow.

"When can you complete the job?" Dayan wanted to know.

Dado assured them that Israeli forces would reach their objectives along a line stretching from Majdal Shams in the far north, though Quneitra, to Butmiya by four o'clock that afternoon.

Eshkol cut in: "If you say four, it could be five or six."

"Sir," the general smiled. "If I say four, I mean two or three."

Deputy Operations Chief Ze'evi was seated next to Eshkol, together with Allon and Moshe Carmel, and listening in on the conversation. "My job was to keep squeezing Eshkol for another hour and then another hour of fighting," Ze'evi later revealed. "The job wasn't easy; the pressures on him from Washington and New York were enormous. And Dayan didn't like the extensions either."

In the end, the defense minister agreed to give the army four additional hours, but not a minute more. At that time he would meet with Gen. Bull and confirm Israel's acceptance of the cease-fire. "Don't even ask for air cover after two o'clock," he concluded.[10]

Israel's decision to prolong the fight coincided with Syria's determination to put up a stronger one. Bolstered by the Security Council's sudden willingness to confront the Israelis and by Russian threats to intervene, Damascus tried to rescind its proclamation of Quneitra's capture. "Our brave forces are still fighting in Quneitra," al-Assad broadcast to Syrian listeners at 11:45 A.M. "Our brave soldiers will not let the enemy conquer the city. Great numbers of enemy tanks have been destroyed." A commentator added: "Our victory in Quneitra today means victory in Tel Aviv tomorrow."

The announcement came too late, however. The Syrian army was in full flight, abandoning its heavy equipment, jamming the roads. Soviet advisers exhorted the troops to remain in their posts, and orders were issued to shoot deserters on sight. All such efforts proved futile, however; the Soviets were ignored while the commanders charged with executing deserters had themselves abandoned the field. Believing that the entire Golan had already fallen, driven by rumors of Israelis wielding nuclear weapons, some 4,000 Syrian soldiers sought refuge in Jordan, and 3,000 in Lebanon.

"We were totally cut off, without radio contact and under heavy bombardment," claimed Marwan Hamdan al-Khuli, an ordnance officer. His platoon had dug in near the Bnot Ya'akov Bridge, untouched by Israeli bombardments, waiting for orders to invade Galilee. "Finally the word came to retreat [but] without knowing why. All we learned we heard on the radio, and from that we began to guess that we'd lost the war." Capt. Muhammad 'Ammar, who had survived the battles around Tel Fakhr, recalled the state of confusion: "The forces that were supposed to block the enemy's advance pulled out without authorization, without coordination. We knew nothing, and had no choice but to fall back. In my platoon alone we had ten killed and four wounded. We had no ammunition and no way of getting more." 8th Brigade commander Ibrahim Isma'il Khahya spoke candidly of his humiliation:

> We received orders to block the roads leading to Quneitra. But then the fall
> of the city was announced and that caused many of my soldiers to leave the
> front and run back to Syria while those roads were still open. They piled onto
> vehicles. It further crushed our morale. I retreated before I ever saw an en-
> emy soldier.

Compounding the confusion was the exodus of 95,000 Syrian civilians from the Golan. "On June 5, we received the order to evacuate," recalled 'Ali al-Darwish, a farmer from the village of al-'Uyun, and a National Guard volunteer. "There was an [Syrian] artillery battalion nearby, and there was a danger that Israeli shells fired at it might hit the villagers. We took nothing with us, only blankets for the children. We hid in caves for five days until the order came to pull out entirely, and we fled on foot to Jordan." 'Abdallah Mar'i Hasan, a Palestinian working for the Syrian administration, insisted on remaining in Quneitra until the morning of June 10. "Only then, when I realized that everyone else had abandoned the city, did I leave, too. I had nothing but the clothes on my back." The Druze and the Circassian communities, whose kinsmen in Israel served loyally in the IDF, alone remained to greet the conquerors.

Most of the refugees converged on Damascus, and yet not even the capital seemed safe from the Israeli onslaught. "The Jews are . . . closing in on Damascus," Chief of Staff Suweidani warned Syria's political leaders; "nobody can stop them. Israel enjoys the support of the Americans and the British and can afford to spurn the UN. We must prepare to defend the capital and to the last drop of blood." And yet the first to flee the city was the general staff, described by one American diplomatic source as "at least cowardly, at most treasonous," followed by government ministers, who rushed to Aleppo with stocks of hoarded gold. "We never had the honor of fighting the Zionist enemy," admitted Mustafa Tlas, who had spent much of the day dodging Israeli jets as he retreated. Though jeeps with bullhorns sped around urging the people to stand and fight, the defense of Damascus was left to a single brigade—the 70th, known for its loyalty to the regime [11]

Following full-tilt on the Syrians' heels, the Israelis descended on Quneitra from three directions—from Mas'ade and Buq'ata in the north, east from Qala', and northeast from Tel Abu Nida'. Other units headed south to Khushniya and north into the foothills abutting the Lebanese border. At the southern tip of the Sea of Galilee, a concentrated artillery barrage on Tawafiq at 1:00 P.M. preceded a paratrooper assault to take the fortress. Thereafter, gambling on the possibility that few, if any, Syrian troops remained in the field, 800 paratroopers were flown by helicopter first to Kafr Harb, then to el-'Al, and finally to Butmiya. So quick was this leapfrogging that commanders often had no idea where they were, only that they had to keep advancing before the cease-fire took effect. The Syrians retreated even more swiftly; most of their positions were deserted.

Yet progress remained relatively slow. The two o'clock deadline was approaching, and even the lead Israeli elements had yet to reach their objectives. Many, believing a cease-fire was imminent, saw no reason to rush. Driving past Nafakh, Yigal Allon halted his jeep and asked one loitering officer—Ron Sariq, a reconnaissance company commander—what he and his men were doing.

"Waiting for orders," came Sariq's reply.

"Don't just stand there, run! Now!" shouted Allon. "Quickly take Quneitra!"[12]

Quneitra was taken at 12:30 P.M. Mendler deferred to a request from Bar-Lev and allowed the Golani Brigade, in honor of its nineteen-year defense of the northern border, to enter the city first. What they found were entire neighborhoods almost completely deserted, their stores and markets full, lunches still hot on the tables. "We could have continued on to Damascus," recalled Col. Benny Inbar, commander of Golani's 51st Battalion. "The road was totally open before us. They [the Syrians] had fled."

Meeting in the Syrian Officers' Club, Elazar urged Rabin to authorize an armored thrust deep into Syria. A 1964 IDF contingency plan, Hatchet (*Garzen*), called for two divisions to conquer the enemy's capital within eighty hours. But Rabin rejected the idea, insisting that there be no more seizure of Syrian territory. The sole exception was Mount Hermon, described by Motti Hod, who was also present at the meeting, as "the eyes of the nation." Part of its summit would be captured as soon as possible and transformed into Israel's highest observation post, with a view of downtown Damascus.[13]

Absent from this crucial consultation was Moshe Dayan. The defense minister was preparing for his rendezvous with Odd Bull. In a rather crude maneuver to gain time, Dayan had arranged for the meeting to be held in Tiberias. But when the chief UN observer arrived there, he found that the venue had been moved to Tel Aviv. The two met, finally, at 3:00 P.M., an hour later than scheduled.

Bull opened by stressing the need to break the cycle in which Israeli forces advanced and the Syrians defended themselves, thus providing the Israelis with a pretext for advancing further. The logic found no sympathy with Dayan, however. The Syrians were still shelling Israeli settlements, he reported; if they stopped, the IDF offensive would halt immediately. "We are not after mileage," he said. Dayan described the cease-fire as absolute—"we are not negotiating and we will agree to no conditions"—but then added major conditions of his own. Israel would accept no excuses for violations, for example, that some Syrian units had yet to receive the order. Moreover, the wording of the cease-fire accord could in no way evoke the General Armistice Agreements of 1949. No UN observers would be allowed near the cease-fire line; Bull would simply have to accept Israel's word that the fighting had indeed halted.[14]

The cease-fire was to go into effect at 6:00 P.M. "Nobody's to say their radio's not working," Dayan instructed Elazar. He ordered Weizman and Ze'evi to draw up a map of Israel's new borders with Syria, scolding them, "and control yourselves!" The Northern Command nevertheless ignored Jerusalem's directives and stretched the deadline by another few hours in order to improve Israel's defensive position. Every unit, every soldier, was pressed into taking strategically valuable hilltops and road junctions. Intelligence officer Ahuvia Tabenkin stuck helmets on his cooks and supply clerks and sent them to sit atop the al-Ruqada cliffs, north of Khushniya. Helicopters continued to ferry troops into the hinterland northeast of Butmiya.

Not all these operations went unopposed, as scattered resistance occasionally reappeared. At one point, the helicopter carrying Elazar was pursued by a Syrian MiG, and was forced to dive sharply through a ravine. The helicopter landed safely, however, at Kibbutz Ein Gev on the southern shore of the Sea of Galilee. Dozens of kibbutz members ran out to greet the general. "That reunion between Dado and the members of Ein Gev was absolutely unforgettable," recalled Yitzhak Hofi, chief of the operations staff, who, along with Bar-Lev, had also been aboard. "Men, women, children, crying, laughing, falling all over him, hugging and kissing him. It must have been their exhilaration over what had happened, relief that the nightmare was now over."[15]

News of Dayan's meeting with Bull, followed by the advent of the cease-fire, defused the volatile situation in the UN. "Israelis played for a time in political maneuvers in the Security Council to a hair-raising proximity to the brink," noted Barbour, and that brinkmanship had clearly paid off. Though Federenko continued to rant against Anglo-American and Israeli imperialism, no resolution was passed condemning Israel. Nor was there a reaction, Arab or Soviet, the following day when Col. Pinchas Noi of the 13th Golani Battalion and his radio operator flew by helicopter to Mount Hermon and planted Israel's flag on the peak.

The focus at the UN was no longer the military situation on the ground but the postwar settlement. Goldberg went from delegation to delegation canvassing their attitudes toward Arab-Israeli negotiations. These, he assumed, would be face-to-face and direct with an option for UN mediation, and result in initial agreements on forces separation and freedom of passage through the Straits. With prophetic understatement, he wrote, "The issue of a simple withdrawal as opposed to withdrawal as part of an overall settlement will be the main and somewhat tricky problem as soon as [the] cease-fire firms up."

World leaders, too, were already looking beyond the battlefield to the subsequent, diplomatic phase. The contentiousness of that stage was evident in Kosygin's subsequent hot line message: "If today all military actions are concluded, it will be necessary to proceed to the next step of evacuating the territory occupied by Israel and the return of troops behind the armistice line." The Soviet leader nevertheless ended on a positive note—"I consider that we should maintain contact with you on this matter"—holding out the possibility for future superpower cooperation. Johnson, for his part, was thinking not only of troop disposition and withdrawal, but also the fundamental question of ending the Arab-Israeli conflict—of changing its context. "It now appears that military action in the Middle East is being concluded," he replied to Kosygin. "I hope our efforts in the days ahead can be devoted to the achievement of a lasting peace throughout the world."[16]

AFTERSHOCKS

Tallies, Postmortems, and the
Old/New Middle East

ONE HUNDRED AND THIRTY-TWO HOURS: That was the duration of the war, one of the shortest in recorded history. In that brief period, the Egyptians lost between 10,000 and 15,000 men, among them 1,500 officers and forty pilots; thousands more were wounded. An additional 5,000 Egyptians were listed as missing. Seven hundred Jordanian soldiers had died, and over 6,000 were wounded or missing. Syria's losses were estimated at 450 dead and roughly four times that number wounded. Israel admitted to 679 dead and 2,563 wounded, though IDF fatality figures were later placed as high as 800—the equivalent, in per capita terms, of 80,000 Americans.[1]

The glaring disparity of the casualty rates—approximately 25 to 1 in Israel's favor—proved even more lopsided in the numbers of prisoners of war. Israel held at least 5,000 Egyptians, including 21 generals, 365 Syrians (of whom only 30 were officers), and 550 Jordanians. Two Soviet advisers also fell prisoner, the IDF claimed. Israeli POW's totaled 15. Though accusations of beatings and even executions were traded by both sides, prisoners were generally well treated. Their exchange, however, dragged on for months. Israel held out for the release of Egyptian Jews imprisoned on spying charges since 1954, and for the remains of several executed agents, among them Eli Cohen. Egypt and Syria were reluctant to repatriate their embittered prisoners, and refused to negotiate directly with Israel.[2]

The widest gap of all, however, was not in human but in material terms. All but 15 percent of Egypt's military hardware, $2 billion worth, was destroyed, and vast stores—320 tanks, 480 guns, 2 SAM missile batteries, and 10,000 vehicles—

became Israeli booty. The Jordanian list was also painfully long: 179 tanks, 53 APC's, 1,062 guns, 3,166 vehicles, nearly 20,000 assorted arms. Of the Arab forces, the Syrians emerged from the war the least impaired, losing 470 guns, 118 tanks, and 1,200 vehicles; another forty tanks were abandoned to the Israelis. In all, the IAF destroyed 469 enemy planes, fifty of them in dogfights, in 3,279 sorties. The figures included 85 percent of Egypt's combat aircraft and all of its bombers. "Never in the history of military aviation has the exercise of air power played so speedy and decisive a part in modern warfare," observed R. Goring-Morris, Britain's air attaché in Tel Aviv, but that part came at a price. Thirty-six planes and eighteen pilots, roughly 20 percent of Israel's air power, had been lost. And while the Soviet Union swiftly replenished Egypt's and Syria's MiG's, Israel's orders for French Mirages and American Skyhawks remained suspended.

Though military casualty rates were, even by contemporary standards, high, those among civilians were remarkably low. Apart from the bombardment of Jerusalem, Israeli border settlements, and Palestinian neighborhoods in Gaza and the West Bank, much of the fighting took place far from major population centers. Nevertheless, large numbers of noncombatants suffered and suffered acutely. Between 175,000 (Israeli estimates) and 250,000 (Jordanian estimates) Palestinians fled the West Bank for Jordan, many of them second-time refugees who were once again billeted in wretched camps. While Israel did little to precipitate this flight, neither did it do anything to stop it or, indeed, to encourage the refugees to return. Rather, initially, the IDF laid ambushes along the banks of the Jordan River to prevent "infiltrators" from crossing back into the West Bank. The ambushes were removed only after Dayan, observing them a week after the war, deemed them inhumane.

Similarly, on the Golan, the exodus of the civilian population was neither impelled nor inhibited by Israel. Though IDF war plans had made no provision for Syrian civilians, the general staff did issue a specific order (No. 121330) stating: "There is to be no expulsion of villagers from the Syrian Heights or from occupied territories in Syria." Damascus later claimed that the villagers had been expelled en masse, but in fact few Israelis even came into contact with civilians, most of whom had fled with the Syrian command, well in advance of the attackers.

After the cease-fire, Israel insisted that the 1967 refugee problem, like that of 1948 before it, would have to be solved within the framework of a comprehensive peace treaty. The Arab states uniformly rejected this demand, and insisted on unconditional repatriation and compensation for the refugees. When, later that summer, Israel was pressed to permit at least some of the Palestinians back into the West Bank, few in fact availed themselves of the offer.[3]

The refugees' plight, however tragic, was soon overshadowed by the persecution of Jews in Arab countries. With news of Israel's victory, mobs attacked Jewish neighborhoods in Egypt, Yemen, Lebanon, Tunisia, and

Morocco, burning synagogues and assaulting residents. A pogrom in Tripoli, Libya, left 18 Jews dead and 25 injured; the survivors were herded into detention centers. Of Egypt's 4,000 Jews, 800 were arrested, including the chief rabbis of both Cairo and Alexandria, and their property sequestered by the government. The ancient communities of Damascus and Baghdad were placed under house arrest, their leaders imprisoned and fined. A total of 7,000 Jews were expelled, many with merely a satchel.[4] Apart from Tunisia's Bourgiba and King Hassan of Morocco, no Arab statesman condemned these outrages. Attempts by both the UN and the Red Cross to intercede on the Jews' behalf were rebuffed.

By comparison, the 1.2 million Palestinians now under Israeli rule were spared systematic persecution. While looting was widespread and acts of vandalism recorded—nearly half the houses in Qalqilya were reportedly damaged, though later repaired by Israel—a military administration was rapidly established for the West Bank and Gaza and a combination of Jordanian and martial law imposed. Palestinian community and religious leaders were, for the most part, retained in their prewar positions, including the Muslim *waqf* atop the Temple Mount—a decision for which Moshe Dayan was criticized by Israeli hawks. Israel nevertheless deviated from its tolerant policy in the Old City of Jerusalem, where hovels of the Mughrabi neighborhood were cleared away to create a prayer plaza in front of the Western Wall. The most controversial decision, however, was the destruction of three villages—Yalu, Beit Nuba, and Imwas—located at a strategic junction in the Latrun Corridor. The Israelis accused the three of abetting the siege of Jerusalem in 1948 and billeting Egyptian commandos in their recent attack on Lod, but even then several troops refused to carry out the demolition order. Ultimately, it was executed, and the Arab inhabitants, though offered compensation, were not allowed to return.

No further acts of retribution were taken against Arabs who, only days before, had celebrated Israel's demise. The revelation that Jordan had destroyed the Old City synagogues and had paved roads and even latrines with Jewish tombstones from the Mount of Olives did not dissuade Dayan from joining 4,000 Muslim worshipers for Friday prayers at the al-Aqsa Mosque.[5]

Casualties, prisoners, refugees—all were ultimately dwarfed by the war's most tectonic outcome. Israel had conquered 42,000 square miles and was now three and a half times its original size. Exceedingly vulnerable before the war, its major cities all within range of Arab guns, the Jewish state now threatened Damascus, Cairo, and Amman. Its own capital, Jerusalem, was united. Though ties had been severed with the Soviet Union and permanent strains left in its relations with France— and in spite of the *Liberty* incident—Israel had earned the solid respect of the United States. "The spirit of the army, indeed of all the people, has to be experienced to be believed," Harry McPherson reported to his president, relating how he had seen a jeep with two Israeli women soldiers, "one with a purple spangled bathing cap on her head, the other with an orange

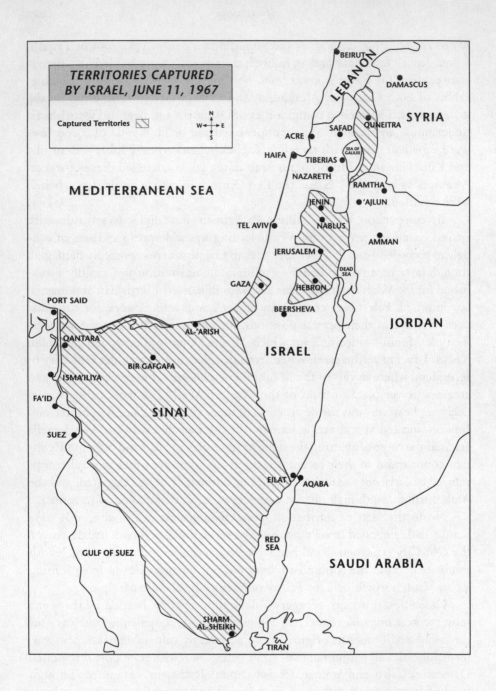

TERRITORIES CAPTURED BY ISRAEL, JUNE 11, 1967

Captured Territories

N
W — E
S

BEIRUT

DAMASCUS

LEBANON

SYRIA

ACRE

SAFAD

QUNEITRA

HAIFA

TIBERIAS

SEA OF GALILEE

NAZARETH

RAMTHA

'AJLUN

JENIN

NABLUS

TEL AVIV

AMMAN

MEDITERRANEAN SEA

JERUSALEM

DEAD SEA

GAZA

HEBRON

BEERSHEVA

JORDAN

PORT SAID

AL-'ARISH

QANTARA

ISRAEL

BIR GAFGAFA

ISMA'ILIYA

FA'ID

SINAI

SUEZ

EILAT

AQABA

RED SEA

SAUDI ARABIA

GULF OF SUEZ

SHARM AL-SHEIKH

TIRAN

turban," riding in the Negev. "After the doubts, confusions, and ambiguities of Vietnam, it was deeply moving to see people whose commitment is total and unquestioning."

Moribund before the war, Israel's economy suddenly flourished as tourists and donations flooded the country, and oil was extracted from Sinai wells. Emigration all but ceased, and thousands of new immigrants hastened to partake of the glory.

Israel indeed basked in that glory as its press for weeks afterward praised the army's audacity, its ingenuity and power. *Ha'aretz* informed its readers of the minting of a new victory coin, and supplied a recipe for "victory cakes" to be baked for homecoming soldiers. "From the podium of the UN, I proclaimed the glorious triumph of the IDF and the redemption of Jerusalem," Abba Eban told a riveted audience in Lod. "Never before has Israel stood more honored and revered by the nations of the world." Less decorously, Haim Bar-Lev told the Cabinet, "We have screwed every Arab country." Always popular, Dayan and Rabin were now elevated to icon-status, and not only among Israelis but throughout the Diaspora where the war had enabled Jews "to walk with their backs straight." To the chief of staff was given the exceptional honor of actually naming the war. Among the titles proposed—The War of Daring, the War of Salvation, the War of the Sons of Light—Rabin chose the least ostentatious, the Six-Day War, evoking the days of creation.

For a moment, the apocalyptic aspect of the Israeli self-view appeared to have been eclipsed by that of the indomitable, the invincible Israeli—but only for a moment. Michael Hadow, the British ambassador, noting the absence of mass celebrations, found "something very inspiring and yet rather terrifying" about the dispassionate way the Israelis went to war, won, and returned home to business as usual. The discomfort many Israelis felt with their victory, the guilt and pain of their losses, poured out in a postwar collection of interviews with kibbutz members, entitled fittingly, *The Seventh Day*. "We weren't especially excited or happy about killing Arabs or knowing that we'd won," recalled Shai, a twenty-seven-year-old member of Kibbutz Afikim, who had led paratroopers at Umm Qatef. "We just felt that we'd done what we had to do. But there's a big difference between that and feeling happy." Similarly, Gal, from Givat Haim, a tank gunner, said, "What have I got against an Arab? Even if I can see that he's got a gun? You shoot at him, you know he's a man, that he's got a family . . . It all goes fine right up to the moment you see someone dead. That's when we began to curse the war." The diary of Rivka Niedt, of Kibbutz Usha, records her feelings upon arriving at al-'Arish: "There's a heavy, thick blackness outside, and an awful noise . . . shots, screams, and short frightening booms . . . Your throat chokes, your eyes cloud over and you run outside . . . but the wind . . . only brings in great gusts of stench from the dead and the clouds of black flies."

Following "Jerusalem of Gold," the most popular Hebrew song to emerge in the years after the war was "The Song of Peace," a threnody of the recently dead:

No one can bring us back
From the dark depths of our grave
Here the thrill of victory means nothing
Nor do songs of praise
Therefore, sing a song for peace
Do not merely whisper a prayer
Better to sing a song for peace
Shouting it loudly.[6]

For Arabs, though, there could be no such ambivalence toward the war. Even the "Six-Day" epithet, with its image of lightning conquests, proved odious to them, and they resorted to more reticent titles—The Setback, The Disaster, or the anodyne June War. No sooner had the shooting stopped than the Arab world embarked on what one Middle East historian called "an audit during a moment of great stress and clarity," examining how "a small state had displayed their historical inadequacy, had seized massive chunks of land, and had devastated the armies whose weapons and machismo had been displayed with great pride for the last decade or so." Intellectuals would evince intense disillusionment with Arab nationalism—as a mass movement, it would never revive—and stress the need for modernization and democracy. Others would advocate an even more militant radicalism on the Vietnamese or Cuban model, or a return to the rigorous fundamentals of Islam. Painful examinations would be made of Arab society, its inherent propensities and weaknesses, and of the Arab personality and psyche.

Arab politicians, on the other hand, persisted in avoiding any responsibility for the defeat, much less engage in introspection. Nasser continued to blame the insubordinate Egyptian officers and the Anglo-American cabal for Egypt's defeat in what he curiously called "Bunche's war." King Hussein waxed fatalistic, telling his people that "I seem to belong to a family which . . . must suffer and make sacrifices for its country without end . . . If you were not rewarded with glory it was not because you lacked courage, but because it is Allah's will." The deepest denial came from Syrian leaders, criticized throughout the Arab world for having done so much to start the war and then so little to fight it. "The Israelis' objective was not to conquer a few miles from Syria but to topple its progressive government," explained Gen. Suweidani. "This they did not accomplish. Therefore we must view ourselves as the victors of this war." The point was refined by Foreign Minister Makhous: "Were Damascus or Aleppo to fall, they could be rebuilt. But there could be no compensation for the loss of the Ba'th, for it is the hope of the Arab nation." Hafez al-Assad declared that "Syria, alone, fought for six days, without letup, with all our might." When one junior officer demanded an investigation of the debacle, Assad reportedly had him shot.[7]

Not until after the 1973 war, with their army's honor restored, did Egyptians begin to speak out about the causes of 1967. Thus, Salah al-Hadidi, chief justice in the trials of officers held accountable for the defeat, wrote that, "I can state that Egypt's political leadership called Israel to war. It clearly provoked

Israel and forced it into a confrontation." Gen. Fawzi singled out "the individu-
alist bureaucratic leadership" and "'Amer's collapse," while Muhammad Sadiq
spoke of "promotions on the basis of loyalty, not expertise, and the army's fear of
telling Nasser the truth." Murtagi credited the Israelis with having better weapons, command, and organization; they seemed to have a stronger will to fight.
Sidqi Mahmud pointed his finger at the hasty decision to oust UNEF, to occupy
Sharm al-Sheikh, and to weather Israel's first strike. "We were totally dependent
on Russian equipment," he testified. "The field marshal was not committed to
the army's affairs." Lack of intelligence was the problem, according to Zakkariya
Muhieddin: "While the Israelis knew the name of every Egyptian on relief, and
his wife's name too, we didn't even know where Moshe Dayan's house was." 'Ali
Sabri faulted the army's refusal to investigate its failures in the Suez and Yemen
wars, and to oust the officers responsible. Shams Badran blamed Nasser: "He
took the decisions that placed the army in a trap. Without consulting with anyone, he led us into the ambush that Israel had laid with American help."[8]

How had it happened? No shortage of pundits rushed to answer that question,
noting the Israelis' superior training and motivation, the Arabs' lack of operational unity and inability to understand their foe. Hadow stressed the personal
element, the stark disparity between the Israeli and the Arab soldier:

> These were not elite professional troops lavishly equipped with the most mod-
> ern equipment, but for the most part civilian reservists, with comparatively
> limited training behind them, who were carried into battle in civilian trans-
> port, and were supplied and supported by essentially civilian services. By com-
> parison, the professional Arab armies showed a total lack of appreciation of
> the essential elements of modern warfare, and an almost equal inability to use
> the sophisticated weapons and equipment provided by their Russian quarter-
> masters. Their leadership on almost all fronts was inept to a degree which
> hardly seems possible after 10 years of preparation and training for a war
> which was to bring about Israel's annihilation.

Moshe Dayan proved less complimentary. His final report to the general
staff criticized Israel's misreading of Nasser's intentions, its overdependence on
the United States and hesitation to act the minute Egypt closed the Straits. Yet
Israel had "ended the Six-Day War with maximum lines on all fronts," in spite of
these shortcomings, he wrote. The reason was that Egypt had failed to appreciate
the advantages of launching a first strike, had failed to gauge the enemy's power
and his willingness to use it. Lulled into arrogance by these errors, the Israelis
would repeat them six years later, in their next major war with the Arabs.[9]

Such analyses perhaps explained how Israel won the war; they could not
account for its outcome. Beyond the goals of eliminating the Egyptian threat and
destroying Nasser's army, no other stage of the conflict was planned or even
contemplated, not the seizure of the entire Sinai Peninsula, not the conquest of
the West Bank, nor the scaling of the Golan Heights. Even the "liberation" of

Jerusalem, as Israelis call it, regarding the event as the most significant of the war and assigning it almost messianic ramifications, came about largely through chance. The vagaries and momentum of war, far more than rational decision making, had shaped the fighting's results. Had Egypt accepted the cease-fire after the first day's fighting, had the Jordanians refrained from seizing Government Hill or had Dayan stuck to his opposition to conquering the Golan (to cite only a few "if"s), the region would have looked much different. Its subsequent history—the upheavals and the breakthroughs, the grueling search for peace—would probably have evolved differently as well.

A similar capriciousness characterized the process leading to the outbreak of the war. This book opened with the well-known image of the butterfly, which, with a mere flap of its wings, triggers a thunderstorm. Starting in November 1966, the Middle East would witness many such "flaps." Take, for example, Ambassador Barbour's tardiness in conveying King Hussein's condolence letter to Eshkol, and the subsequent Samu' raid in which Jordanian and Israeli soldiers inadvertently clashed. There was Jordan's attempt to save face from that defeat by accusing Egypt of "hiding behind UNEF's skirts," and Egypt's resultant interest in ousting the force. Nasser's complex relationship with 'Amer, the political machinations that weakened Eshkol and brought Dayan to the Defense Ministry, elements of honor and chauvinism and fear—each would influence events in profound and unanticipated ways. The last-minute cancellation of Operation Dawn—Egypt's one chance to do to Israel what Israel would soon do to Egypt—poignantly illustrated the process's randomness.

Yet even that chaos had its context. Only within the unique milieu of the Arab-Israeli conflict could elements as diverse as Syrian radicalism and Israeli politicking, inter-Arab rivalry and America's preoccupation with Vietnam, Soviet fears and Egyptian aspirations, combine in a chain reaction culminating in war. And once the war started, that same context allowed for a succession of unexpected events, from the retreat of Arab armies to Israel's attack on the *Liberty*, from the Security Council's paralysis to the Soviets' failure to intervene.

The context facilitated the war, but had the war, in turn, transformed the context? Did it leave the region more or less unchanged, or did it establish an entirely new set of rules and rulers? Were those six explosive days really an act of creation, producing a modern Middle East fundamentally distinct from the old one?

"A Peace of Honor Between Equals"

There had not been just one but several ceremonies held in the newly rededicated Hebrew University amphitheater atop Mount Scopus. Leonard Bernstein had conducted Mahler's 2nd Symphony—the "Resurrection"—and the Mendelssohn Violin Concerto, with solo performances by virtuoso Isaac Stern.

"Jerusalem of Gold" was repeatedly rendered. Now, on June 29, overlooking the Judean desert and the Dead Sea coast so recently occupied by Israeli forces, Yltzhak Rabin received an honorary Doctorate of Philosophy.

Accepting the degree in the name of the entire IDF, Rabin contrasted the exaltation of the home front with the somberness of frontline soldiers "who had seen not only the glories of victory but also its price—the friends who fell next to them, covered in blood." Those soldiers, "aware of the righteousness of our cause, of their deep love of the homeland, and the difficult tasks imposed on them," had demonstrated their moral, spiritual, and psychological worth under the hardest conditions. Many had given their lives to preserve what Rabin called "the right of the people of Israel to live in its own State—free, independent, in peace and tranquillity."

Peace and tranquillity would become a lifelong and elusive goal for Rabin. While political rivals would continue to criticize his performance before and during the war—his breakdown, his inability to stand up to Dayan—the public generally credited him with victory. Riding on that crest, he would soon leave the army and serve successfully as Israel's ambassador in Washington and then, with less aplomb, as Israel's prime minister (1974–77) in the dreary aftermath of the Yom Kippur War. His greatest achievement was to conclude a separation-of-forces agreement in Sinai and so lay the foundation for Israel's subsequent peace treaty with Egypt.

Rabin returned to the prime minister's office in 1992, and embarked on a strategy no less risky than the Six-Day War, seeking a historic reconciliation with the Palestinian people under the leadership of Yasser Arafat—the same Arafat whose guerrilla attacks had helped precipitate the war. The process launched by Rabin and Arafat would earn them each a Nobel Prize (Shimon Peres, Israel's foreign minister, received one as well), but also the enmity of Israelis and Arabs who opposed the process. Palestinian terrorists killed dozens of Israeli civilians and Israeli extremists branded Rabin a traitor. On November 4, 1995, one of those extremists shot and killed the prime minister. Rabin had been addressing a Tel Aviv peace rally. Found in his pocket were the blood-stained lyrics to "The Song of Peace."

The 1967 war, Rabin concluded, had changed the context of the Arab-Israeli conflict, not by making Israel any less repugnant to the Arabs, but by convincing them that it could never be eliminated by force of arms. Many Israeli leaders shared his conviction, and some went even further, believing that for the first time peace was attainable, if purchased with Arab territories.

Ten days before the Mount Scopus ceremony, on June 19, the Cabinet had secretly decided to exchange Sinai and the Golan Heights—some areas would be demilitarized, and free passage through Tiran guaranteed—for peace treaties with Egypt and Syria. Of the territory seized from Egypt, only the Gaza Strip would be incorporated into Israel, and its refugees resettled as part of a regional plan. Fiercely debated, the motion passed by a single vote. But no decision could be reached regarding the future of the West Bank, where many ministers still hoped to create an autonomous Palestinian entity. A consensus was achieved only on Jerusalem, which was to remain Israel's united and sovereign capital.

Prominent among the supporters of the June 19 decision was Abba Eban. He, too, was present at Mount Scopus that day, notwithstanding his reservations about Rabin. The previous week, he had advised his ambassadors: "There is a new reality and it points at talks on peace and security. Those aspects, it must be emphasized, have a territorial dimension. The world and the Arab world must know that there's no turning back the clock to 1957 or 1948." At the same time, he indicated that "everything is fluid, flexible, and open." Eban would adhere to those principles throughout his tenure as foreign minister, until 1974. Originally opposed to creating a Palestinian state in the West Bank and Gaza, he later embraced the idea, warning that the annexation of nearly two million Palestinians would undermine Israel's Jewish majority. Ultimately, Eban would be reconciled with Rabin and with the Israeli public that had so often scoffed at him. Awarded the Israel Prize for Life Achievement in 2001, Abba Eban died the following year, at age eighty-seven.[10]

After the 1967 war, Eban described himself as one of the "politicians" in Israel's leadership who was willing to take advantage of the altered context on the chance that the Arabs would trade territory for peace. Like-minded ministers such as Zalman Aran and Haim Moshe Shapira expressed their willingness to return virtually all the captured land, except Jerusalem, and received support from an unlikely quarter: David Ben-Gurion. Never again to play a significant role in Israeli politics, permanently consigned to his bungalow in Sde Boker, the once-feared martinet cautioned against the demographic dangers of annexation until his death in December 1973, in the shadows of the Yom Kippur War.

But while some decision makers favored far-reaching concessions, others— "security men," Eban dubbed them—doubted the Arabs' readiness to negotiate and, for strategic and ideological reasons, insisted on keeping most of the territories. In the Cabinet, they were led, as previously, by Yigal Allon. The labor minister—later foreign minister—voted against the Cabinet's June 19 resolution, and lobbied for the creation of Israeli settlements in the West Bank. These would form a new defense line down the Jordan Valley, around Jerusalem and southward to the Hebron Hills, delineating "an agreed, independent Arab State, surrounded by Israeli territory." Though Allon would die, aged sixty-two, in 1980, the "Allon Plan" would remain Israel's unofficial policy until the advent of Rabin's negotiations with Arafat.

Also opposed to the June 19 decision was Menachem Begin, whose Gahal (later Likud) party rejected the very notion of territorial concessions. "In my opinion, the concept of autonomy [in the West Bank] will lead to a Palestinian State," he told the Cabinet. The Jewish component of Israeli identity had been stimulated by the conquest of the Biblical homeland—Bethlehem, Jericho, Hebron—and Begin, always attuned to that strain, envisioned creating a Greater

Israel. Ten years later, though, as prime minister, Begin would welcome Anwar Sadat, Nasser's successor, to Israel, and thereafter agreed to return all of Sinai to Egypt and to institute Palestinian autonomy in the West Bank and Gaza. He would resign, his spirit sapped by another Arab-Israeli war—in Lebanon—and die a recluse in 1992.

Seated beside Allon and Begin in the Hebrew University amphitheater were members of the IDF general staff. Among them were those more sympathetic to the "politicians'" stance, generals such as Uzi Narkiss and Yeshayahu Gavish, both of whom went on to become active in public affairs, and Israel Tal, later known as the father of Israel's own battle tank, the *Merkava* (Chariot). None, however, would have the impact on Israeli policy made by the military leaders associated with the "security" school.

David Elazar, for example, was adamant about retaining the Golan Heights he had lobbied so hard to capture. When, shortly after the 1967 war, Palestinian guerrilla attacks resumed from Lebanon and northern Jordan, Dado swore to "make life unbearable" for those countries. "IDF actions are more conducive to quiet than extended constraint is," he said. Forbidden by the government of Golda Meir from launching a preemptive strike on the massing Egyptian and Syrian forces in 1973, Elazar, as chief of staff, was blamed for Israel's early setbacks in that war and ordered to resign. Literally brokenhearted, he died two years later.

Another outspoken opponent of territorial concessions was Ezer Weizman. Leaving the army for politics, he naturally gravitated to Begin's government, in which he served as defense minister. Yet, like Begin, Weizman agreed to Israel's total withdrawal from Sinai. He later switched allegiance to the Labor party and refashioned himself a champion of peace. Elected as Israel's honorific president in 1993, he held the post for seven years, before resigning amid financial scandals.

Finally, there was Ariel Sharon, later to gain fame for his performance in the 1973 war and notoriety as the defense minister who promoted Israel's 1982 invasion of Lebanon. Held indirectly responsible for the massacre of Palestinian refugees by Israel's Lebanese allies the following year, he resigned his post but remained a rigorous foe of forfeiting land, even in return for peace. Yet the same Sharon who promoted the construction of dozens of new settlements in the West Bank and Gaza also uprooted Israeli settlements in Sinai, prior to returning it to Egypt. In 2001, after his election as prime minister, Sharon formed a national unity government with Shimon Peres and other Laborites committed to the near-total withdrawal from the territories.[11]

Israelis were divided over the degree to which the context had changed, whether peace was possible or whether another war lay ahead. In the course of the following decades, many would vacillate between one conclusion and the other. But of all the leaders gathered on Mount Scopus that day in 1967, only one, Moshe Dayan, succeeded in espousing both ideas simultaneously.

"I'm waiting for the phone to ring," Dayan was widely quoted as saying, implying that Israel would be willing to return territories if the Arabs came forward for talks. But in the Cabinet debate on the June 19 resolution, Dayan argued that there was no use discussing the terms for peace since the Arabs would never accept Israel. He protested the decision, saying, "We cannot withdraw from Sinai and the Golan on the basis of a single vote!" Dayan promoted Jewish settlement of the West Bank, but was not averse to establishing a Palestinian state there or to preserving Jordan's status as protector of its Muslim shrines. In Sinai, he opposed settlement building but pushed for the construction of Yamit, the peninsula's largest Jewish town. He stressed the need for Israel "to sit tight and keep ruling" the territories, but in 1970, proposed an Israeli pullback from the Suez Canal as the first step toward nonbelligerency. Six weeks after the end of the Six-Day War, according to the British embassy's count, Dayan voiced no less than six different opinions on peace.

Unpredictable, enigmatic, Dayan would generate further controversy in the 1973 war when he suffered a breakdown similar to Rabin's in 1967, and was forced by popular pressure from the defense ministry. He returned three years later as Begin's foreign minister, and in that capacity spearheaded the negotiations—at first secret and later, at Camp David, overt—with Sadat. Then, angered by Begin's alleged foot-dragging on the Palestinian issue, he quit the government to form his own party dedicated to unilateral withdrawal from the West Bank. The effort was cut short in 1981, however, by Dayan's death from cancer.[12]

Caught between the "politicians" and the "security men," grappling with the protean positions of Dayan, was Israel's prime minister, Eshkol. He had been overshadowed by the military men and haunted by his alleged indecisiveness in the weeks preceding the war. The man who had stood up to the entire general staff, who had bargained with Johnson and called Kosygin's bluff, whose determination to wait three weeks had won much of world opinion and given his army much-needed time to prepare—that man sat unheralded among the Mount Scopus guests.

Eshkol, too, distinguished between Israel's "security" and "political" interests. The former, he maintained, could be satisfied by creating demilitarized zones and forward IDF posts in sensitive areas of the occupied territories, and the latter, by peace treaties with Egypt and Syria on the basis of the prewar borders. Peace could also be reached with Jordan according to the UN Partition lines, and by compensating and resettling the Palestinian refugees.

The linchpin of Eskhol's plan was the Palestinians' willingness to set up a "protected" and potentially independent regime in the West Bank. But his vision could not be realized. Of the eighty West Bank notables interviewed by Israeli fact-finders that summer, few could agree on the nature of Palestinian self-rule, while Palestinians outside the territories violently opposed the concept. Hussein, fearing the threat the proposed state would pose to his kingdom, worked to undermine Eshkol's efforts, and Nasser rejected any arrangement that failed to restore all the occupied territories, including Jerusalem.[13]

Nonetheless, Eshkol refused to give up. He continued to seek Palestinian partners in the West Bank and Arab leaders willing to negotiate directly. He persisted in the belief, as he told Lyndon Johnson, that "the Six-Day War may have possibly, for the first time, stirred in the Middle East the beginnings of a process leading to peace."

The meeting between the president and the prime minister, their first in four years, took place at Johnson's Texas ranch in January 1968. Eshkol stressed the changes that the war had wrought in the region, and the opportunities it had opened. "Our policy is direct negotiations leading to peace treaties. We take this line not because of any obstinate adhesion to any particular formula, but because we believe that face-to-face contact and reasoning together will create a new psychological reality." He continued to evince the dichotomous self-image of Israeli strength and helplessness, praising the IDF while complaining that "one defeat in the field can be fatal for our survival . . . Israel could be exterminated in one day"—still "Samson the nerd." But, at base, Eshkol remained nothing but magnanimous:

> Mr. President, I have no sense of boastful triumph nor have I entered the struggle for peace in the role of victor. My feeling is one of relief that we were saved from disaster in June and for this I thank God. All my thoughts now are turned toward getting peace with our neighbors—a peace of honor between equals.

Just over a year later, Eshkol was dead, the victim of heart failure brought on—Col. Lior persistently believed—by the stresses of the Six-Day War. Strangely, one of the primary sources of that tension, Moshe Dayan, rushed to the foot of the prime minister's deathbed, cried "Eshkol!" and burst sobbing out of the room. Indeed, all of Israel was stunned. The *Ha'aretz* editors, who had once demanded Eshkol's resignation from the Defense Ministry, praised his "ability to run the state with a staff of refinement rather than the stick of wrath," and his "roots as a Jew, an Israeli, and man experienced in the ways of life far beyond politics." Another daily, *Ma'ariv*, acknowledging his leadership in the 1967 war, speculated that, "perhaps only Eshkol, whose personality combined audacity, obstinacy, and weakness, could have weathered the most serious crisis Israel ever faced."

Reactions in the Arab world were less laudatory, of course. Cairo Radio welcomed the demise of a "leader of the gang that built Israel on the body parts of Arab victims," while an Iraqi spokesman eulogized "the cleverest personality ever to conduct war crimes in our captured land." In a communiqué issued from Damascus, al-Fatah claimed credit for killing Eshkol with a surface-to-surface missile. Arafat declared, "our primary goal now is the liberation of Palestine through armed force, even if the struggle continues for tens of years." [14]

Three No's or Three Yeses?

For all appearances, Arab opinion on Israel had only been hardened by the war. There could still be "no peace with Israel, no survival of the influence of imperialism and no existence in our land of the Zionist state," according to an official

Egyptian broadcast. "The Arab masses will never let any responsible Arab person remain alive who would dare negotiate with Israel." The depth of the animosity, the anger, and the shame was expressed by Hazem Nuseibah, a Princeton graduate, a Palestinian who had once served as Jordan's foreign minister. "If the United States believes that because of the enormity of our catastrophe we will forget Palestine and there will be peace in the Middle East, you are making a major mistake," he told Findley Burns. "There will be no peace in the Middle East."

Arab politics, too, appeared to have emerged from the war every bit as implacable as before. On the day that Israel decided to exchange the Golan Heights for peace, the Syrian regime executed twenty officers for sedition, and offered to collaborate with Baghdad in overthrowing King Hussein. Salim Hatum, the former mutineer still living in Amman, was offered amnesty and lured back to Damascus, where Intelligence Chief Jundi personally tortured and killed him. "Nasser is an arch intriguer and a bogus leader," King Faisal told Britain's ambassador to Jidda. "If I'd been in the Jews' place, I'd have done exactly the same thing to him," swore the Saudi monarch who, in 1975, would be shot dead by his own nephew.

The Arab world remained the same, or so it seemed on August 29, when Nasser stepped onto the hot tarmac in Khartoum. The president had arrived in the Sudanese capital for the first pan-Arab summit since 1965, and Nasser's first meeting with Arab leaders since the disaster three months before. Thousands of people thronged the streets to greet him, but Nasser, nervous and pale, still reeled from the summer's events. "I cannot forget those first few days in June," he admitted to his ministers before departing. "I felt a great and indescribable pain. No doubt those days affected all of us, psychologically, materially, spiritually.[15]

Nasser's goal was to regain the lost Arab territories. Any diplomatic solution, he knew, would have to involve cooperation with the United States, but as yet unwilling to accord Israel even oblique recognition, much less peace, Nasser still needed a military option. He had to rebuild his army, and for that he turned to the USSR.

The Soviets, however, were hesitant. Too much of their weaponry had been lost or had fallen into Western hands, and they feared that renewed fighting now, with the Arabs still weak, could result in nuclear war. Visiting Cairo on June 22, President Podgorny agreed to meet Nasser's requests for hundreds of jets, tanks, and advisers, but in return he demanded a port for the Soviet fleet and—more unpalatable for Egypt—a political solution to the Arab-Israeli conflict. "Are you asking for more aircraft with the intention of ultimately annihilating Israel?" inquired Podgorny, and Nasser curtly replied, "any discussion on political concessions is only a reward for aggression and that is illogical both politically and mentally."

The request for arms was reiterated the following month in Moscow by president 'Aref of Iraq and Algeria's Houari Boumedienne, acting as Nasser's emissaries. Brezhnev again demanded a quid pro quo of a land for-non-belligerency arrangement. "Let Israel withdraw and then interpret the resolution the way you want," the party chairman advised them. "Then, when you become strong, do whatever you want." The deal would involve neither peace nor recognition, but again Nasser held firm, declaring, "That which was taken by force will be returned by force," and "the price [of nonbelligerency] will turn our defeat into a double defeat." In the end he got his way: The Soviets agreed to rearm Egypt completely and without preconditions.[16]

With his replenished arsenal, Nasser was able to wage a three-year war of attrition against Israeli forces in Sinai, and so sustain his claim that the June War was merely the first stage in a more protracted struggle. But while Egyptian and Israeli guns pounded one another across the Suez Canal, the superpowers, both in and outside the UN, strove to reach a *modus vivendi* on the Middle East. Nasser could not ignore those efforts. "To my mind the solution of peace, whether Soviet or American, is the way of surrender," he said. "The only way open to us is the road to war." Pursuing that path, he explained to Arab foreign ministers in July, would necessitate a degree of deception:

> We need a period of 2–3 years before we are ready to launch a far-reaching operation to remove the traces of the aggression, but we must hide our preparations under political activity that will convince our friends, and first and foremost the USSR, that we did everything possible within the UN framework and in international negotiations.

The sole exemption to this plan was Jordan, which, dependent on American arms, could not hope to mount a military initiative by 1970. "There is no choice but to give him [Hussein] the freedom to maneuver to regain the West Bank," Nasser confided to Heikal. As long as he refrained from reaching a separate peace agreement with Israel, Hussein was free to explore ways of retrieving the West Bank through American mediation.[17]

Preparing for war and maneuvering around peace—Egypt's "security" and "political" goals; Nasser, too, made the distinction—meant maintaining the level of Arab unity achieved on the eve of the war. A way had to be found of ending the Yemen conflict, of healing the rifts between revolutionary and conservative regimes. In the weeks leading up to Khartoum, Nasser endorsed the resumption of Arab oil shipments to the West; he offered to cease all subversive activity against Arab monarchs and, in return, asked that they aid in salvaging Egypt's economy. To King Hussein, Nasser wrote, "We have entered this war together, lost it together, and we must win it together . . . Egypt is willing to tie its fate completely to that of the brave Jordanian people." In *al-Ahram*, Heikal made the case for Arab co-existence: "It is in the national interest to permit other experiments and different political and social opinions."[18]

Nasser's prodigious efforts succeeded in preserving at least the semblance of Arab unity, but greater energy still would have to be expended to keep his own country united.

Since his resignation, 'Abd al-Hakim 'Amer had secluded himself with sympathizers, chanting "there is no commander but the field marshal" and petitioning for his reinstatement. Fearing widespread sedition, Nasser had offered to restore his former post as vice president, but 'Amer would settle for nothing less than commander in chief. He began to hoard arms, to mobilize officers soon to be cashiered for their failures in the war. A date was set for the coup—September 1, while Nasser was away in Khartoum—but a week before, Nasser determined that his longtime best friend constituted "a danger to peace, the army, and the homeland," and decided to act.

Gen. Fawzi led a handpicked battalion to 'Amer's villa in Giza. Nasser followed the troop with tears in his eyes. "He felt that processions such as this happen only in Greek tragedies and not in the real life of politicians," Heikal wrote. Fawzi confiscated piles of weapons and arrested 300 officers. But the purge was only beginning. Over 1,000 people would be incarcerated, including Generals Murtagi and Sidqi Mahmud, Shams Badran and Salah Nasr, and several hundred members of 'Amer's family. Many would be sentenced to lengthy prison terms, often with hard labor. Yet even those acquitted continued to suffer disgrace. "People would throw bricks through my windows. When I went outside they would curse me bitterly," confessed Gen. 'Abd al-Hamid al-Dugheidi, a senior air force commander who moved from Cairo to Alexandria in order to escape the shame. "Even my own nephew, a child of five, said to me, 'You're a coward, uncle. You ran and abandoned us.'"

The cruelest fate, however, awaited 'Amer. After a prolonged interrogation, the former field marshal and contender for Egypt's leadership became violently ill and died. An official autopsy discovered that the cause of death was aconite poisoning—a dosage of the drug was found taped to 'Amer's stomach—though rumors persisted that he had been shot while trying to escape or executed for threatening to disclose the government's role in the debacle. Nasser, nevertheless, was crushed, confessing, "It would have been far better for me if I had died rather than witness this defeat. And greater even than the defeat itself is my disappointment in my lifelong friend, 'Abd al-Hakim." Others, however, were far less aggrieved. "[It] was the best decision 'Amer ever has taken," Sadat concluded. "If I were him I would have done it on June 5."[19]

These events took a further toll on Nasser, who arrived in Khartoum a physically sick but politically secure ruler, determined to "restore Arab dignity and honor." King Hussein, by comparison, was both ailing and deeply afraid for his crown.

"I have to admit that once June was over, it took me a long time to understand, digest and face up to what had happened," the king confessed in his memoirs. "It was like a dream or worse yet, a nightmare." He, too, had taken steps to repair his army, not so much purging its ranks as reshuffling them to give greater power to royal family members, filling the void left by 'Atif al-Majali, the general who insisted on defending Jerusalem and who collapsed and died shortly after the city's surrender. Hussein had tried to integrate hundreds of PLO fighters now stationed on Jordanian territory, and to shelter hundreds of thousands of Palestinian refugees. Yet he had also mustered the resources to tour Arab and Western capitals, there to deliver hard-line speeches while secretly seeking a "just and honorable peace." At a clandestine meeting in London, he replied to Ya'akov Herzog's question—"Is Your Majesty ready to sign a peace treaty with Israel?"—saying, "Certainly, yes, but . . . I must move together with the entire Arab world."[20]

Peace, Hussein believed, could be achieved only through a summit that authorized him to negotiate for the West Bank's return while protecting him from the Arab radicals. Hussein then convinced an initially skeptical Nasser that a formula could be found for political latitude that did not mean recognizing Israel. Now, together in Khartoum, the two former enemies faced onerous challenges: Algerian and Iraqi demands for continuing the oil embargo and nationalizing Western companies, and Shuqayri's clamoring for guerrilla attacks and a popular uprising in the territories. Syria's delegates described the summit as the springboard for a new military offensive and, finding little support for the initiative, promptly flew back to Damascus.

But Nasser was unfazed. As in his heyday, he dominated the conference, telling participants that Soviet and American plans for ending the state of war "will lead us to surrender and humiliation," while stressing, "There is a difference between political action and the liquidation of the [Palestine] issue." He warned of the danger of creeping Israeli annexation of the West Bank, and urged support for Hussein's efforts to redeem the area, indirectly, through the Americans. Nasser's imprint was discernible in the final communiqué that committed the Arab states to stand united on "political action" to retrieve Arab territories and realize Palestinian rights, while conceding "no recognition of Israel, no peace and no negotiations with her," and taking "all steps necessary to consolidate military preparedness."[21]

Western observers would later debate whether Khartoum was a victory for Arab moderation or radicalism. True, it vetoed any interaction with Israel, but it appeared to open doors to third-party arbitration and the demilitarization of the occupied territories. Hussein claimed the conference had Arab extremists "put on ice," and compelled the Israelis "to prove that they really mean to live in peace . . . and be accepted in this world on which they have encrusted themselves like a scab." Yet, when presented with a Yugoslavian scheme in which Israel would vacate Sinai in return for guarantees of free passage, Nasser turned his back. He reminded his ministers that "our primary intention is to continue to pursue the political solution road in order to gain time for military preparation and to persuade the Soviets to supply us with all the weapons we need." For the Israelis, the "three no's" of Khartoum effectively closed the door on the June 19 resolution. Said Eshkol, "This stand of the Arab Heads of State reinforces Israel's decision not to permit the return of such conditions that enabled our enemies to undermine our security and plot against our sovereignty and existence."[22]

Confusion continued to surround Khartoum, yet certain conclusions were clear. The Arabs' focus had shifted away from liberating Palestine to liberating those areas recently conquered—from "erasing Israel," as Shuqayri put it, to "erasing the traces of the aggression." And for Nasser, who successfully ended the Yemen war and procured $200 million in aid, the summit was unquestionably a triumph, his last.[23]

The next three years would be rife with disappointments for Nasser—military, economic, political. By 1970, the economy was in appalling shape, even by Egyptian standards, and the country was virtually occupied by thousands of Soviet advisers. The attrition war along the Canal had escalated disastrously—the outskirts of Cairo were bombed—without loosening Israel's hold on the territories. In August, Nasser consented to a cease-fire, but a month later he was again thrust into conflict as Palestinian forces in Jordan staged an open revolt against the monarchy. Syrian tanks moved toward the Jordanian border, and the Israelis pledged to help Hussein—the entire region verged on conflagration until Nasser stepped in and mediated a solution in which Arafat and his guerrillas would evacuate Jordan and receive asylum in Lebanon. The Jordanian civil war or, as the Palestinians called it, Black September, utterly drained the already desiccated Nasser. He returned to Cairo on September 28 and went to bed, never to rise again.

Egypt was seized by a paroxysm of anguish unprecedented in its modern history. Kosgyin, notoriously unflappable, was moved to tears by the sight of countless thousands of mourners choking the streets of Cairo. Flags flew at half-mast throughout the Middle East, where the mood was best described by Sadat, Nasser's successor: "My grief for him will live as long as I live, inflaming my heart." Among Israelis, alone, the reaction was muted—not celebratory, but wary of an Arab world without a leader strong enough to make peace as well as war. Many could have subscribed to the words of King Hussein: "The greatness of most world leaders lies in their ideas and actions, but Gamal's greatness empowered his actions and ideas."[24]

Hussein would outlive Nasser by nearly thirty years, navigating his country through social and economic crises and eruptions of Arab-Israeli violence. Abrogating to the PLO his role as representative of the Palestinian people, and surrendering his claim to the West Bank, Hussein tried to mediate between Israeli and Palestinian leaders. Though passively pro-Iraqi in the 1991 Gulf War, he joined Yitzhak Rabin in 1994 in signing the Jordan-Israel peace treaty, and the following year delivered the main eulogy at Rabin's funeral. He died of cancer in February 1999, and was mourned by the entire world, with the exception of many Palestinians.

Hussein, in turn, was survived by one year by Hafez al-Assad, who conspicuously boycotted Khartoum. Ousting Jadid and "Doctors" Makhous and

Atassi, al-Assad achieved supreme power in Syria. He joined Egypt in launching what the Arabs called the October or Ramadan War of 1973, which ended with the IDF on the outskirts of Damascus. Three years later, in an effort to aid Christian militias warring against the PLO, al-Assad sent his troops into Lebanon, where they soon turned on the Christians as well and occupied much of the country. Renowned for his ruthlessness, credited with massacring an estimated 20,000 of his countrymen in an abortive 1982 revolt, he bitterly opposed the Egypt-Israel peace treaty, and continued to support Palestinian guerrillas. And yet al-Assad also negotiated, albeit indirectly, with Rabin and other Israeli leaders. They offered to return most, if not all, of the Golan, but their quid pro quo—peace—proved too steep for Assad.

Yasser Arafat, the longest-lived of all the Arab leaders of 1967, was not even invited to Khartoum. Yet the conference, by negating the possibility of conventional war for the near future, placed him and his guerrillas in the vanguard of the armed struggle. The Palestinians, moreover, were now geographically united (albeit under Israeli rule) as never before since 1948, further galvanizing their national identity. Within two years, Arafat had gained the chairmanship of the PLO—Shuqayri was swiftly forgotten—and mounted numerous high-profile raids, typified by the 1972 massacre of Israeli Olympic athletes in Munich. Two more years passed and the Arab states recognized the PLO as "the sole, legitimate representative of the Palestinian people," and Arafat was invited to address the UN General Assembly. But then the PLO became embroiled in the Lebanese civil war, fighting first the Christians, then the Syrians, and finally the Israelis. Arafat, who had already been banished from Jordan, was now exiled to Tunis where, after declaring his support for Saddam Hussein in the Gulf War and sidelined by a popular revolt in Gaza and the West Bank (the *Intifada*), he seemed to be consigned to obscurity. Rabin revived him, however, and Arafat returned to the territories as president of the newly created Palestinian Authority.[25] The militant who praised the assassins of Sadat in 1981 appeared to be following in his footsteps. Like the Egyptians and Jordanians before him, Arafat would draw on an American peacemaking experience that began, thirty years before, with Lyndon Johnson.

242: Legacy and Reality

The last shot of the war had scarcely been fired, but Arthur Goldberg was already canvassing UN delegations on the possibility of peaceful arrangements; of mediation and direct talks between the parties. Yet very quickly, the difficulty of transforming the latest Arab-Israeli war into a lasting Arab-Israeli peace became apparent.

The Arabs were insisting on the total and unconditional return of their territories, and the Israelis, though willing to cede Sinai and the Golan Heights, had dug in their heels on the West Bank and Jerusalem. America had scant means of influencing the Arabs, and only limited leverage on Israel. "It wasn't Dayan that kept Kosygin out," the president told his advisers shortly after the cease-fire. "The USSR will soon get fed up with Israel's braggadocio." The Soviets, meanwhile, were ready to "pull out all the stops"—Joe Sisco's phrase— to defend the Arabs' rejection of any form of acceptance for the Jewish state. "Israel's keeping the West Bank would create revanchism for the rest of the 20th century," Dean Rusk concluded, "but Israel must be accepted."

Faced with such mountainous challenges, burdened with his own difficulties in Vietnam, Johnson might well have ignored the Middle East. Instead, he embarked on a daring initiative. Addressing an educators' conference on June 19 (again, that date), the president set out the ideas he and his staff had been developing since the very first day of the war. These were framed in five principles that recognized the right of every state in the region to exist, assured the territorial integrity and political independence of all states, and guaranteed freedom of navigation while advocating Middle East arms control and a solution to the refugee problem. Eshkol expressed "deep admiration" for the speech; Eban called it "masterful," and Rostow reported, "as of tonight the Arabs haven't cut the pipelines or our throats."[26] There remained only the Soviets' cooperation to solicit.

The appeal was made in an unlikely venue: a Victorian house in Glassboro, New Jersey. There, on June 23, Johnson raised a number of issues with Premier Kosygin, among them Vietnam and nuclear proliferation, before dealing with the Middle East. Johnson appealed for support for his five principles, and for a "common language of peace." But Kosygin was intractable. He accused the U.S. of encouraging Israeli expansion, of dealing perfidiously with Nasser. "The Arabs are an explosive people," he warned, predicting that the Arabs would "fight with hunting rifles, even their bare hands," to regain their lands unconditionally. In return for Israeli withdrawal from all the territories, the Soviets would at most agree to adjudication of the Straits blockade by the International Court of Justice.

Ten years would pass before Kosygin's ouster by Brezhnev—Podgorny's fall would follow—but in the summer of 1967 the premier's powers were broad. Having failed to fulfill his goals in the Security Council, he requested an emergency General Assembly session to "to bring about the liquidation of the consequences of aggression and the immediate evacuation of Israeli forces behind the armistice lines." U Thant, in what Western observers saw as an effort to atone for his lack of judgment during the crisis, softened the Soviet blow. He merely cited the Uniting for Peace mechanism used when the Security Council was deadlocked, and quietly convened the Assembly.

The session lasted five weeks but failed to uphold the Arab claim that the war had been an act of Israeli aggression. Rather, it produced a Latin American resolution offering UN mediation and the return of all conquered land for recognition of "the right of all states in the area to live in peace and security," and a non-aligned motion demanding immediate and unconditional withdrawal. The Arabs rejected both, however, and the Soviets, exasperated by what they termed "extremist Arab circles," tabled a resolution closely resembling the Latin draft. But this, too, failed to pass. "The Russians seem to have made every mistake that they could," observed Lord Caradon. "Having led the Arabs into battle and having them sustain a resounding defeat, they then showed that they were ready to abandon them." Ambassador Federenko, the demagogue who had once sworn to "humiliate and wipe the floor with the United States," was saddled with the failure and permanently removed from his post.[27]

"We are now in the process of mopping up after Mr. Kosygin's onslaught in the General Assembly," Johnson wrote to Harold Wilson. "The most likely prospect is that the Middle East will go back to the Security Council, where it belongs, and that results will have to be negotiated out behind the scenes." Quiet talks had indeed already begun between Rusk, seeking to wed the "hare" of evacuation to the "horse" of the price the Arabs would pay, and Soviet ambassador Dobrynin, eager to reach any compromise that avoided the word "nonbelligerency." Finally, in early July, Gromyko and Goldberg reached an agreement that stipulated prompt withdrawal "in keeping with the inadmissibility of the conquest of territory by war," and upheld each party's right "to maintain an independent national state of its own and to live in peace and security." UN intervention would be sought in solving the refugee and free passage problems.[28]

The agreement appeared to please nobody. Nasser objected to the absence of a clear reference to withdrawal to the June 4 lines, and to the suggestion of even indirect mediations with Israel. "I cannot accept this," he told the Soviets. "If I did, I could not return home; I could not even face my daughters." The Israelis, for whom even the Latin draft had been insufficiently specific on territory-for-peace, described the agreement "not only as a physical retreat but a diplomatic backtracking to the grave situation that has existed for the last 19 years." Eban protested, "Nothing but a husk will remain of Johnson's principles." By the end of the summer, even the U.S. and the USSR appeared to be distancing themselves from the accord.[29]

The violence in Sinai escalated, meanwhile, climaxing on October 20 in the sinking of the Israeli destroyer *Eilat*—a quarter of its crew was killed—by an Egyptian missile. Israel retaliated by shelling Egypt's principal oil refineries at Suez and setting them ablaze. Sporadic fighting also broke out at various points along the Jordan River. War, much more than a negotiated settlement, seemed near. But the very threat of renewed regional conflict provided a fillip to diplomacy as the Security Council again took up the Middle East.

Success, Goldberg realized, lay in language that intimated both Israel's desire for total peace in return for less than all the territories and the Arabs' demand for complete withdrawal in return for at most nonbelligerency. The démarche, Goldberg's last before resigning over differences with Johnson on Vietnam, required weeks of intensive discussions. To sway the Israelis, Walt

Rostow suggested "we lean against them just enough to keep their thinking from becoming too quickly set in the concrete of their current extended territorial possessions"—to which McPherson warned, "We would have to push them back by military force to accomplish a repeat of 1956; the cut-off of aid would not do it." But having resisted Eisenhower's pressure tactics during Suez, Johnson refused to arm-twist the Israelis. At most he was willing to delay arms shipments to Israel, while urging Eshkol to be "flexible, patient, discreet and generous." As for the Jordanians, "our main purpose must be to let him [Hussein] down as gently as we can from his present conviction that you must pull his chestnuts out of the fire for him," Bundy advised the president. "A formula that is good enough for Kosygin is good enough for Hussein." America could scarcely influence the other Arab delegations, all of which were looking to Egypt's lead. In peacemaking, as previously in war, Nasser held the key.[30]

"This is merely an Israeli resolution camouflaged as an American one," Mahmoud Riad, arriving in New York, protested to Goldberg. "It does not even give us the minimum of erasing the traces of the June aggression." Goldberg responded with several concessions to Egyptian sensibilities, including reference to the "inadmissibility of the acquisition of territory by war" and to a UN "representative" who would "establish contacts" and "promote agreement," rather than a mediator who would facilitate talks. Peace was promised for the Middle East, and territorial integrity and security for all states in the area, without specifying peace with, or recognition of, Israel. Even a non-American sponsor for the resolution, Britain, was found. Finally, only one great stumbling block remained: the extent of Israel's withdrawal—whether from "territories occupied in the recent conflict" or "*the* territories occupied in the recent conflict."

Ultimately, through untiring efforts by Goldberg and Caradon, the Egyptians were persuaded that "territories" indeed meant all the territories—the French and Arabic versions of the text both retained the definite article—while the Israelis were contented by fact that the official English-language version remained obscure. Thus, on November 22, the Security Council unanimously adopted Resolution 242 "Concerning Principles for a Just and Lasting Peace in the Middle East."[31]

Israel accepted the resolution, albeit begrudgingly, as did Jordan. Nasser's response was more equivocal. While endorsing the UN's decision, he reiterated the three no's to his National Assembly, reminding it: "That which was taken by force will be regained by force," and told his generals, "You don't need to pay any attention to anything I may say in public about a peaceful solution." And yet, secretly, he signaled the Americans his openness to a nonbelligerency accord with Israel "with all of its consequences." Iraq and Syria rejected the resolution entirely, denouncing it as "a deception of the people, a recipe for failure," as did the Palestinians, incensed by their exclusion from the text. The PLO, which would approve 242 only twenty years later, declared in 1967: "unresolved, the Palestinian problem will continue to endanger peace and security not only in the Middle East, but in the entire world."[32]

President Johnson was eager to exploit the opportunity he believed 242 created, to cooperate with the UN representative, Swedish diplomat Gunnar Jarring, and to move the Middle East toward peace. Events, however, overwhelmed him. Two months after the Security Council's decision, North Vietnam launched its Tet Offensive, and two months after that, with his foreign policy in ruins and a generation of young Americans reviling him, Lyndon Johnson declined to stand for reelection. The Johnson administration would leave a mixed legacy of good intentions and tragically failed dreams, yet there could be no gainsaying its contribution in laying the cornerstone for future Arab-Israeli agreements. Through seven subsequent presidencies, the United States has continued to champion 242 and the territory-for-peace principle it implies, if never explicitly promises.

Even from the perspective of thirty-five years, the answer to the question, "Did six days of war truly change the Middle East?" remains equivocal. Events in the region that previously converged only toward conflict could also, post-1967, surge in the direction of peace. Diplomatic breakthroughs once deemed inconceivable became almost commonplace in the following years, facilitated by special mediators and leaders of both courage and vision. Violence, nevertheless, continued to plague the lives of millions throughout the Middle East, and to threaten to pitch not only the region, but the entire world, into war.

Along with opportunities for peace, the Six-Day or June War opened the door to even deadlier conflagrations. Basic truths persisted: for all its military conquests, Israel was still incapable of imposing the peace it craved. Though roundly defeated, the Arabs could still mount a formidable military campaign. The status of territories could be negotiated but the essential issues—Israel's right to exist, the demand for Palestinian repatriation and statehood—remained. If the war was indeed a storm that altered the region's landscape, it also exposed the underlying nature of the Arab-Israel conflict—its bedrock. The modern Middle East created in 1967 was therefore a hybrid: a region of incipient promise but also of imminent dangers, a mixture of old contexts and new.

At the time of this writing, the Middle East is once more in the grip of turmoil. The Palestinians have taken up arms, Israel has retaliated, and the peace process has run aground. Familiar patterns of terror and counterstrike, incursion and retribution, have resurfaced. Nor has the bloodshed been confined to the Arab-Israeli arena, but has burst beyond in the form of massive terrorist attacks against the United States and America's reprisals against Islamic extremists. Today, Arab demonstrators, many bearing posters of Nasser, are demanding a showdown with the West and with Israel. The Israelis wait, meanwhile, and weigh the risks of preemption. The war that never quite ended for statesmen, soldiers, and historians, is liable to erupt again.

AFTERWORD

MORE THAN TWO YEARS HAVE PASSED since the outbreak of the latest Middle Eastern turmoil, and there is still no cease-fire in sight. Called by Palestinians the al-Aqsa Intifada, and by the Israelis the "disturbances," the "events," or, simply, the Palestinian terror, the violence that erupted in September 2000, and which has raged ever since, is in every sense a war. No less than in 1948 and 1967, Arabs and Israelis are today once again battling over the final disposition of the area known in Arabic as *Filastin* and in Hebrew as *Eretz Yisrael*—the Land of Israel. As in the processes leading up to previous Arab-Israeli confrontations, mounting violence between Palestinians and Israelis threatens to set the entire region ablaze.

In many respects, the current fighting resembles the civil war in Palestine that broke out in November 1947, following the UN's decision to partition the country into independent Jewish and Arab states. The Zionist leadership accepted the notion of territorial compromise, but the Arabs of Palestine saw no reason to forfeit what they considered their exclusive national rights, and determined to block the partition with attacks against Jewish settlements, road systems, and neighborhoods. Other Arab forces, most prominently those associated with the militant Muslim Brotherhood, aided the Palestinian Arabs from across the border. The Jews, for their part, initially showed restraint, but in April 1948, fearing annihilation, they too went to war. Subsequently, dozens of Arab villages and towns were destroyed, their populations displaced, and their leaders either killed or rendered ineffective. But the Palestinians' defeat generated sympathy throughout the Arab world and intensified the pressure on Arab leaders to intervene against the Jews. The result came one month later with the advent of the first Arab-Israeli war.

A remarkably similar process occurred more than fifty years later, in the latter half of 2000, when the Clinton Administration again proposed to partition the land between the Palestinians and the Jews. Specifically, the United States called for the creation of a Palestinian state in virtually all of the West Bank and the entire Gaza Strip—Israeli settlements would either be removed or concentrated in blocks—with its capital in East Jerusalem. A small number of Palestinian refugees would be repatriated to Israel; the rest were to receive compensation. The Palestinian state would live side by side with Israel in relations of full peace, but while Israeli prime minister Ehud Barak approved the formula, the Palestinian Authority under its president, Yasser Arafat, rejected it. Rather, Arafat demanded the return of all the refugees—a move that, if implemented, would have created a Palestinian majority in Israel. As in 1947–48, the issue was not merely the borders of the Jewish state, but its very existence.

The Palestinians consequently embarked on an armed offensive using tactics reminiscent of those employed in 1947–48—roadside ambushes, snipers, and car bombs—together with the innovation of suicide bombers. Militant Islamic elements once more played a prominent role in the campaign. At first, Israel's reaction was again restrained, but as casualties rapidly mounted, the IDF finally struck back. In April 2002, Israeli forces reoccupied much of the West Bank, causing extensive damage to Palestinian cities and villages, and killing or isolating many Palestinian leaders. As in 1948, the Palestinians' plight aroused sympathy in neighboring Arab countries and placed pressure on their leaders to intercede. Soon Hezbollah guerrillas in Lebanon were launching rockets into northern Israel; the Syrian army went on high alert, as did units in Jordan, Egypt, and Iraq. Israel mobilized its reserves. The region careered toward yet another Arab-Israeli war.

The fighting in 2000–2002 recalled not only the events of 1947–48 but, even more poignantly, those of 1967. That war, this book asserts, was the result of a series of incidents triggered by Palestinian guerrilla raids and Israel's retaliations against them. Today, more than three decades later, the Middle East is still in the grips of a context of conflict in which a single spark can ignite a regional conflagration. Such a spark was kindled in September 2000, when Ariel Sharon, then head of Israel's parliamentary opposition, paid a visit to the Haram al-Sharif, or Temple Mount, in Jerusalem.

Though the visit had been cleared with the Palestinian Authority, many Palestinians viewed it as a provocation and protested against it violently. Firing on the rioters, Israeli forces provided the pretext for launching an *intifada*, or popular uprising, named after the Haram's al-Aqsa mosque. Mass demonstrations of Palestinian youths soon escalated into armed attacks against Israeli targets, most of them civilian, and increasingly fierce countermeasures by Israel. Israeli reprisals in turn instigated unrest in adjacent Arab countries. The "street" was once again agitating—a déjà vu of 1967—and Arab rulers had little choice but to act.

Unlike in 1948 and 1967, however, war between Arabs and Israelis did not erupt in 2002. Though the region has remained in many ways unchanged, several fundamental transformations nevertheless have combined to mitigate the dangers of war.

There is, firstly, the existence of peace treaties between Israel and Egypt and Israel and Jordan. In spite of their failure to bring about any true reconciliation between their signatories, these agreements have nonetheless provided the nations with open channels of communication and venues for reducing tensions. Another change is the emergence of the U.S.-Israeli alliance that not only guarantees Israel a decisive military edge over its enemies, but also affords Washington far-reaching influence over Israeli actions. Finally, there is the nonconventional weaponry now in the arsenals of virtually every Middle Eastern state, which has sharply elevated the stakes in any Arab-Israeli confrontation.

Yet for every change curtailing the chances of war, another could equally contribute to its outbreak. Absent today is the peculiar stability engendered by the Cold War, of a rational counterpart whom the U.S. president might hotline in a crisis, and superpower constraints over key regional players such as Iraq, Iran, and Syria. The once neat division between Arab radicals and Arab conservatives has been replaced by internal fissures within each Arab country—between each regime and its domestic, often Islamic, opposition—and even the lines in the Arab-Israeli conflict have become obscured. Most destabilizing, arguably, is the growth of terrorist organizations, global in outlook and adamant in their theology, transcending all borders and contemptuous of any attempt to restrain them.

These countervailing changes, coupled with the continuing friction surrounding nondemocratic Middle Eastern regimes and Arab resistance to the very *idea* of a Jewish state, might have set the stage for an Arab-Israeli war bigger and possibly more destructive than those of 1948 and 1967. Instead, war in 2002 was averted by the timely intervention of the United States. As tensions in the region spiraled toward an explosion, President George W. Bush strongly advised Syria to rein in its Hezbollah allies and told the Palestinian Authority that its support of terror was totally unacceptable to Americans. At the same time, Washington publicly recognized Israel's right to defend itself and convinced Israelis that they did not stand alone. Bush's actions—admonishing the Arabs and reassuring the Israelis—were precisely those that Lyndon B. Johnson failed to take in 1967, and in 2002 they succeeded in containing, if not defusing, the crisis.

Like Johnson, Bush was engaged in an international struggle with an implacable enemy—no longer communism, of course, but Islamic extremism—but rather than tie his hands as Vietnam once had Johnson's, America's new conflict impelled George Bush to act. The events of September 11, 2001, spurred a radical departure from long-standing American policies toward the Middle East. Having become the victim of large-scale Arab terror, the administration voiced newfound empathy for Israel and its struggle against suicide bombers and gunmen, and went so far as to identify Israel's enemies—Hamas and Islamic Jihad—as America's. Moreover, in declaring war against international terrorism, in dispatching its soldiers thousands of miles to fight in Afghanistan and, avowedly, in Iraq, Washington could hardly deny Israel the ability to strike back in the West Bank and Gaza, its own backyard. Concomitantly, American leaders expressed severe reservations regarding the Arab states, even toward their traditional allies, Egypt and Saudi Arabia, citizens of which were heavily implicated in 9/11. Relations between the U.S. and the Arab world were further strained by the Arabs' reluctance to support a military effort to invade Iraq and oust its dictator, Saddam Hussein.

The success of Bush's effort to rally an anti-Saddam coalition is not, as of this writing, guaranteed. Numerous obstacles, domestic and foreign, stand in the president's way. Nor is it certain whether the toppling of Saddam will install democracy or merely another dictatorship in Iraq, or whether war in the gulf will ultimately enhance or further impair the area's stability. One fact, alone, is incontestable: that the Middle East remains a flash point of multilateral confrontation, a source of seemingly intractable controversies, and a powder keg that the slightest spark could ignite. A context of conflict continues to seize the region, demanding of its leaders almost constant displays of both courage and caution.

November 2002

A CONVERSATION WITH
MICHAEL B. OREN

*Fouad Ajami is professor of Middle East Studies at
The Johns Hopkins University School of Advanced International
Studies and the author of* The Dream Palace of the Arabs.

FOUAD AJAMI: **How old were you in June 1967? I presume you were too
young for this war to be part of your formative experience. I was twenty-
two then, and this was truly a great divide. Do you have early memories
of this war?**

MICHAEL OREN: In 1967, I was twelve years old, very impressionable, and growing up outside New York City. It was a turbulent time throughout the United
States, the time of the civil rights and antiwar movements, of the feminist and
youth revolts. But no single event had a greater influence on my development,
on my identity, than the Six-Day War.

The beginning crisis coincided with my birthday—May 20—and instead
of celebrating, I watched as my parents cried over what they feared was Israel's
imminent destruction. A second Holocaust was about to occur, they believed,
and the world would once again witness it silently. I remember going down to
our synagogue, where the entire community had gathered to pledge its fullest
resources to help ensure Israel's survival.

Then came June 5 and the war that altered not only the Middle East but
also American Jewry. Israel's victory, it was said, allowed American Jews "to
walk with their backs straight" and flex their political muscle as never before.
American Jewish organizations that previously kept Israel at arm's length suddenly proclaimed their Zionism.

For me, personally, the war's impact was especially poignant. I will never
forget my father rushing to the breakfast table, waving a copy of *Life*. On its

Egyptian planes destroyed on the runway. (Israel Government Press Office)

The White House Situation Room. From left to right: McNamara, Katzenbach, Ambassador Thompson (smoking), Walt Rostow, Humphrey, Rusk (seated), Johnson, Bundy. (LBJ Library Photo by Yoichi Okamoto)

The Arabs' UN Ambassadors: Muhammad al-Farra and George Tomeh (above left and right) and Mohamed El Kony (lower right). (Courtesy of Muhammad al-Farra)

Ambassador Arthur Goldberg.
(Courtesy of Muhammad al-Farra)

IDF mechanized troops advance through the West Bank. (Shaham, IDF Archive)

Palestinians flee over the Jordan River. (Associated Press)

'Ata 'Ali speaks with the author outside of Amman, 1999.

Rabbi Goren (with ram's horn) with Israeli soldiers at the Western Wall. (Israel Government Press Office)

Narkiss (left), Dayan (center), and Rabin (right), entering the Lion's Gate. (Ilan Bruner, Israel Government Press Office)

The USS *Liberty:* Some 800 holes were counted in its hull. (USS *Liberty* Homepage)

(Left) June 9: Dayan, Elazar (pointing), Eshkol, Bar-Lev (right, holding map), and Col. Lior (behind Dayan, glasses and cap). (Associated Press)

(Below) Israeli artillery hits Syrian positions at Tawafiq, June 10. (Kidron, IDF Archive)

(Facing page, top)
Egyptian POWs in Sinai. (Tal Shabtai, Israel Government Press Office)

(Facing page, middle)
Suicidal sortie: An Egyptian MIG attacks Israeli troops in Sinai. (Han Micha, Israel Government Press Office)

(Facing page, bottom)
Egyptian wreckage in the Mitla Pass, June 8. "10,000 men lost their lives on that day alone." (Han Micha, Israel Government Press Office)

Dayan and General Odd Bull, the UN chief observer. (Associated Press)

Syria's Hafez al-Assad: "High time to destroy the Zionist presence in the Arab homeland." (Courtesy of Prof. Itamar Rabinovitch)

"I hope our efforts in the days ahead can be devoted to the achievement of a lasting peace." Johnson with Kosygin at Glasboro. (LBJ Library Photo by Yoichi Okamoto)

cover was a photo of an Israeli soldier chest-deep in the Suez Canal, a captured Kalashnikov brandished over his head. "You see that!" he shouted. "That is what we can do!" And then he kissed the picture.

Years later, I met that soldier in person—he's my neighbor in Jerusalem—and told him that it was because of him that I decided right then and there, in 1967, to move to Israel and take part in the drama of Jewish independence. Because of him I, too, would fight in wars and struggle in the face of terror. The man listened to my story, stood, and kissed *me* on the cheek. He understood how the Six-Day War had profoundly changed not only my life but a vast number of lives, in the Middle East and in America.

FOUAD AJAMI: **You rightly observe that wars in history also become wars of history. Where do you see yourself in the battle of Israeli historians?**

MICHAEL OREN: For twenty years now a fierce debate has been raging over the history of the Arab-Israeli conflict, its origins, its escalation, and its wars. The controversy revolves around which party—the Israeli or the Arab—bears greater guilt for initiating and exacerbating the dispute, and for frustrating repeated efforts to resolve it.

On one side of the argument are the self-styled "new historians," mostly Israeli Jews of a distinctly leftist or Marxist orientation, who pin the blame primarily on Israel. The Israelis, they claim, sought to deprive the Palestinians of their homeland and to provoke Arab states into wars of territorial aggrandizement. In making their case, the "new historians" marshal documents from British, American, and Israeli archives, and apply their findings to the current conflict between Israel and the Palestinians. They strive to pass judgment on historical figures—to be, as one of their spokesmen declared, "the hangmen of history."

On the other side of the debate are the more traditional historians who see a prominent Arab role in starting and perpetuating the conflict, who rely not only on English and Hebrew documents but also extensively on Arabic and Russian sources, and who are less judgmental of former decision makers and more inclined to examine historical events on their own merits, free of contemporary influences. The debate surrounding the history of the Arab-Israeli conflict has been one of the most vicious in all of scholarship.

Though I would place myself within the second, traditional, school, in writing *Six Days of War* I nevertheless sought to rise above this fray. My goal was to present a truly comprehensive narrative, one that treated both the Arab and the Israeli sides in a fair and balanced manner, to utilize all of the available sources in all of the relevant languages, and to examine the war in the historical context of 1967, and not of 2002.

Of course, no historian can be entirely objective, and as an Israeli and an American, I take strong stands on issues relating to war and peace in the Middle East. My objective, however, remained to overcome, rather than to indulge, my prejudices—to understand, rather than pass judgment on, the pivotal events of 1967. By creating a new and less polarized paradigm for the study of the Arab-Israeli conflict, I hoped to contribute to the resolution not only of the historiographical debate but ultimately of the conflict itself—to making a peace *of* history the peace *in* history.

FOUAD AJAMI: **I very much admire the serenity and the nonjudgmental quality of your observation that history is made by leaders in real time, not by historians in retrospect. In light of that, would it be fair to say that Egyptian president Nasser wanted the fruits of war but not war itself? As you put it yourself, he did not want war but only kudos. Do you see him as a tragic figure played upon by history and popular pressures?**

MICHAEL OREN: As an Israeli and as a Jew who had grown up hearing of his repeated pledges to destroy the Jewish state and to cast its inhabitants into the sea, I naturally approached the subject of Gamal Abdel Nasser with reservations. Twenty years of studying him, however, beginning with my dissertation on the origins of the Suez crisis, led me to know a more nuanced Nasser—ruthless at times, yes, and cunning, but also incorruptible, charismatic, and committed to the good of his people.

I followed the Egyptian leader's life from its humble beginnings through its formative experiences of the Palestine War, from Nasser's startling rise to power in the Free Officers' revolution of 1952 to his rapid achievements in foreign affairs and domestic reform. I came to appreciate Nasser the man and the vision, and the reasons why both were so fervidly revered by Arabs. But I also saw the personal foibles that gradually undermined so many of his successes. These faults—egoism, and a tendency to confuse rhetoric with reality and to be swayed by public opinion—were dominating Nasser's decision making by the 1960s.

This is not to say that Nasser acted entirely irrationally in 1967. He felt an urgent political need to rid Egypt of UNEF's presence, and he moved to fulfill that need. He evicted UNEF, poured his troops into Sinai, and closed the Straits of Tiran—all while the United States and Israel watched passively and the world seemed unwilling to intervene. The Soviets supported him unreservedly. Nasser had every reason to believe that he had won a bloodless victory, a political triumph that restored him to his former ascendancy in the Arab world.

A more perceptive Nasser, however—a Nasser less prone to believe his own propaganda and the misinformation supplied by his underlings, a Nasser willing to stand up to 'Amer—would have known that the Israelis would not remain inactive indefinitely, and that when they did react, the United States would back them. He would have estimated the glaring deficiencies of his army and those of his allies, and better weathered the disappointment when those deficiencies were starkly exposed on the battlefield.

Was Nasser a tragic figure? I believe he was. In history as in literature, tragic figures are those who initially show great promise and aspire to lofty goals, but who are ultimately defeated by blind ambition and serious deficiencies of character. Nasser was precisely such a figure, and his tragedy is not his alone but of Arabs and Israelis alike.

FOUAD AJAMI: **Moshe Dayan is an intriguing figure in your account, and enigmatic in many ways. He says he waited for the phone to ring from Arab leaders after the guns fell silent, but he also did not want to make territorial concessions. What was he? An opportunist? An adventurer? Was there a method, a deep core, to him?**

MICHAEL OREN: Researching great leaders in history, I get to know them quite intimately—I read their mail—with the one exception of Moshe Dayan. The more I studied him, it seemed, the less I felt I knew him. He was a man of utter contradictions—passionate and cold, creative and close-minded, fearless and fainthearted—with a mind capable of holding not only two but many opposing opinions at once.

These qualities alternatively infuriated and delighted the people around Dayan, instilling in them both admiration and contempt. On historic decisions such as whether or not to conquer the Old City of Jerusalem or the Golan Heights, he went from abject opposition to unqualified support literally within hours. Later, on questions of peace, he resisted territorial concessions, but also returned the Temple Mount/Haram al-Sharif in Jerusalem to the Muslim authorities and offered to withdraw Israeli troops from the Suez Canal in return for an Egyptian pledge of nonbelligerency.

The key, ultimately, to understanding Dayan resides in his prodigious ego. *He*, and nobody else, would give the command to enter the Old City. *He*, and not the Israeli government, would sanction capturing the Golan. And *he* alone would determine the governance of a site holy to three major religions.

As a figure in history, Moshe Dayan leaves an ambiguous legacy, and as an historian, I remain ambivalent toward him. He was a leader of a caliber virtually unknown in the Middle East today, the architect of Israel's greatest military victory and its later peace treaty with Egypt, but also an expert at political machinations and naked displays of power. Hidden behind his trademark eye patch was a mind as enigmatic as it was inaccessible.

FOUAD AJAMI: **The Six-Day War represented the end of the legend of Egypt in Arab life, it has been said. Do you think that Egypt has ever recovered from the bleakness of that defeat?**

MICHAEL OREN: Of great political changes wrought by the 1967 war, few were as traumatic and as momentous as the collapse of Nasserism. Beginning in July

1954, when Nasser officially declared Egypt an Arab country, Egypt conducted an ambitious campaign to unite the Arab world—to realize the dream of pan-Arabism—under its leadership.

Nasser's efforts, building on the widespread understanding of Egypt's historically central role in regional politics, fired the imaginations of Arabs from the Atlantic to the Persian Gulf. Egypt's union with Syria, from 1958 to 1961, seemed to augur a new and cohesive future for the Arab world. But the union dissolved, and another attempt to link up with Iraq similarly foundered, and by 1967, the dream had all but faded. The final blow came on June 5, when the vision of Arab unity was left smoldering among the wrecks of hundreds of Egyptian planes and tanks.

Egypt's defeat opened the door to new and compelling ideologies in the Middle East. Palestinian nationalism rose to the fore, and the PLO under the leadership of Yasser Arafat became a dominant force in Arab politics. More influential still was the rise of Islamic extremism, which also sought to unify the Arab world, albeit as a part of a global Islamic nation, on the basis of common Muslim identity. Here, too, Egypt played a central role as the home of the most powerful purist movement, the Muslim Brotherhood.

In the post-1967 era, and certainly after the 1973 war, Egypt began to play a different role in Arab and Middle East politics—no longer the leader in waging war but the forerunner in the search for peace. The transition was championed by Anwar Sadat, Nasser's successor, and to this day, Egypt's stature is a product not of its military force, prodigious though it remains, but of its potential contribution to regional stability and, ultimately, to peace.

FOUAD AJAMI: **As a historian and an Israeli, have you ever allowed your imagination to conjure up what a defeat would have meant for Israel in the Six-Day War?**

MICHAEL OREN: I read Robert Littell's *If Israel Lost the War* (New York: Coward-McCann, 1969) as a teenager, and it left me sleepless for nights. In vivid prose, the author describes endless columns of burned-out Israeli tanks and trucks, thousands of destitute Israeli POWs, and widespread massacres of Jewish civilians. Especially haunting for me was the final chapter in which Nasser's helicopter flies over the ruins of Tel Aviv, and Moshe Dayan is placed in front of a firing squad.

Defeat for the Israelis might have yielded less apocalyptic results, of course. Failure to react at all to the Tiran blockade would have constituted a severe political defeat for Israel, as would a military confrontation that ended in a standoff like that of 1973. The fact remains, however, that Arab armies in 1967 were poised to inflict existential damage on the Jewish state.

The vast array of Arab forces on all of Israel's borders, combined with the anti-Zionist frenzy sweeping the Arab world, produced a momentum for Israel's destruction that no Arab leader could resist. Irrespective of their specific goals in the war, neither Hussein nor Nasser had the power to rein in their forces once they vanquished the Israel Defense Forces and occupied Israeli territory. In the 1948 war, for example, while a large Arab population remained within Israel, no Jews were allowed to stay in any areas conquered by the Arabs.

Defeat, then, for Israel was simply not an option in 1967, and that realization informed its decisions throughout the crisis, both in the cabinet room and on the battlefield.

FOUAD AJAMI: **The war's legacy, you say, is equivocal. I am reminded here of something the late Chinese premier Zhou En-Lai said when asked about the significance of the French Revolution of 1789: "It's too soon to tell," he answered. Nearly four decades later, is it still too early to tell what the legacy of the Six-Day War is?**

MICHAEL OREN: In addition to Israel's conquest of vast stretches of Arab territory—much of which remains a source of controversy—the 1967 war had several political results that profoundly altered the Middle East.

There was, as mentioned earlier, the collapse of secular pan-Arabism and its replacement by Islamic extremist ideas, the rise of Palestinian nationalism, and the acceleration of the Middle East arms race. On the Israeli side, the war inaugurated Israel's strategic partnership with the United States, richly arming the IDF with American weaponry and according Washington far-reaching control over Jerusalem's policies. Reunited with its biblical homeland in the West Bank (Judea and Samaria), Israel became more "Jewish," spawning Messianic nationalist groups such as Gush Emunim, as well as the secular leftist movements that opposed them.

In spite of these momentous changes, it is nevertheless too early to pass judgment on the war's final legacy. Whether the West Bank and Gaza will form the basis of an independent Palestinian state, whether Israel will return the Golan Heights to Syria in exchange for a full peace treaty, whether Islamic radicalism will sweep the Arab world and trigger another and potentially bloodier Arab-Israeli war—all that is yet to be seen. Though one can posit that it is always premature to decide the ultimate impact of any historic events—we are still witnessing the consequences of World War II—the consequences of the 1967 war to this day remain alarmingly fluid and volatile.

FOUAD AJAMI: **King Hussein, one of your rich cast of characters, died in 1999. Is it fair to say that the man had no choice in 1967: It was either war with Israel, or civil war within his own country and the possible destruction of his dynasty? He lost the West Bank but saved his realm. What do you think?**

MICHAEL OREN: Hussein faced a terrible dilemma in 1967. If Nasser went to war against Israel and Hussein failed to join him, and if Nasser lost the war, then Jordan's Palestinian majority would accuse the king of treason and kill him. But if Nasser won the war against Israel and Hussein failed to join him, then the victorious Egyptian forces would proceed through Israel and march on Amman, where Nasser would kill the monarch.

To escape this bind, Hussein came up with what he believed was a viable solution: Abrogate all responsibility for the crisis and place Jordan's army under direct Egyptian command. Thus, on June 1, the Egyptian general Riad arrived in Jordan to take control of Hussein's military. The scheme seemed to be succeeding when, on June 5, in response to wildly inaccurate reports from Cairo regarding the course of the fighting, Riad ordered Jordanian forces to attack. Having repeatedly petitioned Hussein not to join the fighting, Israel responded with a counterattack that, within forty-eight hours, left most of the West Bank and all of Jerusalem in Israeli hands.

Hussein also allowed himself to be carried away by the war fever—albeit briefly—but he quickly awakened to the hopelessness of Jordan's military situation. Ultimately, it was Hussein's untenable position—a function less of the Arab-Israeli conflict than of the Arab cold war—that made Jordan's loss of the West Bank, and of Jerusalem, unavoidable.

FOUAD AJAMI: **A book of historical research so close to a historian's own world changes the historian and his or her outlook. Could you let your readers in on one or two changes in your outlook that happened by the time the work was completed?**

MICHAEL OREN: Prior to my work on the 1967 war, I believed the politics in the Middle East—as elsewhere in the world—were the product of rational decision making, a reflection of cogent analyses on the part of Arab and Israeli leaders. Today I know differently. Of all the insights I gleaned from my research—the extent of Egyptian war planning, for example, or the depth of Israeli fears—none altered my thinking more than the realization that politics in the Middle East are, more often than not, random and unpredictable, arbitrary in their course and potentially explosive in their outcome.

The deeper I delved into the sources, the more I came to view the Middle East in 1967 as a context of conflict. And in such an unstable and volatile context, it did not take much—a single spark—to ignite a regional conflagration. Such a spark was indeed kindled by Israel's raid on the West Bank village of Samua six months before the war, in November 1966, an incident that touched off a chain reaction of events culminating in Israel's preemptive strike that June. But even if the Samua raid had been averted, some other event would have triggered the war, so combustible was the atmosphere in the Middle East at the time.

Today, more than thirty-five years later, the region remains cast in context of conflict every bit as flammable as that which existed in 1967—if not more so.

Think: In confronting a Middle East crisis today, who could the U.S. president hotline—Osama bin Laden? The peculiar stability of the bipolar Cold War has disappeared, to be replaced by numerous and far less responsible nonconventional powers.

Moreover, were war to break out in the Middle East today, it would not be a classic contest between regular armies fought for the most part in the desert, far from population centers, but rather a ballistic exchange involving a variety of warheads, conventional and nonconventional, aimed at Middle Eastern cities.

That revelation about the context of conflict and its catastrophic potential has had an immense impact on my political thinking. War in the Middle East must at all costs be averted, but by standing up to, rather than mollifying, terror. The context of conflict must be defused, gradually but unstintingly, by guaranteeing basic human rights—above all, women's rights—to all the region's inhabitants. Only then, with deterrence restored and freedom implanted, can Arabs and Israelis, together with the many other Middle East protagonists, begin to address the core issues dividing them. Only then can the universal prerequisites of peace—mutual respect and empathy—take root.

FOUAD AJAMI: **Yitzhak Rabin won the territories of the West Bank and Gaza in 1967, and sought partition in 1992–93. Will his legacy be vindicated in the years to come, or are Israelis and Arabs—more precisely Israelis and Palestinians—doomed to more warfare?**

MICHAEL OREN: Yitzhak Rabin's legacy will be vindicated once the Palestinians—and with them, the rest of the Arab world—reconcile themselves to the existence of a sovereign Jewish state in the Middle East.

Today, a solid majority of Israelis have abandoned the notion of a Greater Israel, and support the creation of a Palestinian state, even at the cost of removing settlements from the West Bank and Gaza. They recognize the reality of a Palestinian people that has suffered injustices in the past and that enjoys a legitimate claim to part of the territory Israelis regard as their historical and spiritual homeland. The Palestinians, however, have yet to reciprocate that recognition. Many still deny that a Jewish people exists, that a Holocaust occurred, or that Jews have lived in the land for centuries.

Once that recognition emerges—once the Palestinian leadership ceases to educate Arab youth for rejection and armed conflict and instills in them the principles of democracy and mutual respect—then most Israelis will vote to withdraw from virtually all of the territories and for generous concessions in Jerusalem as well. Until that happens, unfortunately, no arrangement, whether imposed by the international community or negotiated by Israeli and Palestinian representatives lacking in grassroots support, can succeed. Peace must be built from the bottom up, and until the groundwork for that edifice is laid, violence in the Middle East is almost certain to continue.

FOUAD AJAMI: **Is the Arab rejection of Israel today deeper or more amenable to resolution than it was in 1967?**

MICHAEL OREN: In its attitudes toward Israel, the Arab world today is starkly divided between rulers and the ruled. With few exceptions—Libya, Iraq—Arab governments for the most part accept the notion of negotiating with Israel and talk in terms of future peace arrangements. The leaders of Egypt and Jordan have signed such treaties already and regularly assert their commitment to them.

Arab public opinion, by contrast, is staunchly opposed to any form of recognition of Israel and highly supportive of military measures against the Jewish state. Anti-Zionist propaganda dominates the Arab press and poisons Arabic school textbooks. In Egypt, where the state-run television recently broadcast a multipart movie based on the *Protocols of the Elders of Zion*, a vicious anti-Semitic forgery, the number-one hit song was "I Hate Israel." Forbidden by dictatorial regimes to voice political ideas on any subject *but* Israel and increasingly driven by the lack of basic freedoms to seek Islamic solutions to their problems, Arab populations remain as anti-Israel as they were in 1967.

Altering this situation, generating a readiness for genuine peace and reconciliation, will require a long-term and concerted process of democratization in the Middle East—democracies, historically, rarely make war on one another—and the opening of Arab society to notions of free expression, elected governments, and women's rights. Only then, with the emergence of a strong middle class with a vested interest in stability and a society capable of debating the pros and cons of peace, can a real end to the Arab-Israeli conflict be contemplated.

FOUAD AJAMI: **With your research, you place yourself on that seam between Israelis and Arabs. Based on information from the archives, from the debates, do you think these antagonists know enough about each other?**

MICHAEL OREN: Among the causes of the 1967 war, ignorance was perhaps the most prominent. The Israelis failed to anticipate the degree to which inter-Arab rivalries and Soviet machinations could prod Arab states toward war, and Arab leaders failed to anticipate Israel's readiness to preempt that process militarily. Israeli decision makers were convinced that Nasser sought to destroy the Dimona reactor—the documents prove that he did not—while Nasser believed that Israel would reconcile itself to the loss of free shipping to Eilat.

Though one might expect the Israelis, with their formidable intelligence services and cadres of trained Arabists, to be better informed about their neighbors, the Israeli files reveal a shocking unawareness of political currents and power relationships on the Arab side. The relationship between Nasser and 'Amer, for example, a major determinant in Egyptian policy, was virtually unknown to the Israelis. By the same token, Arab sources abound with myths about the nature of Israeli politics and society. Not a single Arab writer of the 1960s grasped the dynamism of Israel's democracy or gauged the military might that democracy could field.

It remains to be seen whether, nearly four decades and as many wars later, Arabs and Israelis have become better acquainted. Though the advent of modern communications promises to expand such mutual knowledge, in the Middle East the media often serve to spread falsehoods and deepen ignorance. In the end, there is no substitute for face-to-face personal encounters between Arabs and Israelis. Borders of hostility must be broken down before those of peace can arise.

NOTES

The Context

1. Al-Fatah's first operation is described in many sources. The versions vary, however. See, for example, Yezid Sayigh, *Armed Struggle and the Search for State: The Palestinian National Movement, 1949–1993* (Oxford: Clarendon Press, 1997), pp. 107–8, 121. Ehud Yaari, *Strike Terror: The Story of Fatah* (New York: Sabra Books, 1970), pp. 49–79. Salah Khalaf, *My Home My Land, A Narrative of the Palestinian Struggle* (New York: Times Books, 1981), pp. 44–49. Helena Cobban, *The Palestinian Liberation Organization* (Cambridge: Cambridge University Press, 1983), pp. 22–39. Alan Hart, *Arafat: A Political Biography* (London: Sidgwick & Jackson, 1994), pp. 155–56. Ahmad al-Shuqayri, *Mudhakkirat Ahmad al-Shuqayri, 'Ala Tariq al-Hazima, Ma'a al-Muluk wal-Ru'asa'* (Beirut: Dar al-'Awda, 1971), 3, pp. 152–88, 229–56. Arafat quote in Riad El-Rayyes and Dunia Nahas, *Guerrillas for Palestine* (London: Croom Helm, 1976), p. 27.

2. Studies on the origins of Zionism abound. See, for example, David Vital, *The Origins of Zionism: The Formative Years* (Oxford: Oxford University Press, 1982).

3. On Britain's promises to the Jews and the Palestinian Arabs, see Walter Laqueur, *The Israel-Arab Reader* (New York, Citadel Press, 1968), pp. 15–18, and Leonard Stein, *The Balfour Declaration* (London: Mitchell Vallentine, 1961), pp. 309–514, 534–58. See also J. M. Ahmed, *The Intellectual Origins of Egyptian Nationalism* (London: Oxford University Press, 1960).

4. Francis R. Nicosia, *The Third Reich and the Palestine Question* (London: I. B. Tauris, 1985), pp. 177–78. Lukasz Hirszowicz, *The Third Reich and the Arab East* (London: Routledge & K. Paul, 1966), pp. 71, 95, 248. For biographies of Ben-Gurion, see Shabtai Teveth, *Ben-Gurion: The Burning Ground, 1906–1948* (Boston: Houghton Mifflin, 1987), and Michael Bar Zohar, *Ben-Gurion: A Biography* (New York: Adama Books, 1977).

5. Israel Gershoni and James P. Jankowski, *Egypt, Islam and the Arabs: The Search for Egyptian Nationhood, 1900–1930* (Oxford: Oxford University Press, 1986), pp. 40–55, 231–69. Michael Doran, *Pan-Arabism Before Nasser: Egyptian Power Politics and the Palestine Question* (New York: Oxford University Press, 1999), pp. 94–127. Albert Hourani, *A History of the Arab Peoples* (London: Faber and Faber, 1991), pp. 340–64.

6. Yehoshua Porath, *In Search of Arab Unity* (London: Frank Cass, 1986), pp. 290–311. Ahmed M. Gomaa, *The Foundation of the League of Arab States: Wartime Diplomacy and Inter-Arab Politics, 1941 to 1945* (London and New York: Longman, 1977), pp. 98–133.

7. Mary C. Wilson, *King Abdullah, Britain and the Making of Jordan* (Cambridge: Cambridge University Press, 1987), pp. 151–86. On the flight of Palestinian refugees, see also Ilan Pappe, *Britain and the Arab-Israel Conflict, 1948–1951* (London: Macmillan, 1988). Dan Scheuftan, *Ha-Optzia ha-Yardenit: Ha-Yishuv ve-Medinat Yisrael mul ha-Mimshal ha-Hashemi ve ha-Tnua ha-Leumit ha-Falastinit* (Tel Aviv: Yad Tabenkin, Machon Yisrael Galili, 1986). The best treatment of international diplomacy on the Palestine issue can be found in Wm. Roger Louis, *The British Empire in the Middle East, 1945–1951: Arab Nationalism, the United States, and Postwar Imperialism* (Oxford: Oxford University Press, 1984), pp. 381–574.

8. A similar observation was made by the Hebrew University historian J. L. Talmon immediately after the 1967 war: "The Jewish complex grows from a mixture of fear and distrust, on the one hand, and a feeling of power on the other . . . The mixture of hubris and fear is all pervading in Israel. One hears people say in the same breath 'we can reach Cairo within hours; we may be destroyed in half an hour . . .'" See J. L. Talmon, *The Six Days' War in Historical Perspective* (Rehovot, Israel: Yad Chaim Weizmann, 1969), p. 78.

9. Recent writings by revisionist authors have claimed that the Jewish forces in the 1948 war actually outnumbered the Arabs. See, for example, Benny Morris, *The Birth of the Palestinian Refugee Problem*, pp. 20–23. This may be true for the later stages of the conflict, but in its crucial initial phase, in May–June, when Israel's fate hung in the balance, the Arabs invaded with overwhelming force.

10. On the contacts with Husni Za'im, see David Peled, "Ben-Gurion Wasn't Rushing Anywhere," *Ha'aretz* (English edition), Jan. 20, 2000, p. 4, and Itamar Rabinovich, *The Road Not Taken: Early Arab-Israeli Negotiations* (New York: Oxford University Press, 1991), pp. 65–167.

11. On Nuri's secret contacts with the Israelis, see Michael Oren, "Nuri al-Sa'id and Arab-Israel Peace," *Asian and African Studies* 24, no. 3 (1990).

12. Yaacov Ro'i, *From Encroachment to Involvement: A Documentary Study of Soviet Foreign Policy in the Middle East, 1945–1973* (New York: Wiley, 1974), p. 115. Galia Golan, *Soviet Politics in the Middle East: From World War II to Gorbachev* (Cambridge: Cambridge University Press, 1990), pp. 29–37. Naftali Ben-Tsion Goldberg, "SSSR Protiv Izrailia," *Sem Dney*, Aug. 17, 2000, p. 4. M. Prokhorov, ed., *Sovetskii Entsiklopedicheskii Slovar*, 4th ed. (Moscow: Soviet Encyclopedia, 1989), p. 486. Khrushchev quote in Yosef Govrin, *Israeli-Soviet Relations, 1953–1967: From Confrontation to Disruption* (London: Frank Cass, 1990), p. 66.

13. Alpha plan discussed in Evelyn Shuckburgh, *Descent to Suez, 1951–1956* (London: Weidenfeld and Nicolson, 1986), pp. 242–67, and Michael B. Oren, "Secret Efforts to Achieve an Egypt-Israel Settlement Prior to the Suez Campaign," *Middle Eastern Studies* 26, no. 3 (1990).

14. Gamal Abdel Nasser, *The Philosophy of the Revolution* (Washington, D.C.: Public Affairs Press, 1955). Nasser quote from Robert Stephens, *Nasser, A Political Biography* (London: Penguin, 1971), pp. 135–36.

15. Zaki Shalom, *David Ben-Gurion, Medinat Yisrael ve ha-Olam ha-Aravi, 1949–1956* (Sede Boqer: Ha-Merkaz le-Moreshet Ben-Gurion, 1995), p. 39. Michael B. Oren, *Origins of the Second Arab-Israeli War* (London: Frank Cass, 1993), pp. 29–34. Michael B. Oren, "The Egypt-Israel Border War," *Journal of Contemporary History* 24 (1990). V. A. Kirpichenko, *Iz Arkhiva Razvedchika* (Moscow: Mezhdunorodnyie Otnosheniya, 1993), pp. 37–39. On the disputes surrounding the Jordan River and the Hula swamp, see Arnon Soffer, *Rivers of Fire: The Conflicts Over Water in the Middle East* (Lanham, Md.: Rowman and Littlefield, 1999), and Kathryn B. Doherty, *Jordan Waters Conflict* (New York: Carnegie Endowment for International Peace, 1965).

16. Oren, "Secret Efforts to Achieve an Egypt-Israel Settlement Prior to the Suez Campaign."

17. Michael B. Oren, "The Tripartite System in the Middle East, 1950–1956," in Dori Gold, ed., *Arms Control and Monitoring in the Middle East* (Boulder, Colo.: Westview Press, 1990).

18. NAC, MG 26, N1, 29: Pearson Papers: Middle East Crisis, Nov. 20, 1956. ISA, 2459/1: Tekoah to Embassies, Nov. 15, 1956. John Moore, ed., *The Arab-Israel Conflict: Readings and Documents* (Princeton, N.J.: Princeton University Press, 1977), pp. 1045–55. PRO, FO371/121738/189: Dixon to Foreign Office, May 3, 1956. FRUS, XVI, p. 1208. BGA, "Diary: The Diplomatic Battle Over Suez," July 1957. Michael B. Oren, "Faith and Fair-Mindedness: Lester B. Pearson and the Suez Crisis," *Diplomacy and Statecraft* 3, no. 1 (1992); Michael B. Oren, "Ambivalent Adversaries: David Ben-Gurion and Dag Hammarskjold," *Journal of Contemporary History* 27 (1992). Brian Urquhart, *A Life in Peace and War* (New York: Harper & Row, 1987), pp. 193–94.

19. P. J. Vatikiotis, *Nasser and His Generation* (New York: St. Martin's Press, 1978), p. 161.

20. For Arab perceptions of Israel during this period, see Mahmud Husayn, *Al Sira' al-Tabaqi fi Misr min 1945 ila 1970* (Beirut: Dar al-Tali'a, 1971), pp. 250–53. Amin Al-Nafuri, *Tawazun al-Quwwa bayna al-'Arab wa-Isra'il: Dirasa Tahliliyya Istratejiyya li 'Udwan Haziran 1967* (Damascus: Dar al-I'tidal lil-Tiba'a wal-Nashr, 1968), pp. 162–67.

21. Malcolm H. Kerr, *The Arab Cold War: Gamal Abd al-Nasir and His Rivals, 1958–70* (Oxford: Oxford University Press, 1971). Stephens, *Nasser*, pp. 356–57. John Waterbury, *The Egypt of Nasser and Sadat: The Political Economy of Two Regimes* (Princeton, N.J.: Princeton University Press, 1983), pp. 57–82.

22. Alvin Z. Rubinstein, *Red Star on the Nile: The Soviet-Egyptian Influence Relationship Since the June War* (Princeton, N.J.: Princeton University Press, 1977), p. 136.

23. Baruch Gilad, ed., *Teudot le-Mediniyut ha-Hutz shel Medinat Yisrael* 14, 1960 (Jerusalem: Israel Government Printing House, 1997), pp. 16–32. Yitzhak Rabin, *The Rabin Memoirs* (Berkeley: University of California Press, 1996), pp. 55–56. Ze'ev Lachish and Meir Amitai, *Asor Lo Shaket: Prakim be-Toldot Hail ha-Avir ba-Shanim 1956–1967* (Tel Aviv: Misrad ha-Bitahon, 1995), pp. 232–47. Oral history, Col. Shlomo Merom, Dec. 7, 1999. Interview with General Anwar al-Qadi in *al-Ra'i al-'Am*, June 2, 1987.

24. Patrick Seale, *Asad of Syria: The Struggle for the Middle East* (London: I. B. Taurus, 1988), pp. 65–68.

25. *Foreign Relations of the United States 18, 1961–1963: Near East* (Washington: U.S. Government Printing Office, 1995), p. 62. Statistics on U.S. wheat shipments to Egypt and the Chester Bowles quote in William J. Burns, *Economic Aid and American Policy Toward Egypt, 1955–1981* (Albany: State University of New York Press, 1985), pp. 212–16.

26. Ali Abdel Rahman Rahmi, *Egyptian Policy in the Arab World: Intervention in Yemen 1962–1967, A Case Study* (Washington, D.C.: University Press of America, 1983), pp. 189–96. On Nasser's relationship with 'Amer, see 'Abdallah Imam, *Nasir wa-'Amer* (Cairo: Mu'assasat al-Kitab, 1985), pp. 5–32, 67–83. Gen. Muhammad Fawzi, *Harb al-Thalath Sanawat* (Cairo: Dar al-Mustaqbal al-'Arabi, 1980), pp. 33–45. Mohamed Hassanein Heikal, *1967: Al-Infijar* (Cairo: Markaz al-Ahram, 1990), pp. 181, 394–98.

27. Nasser himself would make the Yemen-Vietnam comparison. See LBJ, Lucius Battle Oral History, p. 38.

28. Vatikiotis, *Nasser and His Generation*, pp. 161–62. Anwar El-Sadat, *In Search of Identity: An Autobiography* (New York: Harper & Row, 1977), pp. 162–63. Burns, *Economic Aid and American Policy*, pp. 139–40. Rahmi, *Egyptian Policy in the Arab World*, pp. 189–96. Kennedy quote from *Foreign Relations of the United States 18, 1961–1963*, pp. 752–53.

29. Kennedy quote from *Foreign Relations of the United States 18, 1961–1963*, pp. 280–81. See also Judith A. Klinghoffer, *Vietnam, Jews and the Middle East: Unintended Consequences* (New York: St. Martin's Press, 1999), p. 9. Mordechai Gazit, *President Kennedy's Policy Toward the Arab States and Israel: Analysis and Documents* (Syracuse, N.Y.: Syracuse University Press, 1983). Moshe Ma'oz, *Syria and Israel: From War to Peacemaking* (Oxford: Clarendon Press, 1995), pp. 86–87.

30. Israel's nuclear policy in this period, and its place in Kennedy's foreign policy, are discussed at length in Avner Cohen, *Israel and the Bomb* (New York: Columbia University Press, 1998) and Seymour Hersh, *The Samson Option* (New York: Random House, 1991). Nasser's use of West German and former Nazi scientists is revealed in PRO, FCO 39/233 UAR Internal Political Situation: Who's Who of Nasser's Ex-Nazis, June 26, 1967. See also Martin Van Creveld, *The Sword and the Olive: A Critical History of the Israeli Defense Force* (New York: Public Affairs, 1998), p. 164. Terence Prittie, *Eshkol: The Man and the Nation* (New York: Pitman, 1969), p. 225.

31. Ben-Gurion quotes from, respectively, ISA, Foreign Ministry files, 3329/1: Prime Minister to Director-General of the Foreign Ministry, Nov. 19, 1961, and 723/5/A: Foreign Ministry to Embassy in Washington, May 14, 1963. America's assessment of Egyptian missile capabilities in LBJ, National Intelligence Estimates, boxes 6–7: The Eastern Arab World, Feb. 17, 1966. On Israel's contract with Dassault, see Cohen, *Israel and the Bomb*, p. 116.

32. Ze'ev Schiff, *A History of the Israeli Army, 1874 to the Present* (New York: Macmillan, 1985), pp. 115–17. George W. Gawrych, *The Albatross of Decisive Victory: War and Policy Between Egypt and Israel in the 1967 and 1973 Arab-Israeli Wars* (Westport, Conn.: Greenwood Press, 2000), pp. 23–27. Ze'ev Lachish and Meir Amitai, *Asor Lo Shaket*, pp. 28–31. Aharon Yariv, *Ha'arakha Zehira: Kovetz Ma'amarim* (Tel Aviv: Ma'arakhot, 1998), pp. 123–24. Yair Evron, "Two Periods in the Arab-Israeli Strategic Relations 1957–1967; 1967–1973," in Itamar Rabinovich and Haim Shaked, eds., *From June to October: The Middle East Between 1967 and 1973* (New Brunswick, N.J.: Transaction, 1978), pp. 100, 112–13. S.N. Eisenstadt, *Ha-Hevra ha-Yisraelit* (Jerusalem: Magnes Press of Hebrew University, 1970), pp. 26–33. Klinghoffer, *Vietnam, Jews and the Middle East*, p. 20. Van Creveld, *The Sword and the Olive*, pp. 156–57.

33. Prittie, *Eshkol*, p. 211. Eshkol quotes from Moshe A. Gilboa, *Shesh Shanim, Shisha Yamim–Mekoroteha ve-Koroteha shel Milhemet Sheshet ha-Yamim* (Tel Aviv: Am Oved, 1969), pp. 34, 36.

34. Egyptian quote from Moshe Shemesh, *The Palestinian Entity 1959–1974: Arab Politics and the PLO* (London: Frank Cass, 1989), p. 4. Saudi-Jordanian quote from Asher Susser, *On Both Banks of the Jordan: A Political Biography of Wasfi al-Tall* (London: Frank Cass, 1994), pp. 55–57.

35. Syrian quote from Burns, *Economic Aid and American Policy*, p. 140. Nasser quote from Avraham Sela, *The Decline of the Arab-Israeli Conflict: Middle East Politics and the Quest for Regional Order* (Albany: State University of New York Press, 1998), p. 59. Itamar Rabinovich, *Syria Under the Ba'th 1963–66: The Army-Party Symbiosis* (Jerusalem: Israel Universities Press, 1972), pp. 95–96. Tal quote from Susser, *On Both Banks of the Jordan*, p. 55. See also Leila S. Kadi, *Arab Summit Conferences, and the Palestine Problem, 1945–1966* (Beirut: Palestine Liberation Organization, 1966), pp. 96–109. Fawzi, *Harb al-Thalath Sanawat*, p. 49. Mohamed H. Heikal, *Sanawat al-Ghalayan* (Cairo: Markaz al-Ahram, 1988), pp. 729–30.

36. Syrian quote from Moshe Shemesh, "Hama'avak ha-'Aravi al ha-Mayim Neged Yisrael, 1959–1967," *Iyunim* 7 (1997): 124. Nasser quote from Heikal, *Sanawat al-Ghalayan*, p. 740.

37. David Kimche and Dan Bawly, *The Sandstorm: The Arab-Israeli War of June 1967: Prelude and Aftermath* (London: Secker & Warburg, 1968), p. 25.

38. Mahmoud Riad, *The Struggle for Peace in the Middle East* (New York: Quartet Books, 1981), p. 12. Samir A. Mutawi, *Jordan in the 1967 War* (Cambridge: Cambridge University Press, 1987), pp. 57–58.

39. Quote from Shemesh, *The Palestinian Entity*, p. 38. See also Sela, *The Decline of the Arab-Israeli Conflict*, pp. 62–68. Fawzi, *Harb al-Thalath Sanawat*, pp. 47–48.

40. Ma'oz, *Syria and Israel*, p. 81.

41. The PLO, hailed as "the vanguard of the joint Arab struggle for the liberation of Palestine," was constituted by a Palestinian assembly in Jerusalem on May 28, 1964. See Sayigh, *Armed Struggle and the Search for State*, pp. 95–100. Al-Shuqayri, *Mudhakkirat* 3, p. 144. Avraham Sela, ed., *Political Encyclopedia of the Middle East* (New York: Continuum, 1999), pp. 602–3.

42. LBJ, National Intelligence Estimates, boxes 6–7: The Eastern Arab World, Feb. 17, 1966. Kadi, *Arab Summit Conferences*, pp. 176–77. Al-Shuqayri, *Mudhakkirat* 3, pp. 78–84, 98–106. Heikal, *al-Infijar*, pp. 199–218. Mohamed Ahmed Mahjoub, *Democracy on Trial: Reflections on Arab and African Politics* (London: Andre Deutsch, 1974) pp. 105–14.

43. Oral history interview, Adnan Abu Oudeh, Amman, Nov. 6, 1999. Jadid quotes from Avraham Ben Tzur, *Gormim Sovietiim u-Milhemet Sheshet ha-Yamim: Ma'avakim ba-Kremlin ve-Hashpa'ot be-Azoreinu* (Tel Aviv: Sifriat Poalim, 1975), p. 17. Ma'oz, *Syria and Israel*, p. 84.

44. Bourgiba's plan was designed to paint Israel into a corner. If Israel also accepted the Partition Resolution, sacrificing 30 percent of its territory and accepting the establishment of a Palestinian state, then that would become the basis for negotiations and additional Arab claims. If Israel rejected the plan, the Arab call for war would then be legitimized. For the period of the second and third Arab summits, see Kerr, *The Arab Cold War*, pp. 98–116. Sela, *The Decline of the Arab-Israeli Conflict*, pp. 75–94.

Gilboa, *Shesh Shanim, Shisha Yamim,* p. 40. Heikal, *Al-Infijar,* pp. 137–42. Rahmi, *Egyptian Policy in the Arab World,* pp. 224 27.

45. Nasser quote from Burns, *Economic Aid and American Policy,* p. 159. An alternative translation appears in Richard B. Parker, *The Politics of Miscalculation in the Middle East* (Bloomington: Indiana University Press, 1993), p. 105. Klinghoffer, *Vietnam, Jews and the Middle East,* p. 72. Heikal, *Al-Infijar,* p. 372. See also LBJ, Lucius Battle Oral History, p. 38; David Nes Oral History, pp. 3–5.

46. PRO FCO/39/285, UAR – Economic Affairs: Effects of the Arab-Israeli War on the UAR Economy, Dec. 1, 1967. Kimche and Bawly, *The Sandstorm,* pp. 35–36. Vatikiotis, *Nasser and His Generation,* pp. 202–12. Heikal, *Sanawat,* pp. 733–57, 774–75. Heikal, *Al-infijar,* pp. 175–84. Riad, *The Struggle for Peace in the Middle East,* pp. 15–17. El-Sadat, *In Search of Identity,* pp. 164–65.

47. Ze'ev Ma'oz, "The Evolution of Syrian Power, 1948–1984," in Moshe Ma'oz and Avner Yaniv, eds., *Syria Under Assad: Domestic Constraints and Regional Risks* (London: Croom Helm, 1986), pp. 71–76.

48. Aharon Yariv, *Ha'arakha Zehira,* pp. 159–61, Aharon Yariv, "Ha-Reka la-Milhama," *Dapei Elazar, no. 10, Esrim Shana le-Milhemet Sheshet ha-Yamim* (Tel Aviv: Yad David Elazar, 1988), pp. 15–23. Avi Cohen, *Ha-Hagannah al Mekorot ha-Mayim–Mediniyut Hafalat Hail Ha-Avir le-Tkifa bi-Gvul Yisrael-Suria, 1956–1967* (Tel Aviv: Hail ha-Avir, Misrad ha-Bitahon, 1992), p. 55.

49. On the Syrian-Israeli border war of 1964–65, see PRO, FCO17/565, Israel – Territorial: Hadow to Morris, Feb. 15, 1967. Mustafa Khalil, *Min Milaffat al-Julan: Al-Qism al-Awwal* (Amman: Dar al-Yaqin lil-Tiba'a wal-Nashr, 1970), p. 47. Hanoch Bartov, *Dado: 48 Years and 20 Days* (Tel Aviv: Ma'ariv Books, 1981), pp. 83–92. Shabtai Teveth, *The Tanks of Tammuz* (London: Sphere Books, 1969), pp. 76–95. Cohen, *Ha-Hagannah al Mekorot ha-Mayim,* pp. 86–87, 107–8; Eshkol quote on p. 113.

50. Heikal, *Al-Infijar,* pp. 220–23, 239–46, 333, and Heikal, *The Sphinx and the Commissar: The Rise and Fall of Soviet Influence in the Middle East* (London: Collins, 1978), pp. 166–68. I. Adeed Dawisha, *Egypt in the Arab World: The Elements of Foreign Policy* (New York: Wiley, 1976), pp. 46–47. Lachish and Amitai, *Asor Lo Shaket,* pp. 19–20. Sayigh, *Armed Struggle and the Search for State,* pp. 100–107. ISA, 3975/14, Foreign Ministry files, Diplomatic Relations with the United States, Washington to Foreign Ministry, July 12, 1966. Nasser quotes from Theodore Draper, *Israel & World Politics: Roots of the Third Arab-Israeli War* (New York: Viking, 1967), p. 44, and Stephens, *Nasser,* p. 461.

51. Gen. Odd Bull, *War and Peace in the Middle East: The Experiences and Views of a U.N. Observer* (London: Lee Cooper, 1973), p. 95. Mutawi, *Jordan in the 1967 War,* pp. 38–39, 114. Susser, *On Both Banks of the Jordan,* p. 78.

52. Moshe Zak, *Hussein Ose Shalom* (Ramat Gan: Merkaz Begin-Sadat, 1966), pp. 6–75. Meir Amit, *Rosh be-Rosh: Mabat Ishi al Eruim Gdolim u-Farshiyot Alumot* (Or Yehuda: Hed Arzi, 1999), pp. 94–98. Ben-Gurion quote in *Documents of the Foreign Policy of Israel,* pp. 36–37.

53. Hussein quotes from Susser, *On Both Banks of the Jordan,* pp. 105–6, and Mutawi, *Jordan in the 1967 War,* pp. 66–67. See also William B. Quandt, Fuad Jabber and Ann Mosley Lesche, *The Politics of Palestinian Nationalism* (Berkeley: University of California Press, 1973), pp. 165, 173. Kerr, *The Arab Cold War,* pp. 112–22. Heikal, *Al-Infijar,* pp. 351–53.

54. Eitan Haber, *Ha-Yom Tifrotz Milhama: Zikhronotav shel Tat-Aluf Yisrael Lior, ha-Mazkir Hatzvai shel Rashei ha-Memshala Levi Eshkol ve-Golda Meir* (Tel Aviv: Yediot Ahronot, 1987), pp. 54, 122, 133–34. Matitiahu Mayzel, *Ha-Ma'arakha al ha-Golan–Yuni 1967* (Tel Aviv: Ma'arakhot, 2001), pp. 99–101. The complete Eli Cohen story can be found on the Internet, at www.elicohen.com.

55. Sylvia K. Crosbie, *A Tacit Alliance: France and Israel from Suez to the Six Day War* (Princeton, N.J.: Princeton University Press, 1974), pp. 123–24, 140–48, 170, 224–25. Jean Lacouture, *De Gaulle: The Ruler, 1945–1970* (New York: Norton, 1992), p. 435. ISA, 3975/16, Foreign Ministry files, Diplomatic Relations with the United States: Bitan to Harman, Jan. 19, 1967.

56. Johnson quotes from I. L. Kenen, *Israel's Defense Line: Her Friends and Foes in Washington* (Buffalo, N.Y.: Prometheus Books, 1981), p. 173, and USNA, Middle East Crisis files, 1967, Lot file 68D135, box 1: United States Statements on Israel: Johnson Statements, June 1, 1964. Eshkol quote from Cohen, *Israel and the Bomb*, p. 204.

57. ISA, 3976/9, Foreign Ministry files, Relations with the United States: Eban Conversation with Johnson, Sept. 2, 1966. Lachish and Amitai, *Asor Lo Shaket*, pp. 22–23. Klinghoffer, *Vietnam, Jews and the Middle East*, p. 61. Memorandum of Understanding quoted in Ma'oz, *Syria and Israel*, pp. 86–87.

58. Documents relating to the connection between Vietnam and the Middle East proliferate in the Israeli archives. Though Israel could not come out openly in support of the war—leftist members of the government opposed it—Israeli representatives conveyed strong backing for America's policies in Southeast Asia. See, for example, ISA, 3975/12, Foreign Ministry files, Diplomatic Relations with the United States: Harman to Eban, June 24, 1966; 3975/14, Diplomatic Relations with the United States: Harman to Foreign Ministry, July 4, 1966; 3977/22, Diplomatic Relations with the United States: Report on Eshkol Talk with Feinberg and Ginzburg, April 28, 1966.

59. A survey of Israel's economic crisis appears in PRO FCO17/577: Israel – Defense: Report of Defense Attaché, Nov. 16, 1966. See also Gawrych, *The Albatross of Decisive Victory*, p. 3.

60. Ma'oz, *Syria and Israel*, p. 89.

61. An internal CIA memorandum described the new Syrian government as "unstable, as any foreseeable successor is likely to be. The prospect is one of a succession of extremist military governments . . . The question in regard to Syria's future then is not whether it will be moderate or radical, but what will be the kind and intensity of its radicalism." LBJ, National Security file, Middle East, boxes 145–57: Special Memorandum – Syria's Radical Future. See also, Quandt, Jabber, and Lesche, *The Politics of Palestinian Nationalism*, pp. 166–67. Itamar Rabinovich, "Suria, ha-Yahasim ha-bein-Araviyim u-Frotz Milhemet Sheshet ha-Yamim," in Asher Susser, ed., *Shisha Yamim–Shloshim Shana* (Tel Aviv: Am Oved, 1999), pp. 50–52.

62. On Soviet aid to the Arab world, see PRO, FCO17/112: Soviet Aid to Arab Countries, June 26, 1967 and USNA, Lot files, USUN, box 6: Circular: Foreign Military Assistance to Near East Countries, June 19, 1967. I. L. Blishchenko and V. D. Kudriavtsev, *Agressia Izrailia i Mezhdunarodnoie Pravo* (Moscow: Mezhdunorodnyie Otnosheniya, 1970), pp. 8–11. See also Christoper Andrew and Oleg Gordievsky, *KGB: The Inside Story* (New York: HarperCollins, 1990), pp. 495–98. Oded Eran, "Soviet Policy Between 1967 and 1973," in Rabinovich and Shaked, *From June to October*, pp. 27–30. Kimche and Bawly, *The Sandstorm*, pp. 44–45. Burns, *Economic Aid and American Policy*,

p. 154. On Khrushchev's ouster, see LBJ, Lucius Battle Oral History, pp. 14–15. 'Amer quote from Heikal, *Al-Infijar*, p. 81.

63. NAC, RG 25 box 2827, Syria: New Urge for Industrialization, Feb. 8, 1967. ISA, 4048/1627, Foreign Ministry files, Soviet Foreign Relations: Eban Conversation with Hare, April 27, 1966. Yariv, *Ha'arakha Zehira*, p. 149. Ben Tzur, *Gormim Sovietiim u-Milhemet Sheshet ha-Yamim*, pp. 35–49, 71–72. V. M. Vinogradov, *Diplomatia: liudi i sobytia* (Moscow: Rosspen, 1998), pp. 151–54, 215. O. E. Tuganova, *Mezhdunarodnyie otnoshenia na Blizhnem i Srednem Vostoke* (Moscow: Mezhdunarodnyie Otnoshenia, 1967), pp. 134–35.

64. A. M. Grechko, *Sovetskaia Voiennaia Entsiklopedia 3* (Moscow: Institut Voiennoi Istorii, 1976), p. 508. V. Rumiantsev, "Arabskii Vostok na Novom Puti," *Kommunist* (Moscow) 16 (November 1969), p. 91. I. Ivanov, *Ostorozhno: Sionizm!*, 2nd ed. (Moscow: Politicheskaia Literatura, 1971), p. 3. I. P. Beliaev and E. M. Primakov, *Egipet: Vremia Prezidenta Nasera* (Moscow: Mysl, 1974), p. 324. V. V. Zhurkin and E. M. Primakov, eds., *Mezhdunarodnyie Konflikty* (Moscow: Mezhdunarodnyie Otnoshenia, 1972), p. 129. Govrin, *Israeli-Soviet Relations*, pp. 276–79, 300. Avigdor Dagan, *Moscow and Jerusalem: Twenty Years of Relations Between Israel and the Soviet Union* (London: Abelard-Schuman, 1970), pp. 155–57.

65. Ben Tzur, *Gormim Sovietiim u-Milhemet Sheshet ha-Yamim*, pp. 190–91, 210–11. Atassi quote from Draper, *Israel & World Politics*, p. 35.

66. On U.S. support for Israel *vis-à-vis* Syria, see LBJ, National Security file, Middle East, Israel box 140, 141: Conversation with Foreign Minister Eban, Nov. 3, 1966. ISA, 3977/20, Foreign Ministry files, Relations with the United States: Evron to Bitan, Oct. 25, 1966; President Johnson to Eshkol, Nov. 9, 1966.

67. ISA, 3975/12, Diplomatic Relations with the United States: Rafael to Bitan, June 20, 1966. Haber, *Ha-Yom Tifrotz Milhama*, pp. 127, 139. Parker, *The Politics of Miscalculation*, p. 11. Govrin, *Israeli-Soviet Relations*, pp. 287–89. Tass quote from Dagan, *Moscow and Jerusalem*, p. 176.

68. The Israeli and Syrian versions of the fighting in the Galilee in this period can be found in UN, DAG 13/3.4.0, box 82, Israel/Syria High Level Talks, Cultivation Arrangements: Barromi to the President of Security Council, Jan. 9, 1967, and Tomeh to President of Security Council, Jan. 10, 1967. See also Cohen, *Ha-Hagannah al Mekorot ha-Mayim*, pp. 140–56.

69. Sayigh, *Armed Struggle and the Search for State*, pp. 137–38. Rabin quote from Gilboa, *Shesh Shanim, Shisha Yamim*, pp. 287–89. Syrian quote from BBC, Daily Report, Middle East, Africa, and Western Europe, No. 199, G3.

70. Cohen, *Israel and the Bomb*, p. 261.

71. Amit, *Rosh be-Rosh*, pp. 210–26. Haber, *Ha-Yom Tifrotz Milhama*, pp. 64–65. Klinghoffer, *Vietnam, Jews and the Middle East*, p. 73. On the confluence of Egyptian and Israeli interests in 1966, see ISA, 3975/15, Foreign Ministry files, Diplomatic Relations with the United States: Argov to Harman, March 19, 1966, and 3978/2, United States – Relations with the Middle East. Evron to Gazit, Aug. 25, 1967.

72. 'Ali 'Amer quote from Gilboa, *Shesh Shanim, Shisha Yamim*, p. 65. Nasser quote from Heikal, *Al-Infijar*, pp. 365–66. See also Sela, *The Decline of the Arab-Israeli Conflict*, p. 90. Kerr, *The Arab Cold War*, pp. 122–28. Seale, *Asad of Syria*, p. 126.

73. Suliman Mazhar, *I'tirafat Qadat Harb Yunyu: Nusus Shahadatihim Amama Lajnat Tasjil Ta'rikh al-Thawra* (Cairo: Kitab al-Hurriyya, 1990), p. 88. Makhous quote from

BBC, Daily Report No. 183, G3. Voice of the Arabs and Damascus Radio quotes from BBC, Daily Report No. 183, B1 and Daily Report No. 199, G1.

74. ISA, 3977/20, Foreign Ministry files, Relations with the United States: Handwritten Notes (by Y. Herzog) on LE meeting with Barbour, Nov. 10, 1966. MPA, Party Secretariat Procotols, 2/24/66/88: Eshkol Remarks to the Executive, Dec. 15, 1966. "Notepad" quote from Rafi Man, *Lo Ya'ale al ha-Da'at* (Or Yehuda: Hed Arzi, 1998), p. 242.

75. ISA, 4030/6, Foreign Ministry files, Diplomatic Contacts and Security Council Debate on the Samu' Operation: Harman Conversation with Symes, Nov. 14, 1966; 3977/20, Foreign Ministry files, Relations with the United States, Mr. Bitan's Visit, Nov. 29, 1966.

76. Ezer Weizman, *On Eagles' Wings: The Personal Story of the Leading Commander of the Israeli Air Force* (New York: Macmillan, 1976), p. 206. Haber, *Ha-Yom Tifrotz Milhama*, pp. 106–7. Eshkol remarks to the Cabinet in Zak, *Hussein Ose Shalom*, p. 89.

The Catalysts

1. Descriptions of the Samu' battle from ISA, 3998/5, Foreign Ministry files, Diplomatic Relations with Iran: Y. Rabin to Military Attachés, Nov. 15, 1966. Zak, *Hussein Ose Shalom*, p. 89, Kimche and Bawly, *The Sandstorm*, p. 83. Susser, *On Both Banks of the Jordan*, p. 110. Oral history interviews with Ezer Weizman, March 1, 1999 and Meir Amit, Feb. 9, 1999.

2. NAC, RG 25, box 10050: Political Affairs – Canada's Foreign Policy Trends and Relations – Israel. Middle East Situation – Call By Israeli Ambassador, Dec. 14, 1966. Charles W. Yost, "How It Began," *Foreign Affairs* (January 1968), p. 305. U Thant, *View from the UN* (New York: Doubleday, 1978), pp. 215–17.

3. On the general U.S. reaction to the Samu' raid, see LBJ, National Security file, Middle East, Israel box 140, 141: W. Rostow to the President, Nov. 14, 1966 and ISA, 4030/6, Foreign Ministry files, The Security Council Debate on the Samu' Operation, Nov. 16, 1966; Komer quote from 3977/20, Foreign Ministry files, Relations with the United States: Eban Conversation with Kromer, Dec. 12, 1966. Katzenbach quote from ISA, 3977/20, Foreign Ministry files, Relations with the United States: Eban Conversation with the Acting Secretary of State, Dec. 12, 1966. Rostow quote from ISA, 3977/20, Foreign Ministry files, Relations with the United States, Dec. 12, 1966.

4. Eban's remarks in ISA, 3977/20, Foreign Ministry files, Relations with the United States: Meeting of Foreign Minister Abba Eban with Walt Rostow, Dec. 12, 1966, and Eban Conversation with Kromer, Dec. 12, 1966. Eskhol's letter to Johnson in LBJ, National Security file, Middle East, Israel box 140, 141: Nov. 23, 1966. Johnson's letter to Hussein in LBJ, National Security file, History of the Middle East Crisis, box 17, Nov. 23, 1966. America's refusal to convey the Israeli condolence letter in LBJ, National Security file, Middle East, Israel box 140, 141: Walt Rostow to the President, Nov. 14, 1967, and from oral history interview with Mordechai Gazit, Feb. 4, 1999. National Security file, Middle East, Israel box 140, 141: W. Rostow to the President, Nov. 14, 1966. See also Uriel Dann, *King Hussein and the Challenge of Arab Radicalism: Jordan, 1955–1967* (New York: Oxford University Press, 1989), p.155, and Zak, *Hussein Ose Shalom*, p. 89.

5. Gilboa, *Shosh Shanim, Shisha Yamim*, p. 75. Eshkol quote from MPA, Party Secretariat Protocols, 2/24/66/881 Doo. 15, 1966. Lior quote from Haber, *Ha-Yom Tifrotz Milhama*, p 89

6. Hussein of Jordan, *My "War" with Israel*, as told to Vick Vance and Pierre Lauer (New York: Morrow, 1969), p. 29. Susser, *On Both Banks of the Jordan*, p. 111. Egyptian and Syrian accusations against Hussein in BBC, Daily Report No. 224, B1; Daily Report No. 192, B4–5. Hussein quote in Georgetown University, Special Collections, Findley Burns, Jr., Oral History Recollections, p. 9.

7. Al-Shuqayri, *Mudhakkirat 1*, pp. 271–72. Mutawi, *Jordan in the 1967 War*, pp. 73–74. Oral history interview with Adnan Abu-Oudeh, Amman, Nov. 16, 1999.

8. Indar Jit Rikhye oral history, Feb. 22, 2000. Hussein's letters to Nasser in BBC, Daily Report No. 224, D6-1; his interview with *Christian Science Monitor* in Daily Report No. 192, D2. Edgar O'Balance, *The Third Arab-Israeli War* (London: Faber & Faber, 1972), p. 173. Mutawi, *Jordan in the 1967 War*, p. 81.

9. ISA, 3998/5, Foreign Ministry files, Diplomatic Relations with Iran, Conversation with Dr. Sidriya—Report on Arab Defense Committee Meeting, Dec. 16, 1966. Mutawi, *Jordan in the 1967 War*, p. 82.

10. Sidqi quote in Shmuel Segev, *Sadin Adom* (Tel Aviv: Taversky Press, 1967), pp. 15–16. Predictions of Nasser's fall from power appear in PRO, FCO 39/233 UAR Internal Political Situation: UAR: General Situation. P.W. Unwin, Jan. 20, 1967, and LBJ, National Security file, Country file, Middle East-UAR box 161: CIA Report on Egypt, Oct. 3, 1966, and ISA, 3975/15, Foreign Ministry files, Diplomatic Relations with the United States: Gazit Conversation with Bergus, Feb. 6, 1967. On cuts in Egypt's defense budget, see Salah al-Din al-Hadidi, *Shahid 'ala Harb 67* (Beirut: Dar al-'Awda, 1974), pp. 31–35, and Mazhar, *I'tirafat Qadat Harb Yunyu*, p. 208–9. Information on the El Nasr Automotive plant and the Tesh quote appear in PRO, FCO 39/233, UAR Internal Political Situation, Canadian Embassy, Cairo, to Foreign Ministry, Jan. 19 and March 2, 1967, respectively.

11. Al-Tall remarks in Susser, *Both Banks of the Jordan*, pp. 117–18 and in PRO, FCO 17/231 Jordan-UAR Relations: Amman to Foreign Office, Jan. 9, 1967. Gen. 'Amer's claim in al-Shuqayri, *Mudhakkirat 3*, p. 233. Egyptian charge of Jordanian embezzlement in PRO, FCO 17/231, Jordan-UAR: Amman to Foreign Ministry, Feb. 13, 1967. Nasser's speech in PRO, FCO 17/231, Jordan-UAR Relations: Cairo to Foreign Office, March 15, 1967. Capt. Hamarsha's press conference in USNA, POL 30 Jordan, Cairo to State Department, Feb. 2, 1967. Riyad Hajjaj's press conference in PRO, FCO 17/23, Jordan-UAR Relations: Amman to Foreign Office, March 17, 1967.

12. PRO, FCO 17/231, Jordan-UAR Relations: Morris to Beaumont, March 10, 1967. Descriptions of the Arab Defense Council meeting in USNA Central Foreign Policy files, 1967–1969, POL Arab Jordan, box 1844: Amman to Washington, March 16, 1967. Heikal, *Al-Infijar*, pp. 429–31. Al-Shuqayri, *Mudhakkirat 3*, p. 285. BBC, Daily Report No. 11, B3.

13. Hussein's Jericho speech in BBC, Daily Report No. 41, D1. On Jordan's interpretation of the Egyptian-Syrian treaty, see Mutawi, *Jordan in the 1967 War*, pp. 73–79.

14. Athanasius, a fourth-century church leader, struggled alone against Arianism; he was bishop of Alexandria. "Contra mundum" quote in PRO, FCO 17/494, Israel – Political Affairs : W.H. Fletcher (Cairo) to Foreign Office, June 1, 1967. Akram quote in IDF 192/74, file 1348: The Battle for the Southern Front, p. 55. Sabri and Awad

quotes in Vatikiotis, *Nasser and His Generation*, pp. 166–69. For further descriptions of Nasser in this period, see Andrei Gromyko, *Memoirs* (New York: Doubleday, 1989), p. 272. El-Sadat, *In Search of Identity*, p. 148. Richard B. Parker, *The Six Day War* (Jacksonville: University of Florida Press, 1997), p. 263. Parker, *The Politics of Miscalculation in the Middle East*, pp. 242–45.

15. LBJ, Lucius Battle Oral History, p. 38.

16. YAD, Remarks by Yitzhak Rabin, Feb. 3, 1987. Nasser quote in Kimche and Bawly, *The Sandstorm*, pp. 32–33. 'Abd al-Latif Al-Baghdadi, *Mudhakkirat* (Cairo: al-Maktab al-Misri al-Hadith, 1977), pp. 167–219. Fawzi quote in *Harb al-Thalath Sanawat*, p. 69. Heikal, *Al-Infijar*, p. 457. Wajih Abu Dhikri, *Madhbahat al-Abriya'* (Cairo: Al-Maktab al-Misri al-Hadith, 1988), p. 142. Ramadan, 'Abd al-'Azim. *Tahtim al-Aliha: Qissat Harb Yunyu 1967* (Cairo: Madbuli, 1988), pp. 48–49. Parker, *The Politics of Miscalculation in the Middle East*, p. 91. CIA report cited in USNA, Middle East Crisis, Memos, box 17: Memorandum for the White House, May 24, 1967.

17. USNA, Central Foreign Policy files, 1967–1969, POL 7 ARAB-SUMMIT, box 1844: Damascus to State Department, March 16, 1966. Kerr, *The Arab Cold War*, pp. 125–26. 'Ali 'Ali 'Amer quote from Heikal, *Al-Infijar*, p. 423. Reference to "in the icebox" in LBJ, National Security file, Country file, Middle East-UAR box 161: Lunch with Ambassador Kamel, Jan. 17, 1967. Oral history interview with Gen. Yusuf Khawwash, Nov. 16, 1999. On rumors of revolt in Yemen, see PRO, FCO 39/233, UAR Internal Political Situation: Tennet Minute, March 30, 1967.

18. Profiles of 'Abd al-Hakim 'Amer appear in Berlinti 'Abd al-Hamid, *Al-Mushir wa-Ana* (Cairo: Maktabat Madbuli al-Saghir, 1992), pp. 201–5. Fawzi, *Harb al-Thalath Sanawat*, pp. 33–45, 52–54. Imam, *Nasir wa-'Amer*, pp. 5–13, 39–41, 67–86. Heikal, *Al-Infijar*, pp. 818–22. Birs Zia' al-Din, "'Abd al-Nasir . . . Hakama," in *Ruz al-Yusuf 2464*, Sept. 1, 1975, pp. 42–47. Vatikiotis, *Nasser and His Generation*, pp. 159, 161. Gawrych, *The Albatross of Decisive Victory*, pp. 12–13. Mahjoub, *Democracy on Trial*, p. 134. Wajih Abu Dhikri, *Madhbahat al-Abriya'*, pp. 195–97. Anouar Abdel-Malek, *Egypt: Military Society – The Army Regime, the Left, and Social Change Under Nasser* (New York: Vantage Press, 1968), p. 144. An example of the Soviet communiqués appears in BBC, Daily Report No. 183, B1. 'Mushir' quote from USNA, Central Policy files, 1967–1969, POL 7 UAR, box 2554, Cairo to State Department, April 22, 1967. Nasser's attitudes to 'Amer in El-Sadat, *In Search of Identity*, pp. 168–69 and Richard B. Parker, "The June 1967 War: Some Mysteries Explored," in *Middle East Journal* 46, no. 2 (Spring 1992), p. 194.

19. PRO FCO/39/263 UAR – Relations with the USSR: Mr. Gromyko's Visit to Cairo, March 29, 1967. ISA, Foreign Ministry files, 4083/3, Contacts with the Soviet Union, Raviv to Shimoni, April 1, 1967. Gilboa, *Shesh Shanim, Shisha Yamim*, p. 86. Heikal, *Al-Infijar*, pp. 409–20. Ben Tzur, *Gormim Sovietiim u-Milhemet Sheshet ha-Yamim*, p. 177.

20. USNA, Central Policy files, 1967–1969, POL 7 UAR, box 2554: Battle to Rusk, Feb. 22, 1967. Heikal quotes from *Middle East Record 3, 1967* (Jerusalem: Israel Universities Press, 1971), pp. 49–50. LBJ, Lucius Battle Oral History, p. 36; David G. Nes Papers: Nes To Roger P. Davies, Deputy Assistant Secretary NEA, May 11, 1967. Parker, *The Politics of Miscalculation in the Middle East*, pp. 242–45. The British predictions of Nasser's need for distractions abroad were similar to the Americans'. See ISA, 4080/5, Foreign Ministry files, Contacts with Great Britain, London to FM, May 16, 1967.

21. Heikal, *al-Infijar*, pp. 407–8. Nasser's remarks to 'Aref in BBC, Daily Report, Middle East, Africa, and Western Europe, No. 25, B3–4. Other Nasser quotes in Vatikiotis, *Nasser and His Generation*, pp. 249–51.

22. ISA, Foreign Ministry files, 3977/20, Relations with the United States: Attack on the Northern Border, Jan. 1967. UN, DAG 13/3.4.0, box 82, Israel/Syria High Level Talks, Cultivation Arrangements: Barromi to President of Security Council, Jan. 15, 1967 and Tomeh to President of Security Council Jan. 13, 1967; Comay to the Security Council (Radio Damascus quote), Jan. 17, 1967. Another translation of the Syrian quote can be found in Draper, *Israel & World Politics*, p. 43. USNA, POL 12 SYR – SYR – US, box 2511: 'Asifa Communiqué #56 – *al-Ba'th* and *al-Thawra*, Jan. 15, 1967. PRO, FCO 17/665 Syria – Political Affairs: Damascus to Foreign Office, Jan. 3, 1967.

23. Ma'oz, *Syria and Israel*, p. 82. *Al-Ba'th*, April 10, 1967. Tlas quote from PRO, FO17/671: Syria – Political Affairs: Damascus to Foreign Ministry, March 2, 1967.

24. NAC, RG 25 box 2827, Syria: Present Conflict between the Syrian Government and the I.P.C. (Embassy of Syrian Arab Republic – London), Jan. 3, 1967. Damascus radio quote from BBC, Daily Report, Middle East, Africa, and Western Europe, No. 8, G2. *Al-Ba'th*, March 7, 1967.

25. PRO FCO/39/263 UAR – Relations with the USSR, Speares Minute – Soviet Foreign Minister's Visit to Cairo, April 11, 1967. ISA, 4049/7, Foreign Ministry files, Soviet Relations with Arab Countries, Moscow to Foreign Ministry, Jan. 8, 1967; 3975/15, Foreign Ministry files, Diplomatic Relations with the United States: Argov to Bitan, Feb. 9, 1967 ("small rather than big trouble"); Eban Conversation with Hare, June 27, 1966 ("tensions without explosions"). Anatoly Dobrynin, *In Confidence: Moscow's Ambassador to America's Six Cold War Presidents (1962–1986)* (New York: Random House, 1995), pp. 156–59. Oded Eran, "Soviet Policy Between 1967 and 1973," in Rabinovich and Shaked, eds., *From June to October*, p. 50.

26. USNA Central Foreign Policy files, 1967–1969, POL 12 SY, box 2511: Tel Aviv to Department of State, Jan. 24, 1967; Moscow to Department of State, Feb. 15, 1967. PRO, FO17/672 Syria – Political Affairs: Damascus to Foreign Office, Jan. 27, 1967. ISA, 3977/20, Foreign Ministry files, Relations with the United States: Bitan Conversation with Alfred Atherton, Dec. 12, 1966. Dagan, *Moscow and Jerusalem*, pp. 186–87. Govrin, *Israeli-Soviet Relations 1953–1967*, pp. 276–79. Ben Tzur, *Gormim Sovietiim u-Milhemet Sheshet ha-Yamim*, pp. 131–33, 151.

27. PRO, FCO 17/665 Syria – Political Affairs: Damascus to Foreign Ministry, Jan. 18, 1967; Damascus to Foreign Ministry, Feb. 21, 1967; FO17/671: Syria – Political Affairs: Damascus to Foreign Ministry, Feb. 4, 1967. ISA, 3975/15, Foreign Ministry files, Diplomatic Relations with the United States: North American Desk Memorandum, Feb. 4, 1967. Assassination attempt on al-Assad in BBC, Daily Report, Middle East, Africa, and Western Europe No. 8, G1; arrest of government ministers in 64, G2. See also Itamar Rabinovich, "The Ba'th in Syria," Rabinovich and Shaked, *From June to October*, p. 222.

28. LBJ, National Security file, Middle East Crisis, box 145–57: CIA: Syria – A Center of Instability, March 24, 1967. Assad conversation with 'Awdah in PRO, FO17/671: Syria – Political Affairs: Craig to Moberley, January 24, 1967.

29. The number of complaints submitted to the ISMAC in Frederic C. Hof, *Line of Battle, Order of Peace?* (Washington: Middle East Insight, 1999), p. 14. UN, DAG

13/3.4.0, box 84, Verbatim Records, ISMAC 80th Meeting, Jan. 25, 1967. Syria description of talks in BBC, Daily Report, Middle East, Africa, and Western Europe, No. 19, G1. See also Indar Jit Rikhye, *The Sinai Blunder* (London: Frank Cass, 1980) p. 9.

30. PRO, FCO 17/576: Israel – Defense Attaché, Annexure 1, June 12, 1967. Walid Abu Murshid, Antoine Butrus and Fuad Jabber, "Al-Kitab Al-Sanawi lil-Qadiyya al-Filastiniyya li-'Am 1967," in *Silsilat al-Kitab al-Sanawi lil-Qadiyya al-Filastiniyya 4* (Beirut: Manshurat Mu'assasat al-Dirasa al-Filastiniyya, 1969), pp. 124, 151–54. UN, DAG 13 3.4.0, box 84, IJMAC, Israeli Complaints of March 12 and 26, 1967. Al-Fatah communiqués can be found in USNA, POL 12 SYR – SYR – US, box 2511.

31. UN, DAG 13/3.4.0, box 82: Israeli Complaint S/7853, April 14, 1967.

32. PRO, FO17/671: Syria – Political Affairs: Damascus to Foreign Office, Feb. 27, 1967. USNA Central Foreign Policy files, 1967–1969, POL 12 SY, box 2511: Damascus to Department of State, May 23, 1967. ISA, 3975/15, Foreign Ministry files, Diplomatic Relations with the United States: Argov to Harman, March 19, 1967 (Hoopes quote); 3977/21: Evron to North America Desk, March 16, 1967; Argov to Bitan, March 27, 1967; 7919/1, Levi Eshkol files, Diplomatic Telegrams: U.S.A.: Evron to Levavi, May 17, 1967 (Rostow quote).

33. Evron quote from LBJ, National Security file, Middle East, Israel box 140, 141: W. Rostow to the President, Jan. 16, 1967. Eshkol quote from Haber, *Ha-Yom Tifrotz Milhama*, p. 141; "Syrian syndrome" on p. 99. See also Eyal Sisser, "Bein Yisrael le-Suria: Milhemet Sheshet ha-Yamim ule-Ahareiha," *Iyunim be-Tkumat Yisrael* 8 (1998), pp. 220–21.

34. Al-Shuqayri, *Mudhakkirat 5*, p. 35 ('Ali 'Ali 'Amer quote). Heikal, *Al-Infijar*, p. 434. See also Hisham Sharabi, "Prelude to War: The Crisis of May–June 1967," *The Arab World* 14 (1968). "Takrit ha-7 be-April: 20 Shniyot Aharei – Sheshet ha-Migim she-Kirvu et Sheshet ha-Yamim," *Bamahane* 39 (April 8, 1987).

35. Sidqi quote from Mazhar, *I'tirafat Qadat Harb Yunyu*, pp. 107–8. Heikal, *Al-Infijar*, p. 434. Gilboa, *Shesh Shanim, Shisha Yamim*, p. 94. Al-Shuqayri, *Mudhakkirat 5*, p. 50. Al-Sabbagh, *Mudhakkirat Qadat al-'Askaraiyya al-Misriyya 5*, pp. 14–15. Kimche and Bawly, *The Sandstorm*, p. 86. Cohen, *Ha-Hagannah al Mekorot ha-Mayim*, pp. 178–79. Speeches by the Egyptian delegation to Syria in BBC, Daily Report, Middle East, Africa, and Western Europe, No. 72, B1 and 72, G1.

36. Jordanian claims in BBC, Daily Report, Middle East, Africa, and Western Europe, No. 73, D1. Gilboa, *Shesh Shanim, Shisha Yamim*, p. 83. Nasser's remarks in BBC, Daily Report, Middle East, Africa, and Western Europe, No. 86, B1 –17. Suliman quote from BBC, No. 82, G1.

37. USNA, Central Foreign Policy files, 1967–1969, POL 7 ARAB-SUMMIT, box 1844, Cairo to the Secretary of State, March 27, 1967; 1967–1969, POL Arab-Jordan, box 1844: Amman to Department of State, April 19, 1967. Mutawi, *Jordan in the 1967 War*, p. 101.

38. Ephraim Kamm, *Hussein Poteah be-Milhama: Milhemet Sheshet ha-Yamim be-Eynei ha-Yardenim* (Tel Aviv: Ma'arakhot, Misrad ha-Bitahon, 1974). Mutawi, *Jordan in the 1967 War*, p. 86. Hussein of Jordan, *My "War" with Israel*, pp. 38–39. Heikal, *Al-Infijar*, pp. 435–36. Amman broadcast in BBC, Daily Report, Middle East, Africa, and Western Europe, No. 86, B1 –17.

39. PRO, FCO 17/576: Israel – Defense Attaché, Annexure 1, June 12, 1967. LBJ, National Security file, History of the Middle East Conflict, box 20: United States Policy

and Diplomacy in the Middle East Crisis, May 15–June 10, 1967, pp. 5–6. UN, DAG 13 3.4.0, box 84: Syrian Complaint 7863, April 28, 1967; Israeli Complaint 7880, May 11, 1967.

40. Harman quote in LBJ, National Security file, History of the Middle East Conflict, box 20: United States Policy and Diplomacy in the Middle East Crisis, May 15–June 10, 1967, pp. 8–9. Eban quote from Gilboa, *Shesh Shanim, Shisha Yamim*, p. 97. A similar statement was made by Gideon Rafael, Israel's UN ambassador, to the Security Council. See Parker, *The Politics of Miscalculation*, p. 41.

41. Prittie, *Eshkol*, pp. 105, 183. Haber, *Ha-Yom Tifrotz Milhama*, pp. 140–42. Weizman, *On Eagles' Wings*, pp. 190–91. NAC, RG 25 10082: 20-ISR-9: Visit of Prime Minister Eshkol to Canada, Jan. 15–26, 1968. Oral history interview with Miriam Eshkol, Aug. 30, 1999. See also the essays by Yoav Gelber in http://research.haifa.ac.il/%7Eeshkol/index.html (Levi Eshkol homepage).

42. Robert Slater, *Rabin of Israel: A Biography* (London: Robson Books, 1993), pp. 108–16. Dan Kurzman, *Soldier of Peace: The Life of Yitzhak Rabin* (New York: HarperCollins, 1998), pp. 1–32. Rabin, *The Rabin Memoirs*, p. 61.

43. Michael Brecher, *Decisions in Crisis* (Berkeley: University of California Press, 1980), p. 36. Semyonov quotes in Gilboa, *Shesh Shanim, Shisha Yamim*, p. 87. Parker, *The Politics of Miscalculation*, p. 11.

44. ISA, 3975/15, Foreign Ministry files, Diplomatic Relations with the United States: Harman to Bitan, March 1, 1967; Bitan to Harman, March 6, 1967; Argov to Harman, March 19, 1967. LBJ, National Security file, Middle East, Israel box 140, 141: US Attitudes Toward Military Aid to IS, April 20, 1967; Tel Aviv to Department of State, January 17, 1967 (Barbour quote).

45. *U.S. News & World Report* 62, no. 16 (April 17, 1967), pp. 75–77. Prittie, *Eshkol*, p. 249. Al-Atassi quote from BBC, Daily Report No. 214, G3.

46. LBJ, National Security file, History of the Middle East Conflict, box 20: United States Policy and Diplomacy in the Middle East Crisis, May 15–June 10, 1967, pp. 6–7. Arthur Lall, *The UN and the Middle East Crisis, 1967* (New York: Columbia University Press, 1968), pp. 3–4. Gideon Rafael, *Destination Peace: Three Decades of Israeli Foreign Policy* (New York: Stein and Day, 1981), p. 136. Brian Urquhart, *A Life in Peace and War* (New York: Harper & Row, 1987), p. 20. Tomeh quote in Menachem Mansoor, *Arab World: Political and Diplomatic History, 1900–1967: A Chronological Study* (NCR, Microcard Editors, n.d.), entry for May 13, 1967. See also Yost, "How It Began," pp. 306–7. Rikhye, *Sinai Blunder*, p. 11.

47. LBJ, National Security files, NSC Histories, Middle East Crisis, box 17: Tel Aviv to the Secretary of State, May 12, 1967. Gilboa, *Shesh Shanim, Shisha Yamim*, pp. 98–101. Haber, *Ha-Yom Tifrotz Milhama*, pp. 146–47. *Middle East Record* 3, p. 187. Parker, *The Politics of Miscalculation in the Middle East*, pp. 15–18. Parker, *The Six Day War*, pp. 31–32, 69. Weizman, *On Eagles' Wings*, p. 208.

48. PRO, FO17/666, Syria – Political Affairs: Damascus to Foreign Office, May 14, 1967. ISA, Foreign Ministry files, 3975/17, Bilateral Relations with the U.S.: Harman to Foreign Ministry, May 12, 1967; 7920/4, Levi Eshkol Papers, Prime Minister's Reports and Surveys: Eshkol's Reports to the Ministerial Defense Committee, May 18, 1967. Riad, *The Struggle for Peace in the Middle East*, p. 17. Haber, *Ha-Yom Tifrotz Milhama*, p. 147. Seale, *Asad of Syria*, p. 115. Rikhye, *Sinai Blunder*, p. 10. Al-Atassi quote from Mansoor, *Arab World*, entry for May 13, 1967. Makhous quotes from LBJ,

National Security files, NSC Histories, Middle East Crisis, box 17: The President in the Middle East Crisis, Dec. 19, 1968, and Damascus to the Secretary of State, May 20, 1967.

49. UN, DAG 13/3.4.0, box 84: HJKIMAC, El-Farra to the Secretary General, Feb. 6, 1967; Comay to Secretary General, Feb. 10, 1967; Bull to Sasson, May 15, 1967. LBJ, National Security file, Middle East, Israel box 140, 141. Katzenbach to the President, May 2, 1967. NAC, RG 25, box 10050: Political Affairs – Canada's Foreign Policy Trends and Relations – Israel: Israel's Independence Day Parade, May 15, 1967. ISA, 3977/22, Diplomatic Relations with the United States: Bitan to Evron, April 16, 1967. Teddy Kollek, *For Jerusalem* (London: Weidenfeld and Nicolson, 1978), pp. 187–88. Haber, *Ha-Yom Tifrotz Milhama*, pp. 118–19, 145–46. Rikhye, *Sinai Blunder*, p. 13. Bull, *War and Peace in the Middle East*, p. 70. U Thant, *View from the UN* (New York: Doubleday, 1978), pp. 218–19.

50. Heikal, *Al-Infijar*, pp. 442–44. El-Sadat, *In Search of Identity*, pp. 171–72. Prediction of the U.S. embassy in USNA, Central Policy files, 1967–1969, POL 2 UAR, box 2553: Cairo to the Department of State, April 29, 1967; POL ARAB-ISR, box 9: Paris to the Secretary of State, May 23, 1967. LBJ, National Security files, NSC Histories, Middle East Crisis, box 20: Davis to Rostow, June 2, 1967. On the Soviet interpretation of the absence of tanks and cannons from the Jerusalem parade, see ISA, 4078, Foreign Ministry files, Contacts with the United States with the Entry of Egyptian Forces into Tiran, Evron to Foreign Ministry, May 15, 1967, and USNA, POL ARAB-ISR, box 9: Paris to Teheran, May 15, 1967. Podgorny quotes from Dayan, *My Life*, pp. 309–10 and Heikal, *Al-Infijar*, pp. 445–46.

51. A minor literature has grown up around the reasons for the Soviets' warning to Sadat. See Michael Bar-Zohar, *Embassies in Crisis: Diplomats and Demagogues Behind the Six Day War* (Englewood Cliffs, N.J.: Prentice-Hall, 1970), p. 2. Ali Abdel Rahman Rahmi, *Egyptian Policy in the Arab World: Intervention in Yemen 1962–1967: A Case Study* (Washington D.C.: University Press of America, 1983), pp. 232–35. Nadav Safran, *From War to War: The Arab-Israel Confrontation, 1948–1967* (New York, 1969), pp. 267–77. Anthony Nutting, *Nasser* (New York: Dutton, 1972), pp. 397–98. Parker, *The Politics of Miscalculation in the Middle East*, pp. 18–19, 156–57. Parker, *The Six Day War*, pp. 35–41, 48–49, 70–73. Parker, "The June 1967 War: Some Mysteries Explored," p. 181. Ritchie Ovendale, *The Origins of the Arab-Israeli Wars* (London: Longman, 1984), p. 178. W. W. Rostow, *The Diffusion of Power: An Essay in Recent History* (New York: Macmillan, 1972), p. 257. Seale, *Asad of Syria*, p. 129. Govrin, *Israeli-Soviet Relations*, pp. 308–9. Ben Tzur, *Gormim Sovietiim u-Milhemet Sheshet ha-Yamim*, p. 167. Ilan Asia, *Tismonet Dayan: Arba Milhamot ve-Shalom Ehad—ha-Roved ha-Nistar* (Tel Aviv: Yediot Ahronot, 1995), p. 129. Oral history interviews with Vadim Kirpitchenko, Dec. 25, 2000, and Carin Brutenz, Jan. 21, 2001.

52. A similar interpretation of Soviet decision-making was posited by State Department Middle East expert Harold Saunders shortly after the war: "The Soviet advice to the Syrians [sic] that the Israelis were planning an attack was not far off, although they seem to have exaggerated the magnitude. The Israelis probably were planning an attack—but not an invasion." From LBJ, National Security file, History of the Middle East Crisis, box 17, Saunders to Bundy, June 16, 1967. See also Meir Amit, "Ha-Derekh le-Sheshet ha-Yamim—Sheshet ha-Yamim be-Re'i le-Ahor," *Ma'arakhot* 325 (June–July 1992). ISA, 4083/3, Foreign Ministry files, Contacts with the USSR – Closure of Tiran: Bonn to Foreign Ministry, June 14, 1967; Levanon to Foreign Ministry,

June 23, 1967, "Ideological myopia" from PRO, FCO/39/263, UAR – Relations with the USSR: Mr. Gromyko's Visit to Cairo, April 1, 1967; FCO17/498: Israel –Political Affairs: The Middle East Crisis (Morris), October 23, 1967 ("ideological myopia"). LBJ, National Security files, NSC Histories, Middle East Crisis, box 18: Paris to the Secretary of State, May 23, 1967. Solomon M. Shvarts, *Sovetskii Soiuz l Arabo-Izrailskaia Voina 1967* (New York: Amerikanskii Evreiskii Rabochii Komitet, 1969), pp. 24–26.

53. Shukri Dhabbah, *Wa-Madha Ba'du?* (Cairo: Dar al-Quds, n.d.), pp. 18–24. Eric Rouleau, Jean-Francis Held, Jean and Simone Lacouture, *Israel et les Arabes le 3e Combat* (Paris: Editions du Seuil, 1967), p. 54. Ivan Prokhorovitch Dediulia, "Na Zemle Obetovannoy," *Nezavisimoe Veonnoe Obozrenie*, no. 20 (1998). Syrian claim in Mazhar, *I'tirafat Qadat Harb Yunyu*, pp. 109–10. Parker, *The Six Day War*, pp. 2, 42. Parker, *The Politics of Miscalculation in the Middle East*, p. 5. Heikal, *Al-Infijar*, pp. 448–51.

54. Heikal, *Al-Infijar*, pp. 444–47 ISA, 4078, Foreign Ministry files, Contacts with the United States with the Entry of Egyptian Forces into Tiran, Evron to Foreign Ministry, May 15, 1967.

55. 'Abd al-Muhsin Kamil Murtagi, *Al-Fariq Murtagi Yarwi al-Haqa'iq* (Cairo: Dar al-Watan al-'Arabi, 1976), pp. 27–29, 45–46. Sabr Abu Nidal, *Ma'rakat al-Khamis min Haziran: Awwal Dirasa 'Arabiyya 'Askariyya Shamila lil-Hazima* (Cairo: Al-Mu'assasa al-'Arabiyya lil-Dirasa wal-Nashr, 1971), pp. 26–38. Fawzi, *Harb al-Thalath Sanawat*, pp. 53–66, 117–18. Abu Dhikri, *Madhbahat al-Abriya'*, pp. 111–23. Ramadan, *Tahtim al-Aliha*, pp. 79–80. Mazhar, *I'tirafat Qadat Harb Yunyu*, pp. 208–9. Rikhye, *Sinai Blunder*, p. 147. PRO, FCO 39/233 UAR Internal Political Situation: Cairo to Foreign Office, May 23, 1967. 'Abd al-Mun'im Khalil quote in Al-Sabbagh, *Mudhakkirat Qadat al-'Askaraiyya al-Misriyya 2*.

56. LBJ, National Security file, Country file, Middle East-UAR, box 161: Lunch with Ambassador Kamel, Jan. 17, 1967; Memos to the President (W. Rostow), box 16; Rostow to the President, Feb. 14, 1967. Nasser speech in BBC, Daily Report, Middle East, Africa, and Western Europe, No. 93, B2.

57. Mazhar, *I'tirafat Qadat Harb Yunyu*, pp. 90, 231. 'Amer quote from Mutawi, *Jordan in the 1967 War*, p. 96. Gilboa, *Shesh Shanim, Shisha Yamim*, p. 64. Parker, *The Six Day War*, pp. 41–42. Rikhye oral history, Feb. 22, 2000. PRO, FCO 39/233 UAR Internal Political Situation: Cairo to Foreign Office, Jan. 9, 1967.

58. Heikal, *Al-Infijar*, pp. 448–51. Seale, *Asad of Syria*, pp. 129–30. Robert Stephens, *Nasser: A Political Biography* (London: Penguin, 1971), pp. 470–71. ISA, 6444/4 North America, Telegrams from Foreign Ministry to Embassies, May 19, 1967.

59. 'Abdallah Imam, *'Abd al-Nasir—Kayfa Hakama Misr* (Cairo: Madbuli al-Saghir, 1966), pp. 358–60. 'Abdallah Imam, *'Ali Sabri Yatadhakkar: Bi-Saraha 'an al-Sadat* (Cairo: Dar al-Khayyal, 1997), pp. 122–23, 140. Fawzi, *Harb al-Thalath Sanawat*, pp. 36–39, 40, 52–54. Heikal, *Al-Infijar*, pp. 818–22. Vatikiotis, *Nasser and His Generation*, pp. 159–61. Fawzi, *Harb al-Thalath Sanawat*, pp. 33–45, 52–54. Imam, *Nasir wa-'Amer*, pp. 5–13, 39–41, 67–86. Heikal, *Al-Infijar*, pp. 818–22. Parker, *The Six Day War*, p. 45. Parker, "The June 1967 War: Some Mysteries Explored," p. 194.

60. Fawzi, *Harb al-Thalath Sanawat*, pp. 69–70. Heikal, *Al-Infijar*, pp. 458–59. Murtagi, *Al-Fariq Murtagi Yarwi al-Haqa'iq*, pp. 49–53. Mazhar, *I'tirafat Qadat Harb Yunyu*, pp. 51–52. Parker, *The Politics of Miscalculation in the Middle East*, pp. 61–63.

61. Heikal, *Al-Infijar*, pp. 458–59. Parker, *The Politics of Miscalculation in the Middle East*, pp. 63–64. Description of Fawzi in PRO, FO 39/250: Middle East Crisis: UAR

Attitude Eastern Department Minute, June 23, 1967. In a letter to U.S. Ambassador Arthur Goldberg on May 31, U Thant revealed that he had previously indicated to the Egyptians his recognition of their right to disband UNEF: "In discussion with the Foreign Ministers and Permanent Representatives of the United Arab Republic in the years I have been Secretary-General the subject of the continued presence of the UNEF occasionally came up . . . In the course of these talks, I found that the United Arab Republic took it for granted that if the UAR officially requested withdrawal of the Force, the request would be honoured by the Secretary-General. I had thus given thought to the matter. When, therefore, the request for withdrawal of the Force came, the decision in principle that would have to be taken and the procedure to be followed were perfectly clear to me." See UN, S-0316 box 8, file 8: UNEF-Withdrawals, Correspondence with the United States: U Thant to Goldberg, May 31, 1967. On Egyptian contacts with India and Yugoslavia, see LBJ, National Security files, NSC Histories, Middle East Crisis, box 20: Intelligence Information Cable, June 1, 1967.

62. Murtagi, *Al-Fariq Murtagi Yarwi al-Haqa'iq*, pp. 65–66. Al-Baghdadi, *Mudhakkirat*, p. 174. LBJ, National Security files, NSC Histories, Middle East Crisis, box 17: The President in the Middle East Crisis, Dec. 19, 1968. Qadi quote in Al-Sabbagh, *Mudhakkirat Qadat al-'Askariyya al-Misriyya 1*, p. 7. BBC, Daily Report, Middle East, Africa, and Western Europe, No. 95, B1, B4. 'Amer orders in Heikal, *Al-Infijar*, pp. 452–54. The testimony of Muhammad Ahmad Khamis appears in Darraz, *Dubbat Yunyu Yatakallamun*, pp. 69–75.

63. Al-Hadidi, *Shahid 'ala Harb 67*, p. 112. Ramadan, *Tahtim al-Aliha*, pp. 41–42. PRO, FCO 39/233 UAR Internal Political Situation: Cairo to Foreign Office, May 13, 1967. Fawzi, *Harb al-Thalath Sanawat*, pp. 69–71. Rikhye, *Sinai Blunder*, p. 159. Parker, *The Six Day War*, pp. 43–44. Parker, *The Politics of Miscalculation in the Middle East*, p. 92. Mohamed H. Heikal, *The Sphinx and the Commissar: The Rise and Fall of Soviet Influence in the Middle East* (London: Collins, 1978), p. 175. Asia, *Tismonet Dayan*, p. 127. Sabri quote from Imam, *'Ali Sabri Yatadhakkar*, p. 97. Fawzi quote from Mazhar, *I'tirafat Qadat Harb Yunyu*, pp. 51–52.

64. ISA, 3977/22, Foreign Ministry files, Relations with the United States: Conversation with Ambassador Chuvakhin, May 13, 1967. Gilboa, *Shesh Shanim, Shisha Yamim*, p. 98. Parker, *The Politics of Miscalculation in the Middle East*, pp. 8–9; 248, ft 13. Oral history interview with Arye Levavi, March 4, 1999.

65. ISA, 3977/20, Foreign Ministry files, Diplomatic Relations with the United States, Evron to Gazit, Dec. 12, 1966; 3975/15, Foreign Ministry files, Diplomatic Relations with the United States: Conversation with Bergus, Feb. 16, 1967. NAC, RG 25, box 10050: Political Affairs – Canada's Foreign Policy Trends and Relations – Israel: New York to Ottawa, Sept. 22, 1967. Parker, *The Six Day War*, p. 128. Haber, *Ha-Yom Tifrotz Milhama*, p. 147. Eban, *Personal Witness*, p. 380. Baron, *Hotam Ishi*, p.17.

66. Prittie, Eshkol, pp. 70–71. MPA, Party Secretariat Protocols, 2/24/66/88: Dec. 15, 1966.

The Crisis

1. ISA, 4078/4 Foreign Ministry files, Contacts with the United States on the Entry of Egyptian Forces to the Sinai: Harman Conversation with Rostow, May 15, 1967. Oral history interview with Col. Shlomo Merom, Dec. 7, 1999. Nasser quote from Slater, *Rabin of Israel*, p. 79. Rabin quote from Rabin, *Memoirs*, p. 68. Eshkol quote from oral history interview with Miriam Eshkol, Aug. 30, 1999. See also Parker,

The Six Day War, p. 137. Haber, *Ha-Yom Tifrotz Milhama*, pp. 147–50. Mayzel, *Ha-Ma'arakha al ha-Golan*, pp. 99–103. Slater, *Rabin of Israel*, pp. 88–120. Abraham Rabinovich, *The Battle for Jerusalem, June 5–7, 1967* (Philadephia: Jewish Publication Society of America, 1972), p. 5. Shlomo Nakdimon, *Likrat Sh'at ha-Efes* (Tel Aviv: Ramdor Press, 1968), pp. 17–18. Weizman, *On Eagles' Wings*, p. 208.

2. LBJ, National Security files, NSC Histories, Middle East Crisis, box 17: Department of State to Cairo, May 15, 1967. Appeal to U Thant in Yost, "How It Began," p. 309 and in Rafael, *Destination Peace*, pp. 136–37. Harman's message to Nasser in LBJ, National Security file, History of the Middle East Conflict, box 20: United States Policy and Diplomacy in the Middle East Crisis, May 15–June 10, 1967, pp. 11–12. Amit, *Rosh be-Rosh*, pp. 226–27. ISA, 3977/20, Foreign Ministry files, Relations with the United States: Eban to Washington, London, Paris, May 15, 1967; 6444/4 North America, Telegrams: Foreign Ministry to Embassies, May 19, 1967; 7920/1, Levi Eshkol Papers, Diplomatic Telegrams: Eban to Rafael, May 17, 1967.

3. ISA, 4078/8 U.S. Reactions to the Closing of the Straits, Eban to Harman, May 16, 1967. Rabin, *Memoirs*, pp. 68–70. Slater, *Rabin of Israel*, p. 123. Cairo Radio quote from Mansoor, *Arab World*, entry for May 16. Nasser quote from BBC, Daily Report, The Middle East and Africa, ME/2467/A/2.

4. IDF, 710/70 General Staff Discussion: May 17, 1967. Trevor N. Dupuy, *Elusive Victory: The Arab-Israeli Wars, 1947–1974* (New York: Harper & Row, 1978), p. 239. Van Creveld, *The Sword and the Olive*, p. 179. Haber, *Ha-Yom Tifrotz Milhama*, pp. 150–51. Rabin, *Memoirs*, p. 70. On the PLA in Gaza, see Abu Murshid, Butrus, and Jabber *Silsilat al-Kitab al-Sanawi lil-Qadiyya al-Filastiniyya*, pp. 115–16. See also, interview with Gen. Sidqi al-Ghul, commander of the 4th Division, in *al-Ra'i al-'Am*, June 2, 1987.

5. IDF, 710/70 General Staff Discussion: May 17, 1967; 1977/1786: The Regular Paratrooper Brigade in the Six-Day War, Commander 35th Brigade, p. 619. Haber, *Ha-Yom Tifrotz Milhama*, p. 151. Radio Cairo quote from U Thant, *View from the UN*, p. 219. Syrian quote from Menachem Mansoor, *Arab World: Political and Diplomatic History*, entry for May 16.

6. USNA Central Foreign Policy files, 1967–1969, POL 12 SY, box 2511: Damascus to Department of State, May 18, 1967. PRO, FO17/666, Syria – Political Affairs: Damascus to Foreign Office, April 29, 1967 ; FCO 17/665 Syria – Political Affairs: Damascus to Foreign Office, May 15, 1967. George W. Gawrych, *The Albatross of Decisive Victory*, p. 13. Fred H. Lawson, *Why Syria Goes to War: Thirty Years of Confrontation* (Ithaca, N.Y.: Cornell University Press, 1996), p. 48–50. Patrick Seale, *Asad of Syria: The Struggle for the Middle East*, p. 115.

7. Fawzi, *Harb al-Thalath Sanawat*, pp. 71–72. Murtagi, *Al-Fariq Murtagi Yarwi al-Haqa'iq*, p. 64. Parker, *The Politics of Miscalculation in the Middle East*, pp. 14, 44. Muhammad 'Abd al-Ghani al-Gamasi, *Mudhakkirat al-Gamasi* (Paris: Al-Manshura al Sharqiyya, 1990), p. 19. Ramadan, *Tahtim al-Alihu*, p. 41. Sadiq quote in al-Sabbagh, *Mudhakkirat Qadat al-'Askaraiyya al-Misriyya 4*, pp. 20–21. IDF, 710/70 General Staff Discussion: May 19, 1967. Al-Sabbagh, *Mudhakkirat Qadat al 'Askaraiyya al-Misriyya 1*, p. 7. Mayzel, *Ha-Ma'arakha al ha-Golan*, p. 21. Fawzi quote from testimony of Mahmud Sidqi Mahmud in Mazhar, *I'tirafat Qadat Harb Yunyu*, p. 110. Bull quote appears in Bull, *War and Peace in the Middle East*, p. 104.

8. USNA, Subject-Numeric files, POL ARAB-ISR, box 1789: London to Washington, May 27, 1967. Heikal, *Al-Infijar*, p. 518. Stephens, *Nasser*, pp. 467–68.

9. Fawzi quote in *Harb al-Thalath Sanawat*, p. 72. Murtagi, *Al-Fariq Murtagi Yarwi al-Haqa'iq*, p. 64. 'Amer quote in Mazhar, *I'tirafat Qadat Harb Yunyu*, p. 165. Gawrych, *The Albatross of Decisive Victory*, pp. 13–19. Heikal, *Al-Infijar*, pp. 458–59. Abu Dhikri, *Madhbahat al-Abriya'*, pp. 173–78. Fawzi, *Harb al-Thalath Sanawat*, pp. 92–93. USNA, POL ARAB-IS, box 9: Cairo to the Secretary of State, May 17, 1967.

10. Heikal, *Al-Infijar*, p. 829. Fawzi, *Harb al-Thalath Sanawat*, pp. 48–50. Al-Hadidi, *Shahid 'ala Harb 67*, pp. 85–86. Imam, *'Abd al-Nasir—Kayfa Hakama Misr*, p. 363. Al-Sabbagh, *Mudhakkirat Qadat al-'Askaraiyya al-Misriyya 1*, pp. 15–17. Fawzi quote on p. 18. S. A. El Edroos, *The Hashemite Arab Army, 1908–1979: An Appreciation and Analysis of Military Operations* (Amman: Publishing Committee, 1980), p. 359. O'Balance, *The Third Arab-Israeli War*, pp. 94–95. IDF, 192/74, file 1348: The Battle for the Southern Front, p. 3.

11. PRO FCO17/576: Israel – Defense: Report of Defense Attaché, July 13, 1967. Murtagi, *Al-Fariq Murtagi Yarwi al-Haqa'iq*, pp. 65–68, 121. Fawzi, *Harb al-Thalath Sanawat*, pp. 103–4. Al-Sabbagh, *Mudhakkirat Qadat al-'Askaraiyya al-Misriyya 1*, pp. 15–16. Dupuy, *Elusive Victory*, p. 241. Gilboa, *Shesh Shanim, Shisha Yamim*, p. 116. Parker, "The June 1967 War: Some Mysteries Explored," p. 187.

12. Orders relating to Operation Lion later fell into Israeli hands. They were reproduced in "Hail ha-Avir ba-Milhama," *Bit'on Hail ha-Avir* 3, no. 74/75 (Dec. 1967). Hisham Mustafa Husayn quote in Darraz, *Dubbat Yunyu Yatakallamun*, pp. 23–33. Al-Sabbagh, *Mudhakkirat Qadat al-'Askaraiyya al-Misriyya 1*, p. 23. Muhammad 'Awda and 'Abdallah Imam, *Al-Naksa—Man al-Mas'ul?* (Cairo: Ruz al-Yusuf, 1985), p. 79.

13. Mazhar, *I'tirafat Qadat Harb Yunyu*, pp. 167–68. Murtagi, *Al-Fariq Murtagi Yarwi al-Haqa'iq*, pp. 65–68 (including 'Amer quote). Al-Sabbagh, *Mudhakkirat Qadat al-'Askaraiyya al-Misriyya 10* (testimony of 'Abd al-Mun'im Khalil), p. 8. Heikal article cited in Asia, *Tismonet Dayan*, p. 139. Ramadan, *Tahtim al-Aliha*, pp. 51–54. See also interview with 'Abd al-Muhsin Murtagi in *Akher Sa'a*, July 5, 1974.

14. Heikal, *Al-Infijar*, pp. 457–77. Text of Fawzi's letter to Rikhye appears in UN, S 0316-box 9, file 2: UNEF Withdrawals, Exchange with UAR, Aide-Mémoire, U Thant to UAR, May 17, 1967, and in Rikhye, *Sinai Blunder*, p. 16. Parker, *The Politics of Miscalculation in the Middle East*, p. 68. See also Fawzi, *Harb al-Thalath Sanawat*, pp. 69–71. Riad, *The Struggle for Peace in the Middle East*, p. 18.

15. Urquhart, *A Life in Peace and War*, pp. 136–37, 193–94.

16. UN, S-0316 box 8, file 8: UNEF-Withdrawals, Correspondence with the United States: U Thant to Goldberg, May 31, 1967. Samir N. Anabtawi, "The United Nations and the Middle East Conflict of 1967," *The Arab World* 14 (1968). Oral history interview with Indar Jit Rikhye, Feb. 22, 2000. Quote from Lall, *The UN and the Middle East Crisis*, pp. 12–13. Bull, *War and Peace in the Middle East*, p. 96.

17. Rikhye, *Sinai Blunder*, pp. 13–21. UN, S 0316-box 9, file 2: UNEF Withdrawals, Exchange with UAR, Aide-Mémoire, U Thant to UAR, May 17, 1967. ISA, Foreign Ministry files, 4085/2: Emergency Force, Amir to Rafael, May 17, 1967. Oral history interview with Indar Jit Rikhye, Feb. 22, 2000.

18. UN, S 0316-box 9, file 2: UNEF Withdrawals, Exchange with UAR, Aide-Mémoire, U Thant to UAR, May 17, 1967. Bull, *War and Peace in the Middle East*, p. 96. LBJ, National Security files, NSC Histories, Middle East Crisis, box 21: USUN to the Secretary of State, May 18, 1967 (Bunche quote). Yost, "How It Began," pp. 311–12. Rikhye, *Sinai Blunder*, pp. 21–22. Urquhart, *A Life in Peace and War*, p. 209.

U Thant, *View from the UN*, pp. 221–22. Heikal, *Al-Infijar*, pp. 468–77. Parker, *Six Day War*, p. 86; Parker, *The Politics of Miscalculation in the Middle East*, p. 45. George Tomeh oral history, Nov. 17, 1999.

19. LBJ, National Security file, History of the Middle East Conflict, box 20: United States Policy and Diplomacy in the Middle East Crisis, May 15–June 10, 1967, pp. 12–13. UN, S 0316-box 9, file 2: UNEF Withdrawals, Exchange with UAR, Aide-Mémoire, U Thant to UAR, May 17, 1967. ISA, 4085/2, Foreign Ministry files, Emergency Force: Rafael to Foreign Ministry, May 17, 1967. Yost, "How It Began," p. 312. Rikhye, *Sinai Blunder*, p. 25. Parker, *Six Day War*, pp. 86–89. Rostow, *The Diffusion of Power*, pp. 256–57.

20. UN, S-0316 box 8, file 8: UNEF-Withdrawals, Correspondence with the United States: U Thant to Goldberg, May 31, 1967 (U Thant quote); box 8, file 12: UNEF Withdrawals, Legal Matters: C. A. Stavropoulos, Under-Secretary for Legal Counsel, to U Thant, May 17, 1967. PRO, PREM 13 1617, The Middle East Crisis: Caradon to Foreign Ministry (Conversation with U Thant), May 22, 1967; FCO17/498: Israel – Political Affairs: Record of Meeting, Harold Wilson and U Thant, June 3, 1967.

21. UN, S 0316 box 8, file 11: Verbatim Record of the Meeting of the UNEF Advisory Committee, May 17, 1967. PRO FCO17/498: Israel – Political Affairs: Record of Meeting, Harold Wilson and U Thant, June 3, 1967. Rikhye, *Sinai Blunder*, pp. 26, 54–55, 169. U Thant, *View from the UN* , pp. 222–23. Yost, "How It Began," p. 312.

22. George Tomeh oral history, Nov. 17, 1999. Urquhart, *A Life in Peace and War*, pp. 190–91. LBJ, oral histories, Eugenie Moore Anderson, p. 30.

23. UN, S-0316 box 8, file 8: UNEF-Withdrawals, Correspondence with the United States: U Thant to Goldberg, May 31, 1967. Indar Jit Rikhye oral history, Feb. 22, 2000. NAC, RG 25, box 10050: Political Affairs – Canada's Foreign Policy Trends and Relations – Israel: New York to Ottawa, Sept. 22, 1967.

24. ISA, Foreign Ministry files, 4085/2: Emergency Force: Rafael to Foreign Ministry, May 18, 1967; 7920/1, Levi Eshkol Papers, Diplomatic Telegrams: Rafael to Eban, May 22, 1967. PRO FCO17/498: Israel – Political Affairs: Washington to Foreign Office, June 3, 1967. Rafael, *Destination Peace*, pp. 139–40. U Thant, *View from the UN*, p. 222. Eban, *Personal Witness*, p. 359.

25. Rikhye, *Sinai Blunder*, pp. 32–38. U Thant, *View from the UN*, pp. 222–23.

26. In an angry letter to the *New York Times* on June 11, 1967, Bunche wrote that there was "not a shred of truth" in Nasser's claim that he wanted UNEF retained in Gaza and Sharm al-Sheikh. A similar interpretation of Nasser's thinking during this time was presented by Ambassador Charles Yost to Dr. Ya'akov Herzog of the Israel Foreign Ministry. See ISA, Prime Minister's Office, 7854/6a: Conversation Between Ambassador Charles Yost and Dr. Herzog, July 7, 1969. See also Heikal, *Al-Infijar*, pp. 474–77. Rikhye, *Sinai Blunder*, p. 165. Parker, *Six Day War*, pp. 88–99. UN, S-0316, UNEF-Withdrawals/UN Missions-EIMAC, box 9: Riad to U Thant, May 18, 1967.

27. UN, S 0316-box 9, file 2: UNEF Withdrawals, Exchange with UAR: Riad to U Thant, May 18, 1967; U Thant to Riad, May 18, 1967. Urquhart, *A Life in Peace and War*, p. 210. U Thant, *View from the UN*, pp. 222–23. Heikal, *Al-Infijar*, pp. 474–77.

28. UN, S-0316, UNEF-Withdrawals/UN Missions-EIMAC, box 9: Bull to Bunche, May 19, 1967; Bunche to Rikhye, May 20, 1967. Rikhye, *Sinai Blunder*, pp. 40–45. Indar Jit Rikhye oral history, Feb. 22, 2000. Parker, *Six Day War*, p. 75. Parker, "The June 1967 War: Some Mysteries Explored," pp. 189–90.

29. LBJ, National Security file, History of the Middle East Conflict, box 20: United States Policy and Diplomacy in the Middle East Crisis, May 15–June 10, 1967, p. 14; NSC Histories, Middle East Crisis, box 21: USUN to the Secretary of State, May 18, 1967. U Thant's reports and comments on them in U Thant, *View from the UN*, pp. 227–30. ISA, Foreign Ministry files, 4085/2: Emergency Force, Rafael to Foreign Ministry, May 19, 1967. Rafael, *Destination Peace*, p. 140. Parker, *The Politics of Miscalculation in the Middle East*, p. 71. Urquhart, *A Life in Peace and War*, p. 210. Eban, *Personal Witness*, p. 360. U Thant's reliance on horoscopes from Indar Jit Rikhye oral history, Feb. 22, 2000.

30. FRUS, XVIII, 29–30 (Nasser quote on Dimona), pp. 73–74, 158, 690. Yariv, *Ha'arakha Zehira*, pp. 159–61. Cohen, *Israel and the Bomb*, pp. 259–76. Several respectable authors have posited that Nasser sought to precipitate a conventional showdown with Israel before it could develop non-conventional weapons. My own research, based on dozens of Arabic sources, has shown no evidence whatsoever to support the theory. See Shlomo Aronson with Oded Brosh, *The Politics and Strategy of Nuclear Weapons in the Middle East: Opacity, Theory, and Reality, 1960–1991: An Israeli Perspective* (Albany: State University of New York Press, 1992), pp. 109–18. Hersh, *The Samson Option*, p. 138.

31. ISA, 4085/2, Foreign Ministry files, Emergency Force: Elitzur to Rangoon, May 26, 1967. IDF, 710/70, Gen. Yariv's Briefing to the General Staff, May 19, 1967. Mayzel, *Ha-Ma'arakha al ha-Golan*, pp. 34–36. LBJ, National Security files, NSC Histories, Middle East Crisis, box 17: Tel Aviv to the Secretary of State, May 19, 1967. Yariv, *Ha'arakha Zehira*, pp. 37–40, 162–63. Rabin, *Memoirs*, p. 71. Oral history interview with Col. Shlomo Merom, Dec. 7, 1999. PRO FCO17/498: Israel – Political Affairs: Tel Aviv to Foreign Office, Conversation with Gen. Yariv, June 1, 1967.

32. ISA, 7920/4, Levi Eshkol Papers, Prime Minister's Reports and Surveys: Eshkol's Reports to the Ministerial Defense Committee, May 18, 1967; 4087/6, Foreign Ministry files, Emergency Appeal: Eshkol to Harman, May 17, 1967. Haber, *Ha-Yom Tifrotz Milhama*, p. 153 (Eshkol quote). Rabin, *Memoirs*, pp. 70–71. Kimche and Bawly, *The Sandstorm*, p. 136.

33. ISA, 4078/4 Foreign Ministry files, Contacts with the United States on the Entry of Egyptian Forces to the Sinai: Harman Conversation with Rostow, May 17, 1967. Johnson letter to Eshkol in LBJ, National Security file, History of the Middle East Conflict, box 20: United States Policy and Diplomacy in the Middle East Crisis, May 15–June 10, 1967, p. 13. On Israel's fears of UN pressure on UNEF, see ISA, Foreign Ministry files, 4085/2: Emergency Force: Rafael to Tekoah, May 21, 1967; 4086/5, Foreign Ministry files, Security Council Meetings: Rafael to Eban, May 19, 1967. See also Eban, *Personal Witness*, pp. 36–42. Lyndon Baines Johnson, *The Vantage Point: Perspectives of the Presidency, 1963–1969* (New York: Holt, Rinehart and Winston, 1971), p. 290. William B. Quandt, *Peace Process: American Diplomacy and the Arab-Israeli Conflict since 1967* (Washington, D.C.: The Brookings Institute, 1993), p. 28.

34. ISA, 4078/4 Foreign Ministry files, Contacts with the United States on the Entry of Egyptian Forces to Sinai: Eshkol to Johnson, May 18, 1967; 6444/6 North America, Telegrams, Ministry to Embassies, May 21, 1967; 7919/1, Levi Eshkol files, Diplomatic Telegrams: U.S.A.: Harman to Eban, May 20, 1967 (Harman quote). LBJ, National Security file, History of the Middle East Crisis, box 17: W. Rostow, For the Record, May 16, 1967; Memorandum for the Record (Saunders), May 19, 1967; box 20: United States Policy and Diplomacy in the Middle East Crisis, May 15–June 10,

1967, pp. 20–21 (Rusk quote); NSC Histories, Middle East Crisis, box 17: Summary of Arab-Israel Developments, Night of May 19–20, 1967; Tel Aviv to the Secretary of State, May 21, 1967 (Eban quote). It is not known whether the U.S. granted Israel's request for intelligence regarding the disposition of Jordanian troops. Ambassador Burns strongly recommended against fulfilling it. See USNA, POL ARAB-ISR, box 9: Amman to the Secretary of State, May 25, 1967.

35. ISA, 4084/2, Foreign Ministry files, Relations with France: Eshkol to De Gaulle, May 19, 1967; 4091/23, Exchange of Messages Before the War: Eban to Couve de Murville, May 19, 1967: Eban to Brown, May 19, 1967; 4080/5, Contacts with Great Britain: London to Foreign Ministry, May 18, 1967; 7920/2, Levi Eshkol Papers, Diplomatic Telegrams, USSR: Conversation with the Soviet Ambassador, May 19, 1967. PREM 13 1617, The Middle East Crisis: Record of Conversation between the Foreign Secretary and the Israeli Ambassador, May 19, 1967. Chuvakhin quote from LBJ, National Security file, History of the Middle East Conflict, box 20: United States Policy and Diplomacy in the Middle East Crisis, May 15–June 10, 1967, pp. 20–21, and from ISA, 4078/4 Foreign Ministry files, Contacts with the United States on the Entry of Egyptian Forces to the Sinai: Eban to Harman, May 19, 1967. Haber, *Ha-Yom Tifrotz Milhama,* p. 154 Dagan, *Moscow and Jerusalem,* pp. 211–12.

36. Mansoor, *Arab World,* entries for May 18, 19, 20, 21, 1967. Other references to al-Assad quotes appear in *al-Thawra,* May 20, 1967, and George Khouri, ed., *Al-Watha'iq al-Filastiniyya al-'Arabiyya li-'Am 1967* (Beirut: Mu'assasat al-Dirasa al-Filastiniyya, 1969), pp. 177–79. Makhous quotes in *al-Ba'th,* May 18, 1967, and Draper, *Israel & World Politics,* p. 60. Deportation of Saudi diplomats in USNA Central Foreign Policy files, 1967–1969, POL 12 SY, box 2511: Jidda to the Department of State, May 10, 1967. Hussein quote from *My "War" with Israel,* p. 34. Jordanian quote from Mutawi, *Jordan in the 1967 War,* pp. 88–89, and BBC, Daily Report, Middle East, Africa, and Western Europe, No. A1. *Al-Zaman* quote in LBJ, National Security files, NSC Histories, Middle East Crisis, box 17: Beirut to the Secretary of State, May 19, 1967. See also Husayn Mustafa, *Harb Haziran 1967: Awwal Dirasa 'Askariyyu min Wujhat al-Nazar al-'Arabiyya 2: al-Jabha al-Sharqiyya* (Beirut: Al-Mu'assasa al-'Arabiyya lil-Dirasa wal-Nashr, 1973), pp. 276–79.

37. Rabin quotes from IDF, 710/70 General Staff Discussion: May 19, 1967; Haber, *Ha-Yom Tifrotz Milhama,* p. 155. Slater, *Rabin of Israel,* p. 127. Mayzel, *Ha-Ma'arakha al ha-Golan,* pp. 39–40. Oral history interview with Mordechai Gazit, Feb. 4, 1999. See also Rabin, *The Rabin Memoirs,* p. 72.

38. BGA, Diary, Entry for May 22, 1967. LBJ, National Security files, NSC Histories, Middle East Crisis, box 17: Tel Aviv to the Secretary of State, May 21, 1967 (Eban quote). Rabin, *The Rabin Memoirs,* pp. 73–75. Kurzman, *Soldier of Peace,* pp. 208–9. Slater, *Rabin of Israel,* pp. 126–27. Oral history interview with Miriam Eshkol, Aug. 30, 1999. Eban, *Personal Witness,* pp. 364–65.

39. Dayan, *My Life,* pp. 317–18. Mayzel, *Ha-Ma'arakha al ha-Golan,* pp. 42–43. Dayan quotes from Gilboa, *Shesh Shanim, Shisha Yamim,* p. 66. Shimon Peres, *Battling for Peace: Memoirs* (London: Weidenfeld and Nicolson, 1995) p. 89. Haber, *Ha-Yom Tifrotz Milhama,* p. 152. Kurzman, *Soldier of Peace,* pp. 208–9

40. ISA, 4088/11 the Entry into Sinai of Egyptian Troops and the Closure of the Tiran Straits, Report of Research Branch, May 22, 1967; 7920/4, Levi Eshkol Papers, Prime Minister's Reports and Surveys: Censorship of Information Regarding Ships

Passing Through the Straits of Tiran, May 21, 1967. LBJ, National Security file, History of the Middle East Conflict, box 20: United States Policy and Diplomacy in the Middle East Crisis, May 15–June 10, 1967, pp. 27–28. ISA, 6444/5 North America, telegrams: Foreign Ministry to Embassies May 31, 1967. Rabin, *Memoirs*, p. 72. Haber, *Ha-Yom Tifrotz Milhama*, pp. 155, 161–62 (Eshkol Cabinet quotes). Amit quote from Asia, *Tismonet Dayan*, p. 127. Eshkol Knesset quote from Henry M. Christman, ed., *The State Papers of Levi Eshkol* (New York: Funk & Wagnalls, 1969), p. 88. Israel message to Nasser in Parker, *The Six Day War*, p. 281. See also Prittie, *Eshkol*, p. 88.

41. PRO FCO17/498: Israel – Political Affairs, the Middle East Crisis, October 23, 1967.

42. PRO, FO 17/489, Israel – Political Affairs: Foreign Office to Amman, June 2, 1967. ISA, Foreign Ministry files, 3998/5: Gen. Rabin Conversation with the Shah, April 16, 1967. Heikal, *Al-Infijar*, p. 333. P. J. Vatikiotis, *The History of Egypt: From Muhammad Ali to Sadat* (Baltimore: Johns Hopkins University Press, 1980), p. 313. Randolph S. Churchill and Winston S. Churchill, *The Six Day War* (London: Heinemann Books, 1967), pp. 42–43. Rosemary Higgins, *United Nations Peace-Keeping, 1946–67* (Oxford: Oxford University Press, 1969), pp. 241–415.

43. Fawzi, *Harb al-Thalath Sanawat*, pp. 80–82. Murtagi, *Al-Fariq Murtagi Yarwi al-Haqa'iq*, p. 67. El-Sadat, *In Search of Identity*, p. 172. Heikal, *Al-Infijar*, pp. 514–19. Dhabbah, *Wa-Madha Ba'du?*, pp. 18–24. Abdel Magid Farid, *Nasser: The Final Years* (Reading, U.K.: Ithaca Press, 1994), p. 73. Al-Baghdadi, *Mudhakkirat*, pp. 266–67. Ramadan, *Tahtim al-Aliha*, pp. 55–56. See also L. Carl Brown, "Nasser and the June 1967 War: Plan or Improvisation?" in S. Seikaly, R. Baalbaki and P. Dodd, eds., *Quest for Understanding: Arabic and Islamic Studies in Memory of Malcolm Kerr* (Beirut: American University of Beirut, 1991), p. 127. Parker, *The Politics of Miscalculation in the Middle East*, p. 72.

44. The Bir Gafgafa speech appears in many sources. See, for example, Stephens, *Nasser*, p. 473; U Thant, *View from the UN*, p. 232; and Heikal, *Al-Infijar*, p. 518. Cairo Radio quote from Tim Hewat, ed., *War File: The Voices of the Israelis, Arabs, British and Americans, in the Arab-Israeli War of 1967* (London: Panter Books, 1967), p. 31. Al-Sabbagh, *Mudhakkirat Qadat al-'Askariyya al-Misriyya* 1, p. 24; 5, p. 16. Muhammad 'Abd al-Hafiz's testimony appears in Darraz, *Dubbat Yunyu Yatakallamun*, pp. 135–46. 'Amer's order in Heikal, *Al-Infijar*, p. 518.

45. LBJ, National Security file, History of the Middle East Conflict, box 20: United States Policy and Diplomacy in the Middle East Crisis, May 15–June 10, 1967, pp. 43–44. Hussein quotes from PRO, PREM 13 1617, The Middle East Crisis: Amman to Foreign Office, May 23, 1967, and Kamm, *Hussein Poteah be-Milhama*, p. 203. Mutawi, *Jordan in the 1967 War*, pp. 104–5.

46. Records of U Thant's discussions in Cairo appear in UN, DAG1/5.2.2.1.2.-1: Memoranda by Maj. Gen. Rikhye, May 24, 1967, and in PRO, FCO17/498: Israel–Political Affairs: Record of Meeting, Harold Wilson and U Thant, Washington to Foreign Office, June 3, 1967. Secondary sources on the talks appear in Imam, *'Abd al-Nasir—Kayfa Hakama Misr*, p. 365. Rikhye, *Sinai Blunder*, pp. 66–77. Parker, *The Politics of Miscalculation in the Middle East*, pp. 231–33. U Thant, *View from the UN*, pp. 235–38. See also Riad, *The Struggle for Peace in the Middle East*, p. 20. Dhabbah, *Wa-Madha Ba'du?*, pp. 39–44. Eban, *Personal Witness*, p. 365. Chants of demonstrators at Cairo airport in Mansoor, *Arab World*, entries for May 23 and May 24, 1967. Rikhye quote from oral history interview with Indar Jit Rikhye, Feb. 22, 2000.

47. Rabin, *Memoirs*, p. 83. Haber, *Ha-Yom Tifrotz Milhama*, pp. 164–65.

48. Haber, *Ha Yom Tifrotz Milhama*, pp. 164–65. Rabin, *Memoirs*, pp. 77–78.

49. LBJ, National Security file, History of the Middle East Conflict, box 20: United States Policy and Diplomacy in the Middle East Crisis, May 15–June 10, 1967, pp. 26–34; box 17: May 23, 1967; Memorandum for the President, May 24, 1967 (Rostow quote): Department of State to Tel Aviv, May 23, 1967. ISA, 5937/30: Secret Memoranda Prior to the Six-Day War: Johnson Message to Eshkol, May 22, 1967; 4086/5, Foreign Ministry files, Security Council Meetings, Rafael to Tekoah, May 23, 1967; 7919/1, Levi Eshkol files, Diplomatic Telegrams: U.S.A.: Evron to Bitan, May 21, 1967. Haber, *Ha-Yom Tifrotz Milhama*, p. 165. Eugene V. Rostow, *Peace in the Balance: The Future of American Foreign Policy* (New York: Simon & Schuster, 1972), pp. 259–60.

50. Haber, *Ha-Yom Tifrotz Milhama*, pp. 159, 166–69. Eban, *Personal Witness*, pp. 363–70. Eshkol statement to Knesset in Prittie, *Eshkol*, p. 93. Dayan, *My Life*, pp. 319–20 (Dayan quote). Rabin, *Memoirs*, pp. 78–79. Moshe Raviv, *Israel at Fifty: Five Decades of the Struggle for Peace* (London: Weidenfeld & Nicolson, 1998), pp. 92–93. ISA, 7919/1, Levi Eshkol files, Diplomatic Telegrams: U.S.A.: Harman to Eban, May 22, 1967 (U.S. request for 48-hour delay). Oral history interview with Zorach Warfhaftig, Feb. 23, 1999. See also Brecher, *Decisions in Crisis*, p. 120. Baron, *Hotam Ishi*, pp. 20–21.

51. Rabin quotes from Haber, *Ha-Yom Tifrotz Milhama*, p. 172, and Rabin, *Memoirs*, p. 84. Religious clerics' statement in Mansoor, *Arab World*, entry for May 26, 1967. Lyrics in Rut Leviav "Milhemet Sheshet ha-Yamim: Ha-Festival," *Bamahane* 37 (June 1977).

52. Haber, *Ha-Yom Tifrotz Milhama*, pp. 171–72. Rabin, *Memoirs*, pp. 78–79. Rabin quotes from Ronel Fisher, "Hayta Li Takala, Ze ha-Sipur," *Ma'ariv*, June 6, 1967.

53. Weizman, *On Eagles' Wings*, pp. 211–12. Slater, *Rabin of Israel*, pp. 132–33. Rabin, *Memoirs*, pp. 80–83. Haber, *Ha-Yom Tifrotz Milhama*, pp. 174–75. Kurzman, *Soldier of Peace*, pp. 208–9. Baron, *Hotam Ishi*, pp. 22–23. Shlomo Gazit, *Pta'im be-Malkodet: 30 Shnot Mediniyut Yisrael ha-Shtahim* (Tel Aviv: Zemora-Bitan, 1999), p. 28. USNA, POL ARAB-IS, box 1788: Tel Aviv to Department of State, May 25, 1967.

54. USNA, Lot files, USUN, box 6: CINSTRIKE to AIG, May 25, 1967. Rabin, *Memoirs*, pp. 84–85. Mayzel, *Ha-Ma'arakha al ha-Golan*, pp. 41–44, 170–73. Parker, *The Six Day War*, p. 147. Weizman, *On Eagles' Wings*, pp. 215–16. For an excellent overview of Israeli decision-making in this period, see Ami Gluska, *Imut bein ha-Mateh ha-Klali u-bein Memshelet Eshkol bi-Tkufat ha-Hamtana"—Mai-Yuni, 1967* (Jerusalem: The Leonard Davis Institute for International Relations, 2001).

55. Mazhar, *I'tirafat Qadat Harb Yunyu*, p. 228. Fawzi, *Harb al-Thalath Sanawat*, pp. 106–109. 'Amer quote from Murtagi, *Al-Fariq Murtagi Yarwi al-Haqa'iq*, p. 69. Mahmud Al-Jiyyar, "Rajulun Qatala al-Mushir 'Amer," *Ruz al-Yusuf* 2482 (January 5, 1976), p. 8. Al-Sabbagh, *Mudhakkirat Qadat al 'Askaraiyya al-Misriyya 13*, p. 38. Michael Bar-Zohar, *Embassies in Crisis*, pp. 14–15. Description of posters in Egypt from Parker, *The Politics of Miscalculation in the Middle East*, pp. 76–78; see also *Israel Must Be Annihilated* (Tel Aviv: Zahal Information Office, July 1967). Cairo Radio quote from BBC, Daily Report, The Middle East and Africa, ME/2474/A/1.

56. For examples of the two schools of interpretation, see Heikal, *Al-Infjar*, pp. 573–74, and 'Abd al-Hamid, *Al-Mushir wa-Ana*, pp. 211–22. See also Fawzi, *Harb al-Thalath Sanawat*, pp. 71, 76–80, 105–9. Murtagi, *Al-Fariq Murtagi Yarwi al-Haqa'iq*, p. 67. Fawzi quote from Mazhar, *I'tirafat Qadat Harb Yunyu*, pp. 49–50, 129–30.

57. Fawzi, *Harb al-Thalath Sanawat*, pp. 85–86. Murtagi, *Al-Fariq Murtagi Yarwi al-Haqa'iq*, pp. 71–73. Ramadan, *Tahtim al-Aliha*, pp. 79–80. O'Balance, *The Third Arab-Israeli War*, p. 100. Abu Fadl quote from Parker, *The Politics of Miscalculation in the Middle East*, pp. 94–95. Fawzi and 'Amer quotes from Mazhar, *I'tirafat Qadat Harb Yunyu*, pp. 61–62.

58. Mazhar, *I'tirafat Qadat Harb Yunyu*, p. 227. Murtagi quote from *Al-Fariq Murtagi Yarwi al-Haqa'iq*, pp. 69–70. Sidqi Mahmud quote from Mazhar, *I'tirafat Qadat Harb Yunyu*, p. 111.

59. Mustafa, *Harb Haziran 1967*, pp. 181–82. Al-Shuqayri, *Mudhakkirat 2*, p. 103. El-Sadat, *In Search of Identity*, p. 174. Quotes from Mansoor, *Arab World*, entry for May 24–26, 1967, and Stephens, *Nasser*, p. 479. See also Draper, *Israel & World Politics*, pp. 64–65, 112.

60. LBJ, Office files of George Christian, box 4: Nolte to Rusk, May 24, 1967. Riad, *The Struggle for Peace in the Middle East*, pp. 19–20. Heikal, *Al-Infijar*, pp. 572–73. Johnson statement and *notes verbales* in LBJ, National Security file, History of the Middle East Conflict, box 20: United States Policy and Diplomacy in the Middle East Crisis, May 15–June 10, 1967, pp. 30–33, and Parker, *The Politics of Miscalculation in the Middle East*, pp. 48, 225–27. U.S. Navy spokesman and Humphrey quotes from Mansoor, *Arab World*, entry for May 26, 1967.

61. Descriptions of Kamel appear in Heikal, *Al-Infijar*, pp. 564–65; LBJ, National Security file, Country file, Middle East-UAR box 161: Lunch with Ambassador Kamel, Jan. 17, 1967; History of the Middle East Crisis, box 17: Rostow to Rusk, May 25, 1967. Oral history interview with Walt W. Rostow, July 27, 1999. On Nolte, see PRO FCO/39/261 UAR – Relations with the United States: Record of Conversation with Mr. Richard Nolte, May 18, 1967. Parker, *The Politics of Miscalculation in the Middle East*, pp. 55–56.

62. LBJ, National Security file, History of the Middle East Conflict, box 20: United States Policy and Diplomacy in the Middle East Crisis, May 15–June 10, 1967, pp. 30–33.

63. Fawzi, *Harb al-Thalath Sanawat*, pp. 75–76. Heikal quote in Stephens, *Nasser*, p. 481. Fawzi quote in Heikal, *Al-Infijar*, pp. 567–68. Ramadan, *Tahtim al-Aliha*, pp. 72–76. Eban, *Personal Witness*, p. 383.

64. LBJ, National Security file, History of the Middle East Crisis, box 17: W. Rostow to the President, May 26, 1967.

65. LBJ, National Security file, History of the Middle East Crisis, box 17: State Department Circular, May 18, 1967. ISA, Foreign Ministry files, 4083/3, Contacts with the Soviet Union, Raviv to Shimoni, May 23, 1967; 4048/27, Foreign Ministry files, Diplomatic Relations with the Soviet Union: Moscow to Foreign Ministry, May 24, 1967. Soviet communiqué in LBJ, National Security file, History of the Middle East Crisis, box 19, State Department Activities Report, May 21, 1967. 'Amer's order in Heikal, *Al-Infijar*, p. 454. See also Gilboa, *Shesh Shanim, Shisha Yamim*, pp. 114–15. Riad, *The Struggle for Peace in the Middle East*, pp. 34–35. Dagan, *Moscow and Jerusalem*, pp. 209, 214. Rikhye, *Sinai Blunder*, p. 169.

66. LBJ, National Security file, History of the Middle East Crisis, box 17: Moscow to the Department of State, May 24, 1967. USNA, Middle East Crisis files, 1967, NN3.059.96089, box 1: Chronology of U.S.-Jordanian Consultations on the Middle East, May 22, 1967. Nasser-Pojidaev conversation appears in Parker, *The Politics of Miscalculation in the Middle East*, p. 27, and Heikal, *Al-Infijar*, pp. 519–24.

67. USNA, Central Policy files, 1967–1969, POL 2 UAR, box 2553: Moscow to the Department of State, May 25, 1967. Parker, *The Politics of Miscalculation in the Middle East*, pp. 27, 50; *The Six Day War*, pp. 38–39, 65.

68. Murtagi, *Al-Fariq Murtagi Yarwi al-Haqa'iq*, pp. 78–83. Fawzi, *Harb al-Thalath Sanawat*, pp. 105–9. Mazhar, *I'tirafat Qadat Harb Yunyu*, p. 124. Darraz, *Dubbat Yunyu Yatakallamun*, pp. 36–37. O'Balance, *The Third Arab-Israeli War*, p. 98. UN, S-0316-box 9, file 7, UNEF-Withdrawals: Rikhye to Bunche, May 25, 1967. Oral history interview with Shlomo Merom, Dec. 7, 1999. The presence of a civilian occupation force in Gaza was discovered by the American consul general from Jerusalem while talking to Egyptian POWs. See USNA, Central Foreign Policy files, 1967–1969, POL 27-7 ARAB-ISR, box 1830: Tel Aviv to the Secretary of State, Sept. 13, 1967. Oral history interview with Amin Tantawi, July 4, 2001.

69. Rabin, *Memoirs*, p. 86. Gilboa, *Shesh Shanim, Shisha Yamim*, p. 129. Haber, *Ha-Yom Tifrotz Milhama*, p. 177. Dayan, *My Life*, p. 332. Oral history interview with Meir Amit, Feb. 9, 1999. Yossi Peled, *Ish Tzava* (Tel Aviv: Ma'ariv, 1993), p. 103. Jonathan Netanyahu, *Self-Portrait of a Hero: The Letters of Jonathan Netanyahu* (New York: Random House, 1980), p. 133.

70. Rabin, *Memoirs*, p. 83. Carmit Guy, *Bar-Lev* (Tel Aviv: Am Oved, 1998), p. 125.

71. Haber, *Ha-Yom Tifrotz Milhama*, pp. 185–87. Elinar Ben Akiva and Aner Guvrin, "Sh'at ha-Mirage—Esrim Shana le-Milhemet Sheshet ha-Yamim," *Bit'on Hail ha-Avir* 57 (May 1987). Rabin, *The Rabin Memoirs*, pp. 85–88. Slater, *Rabin of Israel*, p. 134. Parker, *The Six Day War*, pp. 135–36. Oral history interview with Ezer Weizman, March 1, 1999. On Israeli fears for Dimona, see Cohen, *Israel and the Bomb*, pp. 259–76.

72. Haber, *Ha-Yom Tifrotz Milhama*, p. 108. Oral history interview with Miriam Eshkol, Aug. 30, 1999.

73. ISA, 4091/23, Foreign Ministry files, Exchange of Messages Before the War: Eban to Couve de Murville, May 19, 1967. PRO, PREM 13 1617, The Middle East Crisis: Eban to Brown, May 23, 1967 (a similar note was sent by Eban to his French counterpart, Couve de Murville). On the continued supply of French arms to Israel see BGA, Diary, Entry for June 19, 1967. LBJ, National Security file, History of the Middle East Conflict, box 20: United States Policy and Diplomacy in the Middle East Crisis, May 15–June 10, 1967, pp. 50–51. USNA, Subject-Numeric files, POL ARAB-ISR, box 1789: Department of State to London, May 27, 1967. See also Crosbie, *A Tacit Alliance*, 1977.

74. ISA, 5937/30: Secret Memoranda Prior to the Six Day War: Paris to Foreign Ministry, Protocol of Eban Meeting with President de Gaulle, May 25, 1967. Eban, *Personal Witness*, pp. 372–77. Lacouture, *De Gaulle*, p. 439. LBJ, National Security file, History of the Middle East Conflict, box 20: United States Policy and Diplomacy in the Middle East Crisis, May 15–June 10, 1967, pp. 39–40. "Superficial sympathy" quote from PRO, PREM 13 1622: Record of Conversation, President de Gaulle and Prime Minister Wilson, June 19, 1967.

75. Maurice Couve de Murville, *Une politique étrangère 1958–1969* (Paris: Plon, 1971), p. 469. Gilboa, *Shesh Shanim, Shisha Yamim*, p. 141. Raviv, *Israel at Fifty*, pp. 96–97. ISA, 7920/2, Levi Eshkol Papers: Diplomatic Cables – France: Eytan to Levavi: Conversation with Couve, May 24, 1967.

76. PRO, FO17/497: Israel – Political Affairs: Draft Paper for Cabinet – Middle East Crisis, May 24, 1967; CAB 128/42 31st Conclusions: May 24, 1967; PREM 13

1617: The Middle East Crisis, May 23, 1967. ISA, 4080/5, Foreign Ministry files, Contacts with Great Britain: Raviv to Foreign Ministry, May 24, 1967; 7920/1, Levi Eshkol Papers, Diplomatic Telegrams: The Wilson-Eban Conversation, May 24, 1967. LBJ, National Security file, History of the Middle East Conflict, box 20: United States Policy and Diplomacy in the Middle East Crisis, May 15–June 10, 1967, pp. 27–28. Eban, *Personal Witness*, pp. 377–79. Harold Wilson, *The Chariot of Israel: Britain, America, and the State of Israel* (New York: Norton, 1981), pp. 333–34. Wilson quote from www.bemorecreative.com/one/480.htm.

77. First Eban quote from Eban, *Personal Witness*, p. 381. ISA, 4078/7, Foreign Ministry files, Six-Day War: Eban to Washington, Instructions for Conversations with Administration, May 23, 1967 (second Eban quote); New York to Ministry, Rafael Meeting with Goldberg, May 23, 1967; Harman to Rafael, May 23, 1967; Harman to Eban, May 23, 1967.

78. ISA, 5937/30, Secret Memorandum Prior to the Six Day War: Harman to Foreign Ministry, May 24, 1967 (Eisenhower quote); Prime Minister's Office to the Foreign Ministry, May 24, 1967 (Barbour quote). LBJ, National Security file, History of the Middle East Conflict, box 20: United States Policy and Diplomacy in the Middle East Crisis, May 15–June 10, 1967, pp. 52–53. Oral history interview with Meir Amit, Feb. 9, 1999. Eban, *Personal Witness*, pp. 385–86.

79. ISA, 7919/1, Levi Eshkol files, Diplomatic Telegrams: U.S.A.: Eshkol to Eban, May 25, 1967. Eban, *Personal Witness*, pp. 382–83. USNA, POL ARAB-IS, box 1788: Secretary of State to Tel Aviv, Cairo and Damascus, May 25, 1967. Message quoted in Haber, *Ha-Yom Tifrotz Milhama*, p. 187. Amit, *Rosh be-Rosh*, p. 236.

80. LBJ, National Security file, History of the Middle East Conflict, box 20: United States Policy and Diplomacy in the Middle East Crisis, May 15–June 10, 1967, pp. 52–53; Middle East Crisis, box 22–23: Barbour to Rostow, May 23, 1967. PRO, PREM 13 1618, Wilson to Johnson, May 24, 1967. ISA, 3977/22, Foreign Ministry files, Relations with the United States: Bitan Conversation with Barbour, May 23, 1967.

81. LBJ, National Security file, History of the Middle East Crisis, box 17: Saunders to Rostow, May 15, 1967; Memos to the President (W. Rostow), box 16: Saunders to Rostow, May 15, 1967; Middle East, Israel boxes 140, 141: W. Rostow to the President, May 15, 1967. USNA, Lot files, USUN, box 6: CINSTRIKE to AIG ISA, 4078/4 Foreign Ministry files, Contacts with the United States on the Entry of Egyptian Forces to the Sinai: Harman Conversation with Rostow, May 15, 1967.

82. LBJ, National Security file, Middle East Crisis, box 22–23: Saunders to W. Rostow, May 18, 1967; History of the Middle East Conflict, box 17: W. Rostow to the President, May 17, 1967; box 20: United States Policy and Diplomacy in the Middle East Crisis, May 15–June 10, 1967, pp. 10–11, 27–28; Middle East Crisis, boxes 144 and 145: W. Rostow to the President, May 19, 1967. USNA, Middle East Crisis files, 1967, Lot file 68D135, box 2: Rostow to Rusk, May 23, 1967. PRO, PREM 13 1617, The Middle East Crisis: Washington to Foreign Office, May 22, 1967. 7920/2, Levi Eshkol Papers, Diplomatic Telegrams, USSR: Research Branch to Eban, May 24, 1967. See also Johnson, *The Vantage Point*, p. 291.

83. LBJ, National Security file, Memos to the President (W. Rostow), box 16: Overall Arab and Israeli Military Capabilities, May 23, 1967; NSC Histories, Middle East Crisis, box 17: The President in the Middle East Crisis, Dec. 19, 1968. Oral history interview with Robert McNamara, Feb. 11, 2000.

84. LBJ, National Security file, History of the Middle East Crisis, box 17: Rusk to Cairo, May 22, 1967; box 20: United States Policy and Diplomacy in the Middle East Crisis, May 15–June 10, 1967, pp. 44, 51–52. Oral history interview with Walt W. Rostow, July 27, 1999.

85. LBJ, National Security file, History of the Middle East Conflict, United States Policy and Diplomacy in the Middle East Crisis, May 15–June 10, 1967, pp. 32, 37–38, 45–49; box 17: Rusk to Cairo, May 23, 1967. USNA, POL ARAB-ISR: box 7: Rusk – Mideast Sitrep, May 25, 1967; The Department of State to London, May 29, 1967 ("marching orders"); Minutes of the Control Group, box 17: Third Meeting of the Middle East Control Group, May 24, 1967. Rostow, *The Diffusion of Power*, pp. 258–59. Israel's convoy proposal during the Suez crisis in USNA, 976.7301/9-1056: Dulles Conversation with Eban and in PRO, FO371/11191501/2008: Shepherd Minute, Oct. 28, 1956.

86. USNA, Middle East Crisis files, 1967, NN3.059.96089, box 1: Chronology of U.S.-Jordanian Consultations on the Middle East: Rostow Conversation with Harman, May 24, 1967. LBJ, National Security file, History of the Middle East Conflict, box 20: United States Policy and Diplomacy in the Middle East Crisis, May 15–June 10, 1967, pp. 37–38, 52–55; NSC Histories, The Middle East Crisis, box 17: Luncheon Conversation with Saudi Prince Mohammad, May 31, 1967; President's Conversation with the Prime Minister of Canada, May 25, 1967. PRO, PREM 13 1618: Wilson to President Johnson, May 26, 1967; The Middle East Crisis: Washington to Foreign Office, May 24, 1967; CAB 128/42 32nd Conclusions, May 25, 1967. ISA, 7919/1, Levi Eshkol files, Diplomatic Telegrams: U.S.A.: Evron to Eban, May 27, 1967. Dean Rusk, *As I Saw It* (New York: Penguin Books, 1990), p. 384. Quandt, *Peace Process*, pp. 34–35.

87. Rusk, *As I Saw It*, pp. 153, 378, 383. ISA, 3975/14, Foreign Ministry files, Diplomatic Relations with the United States: Evron to Bitan. Meeting Between Eban and Rusk at the Waldorf Astoria, Oct. 7, 1966.

88. LBJ, National Security file, History of the Middle East Conflict, box 20: United States Policy and Diplomacy in the Middle East Crisis, May 15–June 10, 1967, pp. 55–56; box 18: Memorandum of Conversation, the Secretary and Foreign Minister Eban, May 25, 1967. USNA, POL ARAB-ISR, box 17: Rusk to Tel Aviv, Cairo, and Damascus, May 25, 1967; Memoranda of Conversations, UK, USSR, US, Israel, 1967, box 14: Your Conversation with the Israeli Foreign Minister, May 25, 1967; USUN, box 6: CINSTRIKE to AIG, May 26, 1967; Middle East Crisis files, 1967, Chronology, box 7: Tel Aviv to the Secretary of State, May 25, 1967 (Barbour report); POL ARAB-ISR, Cairo, box 1789: Cairo to the Secretary of State, May 26, 1967. ISA, 5937/30 Secret Memoranda Prior to the Six-Day War: Washington to Ministry, Eban Memoranda on a Conversation with Rusk, May 25, 1967; 7919/1, Levi Eshkol files, Diplomatic Telegrams: U.S.A.: Harman to Eshkol, May 26, 1967. Eban, *Personal Witness*, p. 383. Rafael, *Destination Peace*, pp. 143–45 ("horrendous error" quote). Rusk, *As I Saw It*, p. 385. Quandt, *Peace Process*, pp. 38–39. Parker, *Six Day War*, pp. 216–17.

89. ISA, 5937/30 Secret Memoranda Prior to the Six-Day War: Summation of Conversation between Foreign Minister Eban and Undersecretary Rostow during the Evening of May 25, 1967. USNA, POL ARAB-IS: Department of State to Tel Aviv, May 25, 1967; MemCon between Ambassador Dean and Under Secretary Rostow, May 27, 1967; Israeli-U.S. Working Dinner, May 25, 1967. LBJ, National Security files, NSC Histories, Middle East Crisis, box 18: Memorandum of Conversation between Undersecretary

Rostow and Foreign Minister Eban, May 25, 1967. Eban, *Personal Witness*, pp. 383–84. Raviv, *Israel at Fifty*, p. 98.

90. USNA, Memoranda of Conversations, UK, USSR, US, Israel, 1967, box 14: Your Conversation with the Israeli Foreign Minister, May 25, 1967; POL ARAB-ISR, box 17: MemCon between Ambassador Dean and Undersecretary Rostow, May 27, 1967.

91. ISA, 5937/30 Secret Memoranda Prior to the Six-Day War: Note on Thursday dinner at State Department, May 26, 1967. Harman's cable and message to Eban are both cited in Rabin, *The Rabin Memoirs*, pp. 85–89. See also Dayan, *My Life*, p. 328. Slater, *Rabin of Israel*, p. 134. Rafael, *Destination Peace*, p. 145. Parker, *The Six Day War*, pp. 135–36.

92. ISA, 5937/30, Foreign Ministry files, Secret Memoranda Prior to the Six-Day War: Eban to Eskhol, Conversation with Secretary of State Rusk, May 26, 1967; Eban to Eshkol, Meeting with McNamara and Chairman JCS Wheeler, May 26, 1967; 7919/1, Levi Eshkol files, Diplomatic Telegrams: U.S.A.: Evron to Eshkol, May 26, 1967. LBJ, May 27, 1967. Johnson, *Vantage Point*, p. 294. Eban, *Personal Witness*, p. 384. Oral history interview with Robert McNamara, Feb. 11, 2000. Raviv, *Israel at Fifty*, p. 99. McNamara and Wheeler were referring to U.S. intelligence estimates found in LBJ, National Security file, Memos to the President (W. Rostow), box 16: Overall Arab and Israeli Military Capabilities: May 23, 1967.

93. LBJ, National Security file, Memos to the President (W. Rostow), box 16: Rusk to Cairo and Tel Aviv, May 25, 1967; History of the Middle East Conflict, box 20: United States Policy and Diplomacy in the Middle East Crisis, May 15–June 10, 1967, pp. 30–33; NSC Histories, Middle East Crisis, box 17: Department of State to USUN and Cairo, May 25, 1967; box 18: New Delhi to the Secretary of State, May 22, 1967. Heikal, *Al-Infijar*, pp. 564–65.

94. LBJ, Richard Helms Oral History, pp. 11, 37. Oral history interview with Walt W. Rostow, July 27, 1967 and Eugene Rostow, Aug. 5, 1999. Robert A. Caro, *The Years of Lyndon B. Johnson: The Path to Power* (New York: Vintage, 1990), p. xix.

95. ISA, 3975/12, Diplomatic Relations with the United States, Harman to Bitan, June 13, 1966. William B. Quandt, "The Conflict in American Foreign Policy" in Rabinovich and Shaked, *From June to October*, pp. 5–6. Klinghoffer, *Vietnam, Jews and the Middle East*, p. 94. Douglas Little, "The Making of a Special Relationship: The United States and Israel, 1957–68," *International Journal of Middle East Studies* 25, no. 4 (Nov. 1993), pp. 274–75 (Roche quote). R. Evans and R. Novak, *Lyndon B. Johnson: The Exercise of Power* (New York: The New American Library, 1966), p. 175.

96. ISA, 3976/9, Foreign Ministry files, Relations with the United States: Eban Conversation with President Johnson, Sept. 2, 1966; Harman to Eban, June 24, 1966; 3977/15, Foreign Ministry files, United States – Reports and Analyses: Evron to Foreign Ministry, Aug. 25, 1966; 3975/15, Foreign Ministry files, Diplomatic Relations with the United States: Foreign Ministry Memorandum, Feb. 14, 1967 (Johnson quote); Written Communication with Harry McPherson, May 16, 2000. See also LBJ, National Security file, Middle East, Israel box 140, 141: Conflicting U. S. Attitudes Toward Military Aid to Israel, April 20, 1967; U.S.-Israel Relations, Nov. 3, 1967.

97. LBJ, National Security file, Memoranda to the President (W. Rostow), box 16: W. Rostow to the President, May 26, 1967; Congress–Middle East, May 26, 1967; History of the Middle East Crisis, box 17: Memorandum for the President, May 26, 1967. USNA, ARAB-ISR POL, box 1788: Rusk to Tel Aviv, May 26, 1967; Johnson to

Wilson, May 25, 1967 (Also in PRO, PREM 13 1618). ISA, 5937/30 Secret Memorandum Prior to the Six Day War: Evron to Foreign Ministry, May 26, 1967 (Rostow quote). Oral history interview with Walt W. Rostow, July 27, 1967, and Eugene Rostow, Aug. 5, 1999. Parker, *The Six Day War*, pp. 200–202.

98. LBJ, National Security file, Memoranda to the President (W. Rostow), box 16: Minutes of Meeting (Saunders), May 26, 1967; NSC Histories, Middle East Crisis, box 17: Memorandum for the Record, the Arab-Israeli Crisis, May 27, 1967. Quandt, *Peace Process*, pp. 37–40.

99. LBJ, National Security files, NSC Histories, Middle East Crisis, box 17: the President in the Middle East Crisis, Dec. 19, 1968. ISA, 3975/12, Diplomatic Relations with the United States. Eran to Bitan, June 22, 1966; Harman to Bitan, June 13, 1966. LBJ, National Security file, Memos to the President (W. Rostow), box 17: Evron to the President, May 26, 1967. Oral history interview with Mordechai Gazit, Feb. 4, 1999.

100. ISA, 5937/30, Secret Memoranda Prior to the Six-Day War: Evron to Foreign Ministry, May 26, 1967. LBJ, National Security files, NSC Histories, Middle East Crisis, box 17: Walt Rostow to the President, May 26, 1967. Raviv, *Israel at Fifty*, pp. 99–100. Quandt, *Peace Process*, pp. 40, 513–14, ft. 50. Michael Brecher, *Decisions in Israel's Foreign Policy* (New Haven, Conn.: Yale University Press, 1975), pp. 390–91.

101. LBJ, National Security file, History of the Middle East Conflict, box 20: United States Policy and Diplomacy in the Middle East Crisis, May 15–June 10, 1967, pp. 56–59. ISA, 5937/30 Secret Memoranda Prior to the Six-Day War: Evron to Ministry, Report on 1.5 Hour Meeting Between Foreign Minister Eban and President Johnson at the White House, May 26, 1967; 7919/1, Levi Eshkol files, Diplomatic Telegrams: U.S.A.: Eban to Eshkol, May 26, 1967. "A Step-by-Step Account of Moves in Israel Before War with Arabs," *New York Times*, July 10, 1967. Oral history interview with Robert McNamara, Feb. 16, 2000. Eban, *Personal Witness*, pp. 386–91. Raviv, *Israel at Fifty*, pp. 100–101.

102. LBJ, National Security file, History of the Middle East Conflict, box 20: United States Policy and Diplomacy in the Middle East Crisis, May 15–June 10, 1967, pp. 56–57; NSC Histories, Middle East Crisis, box 17: Rusk to Johnson (handwritten note), May 26, 1967. The President in the Middle East Crisis, Dec. 19, 1968 (President's diary); John P. Roche Oral History, pp. 67–68. ISA, 5937/30 Secret Memoranda Prior to the Six-Day War: Evron to Ministry, Report on the 1.5 Hour Meeting Between Foreign Minister Eban and President Johnson at the White House, May 26, 1967. Rafael, *Destination Peace*, p. 145. Raviv, *Israel at Fifty*, pp. 100–101. Quandt, *Peace Process*, p. 514, ft. 53. Eban, *Personal Wtiness*, pp. 389–94. Johnson, *The Vantage Point*, pp. 293–94. Rostow, *The Diffusion of Power*, p. 417. Little, "The United States and Israel, 1957–1968: The Making of a Special Relationship," p. 578.

103. ISA, 5937/30, Secret Memoranda Prior to the Six-Day War: Harman to Ministry, May 27, 1967. USNA, Middle East Crisis files, 1967, Chronology, box 7: Memorandum of Telephone Conversation, Mr. Rostow and Minister Ebron, May 26, 1967. LBJ, National Security files, NSC Histories, Middle East Crisis, box 17: USUN to the Secretary of State, May 27, 1967; Arthur J. Goldberg Oral History, p. 22. Eban, *Personal Witness*, pp. 393–94. Raviv, *Israel at Fifty*, p. 101. Rafael, *Destination Peace*, p. 145.

104. ISA, 4083/3, Foreign Ministry files, Contacts with the USSR – Closure of Tiran: Katz to Foreign Office, May 17, 1967; Katz to Foreign Ministry, May 24, 1967. LBJ, National Security file, History of the Middle East Crisis, box 17: State Department

Circular, May 18, 1967, The Middle East, May, 1967; Moscow to the State Department, May 19, 1967; box 22–23: Arab-Israel Situation Report, May 22, 1967; box 20: United States Policy and Diplomacy in the Middle East Crisis, May 15–June 10, 1967, p. 58; NSC Histories, Middle East Crisis, box 17: London to the Secretary of State, May 25, 1967; box 19: George C. Denney to the Secretary, May 19, 1967 ("brinkmanship" quote). Dagan, *Moscow and Jerusalem*, pp. 209–10.

105. USNA, Middle East Crisis files, 1967, Situation Reports, box 14: Moscow to the Secretary of State, May 24, 1967; Arab-Israeli Crisis, box 9: Moscow to the Secretary of State, May 23, 1967; box 13: Chronology of U.S.-USSR Consultations on the Middle East, May 18 – June 10, 1967; box 4: London to the Secretary of State, May 30, 1967. LBJ, National Security files, NSC Histories, Middle East Crisis, box 18: Paris to the Secretary of State, May 23, 1967; LBJ, National Security files, NSC Histories, Middle East Crisis, box 18: Paris to the Secretary of State, May 24, 1967.

106. LBJ, National Security file, History of the Middle East Crisis, box 19, State Department Activities Report, May 23, 1967. USNA, Middle East Crisis files, 1967, NN3.059.96089, box 1: Chronology of U.S.-Jordanian Consultations on the Middle East: May 23, 1967; Arab-Israeli Crisis, box 9: Moscow to the Secretary of State, May 23, 1967. ISA, Foreign Ministry files, 4083/3, Contacts with the Soviet Union, Katz to Foreign Ministry, May 23, 1967; 7920/2, Levi Eshkol Papers, Diplomatic Telegrams, USSR: Soviet Desk Memorandum, June 4, 1967. Vassiliev, *Russian Policy in the Middle East*, pp. 67–72 (Soviet scholar quote). Dagan, *Moscow and Jerusalem*, p. 214. Riad, *The Struggle for Peace in the Middle East*, pp. 34–35. Soviet statement in Gilboa, *Shesh Shanim, Shisha Yamim*, pp. 114–15.

107. Heikal, *Al-Infijar*, pp. 623–24 (Kosygin quote); Heikal, *The Cairo Documents* (Garden City, New York: Doubleday, 1973) p. 242; Heikal, *The Sphinx and the Commissar*, pp. 178–79; Brown, "Nasser and the June 1967 War," p. 123. Govrin, *Israeli-Soviet Relations*, pp. 311–12. Arkady N. Shevchenko, *Breaking with Moscow* (New York: Alfred A. Knopf, 1985), p. 136. Parker, *The Six Day War*, pp. 38–39. Oral history interview with Gen. Makhmut A. Gareev, May 24, 1999.

108. Heikal, *Al-Infijar*, pp. 614–15, 624–25. Al-Jiyyar, "Rajulan Qatala al-Mushir 'Amer," pp. 9–11. Vatikiotis, *Nasser and His Generation*, p. 163. Fawzi, *Harb al-Thalath Sanawat*, p. 96. Parker, *The Politics of Miscalculation in the Middle East*, pp. 32, 50; Parker, *The Six Day War*, pp. 38–39. Stephens, *Nasser*, p. 484. Klinghoffer, *Vietnam, Jews and the Middle East*, p. 103. Gawrych, *The Albatross of Decisive Victory*, p. 13. 7920/2, Levi Eshkol Papers, Diplomatic Telegrams, USSR: Research Memorandum, May 28, 1967. Badran quote from *Al-Hawadith*, Sept. 2, 1977. Oral history interview with Nikolai Yegoroshev, Dec. 23, 2000.

109. LBJ, National Security file, History of the Middle East Crisis, box 17: Kosygin to Johnson, May 27, 1967. PREM 13 1618: Kosygin to Wilson, May 27, 1967. ISA, 4091/23, Foreign Ministry files, Exchange of Messages Before the War: Kosygin to Eshkol, May 27, 1967. Dagan, *Moscow and Jerusalem*, p. 217.

110. ISA, 4048/27, Foreign Ministry files, Diplomatic Relations with the Soviet Union: Foreign Ministry to Moscow, May 27, 1967; 7920/4, Levi Eshkol Papers, Prime Minister's Reports and Surveys, Meeting of the Cabinet, May 27, 1967. Gilboa, *Shesh Shanim, Shisha Yamim*, p. 152. Nakdimon, *Likrat Sh'at ha-Efes*, pp. 110–13. Oral history interview with Miriam Eshkol, Aug. 30, 1999.

111. Al-Baghdadi, *Mudhakkirat*, p. 274. Fawzi, *Harb al-Thalath Sanawat*, pp. 93–94. Heikal, *Al-Infijar*, pp. 573–74. Riad, *The Struggle for Peace in the Middle East*, p. 23. Mazhar, *I'tirafat Qadat Harb Yunyu*, pp. 144, 149–50. Sela, *The Decline of the Arab-Israeli Conflict*, pp. 90–91. Al-Sabbagh, *Mudhakkirat Qadat al-'Askaraiyya al-Misriyya* 5, pp. 1–3.

112. Mahmud Riad. *Mudhakkirat Mahmoud Riad* 2 (Beirut: Al-Mu'assasa al-'Arabiyya lil-Dirasa wal-Nashr, 1987), p. 63. Al-Sabbagh, *Mudhakkirat Qadat al-'Askaraiyya al-Misriyya* 5, pp. 18–19, 24–25. Fawzi, *Harb al-Thalath Sanawat*, pp. 115–126. Heikal, *Al-Infijar*, pp. 573–74. 'Abd al-Hamid, *Al-Mushir wa-Ana*, pp. 211–22 ('Amer quote to Nasser). 'Amer-Sidqi Mahmud conversation in Mazhar, *I'tirafat Qadat Harb Yunyu*, pp. 141–42. Murtagi, *Al-Fariq Murtagi Yarwi al-Haqa'iq*, pp. 91–93. Parker, *The Six Day War*, p. 45 ('Amer cable to Badran). See also USNA, Central Policy files, 1967–1969, POL 2 UAR: Jidda to the Department of State, May 27, 1967. Oral history interview with 'Abd al-Mun'im Hamza, July 4, 2001.

113. LBJ, National Security file, History of the Middle East Conflict, box 20: United States Policy and Diplomacy in the Middle East Crisis, May 15–June 10, 1967, pp. 43–44; box 18: Tel Aviv to the Secretary of State, May 27, 1967 (Barbour quote); box 17: Arab-Israel Situation Report, May 28, 1967 (*Davar* headline). USNA, Subject-Numeric files, POL ARAB-ISR, box 1789: Baghdad to Department of State, May 27, 1967. Mustafa, *Harb Haziran*, pp. 277–79. Cairo Radio quote in Mutawi, *Jordan in the 1967 War*, pp. 88–89.

114. ISA, 7920/4, Levi Eshkol Papers, Prime Minister's Reports and Surveys, Meeting of the Cabinet, May 27, 1967; 7920/2, Diplomatic Telegrams, USSR: Allon to Eban, May 21, 1967; 3977/22, Foreign Ministry files, Relations with the United States: Foreign Ministry to Embassies, May 27, 1967; 5937/30, Secret Memoranda Prior to the Six-Day War: Evron to Foreign Ministry, May 27, 1967. Haber, *Ha-Yom Tifrotz Milhama*, p. 192. Rabin, *Memoirs*, pp. 89–90. Eban, *Personal Witness*, pp. 396–99. Raviv, *Israel at Fifty*, pp. 102–3. Johnson cables in LBJ, National Security file, National Security Council History, Middle East Crisis 2, box 17: Johnson to Eskhol, May 27, 1967; Johnson to Barbour, May 27, 1967. USNA, POL ARAB-IS, Tel Aviv files, Tel Aviv to the Secretary of State, May 28, 1967 (Allon quote). Aran quote from MPA, Party Secretariat Protocols, 2/24/66/88: June 1, 1967. See also Brecher, *Decisions in Israel's Foreign Policy*, p. 400 and *Decisions in Crisis*, p. 146. Gluska, *Imut bein ha-Mateh ha-Klali u-bein Memshelet Eshkol bi-Tkufat ha-Hamtana*, pp. 17–22.

115. USNA, Pol ARAB-ISR, box 1789: New York to Department of State, May 28, 1967. ISA, 5937/30, Secret Memoranda Prior to the Six-Day War: Evron to Foreign Ministry, May 27, 1967; 4086/2, Foreign Ministry files, Security Council Meetings; M. Aruch: Summary of Security Council Meetings: New York to Foreign Ministry, May 29, 1967. Lall, *The UN and the Middle East Crisis*, pp. 32–39. U Thant, *View from the UN*, pp. 246–47. Haber, *Ha-Yom Tifrotz Milhama*, p. 193. Heikal, *The Sphinx and the Commissar*, p. 177. Rikhye, *Sinai Blunder*, pp. 81–83.

116. LBJ, National Security files, NSC Histories, Middle East Crisis, box 17: Walt Rostow to the President, May 28, 1967; Tel Aviv to the Secretary of State, May 28, 1967; Memos to the President (W. Rostow), box 16: Rostow to the President, May 28, 1967; History of the Middle East Conflict, box 20: United States Policy and Diplomacy in the Middle East Crisis, May 15–June 10, 1967, pp. 66–70. ISA, 7919/1, Levi

Eshkol files, Diplomatic Telegrams: U.S.A.: Evron to Eshkol, May 31, 1967. Haber, *Ha-Yom Tifrotz Milhama*, p. 193. Prittie, *Eshkol*, pp. 99–101.

117. 7920/2, Levi Eshkol Papers, Diplomatic Telegrams, USSR: Paris to Foreign Ministry, June 1, 1967. Grechko quote from Heikal, *Al-Infijar*, pp. 625, 1024. Heikal, *The Sphinx and the Commissar*, pp. 179–80, and Heikal, *The Cairo Documents*, p. 242. Badran quotes from Imam, *Nasir wa-'Amer*, p. 147; *Kayfa Hakama Misr*, p. 261, and Fawzi, *Harb al-Thalath Sanawat*, p. 95. Nasser quote from al-Baghdadi, *Mudhakkirat 2*, p. 274. Atassi quote from Mustafa, *Harb Haziran*, p. 183. See also Parker, *The Six Day War*, pp. 38–39, 44, and *The Politics of Miscalculation in the Middle East*, p. 50. Govrin, *Israeli-Soviet Relations*, pp. 311–12. Stephens, *Nasser*, pp. 483–84.

118. USNA, POL ARAB-IS, box 1788: Rusk to Tel Aviv, May 29, 1967. ISA, 4086/2, Foreign Ministry files, Security Council Meetings; M. Aruch: Summary of Security Council Meetings, May 29, 1967; 7920/1, Levi Eshkol Papers, Diplomatic Telegrams: Rafael to Eban, May 27, 1967. LBJ, National Security files, NSC Histories, Middle East Crisis, box 21: Chronology of the Soviet Delay on the Security Council Meetings (J. Baker), June 26, 1967; box 17: Department of State to Paris, May 25, 1967. Shevchenko, *Breaking with Moscow*, p. 133. Rikhye, *Sinai Blunder*, p. 85. Lall, *The UN and the Middle East Crisis*, pp. 329–32. U Thant, *View from the UN*, p. 246. Federenko quote from Dagan, *Moscow and Jerusalem*, p. 216.

119. UN, S-316 – box 9, file 12, UNEF Withdrawals: U Thant to Eshkol, May 29, 1967. USNA, POL ARAB-ISR, box 1789: Rusk to Certain Embassies, May 26, 1967. LBJ, National Security file, History of the Middle East Crisis, box 17: Walt Rostow to the President, May 26, 1967. Rafael, *Destination Peace*, pp. 147–48. Parker, *The Six Day War*, p. 95. Heikal, *The Sphinx and the Commissar*, p. 177.

Countdown

1. USNA Central Foreign Policy files, 1967–1969, POL Arab-Jordan, box 1844: Amman to the Department of State, May 12, 1967, box 2554: Amman to Department of State, May 23, 1967, Rusk to Jidda and Amman, May 20, 1967. LBJ, National Security files, NSC Histories, Middle East Crisis, box 22: Amman to the Secretary of State, May 3, 1967, box 18: Amman to the Secretary of State, May 23, 1967. Parker, *The Politics of Miscalculation in the Middle East*, p. 8; Parker, *The Six Day War*, p. 157. Zak, *Hussein Ose Shalom*, p. 103.

2. USNA, Subject-Numeric files, Pol ARAB-ISR, box 1789: Amman to Department of State, May 27, 1967 (Touqan quote); Central Foreign Policy files, 1967–1969, POL 12 SY, box 2511: Amman to the Department of State, May 23, 1967. El Edroos, *The Hashemite Arab Army*, pp. 390–92. Al-Rifa'i quote in Mutawi, *Jordan in the 1967 War*, p. 101. Oral history interview with Adnan Abu-Oudeh, Nov. 16, 1999.

3. LBJ, National Security file, History of the Middle East Conflict, box 20: United States Policy and Diplomacy in the Middle East Crisis, May 15–June 10, 1967, pp. 14–15. USNA, Middle East Crisis files, 1967, box 1: Chronology of U.S.-Jordanian Consultations on the Middle East: May 20, 1967; May 23, 1967 ("rock the boat"); ARAB-ISR, box 1789: Amman to Department of State, May 25, 1967 (Burns quote). ISA, 4080/5, Foreign Ministry files, Contacts with Great Britain, Foreign Ministry to London, May 23, 1967. Mustafa, *Harb Haziran*, pp. 277–79. Hussein, *My "War" with Israel*, pp. 38–39. Mutawi, *Jordan in the 1967 War*, pp. 104–5. Heikal, *Al-Infijar*, p. 650.

4. USNA, POL ARAB-ISR, box 9: Amman to the Secretary of State, May 23, 1967, Amman to the Secretary of State, May 27, 1967, Amman to the Secretary of State, May 30, 1967. Hussein quotes from Mutawi, *Jordan in the 1967 War*, pp. 98–99 and from LBJ, National Security file, History of the Middle East Conflict, box 18: Amman to the Secretary of State, May 26, 1967, box 20: United States Policy and Diplomacy in the Middle East Crisis, May 15–June 10, 1967, p. 43. PRO, PREM 13 1617, The Middle East Crisis: Amman to Foreign Office, May 23, 1967.

5. USNA, USNA, Middle East Crisis files, 1967, box 1: Chronology of U.S.-Jordanian Consultations on the Middle East: Amman to the Department of State, May 25, 1967, Amman to the Department of State, May 27, 1967 (Touqan quote); Rusk to Tel Aviv, May 26, 1967 (Hussein oral message), POL ARAB-ISR, box 1789: Subject-Numeric files, box 1788: Amman to the Department of State, May 27, 1967, Central Policy files, 1967–1969, POL 7 UAR, box 2554: Amman to Department of State, May 27, 1967. LBJ, National Security files, NSC Histories, Middle East Crisis, box 17: Amman to the Secretary of State, May 27, 1967. ISA, Foreign Ministry files, 6444/5, North America, telegrams: Foreign Ministry to Embassies, June 1, 1967. Mustafa, *Harb Haziran*, pp. 277–79. Hussein, *My "War" with Israel*, p. 39. Mutawi, *Jordan in the 1967 War*, pp. 105–6. Kamm, *Hussein Poteah be-Milhama*, pp. 203, 277, 283. El Edroos, *The Hashemite Arab Army*, p. 390.

6. Mutawi, *Jordan in the 1967 War*, p. 162. Susser, *On Both Banks of the Jordan*, pp. 122–23. Zak, *Hussein Ose Shalom*, pp. 107–8.

7. Hussein's visit to Cairo has been reconstructed from several sources. See USNA, POL ARAB-ISR, box 9: Amman to the Secretary of State, May 31, 1967. Heikal, *Al-Infijar*, pp. 656–57. Mutawi, *Jordan in the 1967 War*, pp. 108–10. Hussein, *My "War" with Israel*, pp. 43–48. Dhabbah, *Wa-Madha Ba'du?*, pp. 39–41. El Edroos, *The Hashemite Arab Army*, p. 395. Al-Shuqayri, *Mudhakkirat* 3, pp. 191–200. Kimche and Bawly, *The Sandstorm*, p. 106. Kamm, *Hussein Poteah be-Milhama*, p. 283. Mohamad Ibrahim Faddah, *The Middle East in Transition: A Study of Jordan's Foreign Policy* (New York: Asia Publication House, 1974), p. 75. See also Sayigh, *Armed Struggle and the Search for State*, p. 138.

8. Mutawi, *Jordan in the 1967 War*, p. 111; Hussein, *My "War" with Israel*, p. 50; Jum'a quote in Kamm, *Hussein Poteah be-Milhama*, pp. 283–84; LBJ, National Security files, Country file, box 104/107: "Reactions to ME Crisis in UN Circles," June 8, 1967, USNA, Middle East Crisis files, 1967, box 1: Chronology of U.S.-Jordanian Consultations on the Middle East, May 31, 1967; POL ARAB-ISR, box 9: Amman to the Secretary of State ("political and military insurance"), June 1, 1967, Amman to the Secretary of State ("shifted the burden"), June 3, 1967. Cairo Radio quote from El Edroos, *The Hashemite Arab Army*, p. 395.

9. Mutawi, *Jordan in the 1967 War*, pp. 161, 184. Oral history interview with Adnan Abu-Oudeh, Nov. 16, 1999. LBJ, National Security file, NSC Histories, Middle East Crisis, box 21: White House Situation Room to the President, May 30, 1967. USNA, Middle East Crisis files, 1967, box 1: Chronology of U.S.-Jordanian Consultations on the Middle East, Amman to the Department of State, May 31, 1967 ("Pandora's box"); Amman to the Department of State, June 2, 1967 ("August 1914"), Central Foreign Policy file, 1967–1969, box 1789: Egyptian-Jordanian Mutual Defense Treaty—Information Memorandum (Meeker), June 2, 1967. The complete text of the Egyptian-Jordanian Mutual Defense Treaty appeared in the May 31 edition of the *New York Times*.

10. On the Egyptian commando units, see Mutawi, *Jordan in the 1967 War*, p. 129. Shuqayri quotes from Kamm, *Hussein Poteah be-Milhama*, pp. 284–85, and BBC, Daily Report, Middle East, Africa, and Western Europe, No. D-1. Oral history interview with 'Awad Bashir Khalidi, Nov. 16, 1999. See also Uzi Benziman, *Yerushalayim: Ir lelo Homa* (Jerusalem: Schocken, 1973), pp. 23–24.

11. Haber, *Ha-Yom Tifrotz Milhama*, p. 194; Oral history interview with Miriam Eshkol, Aug. 30, 1999; Schiff column in *Ha'aretz*, May 28, 1967.

12. ISA, 7919/1, Levi Eshkol files, Diplomatic Telegrams: U.S.A.: Geva to Rabin, May 26, 1967. LBJ, National Security files, NSC Histories, Middle East Crisis, box 17: Tel Aviv to the Secretary of State, May 28, 1967 (*Ha'aretz* quote). Ariel Sharon, *Warrior* (New York: Simon & Schuster, 1989), pp. 181–84. Haber, *Ha-Yom Tifrotz Milhama*, pp. 194–98. Baron, *Hotam Ishi*, pp. 25–26. Gluska, *Imut bein ha-Mateh ha-Klali u-bein Memshelet Eshkol bi-Tkufat ha-Hamtana*, pp. 23–27. Rabin, *Memoirs*, pp. 92–93, Weizman, *On Eagles' Wings*, pp. 214–16. IDF, 1977/1786: The Regular Paratrooper Brigade in the Six-Day War, Commander 35th Brigade, p. 626. Oral history interviews with Miriam Eshkol, Aug. 30, 1999, with Yeshayahu Gavish, Dec. 7, 1999, with Rehavam Ze'evi, Sept. 9, 2001.

13. Teddy Kollek, *For Jerusalem* (London: Weidenfeld and Nicolson, 1978), p. 190. Dayan, *My Life*, pp. 333–35.

14. BGA, Diary, Entries for May 24, 28, 31, and June 1, 1967, Shabtai Teveth, *Moshe Dayan, Biografia* (Jerusalem: Schocken Press, 1971), pp. 561–62. Peres, *Battling for Peace*, pp. 90–93. Haber, *Ha-Yom Tifrotz Milhama*, p. 182. Moshe Dayan, *Diary of the Sinai Campaign, 1956* (London: Weidenfeld and Nicolson, 1967), p. 180. Zaki Shalom and S. Ilan Troen, "Ben-Gurion's Diary for the 1967 Six-Day War: An Introduction," *Israel Studies* 4, no. 2 (Fall 1999), p. 197.

15. ISA, 4086/8, Foreign Ministry files, Red Cross: Foreign Ministry to Le Hague, May 30, 1967, Stockholm to Foreign Ministry, June 4, 1967; 4087/1: Egyptian Army Entry into Sinai and Closure of the Tiran Straits. Copenhagen to Foreign Ministry, June 3, 1967. PRO, PREM 13 1619, The Middle East Crisis: Tel Aviv to Foreign Office, June 4, 1967. Abraham Rabinovich, *The Battle for Jerusalem, June 5–7, 1967* (Philadelphia: Jewish Publication Society of America, 1972), pp. 23–27, 51, 59. On Weizman's resignation, see Haber, *Ha-Yom Tifrotz Milhama*, pp. 183, 203. Weizman, *On Eagles' Wings*, pp. 217–18. Baron, *Hotam Ishi*, pp. 26–27. Avraham Rabinovich, "The War That Nobody Wanted," *Jerusalem Post*, June 13, 1967.

16. ISA, Foreign Ministry files, 4087/6, Emergency Appeal: Rothschild to Sapir, May 28, 1967, Eytan to Foreign Ministry, May 29, 1967; 4089/8, Foreign Ministry files, Volunteers, Foreign Ministry to South American Embassies, May 28, 1967; 7920/3, Levi Eshkol Papers, Diplomatic Telegrams, General: Bonn to the Foreign Ministry, June 1, 1967. LBJ, National Security files, NSC Histories, Middle East Crisis, box 17: Item for the President's Evening Reading, May 19, 1967. Mansoor, *Arab World*, entry for May 28.

17. Robert J. Donovan, *Six Days in June: Israel's Fight for Survival* (New York: The New American Library, 1967), p. 15. Rabin, *Memoirs*, pp. 93 (Rabin quote), 100. USNA, Summary of MEDAC, box 7: Tel Aviv to the Secretary of State, June 1, 1967. LBJ, National Security file, NSC Histories, Middle East Crisis, box 21: White House Situation Room to the President, May 30, 1967. See also Uzi Narkiss, *Soldier of Jerusalem*, trans. Martin Kett (London: Mitchell Vallentine, 1998), p. 203. Zemer quote from Rabinovich, "The War That Nobody Wanted."

18. UN, S-0316, UNEF-Withdrawals/UN Missions-EIMAC, box 9: Bull to Bunche, May 30, 1967. Eric Hammel, *Six Days in June: How Israel Won the 1967 Arab-Israeli War* (New York: Scribner's, 1992), p. 157. Abu Murshid, Butrus, and Jabber, *Silsilat al-Kitab ul-Sanawi lil-Qadiyya al-Filastiniyya*, p. 117. Eshkol's Knesset speech from Prittie, *Eshkol*, pp. 101 2. Haber, *Ha-Yom Tifrotz Milhama*, p. 209.

19. Hussein speech in BBC, *Daily Report, Middle East, Africa, and Western Europe*, No. B6. On Arab armed forces, see USNA, Summary of MEDAC, box 13: Middle East Sitrep as of June 1; POL ARAB-ISR, box 1789: Amman to Department of State, May 31, 1967. Mustafa, *Harb Haziran*, pp. 169–73, 278–79. LBJ, National Security file, History of the Middle East Conflict, box 20: United States Policy and Diplomacy in the Middle East Crisis, May 15–June 10, 1967, pp. 107–9. Mutawi, *Jordan in the 1967 War*, pp. 112–17. Van Creveld, *The Sword and the Olive*, p. 179. Hammel, *Six Days in June*, pp. 286–87, 388–90. Seale, *Asad of Syria*, p. 117. Schiff, *A History of the Israeli Army*, p. 138. Shmuel Segev, *Sadin Adom*, p. 223. Nasser and Mahmud quotes from Gilboa, *Shesh Shanim, Shisha Yamim*, p. 191.

20. BGA, Diary, June 1, 1967. Haber, *Ha-Yom Tifrotz Milhama*, pp. 200–201. MPA, Meeting of the Executive Committee, June 1, 1967. Teveth, *Moshe Dayan*, pp. 564–65 (Dayan quote). Gluska, *Imut bein ha-Mateh ha-Klali u-bein Memshelet Eshkol bi-Tkufat ha-Hamtana*, pp. 29–33. Rabin, *Memoirs*, p. 94. Golda Meir, *My Life* (New York: G.P. Putnam's Sons, 1975), pp. 362–63. Amos Perlmutter, *The Life and Times of Menachem Begin* (New York: Doubleday, 1987), p. 283. Gawrych, *The Albatross of Decisive Victory*, p. 19. Nakdimon, *Likrat Sh'at ha-Efes*, pp. 61–81, 102. Baron, *Hotam Ishi*, pp. 29–30. MPA, Party Secretariat Protocols, 2/24/66/88: June 1, 1967.

21. Teveth, *Moshe Dayan*, pp. 570–71. Rabin, *Memoirs*, p. 94. Haber, *Ha-Yom Tifrotz Milhama*, p. 184. Mayzel, *Hu-Ma'arakha al ha-Golan*, pp. 241–43. Dayan, *My Life*, pp. 340–41. Ze'evi quote from Michael Shashar, *Sihot im Rehavam – Gandhi – Ze'evi* (Tel Aviv: Yediot Ahronot, 1992), p. 165.

22. PRO PREM 13 1622: The Second Arab-Israel War, 1967: The Preliminaries (Hadow), July 6, 1967 ("terrier at a rat hole"); FCO17/498: Israel – Political Affairs: Tel Aviv to Foreign Ministry, June 3, 1967.

23. LBJ, National Security file, History of the Middle East Conflict, box 20: United States Policy and Diplomacy in the Middle East Crisis, May 15–June 10, 1967, pp. 69–70, 81–88. USNA, POL ARAB-ISR, box 1789: Rusk to Certain Embassies, May 28, 1967; Rusk to Tel Aviv, May 31, 1967; Chronology of U.S. Consultations with Other Governments on the Middle East Crisis, May 15–June 10, 1967. Johnson, *The Vantage Point*, p. 294.

24. LBJ, National Security file, National Security Council History, Middle East Crisis 2, box 17: Walt Rostow to the President, May 30, 1967; Walt Rostow to the President – Report from Barbour, May 28, 1967; Memos to the President (W. Rostow), box 16: Rostow to the President – Conversation with Evron, May 31, 1967. Rabin quote from Rabin, *Memoirs*, pp. 95–96.

25. LBJ, National Security file, Memos to the President (W. Rostow), box 16: Rusk to the President, May 30, 1967; History of the Middle East Crisis, box 19: State Department Activities Report, June 1, 1967; Joint Chiefs of Staff – Memorandum for the Secretary of Defense, June 2, 1967, box 18: Department of State Circular, May 30, 1967; NSC Histories, Middle East Crisis, box 17: The President in the Middle East

Crisis, Dec. 19, 1968 (Rostow quote). USNA, META Agenda, Actions, Minutes, box 15: Memorandum for the Middle East Control Group, May 31, 1967 ("appeal to vanity"). Oral history interview with Walt Whitman Rostow, July 27, 1999. Oral history interview with Robert McNamara, Feb. 11, 2000. Johnson, *The Vantage Point*, p. 295 (Rusk and McNamara memorandum). Rusk, *As I Saw It*, pp. 384–85. Klinghoffer, *Vietnam, Jews and the Middle East*, pp. 109–11. Wheeler quote in Parker, *The Six Day War*, p. 218.

26. LBJ, National Security file, History of the Middle East Crisis, box 17: Saunders to Rostow, May 30, 1967; box 20: United States Policy and Diplomacy in the Middle East Crisis, May 15–June 10, 1967, pp. 61–62, 93–95; NSC Histories, Middle East Crisis, box 18: Memorandum for the Secretary of Defense, June 2, 1967; Pearson to Johnson, June 2, 1967; box 17: The President in the Middle East Crisis, Dec. 19, 1968 (President's diary quote). USNA, Middle East Crisis files, 1967, box 2: The Department of State to Canberra, June 2, 1967, box 13: Memorandum for Mr. Battle (Deane Hinton), June 4, 1967 ("The Belgians are waffling"); History of MADEC (Hinton), June 9, 1967. NAC, RG 25, box 10050: Political Affairs – Canada's Foreign Policy Trends and Relations – Israel: Tel Aviv to Ottawa, May 28, 1967. Parker, *The Politics of Miscalculation in the Middle East*, p. 54. Johnson, *The Vantage Point*, p. 296.

27. PRO, FO17/497: Israel – Political Affairs: Draft Paper for Cabinet – Middle East Crisis: May 28, 1967; PREM 13 1618: Middle East: Memorandum by the Foreign Secretary, May 28, 1967; Note on a Meeting between the Prime Minister and the Foreign Minister, May 28, 1967; CAB 128/42 33rd Conclusions; 128/42 35th Conclusions. USNA, Middle East Crisis files, 1967, box 1: Chronology of U.S.-Jordanian Consultations on the Middle East, June 1, 1967; box 2: London to the Department of State, June 1, 1967. LBJ, National Security file, History of the Middle East Conflict, box 20: United States Policy and Diplomacy in the Middle East Crisis, May 15–June 10, 1967, pp. 93–95; Middle East Crisis 2, box 17: Wilson to Johnson, May 27, 1967; NSC Histories, Middle East Crisis, box 21: White House Situation Room to the President, May 30, 1967 ("going soft"); London to the Secretary of State, June 3, 1967 ("digging in its heels").

28. LBJ, National Security file, History of the Middle East Crisis, box 17: Joint Chiefs of Staff: Military Actions – Straits of Tiran, June 2, 1967. USNA, POL ARAB-ISR, box 1789: First report of Working Group of Economic Vulnerabilities, May 31, 1967. PRO, FO 39/380: Gulf of Aqaba—Political Organization and Guidelines, June 2, 1967; PREM 13 1618: The Middle East Crisis: Annex A—International Action to open the Straits of Tiran, May 28, 1967; FO17/497: Israel – Political Affairs: Draft Paper for Cabinet – Middle East Crisis, June 2, 1967.

29. LBJ, National Security file, History of the Middle East Crisis, box 17: Memorandum for WWR, June 1, 1967; box 18, Joint Chiefs of Staff: Military Actions—Straits of Tiran, May 24, 1967; NSC Histories, Middle East Crisis, box 17: London to the Secretary of State, May 28, 1967. Rusk, *As I Saw It*, p. 365.

30. LBJ, box 1–10, the USS *Liberty*: Department of Defense Press Release, June 8, 1967; box 19: CINCUSNAVEUR Order, May 30, 1967; box 18: Joint Chiefs of Staff: Military Actions—Straits of Tiran, May 25, 1967; box 104/107: The National Military Command Center: Attack on the USS *Liberty*, June 9, 1967.

31. USNA, Pol ARAB-ISR, box 1789: Cairo to the Department of State, May 27, 1967, and LBJ, National Security file, History of the Middle East Crisis, box 17: Cairo to the Department of State, May 26, 1967; Damascus to the Department of State, May

26, 1967; Amman to the Department of State, June 3, 1967; Amman to the Secretary of State, June 4, 1967; box 20: United States Policy and Diplomacy in the Middle East Crisis, May 15–June 10, 1967, pp. 71–73 (Porter quote). See also LBJ, National Security file, NSC Histories, Middle East Crisis, box 17: Cairo to the Secretary of State, May 28, 1967; Amman to the Secretary of State, June 2, 1967; Beirut to the Secretary of State, May 29, 1967. Parker, *The Politics of Miscalculation in the Middle East*, pp. 53, 233.

32. USNA, POL ARAB-ISR, box 1789; Rusk to Harmel, May 28, 1967; Arab-Israeli Crisis, Minutes of the Control Group, box 17: 5th Meeting of Control Group, May 28, 1967 ("full speed ahead"); box 13: Summary of MEDAC: Middle East Sitrep as of June 1, 1967. LBJ, National Security file, History of the Middle East Conflict, box 18: Memo for the President: Today's Security Council Meeting, May 31, 1967; NSC Histories, Middle East Crisis, box 17: Secretary of State to Ambassador Goldberg, May 30, 1967; box 23: Circular to Arab Capitals (Rusk), June 3, 1967; box 21: Arab-Israeli Situation Report, June 2, 1967; Arab-Israeli Situation Report, June 3, 1967; Chronology of the Soviet Delay on the Security Council Meetings (J. Baker), June 6, 1967; White House Situation Room to the President, May 30, 1967; Memorandum to the President: Security Council Meeting, June 3, 1967 ("drowned Vietnam in blood"). Rikhye, *Sinai Blunder*, pp. 82–84. Lall, *The UN and the Middle East Crisis*, pp. 40–43. Rusk response to Middle East ambassadors in Parker, *The Politics of Miscalculation in the Middle East*, pp. 121–22.

33. LBJ, National Security file, History of the Middle East Crisis, box 17: Johnson to Kosygin, May 28, 1967; Rusk to Gromyko, May 28, 1967; box 20: Nathaniel Davis, Memorandum for Mr. Rostow, May 29, 1967.

34. LBJ, National Security file, History of the Middle East Conflict, box 18: Text of Cable from Mr. Yost, June 1, 1967; box 20: United States Policy and Diplomacy in the Middle East Crisis, May 15–June 10, 1967, pp. 88–92. Mahmoud Riad, *Mudhakkirat Mahmoud Riad 1, 1948–1976: al-Bahth 'an al-Salam fi al-Sharq al-Awsat* (Beirut: al-Mu'assasa al-'Arabiyya lil-Dirasa wal-Nashr, 1987), p. 312. Imam, *'Abd al-Nasir—Kayfa Hakama Misr*, p. 366. Parker, *The Politics of Miscalculation in the Middle East*, pp. 56, 233–39. Rouleau et Lacouture, *Israel et les Arabes le 3e Combat*, p. 83.

35. LBJ, National Security file, History of the Middle East Conflict, box 17: W. Rostow to the President, May 23, 1967; Rusk to Cairo, May 29, 1967; Anderson to the President, June 1, 1967; box 20: United States Policy and Diplomacy in the Middle East Crisis, May 15–June 10, 1967, pp. 88–89; NSC Histories, Middle East Crisis, box 17: The President in the Middle East Crisis, Dec. 19, 1968; box 18: Scenario: June 4–11, June 3, 1967; box 23: Cairo to the Secretary of State, June 4, 1967. USNA, Middle East Crisis files, 1967, box 17: Eighth Control Group Meeting, June 3, 1967; Ninth Control Group Meeting, June 4, 1967. PRO, FCO/39/261 UAR – Relations with the US: Washington to Foreign Ministry, June 4, 1967. Imam, *'Abd al-Nasir—Kayfa Hakama Misr*, pp. 366–67. Heikal, *Al-Infijar*, pp. 680–84. Parker, *The Politics of Miscalculation in the Middle East*, pp. 235–41.

36. USNA, Middle East Crisis files, Maritime Declaration, box 13: Memorandum of Conversation, June 2, 1967; box 2: Grey to Rusk, June 2, 1967. LBJ, National Security file, History of the Middle East Crisis, box 17: Memorandum for WWR, June 1, 1967; Miscellaneous Reports, box 15: Battle to Rusk, June 2, 1967; NSC Histories, Middle East Crisis, box 23: Tel Aviv to the Secretary of State, June 4, 1967 (Barbour quote); Circular to All American Diplomatic Posts, June 2, 1967 (Rusk quote).

37. Oral history interview with Meir Amit, Feb. 9, 1999; all quotes from Amit's Report on Visit to the United States, June 4, 1967, access to which was furnished during the interview. ISA, 6444/5 North America, telegrams. Ministry to Embassies, Head of the Mossad to the Mossad, June 1, 1967; Head of the Mossad to the Mossad, June 2, 1967. LBJ, National Security file, NSC Histories, Middle East Crisis, box 18: Walt Rostow to the President, June 2, 1967. Oral history interview with Robert McNamara, Feb. 11, 2000. Quandt, *Peace Process*, pp. 43–45. Parker, *The Six Day War*, pp. 124–25; 136. Amit, "Ha-Derekh le-Sheshet ha-Yamim."

38. LBJ, National Security file, History of the Middle East Conflict, box 20: United States Policy and Diplomacy in the Middle East Crisis, May 15–June 10, 1967, pp. 96–97.

39. Oral history interview with Shlomo Merom, Dec. 7, 1999. Eshkol quote from Dayan, *My Life*, p. 338.

40. PRO, FCO 17/506: Israel – Political Affairs (External): Tel Aviv to Foreign Ministry, June 2, 1967. Teveth, *Moshe Dayan*, pp. 67, 104 ("a liar, a braggart"), 134, 440–41, 556–57. Amit, *Rosh be-Rosh*, pp. 85–87. Rafael quotes from Rafael, *Destination Peace*, p. 283, and http://www.us-israel.org/jsource/biography/Dayan.html. See also Moshe Dayan, *Avnei Derekh* (Tel Aviv: Yediot Ahronot, 1976) pp. 39–40.

41. Gal quote in Yisrael Harel, *Sha'ar ha-Arayot—Ha-Krav al Yerushalayim be-Havayat Lohamei Hativat ha-Tzanhanim* (Tel Aviv: Ma'arkhot, n.d.), p. 209. Baron, *Hotam Ishi*, pp. 28–29, 43–44. Haber, *Ha-Yom Tifrotz Milhama*, pp. 203, 249. Dayan, *My Life*, pp. 338–39.

42. LBJ, National Security file, Middle East Crisis, box 18: W. Rostow to the President, June 2, 1967; NSC Histories, Middle East Crisis, box 17: The President in the Middle East Crisis, Dec. 19, 1968 (Rostow quote). USNA, Middle East Crisis files, 1967, box 17: Ninth Control Group Meeting, June 3, 1967. ISA, 4091/23, Foreign Ministry files, Exchange of Messages Before the War: Kosygin to Eshkol, June 2, 1967; 7919/1, Levi Eshkol files, Diplomatic Telegrams: U.S.A.: Geva to Rabin, May 26, 1967; Evron to Levavi, May 27, 1967; Evron to Bitan, May 29, 1967. PRO, FO 17/489, Israel – Political Affairs: Foreign Ministry to Washington, June 2, 1967. Oral history interview with Avraham Liff, Sept. 13, 1999. Oral history interview with Shlomo Merom, Dec. 7, 1999. Quandt, *Peace Process*, pp. 46–47.

43. USNA, Summary of MEDAC, box 13: Middle East Sitrep as of June 1 (Eban quote). Baron, *Hotam Ishi*, pp. 28–29. Gluska, *Imut bein ha-Mateh ha-Klali u-bein Memshelet Eshkol bi-Tkufat ha-Hamtana*, pp. 38–44. Mayzel, *Ha-Ma'arakha al ha-Golan*, pp. 48–50. Haber, *Ha-Yom Tifrotz Milhama*, pp. 206–12. Dayan, *My Life*, pp. 338–39. Yariv, *Ha'arakha Zehira*, pp. 57–58. Bartov, *Dado*, p. 94. Rabin, *Memoirs*, pp. 96–97. Sharon, *Warrior*, pp.185–86.

44. ISA, 7919/1, Levi Eshkol files, Diplomatic Telegrams: U.S.A.: Harman to Bitan, May 24, 1967; Rafael to Eban, June 4, 1967. Haber, *Ha-Yom Tifrotz Milhama*, p. 203. Dayan, *My Life*, pp. 340–41. Rabin, *Memoirs*, p. 97. Baron, *Hotam Ishi*, p. 35. Fortas quote from Eban, *Personal Witness*, p. 405. Quandt, *Peace Process*, p. 47, and Laura Kalman, *Abe Fortas: A Biography* (New Haven, Conn.: Yale University Press, 1990), pp. 300–301. A different version of the quote appears in Parker, *The Politics of Miscalculation in the Middle East*, pp. 119–20. Goldberg quote from Parker, *The Six Day War*, pp. 149–50 and in Rafael, *Destination Peace*, pp. 153–54.

45. Baron, *Hotam Ishi*, pp. 36–39. David Rozner, "H-5 be-Yuni 1967 be-Kahir," *Bamahane* 35 (May 1968), p. 20. Dupuy, *Elusive Victory*, p. 244. Churchill and Churchill,

The Six Day War, pp. 97–98. Dayan, *My Life*, p. 341. Oral history interview with Israel Tal, Aug. 23, 1999. Dayan's comments to reporters in PRO, FO 17/489, Israel–Political Affairs: Tel Aviv to Foreign Ministry, June 3, 1967, and Hadow's reactions in PREM 13 1619, The Middle East Crisis: Tel Aviv to Foreign Ministry, June 3, 1967, and PREM 13 1622, The Second Arab-Israel War, 1967: The Preliminaries, July 6, 1967.

46. Dayan remarks to General Staff, Zak, *Hussein Ose Shalom*, p. 109. Dayan conversation with Elazar in Bartov, *Dado*, pp. 93–96; in Dayan, *My Life*, p. 348; and in Baron, *Hotam Ishi*, pp. 47–48. See also YAD, Interview with Ephraim Reiner, June 20, 1996. Mayzel, *Ha-Ma'arakha al ha-Golan*, pp. 46–47 (Rabin quote), 102, 115–23, 154–63, 174–83. Yehezkel Hame'iri, *Mi-Shnei Evrei ha-Rama* (Tel Aviv: Levin-Epstein, 1970), p. 41. Rabin, *Memoirs*, p. 103. Dayan conversation with Narkiss in Narkiss, *Soldier of Jerusalem*, p. 204. See also IDF, 901/67/1, Central Command: The Six-Day War, Concluding Report 1, p. 142. Rabinovich, *The Battle for Jerusalem*, p. 60. Mayzel, *Ha-Ma'arakha al ha-Golan*, pp. 51–52. Zak, *Hussein Ose Shalom*, p. 109. Oral history interview with Rehavam Ze'evi, Sept. 9, 2001.

47. LBJ, National Security file, History of the Middle East Conflict, box 20: United States Policy and Diplomacy in the Middle East Crisis, May 15–June 10, 1967, pp. 97–98; box 18: Johnson to Eshkol, June 3, 1967; Intelligence Information Cable: France, June 3, 1967. ISA, 7920/2, Levi Eshkol Papers, Diplomatic Telegrams, France: Meroz to Eban, June 3, 1967. Mansoor, *Arab World*, entry for June 2. De Gaulle-Eytan conversation in Gilboa, *Shesh Shanim, Shisha Yamim*, p. 143. Haber, *Ha-Yom Tifrotz Milhama*, p. 214.

48. Dayan, *My Life*, p. 342. Haber, *Ha-Yom Tifrotz Milhama*, pp. 216–18. Amit, Report on Visit to the United States, June 4, 1967. Information on the *Dolphin* in ISA, 7919/1, Levi Eshkol files, Diplomatic Telegrams: U.S.A.: Bitan to Evron, May 24, 1967, and in PRO, PREM 13 1619: The Middle East Crisis – Summary of telegrams, June 3, 1967.

49. Dayan, *My Life*, pp. 343–47. Haber, *Ha-Yom Tifrotz Milhama*, p. 221. Zorach Warhaftig, *Hamishim Shana ve-Shana: Pirkei Zikhronot* (Jerusalem: Yad Shapira, 1998), pp. 178–82.

50. Mazhar, *I'tirafat Qadat Harb Yunyu*, pp. 181–82. Fawzi, *Harb al-Thalath Sanawat*, pp. 122–30. Imam, *Nasir wa-'Amer*, pp. 143–49. 'Abd al-Hamid, *Al-Mushir wa-Ana*, p. 125. Murtagi, *Al-Fariq Murtagi Yarwi al-Haqa'iq*, p. 109. Heikal, *Al-Infijar*, p. 699. El-Sadat, *In Search of Identity*, p. 174. Parker, *The Politics of Miscalculation in the Middle East*, p. 57. Nasser-Sidqi conversation in Al-Sabbagh, *Mudhakkirat Qadat al-'Askariyya al-Misriyya* 2, pp. 5–6; see also 4, pp. 13–19, and 5, pp. 22–23. BBC, Daily Report, Middle East, Africa and West Europe, No. 196, B4. Interview with General Hudud in *Al-Hawadith* (Lebanon), Sept. 8, 1972—cited in Yariv, *Ha'arakha Zehira*, p. 155.

51. Al-Baghdadi, *Mudhakkirat*, p. 274. Al-Sabbagh, *Mudhakkirat Qadat al-'Askariyya al-Misriyya* 4, p. 19; 5, pp. 21–23. PRO, FCO/39/286 UAR – Economic Affairs: Foreign Office to Washington, June 3, 1967; PREM 13 1619, The Middle East Crisis: Foreign Office to Washington, June 3, 1967. Farid, *Nasser*, p. 20. Mahjoub, *Democracy on Trial*, p. 114. Ben D. Mor, "Nasser's Decision-Making in the 1967 Middle East Crisis: A Rational-choice Explanation," *Journal of Peace Research* 28, no. 4 (1991), pp. 359–75. Nasser's interviews with the British press appear in Mansoor, *Arab World*, entry for June 3.

52. PRO, FCO 17/494, Israel – Political Affairs: Cairo to Foreign Office, June 2, 1967 (Tesh quote); FCO 39/233 UAR Internal Political Situation: Canadian Embassy, Cairo to Foreign Office, June 2, 1967. USNA, Central Policy files, 1967–1969, POL 2 UAR, box 2553: Alexandria to the Department of State, May 31, 1967. LBJ, National Security file, History of the Middle East Conflict, box 20: United States Policy and Diplomacy in the Middle East Crisis, May 15–June 10, 1967, pp. 82–83. UN, DAG 1/ 5.2.2.1.2-2, Middle East: El Kony to the Secretary-General, June 2, 1967. Nasser quote in BBC, Daily Report, Middle East, Africa, and Western Europe, No. B4. See also Stephens, *Nasser*, p. 480.

53. Fawzi, *Harb al-Thalath Sanawat*, pp. 109–11, 128–30. Nasser and ʿAmer exchange in ʿAbd al-Hamid, *Al-Mushir wa-Ana*, pp. 125, 212–13. Mazhar, *Iʾtirafat Qadat Harb Yunyu*, pp. 181–82. Imam, *Nasir wa-ʿAmer*, pp. 143–49. Murtagi, *Al-Fariq Murtagi Yarwi al-Haqaʾiq*, p. 109. Heikal, *Al-Infijar*, p. 699. Mahmud Murad "Harb Haziran," *Al-Majalla al-ʿAskariyya* 19, no. 1 (Aug. 1968), pp. 45–46. Al-Sabbagh, *Mudhakkirat Qadat al-ʿAskariyya al-Misriyya* 2, pp. 14–15. Abu Dhikri, *Madhbahat al-Abriyaʾ*, pp. 156–62. USNA, Central Policy files, 1967–1969, POL Arab-ISR, box 7: Alexandria to the Department of State, May 16, 1967.

54. ʿAbd al-Hamid, *Al-Mushir wa-Ana*, pp. 212–13. Fawzi, *Harb al-Thalath Sanawat*, pp. 115–16. Imam, *Nasir wa-ʾAmer*, pp. 146–48. Gawrych, *The Albatross of Decisive Victory*, pp. 20–21. ʿAmer quotes from Murtagi, *Al-Fariq Murtagi Yarwi al-Haqaʾiq*, pp. 94–95, 98. Amin al-Nafuri, *Tawazun al-Quwwa bayna al-ʿArab wa-Israʾil*, pp. 212–13.

55. Murtagi, *Al-Fariq Murtagi Yarwi al-Haqaʾiq*, pp. 51, 107. Fawzi, *Harb al-Thalath Sanawat*, pp. 92–93, 104, 123–26. Walter Laqueur, *The Road to Jerusalem: The Origins of the Arab-Israeli Conflict, 1967* (London: Weidenfeld and Nicolson, 1968), pp. 288–93. Al-Shuqayri, *Mudhakkirat* 5, pp. 76–77. Oral history interview with General Yeshayahu (Shaike) Gavish, Dec. 7, 1999. USNA, ARAB-IS, box 14: Memorandum for the files – Captured UAR Battle Order, June 2, 1967. Versions of the War Order also appear in Gilboa, *Shesh Shanim, Shisha Yamim*, p. 193, and Kimche and Bawly, *The Sandstorm*, pp. 109–10.

56. Mutawi, *Jordan in the 1967 War*, pp. 112–18. Mustafa, *Harb Haziran*, pp. 278–79. Kamm, *Hussein Poteah be-Milhama*, pp. 121, 127, 140–41. Hammel, *Six Days in June*, p. 293. Bull, *War and Peace in the Middle East*, p. 111. Rabinovich, *The Battle for Jerusalem*, pp. 62–64, 73. Oral history interview with Yusuf Khawwash, Nov. 16, 1999; Mahmud Abu Faris, Nov. 17, 1999. El Edroos, *The Hashemite Arab Army*, p. 359.

57. Mutawi, *Jordan in the 1967 War*, pp. 112–18, 122. Hussein, *My "War" with Israel*, pp. 54–59. USNA, Summary of MEDAC, box 13: Middle East Sitrep as of June 4. The orders for Operation Tariq, discovered by Israeli forces during the war, can be found at the IDF Intelligence Library: The Six Day War, file 1, Jordan, Document 59/ 1/67, Col. ʿAbd al-Rahim Fakhr al-Din, May 22, 1967. The orders are also discussed in PRO, PREM 13 1622: Record of Conversation between the Foreign Secretary and the Israeli Ambassador, June 30, 1967. Hussein quote in PRO, PREM 13 1619: The Middle East Crisis, Amman to Foreign Office, June 4, 1967.

58. USNA, Summary of MEDAC, box 13: Middle East Sitrep as of June 1. Tlas quote from PRO, FO 17/671: Syria – Political Affairs, Damascus to Foreign Office, June 3, 1967. Murtagi, *Al-Fariq Murtagi Yarwi al-Haqaʾiq*, pp. 52, 104. Mutawi, *Jordan in the 1967 War*, p. 112. Al-Shuqayri, *Mudhakkirat* 5, pp. 215–20. See also Hani al-Shumʿa, *Maʿarik Khalida fi Taʾrikh al-Jaysh al-ʿArabi al-Suri* (Damascus: Al-Tibaʿa al-Suriyya, 1988).

59. USNA Central Foreign Policy files, 1967–1969, POL 12 SY, box 2511: Beirut to the Department of State, June 3, 1967. ISA, Foreign Ministry files, 4083/3, Contacts with the Soviet Union, Raviv to Shimoni, June 7, 1967. Mustafa, *Harb Haziran*, pp. 169–73. Segev, *Sadin Adom*, p. 223. Gilboa, *Shesh Shanim, Shisha Yamim*, pp. 230–32. Hame'iri, *Mi-Shnei Evrei ha-Rama*, pp. 55–57. Mayzel, *Ha-Ma'arakha al ha-Golan*, pp. 133–41. For documents on Operation Victory, see IDF Intelligence Library, The Six Day War, file 1: Syria, Defense Ministry Document No. 26/123 Southwest Area Command, Operations Branch to 8th Brigade Operations, by Col. K.M. Ahmad, Signed General Muhamad Ahmad Ayd, 123rd Brigade Commander, June 3, 1967. See also Hame'iri, *Mi-Shnei Evrei ha-Rama*, pp. 55–57, and O'Balance, *The Third Arab-Israeli War*, p. 229.

60. USNA, USUN, box 6: CINSTRIKE to AIG, May 24, 1967. Oral history interview with Fayiz Fahed Jaber, Nov. 17, 1999. Mustafa Khalil, *Suqut al-Julan* (Amman: Dar al-Yaqin lil-Tiba'a wal-Nashr, n.d.), pp. 25–26, 174, 248–49, 254. IDF Intelligence Library, Internal Syrian Army Papers: The Southwestern Front, June 9, 1967. Mayzel, *Ha-Ma'arakha al ha-Golan*, p. 130. Oral history interviews with Ibrahim Isma'il Khahya and Muhammad 'Ammar, Jan. 10, 2001; with Marwan Hamdan al-Khuli, Jan. 11, 2001. Sisser, "Bein Yisrael le-Suria," pp. 224–25. Tlas quote from Parker, *The Politics of Miscalculation in the Middle East*, p. 162; also cited in Gilboa, *Shesh Shanim, Shisha Yamim*, p. 191.

61. LBJ, National Security file, NSC Histories, Middle East Crisis, box 17: Beirut to the Secretary of State, June 2, 1967; box 18: Sanaa to the Secretary of State, May 23, 1967. Heikal, *Al-Infijar*, pp. 694–95. PRO, FO 17/489, Israel – Political Affairs: Cairo to Foreign Office, June 3, 1967 (Nasser threat to close the Suez Canal). USNA, POL ARAB-ISR, box 1789: Amman to the Department of State, May 27, 1967 (Jum'a quote). Mansoor, *Arab World*, entries for June 2, 3, 4 (Boumedienne quote). Arab military figures, from Rabin, *Memoirs*, p. 100. 'Aref quote from BBC, Daily Report, Middle East, Africa, and Western Europe, No. 1.

62. USNA, Middle East Crisis files, Maritime Declaration, box 13: Memorandum of U.S.-British Conversation, June 2, 1967; META Agenda, Actions, Minutes, box 15: Memorandum for the Middle East Control Group, May 31, 1967; Intelligence Notes, box 11: Hughes to the Secretary of State, June 5, 1967. PRO, FO17/497: Israel – Political Affairs: Draft Paper for Cabinet – Middle East Crisis—Conversation between the Prime Minister and the President at the White House, June 2, 1967; PREM 13 1619, The Middle East Crisis: Prime Minister to the Foreign Secretary, June 3, 1967. LBJ, National Security file, History of the Middle East Conflict, box 20: United States Policy and Diplomacy in the Middle East Crisis, May 15–June 10, 1967, pp. 95–96; NSC Histories, Middle East Crisis, box 21: Arab-Israeli Situation Report, May 31, 1967. ISA, Foreign Ministry files, 4083/3, Contacts with the Soviet Union: Ankara to Tekoah – Soviet Ships in the Mediterranean, June 1, 1967. The passage of Soviet ships through the Dardanelles was widely reported in the Middle East; see Mansoor, *The Arab World*, entries for June 2, 3, 4, 1967.

63. LBJ, National Security file, History of the Middle East Conflict, box 20: United States Policy and Diplomacy in the Middle East Crisis, May 15–June 10, 1967, pp. 86–89, 103–5; NSC Histories, Middle East Crisis, box 21: Arab-Israeli Situation Report, May 31, 1967; box 18: Saunders to Walt Rostow, May 31, 1967 ("parade of horribles"); Memorandum for the Secretary of Defense, June 2, 1967; box 17: USUN to the Secre-

tary of State, May 29, 1967. USNA, Arab-Israel Crisis, Miscellaneous Reports, box 15: Memorandum for the Secretary of Defense, May 25, 1967. PRO FCO/39/261, UAR – Relations with the United States: Washington to the Foreign Office, June 4, 1967; PREM 13 1619, The Middle East Crisis: Washington to the Foreign Office, June 4, 1967. ISA, 7919/1, Levi Eshkol files, Diplomatic Telegrams: U.S.A.: Evron to Eshkol, May 31, 1967. Oral history interview with Walt Rostow, July 27, 1999; with Eugene Rostow, Aug. 5, 1999.

64. LBJ, National Security files, NSC Histories, Middle East Crisis, box 17: Reflections Pre-Eban (Saunders), May 25, 1967; box 18: Arab-Israel: Where We Are and Where We're Going (Saunders), May 31, 1967. USNA, Middle East Crisis files, 1967, box 17: Ninth Control Group Meeting, June 4, 1967; Arab-Israeli Crisis, Intelligence Notes, box 11: Denny to Rusk, June 2, 1967; Battle to the Secretary of State, June 2, 1967. LBJ, National Security file, History of the Middle East Conflict, box 18: Walt Rostow to the President, June 4, 1967; Saunders to Walt Rostow, May 31, 1967. Rusk quote from Parker, *The Politics of Miscalculation in the Middle East*, pp. 121–22, and from Rusk, *As I Saw It*, p. 385. Feinberg quote from Quandt, *Peace Process*, p. 48.

65. USNA, Middle East Crisis files, 1967, box 13: Circular to All American Diplomatic Posts (Rusk), June 4, 1967. Murtagi, *Al-Fariq Murtagi Yarwi al-Haqa'iq*, pp. 110–15. Imam, *Nasir wa-'Amer*, pp. 156–57 (Dugheidi quote). Fawzi, *Harb al-Thalath Sanawat*, pp. 132–34. Al-Sabbagh, *Mudhakkirat Qadat al-'Askariyya al-Misriyya 5*, pp. 24–25. 'Imad Al-'Ilmi, *Harb 'Am 1967* (Acre: Al-Aswar lil-Thaqafa, 1990), p. 114. USNA, Central Policy files, 1967–1969, POL 2 UAR, box 2553: Jidda to the Department of State, Aug. 29, 1967. Bar-Zohar, *Embassies in Crisis*, p. 176. Murtagi communiqué in Lall, *The UN and the Middle East Crisis*, p. 48, and in Rikhye, *Sinai Blunder*, pp. 95–97.

66. Rikhye, *Sinai Blunder*, pp. 96–100. Donovan, *Six Days in June*, p. 78.

67. Mutawi, *Jordan in the 1967 War*, p. 122. El Edroos, *The Hashemite Arab Army*, p. 373. Hussein, *My "War" with Israel*, p. 59.

68. ISA, Foreign Ministry files, 4083/3, Contacts with the Soviet Union: Katz to Foreign Ministry, June 4, 1967; 7920/2, Levi Eshkol Papers, Diplomatic Telegrams, USSR: Katz to Foreign Ministry, May 24, 1967; Katz to Levavi, June 4, 1967. Dagan, *Moscow and Jerusalem*, p. 224.

69. Baron, *Hotam Ishi*, pp. 47–48. BGA, Diary, Entry for June 4, 1967. YAD, Remarks by Yitzhak Rabin, Feb. 3, 1987. Rabin, *Memoirs*, pp. 98–100. Slater, *Rabin of Israel*, p. 133. Nachshon quote in IDF, 1977/1786: The Regular Paratrooper Brigade in the Six-Day War, Commander 35th Brigade, p. 619. Dayan, *My Life*, pp. 349–50. Haber, *Ha-Yom Tifrotz Milhama*, pp. 222–24. Mayzel, *Ha-Ma'arakha al ha–Golan*, pp. 51–52. ISA, Foreign Ministry files, 4089/4, Prime Minister's Memoranda; Eshkol to Kosygin, June 5, 1967; Eshkol to Johnson, June 5, 1967. Similar letters were sent to Lester Pearson and Charles de Gaulle; see NAC, RG 25, box 10050: Political Affairs – Canada's Foreign Policy Trends and Relations – Israel: Tel Aviv to Ottawa, June 5, 1967 and ISA, 7920/2, Levi Eshkol Papers, Diplomatic Telegrams, France: Eshkol to de Gaulle, June 5, 1967.

The War: Day One, *June 5*

1. PRO FCO17/576: Israel – Defense: Report of Air Attaché, July 13, 1967. USNA, Middle East Crisis, 1967, Cir/Military files, box 6: CINSTRIKE to AIG 930, May 24, 1967. 'Isam Darraz, *Dubbat Yunyu Yatakallamun: kayfa Shahada Junud Misr Hazimat 67*

(Cairo: al-Manar al-Jadid lil-Sahafa wal-Nashr, n.d.), pp. 89–94. Ze'ev Schiff, *Tzahal be Hailo: Encyclopedia le-Tzava u-le-Bitahon* (Tel Aviv: Revivim, 1981), pp. 98–99 (Hod quote). Ehud Yanay, *No Margin for Error: The Making of the Israeli Air Force* (New York: Pantheon Books, 1993), pp. 234–36 (including the Harlev quote). "Hail ha-Avir ba-Milhama," *Bit'on Hail ha-Avir.* 'Imad Al-'Ilmi, *Harb 'Am 1967* (Acre: Al-Aswar lil-Thaqafa, 1990), pp. 90–91. Gawrych, *The Albatross of Decisive Victory,* pp. 14, 25. Al-Sabbagh, *Mudhakkirat Qadat al-'Askaraiyya al-Misriyya 5,* p. 20. Shmuel M. Katz, *Soldier Spies: Israeli Military Intelligence* (Novato, Calif.: Presidio Press, 1992), pp. 150–201. Oral history interview with Motti Hod, March 9, 1999. A profile of Wolfgang Lotz and other Israeli intelligence sources in Egypt appears in http://www.us-israel.org/jsource/biography/Lotz.html.

2. Fawzi, *Harb al-Thalath Sanawat,* pp. 132–35. Heikal, *Al-Infijar,* pp. 822–27. *Al-Hawadith,* interview with Shams Badran, Sept. 2, 1977, p. 21. Ramadan, *Tahtim al-Aliha,* pp. 93–94. Riad, *The Struggle for Peace in the Middle East,* p. 24. 'Abd al-Hamid, *Al-Mushir wa-Ana,* pp. 217–20. Israel Intelligence Library, Internal Jordanian Army Papers: Series of Events on the Jordanian Front, June, 1967. "Hail ha-Avir ba-Milhama," *Bit'on Hail ha-Avir.* Rozner, "Ha-5 be-Yuni 1967 be-Kahir." Dupuy, *Elusive Victory,* p. 242. 'Awda and Imam, *Al-Naksa—Man al-Mas'ul?,* p. 87. 'Afifi quote in Al-Sabbagh, *Mudhakkirat Qadat al-'Askaraiyya al-Misriyya 3,* pp. 7–8; see also 4, pp. 15–6, and 5, pp. 33–39.

3. YAD, Remarks by Yitzhak Rabin, Feb. 3, 1987, p. 24. Rabinovich, *The Battle for Jerusalem,* p. 67. Weizman quote from Weizman, *On Eagles' Wings,* p. 221.

4. YAD, Conference on the Six-Day War sponsored by the Center for the History of Defensive Force, Feb. 3, 1987, remarks by Motti Hod. P3RO FCO17/576: Israel – Defense: Report of Air Attaché, July 13, 1967. "Hail ha-Avir ba-Milhama," *Bit'on Hail ha-Avir.* Fawzi, *Harb al-Thalath Sanawat,* pp. 88–89. Al-'Ilmi, *Harb 'Am 1967,* p. 239. Weizman, *On Eagles' Wings,* pp. 192, 223–24. Rabin, *Memoirs,* p. 104. Yanay, *No Margin for Error,* p. 217. Gawrych, *The Albatross of Decisive Victory,* p. 14. Dupuy, *Elusive Victory,* p. 245. O'Balance, *The Third Arab-Israeli War,* pp. 53, 59.

5. Van Creveld, *The Sword and the Olive,* p. 162. Dupuy, *Elusive Victory,* p. 246. PRO FCO17/576: Israel – Defense: Report of Air Attaché, July 13, 1967. *Bit'on Hail ha-Avir 20,* no. 74/75 (Dec. 1967). Hammel, *Six Days in June,* pp. 167–68. Zaki quote from Darraz, *Dubbat Yunyu Yatakallamun,* pp. 7–8. Bin-Nun quote from "First Strike," *Jerusalem Post,* June 5, 1997.

6. LBJ, National Security files, NSC Histories, The Middle East Crisis, box 23: Cairo to the Secretary of State, June 5, 1967. Ben Akiva and Guvrin, "Sh'at ha-Mirage—Esrim Shana le-Milhemet Sheshet ha-Yamim." Dayan, *My Life,* pp. 351–53. Schiff, *Tzahal be-Hailo,* pp. 103–4. Haber, *Ha-Yom Tifrotz Milhama,* pp. 226–67. Fawzi, *Harb al-Thalath Sanawat,* pp. 140–41. Al-Sabbagh, *Mudhakkirat Qadat al-'Askaraiyya al-Misriyya 5,* p. 31. Riad, *The Struggle for Peace in the Middle East,* pp. 25–26. Hammel, *Six Days in June,* pp. 168–70. Yanay, *No Margin for Error,* p. 243. Dupuy, *Elusive Victory,* pp. 245–46. O'Balance, *The Third Arab-Israeli War,* pp. 65–67. M. Naor, and Z. Aner, eds., *Yemei Yuni – Teurim min ha-Milhama 1967* (Tel Aviv: Ma'arakhot, 1967), p. 77. PRO FCO17/576: Israel – Defense: Report of Air Attaché, July 13, 1967. Rozner, "H-5 be-Yuni 1967 be-Kahir." Oral history interview with Motti Hod, March 9, 1999; with Sa'id Ahmad Rabi', July 4, 1999.

7. Darraz, *Dubbat Yunyu Yatakallamun,* pp. 7–12 (Zaki testimony and quote), 25–33 (Hashim Mustafa Hassan testimony). Khouri, *Al-Watha'iq al-Filastiniyya,* pp. 314–

16. Israel Intelligence Library, Internal Jordanian Army Papers: Series of Events on the Jordanian Front, June, 1967. V.A. Zolotarev, main ed., *Rossia (SSSR) v' lokal'nykh voinakh i voennykh konfliktakh vtoroi poliviny XX veka* (Moscow: Kuchkovo Pole, 2000), pp. 183–84 (Tarasenko quote). Imam, '*Abd al-Nasir—Kayfa Hakama Misr*, pp. 366–67. Fawzi, *Harb al-Thalath Sanawat*, pp. 143–45. Al-Sabbagh, *Mudhakkirat Qadat al-'Askaraiyya al-Misriyya* 5, pp. 26–27 (Sidqi quote). Murtagi, *Al-Fariq Murtagi Yarwi al-Haqa'iq*, p. 127. Mazhar, *I'tirafat Qadat Harb Yunyu*, pp. 122–23. Ramadan, *Tahtim al-Aliha*, pp. 97–98. Riad, *The Struggle for Peace in the Middle East*, p. 24. Hussein, *My "War" with Israel*, pp. 60–61. Dupuy, *Elusive Victory*, p. 267. Joseph Finklestone, *Anwar Sadat: Visionary Who Dared* (London: Frank Cass, 1996), p. 57. USNA, Central Policy files, 1967–1969, POL 2 UAR, box 2553: Cairo to the Department of State, June 5, 1967. Oral history interview with Eric Rouleau, Dec. 18, 2000.

8. Heikal, *Al-Infijar*, pp. 830–33. Al-Jiyyar, "Ayyam al-Naksa fi Bayt 'Abd al-Nasir," *Ruz al-Yusuf* 2482 (January 5, 1976), p. 8. Riad, *The Struggle for Peace in the Middle East*, pp. 23–24. El-Sadat, *In Search of Identity*, p. 175. Cairo Radio quotes from BBC, *Daily Report, Middle East, Africa, and Western Europe*, B4, B5. Oral history interview with Israel Tal, Aug. 23, 1999; with Yeshayahu Gavish, Dec. 7, 1999.

9. IDF, 192/74, file 1348: The Battle for the Southern Front, n.d., p. 3; 1977/17: Ugdah 84, Hativa 35, in the Six-Day War, pp. 637–42; 1977/1786: The Regular Paratrooper Brigade in the Six-Day War, Commander 35th Brigade, 605, 625 (Tal quote); IDF, 717/77, file 86: Battle for the Southern Front, p. 353. Rabin, *Memoirs*, p. 102. Dayan, *My Life*, pp. 359–60. Segev, *Sadin Adom*, p. 83.

10. IDF 1977/17: Ugdah 84, 35th Brigade in the Six-Day War, pp. 646–48; Eytan quote on p. 650; 717/77, file 86: Battle for the Southern Front, p. 367 (description of Jiradi battle). Dupuy, *Elusive Victory*, pp. 249–52. Hammel, *Six Days in June*, pp. 144, 176–79. Churchill and Churchill, *The Six Day War*, p. 106. Fawzi, *Harb al-Thalath Sanawat*, p. 147. Gawrych, *Albatross of Decisive Victory*, p. 44. Gonen quote from Shabtai Teveth, *The Tanks of Tammuz* (London: Sphere Books, 1969), pp. 108–9. Gonen press comment from O'Balance, *The Third Arab-Israeli War*, p. 109. Tal quote from Churchill and Churchill, *The Six Day War*, pp. 108–9. Peled, *Ish Tzava*, p. 105. Oral history interview with 'Izzat 'Arafa, July 6, 2001.

11. Sharon, *Warrior*, pp. 191–92. Dupuy, *Elusive Victory*, pp. 257–61. Hammel, *Six Days in June*, pp. 202–14, 228–31. O'Balance, *The Third Arab-Israeli War*, pp. 120–27.

12. LBJ, National Security files, NSC Histories, Middle East Crisis, box 21: Jerusalem to the Secretary of State, May 23, 1967. USNA, Summary of MEDAC, box 13: Middle East Sitrep as of June 4. The document reports that "Israel did not return the [Jordanian] fire and [we] do not yet attribute much importance to such incidents on that front." PRO, FO 17/489, Israel – Political Affairs: Jerusalem to the Foreign Office, June 5, 1967. IDF, 901/67/1 Central Command: The Six-Day War, Concluding Discussion 1; pp. 2 (Narkiss quote), 66, 142; 2, p. 3; 192/74/1076 Round Table Discussion on the Liberation of Jerusalem, n.d. Weizman, *On Eagles' Wings*, p. 210. O'Balance, *The Third Arab-Israeli War*, pp. 177–78. Ammunition Hill Archive, Museum of the Tourjeman Post: Interview with Yoram Galon, Sept. 27, 1983.

13. IDF, 901/67/1 Central Command: The Six-Day War, Concluding Discussion 2, p. 2 (Narkiss quote); 192/74/1076 Round Table Discussion on the Liberation of Jerusalem, n.d. Uzi Narkiss, *Soldier of Jerusalem*, pp. 200–203. Rabinovich, *The Battle for Jerusalem*, pp. 12–13.

14. IDF, 901/67/1 Central Command, Six Day War, Concluding Report, Part A, p. 142 (Narkiss quote). Dupuy, *Elusive Victory*, p. 284. Hammel, *Six Days in June*, p. 290.

15. LBJ, National Security file, History of the Middle East Conflict, box 20: United States Policy and Diplomacy in the Middle East Crisis, May 15–June 10, 1967, p. 125. ISA, 6444/6, Foreign Ministry files, North America Telegrams: Foreign Ministry to Embassies, June 5, 1967. Haber, *Ha-Yom Tifrotz Milhama*, p. 222 (Dayan quote). Bull, *War and Peace in the Middle East*, pp. 42–43, 113. Rabinovich, *The Battle for Jerusalem*, pp. 80–83. Rabin, *Memoirs*, p. 105. Narkiss quote from Schiff, *A History of the Israeli Army*, p. 132. Eban, *Personal Witness*, p. 409. Israel cable to Hussein in ISA, 6444/6 North America, telegrams: Foreign Ministry to Embassies, June 5, 1967.

16. Mustafa, *Harb Haziran*, pp. 16–18. Darraz, *Dubbat Yunyu Yatakallamun*, pp. 34–48. Hussein, *My "War" with Israel*, pp. 60–64. Mutawi, *Jordan in the 1967 War*, pp. 116–17, 125–26. Kamm, *Hussein Poteah be-Milhama* (Abu Nawwar quote), p. 142. Col. Ephraim Kamm, "Haf'alat ha-Zira ha-Mizrahit be-Milhemet Sheshet ha-Yamim," *Ma'arakhot* 325 (June 1992), pp. 16–17. El Edroos, *The Hashemite Arab Army*, p. 379. Israel Intelligence Library, Internal Jordanian Army Papers: Series of Events on the Jordanian Front, June, 1967. Oral history interview with 'Awad Bashir Khalidi, Nov. 17, 1999; with Shafiq 'Ujeilat, Nov. 17, 1999; with Yusuf Khawwash, Nov. 16, 1999.

17. LBJ, National Security files, NSC Histories, Middle East Crisis, box 23: Amman to the Secretary of State, June 5, 1967. ISA, 4078/7, Foreign Ministry files, Contacts with the United States with the Entry of Egyptian Forces into Tiran: Evron to Foreign Ministry, June 5, 1967 (Hussein quote to American ambassador). O'Balance, *The Third Arab-Israeli War*, p. 181 (another version of Hussein's response). Israel Intelligence Library, Internal Jordanian Army Papers: Sequence of Events on the Jordanian Front, June, 1967. Hussein, *My "War" with Israel*, pp. 64–65, 71 (Nasser quote). Rabin, *Memoirs*, p. 188. Mutawi, *Jordan in the 1967 War*, pp. 123, 130. Dann, *King Hussein and the Challenge of Arab Radicalism*, p. 163.

18. IDF 901/67/1 Central Command: The Six-Day War, Concluding Discussion 1: Testimony of Col. Reuben Davidi, artillery corps, p. 64. PRO FCO17/576: Israel – Defense: Report of Air Attaché, July 13, 1967. LBJ, National Security Council files, History of the Middle East Crisis, box 18: McPherson to the President, June 11, 1967; NSC Histories, Middle East Crisis, box 17: Amman to the Secretary of State, June 5, 1967 (remark of Soviet ambassador). Mustafa, *Harb Haziran*, pp. 40–41, 264–65. Mayzel, *Ha-Ma'arakha al ha-Golan*, p. 194. Schiff, *Tzahal be-Hailo*, pp. 104–5. Yanay, *No Margin for Error*, pp. 249–50. Dayan, *My Life*, p. 353. Orders to Jordanian commanders in Kamm, *Hussein Poteah be-Milhama*, pp. 188, 195.

19. USNA, Central Foreign Policy files, 1967–1969, POL 27-7 ARAB-ISR, box 1830: Jerusalem to Department of State, June 5, 1967. Rabinovich, *The Battle for Jerusalem*, pp. 151, 352. Teddy Kollek, *For Jerusalem*, pp. 190–91. Bull, *War and Peace in the Middle East*, p. 113. PRO, FO 17/489, Israel – Political Affairs: Jerusalem to Foreign Office, June 5, 1967. Ammunition Hill Archive, Museum of the Tourjeman Post: Interview with Eliezer Amitai, n.d. Amitai quote from IDF, IDF 901/67/1 Central Command: The Six-Day War, Concluding Discussion 1, p. 43.

20. Baron, *Hotam Ishi*, pp. 56–57. Dayan, *My Life*, pp. 358–59. Hammel, *Six Days in June*, p. 295. On the continued flow of French arms to Israel, see LBJ National Security file, Middle East Crisis, box 104, 107: Paris to the Department of State, June 8, 1967. PRO, PREM 13 1620, Middle East Crisis: Paris to Foreign Office, June 9, 1967.

21. PRO, FCO 17/275: Amman to Foreign Ministry, Air Attaché's Report on the Jordan-Israel Battles, June 5, 1967; FCO 17/490, Israel – Political Affairs: Report of the Air Attaché, July 13, 1967. Israel Intelligence Library, Internal Jordanian Army Papers: Sequence of Events on the Jordanian Front, June 1967. Hussein, *My "War" with Israel*, pp. 72–73, 111. Mustafa, *Harb Haziran*, pp. 9–12. Mutawi, *Jordan in the 1967 War*, pp. 125–26. Dayan, *My Life*, pp. 353–54. Yanay, *No Margin for Error*, pp. 253–54. Mayzel, *Ha-Ma'arakha al ha-Golan*, p. 50. Kamm, *Hussein Poteah be-Milhama*, p. 196. Bull, *War and Peace in the Middle East*, p. 112. O'Balance, *The Third Arab-Israeli War*, pp. 69–71. Tal quote from Al-Shuqayri, *Mudhakkirat 5*, pp. 279–80.

22. Rabinovich, *The Battle for Jerusalem*, p. 97. Quote from Ari Milstein, "Ha-Til she-Haras et Emdot ha-Ligion," *Bamahane* 34 (May, 1977). Ben-Or quote from Schiff, *Tzahal be-Hailo*, pp. 102–3.

23. Gilboa, *Shesh Shanim, Shisha Yamim*, p. 222. Zak, *Hussein Ose Shalom*, p. 110 (Beiberman and Jum'a quotes). Dome of the Rock announcement in Rabinovich, *The Battle for Jerusalem*, p. 117.

24. El Edroos, *The Hashemite Arab Army*, p. 374. Oral history interview with Badi 'Awad, Nov. 21, 1999. Bull's protest appears in UN, DAG 13 3.4.0: 84: Chairman IJMAC to Chief of Staff UNTSO, May 11, 1967.

25. Israel Intelligence Library, Internal Jordanian Army Papers: Sequence of Events on the Jordanian Front, June, 1967. Bull, *War and Peace in the Middle East*, pp. 114–15. De Carvalho quote from *Life: Special Edition – Israel's Swift Victory* (1967), p. 50. Narkiss quote from IDF, 901/67/1 Central Command: The Six-Day War, Concluding Discussion 1; 192/74/1076 Round Table Discussion on the Liberation of Jerusalem, n.d. Rabinovich, *The Battle for Jerusalem*, pp. 116–22. Hammel, *Six Days in June*, pp. 293–94. Dupuy, *Elusive Victory*, p. 294. Michael Shashar, *Milhemet ha-Yom ha-Shvi'i: Yoman ha-Mimshal ha-Tzvai be-Yehuda ve-Shomron* (Tel Aviv: Hoza'at Poalim, 1997), p. 133.

26. IDF, Central Command: The Six-Day War, Concluding Discussion 2, p. 29. Baron, *Hotam Ishi*, pp. 56–58. Narkiss, *Soldier of Jerusalem*, pp. 203–6. Bartov, *Dado*, p. 97. Hammel, *Six Days in June*, pp. 307–8, 362–66. Mayzel, *Ha-Ma'arakha al ha-Golan*, p. 196. Mustafa, *Harb Haziran 1967*, pp. 279–81. Dupuy, *Elusive Victory*, p. 294. All quotes from Haber, *Ha-Yom Tifrotz Milhama*, pp. 227–28. Oral history interview with Rehavam Ze'evi, Sept. 9, 2001.

27. IDF, 901/67/1 Central Command: The Six-Day War, Concluding Discussion 2, pp. 43–44; 192/74/1076 Round Table Discussion on the Liberation of Jerusalem, n.d., p. 49 (Dreizin quote). ISA, Foreign Ministry files, 4086/1: Government House, Foreign Ministry to New York, June 6, 1967. Slater, *Rabin of Israel*, p. 135. Narkiss, *Soldier of Jerusalem*, pp. 206–7. U Thant, *View from the UN*, p. 255. Hammel, *Six Days in June*, pp. 300–304. Rabinovich, *The Battle for Jerusalem*, pp. 123–31, 138–48. Dupuy, *Elusive Victory*, pp. 294–95. Oral history interview with Rafi Benvenisti, Jan. 1, 1999; with 'Ata 'Ali, Nov. 18, 1999.

28. Hammel, *Six Days in June*, pp. 84–85, 117. Rabinovich, *The Battle for Jerusalem*, pp. 49–50. IDF, 901/67/1 Central Command: The Six-Day War, Concluding Discussion 2, pp. 5, 76; 192/74/1076 Round Table Discussion on the Liberation of Jerusalem, n.d., p. 50 (Gal quote); 901/67/ Central Command: The Six-Day War, Concluding Discussion 2, p. 39 (Ben-Ari quote). Israel Intelligence Library, Internal Jordanian Army Papers: Sequence of Events on the Jordanian Front, June, 1967. Motta Gur, *Har ha-Bayyit be-Yadeinu!: Kravot ha-Tzanhanim be-Yerushalayim be-Milhemet*

Sheshet ha-Yamim (Tel Aviv: Ma'arakhot, 1974), pp. 53–54 (Gur quote), 75–80. Oral history interview with Shimon Kahaner, Oct. 18, 2000.

29. IDF 901/67/1 Central Command: The Six-Day War, Concluding Discussion 2, p. 40 (Ben-Ari quote); 192/74/1076 Round Table Discussion on the Liberation of Jerusalem, n.d., p. 57 (Gal quote). Hammel, *Six Days in June*, pp. 315–18. Rabinovich, *The Battle for Jerusalem*, pp. 195–96. El Edroos, *The Hashemite Arab Army*, p. 377.

30. Elad quoted in El Edroos, *The Hashemite Arab Army*, p. 384. Ami Shamir, "Im ha-Koah she-Ala al Jenin," *Lamerhav*, no. 3014 (June 8, 1967), p. 4. Eitan Haber and Ze'ev Schiff, eds., *Lexicon le-Bithon Yisrael* (Tel Aviv: Mahadurat Davar, 1976), p. 423. Mutawi, *Jordan in the 1967 War*, pp. 116–17. Kamm, *Hussein Poteah be-Milhama*, pp. 205–6, 303. Hussein, *My "War" with Israel*, pp. 76–78. Mustafa, *Harb Haziran 1967*, pp. 279–81. Moshe Bar Kokhva, *Merkavot ha-Plada* (Tel Aviv: Ma'arakhot, 1989), pp. 151–52. Interview with 'Awad Bashir Khalidi, Nov. 17, 1999.

31. IDF, Central Command: The Six-Day War, Concluding Discussion 2, pp. 29–40. Israel Intelligence Library, Internal Jordanian Army Papers: Sequence of Events on the Jordanian Front, June, 1967. Kamm, "Haf'alat Hazira ha-Mizrachit be-Milhemet Sheshet ha-Yamim," p. 21; *Hussein Poteah be-Milhama*, pp. 190–92. Sadiq al-Shara', *Hurubuna ma'a Isra'il* (Amman: Dar al-Shuruq lil-Nashr wal-Tawzi', 1997), p. 491. Mutawi, *Jordan in the 1967 War*, pp. 76–78, 135. Hussein, *My "War" with Israel*, pp. 76–78. Mustafa, *Harb Haziran 1967*, pp. 279–81. Hammel, *Six Days in June*, pp. 362–66. Dupuy, *Elusive Victory*, pp. 309–11. Bar Kokhva, *Merkavot ha-Plada*, pp. 152–67.

32. USNA Central Foreign Policy files, 1967–1969, POL 12 SY, box 2511: Beirut to State Department, June 19, 1967. LBJ, National Security file, NSC Histories, Middle East Crisis, box 23: Damascus to the Secretary of State, June 5, 1967. PRO, FO 17/490, Israel – Political Affairs: Damascus to Foreign Ministry, June 5, 1967. Schiff, *Tzahal be-Hailo*, p. 108. Yanay, *No Margin for Error*, pp. 253–54. Dayan, *My Life*, pp. 353–54. O'Balance, *The Third Arab-Israeli War*, pp. 61–62. Mayzel, *Ha-Ma'arakha al ha-Golan*, p. 197. Hame'iri, *Mi-Shnei Evrei ha-Rama*, pp. 66–67. Mustafa, *Harb Haziran 1967*, pp. 142–45, 270–71. Al-'Ilmi, *Harb 'Am 1967*, pp. 190–91.

33. Mustafa, *Harb Haziran 1967*, pp. 184–85. PRO, FO 17/490, Israel – Political Affairs: Damascus to Foreign Ministry, June 5, 1967. Israel Intelligence Library : Internal Syrian Army Papers: The Southwestern Front, June 29, 1967; The Six Day War, file 1, Syria, Defense Ministry Document No. 25/3 to Col. Ahmad al-Amir Mahmud, commander of the 12th Brigade Attack Group, June 5, 1967. Baron, *Hotam Ishi*, p. 58. Bartov, *Dado*, p. 96. Draper, *Israel & World Politics*, p. 114. David Dayan, *Me-Hermon ad Suez: Korot Milhemet Sheshet ha-Yamim* (Ramat Gan: Masada Press, 1967), pp. 202–5. Khalil, *Suqut al-Julan*, pp. 139–41. Mustafa Tlas, *Mir'at Hayati*, (Damascus: Tlasdar, 1995), pp. 854–55. Atassi quote from Khouri, *Al-Watha'iq al-Filastiniyya*, p. 292. Assad quote from Hame'iri, *Mi-Shnei Evrei ha-Rama*, pp. 69–70.

34. Baron, *Hotam Ishi*, p. 58. Dayan, *My Life*, p. 375. YAD, Ramat Efal, Israel: Remarks by Matti Mayzel, June 20, 1966. Mayzel, *Ha-Ma'arakha al ha-Golan*, pp. 196–200.

35. LBJ, National Security file, History of the Middle East Conflict, box 18: Walt Rostow's Recollections of June 5, 1967 Security Council Meeting, Nov 17, 1968; box 19: Daily Brief for the President, June 5, 1967; box 20: United States Policy and Diplomacy in the Middle East Crisis, May 15–June 10, 1967, pp. 106–108; NSC Histories, Middle East Crisis, box 23: Circular, All American Diplomatic Posts, June 5, 1967; box

18: Memorandum for the Record, "Who Fired the First Shot?" Dec. 19, 1968. USNA, Middle East Crisis files, 1967, Chronology, box 8: Tel Aviv to the Secretary of State, June 5, 1967; box 17: The President in the Middle East Crisis, Dec. 19, 1968 ("All HELL broke lose"); box 21: Memorandum for Mr. W.W. Rostow (Davis), June 5, 1967; Arab-Israeli Situation Report, June 5, 1967 ("reduced by a coefficient of ten"). Quandt, *Peace Process*, p. 520, ft. 5. Oral history interview with Robert McNamara, Feb. 11, 2000. Johnson quote from Johnson, *Vantage Point*, p. 297. Rusk quote from Rusk, *As I Saw It*, pp. 386–87.

36. LBJ: National Security file, History of the Middle East Crisis, box 19: Kosygin to Johnson, June 5, 1967; Rusk to Gromyko, June 5, 1967; Johnson to Kosygin, June 5, 1967. PRO, FO 17/490, Israel – Political Affairs: Washington to Foreign Ministry, June 5, 1967. USNA, Middle East Crisis files, 1967, Situation Reports, box 13: Chronology of U.S.-USSR Consultations on the Middle East, May 18 – June 10, 1967. PRO, FO 17/490, Israel – Political Affairs, Washington to Foreign Office, June 5, 1967. Johnson and McNamara quotes from Johnson, *The Vantage Point*, p. 287, and Robert S. McNamara, *In Retrospect: The Tragedy and Lessons of Vietnam* (New York: Times Books, 1995), pp. 278–79. Quandt, *Peace Process*, pp. 50–51. Alvin Z. Rubinstein, *Red Star on the Nile*, pp. 9–10. Johnson message to Eshkol in Eban, *Personal Witness*, p. 409.

37. USNA, Middle East Crisis, Chronology June 4th – 7th, box 15: Tel Aviv to Department of State, June 5, 1967; Memorandum for the Middle East Task Force, May 29, 1967 (Rostow quote). LBJ, National Security file, National Security Council Histories, Middle East Crisis, 1967, 1, box 17: Saunders to Rostow, May 15, 1967; The President in the Middle East Crisis, Dec. 19, 1968 (Walt Rostow quote); History of the Middle East Conflict, box 18: Walt Rostow's Recollections of June 5, 1967 Security Council Meeting, Nov 17, 1968; Tel Aviv to the Department of State, June 5, 1967; Memos to the President (W. Rostow), box 17: Rostow to the President, June 5, 1967. PRO, FO 17/490, Israel – Political Affairs: Rostow to Certain Embassies, June 5, 1967.

38. USNA, Summary of MEDAC, box 13: Rusk to Johnson, June 5, 1967; Middle East Crisis files, 1967, box 2: Nairobi to the Department of State, June 5, 1967 (see also cables from Tokyo, Adis Ababa, and Lisbon); Central Foreign Policy files, 1967–1969, POL 12 SY, box 2511 Beirut to the Department of State, June 5, 1967. LBJ, National Security file, The Middle East Crisis, box 20: United States Policy and Diplomacy in the Middle East Crisis, May 15–June 10, 1967, pp. 112–18; History of the Middle East Crisis, box 18: Califano to Johnson, June 5, 1967; White House Communiqué, June 5, 1967; NSC Histories, Middle East Crisis, box 21: Arab-Israeli Situation Report, June 6, 1967; box 23: Circular, All American Diplomatic Posts, June 5, 1967; Circular, London to Washington, June 5, 1967. Rikhye, *Sinai Blunder*, pp. 99–100. Draper, *Israel & World Politics*, p. 111.

39. PRO, FO, 7/490, Israel – Political Affairs, New York to Foreign Ministry, June 5, 1967 (Egyptian complaint to the Security Council). ISA, 4086/4, Foreign Ministry files, Security Council Meetings, Eban to Levavi, June 5, 1967. LBJ, National Security file, NSC Histories, Middle East Crisis, box 23: USUN to the Secretary of State, June 5, 1967. UN, DAG 1/5.2.2.1.2-2 El Kony to the Secretary-General, June 5, 1967. U Thant, *View from the UN*, pp. 253–54 (Bunche quote). Lall, *The UN and the Middle East Crisis*, pp. 46–50. Rafael, *Destination Peace*, pp. 154–55. El Kony quote in Shevchenko, *Breaking with Moscow*, p. 133. Oral history interview with George Tomeh, Nov. 17, 1999; with Dr. Muhammad al-Farra, Nov. 16, 1999.

40. LBJ, National Security file, History of the Middle East Crisis, box 17: W. Rostow to the President, May 26, 1967; Arthur J. Goldberg Oral History, pp. 20–21; Eugenie Moore Anderson Oral History, p. 34; box 20: United States Policy and Diplomacy in the Middle East Crisis, May 15–June 10, 1967, p. 109. ISA, Foreign Ministry files, 3979/10, Goldberg: Evron to Bitan. March 2, 1967. Donovan, *Six Days in June*, pp. 100–101. For a general biography of Goldberg, see David L. Stebenne, *Arthur J. Goldberg: New Deal Liberal* (New York: Oxford University Press, 1996).

41. LBJ, National Security file, NSC Histories, Middle East Crisis, box 20: The Cease-Fire Negotiations in New York, Nov. 7, 1968; box 21: State of Play in New York (Davis), May 26, 1967; Report by Bureau of International Organizations Affairs (Arthur Day), n.d; Arthur J. Goldberg Oral History, p. 17. PRO, FCO 17/494, Israel – Political Affairs: Hayman Minute, June 5, 1967. Lall, *The UN and the Middle East Crisis*, pp. 50–59. Wilson, *The Chariot of Israel*, pp. 348–50. Federenko quote from Dagan, *Moscow and Jerusalem*, pp. 228–29.

42. ISA, 4086/4, Foreign Ministry files, Security Council Meetings: Eban to Rafael, June 5, 1967.

43. IDF, 522/69/212: General Operations Survey, n.d. Hammel, *Six Days in June*, pp. 232–40. Dupuy, *Elusive Victory*, pp. 259–61. Sharon, *Warrior*, pp. 189, 191. O'Balance, *The Third Arab-Israeli War*, pp. 124–26. Egyptian Military Orders in Khouri, *Al-Watha'iq al-Filastiniyya*, pp. 314–15. Bahgat quote in Darraz, *Dubbat Yunyu Yatakallamun*, pp. 81–82. Murtagi, *Al-Fariq Murtagi Yarwi al-Haqa'iq*, p. 62.

44. Most of the UNEF casualties were members of the Indian contingent caught in an Israeli artillery barrage. India protested the action. See Mansoor, *Arab World*, entry for June 5. Yahya Sa'ad Basha's testimony appears in Darraz, *Dubbat Yunyu Yatakallamun*, pp. 49–54. Baron, *Hotam Ishi*, pp. 50–52. Teveth, *The Tanks of Tammuz*, pp. 194–95. Oral history interview with Rafael Eytan, Feb. 24, 1999. IDF, 1977/71786: The Regular Paratrooper Brigade in the Six Day War, Commander 35th Brigade (Eytan quote); 717/77, file 86: Battle for the Southern Front, 375 (description of the al-'Arish battle).

45. LBJ National Security file, box 104, 107. Middle East Crises Joint Embassy Memorandum, June 5, 1967. Israel Intelligence Library, Internal Jordanian Army Papers: Sequence of Events on the Jordanian Front, June, 1967. Mustafa, *Harb Haziran*, pp. 80–84. Mutawi, *Jordan in the 1967 War*, pp. 125–26. *Al-Watha'iq al-Urduniyya, 1967* (Amman: Da'irat al-Matbu'at wal-Nashr, 1967), pp. 491–92. Hammel, *Six Days in June*, pp. 362–66. Kamm, *Hussein Poteah be-Milhama*, pp. 189–97 ('Ajluni quote on pp. 192–93). Dupuy, *Elusive Victory*, pp. 308–9. 'Alayyan quote in El Edroos, *The Hashemite Arab Army*, p. 386. Israeli official history quote in Yosef Eshkol, ed., *Milhemet Sheshet ha-Yamim* (Tel Aviv, Misrad ha-Bitahon, 1967), p. 85. YAD, interview with Ephraim Reiner, June 20, 1996.

46. IDF, Central Command: The Six-Day War, Concluding Report, Part B, pp. 3, 32. Kamm, *Hussein Poteah be-Milhama*, p. 150. Dupuy, *Elusive Victory*, pp. 295–97. PRO, FCO 17/493, Israel – Political Affairs: Foreign Office to Amman, June 7, 1967. Hammel, *Six Days in June*, p. 361. Rabinovich, *The Battle for Jerusalem*, pp. 188–93. 'Awda and Imam, *Al-Naksa—Man al-Mas'ul?*, pp. 117–31. Marsi testimony appears in Darraz, *Dubbat Yunyu Yatakallamun*, pp. 34–48. Bar-Lev quote from Haber, *Ha-Yom Tifrotz Milhama*, p. 228. Gur quote from Gur, *Har ha-Bayyit be-Yadeinu!*, pp. 58–59, 86–89. Oral history interview with Muhammad Fallah al-Fayiz, Nov. 21, 1999.

47. Mustafa, *Harb Haziran*, pp. 57–58, 71–74. Israel Intelligence Library, Internal Jordanian Army Papers: Sequence of Events on the Jordanian Front, June, 1967. Oral history interview with 'Ata 'Ali, Nov. 18, 1999. Mutawi, *Jordan in the 1967 War*, p. 132. Dupuy, *Elusive Victory*, pp. 292–96. Hammel, *Six Days in June*, pp. 300, 309–10. El Edroos, *The Hashemite Arab Army*, pp. 379–80.

48. For Eshkol's reply to Allon and Begin, see Ammunition Hill Archive, Begin to Motta Gur, June 15, 1992. Zak, *Hussein Ose Shalom*, p. 110. Hussein, *My "War" with Israel*, p. 73. Benziman, *Ir lelo Homa*, pp. 13–14. Nadav Shragai, *Har ha-Meriva: Ha-Ma'avak al Har ha-Bayyit, Yehudim ve-Muslemim, Dat ve-Politika Meaz 1967* (Jerusalem: Keter, 1995), pp. 18–20. Lior quote in Haber, *Ha-Yom Tifrotz Milhama*, p. 228.

49. Baron, *Hotam Ishi*, pp. 58–59. Dayan, *My Life*, pp. 358–59. Dayan quote from Bartov, *Dado*, p. 97. All other quotes from Haber, *Ha-Yom Tifrotz Milhama*, pp. 228–31. Benziman, *Ir lelo Homa*, pp. 14–19. Eban, *Personal Witness*, p. 412.

50. *Al-Watha'iq al-Urduniyya*, pp. 46–47. Mansoor, *Arab World*, entry for June 5, 1967.

51. Fawzi, *Harb al-Thalath Sanawat*, pp. 143–46, 155–56. Imam, *'Abd al-Nasir—Kayfa Hakama Misr*, pp. 162–63. Murtagi, *Al-Fariq Murtagi Yarwi al-Haqa'iq*, p. 67. Al-Jiyyar, "Ayyam al-Naksa fi Bayt 'Abd al-Nasir." El-Sadat, *In Search of Identity*, p. 172. Heikal, *Al-Infijar*, pp. 830–33. Riad, *The Struggle for Peace in the Middle East*, p. 26. U Thant, *View from the UN*, p. 257. Dupuy, *Elusive Victory*, p. 267. Hammel, *Six Days in June*, p. 244. El-Sadat, *In Search of Identity*, p. 175. Rubinstein, *Red Star on the Nile*, pp. 9–10. Voice of the Arabs quote from BBC, Daily Report, Middle East, Africa, and Western Europe, B3.

52. PRO, FO 17/490, Israel – Political Affairs: Washington to Foreign Ministry, June 5, 1967; PREM 13 1622: The Second Arab-Israel War, 1967: The Preliminaries (Hadow), July 6, 1967. Schiff, *A History of the Israeli Army*, p. 131. O'Balance, *The Third Arab-Israeli War*, p. 75. Ayyub quote from oral history interview with Fayiz Fahed Jaber, Nov. 21, 1999. Eshkol quote from Prittie, *Eshkol*, pp. 109–10.

53. USNA, Middle East Crisis, box 18: Tel Aviv to the Department of State, Chronology June 4th – 7th, June 7, 1967. LBJ, National Security file, History of the Middle East Crisis, box 18: W. Rostow to the President, June 5, 1967; Tel Aviv to the Secretary of State, June 5, 1967 ("push all the buttons").

Day Two, June 6

1. IDF, 192/74, file 1348: The Battle for the Southern Front, n.d., p. 3; 717/77, file 32: Summary of the Battle for the Southern Front, p. 29. Dayan, *My Life*, p. 355. Fawzi, *Harb al-Thalath Sanawat*, pp. 146–47. Dupuy, *Elusive Victory*, pp. 254–55, 263–64. Teveth, *The Tanks of Tammuz*, pp. 195–200. Hammel, *Six Days in June*, pp. 214–17. O'Balance, *The Third Arab-Israeli War*, pp. 134–36, 141–42. Shlomo Gazit, *Pta'im be-Malkodet*, p. 28. Peled, *Ish Tzava*, p. 107. Shadmi quote from Eran Sorer *Derekh ha-Mitla* (Ramat Gan: Masada, 1967), p. 35. Oral history interview with Meir Pa'il, Dec. 6, 2000.

2. Sorer, *Derekh ha-Mitla*, pp. 54–58. The testimonies of 'Adel Mahjub, Hasan Bahgat, and 'Azzam Shirahi appear in Darraz, *Dubbat Yunyu Yatakallamun*, pp. 79–86, 89–94, and 97–103, respectively.

3. IDF, 717/77, file 32: Summary of the Battle for the Southern Front, p. 31. LBJ, National Security file, Middle East Crisis, box 104, 107: Intelligence Cable, June 6,

1967; NSC Histories, Middle East Crisis, box 23: Rabat to the Secretary of State, June 6, 1967; Paris to the Secretary of State, June 8, 1967. PRO, FCO 17/492, Israel – Political Affairs, Khartoum to Foreign Ministry, June 5, 1967; 17/492, Israel – Political Affairs, Tunis to Foreign Ministry, June 5, 1967; 17/495, Israel – Political Affairs: Hanoi to Foreign Ministry, June 5, 1967 (Ho Chi Minh cable). ISA, Foreign Ministry files, 4083/3, Contacts with the Soviet Union: Moscow to Foreign Ministry, June 5, 1967 (Soviet statement). Ramadan, *Tahtim al-Aliha*, pp. 99–100. Mansoor, *Arab World*, entries for June 5 and 6, 1967.

4. IDF, 171/77/48: Debriefing on Battles on the Southern Front, p. 135. USNA, Middle East Crisis files, 1967, Chronology, box 12: Tel Aviv to the Secretary of State, June 6, 1967. Baron, *Hotam Ishi*, pp. 61–63. Rabin, *Memoirs*, p. 107 (Dayan quote). O'Balance, *The Third Arab-Israeli War*, pp. 73–74. Rabinovich, *The Battle for Jerusalem*, p. 183. Dayan, *My Life*, pp. 364–65.

5. *Al-Hawadith*, interview with Shams Badran, Sept. 2, 1977. Heikal, *Al-Infijar*, p. 822. El-Sadat, *In Search of Identity*, p. 176. Fawzi, *Harb al-Thalath Sanawat*, pp. 151–52. Mazhar, *I'tirafat Qadat Harb Yunyu*, pp. 90–91. Imam, *'Abd al-Nasir—Kayfa Hakama Misr*, p. 167. Al-'Ilmi, *Harb 'Am 1967*, pp. 146–48. For examples of Cairo's victory broadcasts see Mansoor, *Arab World*, entry for June 6, 1967.

6. Mazhar, *I'tirafat Qadat Harb Yunyu*, pp. 152–53 ('Amer order to Sidqi Mahmud), 221–22 (Murtagi quote). Fawzi, *Harb al-Thalath Sanawat*, pp. 152–53 ('Amer remark to Fawzi). Moshe Seren, "Tvusat Mitzrayim be-Enei ha-Aravim," *Ma'arakhot* 200 (June 1969). Imam, *'Abd al-Nasir—Kayfa Hakama Misr*, p. 164. Al-Sabbagh, *Mudhakkirat Qadat al-'Askaraiyya al-Misriyya* 1, pp. 26–27. Parker, *The Politics of Miscalculation in the Middle East*, p. 88. IDF, 717/77, file 32: Summary of the Battle for the Southern Front, p. 33. 'Amer quote in Ramadan, *Tahtim al-Aliha*, p. 114. For 'Uthman Nassar story, see PRO FCO/39/243 UAR – Political Affairs: *Egypt Gazette* clipping, Feb. 11, 1968. Muhammad Ahmad Khamis' testimony appears in Darraz, *Dubbat Yunyu Yatakallamun*, pp. 69–75.

7. IDF, 171/77/48: Debriefing on Battles on the Southern Front, p. 121. Dayan, *My Life*, p. 366.

8. IDF, 171/77/48: Debriefing on Battles on the Southern Front, p. 41; Summary of the Battle for the Southern Front, p. 39. Oral history interview with Yeshayahu Gavish, Dec. 7, 1999; Israel Tal, Aug. 23, 1999. Hammel, *Six Days in June*, pp. 248–50. Dupuy, *Elusive Victory*, p. 271.

9. Heikal, *Al-Infijar*, pp. 728–29 (Pojidaev quote). Parker, "The June 1967 War: Some Mysteries Explored," pp. 183–85. LBJ, National Security files, NSC Histories, Middle East Crisis, box 23: Washington to Amman and London, June 10, 1967. Riad, *Mudhakkirat* 1, pp. 310–12. Nasser communiqué in USNA, USUN, box 6: Circular: Middle East Sitrep as of June 7; Middle East Crisis files, box 4: London to the Secretary of State, June 8, 1967. PRO, PREM 13 1621: Amman to Foreign Office, June 14, 1967. See also Arye Shalev, "Ha-Milhama ve-Totzoteha be-Eynei ha-Aravim," *Dapei Elazar*, no. 10, *Esrim Shana le-Milhemet Sheshet ha-Yamim* (Tel Aviv: Yad David Elazar, 1988), p. 65.

10. LBJ, National Security file, Middle East Crisis, box 23: Cairo to the Department of State, June 6, 1967 (Nolte cable); box 104, 107: Cairo to the Department of State, June 6, 1967 (Nolte-Riad discussion); Intelligence Information Cable, June 6, 1967; Jidda to the Department of State, June 6, 1967; LBJ, National Security file, NSC Histories, Middle East Crisis, box 23: Amman to the Secretary of State, June 6,

1967. Thompson quote from *Life: Special Edition – Israel's Swift Victory* (1967), p. 70. BBC, Daily Report, Middle East, Africa, and Western Europe, B4 –5. Radio Damascus report in Hame'iri, *Mi-Shnei Evrei ha-Rama*, p. 20. Radio Algiers broadcast in Mansoor, *Arab World*, entry for June 6, 1967. Murad, "Harb Haziran," pp. 47–48.

11. USNA, USUN, box 6: Circular: Middle East Sitrep as of June 7. Reports on attacks on U.S. embassies and consulates appear in LBJ, National Security file, History of the Middle East Crisis, box 19: Daily Brief, June 6, 1967; Miscellaneous files, box 16: Oil Exporters Actions During Crisis as of June 23, 1967; Country file, box 104, 107: Middle East Crisis (see reports from Benghazi, Aleppo, Tunis, Algiers, Damascus); The box also contains Nolte's cable to the State Department. LBJ, National Security file, NSC Histories, Middle East Crisis, box 23: Damascus to the Secretary of State, June 6, 1967. PRO, FCO 17/493, Israel – Political Affairs: Damascus to Foreign Office, June 6, 1967. Mahjoub, *Democracy on Trial*, pp. 118–19. Riad, *Mudhakkirat 2*, pp. 96 (Nasser quote regarding Jordan and Hussein), 313; Riad, *The Struggle for Peace in the Middle East*, pp. 26–27.

12. Israel Intelligence Library, Internal Jordanian Army Papers: Sequence of Events on the Jordanian Front, June, 1967. El Edroos, *The Hashemite Arab Army*, p. 397. Mutawi, *Jordan in the 1967 War*, pp. 116–17. Kamm, *Hussein Poteah be-Milhama*, pp. 215–16, 220–24, 230, 242. Dupuy, *Elusive Victory*, p. 310. Hammel, *Six Days in June*, pp. 366–74. Hussein quote from Hussein, *My "War" with Israel*, p. 79. Mustafa, *Harb Haziran*, pp. 99–103. Bar Kokhva quote from Bar Kokhva, *Merkavot ha-Plada*, pp. 163–64. Shmuel Katz and Aharon Megged, *Me-Har Grizim ad Har Hermon: Rishumei Pikud ha-Tzafon be-Milhemet Sheshet ha-Yamim* (Tel Aviv: Misrad ha-Bitahon, 1967), pp. 5–56. Interview with 'Awad Bashir Khalidi, Nov. 17, 1999.

13. IDF, 192/74/1076 Round Table Discussion on the Liberation of Jerusalem, n.d. Rabinovich, *The Battle for Jerusalem*, pp. 235–36. Israel Intelligence Library, Internal Jordanian Army Papers: Sequence of Events on the Jordanian Front, June, 1967.

14. IDF, 901/67/1 Central Command: The Six-Day War, Concluding Report, Part B, Testimony of Gen. Narkiss, p. 76; 192/74/1076 Round Table Discussion on the Liberation of Jerusalem, n.d. Israel Intelligence Library, Internal Jordanian Army Papers: Sequence of Events on the Jordanian Front, June, 1967. Rabinovich, *The Battle for Jerusalem*, pp. 163–64.

15. IDF, 192/74/1076 Round Table Discussion on the Liberation of Jerusalem, n.d; Central Command: The Six Day War, Summary Report, Part B. Rabinovich, *The Battle for Jerusalem*, pp. 228–59. El Edroos, *The Hashemite Arab Army*, p. 397. Mutawi, *Jordan in the 1967 War*, pp. 116–17. Kamm, *Hussein Poteah be-Milhama*, pp. 215–16, 220–24, 242. Gur, *Har ha-Bayyit be-Yadeinu!* pp. 93–159. Dupuy, *Elusive Victory*, pp. 298–301. Hammel, *Six Days in June*, pp. 332–35. Narkiss, *Soldier of Jerusalem*, p. 208. Mustafa, *Harb Haziran*, pp. 57–58, 71–74. Oral history interview with 'Awad Bashir Khalidi, Nov. 17, 1999; with Mahmud Abu Faris, Nov. 17, 1999. Miller quote from Yisrael Harel, *Sha'ar ha-Arayot*, p. 101. Kirshan quotes from Kamm, *Hussein Poteah be-Milhama*, pp. 154–68.

16. IDF, 192/74/1076 Round Table Discussion on the Liberation of Jerusalem, n.d; Central Command: The Six Day War, Summary Report, Part B. Gur, *Har ha-Bayyit be-Yadeinu!*, pp. 161–258; Gur and Narkiss quotes on p. 258. ISA, 7920/1, Levi Eshkol Papers, Diplomatic Telegrams: Herzog to Eban, June 6, 1967. Oral history interview with Mahmud Abu Faris, Nov. 17, 1999; with Ghazi Isma'il Ruba'iyya, Nov.

21, 1999; with Shimon Kahaner, Oct. 18, 2000. Hammel, *Six Days in June*, pp. 330–31. Rabinovich, *The Battle for Jerusalem*, pp. 267–91, 298 300. El Edroos, *The Hashemite Arab Army*, p. 397. Mutawi, *Jordan in the 1967 War*, pp. 116–17. Kamm, *Hussein Poteah be-Milhama*, pp. 173–75 (Kranshur quote). Dupuy, *Elusive Victory*, pp. 298–301. Fradkin quote from Harel, *Sha'ar ha-Aruyot*, p. 214; Eilam quote on pp. 219–20.

17. IDF, 192/74/1076 The Six Day War, Summary Report, Part B. El Edroos, *The Hashemite Arab Army*, p. 397. Israel Intelligence Library, Internal Jordanian Army Papers: Sequence of Events on the Jordanian Front, June, 1967. Hammel, *Six Days in June*, pp. 316–20, 335–37. Rabinovich, *The Battle for Jerusalem*, pp. 267–91, 298–300, 335–42. Mutawi, *Jordan in the 1967 War*, pp. 116–17, 134. Dupuy, *Elusive Victory*, p. 299. Yusuf Khawwash, *Al-Jabha al-Urduniyya, Harb Haziran* (Amman: Dar al-Yaqin lil-Tiba'a wal-Nashr, 1980), n.p.

18. USNA, Middle East Crisis files, 1967, box 1: Chronology of U.S.-Jordanian Consultations on the Middle East, June 6, 1967; box 12: Tel Aviv to the Secretary of State, June 6, 1967 (Barbour quote); Amman to the Secretary of State, June 6, 1967 (Hussein quote); box 9: Tel Aviv to the Secretary of State, June 7, 1967. PRO, FO 17/490, Israel – Political Affairs: Amman to Foreign Ministry, June 6, 1967. LBJ, National Security file, History of the Middle East Conflict, box 20: United States Policy and Diplomacy in the Middle East Crisis, May 15–June 10, 1967, pp. 126–29. ISA, 7920/4, Levi Eshkol Papers, Prime Minister's Speeches, Surveys, and Reports: Bitan to Harman, Evron, Eban: June 6, 1967; 6444/6, Foreign Ministry files, North America Telegrams: Lourie to Foreign Ministry, June 6, 1967. Riyad quote from Hussein, *My "War" With Israel*, p. 81.

19. LBJ, National Security file, History of the Middle East Crisis, box 21: CIA Intelligence Memorandum, Arab-Israeli Situation Report June 8, 1967. For example of the text of the Hussein-Nasser conversation, see Donovan, *Six Days in June*, pp. 109–10. See also Hussein, *My "War" With Israel*, pp. 82–87. Mutawi, *Jordan in the 1967 War*, p. 159. Al-Ahram confirmation in Khouri, *Al-Watha'iq al-Filastiniyya*, pp. 316–17.

20. Mutawi, *Jordan in the 1967 War*, pp. 128–29, 138–39, 155. Mustafa, *Harb Haziran*, pp. 267, 279–80. Al-Shuqayri, *Mudhakkirat 5*, p. 296. Israel Intelligence Library, Internal Jordanian Army Papers: Sequence of Events on the Jordanian Front, June, 1967. Hussein's cable to Nasser in Hussein, *My "War" With Israel*, pp. 87–88, and in Kamm, *Hussein Poteah be-Milhama*, p. 294. Oral history interview with Munir Zaki Mustafa, July 5, 2001.

21. IDF, 192/74/1076 Round Table Discussion on the Liberation of Jerusalem, n.d; Central Command: The Six Day War, Summary Report, Part B. Oral history interview with Suliman Marzuq, Nov. 17, 1999. Hammel, *Six Days in June*, pp. 334–40. Rabinovich, *The Battle for Jerusalem*, pp. 357–70. El Edroos, *The Hashemite Arab Army*, p. 397. Mutawi, *Jordan in the 1967 War*, p. 134. Kamm, *Hussein Poteah be-Milhama*, p. 304. Dupuy, *Elusive Victory*, pp. 298 301. Bartov, *Dado*, p. 97. Hussein and Riad quotes from Hussein, *My "War" With Israel*, pp. 89–91 and 107, respectively.

22. IDF, 192/74/1076 Round Table Discussion on the Liberation of Jerusalem, n.d. Gur, *Har ha-Bayyit be-Yadeinu!*, pp. 387–407. Oral history interview with 'Ata 'Ali, Nov. 18, 1999.

23. ISA, 7920/4, Levi Eshkol Papers, Prime Minister's Speeches, Surveys, and Reports: Eshkol's Remarks to the Knesset Defense and Foreign Affairs Committee,

June 7, 1967. Bartov, *Dado*, p. 90. Oral History with Ya'akov Eshkoli, Feb. 7, 2000. Baron, *Hotam Ishi*, pp. 76, 83. Lior quote from Haber, *Ha-Yom Tifrotz Milhama*, p. 241. Dayan quotes from YAD, Interviews with Ephraim Reiner, Haim Nadel and Matti Mayzel, June 20, 1996. BGA, Diary, Entry for June 6, 1967.

24. PRO, FCO 17/493, Israel – Political Affairs: Damascus to Foreign Office, June 6, 1967. Mustafa, *Harb Haziran*, pp. 188–93 (including al-Assad quote). Aktum quote in Yehezkel Hame'iri, *Mi-Shnei Evrei ha-Rama* (Tel Aviv: Levin-Epstein, 1970), p. 16. Ha-Merkaz le-Moreshet ha-Modi'in: Report on Syrian artillery barrage, top secret, signed by Col. Muhammad Rafiq Qu'ad. Khouri, *Al-Watha'iq al-Filastiniyya*, p. 342. Heikal, *Al-Infijar*, pp. 755–56. YAD, Interview with Haim Nadel, June 20, 1996. Dupuy, *Elusive Victory*, pp. 317–19. Mayzel, *Ha-Ma'arakha al ha-Golan*, p. 203. Ezra Sadeh, *Amud Ha-Esh: Yoman ha-Milhama shel Yirmi* (Tel Aviv: Yosef Shimoni, n.d.), pp. 189–90. Yehuda Harel, *El Mul Golan* (Givatayim: Masada Press, 1967), pp. 86–98. Meir Hareuveni and Meir Arye, eds., *Ha-Hativa Shelanu be-Milhemet Sheshet ha-Yamim* (Tel Aviv: Misrad ha-Bitahon, 1968), pp. 56–57. Dayan, *Me-Hermon ad Suez*, pp. 209–11 (Yossi quote).

25. Israel Intelligence Library, Internal Syrian Army Papers: The Southwestern Front, June 29, 1967. Khalil, *Suqut al-Julan*, p. 148. Mayzel, *Ha-Ma'arakha al ha-Golan*, pp. 140–43. Syrian communiqué in Hame'iri, *Mi-Shnei Evrei ha-Rama*, pp. 77–78.

26. Baron, *Hotam Ishi*, pp. 60–61, 66. Bartov, *Dado*, p. 99. Mayzel, *Ha-Ma'arakha al ha-Golan*, pp. 188–91, 204–8. Rabin quote from *Memoirs*, p. 112.

27. IDF, 192/74/1076 Round Table Discussion on the Liberation of Jerusalem, n.d LBJ National Security file, box 104, 107. Middle East Crisis: Department of State to Tel Aviv and Amman, June 6, 1967; History of the Middle East Conflict, box 20: United States Policy and Diplomacy in the Middle East Crisis, May 15–June 10, 1967, pp. 126–29. BGA, Diary, Entry for June 6, 1967. Baron, *Hotam Ishi*, pp. 61–64 (Dayan quotes). Narkiss, *Soldier of Jerusalem*, p. 209. Benziman, *Ir lelo Homa*, pp. 19–20. Shragai, *Har ha-Meriva*, pp. 16–17.

28. ISA, 7920/4, Levi Eshkol Papers, Prime Minister's Speeches, Surveys, and Reports: Bitan to Harman, Evron, Eban, Rafael, June 7, 1967; 7920/3, Diplomatic Telegrams, General: Rome to the Foreign Ministry, June 6, 1967. Haber, *Ha-Yom Tifrotz Milhama*, pp. 231–33. Rabin, *Memoirs*, p. 107. Begin quote from Ammunition Hill Archive, Begin to Motta Gur, June 15, 1992. BGA, Diary, June 6, 1967. Senior defense official quoted in USNA, Middle East Crisis files, 1967, Miscellaneous Documents, box 14: Houghton to Morehouse, June 6, 1967.

29. ISA, 4086/4, Foreign Ministry files, Security Council Meetings 2: Eban to Levavi, June 6, 1967; Security Council Meetings: Herzog to Eban, June 6, 1967; 7920/1, Levi Eshkol Papers, Diplomatic Telegrams: Herzog to Eban, June 6, 1967; Tekoah to Rafael, June 6, 1967.

30. ISA, 7920/1, Levi Eshkol Papers, Diplomatic Telegrams: Rafael to Tekoah, June 5, 1967. Text of Eban speech appears in PRO, FCO 17/492, Israel – Political Affairs: New York to Foreign Ministry, June 6, 1967. Eban, *Personal Witness*, pp. 413–16. Raviv, *Israel at Fifty*, pp. 109–10. Rafael, *Destination Peace*, pp. 158–60 (including Goldberg quote). Donovan, *Six Days in June*, p. 133.

31. ISA, 4086/4, Foreign Ministry files, Security Council Meetings 2: Eban to Eshkol, June 6, 1967; 7919/1, Levi Eshkol files, Diplomatic Telegrams: U.S.A.: Bitan to Harman, June 6, 1967; 7920/4, Prime Minister's Speeches, Surveys, and Reports:

Eshkol's Remarks to the Knesset Defense and Foreign Affairs Committee, June 7, 1967. LBJ National Security files, box 104, 107. Middle East Crisis: Donnelly to Rusk, Aug. 6, 1967 (analysis of White House mail); History of the Middle East Conflict, box 20: United States Policy and Diplomacy in the Middle East Crisis, May 15–June 10, 1967, p. 129; Country file, box 104, 107: Rostow to the President, June 6, 1967 (Eshkol message); NSC Histories, Middle East Crisis, box 17: The President in the Middle East Crisis, Dec. 19, 1968 (Rusk quote); box 18: Rostow to the President, June 6, 1967. Eban, *Personal Witness*, pp. 417–18. Johnson, *Vantage Point*, p. 229. Quandt, *Peace Process*, p. 522, ft. 20. BGA, Diary, Entry for June 7, 1967.

32. LBJ, National Security file, History of the Middle East Crisis, box 18: New York to the Department of State, June 6, 1967; Country file, box 104, 107: New York to the Department of State, June 6, 1967; NSC Histories, Middle East Crisis, box 20: The Cease-Fire Negotiations in New York, Nov. 7, 1968; Memorandum of Conversation: The Hotline Exchanges, Nov. 4, 1968; box 23: Kuwait to the Secretary of State, June 6, 1967; Secretary of State to Tel Aviv, June 6, 1967. PRO, FCO 17/492, Israel – Political Affairs: New York to Foreign Office, June 6, 1967; FCO 17/493, Israel – Political Affairs: New York to Foreign Office, June 6, 1967. ISA, 7920/1, Levi Eshkol Papers, Diplomatic Telegrams: Rafael to Levavi, June 6, 1967; 4086/4, Foreign Ministry files, Security Council Meetings 2: Eban to Eshkol, June 6, 1967. Vassiliev, *Russian Policy in the Middle East*, p. 68. Arthur J. Goldberg Papers, "Behind Goldberg's UN Victory," in *New York Post*, June 7, 1967. Johnson quote in Donovan, *Six Days in June*, p. 130. Semyonov quote from Shevchenko, *Breaking with Moscow*, pp. 34–35.

33. USNA, Central Foreign Policy files, 1967–1969, POL 77-14 ARAB-ISR, box 1832: Goldberg to Rusk, June 6, 1967. PRO, FCO 17/494, Israel – Political Affairs: Hayman Minute, June 8, 1967. LBJ, National Security file, Country file, box 104, 107: Davis to Rostow, June 6, 1967. PRO, FCO 17/492, Israel – Political Affairs: New York to Foreign Office, June 6, 1967. LBJ, National Security file, NSC Histories, Middle East Crisis, box 23: Washington to Amman and London, June 10, 1967. Riad, *The Struggle for Peace in the Middle East*, p. 27 (Riad quote). Murtagi, *Al-Fariq Murtagi Yarwi al-Haqa'iq*, p. 154. Lall, *The UN and the Middle East Crisis*, pp. 59–62. U Thant, *View from the UN*, pp. 258–59. Mutawi, *Jordan in the 1967 War*, p. 158. Muhammad El-Farra, *Years of Decision* (London: KPI, 1987) pp. 1–22, 50–57. Oral history interview with Muhammad al-Farra, Nov. 17, 1999.

34. ISA, 7920/4, Levi Eshkol Papers, Prime Minister's Speeches, Surveys, and Reports: Bitan to Harman, Evron, Eban, and Rafael, June 6, 1967; 7920/3, Diplomatic Telegrams, Negotiations: Harman to the Prime Minister, June 6, 1967. IDF, 717/77, file 32: Summary of the Battle for the Southern Front, p. 29. Rabin quote from *Memoirs*, p. 113. Baron, *Hotam Ishi*, pp. 65–66. Warhaftig, *Hamishim Shana ve-Shana*, p. 190. Haber, *Ha-Yom Tifrotz Milhama*, pp. 240–41 (Eshkol quote).

35. Nasser letter in Hussein, *My "War" with Israel*, pp. 92–93. Hussein quote in Kamm, *Hussein Poteah be-Milhama*, p. 296. Mutawi, *Jordan in the 1967 War*, pp. 129–30. PRO, FCO/17/275 Defense Attaché's Report on the Jordan-Israel Battles (Colonel J.F. Weston-Simons), Amman to Foreign Office, June 7, 1967. Israel Intelligence Library, Internal Jordanian Army Papers: Series of Events on the Jordanian Front, June, 1967. Oral history interview with Shafic 'Ujeilat, Nov. 17, 1999.

36. LBJ, National Security file, History of the Middle East Conflict, box 20: United States Policy and Diplomacy in the Middle East Crisis, May 15–June 10, 1967, p. 129.

Hussein, *My "War" with Israel*, p. 95. Kamm, *Hussein Poteah be-Milhama*, pp. 296, 304. Mutawi, *Jordan in the 1967 War*, pp. 129, 139–40, 156. Hammel, *Six Days in June*, p. 375. Israel Intelligence Library, Internal Jordanian Army Papers: Sequence of Events on the Jordanian Front, June, 1967. Oral history interview with Yusuf Khawwash, Nov. 16, 1999.

Day Three, June 7

1. Hussein cable to Nasser in Hussein, *My "War" with Israel*, pp. 93–94. Hussein's orders in USNA, Middle East Crisis files, 1967, Misc. Documents, box 14: Morehouse to Houghton, June 7, 1967. El Edroos, *The Hashemite Arab Army*, pp. 398–99. Dupuy, *Elusive Victory*, p. 302. IDF, 901/67/1 Central Command: Six Day War, Concluding Report, Part A. Oral history interview with 'Ata 'Ali, Nov. 18, 1999; with Badi 'Awad, Nov. 21, 1999. Mutawi, *Jordan in the 1967 War*, p. 140.

2. USNA, Middle East Crisis files, 1967, box 1: Chronology of U.S.-Jordanian Consultations on the Middle East, June 7, 1967. Cable from Cairo in Hussein, *My "War" with Israel*, pp. 94–95. Kamm, *Hussein Poteah be-Milhama*, pp. 243–46 (al-Darubi quote). Hammel, *Six Days in June*, pp. 366–74. Benziman, *Ir lelo Homa*, pp. 22–25, 29. Bartov, *Dado*, p. 98. Oral history interview with Adnan Abu Oudeh, Nov. 16, 1999.

3. LBJ, National Security file, History of the Middle East Conflict, box 20: United States Policy and Diplomacy in the Middle East Crisis, May 15–June 10, 1967, pp. 129 (Barbour quote), 132–33. USNA, Middle East Crisis files, 1967, box 1: Chronology of U.S.-Jordanian Consultations on the Middle East, June 7, 1967. ISA, 4086/4, Foreign Ministry files, Security Council Meetings 2. Director-General's Office to Levavi and the Defense Ministry. Haber, *Ha-Yom Tifrotz Milhama*, p. 238. Zak, *Hussein Ose Shalom*, pp. 110–15.

4. IDF, 192/74/1076 Rav Siah ba-Nose: Shihrur Yerushalayim: n.d Baron 67. 901/67/1 Central Command: Six Day War, Concluding Report, Part A (Bar-lev and Narkiss quotes). Gur, *Har ha-Bayyit be-Yadeinu!*, pp. 284, 309; Gur quote on p. 287. Dupuy, *Elusive Victory*, pp. 303–4. Hammer, *Six Days in June*, p. 350. Haber, *Ha-Yom Tifrotz Milhama*, p. 233. Rabinovich, *The Battle for Jerusalem*, pp. 410–19; Gur quote on p. 419. Benziman, *Ir lelo Homa*, pp. 20–21. Shragai, *Har ha-Meriva*, p. 21. Baron, *Hotam Ishi*, p. 67 (Dayan quote). Oral history interview with Mahmud Abu Faris, Nov. 17, 1999.

5. Kollek, *For Jerusalem*, p. 194. Biographical information on Kollek, Herzog and Goren from the Jewish Agency Zionist Education website, www.jajz-ed.org.il.

6. USNA, Middle East Crisis files, 1967, box 1: Chronology of U.S.-Jordanian Consultations on the Middle East, June 7, 1967. PRO, PREM 13 1620, Middle East Crisis: Foreign Office to Amman, June 7, 1967; Amman to Foreign Office, June 7, 1967; FCO 17/493, Israel – Political Affairs: Foreign Office to Amman, June 7, 1967; Tel Aviv to Foreign Office, June 7, 1967. ISA, 7920/1, Levi Eshkol Papers, Diplomatic Telegrams: Eban to Eshkol, June 7, 1967; 7920/4, Prime Minister's Speeches, Surveys, and Reports: Eshkol's Remarks to the Knesset Defense and Foreign Affairs Committee, June 7, 1967; Remez to Levavi, June 7, 1967.

7. IDF, 901/67/1: Central Command: Six Day War, Concluding Report, Part A; 192/74/1076: Roundtable Discussion on the Liberation of Jerusalem, n.d. (Achman quote). Gur, *Har ha-Bayyit be-Yadeinu!*, pp. 316–24. Benziman, *Ir lelo Homa*, p. 29. O'Balance, *The Third Arab-Israeli War*, pp. 208–11. Harel, *Sha'ar ha-Arayot*, pp. 160–62. Hammel, *Six Days in June*, pp. 335–36 (Goren quote).

8. Uzi Narkiss, "Kakh Uhda Yerushalayim," *Bamahane* 34 (May 1987); *Soldier of Jerusalem*, p. 209 (Narkiss quote). Dayan quote from Mansoor, *Arab World*, entry for June 7, 1967. Rabin quotes from Rabin, *Memoirs*, pp. 111–12, and Slater, *Rabin of Israel*, p. 142. Donovan, *Six Days in June*, p. 120. Nadav Shragai, *Har ha-Meriva*, pp. 23–24, 28–30.

9. Haber, *Ha-Yom Tifrotz Milhama*, pp. 242–45. Eban, *Personal Witness*, p. 419. Warhaftig, *Hamishim Shana ve-Shana*, pp. 204–6.

10. USNA, Middle East Crisis, Chronology June 4th – 7th, box 1: Amman to the Department of State, June 6, 1967; Miscellaneous Documents, box 14: Morehouse to Houghton, June 7, 1967 (officer's description of Hussein). Israel Intelligence Library, Internal Jordanian Army Papers: Sequence of Events on the Jordanian Front, June, 1967. Dayan, *My Life*, p. 370. Susser, *On Both Banks of the Jordan*, p. 17. Narkiss, *Soldier of Jerusalem*, p. 209. Al-Shara', *Hurubuna ma'a Isra'il*, p. 494. Kamm, *Hussein Poteah be-Milhama*, p. 296.

11. IDF, 717/77, file 32: Summary of the Battle for the Southern Front, pp. 57–62. USNA, Lot files, USUN, box 6: Circular: Middle East Sitrep as of June 7. LBJ, National Security file, History of the Middle East Crisis, box 21: CIA Intelligence Memorandum, Arab-Israeli Situation Report, June 8, 1967; box 104, 107: Cincstrike and Eucom for Polad, June 8, 1967. Fawzi, *Harb al-Thalath Sanawat*, pp. 151–56. Rabin, *Memoirs*, pp. 107–8. Hammel, *Six Days in June*, pp. 251–53. Baron, *Hotam Ishi*, pp. 67, 71. Slater, *Rabin of Israel*, p. 150. Schiff, *A History of the Israeli Army*, p. 133. Al-Sabbagh, *Mudhakkirat Qadat al-'Askaraiyya al-Misriyya* 1, pp. 28–29. Al-Sabbagh, *Mudhakkirat Qadat al-'Askaraiyya al-Misriyya* 10, pp. 9–10 (Khalil quote). Mahmud 'Abd al-Hafiz's testimony appears in Darraz, *Dubbat Yunyu Yatakallamun*, pp. 135–46. Interview with Sidqi al-Ghul in *al-Ra'i al-'Am*, June 2, 1987. Oral history interview with Meir Pa'il, Dec. 6, 2000.

12. ISA, Foreign Ministry files, 4085/1: Emergency Situation 1967 – Prisoners, June 14, 1967. USNA, Middle East Crisis files, 1967, Chronology, box 8: Tel Aviv to the Secretary of State, June 8, 1967. Dupuy, *Elusive Victory*, pp. 271–75. Fawzi, *Harb al-Thalath Sanawat*, pp. 151–56. Al-Sabbagh, *Mudhakkirat Qadat al-'Askaraiyya al-Misriyya* 5, p. 28. Rabin, *Memoirs*, pp. 107–8. Hammel, *Six Days in June*, pp. 251–53. Baron, *Hotam Ishi*, pp. 67, 71. Slater, *Rabin of Israel*, p. 150. Schiff, *A History of the Israeli Army*, p. 133. Sharon, *Warrior*, pp. 194–95. O'Balance, *The Third Arab-Israeli War*, pp. 144–45. Mahmud 'Abd al-Hafiz's testimony appears in Darraz, *Dubbat Yunyu Yatakallamun*, pp. 135–46. Asher quote from Avraham Shapira, ed., *The Seventh Day: Soldiers Talk About the Six-Day War* (New York: Scribners, 1970), p. 66. Oral history interview with Mahmud al-Suwarqa, July 7, 2001.

13. The testimonies of 'Azzam Shirahi and Dr. 'Abd al-Fattah al-Tarki appear in Darraz, *Dubbat Yunyu Yatakallamun*, pp. 89–94 and 107–18, respectively. Oral history interview with Amin Tantawi, July 4, 2001.

14. Mazhar, *I'tirafat Qadat Harb Yunyu*, p. 177. Fawzi, *Harb al-Thalath Sanawat*, pp. 151–53. Murtagi, *Al-Fariq Murtagi Yarwi al-Haqa'iq*, p. 163. Quote from Ramadan, *Tahtim al-Aliha*, p. 105. Oral history interview with Al-Shirbini Sa'id Hamada, July 5, 2001.

15. LBJ, National Security file, History of the Middle East Crisis, box 19: CIA, Office of National Estimate—Current Soviet Attitudes, June 9, 1967; State Department Activities Report, June 7, 1967; Country file, box 104, 107: Davis to Rostow, June 6, 1967; New York to the Department of State, June 8, 1967; Soviet Official's

Comments on Soviet Policy on the Middle Eastern War, June 8, 1967. Heikal, *Al-Infijar*, pp. 728–31. Parker, *The Politics of Miscalculation in the Middle East*, pp. 33–34. Segev, *Sadin Adom*, p. 132. Pravda quote from ISA, Foreign Ministry files, 4083/3, Contacts with the Soviet Union, Moscow to Foreign Ministry, June 6, 1967. Dagan, *Moscow and Jerusalem*, pp. 226–27 (Chuvakhin quote and Kosygin's letter to Eshkol). Al-'Ilmi, *Harb 'Am 1967*, pp. 203–7. I. I. Mintz, *Sionizm: Teoria i Praktika* (Moscow: Izdetelstvo Politicheskoy Literatury, 1970), pp. 111–12. See also Yosef Argaman, "Nasser Metzaltzel le-Hussein: Ha-Siha," *Bamahane* 18 (January 1989).

16. ISA, 7920/2, Levi Eshkol Papers, Diplomatic Telegrams, USSR: Tekoah to New York, June 7, 1967 (Kosygin cable to Eshkol). PRO, FCO 17/493, Israel – Political Affairs: Kosygin to Wilson, June 7, 1967. Eshkol in Dagan, *Moscow and Jerusalem*, pp. 229–30. Haber, *Ha-Yom Tifrotz Milhama*, pp. 243–44. Wilson, *Chariot of Israel*, pp. 351–52.

17. Mazhar, *I'tirafat Qadat Harb Yunyu*, pp. 188–90. Fawzi, *Harb al-Thalath Sanawat*, pp. 155–61. Murtagi, *Al-Fariq Murtagi Yarwi al-Haqa'iq*, pp. 164–65. Ramadan, *Tahtim al-Aliha*, pp. 136–37 (including orders to the 4th Division).

18. UN, DAG 1/5.2.2.1.2-2, The Middle East, Eban to the Secretary-General, June 7, 1967. Baron, *Hotam Ishi*, pp. 73–74 (Dayan quote). Haber, *Ha-Yom Tifrotz Milhama*, pp. 237–40, 244 (Lior, Allon, Eshkol and Tekoah quotes). Zak, *Hussein Ose Shalom*, pp. 110–15. PRO, FCO 17/494, Israel – Political Affairs: Hayman Minute, June 8, 1967.

19. LBJ, National Security file, Country file, box 104, 107: Minutes of the NSC Meeting, June 7, 1967; Rostow to the President, June 7, 1967; History of the Middle East Crisis, box 19: Bundy to the President, June 9, 1967; Guidelines for U.S. Position and Action in Connections with the Present ME Situation, by Nadav Safran and Stanley Hoffman, June 8, 1967. USNA, POL AR-ISR, Mintues of the Control Group, box 17: Twelfth Control Group Meeting, June 7, 1967.

20. LBJ National Security file, Country file, Middle East Crisis, box 104, 107: Tel Aviv to the Department of State, June 7, 1967 (Barbour quote); USNA, Middle East Crisis, Chronology June 4th – 7th, box 8: Tel Aviv to the Department of State, June 7, 1967 (report from Tel Aviv); USUN, box 6: Circular: Middle East Sitrep as of June 7. USNA, POL ARAB-ISR, United Nations files, box 1: Tel Aviv to the Secretary of State, June 8, 1967. ISA, Foreign Ministry files, 4089/15: Rome to Foreign Ministry, June 7, 1967. PRO, FO 17/11, American Middle East Policy, Urwick to Morris, June 7, 1967 (Bank of Israel plans). See also Reuven Pedatzur, "Coming Back Full Circle: The Palestinian Option of 1967," *Middle East Journal* 49, no. 2 (Spring 1995).

21. USNA, Arab-Israeli Crisis, box 17: Minutes of the Control Group, June 7, 1967. LBJ, National Security file, Country file, box 104, 107: Rusk to London, June 7, 1967 ("territorial integrity"); Minutes of the NSC Meeting, June 7, 1967 ("attorneys for Israel"); Memorandum for Mr. Bundy, June 7, 1967; CIA Intelligence Memorandum: Impact on Western Europe and Japan of a Denial of Arab oil, June 7, 1967; Mrs. Arthur Krim to Walt Rostow, June 7, 1967. Draper, *Israel & World Politics*, p. 117. William B. Quandt, "The Conflict in American Foreign Policy," in Rabinovich and Shaked, *From June to October*, p. 5.

22. Oral history interview with Rafi Benvenisti, Jan. 1, 1999. Susser, *On Both Banks of the Jordan*, pp. 19–20. Hammel, *Six Days in June*, pp. 377–80. Donovan, *Six Days in June*, p. 121. Kamm, *Hussein Poteah be-Milhama*, p. 217. Dupuy, *Elusive Victory*,

pp. 301–2. Shashar, *Milhemet ha-Yom ha-Shvi'i*, p. 20. Ram quote from Bartov, *Dado*, p. 98. Dayan, *My Life*, p. 370. Al-Shara', *Hurubuna ma'a Isra'il*, pp. 493–95.

23. Hammel, *Six Days in June*, pp. 254–59. Sorer, *Derekh ha-Mitla*, pp. 37–38. Dupuy, *Elusive Victory*, pp. 273–75. *The Six Days' War* (Tel Aviv: Ministry of Defense, 1967), p. 36. Al-'Ilmi, *Harb 'Am 1967*, pp. 176–85.

Day Four, June 8

1. USNA, Middle East Crisis files, 1967, box 1: Chronology of U.S.-Jordanian Consultations on the Middle East, June 8, 1967. PRO, PREM 13 1620 Middle East Crisis: Amman to Foreign Office, June 10, 1967. UN, DAG 1/5.2.2.1.2-2, Middle East: Minister of Foreign Affairs of Jordan to the Secretary-General, June 8, 1967. Hussein, *My "War" with Israel*, p. 88. Khalid Fakhida, "Al-Fariq Haditha lil-Hadath: Sharakna fi Harb '67 Irda'an li-'Abd al-Nasir wa-Man'an min 'Takhwin' al-Urdun," *al-Hadath*, no. 265 (Jan. 29, 2001).

2. Hammel, *Six Days in June*, pp. 258–59. Mustafa, *Harb Haziran*, pp. 118–19. "Hail ha-Avir ba-Milhama," *Bit'on Hail ha-Avir* 3, no. 74/75 (December 1967), p. 265. IDF, 901/67/1 Central Command: The Six-Day War, Concluding Report, Part A, 3 (Narkiss quote), p. 38 (evaluation of Jordanian soldiers). Mutawi, *Jordan in the 1967 War*, p. 140.

3. IDF, 717/77, file 32: Summary of the Battle for the Southern Front, pp. 31 (Dayan quote), 63, 399 (Even quote). LBJ, National Security file, History of the Middle East Crisis, box 21: CIA Intelligence Memoranda, Arab-Israeli Situation Report, June 8, 1967; box 104, 107. Middle East Crisis: Joint Embassy Memorandum, June 8, 1967 (Yariv quote). 'Amer, Murtagi and Muhsin quotes from Al-Sabbagh, *Mudhakkirat Qadat al-'Askaraiyya al-Misriyya 1*, pp. 30–31. Rabin quote in Haber, *Ha-Yom Tifrotz Milhama*, p. 245. Dupuy, *Elusive Victory*, pp. 264, 276–77. Hammel, *Six Days in June*, pp. 268–69. Dayan, "Before and After the Battle," in *The Six Days' War* (Tel Aviv: Ministry of Defense, 1967), p. 36. Riad, *The Struggle for Peace in the Middle East*, p. 32. Fawzi, *Harb al-Thalath Sanawat*, p. 148. Aviezer Golan, *Albert* (Tel Aviv: Yediot Ahronot, 1977), p. 118. Sorer, *Derekh ha-Mitla*, pp. 37–39, 93–101.

4. Dayan, *My Life*, p. 367. Slater, *Rabin of Israel*, p. 150. Schiff, *A History of the Israeli Army*, p. 133. Hammel, *Six Days in June*, pp. 264–78. Dupuy, *Elusive Victory*, pp. 274–75. Oral history interviews with Yeshayahu Gavish, Dec. 7, 1999; with Meir Pa'il, Dec. 6, 2000; with Rehavam Ze'evi, Sept. 9, 2001.

5. LBJ National Security file, Middle East Crisis, box 104, 107: Tel Aviv to the Department of State, June 8, 1967; box 20: United States Policy and Diplomacy in the Middle East Crisis, May 15–June 10, 1967, pp. 140–41; box 23: Tel Aviv to the Secretary of State, June 8, 1967; Beirut to the Secretary of State, June 8, 1967; NSC Histories, Middle East Crisis, box 23: Tel Aviv to the Secretary of State, June 8, 1967. USNA, Middle East Crisis files, 1967, Situation Reports, box 14: Middle East Sitrep as of June 7. Al-Shuqayri, *Mudhakkirat 5*, p. 330. Hart, *Arafat*, pp. 199–200. Kimche and Bawly, *The Sandstorm*, pp. 200–201. Mustafa, *Harb Haziran*, pp. 193–94. Khouri, *Al-Watha'iq al-Filastiniyya*, p. 354. Khalil, *Suqut al-Julan*, pp. 100–101. Mayzel, *Ha-Ma'arakha al ha-Golan*, p. 438. Syrian army record in Israel Intelligence Library: Internal Syrian Army Papers: The Southwestern Front, June 29, 1967.

6. Baron, *Hotam Ishi*, p. 83. Eshkoli and Eshkol quotes from *Eretz ha-Golan*, no. 100 (1985), pp. 32–33. Warhaftig, *Hamishim Shana ve-Shana*, pp. 186–89. Haber, *Ha-Yom*

Tifrotz Milhama, pp. 244–46 (Aran quote). Gilboa, *Shesh Shanim, Shisha Yamim*, p. 232. *Ha'aretz* quote from USNA, POL ARAB-ISR, United Nations files, box 1: Tel Aviv to the Secretary of State, June 8, 1967. Bar-Lev quote from Guy, *Bar-Lev*, p. 139. Dayan quote from YAD, Interview with Matti Mayzel, June 20, 1996.

7. Rabin, *Memoirs*, p. 113. Elazar quotes from YAD, Interview with Haim Nadel, June 20, 1996, from Bartov, *Dado*, pp. 99–101, Mayzel, *Ha-Ma'arakha al ha-Golan*, pp. 225–27. Golan, *Albert*, pp. 124–25. Allon and Ber quotes from Haber, *Ha-Yom Tifrotz Milhama*, p. 247. Oral history interview with Rehavam Ze'evi, Sept. 9, 2001.

8. LBJ National Security file, Middle East Crisis, box 104, 107: Joint Embassy Memorandum, June 8, 1967; Report of the American Consulate in Jerusalem, June 8, 1967 ("an apparent prelude..."); The Secretary of State to Tel Aviv, June 8, 1967. Eban, *Personal Witness*, p. 424. IDF, 901/67/1 Central Command: The Six-Day War, Concluding Report, Part A, pp. 9–10. Eban, *Personal Witness*, p. 423 (Bundy quote).

9. LBJ National Security file, Middle East Crisis, box 19: NSC Special Committee Meeting (handwritten notes). June 8, 1967; box 104, 107: Rusk to Embassies, June, 1967; Tripoli to the Department of State, June 8, 1967; box 20: United States Policy and Diplomacy in the Middle East Crisis, May 15–June 10, 1967, pp. 132–33, 140–41. USNA, Middle East Crisis files, 1967, Situation Reports, box 13: The Secretary of State to King Faisal, June 8, 1967. UN, DAG 1/5.2.2.1.2-2, Middle East: Goldberg to U Thant, June 9, 1967.

10. LBJ, National Security file, History of the Middle East Crisis, box 19: JCS to USCINCEUR, June 8, 1967; box 104, 107, The National Military Command Center: Attack on the USS *Liberty*, June 9, 1967; Department of Defense: USS *Liberty* Incident, June 15, 1967. USNA, Chairman Wheeler files, box 27: The Court of Inquiry Findings, June 22, 1967.

11. IDF, 2104/92/47: *Attack on the Liberty*, IDF Historical Department, Research and Instruction Branch, June 1982 (hereafter IDF, *Attack on the Liberty*). The Israeli fighter pilot originally thought that the ship had fired at him, and Israeli destroyers were ordered to find it. The orders were rescinded, however, following further debriefing of the pilot. See also ISA, 4079/26 Foreign Ministry files, the *Liberty* Incident; IDF Preliminary Inquiry file 1/67 Col. Y. Yerushalmi, July 24, 1967. Report by Carl F. Salans, Department of State Legal Advisor, September 21, 1967, to the Undersecretary of State. (Document available on the USS *Liberty* site—www.halcyon.com/jim/uss*Liberty*/*Liberty*.htm)

12. USNA, Middle East Crisis files, 1967, USUN, box 6: CINSTRIKE to AIG, June 2, 1967; Cir/Military files, box 6: CINSTRIKE to AIG 930, May 24, 1967; INR Reseach Reports: ALUSNA to COMSIXTHFLEET: June 8, 1967. LBJ, National Security file, History of the Middle East Crisis, box 20: United States Policy and Diplomacy in the Middle East Crisis, May 15–June 10, 1967, pp. 87–88. On the naval liaison, see LBJ, National Security file, NSC Histories, Middle East Crisis, box 17: Tel Aviv to the Secretary of State, May 27, 1967. Ben-Gurion Archive, Diary, Entry for May 26, 1967. See also A. Jay Cristol, *The Liberty Incident*, unpublished doctoral dissertation, University of Miami, 1997, pp. 25–26. British Public Record Office, FCO17/498, Israel—Political Affairs: Tel Aviv to Foreign Office, June 5, 1967. Shlomo Erell, *Lefanekha ha-Yam: Sipuro shel Yamai, Mefaked u-Lohem* (Tel Aviv: Misrad ha-Bitahon, 1998), pp. 268–75. Rabin, *Memoirs*, pp. 100, 110; Hirsh Goodman and Ze'ev Schiff, "The Attack on the *Liberty*," *The Atlantic Monthly*, September 1984, p. 81.

13. ISA, 4079/26 Foreign Ministry files, the *Liberty* Incident; IDF Preliminary Inquiry file 1/67 Col. Y. Yerushalmi, July 24, 1967. IDF, 717/77, file 32: Summary of the Battle for the Southern Front, p. 34. The *Liberty* was also sailing near 'Point Boaz,' the location at which Israeli aircraft entered and exited Sinai—another reason for the heavy air traffic that morning. See IDF, *Attack on the Liberty*, p. 39, n. 14.

14. ISA, 4079/26 Foreign Ministry files, the *Liberty* Incident; IDF Preliminary Inquiry file 1/67 Col. Y. Yerushalmi, July 24, 1967. See also Rabin, *The Rabin Memoirs*, pp. 108–9. Oral history interview with Mordechai Hod, March 9, 1999. Yanay, *No Margin for Error*, p. 257. On issue of whether the Israelis consulted Commander Castle, see the protocol of the official U.S. Naval Board of Inquiry posted on the USS *Liberty* website.

15. The Israeli pilot mistook the "G" on the *Liberty*'s hull for a "C." IDF, Attack on the *Liberty*; Israeli Air Force Historical Branch, Transcript of the Ground-To-Air Communications, the *Liberty* Incident. ISA, 4079/26 Foreign Ministry files, the *Liberty* Incident; IDF Preliminary Inquiry file 1/67 Col. Y. Yerushalmi, 24 July, 1967. USNA, Chairman Wheeler files, box 27: The Court of Inquiry Findings, June 22, 1967. Rabin quote from *Memoirs*, pp. 109, 127. LBJ, Country files, box 104, 107, The National Military Command Center: Attack on the USS *Liberty*, June 9, 1967; NSC Histories, box 18: CINCEURUR to RUDLKD/CINSUSNAVEUR, June 8, 1967; COMSIXTHFLT to RUFPBK/USCINCEUR, June 8, 1967; USDOA Tel Aviv to RUDLKD/CINCUSNAVEUR, June 15, 1967. See also Cristol, *Liberty Incident*, p. 55. James M. Ennes, Jr., *Assault on the Liberty: The True Story of the Israeli Attack on an American Intelligence Ship* (New York: Random House, 1979), pp. 72–117. Prostinak quote provided by Marvin Nowicki in a personal letter to Jay Cristol, dated March 3, 2000; conveyed to the author on May 31, 2001.

16. LBJ, National Security file, History of the Middle East Crisis, box 19: Memorandum for the Record, Washington-Moscow "Hot-line" Exchange, Oct. 22, 1968; box 20: United States Policy and Diplomacy in the Middle East Crisis, May 15–June 10, 1967, pp. 143–44. Johnson, *Vantage Point*, p. 301.

17. LBJ, National Security files, History of the Middle East Crisis, box 20: United States Policy and Diplomacy in the Middle East Crisis, May 15–June 10, 1967, pp. 143–44; boxes 1, 3, 4, 5, 6, 7, 8, 9, 10: Memorandum for the Record (E. Rostow), June 9, 1967 (Operation Frontlet); Department of Defense Press Release, June 8, 1967; box 19: JCS to USCINCEUR, June 8, 1967. USNA, Middle East Crisis files, 1967, Chronology, box 7: Tel Aviv to the Secretary of State, June 8, 1967 (Barbour quote). Compensation package described in U.S. Department of State Bulletin 58, no. 1512, June 17, 1968, and 60, no. 1562, June 2, 1969, and U.S. Department of State Daily News Briefing, DPC 2451, December 18, 1980. See also Phil G. Goulding, *Confirm or Deny—Informing the People on National Security* (New York: Harper and Row, 1970), pp. 123–30.

18. USNA, box 16: Diplomatic Activity in Connection with the USS *Liberty* Incident, June 14, 1967. LBJ, Country files, box 104, 107, Middle East Crisis: Eshkol to Johnson; Memos to the President (W. Rostow), June 8, 1967; box 17: Barbour to Department of State, June 8, 1967; box 19: NSC Special Committee Meeting (handwritten notes), June 9, 1967. ISA, 4079/26 Foreign Ministry files, the *Liberty* Incident: Harman to Foreign Ministry, June 10, 1967; Eban to Johnson, June 9, 1967; Evron to Johnson, June 8, 1967. Barbour and Nolte quotes in LBJ, National Security file, box 20: United States Policy and Diplomacy in the Middle East Crisis, May 15–June 10, 1967, pp. 143–44; box 104, 107, Middle East Crisis: Cairo to the Department of State, June 9,

1967. Clark Clifford with Richard Holbrooke, *Counsel to the President* (New York: Random House, 1991), pp. 446–47.

19. ISA, 4079/26 the *Liberty* Incident: Bitan to Harman, June 18, 1967; IDF Preliminary Inquiry file 1/67 Col. Y. Yerushalmi, July 24, 1967. LBJ, National Security file, Country files, box 104, 107: Middle East Crisis: Diplomatic Activity in Connection with the USS *Liberty* Incident, June 14, 1967. Erell, *Lefanekha ha-Yam*, pp. 275–77.

20. USNA, Chairman Wheeler files, box 27: The Court of Inquiry Findings, June 22, 1967. LBJ, National Security file, Special Committee, box 1–10: Why the USS *Liberty* Was Where It Was, June 10, 1967; W. Rostow to the President, June 13, 1967 (Evron quote); NSA Declassified Report: Attack on the U.S.S. *Liberty*, July 11, 1983. Cristol, *Liberty Incident*, pp. 86–105. Rusk, *As I Saw It*, p. 388. The complete protocol of the U.S. Naval Inquiry can be found on the USS *Liberty* website.

21. Conspiracy theories on the *Liberty* affair can be found in Ennes, *Assault on the Liberty*, pp. 254–59. Anthony Pearson, *Conspiracy of Silence: The Attack on the U.S.S. Liberty* (London: Quartet Books, 1978). Donald Neff, *Warriors for Jerusalem: The Six Days That Changed the Middle East* (Brattleboro, Vt.: Amana Books, 1988), p. 253. John Loftus and Mark Aarons, *The Secret War Against the Jews: How Western Espionage Betrayed the Jewish People* (New York: St. Martin's Press, 1997), p. 267. Richard Deacon, *The Israeli Secret Service* (London: Sphere Books, 1979), pp. 192–97. For the Arab interpretation of the affair, see Riad, *Mudhakkirat 1*, p. 312. Heikal, *Al-Infijar*, pp. 731–32. Mazhar, *I'tirafat Qadat Harb Yunyu*, pp. 86–88. El-Farra, *Years of No Decision*, pp. 58–68. Fawzi, *Harb al-Thalath Sanawat*, pp. 135–36. Salah al-Din Al-Ashram, "Al-Tawatu' al-Anklo-Amriki ma'a Isra'il," *Al-Majalla al-'Askariyya* 6, no. 18 (1967). I. P. Beliaev and E.M. Primakov, *Egipet: vremia prezidenta Nasera* (Moscow: Mysl', 1974), p. 50. L. Sheidin, "Imperialisticheskii zagovor na Blizhnem Vostoke," *Kommunist*, no. 11 (July 1967), pp. 107–17.

22. LBJ, National Security file, Country file, box 104, 107: Davis to Rostow, June 8, 1967; NSC Histories, Middle East Crisis, box 21: Report by Bureau of International Organizations Affairs (Arthur Day), n.d. (Goldberg quote); USUN to the Secretary of State, June 8, 1967; CIA to the White House Situation Room, June 8, 1967 ("We have no other choice"); NSC Histories, Middle East Crisis, box 20: Memorandum of Conversation: The Hotline Exchanges, Nov. 4, 1968. USNA, Central Foreign Policy files, 1967–1969, POL 77-14 ARAB-ISR, box 1832: Goldberg to Rusk, June 8, 1967. PRO, FCO 17/494, Israel – Political Affairs: Hayman Minute, June 8, 1967. ISA, 7920/1, Levi Eshkol Papers, Diplomatic Telegrams: Eban to Eshkol, June 8, 1967; 7919/1, Diplomatic Telegrams: U.S.A.: Eban to Eshkol, June 8, 1967 (Goldberg advice to Eban). Lall, *The UN and the Middle East Crisis*, pp. 66–67. Rafael, *Destination Peace*, pp. 160–61. Federenko and Rafael quotes from Dagan, *Moscow and Jerusalem*, p. 232.

23. Mahmud al-Jiyyar, "Rajulan Qatala al-Mushir 'Amer," in *Ruz al-Yusuf* 2482 (January 5, 1976), pp. 8–9. El-Sadat, *In Search of Identity*, pp. 176–77. Riad, *The Struggle for Peace in the Middle East*, pp. 28–30. Cairo Radio broadcasts in IDF, Historical Branch, 192/74/1349: Cease-Fire Orders in the Egyptian, Jordanian, and Syrian Sectors, p. 26. Nasser quote from Ramadan, *Tahtim al-Aliha*, p. 171. Salah Nasser quote in LBJ, National Security file, Middle East Crisis, box 104, 107: Cairo to the Department of State, June 8, 1967.

24. USNA, Central Foreign Policy files, 1967–1969, POL 27-7 ARAB-ISR, box 1830: Department of the Army to the Department of State, June 16, 1967. Muhammad

Ahmad Khamis's testimony appears in Darraz, *Dubbat Yunyu Yatakallamun*, pp. 69–75; Yahya Sa'ad Basha's testimony appears on pp. 49–54. Oral history interview with Fu'ad Hijazi, July 5, 1967. Al-Sabbagh, *Mudhakkirat Qadat al-'Askuruiyya al-Misriyya* 10, p. 11 (Khalil quote). Ramadan, *Tahtim al-Aliha*, pp. 110–11. Interview with Sidqi al-Ghul in *al-Ra'i al-'Am*, June 1, 1987. David Pryce-Jones, *The Closed Circle: An Interpretation of the Arabs* (London: Paladin, 1990), p. 8. Nolte quote in LBJ, National Security file, NSC Histories, Middle East Crisis, box 23: Cairo to the Secretary of State, June 8, 1967.

25. LBJ, National Security file, NSC Histories, Middle East Crisis, box 23: UNUS to the Secretary of State, June 8, 1967. Mahmud Al-Jiyyar, "Rajulan Qatala al-Mushir 'Amer," p. 9. Riad, *The Struggle for Peace in the Middle East*, p. 30. Lall, *The UN and the Middle East Crisis*, pp. 67–72. El Kony quote from oral history interview with Muhammad al-Farra, Nov. 17, 1999; El Kony statement to the Security Council in IDF, Historical Branch, 192/74/1349: Cease-Fire Orders in the Egyptian, Jordanian, and Syrian Sectors, p. 26. Supreme Headquarters communiqué in BBC, Daily Report, Middle East, Africa, and Western Europe, B1.

26. LBJ, National Security file, NSC Histories, Middle East Crisis, box 23: Tel Aviv to the Secretary of State, June 8, 1967 (Chuvakhin quote). Baron, *Hotam Ishi*, pp. 83–85. Hame'iri, *Mi-Shnei Evrei ha-Rama*, pp. 25–26. Gilboa, *Shesh Shanim, Shisha Yamim*, p. 235. Bartov, *Dado*, p. 101. Dayan, *My Life*, pp. 364–67. Rabin, *Memoirs*, p. 113. Hammel, *Six Days in June*, p. 278. Dupuy, *Elusive Victory*, p. 277. Mayzel, *Ha-Ma'arakha al ha-Golan*, pp. 258 (Eshkol "bulldog" quote), 264–65. Dayan quotes from Baron, *Hotam Ishi*, pp. 85–86, and Hame'iri, *Mi-Shnei Evrei ha-Rama*, pp. 30–31. Haber, *Ha-Yom Tifrotz Milhama*, pp. 244 (Chuvakhin quote), 240–50. Protocol of the Ministerial Defense Committee appears in Warhaftig, *Hamishim Shana ve-Shana*, pp. 189–91.

27. Baron, *Hotam Ishi*, pp. 86–87. Bartov, *Dado*, p. 101. Hame'iri, *Mi-Shnei Evrei ha-Rama*, pp. 27, 54, 98.

Day Five, June 9

1. Dayan, *My Life*, p. 382. Rabin, *Memoirs*, p. 116. Warhaftig, *Hamishim Shana ve-Shana*, p. 200. Bartov, *Dado*, pp. 101–2. Mayzel, *Ha-Ma'arakha al ha-Golan-Yuni*, pp. 230–32. YAD, interview with Ephraim Reiner, June 20, 1996. Baron, *Hotam Ishi*, pp. 76–77, 80 (Dayan quote).

2. Bartov, *Dado*, p. 103. Nasser cable and Dayan's notes on it, in Baron, *Hotam Ishi*, pp. 87–88 and in Haber, *Ha-Yom Tifrotz Milhama*, pp. 252–53. Halahmi and Yariv quotes from Amos Gilboa, "Milhemet Sheshet Ha-Yamim 30 Shana," *Ma'ariv*, June 6, 1997. Oral history interview with Miriam Eshkol, Aug. 30, 1999. Radio Damascus quote in Hame'iri, *Mi-Shnei Evrei ha-Rama*, p. 33. Rabin quote from *Memoirs*, pp. 115–16.

3. Dayan-Elazar dialogue in Bartov, *Dado*, p. 103 and in Baron, *Hotam Ishi*, pp. 90–91. Mayzel, *Ha-Ma'arakha al ha-Golan*, pp. 232–33, 255–57, 272–74. Oral history interview with Miriam Eshkol, Aug. 30, 1999. Lior and Eshkol quotes in Haber, *Ha-Yom Tifrotz Milhama*, pp. 250–51. ISA, 4086/6, Foreign Ministry files, Security Council Meetings: Rafael to Tekoah, June 9, 1967. Rabin quote from *Memoirs*, pp. 115–16.

4. IDF Intelligence Library, Internal Syrian Army Papers: The Southwestern Front, June 29, 1967. Mustafa, *Harb Haziran*, pp. 248–50. Khalil, *Suqut al-Julan*, pp. 189–90. Mayzel, *Ha-Ma'arakha al ha-Golan*, pp. 145–46. O'Balance, *The Third Arab-Israeli War*,

pp. 232–33. Or Kashti, "Mesima Bilti Efsharit," *Bamachane* 37 (May 1992). Hame'iri, *Mi-Shnei Evrei ha-Rama*, pp. 20–25; Suweidani quote on p. 100.

5. IDF 522/69, file 212: Special Operations Survey, p. 9. PRO, FCO17/576: Israel – Defense: Report of Defense Attaché, July 13, 1967. Aharon Meged, "Sh'ot ha-Tofet shel Tel Fakhr," *Bamahane 31–32* (April 1967). Mayzel, *Ha-Ma'arakha al ha-Golan*, pp. 295–306; Horowitz quotes on pp. 391–94. Hammel, *Six Days in June*, pp. 413–14. Dupuy, *Elusive Victory*, pp. 322–23. O'Balance, *The Third Arab-Israeli War*, pp. 438–41. Dayan, *Me-Hermon ad Suez*, pp. 21–29. Yosef Eshkol, ed., *Milhemet Sheshet ha-Yamim* (Tel Aviv: Misrad ha-Bitahon, 1967), p. 104. Hareuveni and Arye, eds., *Ha-Hativa Shelanu be-Milhemet Sheshet ha-Yamim*, pp. 60–65. Harel, *El Mul Golan*, pp. 117–20. Ya'akov Horesh, *47 Madregot* (Tel Aviv: Yaron Golan, 1993), p. 16. Mendler quotes in Hame'iri, *Mi-Shnei Evrei ha-Rama*, pp. 18, 21. Golan, *Albert*, pp. 121–29. Oral history interview with Elad Peled, Jan. 28, 2001.

6. IDF Intelligence Library, Internal Syrian Army Papers: The Southwestern Front, June 29, 1967 (including Khalili quote). Mayzel, *Ha-Ma'arakha al ha-Golan*, pp. 283–86, 307–19. Eshkol, *Milhemet Sheshet ha-Yamim*, p. 106. Harel, *El Mul Golan*, pp. 121–26. Mustafa, *Harb Haziran*, pp. 208–20. Hani al-Shum'a, *Ma'arik Khalida fi Ta'rikh al-Jaysh al-'Arabi al-Suri* (Damascus: Al-Tiba'a al-Suriyya, 1988), pp. 63–74. Hammel, *Six Days in June*, pp. 399, 406–13. O'Balance, *The Third Arab-Israeli War*, pp. 240–42. Shmuel Katz and Aharon Megged, *Me-Har Grizim ad Har Hermon: Rishumei Pikud ha-Tzafon be-Milhemet Sheshet ha-Yamim* (Tel Aviv: Misrad ha-Bitahon, 1967), pp. 56–58. Khalil, *Suqut al-Julan*, pp. 197–204. M. Naor and Z. Aner, eds., *Yemei Yuni-Teurim min ha-Milhama 1967* (Tel Aviv: Ma'arakhot, 1967), pp. 240–41. Dangor quote from Hareuveni and Arye, *Ha-Hativa Shelanu be-Milhemet Sheshet ha-Yamim*, pp. 67–68. Dayan, *Me-Hermon ad Suez*, pp. 228–29 (Ben Basat quote), 240 (Ben Harush quote). Hame'iri, *Mi-Shnei Evrei ha-Rama*, pp. 116–19, 125–28, 133 (Mendler quote), 138–40 (Takum and Haliq quotes), 143 (Hamawi quote).

7. Mansoor, *Arab World*, entry for June 9, 1967. Mayzel, *Ha-Ma'arakha al ha-Golan*, p. 147. Rabin, *Memoirs*, p. 117. Assad quote from Hame'iri, *Mi-Shnei Evrei ha-Rama*, p. 181.

8. USNA, Central Foreign Policy files, 1967–1969, POL 27-7 ARAB-ISR, box 1830: Cairo to the Department of State, Aug. 12, 1967. PRO, FCO 39/241, UAR – Political Affairs: Cairo to Foreign Office, July 25, 1967. LBJ, National Security file, Memos to the President (W. Rostow), box 17: W. Rostow to the President, June 17, 1967; Cairo to the Secretary of State, June 8, 1967. Dayan, *My Life*, p. 365. Schiff, *A History of the Israeli Army*, p. 113. Lufti Al-Khuli, *Harb Yunyu 1967 ba'da 30 Sana* (Cairo: Markaz Al-Ahram, 1997), pp. 109–11. Ramadan, *Tahtim al-Aliha*, pp. 144–45. Fawzi, *Harb al-Thalath Sanawat*, p. 193. Riad, *Mudhakkirat Mahmud Riad*, p. 83. Al-'Ilmi, *Harb 'Am 1967*, p. 161. El-Sadat, *In Search of Identity*, p. 184. Mahjoub, *Democracy on Trial*, pp. 115–16 (Nasser quote), pp. 120–21. Oral history interview with Eric Rouleau, Dec. 18, 2000. On the Soviet resupply of Egypt, see Valerii Yeryomenko, "Imenno Sovyetski Soyuz spas arabskuyu koalitziyu vo vremya Shestidnevnoi voiny," *Nezavisimoe Veonnoe Obozrenie*, no. 20 (1998).

9. LBJ, National Security file, History of the Middle East Crisis, box 21: CIA Intelligence Memorandm, Arab-Israeli Situation Report, June 9, 1967. PRO FCO/39/263 UAR – Relations with the USSR: Effects of the Arab-Israeli War on the UAR Economy, Dec. 1, 1967. Shamir, "Nasser and Sadat, 1967–1973," in Rabinovich and

Shaked, eds., *From June to October*, p. 203. Riad, *The Struggle for Peace in the Middle East*, p. 40. Farid, *Nasser*, p. 76. Al-Sabbagh, ed., *Mudhakkirat Qadat al-'Askaraiyya ul-Misriyya 12*, pp. 56–57 (Nasser conversation with Madkur Abu al-'Izz). Vatikiotis, *Nasser and His Generation*, p. 315. Heikal, *Al-Infijar*, pp. 822, 840–46; Nasser remarks to 'Amer on pp. 835 and 840–41.

10. LBJ, National Security file, History of the Middle East Crisis, box 21: CIA Intelligence Memorandum, Arab-Israeli Situation Report, June 9, 1967; box 23: Amman to the Secretary of State, June 10, 1967. USNA, USUN, box 6: Circular: Middle East Sitrep as of June 9; USNA, Central Policy files, 1967–1969, POL 7 UAR, box 2554: Athens to the Department of State, June 16, 1967. Riad, *The Struggle for Peace in the Middle East*, p. 31. El-Sadat, *In Search of Identity*, p. 179. Stephens, *Nasser*, p. 506. Hussein quote from Kamm, *Hussein Poteah be-Milhama*, pp. 299–300. Nasser's communiqué in Mansoor, *Arab World*, entry for June 9, 1967. FCO 39/233 UAR Internal Political Situation: Cairo to the Foreign Office, June 19, 1967 (Tesh). BGA, Diary, Entry for June 9, 1967. Thompson quote from *Life: Special Edition – Israel's Swift Victory* (1967), p. 71. Oral history interview with Eric Rouleau, Dec. 18, 2000. Cairo Radio announcement in Daily Report, Middle East, Africa, and Western Europe, B1. Nasser speech from *Watha'iq 'Abd al-Nasir 1* (Cairo: Markaz al-Ahram, 1973), p. 226, and Dan Hofstadter, ed., *Egypt and Nasser 3, 1967–72* (New York: Facts on File, 1973), pp. 40–42.

11. LBJ, National Security file, NSC Histories, Middle East Crisis, box 21: Chronology of the Soviet Delay on the Security Council Meetings (J. Baker), June 26, 1967 (Federenko quote); Memorandum for Mr. W.W. Rostow (Davis), June 9, 1967; Tel Aviv to the Secretary of State, June 8, 1967 (Barbour quote). ISA, 4086/6, Foreign Ministry files, Security Council Meetings: Rafael to Tekoah, June 9, 1967. PRO FO17/ 495: Israel Political Affairs: Tel Aviv to Foreign Office, June 9, 1967. UN, DAG 1/5.2.2.1.2-2, Middle East: Rafael to the Secretary-General, June 9, 1967; Tomeh to the Secretary-General, June 9, 1967. Rafael, *Destination Peace*, p. 163 (Rafael quote to Nesterenko). Lall, *The UN and the Middle East Crisis*, pp. 77–78 (Rafael quote in the Security Council). Mansoor, *Arab World*, entry for June 9, 1967 (Tomeh and Rafael quotes).

12. USNA, POL ARAB-ISR, Tel Aviv file, box 6: Tel Aviv to the Secretary of State, June 10, 1967. LBJ, National Security file, History of the Middle East Conflict, box 20: United States Policy and Diplomacy in the Middle East Crisis, May 15–June 10, 1967, pp. 145–46 (Rusk cable), pp. 148–52; box 19: NSC Special Committee Meeting (handwritten notes), June 9, 1967; NSC Histories, Middle East Crisis, box 23: Secretary of State to Tel Aviv, June 9, 1967 (Rusk quote); box 17: The President in the Middle East Crisis, Dec. 19, 1968. ISA, 7919/1, Levi Eshkol files, Diplomatic Telegrams: U.S.A.: Harman to Eshkol, June 9, 1967.

13. Baron, *Hotam Ishi*, pp. 94–95. Haber, *Ha-Yom Tifrotz Milhama*, pp. 253–56. BGA, Diary, Entries for June 9 and 11, 1967. Mayzel, *Ha-Ma'arakha al ha-Golan*, pp. 317–18. All quotes from Warhaftig, *Hamishim Shana ve-Shana*, pp. 196–99.

14. Bartov, *Dado*, pp. 104–5. Baron, *Hotam Ishi*, p. 96. Hareuveni and Arye, *Ha-Hativa Shelanu be-Milhemet Sheshet ha-Yamim*, p. 60. Naor and Aner, *Yemei Yuni*, p. 239. Elazar quote from Rabin, *Memoirs*, pp. 116–17, and from Arye Yitzhaki, "Ha-Ma'arakha le-Kibush ha-Golan be-Milhemet Sheshet ha-Yamim," *Ariel*, no. 50–51 (1987). IDF Intelligence Library, Internal Syrian Army Papers: The Southwestern Front, June 29, 1967. Mayzel, *Ha-Ma'arakha al ha-Golan*, pp. 147, 293. Hammel, *Six Days in June*, p. 423. Eshkol and Dayan quotes from Haber, *Ha-Yom Tifrotz Milhama*, pp. 255–56. Assad quote from Hame'iri, *Mi-Shnei Evrei ha-Rama*, p. 123.

Day Six, *June 10*

1. Hame'iri, *Mi-Shnei Evrei ha-Rama*, pp. 168–70, 179 (Rabin-Elazar conversation), 180 (Elazar order to his officers). Bartov, *Dado*, p. 105. Mayzel, *Ha-Ma'arakha al ha-Golan*, pp. 331–32; Finkelstein quote on pp. 407–8. Hammel, *Six Days in June*, pp. 417–18.

2. Dayan, *Me-Hermon ad Suez*, pp. 254–57. Mayzel, *Ha-Ma'arakha al ha-Golan*, p. 286. Hammel, *Six Days in June*, pp. 417–18. Rabin, *Memoirs*, pp. 117–18. Mendler quote from Gilboa, *Shesh Shanim, Shisha Yamim*, p. 242. Eshkol, ed., *Milhemet Sheshet ha-Yamim*, p. 108. Radio Damascus quote from Hame'iri, *Mi-Shnei Evrei ha-Rama*, p. 214.

3. USNA Central Foreign Policy files, 1967–1969, POL 12 SY, box 2511: Goldberg to Rusk, June 10, 1967. Hame'iri, *Mi-Shnei Evrei ha-Rama*, p. 190. Mustafa, *Harb Haziran*, pp. 229–32.

4. LBJ, National Security file, NSC Histories, Middle East Crisis, box 21: Chronology of the Soviet Delay on the Security Council Meetings (J. Baker), June 26, 1967; Report by Bureau of International Organizations Affairs (Arthur Day), n.d. ISA, 4086/6, Foreign Ministry files, Security Council Meetings: Rafael to Eban, June 10, 1967; Rafael to Tekoah, June 10, 1967. UN, DAG 13/3.4.0: 83 Chief of Staff, UNTSO to Chairman, ISMAC, June 10, 1967; Mission and Commissions: Chron-9/06 to 24/06, June 10, 1967. Rafael, *Destination Peace*, pp. 163–64. Bull, *War and Peace in the Middle East*, p. 120. Dagan, *Moscow and Jerusalem*, p. 232. Lall, *The UN and the Middle East Crisis*, pp. 77–94 (includes Federenko quote).

5. LBJ, National Security file, Middle East Crisis: Soviet Official's Comments on Soviet Policy on the Middle Eastern War, June 8, 1967; box 19: State Department Activities Report, June 9, 1967. N.S. Khrushchev, *Vospominaniya 3: Vremia. Lyudi. Vlast'*, pp. 461–62. Schevchenko, *Breaking with Moscow*, p. 135.

6. LBJ National Security file, Middle East Crisis: Soviet Role in the Middle East Crisis, June 14, 1967; box 23: USUN to the Secretary of State, June 8, 1967. USNA, POL ARAB-IS, Chronology, box 8: Ankara to the Secretary of State, June 8, 1967; box 9: Moscow to the Secretary of State, June 6, 1967. ISA, 4048/27, Foreign Ministry files, Diplomatic Relations with the Soviet Union: Bonn to Foreign Ministry, June 8, 1967; 4079/11, Foreign Ministry files, Contacts with the United States with the Entry of Egyptian Forces into Tiran: Foreign Ministry to Embassies, June 8, 1967. PRO, FO17/496: Israel – Political Affairs: NATO Intelligence Assessment, June 10, 1967; PREM 13 1622: The Soviet Role in the Middle East Crisis, July 20, 1967 ("bad six weeks"). Dagan, *Moscow and Jerusalem*, pp. 234–35. I. L. Blishchenko and V. D. Kudriavtsev, *Agressia Izrailia i Mezhdunarodnoie Pravo* (Moscow: Mezhdunorodnyie Otnosheniya, 1970) p. 11. Vassiliev, *Russian Policy in the Middle East*, p. 70 (Soviet official quote). Rumors of Soviet intervention in Isabella Ginor, "The Russians Were Coming: The Soviet Military Threat in the 1967 Six-Day War," *Middle East Review of International Affairs* 4, no. 4 (Dec. 2000). A. Khaldeev, "Nesostoiavshiisia desant," *Vesti* (Israel), Sept. 14, 2000.

7. LBJ, National Security file, History of the Middle East Crisis, box 19: Memorandum for the Record, Washington-Moscow "Hot-line" Exchange, Oct. 22, 1968; Kosygin to Johnson, June 10, 1967 (10:00 A.M.); Johnson to Kosygin (10:58 A.M.); Movements of Sixth Fleet, June 10, 1967; NSC Histories, Middle East Crisis, box 20: Memorandum of Conversation: The Hotline Exchanges, Nov. 4, 1968 (Thompson quote).

Sedov quote in USNA, Middle East Crisis, Miscellaneous Reports, box 15: Garthoff to Kohler, June 10, 1967. PRO, PREM 13 1620, Middle East Crisis: Moscow to the Foreign Office, Text of Communiqué from the Representatives of Ten Socialist Countries, June 10, 1967. Dobrynin, *In Confidence*, p. 160. Vassiliev, *Russian Policy in the Middle East*, p. 69. Quandt, *Peace Process*, p. 52. P. Demchenko, *Arabskii Vostok v chas ispytanii* (Moscow: Politicheskaia Literarura, 1967), pp. 118–19. LBJ, Richard Helms Oral History; Llewellyn Thompson Oral History. Oral history interview with Robert McNamara, Feb. 11, 2000.

8. LBJ, National Security file, History of the Middle East Conflict, United States Policy and Diplomacy in the Middle East Crisis, May 15–June 10, 1967, pp. 147–49; NSC Histories, Middle East Crisis, box 23: Tel Aviv to the Secretary of State, June 10, 1967; Washington to Tel Aviv, June 10, 1967 (Eban and Barbour quotes). USNA, Central Foreign Policy files, 1967–1969, POL 77-14 ARAB-ISR, box 1832: Department of State to Tel Aviv, June 10, 1967. ISA, 4078, Foreign Ministry files, Contacts with the United States with the Entry of Egyptian Forces into Tiran: Rafael to Eban, June 10, 1967; 7919/1, Levi Eshkol files, Diplomatic Telegrams: U.S.A.: Harman to Eban, June 10, 1967; Evron to Eban, June 10, 1967. Rabin, *Memoirs*, pp. 116–17. Parker, *The Six Day War*, p. 233. Baron, *Hotam Ishi*, p. 97. Goldberg quote in Rafael, *Destination Peace*, pp. 164–65. I. I. Mintz., *Sionizm: Teoria I Praktika* (Moscow: Izdetelstvo Politicheskoy Literatury, 1970), pp. 111–12.

9. ISA, 4083/3, Foreign Ministry files, Contacts with the Soviet Union: Katz to Foreign Ministry, June 10, 1967; 7920/2, Levi Eshkol Papers, Diplomatic Telegrams, USSR: Katz to the Prime Minister, June 10, 1967. LBJ, National Security file, NSC Histories, Middle East Crisis, box 23: Washinton to Tel Aviv, June 9, 1967. Mintz, *Sionizm*, p. 113. Dagan, *Moscow and Jerusalem*, p. 232. Parker, *The Six Day War*, p. 230. Mintz, *Sionizm*, p. 113. Chuvakhin quote from Eban, *Personal Witness*, pp. 425–26. See also Eban, *Diplomacy for the Next Century*, pp. 101–2.

10. Hame'iri, *Mi-Shnei Evrei ha-Rama*, pp. 187–88 (text of meeting with Eshkol, Dayan, and Elazar), 204–5. Bartov, *Dado*, p. 106. Warhaftig, *Hamishim Shana ve-Shana*, pp. 191–92, 200. Baron, *Hotam Ishi*, pp. 97–98. Mayzel, *Ha-Ma'arakha al ha-Golan*, pp. 332–33, 342–43. Rabin, *Memoirs*, pp. 117–18. Amos Gilboa, "Milhemet Sheshet Ha-Yamim 30 Shana," *Ma'ariv*, June 6, 1997. Ze'evi quote from Shashar, *Sihot im Rehavam–Gandhi–Ze'evi*, p. 166.

11. USNA, Central Foreign Policy files, 1967–1969, POL Arab-Jordan, box 1844: Amman to the Department of State, June 10, 1967. PRO FCO17/576: Israel – Report of Defense Attaché, July 13, 1967. Rabin, *Memoirs*, p. 118. Mayzel, *Ha-Ma'arakha al ha-Golan*, pp. 81, 335, 338–39. Ezra Sadeh, *Amud Ha-Esh: Yoman ha-Milhama shel Yirmi* (Tel Aviv: Yosef Shimoni, n.d.), pp. 203–4. Oral history interviews with Ibrahim Isma'il Khahya and Muhammad 'Amer, Jan. 10, 2001; with Marwan Hamdan al-Khuli, Jan. 11, 2000. Suweidani quote from Hame'iri, *Mi-Shnei Evrei ha-Rama*, p. 212. Mustafa Tlas, *Mir'at Hayati* (Damascus: Tlasdar, 1995), p. 857. Darwish and Hassan quotes from Saqr Abu Fakhr, "Al-Julan: Shahadat Nazihin 'an Ayyam al-Harb wal-Hadir," *Majallat al-Dirasat al-Filastiniyya* 42 (Spring 2000) pp. 135–39.

12. Eshkol, *Milhemet Sheshet ha-Yamim*, pp. 108–9. Hammel, *Six Days in June*, pp. 419–20. Harel, *El Mul Golan*, p. 130. PREM 13 1620, Middle East Crisis: New York to Foreign Office, June 10, 1967. Mayzel, *Ha-Ma'arakha al ha-Golan*, pp. 418–20. Hame'iri, *Mi-Shnei Evrei ha-Rama*, pp. 165–67. Allon quote from YAD, Remarks by Ephraim Reiner June 20, 1996.

13. Bartov, *Dado*, pp. 107–9. Baron, *Hotam Ishi*, p. 98. Mayzel, *Ha-Ma'arakha al ha-Golan*, pp. 109–14, 359. Ma'oz, *Syria and Israel*, pp. 101–2. Schiff, *A History of the Israeli Army*, p. 141. Golan, *Albert*, pp. 134–35. Inbar quote from Ran Bin-Nun, *Krav ha-Havka'a shel Hativat 'Golani' be-Milhemet Sheshet ha-Yamim*, unpublished thesis, Kedourie School, Feb. 1988, p. 12.

14. UN, DAG 13/3.4.0.:83: Mission and Commissions: Chron-9/06 to 24/06, O'Hora to the Chief of Staff, June 10, 1967. ISA, 4086/6, Foreign Ministry files, Security Council Meetings: Sasson to Washington, June 10, 1967. Baron, *Hotam Ishi*, pp. 98–99. Hame'iri, *Mi-Shnei Evrei ha-Rama*, p. 187. Mayzel, *Ha-Ma'arakha al ha-Golan*, p. 342.

15. Hame'iri, *Mi-Shnei Evrei ha-Rama*, p. 187. YAD, Interview with Ephraim Reiner, June 20, 1996; with Elad Peled, June 20, 1967. Hofi quote from Bartov, *Dado*, p. 108. Mayzel, *Ha-Ma'arakha al ha-Golan*, pp. 343–44, 354–57. Oral history interview with Yitzhak Hofi, July 14, 1999.

16. ISA, 4086/6, Foreign Ministry files, Security Council Meetings: New York to Foreign Ministry, June 10, 1967. USNA, Middle East Crisis files, 1967, Chronology, box 7: Tel Aviv to the Secretary of State, June 10, 1967. PRO, PREM 13 1620, Middle East Crisis: New York to Foreign Office, June 11, 1967. LBJ, National Security file, History of the Middle East Conflict, box 20: United States Policy and Diplomacy in the Middle East Crisis, May 15–June 10, 1967, p. 152 (Barbour quote); NSC Histories, Middle East Crisis, box 21: Report by Bureau of International Organizations Affairs (Arthur Day), n.d. (Goldberg quote); box 19: Kosgyin to Johnson, June 10, 1967; Johnson to Kosygin, June 10, 1967. Rabin, *Memoirs*, p. 118. Baron, *Dado*, pp. 101–2.

Aftershocks

1. USNA, Middle East Crisis files, box 4: Circular to all American Diplomatic Posts, June 12, 1967. Hammel, *Six Days in June*, p. 383. Schiff, *A History of the Israeli Army*, pp. 135, 141. Mutawi, *Jordan in the 1967 War*, p. 164. Mustafa, *Harb Haziran*, pp. 242–44. Fawzi, *Harb al-Thalath Sanawat*, pp. 160–61. Donovan, *Six Days in June*, p. 123. Mayzel, *Ha-Ma'arakha al ha-Golan*, p. 425. Adnan Abu Oudeh, *Jordanians, Palestinians, and the Hashemite Kingdom in the Middle East Peace Process* (Washington, D.C.: United States Institute of Peace, 1998), p. 137.

2. USNA, USUN, box 6: Circular to All American Diplomatic Posts, June 10, 1967; POL 27-7 ARAB-ISR, box 1830: Cairo to the Secretary of State, Aug. 31, 1967. LBJ, National Security file, History of the Middle East Crisis, box 21: CIA Intelligence Memorandum, Arab-Israeli Situation Report, June 11, 1967. PRO, FCO17/ 577: Report of Air Attaché, Aug. 8, 1967. ISA, 4086/8, Foreign Ministry files, Red Cross: Foreign Ministry Circular, June 7, 1967; 4089/3, Foreign Ministry files, Report on the Gossing Visit, July 26, 1967. Schiff, *A History of the Israeli Army*, p. 135. Mayzel, *Ha-Ma'arakha al ha-Golan*, p. 425. Mutawi, *Jordan in the 1967 War*, p. 164. Kimche, *The Sandstorm*, p. 237. Shashar, *Milhemet ha-Yom ha-Shvi'i*, p. 45.

3. USNA, Central Foreign Policy files, 1967–1969, POL 27-7 ARAB-ISR, box 1830: Amman to the Secretary of State, June 30, 1967. ISA, Foreign Ministry files, 4089/2, Refugees: Jerusalem to Embassies, June 23, 1967; Comay to Bitan, July 3, 1967. PRO, FCO17/577: Israel – Defense: Report of Defense Attaché, Oct. 9, 1967; PREM 13 1623: Record of Meeting, The Foreign Secretary and the Israeli Ambassador, July 30, 1967. Shashar, *Milhemet ha-Yom ha-Shvi'i*, pp. 24, 66–67, 76–77, 105, 165,

212. Gazit, *Pta'im be-Malkodet*, pp. 29, 36–39, 48–49. Mayzel, *Ha-Ma'arakha al ha-Golan*, p. 82. Susser, *On Both Banks of the Jordan*, p. 25. Abu Murshid, Butrus, and Jabber, *Silsilat al-Kitab al-Sanawi lil-Qadiyya al-Filastiniyya*, pp. 509–10, 532, 540–41, Yosef Levita, "Ma Ya'ase Zahal ha-Shalal," *Bamahane* 48 (August, 1967). IDF order in Mayzel, *Ha-Ma'arakha al ha-Golan*, p. 364; see also pp. 433–35.

4. LBJ, National Security file, Memos to the President, box 22: Wine to E. Rostow, Aug. 16, 1967. USNA, Central Foreign Policy files, 1967–1969, POL 27-7 ARAB-ISR, box 1830: The Hague to the Secretary of State, July 7, 1967; POL 12 SY, box 2511: Beirut to the Secretary of State, Sept. 6, 1967. ISA, Foreign Ministry file 4091/7: Speeches and Decisions (Comay): Foreign Ministry to Washington, June 16, 1967; 4085/1: Emergency Situation 1967 – Prisoners: Geneva to Tekoah, June 13, 1967. PRO, FCO17/531 Israel – Political Affairs (External): Condition of the Jews of the Arab States in the Light of the Six-Day War, Sept. 27, 1967.

5. USNA, Central Foreign Policy files, 1967–1969, POL 27-7 ARAB-ISR, box 1830: Jerusalem to the Secretary of State, June 13, 1967; Jerusalem to the Secretary of State, June 23, 1967; Jerusalem to the Secretary of State, Aug. 30, 1967. Abu Murshid, Butrus, Jabber, *Silsilat al-Kitab al-Sanawi lil-Qadiyya al-Filastiniyya*, pp. 525, 531. Shashar, *Milhemet ha-Yom ha-Shvi'i*, pp. 66–69, 131–32, 148. Dayan, *My Life*, pp. 393, 403. Susser, *On Both Banks of the Jordan*, pp. 24–26, 36.

6. LBJ, National Security Council file, History of the Middle East Crisis, box 18: McPherson to the President, June 11, 1967. Eban quote in *Ha'aretz*, June 11, 1967; "victory cake" recipe in June 12, 1967. Slater, *Rabin of Israel*, p. 148. PRO, PREM 13 1622: The Second Arab-Israel War (Hadow), July 6, 1967. Avraham Shapira, ed., *The Seventh Day*, pp. 100, 124–25. Lyrics to "Song of Peace" by Yankele Rotblitt; translation by Michael Oren.

7. Haber, *Ha-Yom Tifrotz Milhama*, p. 256 (Bar-Lev quote). Fuad Ajami, *The Arab Predicament: Arab Political Thought and Practice Since 1967* (Cambridge: Cambridge University Press, 1981), pp. 12 (Middle East historian's quote), 25–40, 50–62. Ramadan, *Tahtim al-Aliha*, p. 88. Hussein, *My "War" with Israel*, p. 97. Riad, *Mudhakkirat 2*, pp. 310–12. Al-Khuli, *Harb Yunyu 1967*, pp. 50–66, 81–101. Gawrych, *The Albatross of Decisive Victory*, pp. 84–88. USNA Central Foreign Policy files, 1967–1969, POL Arab-Jordan, box 1844: Beirut to the Secretary of State, June 10, 1967 (reference to Assad). Suweidani and Makhous quotes in Khalil, *Shukut al-Julan*, pp. 190–92. Assad quote in Hani al-Shum'a, *Ma'arik Khalida fi Ta'rikh al-Jaysh al-'Arabi al-Suri*, p. 35.

8. Hadidi quote in Al-Sabbagh, *Mudhakkirat Qadat al-'Askaraiyya al-Misriyya 3*, p. 17. Fawzi quote in Ramadan, *Tahtim al-Aliha*, p. 109. Al-Sabbagh, *Mudhakkirat Qadat al-'Askaraiyya al-Misriyya 4*, p. 32 (Sadiq quote). Mazhar, *I'tirafat Qadat Harb Yunyu*, pp. 157–58 (Sidqi Mahmud quote), 193–95. Muhieddin quote from LBJ National Security file, Memos to the President, box 20: CIA Intelligence Cable: Egypt, July 31, 1967. Imam, *'Ali Sabri Yatadhakkar*, pp. 89–90. Badran, *Al-Hawadith*, Sept. 2, 1977, p. 19.

9. PRO, PREM 13 1622: The Second Arab-Israel War (Hadow), July 6, 1967. Moshe Dayan, "Before and After the Battle," pp. 11–18. Dayan, *My Life*, pp. 382–83. For further explanations of Israel's victory, see IDF, 717/77, file 86: Battle for the Southern Front, General Tal on the Lessons of War, pp. 113–16.

10. LBJ, National Security file, NSC Histories, Middle East Crisis, box 17: The President in the Middle East Crisis, Dec. 19, 1968; box 21: Memos to the President:

CIA Intelligence Cable, July 11, 1967. PRO, FCO 27/1 Arab-Israel Dispute—Peace Negotiations: The Middle East Situation, Aug. 14, 1967. ISA, 4078/7, Foreign Ministry files, Contacts with the United States with the Entry of Egyptian Forces into Tiran: Eban to Harman and Rafael, June 12, 1967 (Eban quote); Eban to Harman and Rafael, June 26, 1967 ("Constructive deadlock"). Rafael, *Destination Peace*, p. 177. Gazit, *Pta'im be-Malkodet 32*, pp. 136–37. Pedatzur, "Coming Back Full Circle." Mayzel, *Ha-Ma'arakha al ha-Golan*, pp. 381–83. Rabin quote from Beni Michelson, Avraham Zohar, and Effi Meltzer, eds., *Ha-Ma'avak le-Bithon Yisrael* (Tel Aviv: Ha-Amuta ha-Yisraelit le-Historia Tzva'it leyad Universitat Tel Aviv, 2000), pp. 150–51. Eban quote from ISA, 4078/7, Foreign Ministry files, Contacts with the United States with the Entry of Egyptian Forces into Tiran: Eban Conversation with Goldberg, July 18, 1967.

11. BGA, Diary: Entry for June 11, 1967. Bartov, *Dado*, pp. 112–13. Gazit, *Pta'im be-Malkodet*, pp. 144–46. Shashar, *Milhemet ha-Yom ha-Shvi'i*, p. 175. Profiles of Yigal Allon, Menachem Begin, David Elazar, Ezer Weizman, and Ariel Sharon can be found at www.us-israel.org/jsource/biography. Allon and Begin quotes from www.research.haifa.ac.il/~eshkol/peace.

12. PRO, FCO 17/507: Israel – Political Affairs (External): Tel Aviv to the Foreign Office, July 27, 1967; FCO 17/506: Tel Aviv to the Foreign Office, Sept. 13, 1967. Dayan quotes from Mayzel, *Ha-Ma'arakha al ha-Golan*, pp. 381–82, and Gazit, *Pta'im be-Malkodet*, p. 141.

13. ISA, 4078/5, Foreign Ministry files, Contacts with the United States After the Six-Day War, North America Desk to Eban, June 26, 1967. Oral history interview with David Kimche, Aug. 26, 1999. Sadia Touval, *The Peace-Brokers: Mediators in the Arab-Israeli Conflict, 1948–1979* (Princeton: Princeton University Press, 1982) pp. 134–53. See also article by Moshe Sasson at www.research.haifa.ac.il/~eshkol/peace. Susser, *On Both Banks of the Jordan*, p. 37.

14. LBJ, National Security Council file, History of the Middle East Crisis, box 18: McPherson to the President, June 11, 1967. PRO, PREM 13 1623: Tel Aviv to Foreign Office, Oct. 16, 1967. Eshkol quotes from FRUS, XX, *Arab-Israeli Dispute, 1967–1968* (Washington, D.C.: United States Government Printing Office, 2001), pp. 80, 82, 83, 87. *Ha'aretz*, Feb. 27, 1967. *Ma'ariv*, Feb. 27, 1967. Oral history interview with Miriam Eshkol, Aug. 30, 1999. Arab reactions to Eshkol's death, including Arafat quote, from Moshe Dayan Center Library, Tel Aviv University, Ramat Aviv, Israel (translations of Arabic press).

15. Egyptian broadcasts in BBC, Daily Report, Middle East, Africa, and Western Europe, B 2 and 137. USNA Central Foreign Policy files, 1967–1969, POL Arab-Jordan, box 1844: Beirut to the Secretary of State, June 19, 1967; Beirut to the Secretary of State, July 30, 1967; USUN, box 6: USUN to the Secretary of State, June 27, 1967; Middle East Crisis files, 1967, box 1: Amman to the Secretary of State, June 10, 1967 (Nuseibeh quote). Feisal quote in PRO, PREM 13 1622: Jedda to Foreign Office, June 26, 1967. Nasser quote from Riad, *Mudhakkirat 2*, pp. 80–81.

16. Farid, *Nasser*, pp. 4–5, 11 (Podgorny quote), 24–47 (including Brezhnev quote). Heikal, *Al-Infijar*, pp. 777–91 (including Nasser quote "any concession . . ."). Fawzi, *Harb al-Thalath Sanawat*, pp. 193–97. Riad, *The Struggle for Peace in the Middle East*, pp. 42–50; *Muthakkirat 2*, pp. 84–85, 97–98 (Nasser 's "That which was taken by war" and "double defeat" quotes), pp. 110–15. Raphael Israeli, *Man of Defiance: A Political Biography of Anwar Sadat* (Totowa, N.J.: Barnes and Noble, 1985), p. 42. PRO, FCO 39/

233 UAR Internal Political Situation: Canadian Embassy, Cairo, to the Foreign Office, June 22, 1967. LBJ, National Security file, Memos to the President (W. Rostow), box 19: Goodpaster Memorandum for the Record, July 12, 1967. ISA, 40/8/5, Foreign Ministry files, U.S. – Borders: Lourie to Foreign Ministry, June 22, 1967.

17 Heikal, *Al-Infijar*, pp. 896–97 (all Nasser quotes). Fawzi, *Harb al-Thalath Sanawat*, pp. 199–201. Riad, *Mudhakkirat 2*, pp. 97–98; Riad, *The Struggle for Peace in the Middle East*, pp. 48–49. PRO, FCO 39/250 Middle East Crisis: UAR Attitude, July 10, 1967. LBJ National Security file, Memos to the President, box 19: Extracts from a Cable from Ambassador Burns, July 19, 1967.

18. Riad, *The Struggle for Peace in the Middle East*, pp. 109–31. Nasser message to Hussein in Kamm, *Hussein Poteah be-Milhama*, p. 301. Heikal column in BBC, Daily Report, Middle East, Africa and West Europe, no. 138, d 3. Daniel Dishon, "Inter-Arab Relations," in Rabinovich and Shaked, eds., *From June to October*, p. 159.

19. Ramadan, *Tahtim al-Aliha*, pp. 196–273. Heikal, *Al-Infijar*, pp. 922–28. Farid, *Nasser*, pp. 41, 75. Fawzi, *Harb al-Thalath Sanawat*, pp. 166–79. Riad, *The Struggle for Peace in the Middle East*, pp. 33–34. Imam, *'Abd al-Nasir—Kayfa Hakama Misr*, pp. 212–39. USNA, Central Policy files, 1967–1969, POL UAR, box 2552: Memorandum of Conversation with Habib Bourgiba, Sept. 28, 1967; POL 2 UAR, box 2553: Amman to the Secretary of State, Oct. 3,1967. PRO, FCO 39/233, North and East African – Political Affairs: Washington to the Foreign Office; June 14, 1967; FCO 39/235, UAR – Political Affairs: Cairo to the Foreign Office, June 11, 1967. Al-Dugheidi quote in Al-Sabbagh, *Mudhakkirat Qadat al-'Askaraiyya al-Misriyya 3*, pp. 9–10. Nasser quote from Mahjoub, *Democracy on Trial*, p. 134. Sadat quote from Finkelstone, *Anwar Sadat*, p. 58. See also Jamal Hamad, *Al-Hukuma al-Khafiyya – Fi 'Ahd 'Abd al-Nasir* (Cairo: Al-Zahra lil-I'lam al-'Arabi, 1988).

20. Hussein, *My "War" with Israel*, p. 88. Dupuy, *Elusive Victory*, pp. 282–83. Mutawi, *Jordan in the 1967 War*, pp. 164–65. Kamm, *Hussein Poteah be-Milhama*, pp. 300–301. LBJ, National Security file, History of the Middle East Crisis, box 21: CIA Intelligence Memorandum, Arab-Israeli Situation Report, June 9, 1967. PRO, PREM 13 1622: Amman to Foreign Office; June 17, 1967; New York to Foreign Office, June 26, 1967; Foreign Office to Amman, July 6, 1967 ("Just and honorable peace"). Secret talks in London in Zak, *Hussein Ose Shalom*, p. 21.

21. Khartoum communiqué in PREM 13 1623: Khartoum to Foreign Office, Sept. 2, 1967; Arabic text in Khouri, *Al-Watha'iq al-Filastiniyya*, pp. 667–68. Sela, *The Decline of the Arab-Israeli Conflict*, pp. 104, 108. Kimche, *The Sandstorm*, pp. 265–67. Kamm, *Hussein Poteah be-Milhama*, pp. 298–99. Mutawi, *Jordan in the 1967 War*, pp. 176–77. Riad, *The Struggle for Peace in the Middle East*, p. 51; *Mudhakkirat 2*, pp. 119–21. Mahjoub, *Democracy on Trial*, pp. 137–48.

22. LBJ, National Security file, Country file, Middle East-UAR box 161: Cairo's Moderation Since Khartoum, Sept. 28, 1967; Memos to the President, box 20: CIA Intelligence Cable: Egypt, Feb. 16, 1968 (Nasser quote). PRO, CAB 128/42 54th Conclusions: Sept. 7, 1967; FCO/39/245 UAR – Political Affairs (External): Cairo to Foreign Office, Sept. 5, 1967; PREM 13 1623: Washington to the Foreign Office, June 22, 1967 (Yugoslavian plan); Tel Aviv to the Foreign Office, Sept. 4, 1967 (Eshkol quote). ISA, Foreign Ministry files, 3978/2, United States – Relations with the Middle East: Ben Aharon to the Foreign Ministry, Oct. 4, 1967. Muhammad 'Izza Daruze, *Fi Sabil Qadiyyat Filastin wal-Wahda al-'Arabiyya wamin Wahi al-Nakba wa-liajli mu'alijiha:*

rasa'il wa-Maqalat wa-Buhuth wa-Muqabalat wa-Ta'aqibat, Beirut 1948–1972 (Beirut: al-Maktaba al-'Asriyya, 1972), pp. 85–87. Hussein quote from *My "War" with Israel*, p. 120. Gazit, *Pta'im be-Malkodet*, pp. 143–44.

23. PRO, FCO17/513 Israel – Political Affairs (External): Washington to the Foreign Office, Sept. 5, 1967. Mohamed Hassanein Heikal, *The Road to Ramadan* (London: Collins Press, 1975), pp. 52–53. Al-Shuqayri, *Mudhakkirat* 5, pp. 109–10. Yoram Meital, "The Khartoum Conference and Egyptian Policy After the 1967 War: A Reexamination," *The Middle East Journal* 54, no. 1 (Winter 2000). Al-Khuli, *Harb Yunyu*, pp. 171–77, 187.

24. Heikal, *The Road to Ramadan*, pp. 102–13. Arab reactions to Nasser's death, including Sadat and Hussein quotes, from Moshe Dayan Center Library, Tel Aviv University, Ramat Aviv, Israel (translations of Arabic press). Israeli reactions in BBC, Daily Report, Middle East, Africa, and Western Europe, 3495/E/5.

25. Biographical information for Hussein, al-Assad, and Arafat can be found at, respectively, www.kinghussein.gov.jo/, www.defencejournal.com/globe/2000/aug/hafez.htm, and www.p-p-o.com/.

26. LBJ, National Security file, History of the Middle East Crisis, box 19: NSC Special Committee Meeting, June 12, 1967 (Johnson and Sisco quotes); NSC Histories, Middle East Crisis, box 17: The President in the Middle East Crisis, Dec. 19, 1968 (Rusk quote); Rostow to the President, June 20, 1967 (Eshkol and Eban quotes and "cut the pipelines"); PRO, PREM 13 1622: Washington to the Foreign Office, June 27, 1967. ISA, 4078/5, Foreign Ministry files, Contacts with the United States After the Six-Day War: Evron to Eban, June 28, 1967.

27. LBJ, National Security file, Country file, Addendum: Minutes of Meeting, LBJ and Kosygin, June 22, 1967; Europe and the USSR, box 229: President's Meeting with Chairman Kosygin (Zbigniew Brzezinski), June 22, 1967; Memos to the President (W. Rostow), box 18: Rostow to the President, July 21, 1967; NSC Histories, Middle East Crisis , box 20: Davis to Rostow, June 16, 1967; box 21: CIA Intelligence Memorandum, June 15, 1967 (Federenko quote). PRO, PREM 13 1622: Middle East Situation, June 14, 1967 ("consequences of aggression"). CAB 128/42 50th Conclusions: July 20, 1967. PRO, FCO 17/523: Israel – Political Affairs (External); New York to the Foreign Office, July 21, 1967 (Caradon quote); FCO 17/505: Washington to the Foreign Office, July 27, 1967 ("extremist Arab circles"). Eban, *Personal Witness*, pp. 433–40. Dobrynin, *In Confidence*, pp. 162–63. Lall, *The UN and the Middle East Crisis*, pp. 153–81, 218–27 (Federenko quote). Lawrence L. Whetten, *The Canal War: Four-Power Conflict in the Middle East* (Cambridge: The MIT Press, 1974), pp. 46–48.

28. LBJ, National Security file, History of the Middle East Crisis, box 18: CIA: Special Assessments on the Middle East Situation, July 7, 1967. PRO, PREM 13 1622: Johnson to Wilson, July 6, 1967; PREM 13 1623: Goldberg/Gromyko draft (n.d.); FCO 17/523: Israel – Political Affairs (External): Dobrynin Meeting with Rusk, July 9, 1967.

29. ISA, 4078/7, Foreign Ministry files, Contacts with the United States with the Entry of Egyptian Forces into Tiran: Eban Conversation with Goldberg, July 21, 1967 (Eban quote); 4088/7, General Assembly Discussions: Rafael to Eban, July 9, 1967; 3976/12, Diplomatic Relations with the United States: Tekoah to Rafael, Aug. 16, 1967 ("physical retreat"). Mahjoub, *Democracy on Trial*, p. 133 (Nasser quote). Lall, *The UN and the Middle East Crisis*, p. 212.

30. LBJ, National Security file, History of the Middle East Crisis); Memos to the President, box 20: Rostow to the President ("lean on them"), June 27, 1967; NSC Histories, box 18: McPherson to the President, June 11, 1967; Country file – Middle East, box 148: Memorandum for the President – Handling Hussein, Bundy to the President, June 27, 1967. USNA, Central Policy files, 1967–1969, POL 2 UAR, box 2553: New York to the Department of State, Nov. 1, 1967. PRO, FCO 17/505: Israel – Political Affairs (External): Johnson Oral Message to Eshkol, July 31, 1967. Mutawi, *Jordan in the 1967 War*, pp. 178–79. Riad, *The Struggle for Peace in the Middle East*, pp. 64–68.

31. PRO FCO/39/245 UAR – Political Affairs (External): Cairo to the Foreign Office, Nov. 5, 1967; CAB 128/42 68th Conclusions: Nov. 23, 1967. LBJ, National Security file, Memos to the President, box 23: Walt Rostow to the President, Oct. 5, 1967; Arthur J. Goldberg Oral History, pp. 17, 24–25. Riad quote from *Mudhakkirat 2*, pp. 136–37, 151–52. *UN Security Council Resolution 242: The Building Block of Peacemaking. A Washington Institute Monograph* (Washington, D.C.: The Washington Institute for Near East Policy, 1993). Oral history interview with Muhammad al-Farra, Nov. 17, 1999; with George Tomeh, Nov. 17, 1999. Lall, *The UN and the Middle East Crisis*, pp. 254–55. Eban, *Personal Witness*, pp. 456–59. Rafael, *Destination Peace*, pp. 186–90. Quandt, *Peace Process*, pp. 154–57.

32. Nasser quotes from PRO FCO/39/246 UAR – Political Affairs (External): Cairo to the Foreign Office, Nov. 24, 1967; Heikal, *The Road to Ramadan*, p. 54, and LBJ, National Security file, Country file, Middle East-UAR box 161: Rostow to the President, Dec. 18, 1967. Syrian quote from *al-Ba'th*, Nov. 30, 1967. PLO declaration from Moshe Dayan Center Library, Tel Aviv University, Ramat Aviv, Israel (translations of Arabic press), summary for Nov. 23, 1967.

BIBLIOGRAPHY AND SOURCES

Archives

Abba Eban Papers, Hebrew University, Jerusalem, Israel

Ammunition Hill Archive, Jerusalem, Israel

Ben-Gurion Archives, Sde Boker, Israel

Galili Institute for the Research of War and Defense, Ramat Efal, Israel

Findley Burns, Jr., Oral Recollections, Georgetown University, Special Collections, Washington, D.C.

Arthur J. Goldberg Papers, Library of Congress, Washington, D.C.

Israel Defense Forces Archives, Givatayim, Israel

Israel Intelligence Library (Center for the Legacy of Intelligence), Herzliya, Israel

Israel State Archives (ISA), Jerusalem, Israel

Jerusalem Post Archives

Levi Eshkol Papers, Jerusalem, Israel

Lyndon Baines Johnson Presidential Library (LBJ), Austin, Texas, U.S.A.

Mapai Party Archives (MPA), Beit Berl, Israel

Moshe Dayan Center Library, Tel Aviv University, Ramat Aviv, Israel

National Archives of Canada (NAC), Ottawa

Public Record Office (PRO), London, U.K.

Shiloah Center Archive, Tel Aviv University, Ramat Aviv, Israel

Soviet Foreign Ministry Archives (SFM), Moscow

United Nations Archives (UN), New York, N.Y.

United States National Archives (USNA), Washington, D.C.

Yad Tabenkin Archive (YAD), Ramat Efal, Israel

Bound collections of documents and transcripts

British Broadcasting Service World Monitoring Service
Documents of the Foreign Policy of Israel
Foreign Relations of the United States (FRUS)
Middle East Record 3 (1967) (Jerusalem: Israel Universities Press, 1971)
The Department of State During the Administration of President Lyndon B. Johnson,
    November 1963–January 1969, 1: Administrative History

Oral History Interviews

Name	Position in 1967	Date of Interview
EGYPT		
Amin Tantawi	Company Commander, 4th Division	July 4, 2001
Al-Shirbini Sa'id Hamada	Operations Officer, 14th Armored Brigade	July 5, 2001
'Abd al-Mun'im Hamza	Military Intelligence	July 4, 2001
'Izzat 'Arafa	Battalion Commander, 7th Division	July 6, 2001
Fu'ad Hijazi	Officer, 37th Commando Battalion	July 5, 2001
Mahmud al-Suwarqa	Driver, 6th Division	July 7, 2001
'Isam Darraz	Historian	July 7, 2001
Munir Zaki Mustafa	Egyptian physician attached to Saudi forces in Jordan	July 5, 2001
Sa'id Ahmad Rabi'	Company Commander, Anti-Aircraft	July 4, 2001
JORDAN		
Adnan Abu-Oudeh	Military Intelligence	Nov. 16, 1999
Shafiq 'Ujeilat	Armored Corps, Intelligence	Nov. 17, 1999
'Ata 'Ali Haza'	Brigade Commander, Jerusalem	Nov. 18, 1999
Badi 'Awad	Battalion Commander, Jerusalem	Nov. 21, 1999
Mahmud Abu Faris	Company Commander, Jerusalem	Nov. 17, 1999
Muhammad al-Farra	Ambassador to the UN	Nov. 17, 1999
Muhammad Fallah al-Fayiz	Commander, Airborne Battalion	Nov. 21, 1999
Fayiz Fahed Jaber	Deputy Commander, Intelligence	Nov. 21, 1999
'Awad Khalidi	Battalion Commander, Jerusalem Corridor	Nov. 18, 1999
'Awad Bashir Khalidi	Colonel, Infantry Brig., Jerusalem Corridor	Nov. 17, 1999
Yusuf Khawwash	General, Jordanian Representative, United Arab Command, Cairo	Nov. 16, 1999
Suliman Marzuq	King Hussein's personal driver	Nov. 17, 1999
Ghazi Isma'il Ruba'iyya	Platoon commander, Jerusalem	Nov. 21, 1999
SYRIA		
Muhammad 'Amer	Captain, Infantry	Jan. 10, 2001
Ibrahim Isma'il Khahya	Commander, 8th Infantry Brigade	Jan. 10, 2001

Marwan Hamdan al-Khuli	Captain, Ordnance Corps	Jan. 11, 2001
George Tomeh	Ambassador to the UN	Nov. 17, 1999

PALESTINE

Sadiq Juda	Volunteer, Palestinian forces attached to the Iraqi army	July 5, 2001

ISRAEL

Meir Amit	Chief, Mossad	Feb. 9, 1999
Rafi Benvenisti	Commander, Jerusalem Line	Jan. 1, 1999
Abba Eban*	Foreign Minister	Nov. 26, 2000
Rafael Eitan	Commander, 35th Airborne Brigade	March 2, 1999
Miriam Eshkol	Wife, Private Secretary of Levi Eshkol	Aug. 30, 1999
Ya'akov Eshkoli	Resident of Kfar Giladi; northern settlements leader	Dec. 11, 1999
Yeshayahu Gavish	Chief, Southern Command	Dec. 7, 1999
Mordechai Gazit	Israel Foreign Ministry	Feb. 4, 1999
Shlomo Gazit	IDF Intelligence, Head of Research Branch	March 9, 1999
Motti Hod	Commander, Israel Air Force	
Yitzhak Hofi	IDF, Deputy Chief of Operations	July 14, 1999
Shimon Kahaner	IDF, Deputy Battalion Commander, 55th Paratroop Brigade	Oct. 18, 2000
David Kimche	Mossad/IDF Intelligence	Aug. 26, 1999
Arye Levavi	Director-General, Israel Foreign Ministry	Nov. 4, 1999
Avraham Lif	Strategic Planning, IDF Intelligence	Sept. 13, 1999
Shlomo Merom	IDF Intelligence, Southern Command	Dec. 7, 1999
Meir Pa'il	Deputy Commander, Tal *Ugdah*	Dec. 6, 2000
Elad Peled	*Ugdah* (Divisional) Commander	Jan. 28, 2001
Israel Tal	*Ugdah* (Divisional) Commander	Aug. 23, 1999
Zorach Warhaftig	Minister of Religious Affairs (National Religious party)	
Ezer Weizman	IDF, Chief of Operations	Jan. 13, 1999
Rehavam Ze'evi	IDF, Deputy Chief of Operations	Sept. 9, 2001

FORMER SOVIET UNION

Karen Brutents	Member, Supreme Soviet	Jan. 21, 2001
General Makhmut A. Gareev	Soviet military adviser, Egypt	May 24, 1999
Lt. Gen. Vadim Kirpitchenko	Director, KGB liaison desk with Egyptian and Syrian security services	Dec. 25, 2000
Nikolai Yegoroshev	Member, Supreme Soviet	Dec. 23, 2000

FRANCE

Eric Rouleau	Middle East correspondent, *Le Monde*	Dec. 17, 2000

UNITED STATES

Robert McNamara	Secretary of Defense	Feb. 11, 1999
Harry McPherson*	White House counsel	May 14, 1999
Anthony "Bud" Perna	Colonel, U.S. Air Force	Dec. 10, 2000
	U.S. Military Attaché to Israel	
Indar Jit Rikhye	Commander, United Nations	Feb. 22, 1999
	Emergency Force	
Eugene V. Rostow	Undersecretary of State	Aug. 5, 1999
Walt Whitman Rostow	National Security Affairs Advisor	July 27, 1999
Joseph Sisco	Undersecretary of State for	Aug. 6, 1999
	Near Eastern Affairs	

*Responded to written questions

Books in English, French, and Spanish

Abdel-Malek, Anouar. *Egypt: Military Society—The Army Regime, the Left, and Social Change Under Nasser.* New York: Vantage Press, 1968.

Abu-Lughod, I., ed. *The Arab-Israeli Confrontation of June 1967: An Arab Perspective.* Evanston, Ill.: Northwestern University Press, 1970.

Abu Oudeh, Adnan. *Jordanians, Palestinians, and the Hashemite Kingdom in the Middle East Peace Process.* Washington, D.C.: United States Institute of Peace, 1998.

Ahmed, J. M. *The Intellectual Origins of Egyptian Nationalism.* London: Oxford University Press, 1968.

Ajami, Fuad. *The Arab Predicament: Arab Political Thought and Practice Since 1967.* Cambridge: Cambridge University Press, 1981.

Andrew, Christopher, and Oleg Gordievsky. *KGB: The Inside Story.* New York: HarperCollins, 1990.

Aronson, Shlomo, with Oded Brosh. *The Politics and Strategy of Nuclear Weapons in the Middle East: Opacity, Theory, and Reality, 1960-1991: An Israeli Perspective.* Albany: State University of New York Press, 1992.

Bartov, Hanoch. *Dado: 48 Years and 20 Days.* Tel Aviv: Maariv Books, 1981.

Bar-Zohar, Michael. *Ben-Gurion: A Biography.* New York: Adama Books, 1978.

———. *Embassies in Crisis: Diplomats and Demagogues Behind the Six Day War.* Englewood Cliffs, N.J.: Prentice-Hall, 1970.

Beliaev, I. P., T. Kolesnichenko, and Y. M. Primako. *Soviet Review of the Israeli-Arab June 1967 Conflict.* Washington, D.C.: Joint Publications Research Service, 1968.

Black, Ian, and Benny Morris. *Israel's Secret Wars: The Untold History of Israeli Intelligence.* London: Hamish Hamilton, 1991.

Brecher, Michael. *Decisions in Crisis.* Berkeley: University of California Press, 1980.

———. *Decisions in Israel's Foreign Policy.* New Haven, Conn.: Yale University Press, 1975.

Bull, Gen. Odd. *War and Peace in the Middle East: The Experiences and Views of a U.N. Observer.* London: Lee Cooper, 1973.

Burns, William J. *Economic Aid and American Policy Toward Egypt, 1955–1981.* Albany: State University of New York Press, 1985.

Caro, Robert A. *The Years of Lyndon B. Johnson: The Path to Power.* New York: Vintage, 1990.

Christman, Henry M., ed. *The State Papers of Levi Eshkol.* New York: Funk & Wagnall's, 1969.

Churchill, Randolph S., and Winston S. Churchill. *The Six Day War.* London: Heinemann Books, 1967.

Clifford, Clark (with Richard Holbrooke). *Counsel to the President.* New York: Random House, 1991.

Cobban, Helena. *The Palestinian Liberation Organization.* Cambridge: Cambridge University Press, 1983.

Cockburn, Andrew and Leslie. *Dangerous Liaison.* New York: HarperCollins, 1991.

Cohen, Avner. *Israel and the Bomb.* New York: Columbia University Press, 1998.

Copeland, Miles. *The Game of Nations: The Amorality of Power Politics.* London: Weidenfeld & Nicolson, 1969.

Couve de Murville, Maurice. *Une politique étrangère 1958–1969.* Paris: Plon, 1971.

Cristol, A. Jay. *The Liberty Incident,* unpublished doctoral dissertation, University of Miami, 1997.

Crosbie, Sylvia K. *A Tacit Alliance: France and Israel from Suez to the Six Day War.* Princeton, N.J.: Princeton University Press, 1974.

Dagan, Avigdor. *Moscow and Jerusalem: Twenty Years of Relations Between Israel and the Soviet Union.* London: Abelard-Schuman, 1970.

Dann, Uriel. *King Hussein and the Challenge of Arab Radicalism: Jordan, 1955–1967.* New York: Oxford University Press, 1989.

Dawisha, I. Adeed. *Egypt in the Arab World: The Elements of Foreign Policy.* New York: Wiley, 1976.

Dayan, Moshe, *Diary of the Sinai Campaign, 1956.* London: Wiedenfeld & Nicolson, 1967.

———. *The Story of My Life.* London: Sphere Books, n.d.

Deacon, Richard. *The Israeli Secret Service.* London: Sphere Books, 1979.

Dekmejian, R. Hrair. *Egypt Under Nasir: A Study in Political Dynamics.* Albany: State University of New York Press, 1971.

Dobrynin, Anatoly. *In Confidence: Moscow's Ambassador to America's Six Cold War Presidents (1962–1986).* New York: Random House, 1995.

Doherty, Kathryn B. *Jordan Waters Conflict.* Carnegie Endowment for International Peace, no. 533. New York, 1965.

Donovan, Robert J. *Six Days in June: Israel's Fight for Survival.* New York: New American Library, 1967.

Doran, Michael. *Pan-Arabism Before Nasser: Egyptian Power Politics and the Palestine Question.* New York: Oxford University Press, 1999.

Draper, Theodore. *Israel and World Politics: Roots of the Third Arab-Israeli War.* New York: Viking, 1967.

Dupuy, Trevor N. *Elusive Victory: The Arab-Israeli Wars, 1947–1974.* New York: Harper & Row, 1978.

Eban, Abba. *Diplomacy for the Next Century.* New Haven, Conn.: Yale University Press, 1998.

———. *Personal Witness: Israel Through My Eyes.* New York: Putnam, 1992.

El Edroos, S. A. *The Hashemite Arab Army, 1908–1979: An Appreciation and Analysis of Military Operations.* Amman, Jordan: Publishing Committee, 1980.

El-Farra, Muhammad. *Years of Decision.* London: KPI, 1987.

El-Rayyes, Riad, and Dunia Nahas. *Guerrillas for Palestine.* London: Croom Helm, 1976.

El-Sadat, Anwar. *In Search of Identity: An Autobiography*. New York: Harper & Row, 1977.

Ennes, James M. *Assault on the Liberty*. New York: Random House, 1980.

Evans, R., and R. Novak. *Lyndon B. Johnson: The Exercise of Power*. New York: New American Library, 1966.

Eveland, Wilbur Crane. *Ropes of Sand*. New York: Norton, 1969.

Faddah, Mohamad Ibrahim. *The Middle East in Transition: A Study of Jordan's Foreign Policy*. New York: Asia Publication House, 1974.

Farid, Abdel Magid. *Nasser: The Final Years*. Reading, U.K.: Ithaca Press, 1994.

Finklestone, Joseph. *Anwar Sadat: Visionary Who Dared*. London: Frank Cass, 1996.

Gawrych, George W. *The Albatross of Decisive Victory: War and Policy Between Egypt and Israel in the 1967 and 1973 Arab-Israeli Wars*. Westport, Conn.: Greenwood Press, 2000.

Gazit, Mordechai. *President Kennedy's Policy Toward the Arab States and Israel: Analysis and Documents*. Syracuse, N.Y.: Syracuse University Press, 1983.

Gershoni, Israel, and James P. Jankowski. *Egypt, Islam, and the Arabs: The Search for Egyptian Nationhood, 1900–1930*. New York: Oxford University Press, 1986.

Glassman, Jon D. *Arms for the Arabs*. Baltimore: Johns Hopkins University Press, 1975.

Ghobashi, Omar Z. *The Development of the Jordan River*. New York: Arab Information Center, 1961.

Golan, Galia. *Soviet Politics in the Middle East: From World War II to Gorbachev*. Cambridge: Cambridge University Press, 1990.

Gold, Dori, ed. *Arms Control and Monitoring in the Middle East*. Boulder, Colo.: Westview Press, 1990.

Gomaa, Ahmed M. *The Foundation of the League of Arab States: Wartime Diplomacy and Inter-Arab Politics, 1941 to 1945*. London and New York: Longman, 1977.

Goulding, Phil G. *Confirm or Deny—Informing the People on National Security*. New York: Harper & Row, 1970.

Govrin, Yosef. *Israeli-Soviet Relations, 1953–1967: From Confrontation to Disruption*. London: Frank Cass, 1990.

Gromyko, Andrei. *Memoirs*. New York: Doubleday, 1989.

Hammel, Eric. *Six Days in June: How Israel Won the 1967 Arab-Israeli War*. New York: Scribner's, 1992.

Hart, Alan. *Arafat: A Political Biography*. London: Sidgwick & Jackson, 1994.

Heikal, Mohamed Hassanein. *The Cairo Documents*. Garden City, N.Y.: Doubleday, 1973.

———. *The Road to Ramadan*. London: Collins, 1975.

———. *The Sphinx and the Commissar: The Rise and Fall of Soviet Influence in the Middle East*. London: Collins, 1978.

Hersh, Seymour M. *The Samson Option: Israel, America, and the Bomb*. London: Faber & Faber, 1991.

Hewat, Tim, ed. *War File: The Voices of the Israelis, Arabs, British and Americans, in the Arab-Israeli War of 1967*. London: Panter Books, 1967.

Higgins, Rosalyn. *United Nations Peace-Keeping, 1946–67*. London: Oxford University Press, 1969-1987.

Hirszowicz, Lukasz. *The Third Reich and the Arab East*. London: Routledge & K. Paul, 1966.

Hof, Frederic C. *Line of Battle, Order of Peace?* Washington: Middle East Insight, 1999.

Hofstadter, Dan, ed. *Egypt and Nasser 3, 1967–72*. New York: Facts on File, 1973.

Hourani, Albert. *A History of the Arab Peoples*. London: Faber & Faber, 1991.

Howard, M., and R. Hunter. "Israel and the Arab World." *Adelphi Papers* 41 (1974).

Hussein of Jordan. *My "War" with Israel* (as told to Vick Vance and Pierre Lauer). New York: Morrow, 1969.

Israel Must Be Annihilated. Tel Aviv: Zahal Information Office, 1967.

Israeli, Raphael. *Man of Defiance: A Political Biography of Anwar Sadat*. Totowa, N.J.: Barnes & Noble, 1985.

Jalil, Mustafa. *La Guerra Nunca Exista*. (n.d.)

Johnson, Lyndon Baines. *The Vantage Point: Perspectives of the Presidency, 1963–1969*. New York: Holt, Rinehart & Winston, 1971.

Kadi, Leila S. *Arab Summit Conferences and the Palestine Problem, 1945–1966*. Beirut: Palestine Liberation Organization, 1966.

Kalman, Laura. *Abe Fortas: A Biography*. New Haven, Conn.: Yale University Press, 1990.

Katz, Shmuel M. *Soldier Spies: Israeli Military Intelligence*. Novato, Calif.: Presidio Press, 1992.

Kenen, I. L. *Israel's Defense Line: Her Friends and Foes in Washington*. Buffalo, N.Y.: Prometheus Books, 1981.

Kerr, Malcolm H. *The Arab Cold War: Gamal Abd al-Nasir and His Rivals, 1958–70*. London: Oxford University Press, 1971.

Khalaf, Salah. *My Home, My Land: A Narrative of the Palestinian Struggle*. New York: Time Books, 1981.

Khour, Fred. J. *The Arab-Israeli Dilemma*. Syracuse, N.Y.: Syracuse University Press, 1976.

Kimche, David, and Dan Bawly. *The Sandstorm: The Arab-Israeli War of June 1967: Prelude and Aftermath*. London: Secker & Warburg, 1968.

Klinghoffer, Judith A. *Vietnam, Jews, and the Middle East: Unintended Consequences*. New York: St. Martin's Press, 1999.

Kollek, Teddy. *For Jerusalem*. London: Weidenfeld & Nicolson, 1978.

Kosygin, A. N. *Selected Speeches and Writings*. Oxford: Pergamon Press, 1981.

Kurzman, Dan. *Soldier of Peace: The Life of Yitzhak Rabin*. New York: HarperCollins, 1998.

Lacouture, Jean. *De Gaulle: The Ruler, 1945–1970*. New York: Norton, 1992.

Lall, Arthur. *The UN and the Middle East Crisis, 1967*. New York: Columbia University Press, 1968.

Laqueur, Walter. *The Israel-Arab Reader*. New York: Citadel Press, 1968.

———. *The Road to Jerusalem: The Origins of the Arab-Israeli Conflict, 1967*. New York: Macmillan, 1968.

Lawson, Fred H. *Why Syria Goes to War: Thirty Years of Confrontation*. Ithaca, N.Y.: Cornell University Press, 1996.

Life: Special Edition – Israel's Swift Victory (1967).

Loftus, John, and Mark Aarons. *The Secret War Against the Jews: How Western Espionage Betrayed the Jewish People*. New York: St. Martin's Press, 1997.

Louis, William Roger. *The British Empire in the Middle East, 1945–1951: Arab Nationalism, the United States, and Postwar Imperialism*. Oxford: Oxford University Press, 1984.

Lowi, Miriam. *Water and Power: The Realities of a Scarce Resource in the Jordan River Basin*. Cambridge: Cambridge University Press, 1993.

Mahjoub, Mohamed Ahmed. *Democracy on Trial: Reflections on Arab and African Politics.* London: Andre Deutsch, 1974.

Mansoor, Menachem. *Arab World: Political and Diplomatic History, 1900–1967: A Chronological Study.* NCR, Microcard Editors, n.d..

Ma'oz, Moshe. *Syria and Israel: From War to Peacemaking.* Oxford: Clarendon Press, 1995.

Ma'oz, Moshe, and Avner Yaniv. *Syria Under Assad: Domestic Constraints and Regional Risks.* London: Croom Helm, 1986.

Marshall, S. L. A. *Swift Sword: The Historical Record of Israel's Victory, June 1967.* New York: American Heritage Publishing, 1967.

McNamara, Robert S. *In Retrospect: The Tragedy and Lessons of Vietnam.* New York: Time Books, 1995.

Meir, Golda. *My Life.* New York: Putnam's, 1975.

Moore, John, ed. *The Arab-Israel Conflict: Readings and Documents.* Princeton, N.J.: Princeton University Press, 1977.

Morris, Benny. *The Birth of the Palestinian Refugee Problem.* Cambridge: Cambridge University Press, 1988.

Moskin, J. Robert. *Among Lions: The Battle for Jerusalem, June 5–7, 1967.* New York: Ballantine Books, 1982.

Mutawi, Samir A. *Jordan in the 1967 War.* Cambridge: Cambridge University Press, 1987.

Narkiss, Uzi. *Soldier of Jerusalem,* trans. Martin Kett. London: Mitchell Vallentine, 1998.

Nasser, Gamal Abdel. *The Philosophy of the Revolution.* Washington, D.C.: Public Affairs Press, 1955.

Nassit, Ramses. *U Thant in New York, 1961–1971: A Portrait of the Third UN Secretary-General.* New York: St. Martin's Press, 1988.

Neff, Donald. *Warriors for Jerusalem: The Six Days That Changed the Middle East.* Brattleboro, Vt.: Amana Books, 1988.

Netanyahu, Jonathan. *Self-Portrait of a Hero: The Letters of Jonathan Netanyahu.* New York: Random House, 1980.

Nicosia, Francis, R. *The Third Reich and the Palestine Question.* London: I. B. Tauris, 1985.

Nutting, Anthony. *Nasser.* New York: Dutton, 1972.

O'Balance, Edgar. *The Third Arab-Israeli War.* London: Faber & Faber, 1972.

Oren, Michael B. *The Origins of the Second Arab-Israeli War: Egypt, Israel, and the Great Powers, 1952–1956.* London: Frank Cass, 1992.

Ovendale, Ritcie. *The Origins of the Arab-Israeli Wars.* London: Longman, 1984.

Pappe, Ilan. *Britain and the Arab-Israel Conflict, 1948–1951.* London: Macmillan, 1988.

Parker, Richard B. *The Politics of Miscalculation in the Middle East.* Bloomington: Indiana University Press, 1993.

———. *The Six Day War.* Jacksonville: University of Florida Press, 1997.

Péan, Pierre. *Les deux bombes.* Paris: Fayard, 1981.

Pearson, Anthony. *Conspiracy of Silence: The Attack on the U.S.S. Liberty.* London: Quartet Books, 1978.

Peres, Shimon. *Battling for Peace: Memoirs.* London: Weidenfeld & Nicolson, 1995.

Perlmutter, Amos. *The Life and Times of Menachem Begin.* New York: Doubleday, 1987.

Porath, Yehoshua. *In Search of Arab Unity.* London: Frank Cass, 1986.

Primakov, Y. M. *Anatomy of the Middle East Conflict*. Moscow: Nauka, 1979.

Prittie, Terence. *Eshkol: The Man and the Nation*. New York: Pitman, 1969.

Pryce-Jones, David. *The Closed Circle: An Interpretation of the Arabs*. London: Paladin, 1990.

Quandt, William B. *Peace Process: American Diplomacy and the Arab-Israeli Conflict Since 1967*. Washington, D.C.: Brookings Institute, 1993.

Quandt, William B., Fuad Jabber, and Ann Mosley Lesche. *The Politics of Palestinian Nationalism*. Berkeley: University of California Press, 1973.

Rabin, Yitzhak. *The Rabin Memoirs*. Berkeley: University of California Press, 1996.

Rabinovich, Abraham. *The Battle for Jerusalem, June 5–7, 1967*. Philadelphia: Jewish Publication Society of America, 1972.

Rabinovich, Itamar. *The Road Not Taken: Early Arab-Israeli Negotiations*. New York: Oxford University Press, 1991.

———. *Syria Under the Ba'th 1963–66: The Army-Party Symbiosis*. Jerusalem: Israel Universities Press, 1972.

Rabinovitch, Itamar, and Haim Shaked, eds. *From June to October: The Middle East Between 1967 and 1973*. New Brunswick, N.J.: Transaction, 1978.

Rafael, Gideon. *Destination Peace: Three Decades of Israeli Foreign Policy*. New York: Stein & Day, 1981.

Rahmi, Ali Abdel Rahman. *Egyptian Policy in the Arab World: Intervention in Yemen 1962–1967, A Case Study*. Washington, D.C.: University Press of America, 1983.

Ranelagh, John. *The Agency: The Rise and Decline of the CIA*. New York: Simon & Schuster, 1988.

Raviv, Dan, and Yossi Melman. *Friends in Deed: Inside the U.S.-Israel Alliance*. New York: Hyperion, 1994.

Raviv, Moshe. *Israel at Fifty: Five Decades of the Struggle for Peace*. London: Weidenfeld & Nicolson, 1998.

Riad, Mahmoud. *The Struggle for Peace in the Middle East*. New York: Quartet Books, 1981.

Rikhye, Indar Jit. *The Sinai Blunder*. London: Frank Cass, 1980.

Ro'i, Yaacov. *From Encroachment to Involvement: A Documentary Study of Soviet Foreign Policy in the Middle East, 1945–1973*. New York: Wiley, 1974.

Rostow, Eugene V. *Peace in the Balance: The Future of American Foreign Policy*. New York: Simon & Schuster, 1972.

Rostow, W. W. *The Diffusion of Power: An Essay in Recent History*. New York: Macmillan, 1972.

Rouleau, Eric, Jean-Francis Held, and Jean and Simone Lacouture. *Israel et les Arabes le 3e Combat*. Paris: Editions du Seuil, 1967.

Rubinstein, Alvin Z. *Red Star on the Nile: The Soviet-Egyptian Influence Relationship Since the June War*. Princeton, N.J.: Princeton University Press, 1977.

Rusk, Dean. *As I Saw It*. New York: Penguin Books, 1990.

Safran, Nadav. *From War to War: The Arab-Israel Confrontation, 1948–1967*. New York: Pegasus, 1969.

Saliba, Samir Nicolas. *The Jordan River Dispute*. The Hague: M. Nijhoff, 1968.

Sayed-Ahmed, Muhammad Abd el-Wahab. *Nasser and American Foreign Policy, 1952–1956*. London: LAAM, 1989.

Schiff, Ze'ev. *A History of the Israeli Army, 1874 to the Present*. New York: Macmillan, 1985.

Seale, Patrick. *Asad of Syria: The Struggle for the Middle East.* London: Taurus, 1988.

Seikaly, S., R. Baalbaki, and P. Dodd, eds. *Quest for Understanding: Arabic and Islamic Studies in Memory of Malcolm Kerr.* Beirut: American University of Beirut, 1991.

Sela, Avraham. *The Decline of the Arab-Israeli Conflict: Middle East Politics and the Quest for Regional Order.* Albany: State University of New York Press, 1998.

Sela, Avraham, ed. *Political Encyclopedia of the Middle East.* New York: Continuum, 1999.

Shapira, Avraham, ed. *The Seventh Day: Soldiers Talk About the Six-Day War.* New York: Scribners, 1970.

Sharon, Ariel. *Warrior.* New York: Simon & Schuster, 1989.

Shemesh, Moshe. *The Palestinian Entity 1959–1974: Arab Politics and the PLO.* London: Frank Cass: 1989.

Shevchenko, Arkady N. *Breaking with Moscow.* New York: Knopf, 1985.

Shuckburgh, Evelyn. *Descent to Suez, 1951–1956.* London: Weidenfeld & Nicolson, 1986.

Slater, Robert. *Rabin of Israel: A Biography.* London: Robson Books, 1993.

Soffer, Arnon. *Rivers of Fire: The Conflicts over Water in the Middle East.* Lanham, Md.: Rowman & Littlefield, 1999.

Stebenne, David L. *Arthur J. Goldberg: New Deal Liberal.* New York: Oxford University Press, 1996.

Stein, Leonard. *The Balfour Declaration.* London: Mitchell Vallentine, 1961.

Stephens, Robert. *Nasser: A Political Biography.* London: Penguin, 1971.

Steven, G. A. *Jordan River Partition.* Stanford: Hoover Institute Studies, 1965.

Susser, Asher. *On Both Banks of the Jordan: A Political Biography of Wasfi al-Tall.* London: Frank Cass, 1994.

Talmon, Jacob Leib. *The Six Days' War in Historical Perspective.* Rehovot, Israel: Yad Chaim Weizmann, 1969.

Teveth, Shabtai. *Ben-Gurion: The Burning Ground, 1906–1948.* Boston: Houghton Mifflin,1987.

———. *The Tanks of Tammuz.* London: Sphere Books, 1969.

Touval, Sadia. *The Peace-Brokers: Mediators in the Arab-Israeli Conflict, 1948–1979.* Princeton, N.J.: Princeton University Press, 1982.

UN Security Council Resolution 242: The Building Block of Peacemaking. A Washington Institute Monograph. Washington, D.C.: The Washington Institute for Near East Policy, 1993.

U Thant. *View from the UN.* New York: Doubleday, 1978.

Urquhart, Brian. *Hammarskjold.* New York: Alfred A. Knopf, 1972.

———. *A Life in Peace and War.* New York: Harper & Row, 1987.

Van Creveld, Martin. *The Sword and the Olive: A Critical History of the Israeli Defense Force.* New York: Public Affairs, 1998.

Vassiliev, Alexei. *Russian Policy in the Middle East: From Messianism to Pragmatism.* Reading, U.K.: Ithaca Press, 1993.

Vatikiotis, P. J. *The History of Egypt: From Muhammad Ali to Sadat.* Baltimore: Johns Hopkins University Press, 1980.

———. *Nasser and His Generation.* New York: St. Martin's Press, 1978.

Vital, David. *The Origins of Zionism: The Formative Years.* Oxford: Clarendon Press, 1982.

Waterbury, John. *The Egypt of Nasser and Sadat: The Political Economy of Two Regimes.* Princeton, N.J.: Princeton University Press, 1983.

Weizman, Ezer. *On Eagles' Wings: The Personal Story of the Leading Commander of the Israeli Air Force.* New York: Macmillan, 1976.

Whetten, Lawrence L. *The Canal War: Four-Power Conflict in the Middle East.* Cambridge: MIT Press, 1974.

Wilson, Harold. *The Chariot of Israel: Britain, America, and the State of Israel.* New York: Norton, 1981.

Wilson, Mary C. *King Abdullah, Britain and the Making of Jordan.* Cambridge: Cambridge University Press, 1987.

Yaari, Ehud. *Strike Terror: The Story of Fatah.* New York: Sabra Books, 1970.

Yanay, Ehud. *No Margin for Error: The Making of the Israeli Air Force.* New York: Pantheon Books, 1993.

Articles in English

Abu-Jaber, Kamel S. United States Policy Toward the June Conflict. *The Arab World* 14 (1968).

Anabtawi, Samir N. The United Nations and the Middle East Conflict of 1967. *The Arab World* 14 (1968).

Dayan, Moshe. Before and After the Battle in *The Six Days' War.* Tel Aviv: Ministry of Defense, 1967.

Evans, Rowland, and Robert Novak. Remembering the Liberty. *Washington Post,* Nov. 6, 1991.

Fishel, Reverdy S. The Attack on the Liberty: An "Accident"? *International Journal of Intelligence and Counterintelligence* 8, no. 3 (Fall 1995).

Ginor, Isabella. The Russians Were Coming: The Soviet Military Threat in the 1967 Six-Day War. *Middle East Review of International Affairs* 4, no. 4 (Dec. 2000).

Goodman, Hirsh, and Ze'ev Schiff. The Attack on the Liberty. *Atlantic Monthly,* Sept. 1984.

The June War: Whose Conspiracy? *Journal of Palestine Studies* 21, no. 4 (Summer 1992).

Little, Douglas. The Making of a Special Relationship: The United States and Israel, 1957-68. *International Journal of Middle East Studies* 25, no. 4 (Nov. 1993).

Meital, Yoram. The Khartoum Conference and Egyptian Policy After the 1967 War: A Reexamination. *Middle East Journal* 54, no. 1 (Winter 2000).

Mor, Ben D. Nasser's Decision-Making in the 1967 Middle East Crisis: A Rational-choice Explanation. *Journal of Peace Research* 28, no. 4 (1991).

Oren, Michael B. Ambivalent Adversaries: David Ben-Gurion and Dag Hammarskjold. *Journal of Contemporary History* 27 (1992).

———. The Egypt-Israel Border War. *Journal of Contemporary History* 24 (1990).

———. Faith and Fair-Mindedness: Lester B. Pearson and the Suez Crisis. *Diplomacy and Statecraft* 3, no. 1 (1992).

———. Nuri al-Sa'id and Arab-Israel Peace. *Asian and African Studies* 24, no. 3 (1990).

———. Secret Efforts to Achieve an Egypt-Israel Settlement Prior to the Suez Campaign. *Middle Eastern Studies* 26, no. 3 (1990).

Parker, Richard B. The June 1967 War: Some Mysteries Explored. *Middle East Journal* 46, no. 2 (Spring 1992).

Pedatzur, Reuven. Coming Back Full Circle: The Palestinian Option of 1967. *Middle East Journal* 49, no. 2 (Spring 1995).

Peled, David. Ben-Gurion Wasn't Rushing Anywhere. *Ha'aretz* (English ed.), Jan. 20, 2000, p. 4.

Rabinovich, Avraham. The War that Nobody Wanted. *Jerusalem Post Magazine*, June 13, 1967.

Report by Carl F. Salans, Department of State Legal Adviser, Sept. 21, 1967, to the Undersecretary of State. "The *Liberty*": Discrepancies Between the Israeli Inquiry and the U.S. Navy Inquiry. (*Liberty* Website)

Shalom, Zaki. Lyndon Johnson's Meeting with Abba Eban, May 26, 1967: An Introduction. *Israel Studies* 4, no. 2 (Fall 1999).

Shalom, Zaki, and S. Ilan Troen. Ben-Gurion's Diary for the 1967 Six-Day War: An Introduction. *Israel Studies* 4, no. 2 (Fall 1999).

Sharabi, Hisham. Prelude to War: The Crisis of May-June 1967. *The Arab World* 14 (1968).

Schiff, Ze'ev. The Dispute on the Syrian-Israeli Border. *New Outlook* 10, no. 2 (Feb. 1967).

Shlonim, Shlomo. Origins of the 1950 Tripartite Declaration on the Middle East. *Middle Eastern Studies* 23, no. 1 (July 1987).

Yost, Charles W. How It Began. *Foreign Affairs*, Jan. 1968.

Books in Hebrew

Allon, Yigal. *Kelim Shluvim*. Tel Aviv: Am Oved, 1980.

Amit, Meir. *Rosh be-Rosh: Mabat Ishi al Eruim Gdolim u-Farshiyot Alumot*. Or Yehuda: Hed Arzi, 1999.

Asia, Ilan. *Tismonet Dayan: Arba Milhamot ve-Shalom Ehad—ha-Roved ha-Nistar*. Tel Aviv: Yediot Ahronot, 1995.

Bar Kokhva, Moshe. *Merkavot ha-Plada*. Tel Aviv: Ma'arakhot, 1989.

Baron, Arye. *Hotam Ishi: Moshe Dayan be-Milhemet Sheshet ha-Yamim ve-Aharciha*. Tel Aviv: Yediot Ahronot, 1997.

Ben Tzur, Avraham. *Gormim Sovietiim u-Milhemet Sheshet ha-Yamim: Ma'avakim ba-Kremlin ve-Hashpa'ot be-Azoreinu*. Tel Aviv: Sifriat Poalim, 1975.

Benziman, Uzi. *Yerushalayim: Ir lelo Homa*. Jerusalem: Schocken, 1973.

Cohen, Avi. *Ha-Haganah al Mekorot ha-Mayim–Mediniyut Hafalat Hail ha-Avir le-Tkifa bi-Gvul Yisrael-Suria, 1956-1967*. Tel Aviv: Hail ha-Avir, Misrad ha-Bitahon, 1992.

Dayan, David. *Me-Hermon ad Suez: Korot Milhemet Sheshet ha-Yamim*. Ramat Gan: Masada Press, 1967.

Dayan, Moshe. *Avnei Derekh*. Tel Aviv: Yediot Ahronot, 1976.

Eisenstadt, S. N. *Ha-Hevra ha-Yisraelit*. Jerusalem: Magnes Press of the Hebrew University, 1970.

Erell, Shlomo. *Lefanekha ha-Yam: Sipuro shel Yamai, Mefaked u-Lohem*. Tel Aviv: Misrad ha-Bitahon, 1998.

Eshkol, Yosef, ed. *Milhemet Sheshet ha-Yamim*. Tel Aviv: Misrad ha-Bitahon, 1967.

Gazit, Shlomo. *Pta'im be-Malkodet: 30 Shnot Mediniyut Yisrael ba-Shtahim*. Tel Aviv: Zemora-Bitan, 1999.

Gilad, Baruch, ed. *Teudot le-Mediniyut ha-Hutz shel Medinat Yisrael 14*, 1960. Jerusalem: Israel Government Printing House, 1997.

Gilboa, Moshe A. *Shesh Shanim, Shisha Yamim–Mekoroteha ve-Koroteha shel Milhemet Sheshet ha-Yamim*. Tel Aviv: Am Oved, 1969.

Gluska, Ami. *Imut bein ha-Mateh ha-Klali u-bein Memshelet Eshkol bi-Tkufat ha-Hamtana"—Mai-Yuni, 1967*. Jerusalem: Leonard Davis Institute for International Relations, 2001.

Golan, Aviezar. *Albert*. Tel Aviv: Yediot Ahronot, 1977.

Gur, Motta. *Har ha-Bayyit be-Yadeinu!: Kravot ha-Tzanhanim be-Yerushalayim be-Milhemet Sheshet ha-Yamim*. Tel Aviv: Ma'arakhot, 1974.

Guy, Carmit. *Bar-Lev*. Tel Aviv: Am Oved, 1998.

Haber, Eitan. *Ha-Yom Tifrotz Milhama: Zikhronotav shel Tat-Aluf Yisrael Lior, ha-Mazkir Hatzvai shel Rashei ha-Memshala Levi Eshkol ve-Golda Meir*. Tel Aviv: Yediot Ahronot, 1987.

Haber, Eitan, and Ze'ev Schiff, eds. *Lexicon le-Bithon Yisrael*. Tel Aviv: Mahadurat Davar, 1976.

Hame'iri, Yehezkel. *Mi-Shnei Evrei ha-Rama*. Tel Aviv: Levin-Epstein, 1970.

Harel, Yehuda. *El Mul Golan*. Givatayim: Masada Press, 1967.

Harel, Yisrael. *Sha'ar ha-Arayot—Ha-Krav al Yerushalayim be-Havayat Lohamei Hativat ha-Tzanhanim*. Tel Aviv: Ma'arkhot, n.d.

Hareuveni, Meir, and Meir Arye, eds. *Ha-Hativa Shelanu be-Milhemet Sheshet ha-Yamim*. Tel Aviv: Misrad ha-Bitahon, 1968.

Horesh, Ya'akov. *47 Madregot*. Tel Aviv: Yaron Golan, 1993.

Kamm, Ephraim. *Hussein Poteah be-Milhama: Milhemet Sheshet ha-Yamim be-Eynei ha-Yardenim*. Tel Aviv: Ma'arakhot, Misrad ha-Bitahon, 1974.

Katz, Shmuel, and Aharon Megged. *Me-Har Grizim ad Har Hermon: Rishumei Pikud ha-Tzafon be-Milhemet Sheshet ha-Yamim*. Tel Aviv: Misrad ha-Bitahon, 1967.

Lachish, Ze'ev, and Meir Amitai. *Asor Lo Shaket: Prakim be-Toldot Hail ha-Avir ba-Shanim 1956-1967*. Tel Aviv: Misrad ha-Bitahon, 1995.

Man, Rafi. *Lo Ya'ale al ha-Da'at*. Or Yehuda: Hed Artzi, 1998.

Mayzel, Matitiahu. *Ha-Ma'arakha al ha-Golan–Yuni 1967*. Tel Aviv: Ma'arakhot, 2001.

Michelson, Beni, Avraham Zohar, and Effi Meltzer, eds. *Ha-Ma'avak le-Bithon Yisrael*. Tel Aviv: Ha-Amuta ha-Yisraelit le-Historia Tzva'it leyad Universitat Tel Aviv, 2000.

Nakdimon, Shlomo. *Likrat Sh'at ha-Efes*. Tel Aviv: Ramdor Press, 1968.

Naor, M., and Z. Aner, eds. *Yemei Yuni–Teurim min ha-Milhama 1967*. Tel Aviv: Ma'arakhot, 1967.

Pedatzur, Reuben. *Nitzhon ha-Mevukha*. Tel Aviv: Bitan/Yad Tabenkin, 1996.

Peled, Yossi. *Ish Tzava*. Tel Aviv: Ma'ariv, 1993.

Rosental, Yemima, ed., *Teudot Le-Mediniyut ha-Hutz shel Medinat Yisrael 3: December 1948 - July 1949*. Jerusalem: Israel Government Press, 1985.

Sadeh, Ezra. *Amud ha-Esh: Yoman ha-Milhama shel Yirmi*. Tel Aviv: Yosef Shimoni, n.d..

Scheuftan, Dan. *Ha-Optzia ha-Yardenit: Ha-Yishuv ve-Medinat Yisrael mul ha-Mimshal ha-Hashemi ve ha-Tnua ha-Leumit ha-Falastinit*. Tel Aviv: Yad Tabenkin, Machon Yisrael Galili, 1986.

Schiff, Ze'ev. *Tzahal be-Hailo: Encyclopedia le-Tzava u-le-Bitahon*. Tel Aviv: Revivim, 1981.

Shashar, Michael. *Milhemet ha-Yom ha-Shvi'i: Yoman ha-Mimshal ha-Tzvai be-Yehuda ve-Shomron.* Tel Aviv: Hoza'at Poalim, 1997.

———. *Sihot im Rehavam–Gandhi–Ze'evi.* Tel Aviv: Yediot Ahronot, 1992.

Shragai, Nadav. *Har ha-Meriva: Ha-Ma'avak al Har ha-Bayyit, Yehudim ve-Muslemim, Dat ve-Politika Meaz 1967.* Jerusalem: Keter, 1995.

Segev, Shmuel. *Sadin Adom.* Tel Aviv: Taversky Press, 1967.

Shalev, Arye. Ha-Milhama ve-Totzoteiha be-Eynei ha-Aravim. *Dapei Elazar 10, Esrim Shana le-Milhemet Sheshet ha-Yamim.* Tel Aviv: Yad David Elazar, 1988.

Shalom, Zaki. *David Ben-Gurion, Medinat Yisrael ve hu-Olam ha-Aravi, 1949–1956.* Sede Boqer: Ha-Merkaz le-Moreshet Ben-Gurion, 1995.

Sorer, Eran. *Derekh ha-Mitla.* Ramat Gan: Masada, 1967.

Susser, Asher. *Shisha Yamim–Shloshim Shana.* Tel Aviv: Am Oved, 1999.

Teveth, Shabtai. *Moshe Dayan, Biografia.* Jerusalem: Schocken Press, 1971.

Warhaftig, Zorach. *Hamishim Shana ve-Shana: Pirkei Zikhronot.* Jerusalem: Yad Shapira, 1998.

Yariv, Aharon. *Ha'arakha Zehira: Kovetz Ma'amarim.* Tel Aviv: Ma'arakhot, 1998.

Zak, Moshe. *Hussein Ose Shalom.* Ramat Gan: Merkaz Begin-Sadat, 1966.

Articles in Hebrew

Amit, Meir. Ha-Derekh le-Sheshet ha-Yamim—Sheshet ha-Yamim be-Re'i le-Ahor. *Ma'arakhot* 325 (June–July 1992).

Argaman, Yosef. Nasser Metzaltzel le-Hussein: Ha-Siha. *Bamahane* 18 (Jan. 1989).

Ba-Avir bein New York le-London–Megale ha-Melekh Hussein et Sibat Mapalato. *Bit'on Hail ha-Avir* 3, no. 74/75 (Dec. 1967).

Ben Akiva, Elinar and Aner Guvrin. Sh'at ha-Mirage—Esrim Shana le-Milhemet Sheshet ha-Yamim. *Bit'on Hail ha-Avir* 57 (May 1987).

Ben, Aluf. Lo Huzkar be-Albomei ha-Nitzahon. *Bamahane* 37 (May, 1992).

Ben Tzadaf, Evyatar. Elze Min Tzava Haya. *Bamahane* 47 (Feb. 1992).

Bin-Nun, Ran. Krav ha-Havka'a shel Hativat 'Golani' be-Milhemet Sheshet ha-Yamim. Unpublished thesis, Kedourie School, Feb. 1988.

Hail ha-Avir ba-Milhama. *Bit'on Hail ha-Avir* 3, no. 74/75 (Dec. 1967).

Ha-Shita – Pashtut. *Bit'on Hail ha-Avir* 3, no. 74/75 (Dec. 1967).

Eruei ha-Hodesh–Ashan ve-Esh be-Kav Hafsakat-Ha-Esh. *Skira Hodshit* 9–10. (Sept.–Oct. 1967).

Kamm, Ephraim Col. Haf'alat ha-Zira ha-Mizrahit be-Milhemet Sheshet ha-Yamim. *Ma'arakhot* 325 (June 1992).

Kashti, Or. Mesima Bilti Efsharit. *Bamahane* 37 (May 1992).

Leviav, Rut. Milhemet Sheshet ha-Yamim: Ha-Festival. *Bamahane* 37 (June 1977).

Levita, Yosef. Ma Ya'ase Zahal ba-Shalal. *Bamahane* 48 (Aug. 1967).

Meged, Aharon. Sh'ot ha-Tofet shel Tel Fakhr. *Bamahane* 31–32 (April 1967).

Me-Kuneitra ad Kantara: Reayon im ha-Ramatkal. *Bamahane* 42 (June 1967).

Milhemet Sheshet ha-Yamim: Hizdamnut velo Pitron. *Skira Hodshit* 3–4 (May 1987).

Milhemet Sheshet ha-Yamim: Teur ha-Peulot bekhol ha-Hazitot. *Skira Hodshit* 5–7 (May–July 1967).

Milstein, Ari. Ha-Til she-Haras et Emdot ha-Ligion. *Bamahane* 34 (May 1977).

Narkiss, Uzi. Kakh Uhda Yerushalayim. *Bamahane* 34 (May 1987).

Reayon im Rav Aluf Yitzhak Rabin. *Bamahane* 13 (June 1977).

Reayon im Ya'akov Eshkoli. *Eretz ha-Golan* 100 (1985).

Rozner, David. Ha-5 be-Yuni 1967 be-Kahir. *Bamahane* 35 (May 1968).

Seren, Moshe (Captain Moshe: an assumed name). Tvusat Mitzrayim be-Eynei ha-Aravim. *Ma'arakhot* 200 (June 1969).

Shamir, Ami. Im ha-Koah she-Ala al Jenin. *Lamerhav* 3014 (June 8, 1967).

Shapira, Boaz. Mesokim be-Um Katef. *Bamahane* 37 (June 1977).

Shemesh, Moshe. Ha-Ma'avak ha-Aravi al ha-Mayim Neged Yisrael, 1959-1967. *Iyunim* 7 (1997).

Sisser, Eyal. Bein Yisrael le-Suria: Milhemet Sheshet ha-Yamim ule-Ahareiha. *Iyunim be-Tkumat Yisrael* 8 (1998).

Takrit ha-7 be-April: 20 Shniyot Aharei–Sheshet ha-Migim she-Kirvu et Sheshet ha-Yamim. *Bamahane* 39 (April 8, 1987).

Yariv, Aharon. Ha-Reka la-Milhama. *Dapei Elazar 10, Esrim Shana le-Milhemet Sheshet ha-Yamim.* Tel Aviv: Yad David Elazar, 1988.

Yitzhaki, Arye. Ha-Ma'arakha le-Kibush ha-Golan be-Milhemet Sheshet ha-Yamim. *Ariel* 50-51 (1987).

Hebrew Newspapers

Ha'aretz
Ma'ariv
Davar
Yediot Ahronot

Books and Articles in Arabic

'Abd al-Hamid, Berlinti. *Al-Mushir wa-Ana*. Cairo: Maktabat Madbuli al-Saghir, 1992.

'Abd al-Nasir wa-Zu'ama' 'Arab "Baraku" Ijra'at al-Husayn Didda al-Fida'iyyin. *al-Hadath* 6, no. 265 (Jan. 29, 2001).

Abu Fakhr, Saqr. Al-Julan: Shahadat Nazihin 'an Ayyam al-Harb wal-Hadir. *Majallat al-Dirasat al-Filastiniyya* 42 (Spring 2000).

Abu Murshid, Walid, Antoine Butrus, and Fuad Jabber. Al-Kitab Al-Sanawi lil-Qadiyya al-Filastiniyya li-'Am 1967. *Silsilat al-Kitab al-Sanawi lil-Qadiyya al-Filastiniyya* 4. Beirut: Manshurat Mu'assasat al-Dirasa al-Filastiniyya, 1969.

Abu Nidal, Sabr. *Ma'rakat al-Khamis min Haziran: Awwal Dirasa 'Arabiyya Askariyya Shamila lil-Hazima.* Cairo: Al-Mu'assasa al-'Arabiyya lil-Dirasa wal-Nashr, 1971.

Abu Dhikri, Wajih. *Madhbahat al-Abriya'*. Cairo: Al-Maktab al-Misri al-Hadith, 1988.

Al-Ashram, Salah al-Din. Al-Tawatu' al-Anklo-Amriki ma'a Isra'il. *Al-Majalla al-'Askariyya* 6, no. 18 (1967).

Al-Baghdadi, 'Abd al-latif. *Mudhakkirat*. Cairo: al-Maktab al-Misri al-Hadith, 1977.

Al-Dajani, Ahmad Sidqi. *Min al-Muqawama ila al-Thawra al-Shabbiyya fi Filastin*. Cairo: Maktabat al-Anklu al-Misriyya, 1969.

Al-Gamasi, Muhammad 'Abd al-Ghani. *Mudhakkirat al-Gamasi*. Paris: Al-Manshura al-Sharqiyya, 1990.

al-Hadidi, Salah al-Din. *Shahid 'ala Harb 67*. Beirut: Dar al-'Awda,1974.

Al-'Ilmi, 'Imad. *Harb 'Am 1967*. Acre: Al-Aswar lil-Thaqafa, 1990.

Al-Jiyyar, Mahmud. Ayyam al-Naksa fi Bayt 'Abd al-Nasir. *Ruz al-Yusuf* 2484 (Jan. 19, 1976).

———. Rajulan Qatala al-Mushir 'Amer. *Ruz al-Yusuf* 2482 (Jan. 5, 1976).

Al-Khuli, Lutfi. *Harb Yunyu 1967 ba'da 30 Sana*. Cairo: Markaz Al-Ahram, 1997.

Al-Munjid, Salah al-Din. *'Umdat al-Nukhba*. Beirut: Dar al-'Awda, 1967.

Al-Naturi, Amin. *Tawazun al-Quwwa bayna al-'Arab wa-Isra'il: Dirasa Tahliliyya Istratejiyya li-'Udwan Haziran 1967*. Damascus: Dar al-I'tidal lil-Tiba'a wal-Nashr, 1968.

Al-Sabbagh, Muhammad, ed. *Mudhakkirat Qadat al-'Askariyya al-Misriyya 1967-1972 fi A'qab al-Naksa*. Cairo: Dar al-Khayyal, in press.

Al-Shara', Sadiq. *Hurubuna ma'a Isra'il*. Amman: Dar al-Shuruq lil-Nashr wal-Tawzi', 1997.

Al-Shum'a, Hani. *Ma'arik Khalida fi Ta'rikh al-Jaysh al-'Arabi al-Suri*. Damascus: Al-Tiba'a al-Suriyya, 1988.

Al-Shuqayri, Ahmad. *Mudhakkirat Ahmad al-Shuqayri, 'Ala Tariq al-Hazima, Ma'a al-Muluk wal-Ru'asa'. Vol. 3. Min al-Qimma ila al-Hazima, Ma'a al-Muluk wal-Ru'asa'*. Beirut: Dar al-'Awda, 1971. *Vol. 5, 2: Al-Hazima al-Kubra Ma'a al-Muluk wal-Ru'asa': Min Bayt 'Abd al-Nasir ila Ghurfat al-'Amaliyyat*. Beirut: Dar al-'Awda, 1972.

Al-'Uthm, Sadiq Jalal. *Al-Naqd al-Dhati ba'da al-Hazima*. Acre: Dar al-Jalil lil-Tiba'a wal-Nashr, 1969.

Al-Watha'iq al-Urduniyya, 1967. Amman: Da'irat al-Matbu'at wal-Nashr, 1967.

'Awda, Muhammad, and 'Abdallah Imam. *Al-Naksa—Man al-Mas'ul?* Cairo: Ruz al-Yusuf, 1985.

Badran, Shams. Interview. *Al-Hawadith*. Sept. 2, 1977.

Darraz, 'Isam. *Dubbat Yunyu Yatakallamun: Kayfa Shahada Junud Misr Hazimat 67*. Cairo: al-Manar al-Jadid lil-Sahafa wal-Nashr, n.d.

Daruze, Muhammad 'Izza. *Fi Sabil Qadiyyat Filastin wal-Wahda al-'Arabiyya wamin Wahi al-Nakba wa-liajli mu'alijiha: rasa'il wa-Maqalat wa-Buhuth wa-Muqabalat wa-Ta'aqibat, Beirut 1948-1972*. Beirut: al-Maktaba al-'Asriyya, 1972.

Dhabbah, Shukri. *Wa-Madha Ba'du?* Cairo: Dar al-Quds, n.d.

Fakhida, Khalid. *Al-Fariq Haditha lil-Hadath: Sharakna fi Harb '67 Irda'an li-'Abd al-Nasir wa-Man'an min 'Takhwin' al-Urdun*. *al-Hadath* 265 (Jan. 29, 2001).

Fawzi, Gen. Muhammad. *Harb al-Thalath Sanawat*. Cairo: Dar al-Mustaqbal al-'Arabi, 1980.

Gohar, Sami. *Al-Samitun Yatakallamun*. Cairo: al-Manar al-Jadid lil-Sahafa wal-Nashr, 1975.

Hamad, Jamal. *Al-Hukuma al-Khafiyya–Fi 'Ahd 'Abd al-Nasir*. Cairo: Al-Zahra lil I'lam al-'Arabi, 1988.

Husayn, Mahmud. *Al-Sira' al-Tabaqi fi Misr min 1945 ila 1970*. Beirut: Dar al-Tali'a, 1971.

Heikal, Mohamed Hassanein. *1967: Al-Infijar*. Cairo: Markaz al-Ahram, 1990.

———. *Sanawat al-Ghalayan*. Cairo: Markaz al-Ahram, 1988.

Imam, 'Abdallah. *'Abd al-Nasir—Kayfa Hakama Misr*. Cairo: Madbuli al-Saghir, 1966.

———. *'Ali Sabri Yatadhakkar: Bi-Saraha 'an al-Sadat*. Cairo: Dar al-Khayyal, 1997.

———. *Nasir wa-'Amer*. Cairo: Mu'assasat al-Kitab, 1985.

Khalil, Mustafa. *Min Milaffat al-Julan: Al-Qism al-Awwal*. Amman: Dar al-Yaqin lil-Tiba'a wal-Nashr, 1970.

————. *Suqut al-Julan*. Amman: Dar al-Yaqin lil-Tiba'a wal-Nashr, n.d.

Khawwash, Yusuf. *Al-Jabha al-Urduniyya, Harb Haziran*. Amman: Dar al-Yaqin lil-Tiba'a wal-Nashr, 1980.

Mazhar, Suliman. *I'tirafat Qadat Harb Yunyu: Nusus Shahadatihim Amama Lajnat Tasjil Ta'rikh al-Thawra*. Cairo: Kitab al-Hurriyya,1990.

Murad, Mahmud. Harb Haziran. *Al-Majalla al-'Askariyya* 19, no. 1 (Aug. 1968).

Murtagi, 'Abd al-Muhsin Kamil. *Al-Fariq Murtagi Yarwi al-Haqa'iq*. Cairo: Dar al-Watan al-'Arabi, 1976.

Mustafa, Husayn. *Harb Haziran 1967: Awwal Dirasa 'Askariyya min Wujhat al-Nazar al-'Arabiyya. 2: al-Jabha al-Sharqiyya*. Beirut: Al-Mu'assasa al-'Arabiyya lil-Dirasa wal-Nashr, 1973.

Khouri, George, ed. *Al-Watha'iq al-Filastiniyya al-'Arabiyya li-'Am 1967*. Beirut: Mu'assasat al-Dirasa al-Filastiniyya, 1969.

Ramadan, 'Abd al-'Azim. *Tahtim al-Aliha: Qissat Harb Yunyu 1967*. Cairo: Madbuli, 1988.

Riad, Mahmoud. *Mudhakkirat Mahmoud Riad, 1948-1976, al-Juz' al-Awwal: al-Bahth 'an al-Salam fi al-Sharq al-Awsat*. Beirut: al-Mu'assasa al-'Arabiyya lil-Dirasa wal-Nashr, 1987.

————. *Mudhakkirat Mahmud Riad, 2*. Beirut: Al-Mu'asassa al-'Arabiyya lil-Dirasa wal-Nashr, 1987.

Tlas, Mustafa. *Mir'at Hayati*. Damascus: Tlasdar, 1995.

Watha'iq 'Abd al-Nasir 1. Cairo: Markaz al-Ahram,1973.

Zia' al-Din, Birs. 'Abd al-Nasir . . . Hakama. *Ruz al-Yusuf 2464* (Sept. 1, 1975).

Arabic Newspapers

Akher Sa'a (Egypt)
Al-Ahram (Egypt)
Al-Ba'th (Syria)
Al-Difa'i (Jordan)
Al-Hawadith (Lebanon)
Ruz al-Yusuf (Egypt)
al-Ra'i al-'Am (Egypt)

Books and Articles in Russian

Beliaev, I. P., and E. M. Primakov. *Egipet: vremia prezidenta Nasera*. Moscow: Mysl', 1974.

Blishchenko, I. L., and V. D. Kudriavtsev. *Agressia Izrailia 1 Mezhdunarodnoie Pravo*. Moscow: Mezhdunorodnye Otnoshenia, 1970.

Dediulia, Ivan Prokhorovitch. Na Zemle Obetovannoy. *Nezavisimoe Veonnoe Obozrenie* 20 (1998).

Demchenko, P. *Arabskii Vostok v chas ispytanii*. Moscow: Politicheskaia Literarura, 1967.

Goldberg, Naftali Ben-Sion. SSR Protiv Izrailia. *Sem' Dney*, Aug. 17, 2000.

Grechko, A. M. *Sovetskaia Voiennaia Entsiklopedia, Vol. 3*, (Moscow: Institut Voiennoi Istorii, 1976.

Ivanov, Iuri. *Ostorozhno: Sionizm! Ocherki po ideologii, organizatsii i praktike sionizma*. Moscow: Politicheskaia Literatura, 1971.

Khaldeev, A. Nesostoiavshiisia desant. *Vesti* (Israel), Sept. 14, 2000.

Khrushchev, Nikita. *Vospominania 3: Vremya. Lyudi. Vlast'*. Moscow: Moskovskie novosti. Informatzionno-izdatel'skaya kompania, 1999.

Kirpichenko, V. A. *Iz Arkhiva Razvedchika*. Moscow: Mezhdunorodnye Otnoshenia, 1993.

Mintz, I. I. *Sionizm: Teoria i Praktika.* Moscow. Izdetelstvo Politicheskoi Literatury, 1970.

Pokormiak, N. V. *Izrail': kursom militarizma i agressii*. Moscow: Ministerstvo Oborony SSSR, 1982.

Prokhorov, A. M., ed. *Sovetskaia Entsiklopedia Slovar*, 4th ed. Moscow: Sovetskaia Entsiklopedia, 1989.

———. *Bol'shaia Sovetskaia Entsiklopedia*. Moskva: Sovetskaia Entsiklopedia, 1978.

Rumiantsev, V. Arabskii Vostok na Novom Puti. *Kommunist* (Moscow) 16 (Nov. 1969): 90-101.

Sheidin, L. Imperialisticheskii zagovor na Blizhnem Vostoke. *Kommunist* 11 (July 1967): 107-17.

Shvarts, Solomon M. *Sovetskii Soiuz i Arabo-Izrail'skaia Voina 1967*. New York: Amerikanskii Evreiskii Rabochii Komitet, 1969.

Tuganova, O. E. *Mezhdunarodnie otnoshenia na Blizhnem i Srednem Vostoke*. Moscow: Mezhdunarodnye Otnoshenia, 1967.

Vinogradov, V. M. *Diplomatia: liudi i sobytia*. Moscow: Rosspen, 1998.

Yeryomenko, Valerii. Imenno Sovyetskii Soyuz spas arabskuyu koalitziyu vo vremia Shestidnevnoi voiny. *Nezavisimoe Veonnoe Obozrenie* 20 (1998).

Zhurkin V. V. and E. M. Primakov, eds. *Mezhdunarodnye Konflikty*. Moscow: Mezhdunarodnye Otnoshenia, 1972.

Zolotarev, V. A., ed. *Rossia (SSSR) v' lokal'nykh voinakh i voennykh konfliktakh vtoroi poloviny XX veka*. Moscow: Kuchkovo Pole, 2000.

Internet Sites:

www.bemorecreative.com/one/480.htm
    Quotes from Harold Wilson
www.geocities.com/CapitolHill/Lobby/5270/index2.htm
    Biography of Gamal Abdel Nasser
www.defencejournal.com/globe/2000/aug/hafez.htm
    Biography of Hafez al-Assad
www.elicohen.com
    Biography of Eli Cohen
www.us-israel.org/jsource/biography
    Biographies of Levi Eshkol, Moshe Dayan, and Wolfgang Lotz
www.jajz-ed.org.il
    Biographies of Teddy Kollek, Chaim Herzog, and Rabbi Shlomo Goren
www.halcyon.com/jim/ussliberty/liberty.htm
    USS *Liberty* page
www.kinghussein.gov.jo/
    Biography of King Hussein
www.p-p-o.com/
    Biography of Yasser Arafat

INDEX

NOTE: Entries beginning with numbers can be found under the spelling of the
number (i.e., 7th Brigade is alphabetized under "Seventh").
Page numbers in *italics* refer to maps.